ISBN 978-1-5283-3769-4
PIBN 10912338

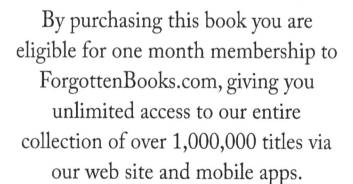

English
Français
Deutsche
Italiano
Español
Português

www.forgottenbooks.com

Mythology Photography **Fiction**
Fishing Christianity **Art** Cooking
Essays Buddhism Freemasonry
Medicine **Biology** Music **Ancient**
Egypt Evolution Carpentry Physics
Dance Geology **Mathematics** Fitness
Shakespeare **Folklore** Yoga Marketing
Confidence Immortality Biographies
Poetry **Psychology** Witchcraft
Electronics Chemistry History **Law**
Accounting **Philosophy** Anthropology
Alchemy Drama Quantum Mechanics
Atheism Sexual Health **Ancient History**
Entrepreneurship Languages Sport
Paleontology Needlework Islam
Metaphysics Investment Archaeology
Parenting Statistics Criminology
Motivational

ANNUAL REPORT

OF THE

SUPERINTENDENT OF EDUCATION

ON THE

PUBLIC SCHOOLS OF NOVA SCOTIA,

For the Year ending 31st October,

1892.

HALIFAX, N. S.:
COMMISSIONER OF PUBLIC WORKS AND MINES
QUEEN'S PRINTER.
1893.

WM. MACNAB, PRINTER, NO. 3 PRINCE STREET.

EDUCATION OFFICE,

HALIFAX, March, 1893.

SIR,—

I have the honor to transmit herewith, to be laid before His Honor the Lieutonant-Governor, my report on the Public Schools of Nová Scotia, for the School year ended October 31, 1892.

I am, with respect,

Your obedient servant,

A. H. MACKAY,
Superintendent of Education.

To the HON. W. S. FIELDING, M.P.P.,
Provincial Secretary.

70360

GENERAL CONTENTS.

PART I.—GENERAL REPORT.

PART III.—APPENDICES.

PART I.

GENERAL REPORT, 1892.

ANNUAL REPORT

ON THE

PUBLIC SCHOOLS OF NOVA SCOTIA,

1891-2.

To His Honor, Malachy Bowes Daly, Esq.,

Lieutenant-Governor of the Province of Nova Scotia:

MAY IT PLEASE YOUR HONOR,—

I beg, in accordance with the law, to submit my annual report on the Public Schools of the Province, for the year ended 31st October, 1892.

As the statistics following will show in detail, there has been improvement in nearly every item of the customary tabulation.

The decrease in the total number of sections, even although new ones were formed, indicates a tendency to the consolidation of weak sections into larger and more effective ones. In some portions of the province it may be necessary, in the true interests of the people, for the Government to adopt special measures to accelerate this movement.

The total number of schools in operation and of teachers employed increased by about forty.

The pupils increased by over a thousand.

Their attendance was not only more regular than during the previous year, but more regular on the average of summer and winter terms, than during any previous year.

The grand total days' attendance at school shows an increase of over 100,000 during the Summer, and over 200,000 during the Winter.

The average salaries of first-class male teachers increased by about forty dollars, and of first-class female teachers, about ten dollars; while the average salaries of the lower classes of teachers, male and female, as a general rule, decidedly diminished. This appears to indicate a growing appreciation on the part of our people for superior teachers, and a corresponding diminution of esteem for the work of the lower grades.

The Government increased its expenditure by over $2500. The people directly, through the county and sectional assessments, gave about $19,000 more than during the previous year, the increase being specially due to the repair and erection of buildings, which are markedly improving.

STATISTICAL ABSTRACT.

1.—School Sections.

Total number in Province	....	1905
" " 1891	....	1908

Decrease	 3

	Winter.	Summer.	Year
No. of Sections without Schools	267	151	73
" " " 1891	293	175	87

Decrease .... 26 Decrease, 24 Decrease, 14

2.—No. of Schools, Pupils, Teachers, &c.

	Winter.	Summer.
Total No. Schools in operation	2158	2281
" " " 1891	2120	2236

Increase................. 38 Increase, 45

Total No. Registered Pupils	82965	87189
" " " 1891	81304	85792

Increase .... 1661 Increase, 1397

Total No. of different pupils during year	102586
" " " " 1891	101724

Increase............................. 862

Total No. of Teachers and Licensed Assistants employed	2196	2340
" " " 1891	2158	2300

Increase .... 38 Increase, 40

3.—Proportion of Population at School, &c.

	Winter Term.	Summer Term
Proportion of Population at School	1 in 5.4	1 in 5.1
" " " 1891	1 in 5.4	1 in 5.1

Proportion of Population at School during year	1 in 4.3
" " " " 1891	1 in 4.3

No of Pupils daily present on an average for time in session	49493.6	52456.8
" " " " 1891	47874.7	50819.6

Increase............... 1618.9 Increase 1637.2

	Winter Term.	Summer Term.
No. of Pupils daily present on full term average........................	47132.6	49922.5
" " ' " 1891	46215.7	48391.1
Increase...............	916.9 Increase,	1531.4
Percentage of Pupils daily present on average for time Schools were in session........................	59.6	60
" " " " 1891	58.8	59 2
Increase...............	.8 Increase,	.8
Percentage of Pupils daily present on an average for full term.........	56.8	57.2
" ". " " 1891	56.8	56.4
	Increase,	.8
Grand total days' attendance.........5494836		5240241
" " " 1891.....5271436		5104241
Increase...............	223400 Increase,	136000

4.—Classification of Teachers.

	Winter Term.	Summer Term.
Academic Class (Grade A)............	47	46
" " " 1891.......	46	46
Increase..............	1	
First Class (Grade B) Male Teachers..	161	160
" " " " 1891	170	161
Decrease...............	9 Decrease,	1
First Class (Grade B) Female Teachers.	147	167
" " " " 1891	154	144
Decrease..............	7 Increase,	23
Second Class (Grade C) Male Teachers.	210	194
" " " " 1891	203	199
Increase..............	7 Decrease,	5
Second Class (Grade C) Female Teachers	812	896
" " " " 1891	816	870
Decrease..............	4 Increase,	26
Third Class (Grade D) Male Teachers...	151	153
" " " " 1891	155	157
Decrease..............	4 Decrease,	4

	Winter Term.	Summer Term.
Third Class (Grade D) Female Teachers...	648	707
" " " " 1891..	596	703
Increase..................	52 Increase,	4
Total No. Male Teachers...............	567	550
" " 1891............	572	561
Decrease..................	5 Decrease,	11
Total No. Female Teachers.............	1609	1773
" " " 1891..........	1568	1719
Increase.................	41 Increase,	54

5.—PERIOD OF SERVICE OF TEACHERS.

	Winter Term.	Summer Term.
No. of Teachers engaged in same sections..	1112	1394
" " " " 1891..	1094	1326
Increase..................	18 Increase,	68
No. of Teachers removed to another section	775	796
" " " " 1891	775	751
	Increase.	45
No. of new Teachers....................	289	133
" " 1891	271	203
Increase..................	18 Increase,	70

6.—SUMMARY OF GOVERNMENT EXPENDITURE ON PUBLIC SCHOOLS.

	Winter Term.	Summer Term.
Common Schools..................	$82,000.00	$85,498.85
" " 1891...............	82,000.00	85,487.58
Increase..		11.27
County Academies.............................		$12976 18
" " 1891.........................		14123 33
Decrease		1147 15
Government Expenditure assignable to Counties		$180475 03
" " " " 1891..		181610 91
Decrease.........................		1135 88
Inspection of School..........................		$13050 00
" " 1891.........		12800 00
Increase		250 00

Examination of Teachers	$995	15
" " 1891	861	84
Increase	133	31
Travelling Expenses Normal School Pupils	$758	55
" " " " " 1891	701	10
Increase	57	45
Salaries	$3800	00
" 1891	3000	00
Increase	800	00
Travelling Expenses Superintendent	$400	00
" " " 1891	400	00
Office Expenses	$1265	59
" 1891	1528	27
Decrease		262.68
Government Expenditure not assignable to Counties	$20269	29
" " " 1891	19291	21
Increase	978	08
Total Government Expenditure in aid of Public Schools	$200744	32
" " " 1891	200902	12
Decrease	157	80
Institution for Deaf and Dumb	$3090	00
" " 1891	1620	00
Increase	1470	00
Halifax School for the Blind	$1575	00
" " 1891	1387	50
Increase	187	50
Manual Training School	$750	00
" " 1891		
Increase	750	00
Normal and Model Schools	$6995	00
" " 1891	6950	00
Increase	45	00

School of Agriculture $1569 76
"   "   1891........................ 1682 84

Decrease 113 08

Government Night Schools....................... $1705 65
"   "   1891.... .... 1362 55

Increase........................... 343 10

Total Government Expenditure for Education........ $216429 73
"   "   "   "   1891..... 213905 01

Increase........................... 2524 72

7.—TOTAL EXPENDITURE FOR PUBLIC EDUCATION.

Gov't. Expend. for Public Schools........ $200744 32
"   "   Inst. for Deaf and Dumb.. 3090 00
"   "   Halifax School for the Blind 1575 00
"   "   Manual Training School... 750 00
"   "   Normal and Model Schools 6995 00
"   "   School of Agriculture..... 1569 76
"   "   Gov't. Night Schools..... 1705 65
                                                    ——————— $216429 73

Local Expenditure—County Fund...... $120127 75
Ass'mnt on Sections for support of Schools 313229 32
"   "   Buildings and Repairs... 96788 05
                                                    ——————— 530145 12

Total Expenditure for Public Education........... 746574 85
"   "   "   "   1891........ 725284 03

Increase........................... $ 21290 82

SCHOOL STATISTICS.

These will be found in detail in Tables I-VI, but for convenient reference a summary and comparative view of those of chief importance have been presented in the foregoing abstract.

Sections without Schools.—Only seventy-three sections, embracing a few new ones in which school organization had not been fully perfected at the end of the year, are reported as having had no schools in operation during either of the terms. This gratifying result is largely due to the persevering efforts of the Inspectors to extend the benefits of our school system to the remote and thinly populated parts of their respective districts. The sections without schools are thus distributed among the various counties :—

Annapolis	5
Antigonish	1
Cape Breton	12
Colchester	3
Cumberland	6
Digby	2
Guysboro	3
Halifax	6
Hants	3
Inverness	6
Kings	2
Lunenburg	3
Pictou	2
Queens	3
Richmond	4
Shelburne	3
Victoria	6
Yarmouth	3

Number of Schools and Teachers.—In the winter term 2196 teachers were employed and 2158 schools were in operation, increases over the preceding year of 38 in both cases. In the summer term there were 2281 schools, employing 2340 teachers, an increase of 45 schools and of 40 teachers as compared with the corresponding term of 1890-91.

Attendance.—The following is a statement of the registered attendance of pupils from 1866 to 1892 inclusive :—

YEARS.	No. of Pupils registered in Winter.	No. of Pupils registered in Summer.	No. different Pupils registered during the year.
1866..........	45131	56017	71059
1867..........	61818	70075	83048
1868..........	65983	72141	88707
1869..........	72756	75523	93732
1870..........	74321	76237	94496
1871..........	74759	77235	92858
1872..........	70780	76496	91637
1873..........	70320	78266	93759
1874..........	72645	79910	93510
1875..........	76349	81878	94029
1876..........	77593	82034	94162
1877..........	80788	83941	100710
1878..........	81523	84169	101538
1879..........	81640	84356	99094
1880..........	73978	78808	93700
1881..........	77468	80189	98148
1882..........	76888	81196	95912
1883..........	79091	81863	98307
1884..........	80041	84266	101069
1885..........	81472	86578	103288
1886..........	84570	86858	105410
1887..........	84217	86731	105137
1888..........	82486	86582	105231
1889..........	82371	86488	103688
1890..........	82794	88170	103597
1891..........	81304	85792	101724
1892..........	82965	87189	102586

The following is a statement of the registration of the past two years by counties :

	1891.	1892.
Annapolis..............	4729	4601
Antigonish.............	3756	3740
Cape Breton...........	7147	7207
Colchester.............	6514	6426
Cumberland...........	8310	8388
Digby.................	4748	4834
Guysboro	3854	4047
Halifax Co.............	6754	6692
" City.............	7299	7550
Hants	5477	5371
Inverness	6371	6496
Kings	5346	5345
Lunenburg.............	7164	7472
Pictou	7425	7500
Queens................	2265	2193
Richmond	2872	3086
Shelburne.............	3618	3680
Victoria...............	2918	2857
Yarmouth	5157	5101

The Provincial average of attendance (1 in 4.3) was exceeded in the following Counties :—Inverness and Shelburne, 1 in 4.; Cumberland, Digby, Hants and Lunenburg, 1 in 4.1 ; Annapolis, Colchester, Guysboro and Kings, 1 in 4.2 ; Antigonish, Victoria and Yarmouth make the Provincial average, 1 in 4.3. The following fall below the general average : Pictou, Queens and Richmond, 1 in 4.6 ; Cape Breton, 1 in 4.7 ; Halifax County, 1 in 4.9 ; Halifax City, 1 in 5.1.

Regularity of Attendance.—The following table shows the percentage of registered pupils daily present on an average during the period the several schools were open for the respective terms of the past ten years :

	Winter.	Summer.
1883	56.9	56.5
1884	57.8	57.2
1885	57.6	58.
1886	59.7	59.5
1887	57.9	59.2
1888	57.6	57.6
1889	60.4	58.1
1890	58.3	57.7
1891	58.8	59.2
1892	59.6	60.

When reduced to the basis of the full number of teaching days in the respective terms, the percentages stand as follows :

	Winter Term.	Summer Term.
1883	53.7	52.7
1884	54.8	53.6
1885	54.7	54.8
1886	57.1	57.1
1887	56.7	56.8
1888	55.3	55.4
1889	57.9	55.9
1890	56.2	54.5
1891	56.8	56.4
1892	56.8	57.2

These percentages measure both the regularity of attendance and the length of time during which the schools were in operation.

PERIOD OF SERVICE, SEX, AND SALARIES OF TEACHERS.

During the winter term 1112 teachers continued to teach in the same section in which they taught the preceding term; 775 removed to other sections; 289 engaged in teaching for the first time. During the summer term the corresponding figures were 1394, 796, and 133.

Of the 203 male teachers of the academic and first classes (grades A and B) in charge of schools during the summer term, 92 have been in service for upwards of *seven* years; 17 for upwards of *five* years, and 37 for upwards of *three* years. Altogether, of the 203 male teachers of the higher grades (A and B) 146 have been in service for upwards of *three* years.

Of the 1,066 female teachers of the first and second classes (grades B and C) employed during the summer term, 297 have been in service upwards of *seven* years; 173 for upwards of *five* years, and 226 for upwards of *three* years. Altogether, of the 1,066 teachers of these grades, 696 have been in service for more than *three* years.

In regard to sex, the teachers in the public schools (an average between the two terms being taken) are classed as follows:—Male, 558; Female, 1,691. As compared with the preceding year, the number of male teachers has decreased by 8, and that of female teachers increased by 48.

The average salary throughout the Province for male teachers of the first class was $488.95, as compared with $448.59 in 1890-91. The highest averages paid such teachers were in Halifax City, $917.86; Colchester, $670.21; Pictou, $655.08. The average of salaries was above the general average in the following other counties:—Cumberland $582.88; Yarmouth, $540.81; Halifax Co. $539.83; Guysboro, $522.08

The Provincial average for female teachers of the first class was $295.77 as compared with $286.03 of the previous year. The three highest averages were in Halifax City, $470; Cape Breton, $388.44; Yarmouth, $318.68. The general average was exceeded in Kings, $314.08; Pictou and Halifax Co., $312.58; Colchester, $305.88.

The general average for male teachers of the second class was $255.45, as compared with $260.57 in 1891. The three highest averages were Digby, $359.06; Shelburne, $296.79; Yarmouth, $296.06.

The Provincial average for female teachers of the second class was $224.24, as compared with $223.06 in 1891. The three highest averages were:—Halifax City, $362.00; Yarmouth, $257.97; Halifax Co., $252.06.

The Provincial average for male teachers of the third class was $180.05, as compared with $185.93 in 1891. The three highest averages were:—Cumberland, $316.04; Yarmouth, $256.04; Digby, $237.70.

The Provincial average for female teachers of the third class was $158.43, as compared with $163.56 in 1891. The three highest averages were:—Halifax City, $300.00; Yarmouth, $173.65; Queens, $168.54.

EXAMINATION FOR TEACHERS' LICENSES.

Table X contains in detail the statistics of the last annual examination for teachers' licenses. The following is a summary:—

In 1892 the total number of candidates examined, 1431; in 1891, 1334; increase, 97.

Number of candidates examined for Academic Licenses in 1892, 22; in 1891, 11; increase, 11.

Number examined for First Class License (Grade B,) 1892, 196; in 1891, 165; increase, 31. Licenses issued in 1892, 56; in 1891, 46; increase, 10. Divided between the sexes the results stand as follows: Total number of male candidates, 1892, 104; in 1891, 87; increase, 17. Number of licenses issued to male candidates, 1892, 30; 1891, 20; increase, 10. Total number of female candidates, 1892, 92; 1891, 78; increase, 14. Number of licenses issued to female candidates, 1892, 26; 1891, 26.

Total number of candidates examined for Second Class (Grade C,) 1892, 742; in 1891, 703; increase, 39. Total number of licenses issued to Second Class candidates, 1892, 238; in 1891. 225; increase, 13. Sub-divided in relation to sex these items stand: Number of male candidates 1892, 152; 1891, 175; decrease, 23. Number of licenses issued to male candidates 1892, 48; 1891, 70; decrease, 22. Total number of female candidates 1892, 590; 1891, 528; increase, 62. Number of licenses issued to female candidates 1892, 190; 1891, 155; increase, 35.

Total number of candidates for Third Class (Grade D) licenses, 1892, 471; 1891, 455; increase, 16. Total number of licenses issued to Third Class candidates, 1892, 121; 1891, 103; increase, 18. Analyzed in relation to sex these items stand: number of male candidates, 1892, 96; 1891, 102; decrease, 6. Number of licenses issued to male candidates, 1892, 19; 1891, 23; decrease, 4. Total number of female candidates, 1892, 375; 1891, 353; increase 22. Number of licenses issued to female candidates, 1892, 102; 1891, 80; increase, 22.

Of the whole number of applicants for licenses, 420 received the class applied for, in comparison with 379 in 1891, an increase of 41. 831 received licenses of some grade as compared with 698 in 1891, a increase of 133, while 600 failed to obtain licenses of any kind, in comparison with 636 in 1891. Of the candidates obtaining license, 180 simply maintained the grade previously held, a comparative increase of 44, while 29 sank to a lower class. The number of candidates holding license prior to the examination and succeeding in obtaining an advance of grade was 175, as compared with 150 in 1891, an increase of 25. The number obtaining for the first time licenses of some class was 447, as compared with 392, an increase of 55.

The examinations are uniform for each class of license respectively, and are conducted by printed questions and written answers. The written papers are valued (in parts of 100) by the Provincial Examiners, who have no means of knowing either the personality or the residence of the candidate. Licenses valid throughout the Province are issued under the seal of the Council of Public Instruction to all successful candidates. For the due protection of the interests both of the Province and of candidates, awards are in all cases made in strict accordance with the published Standards of Examination. All possible pains are taken that the questions of a given year, while avoiding repetition, shall not differ too sharply in point of difficulty from those of the preceding examination, proper allowance of course being made for the general progress of education in the country. The following table, showing the *percentages* of successful applicants in each of the three lower classes during the past twelve years, will be of interest. It may be observed that, as a rule, whenever the number of applicants for any grade has been exceptionally large, the percentage for that year shows a more or less marked decline.

	First Class, Grade B.		Second Class, Grade C.		Third Class, Grade D.	
Percentage of applicants who received the License applied for.						
	Male.	Female.	Male.	Female.	Male.	Female.
1881	41	57	44	45	41	39
1882	49	45	38	36	25	40
1883	45	59	36	35	29	45
1884	49	53	32	41	36	50
1885	43	58	43	41	34	35
1886	45	41	40	40	30	23
1887	33	26	40	33	27	21
1888	55	51	34	33	31	34
1889	23	28	27	26	32	34
1890	52	56	33	31	37	35
1891	23	33	40	29	22	22
1892	29	28	31	32	20	27

STUDIES OF PUPILS.

Table VI contains a statement of the number of pupils receiving instruction in the various branches, according to the provisions of the Course of Study for Common Schools and that for High Schools respectively. The following summary is given to promote convenience, but the details as furnished in the table will repay investigation.

COMMON SCHOOL COURSE—(Eight Grades.)

	Winter Term.	Summer Term.
Total Registration...................	82,965	87,189
Oral Lessons on Health................	47,995	51,701
" " Temperance	46,244	49,523
" " Moral and Patriotic Duties	42,705	47,116
" Nature (familiar objects, phenomena and laws)...	53,262	57,572
Singing (theory)......................	13,832	13,338
" (by rote)......................	29,163	27,504
Reading, Grades I–VIII..........	78,054	80,213
Spelling, " II–VIII..........	67,340	62,446
Language, " I–VI.	54,497	60,028
Grammar, " VII and VIII......	17,152	13,850
Composition, " " "	11,803	10,219
Geography, " III–VIII..........	48,911	46,172
History, " V–VIII..........	29,039	26,322
Arithmetic, " I–VIII..........	75,770	78,622
Algebra, Grade VIII..............	5,476	4,657
Geometry, " "	2,862	2,730
Writing, Grades I–VIII..........	74,682	76,564
Drawing, " I–VIII..........	38,634	43,508
Book-keeping, Grade VIII...............	4,323	2,693
Latin, " " ...!..........	201	168

HIGH SCHOOL COURSE.—(3 Years.)

(Attendance in the County Academies is included.)

	Winter Term.	Summer Term.
English Language..............	3414	2724
English Literature..............	1071	652
Geography	3325	2998
History....	3337	3139
Arithmetic....	3390	3194
Geometry	3183	3061
Algebra	3312	3059
Practical Mathematics...........	342	377
Drawing	1165	1401
Book-keeping..................	2428	2004
Physics.......................	800	520
Botany........................ ...	632	1678
Chemistry (Inorganic)...........	727	518
Chemistry (Agricultural)	187	170
Physiology	341	342
Geology	21	37
Latin	1386	1323
Greek	269	219
French........................	643	725
German	68	32

EXPENDITURE :—(See Tables XIII., XIV., XV.)

The total Government expenditure for Education was $216,329.73, as compared with $213,905.01, an increase of $2524.72. The principal item of expenditure, the total of grants to teachers, is now fixed by law.

The following are the aggregates of teachers' grants for the past fourteen years :—

1878............................	$150,455 97
1879............................	151,655 38
1880......	143,493 92
1881.....	148,173 50
1882...........................	149,058 22
1883.............................	149,761 50
1884............................	153,694 00
1885............................. ...	160,513 55
1886......	167,184 97
1887.............................	172,067 28
1888............................	167,504 81
1889	167,500 00
1890........	167,500 00
1891.............................	167,487 58
1892.............................	167,498 85

A detailed statement of the distribution of the grants for the winter term of 1891-92 was published, as the law directs, in the *Journal of Education* for August last. A similar statement for the summer term is awaiting publication in the forthcoming issue of that periodical in April.

COUNTY.

The provisions of the law for the levying and apportionment of the County Fund are as follows:—

" The Clerk of the Municipality in each county, except as hereinafter provided in relation to the City of Halifax, shall add to the sum annually voted for general municipal purposes, at the regular meeting of the Council, a sum sufficient, after deducting costs of collecting and probable loss, to yield an amount equal to thirty cents for every inhabitant of the Municipality, according to the last census preceding the issue of the municipal rate-roll; and the sum so added shall form and be a portion of the municipal rates. One-half the sum thus raised shall be paid semi-annually by the Municipal Treasurer upon the order of the Superintendent of Education."

" One-half of the amount provided to be raised annually, as aforesaid, shall, at the close of each half year, be apportioned to the Trustees of Schools conducted in accordance with this chapter, to be applied to the payment of teachers' salaries; and each school shall be entitled to participate therein at the rate of twelve and a half dollars per term for each licensed teacher employed, and the balance of the municipal fund shall be distributed among the schools according to the average number of pupils in attendance and the length of time in operation, but shall receive no allowance for being in session more than the prescribed number of days in any one half year."

The gross annual amount of the County Fund for the entire Province is now $120,127.75. Under the above provisions, as modified by the Acts in relation to the education of the Blind and of the Deaf and Dumb, the County Fund for 1891-92 was appropriated as follows :

Paid to trustees in proportion to the average number of
    pupils and length of time schools were in operation $65,512 41
Paid to trustees in respect to teachers employed....... 50,647 84
Paid to Halifax School for the Blind................. 1,237 50
Paid Institution for the Deaf and Dumb............. 2,730 00

SECTIONAL.

The total sectional assessments for the direct support of schools, as reported, amount to $313,229.32, a decrease of $28,426.43. The sum levied throughout the Province for building and repair of school houses was $96,788.05, an increase of $45,366.12. This makes a net increase of $16,939.69.

HIGH SCHOOL WORK.

The changes made in the Statutes and Regulations during the year necessitated a complete revision of all the forms and much of the usual routine of the Department. With the utmost application the details involved by these changes can hardly be matured in time for the successive events of the coming year. This state of affairs combined with the increase of correspondence always incident on extensive changes, prevented me from visiting officially all of the County Academies. Only those whose claims to their academic grants required close investigation were thus examined. Several academies and other schools were visited incidentally as matters of special urgency called me to one part of the province or another. My impressions thus formed were in accord with the inferences naturally deducible from the tables of statistics here presented. There has been a steady advance in the high schools as well as in the common schools.

This fact appears also to be indicated in a decisive manner by the fine buildings which the people are spontaneously raising in the different quarters of the province for the higher educational work as well as for the lower.

The citizens of Digby with a public spirit not excelled in the most wealthy communities have signalized their appreciation of the public educational system by the erection and completion of a costly and ornamental brick structure for its Common Schools and the County Academy. The citizens of Amherst are doing the same, but apparently with the well founded intention of excelling all who have gone before them. And the prospects are, that the coming year will not be without its contribution to the superior class of school buildings in the province.

SCHOOL INSPECTION

requires a word. On our staff of inspectors we have men who are worth more to our country than unobserving people can easily understand. These men combine in an admirable manner, promptness of action, firmness, suavity, and a deep interest in the educational development of their inspectorates. Their steady and well directed energy has in a few years wrought remarkable changes in the general habits and status of teachers and schools in their respective districts. That this is partly due to the personality of the inspector can be easily seen by comparing the general aspect of the profession in different inspectorates after making due allowance for the local constant, and by observing its fluctuations from year to year. The Provincial examination mill grinds out the various classes of teachers with a sort of mechanical uniformity. But the uniformity is by no means uniform. For acclimatization in different inspectorates tends to develop different points of character. The inspector is a bishop in his district; and the right man has a bishop's influence

over teachers and ratepayers, given him the time to make an acquaintance with his diocese.

During the year the work of inspectors was increased in some respects on account of the necessity of instructing many people in the details of the revised order of things. I therefore recommended a single annual inspection of schools known to be running in good order, for the purpose of giving time for the more frequent inspection of schools and localities requiring correction, direction or stimulus. With such men as I hope our staff of inspectors will always continue to be, this method will be much more useful than the imperative two inspections of every school each year, especially under the new regulations. As the statute expressly gave the Superintendent some such power under the two term system, it was not deemed necessary to seek for an amendment of the Act adapted. more especially to the one term system.

Summary of Changes.

There are special reasons why my report should be as brief as possible on this occasion. I make no attempt, therefore, to re-state the reasons for the changes which have been made. Those intimately acquainted with the working of our system know enough already. Others, by referring to the excellent Annual Reports of my predecessor, will find the justification of many of them repeatedly stated in the most convincing manner, in the case of some of them for a period extending over the last ten or eleven years. Signs of the times were above the horizon for years. The only explanation I have to make is as to the manner, not to the matter. It appeared to me most desirable to minimize the period of reconstruction by making as many changes as were specially required simultaneously. These being once accomplished, the trimming of the system will not interfere with its free development. I have gratefully to acknowledge the unexpected courtesy with which our people have to date received the intimation of these changes, the details of the working of which must to very many yet appear obscure. I beg simply to have it remembered, that the coming year will test what has been done under the most trying circumstances. I have the fullest confidence that the result will be fairly successful. I shall, therefore, merely enumerate the leading changes, while I hope to have the consolidated Regulations published for complete information in the April edition of the Department's official organ, the Journal of Education.

1. The school term, one year, opening in August, closing in July, with a summer vacation of six weeks between the dates of closing and opening.

2. The engagement of teachers for a period less than one year illegal, except by express authority from the Inspector under special circumstances.

3. The opening of every school to be immediately reported to the Inspector on the pain of the loss of grants for days taught before notification. ,

4. Annual meeting of section on the last Monday in June (except when special arrangements are made for sections or districts by the C. P. I).

5. Provincial Grants payable in February and July; County Grants payable in July.

6. Registers modified to give fuller statistics.

7. Returns in full to be made only annually.

8. The High School course of study and the syllabus of the " Teachers' Examination" unified.

9. Provincial classification and certification of High School scholarship, admitting to Universities, Normal Schools, Teaching, profession, etc.

10. Candidates for Teachers' licenses having all the other qualifications can obtain licenses whenever they attain the age limit.

11. Premium on Normal School training equal to one grade in class of license.

12. Normal School devoted to professional training and special teaching.

13. Temperance teaching made compulsory in all schools ; the text books for pupils prepared and prescribed ; the examination of all teachers on Hygiene and Temperance ; the exacting of more specific certification as to the good moral character of candidates for the profession.

14. In the common schools, more attention directed to music, writing, drawing, and the practical use of the English language. Memory work, as in Geography and History, lessened. Lessons on Nature made strictly observational—" cram" specially prohibited. In the high schools, the outlining of a higher or post-graduate high school grade for institutions wishing to do such work. The bifurcation of this portion of the course into classical and scientific sides forming the scholarship basis of classical and scientific academic headmaster's licenses. Further, the reduction of the number of examination papers for this grade, from about *thirty*, which for the last twenty-eight years included *both* classical and scientific subjects, to *twenty* on *either* a classical or scientific group. Still further, candidates may pass on these twenty papers in two annual stages. For instance, if an aggregate of 1,000 be made on *ten* or more papers,

one year, the candidate will be required to pass only on papers omitted or "not passed" at the next examination.

By thus narrowing the scope of the students' work to fewer subjects than usual, and by allowing options to accommodate the natural bias of different minds, it is expected in the long run to produce higher and more varied species of scholarship, without so much risk of undue mental application.

THE NORMAL SCHOOL.

The province has already vested a large amount of money in a splendid building, which is shown in our frontispiece. It is our duty from every point of view to make that investment pay as well as possible. Under the past regime the school did good work, as can be evidenced by the higher appreciation of the people as a general rule for Normal School trained teachers. The teacher with genius is of course born, but that the teacher is an exception to the general law that special training is useful, even the genuises must admit. Heretofore our Provincial Normal School was tremendously handicapped. The student who attended it received no more consideration from the government which called it into existence than the law student or theologian who was straining every nerve solely to reach his final profession. I do not mean that these students were not doing what was right. Many of them did excellent service while in the profession, and rightly left it when there was a stronger call for them in another sphere.

Secondly, the government subsidized heavily a number of academies to do very nearly similiar work unburdened by practical training in teaching which counted for nothing in obtaining a license. And thirdly, the Academic Course preparing directly for high university prizes, tended still further to attract the abler students from the Normal School. The good work which it has done while thus handicapped demonstrates an ability in its staff of instructors of which any institution may be proud.

In my next report I hope to be able to say, that our Provincial Normal School, in addition to more fully developing the training in "general and special methodology," in elocution, music, drawing and calisthenics, is also giving a superior course in manual training in wood work, in practical physics and chemistry, and in advanced practical work in the natural sciences bearing on agriculture and other industries. Wood work, not for the purpose of making the teacher a mechanic, but for the purpose of training the hand to execute with precision what a drawing or the mind marks out. Not to enable him or her to make apparatus for the school room or become the trustees' carpenter. Rather to enable the teacher to understand how things may be done, to suggest possibilities, to have it in the air of the school room that manual labor may be as worthy a way of utilizing life as any other kind of labor ; that science, and art, and the farm, and the work-bench are as noble arenas for man's energies as quill-driving or money changing. In other words it is desirable that the training of the teacher will not tend to draw all the clever pupils in the one direction of book-learning and the so-called professions as hitherto, while the knowledge of *things* is so all-important and the industrial vocations so necessary.

But more. With the new building for the Provincial School of Agriculture so near the Normal School, and so luxuriously fitted up with laboratory accommodations (see Appendix E.) for the study of Botany, Entomology, Zoology, and the higher Chemical Analysis, our teachers will have an opportunity of obtaining practical knowledge with the microscope, the scalpel and the chemical balance. With such training superadded to his academic education the teacher will be able to go into a country section with at least a rudimentary knowledge of what is in *it*, as well as of what is in books. His nose will not be continually uptilted above the plane of the horizon with the eyes of his imagination looking down on a far off Eldorado, while he sees nothing around his feet except a desert of rubbish and common place. The upas air of discontent need not taint the nascent ideals of the embryo citizens within his school room. For weed and blade and wild-flower are ever revealing new lights to him. The mossy bank and the lichened-draped trees teach him poetry and science. The droning beetle and the plundering bug can not out manœuvre him. The gravel bank preaches sermons for him of antiquity, more hoary than antiquity. The pebbles by the brook tell their fairy tales of travel when there were no human eyes to follow them, of the times when the foundations of the earth were laid with ceremonials grand and weird but spectatorless. Under such a teacher the dreariest woodland or the rockiest coast would be glorified to the young, who would thus better learn to live in, love and die for such a country. This sentiment has also a practical side. For even a fair elementary knowledge of the *things* in a school section would make the teacher a local seer, who could throw light on much of the ordinary difficulties of the industries of the community. Such a training will enable the teacher and people to sympathise with and aid each other more than is otherwise possible. The clever boys will not be crowded on by the sentiment displayed too often by the former teacher, to forsake industrial work for some clerical profession. For industrial work will be seen in its true light to be compatible with the most perfect physical health, and the enjoyment of the fullest pleasure in the contemplation of the science, the poetry, the beauty, the love and the light in the infinite realm of our environment, while it also contributes directly to the welfare of every element of our common country. Can we not expect our Normal School to develop more of this character in the scholarly men and women they may send out in future; not simply scholars who have managed to think over again what others have thought, but those who are able to explore a new world and understand it. Scholars also, with some training in the fine arts. who with pencil as well as with pen can interest their pupils, picture facts, educate fancy, and open as many avenues as possible for useful and happy lives to the youth of our country.

EDUCATIONAL CONVENTIONS.

During the year, I had the pleasure of attending a large and enthusiastic convention of the Teachers' Association of Kings and Hants, at Hantsport; and another of Annapolis and Digby at Digby. In Appendix E, I publish as a matter of record, reports of these conventions, as they appeared in the EDUCATIONAL REVIEW.

The first meeting of a Dominion Association of teachers at Montreal in July last, is a very important incident in the history of our educational development. Such interprovincial intercourse will undoubtedly be useful more or less to all the provinces; while there are looming up some important educational problems which can be solved only by the co-operation of provincial and perhaps national educational authorities. A report of this convention, also taken from the EDUCATIONAL REVIEW, will be found in Appendix E.

EDUCATIONAL EXHIBIT.

Dr. Saunders, the Canadian Commissioner for the World's Columbian Exposition at Chicago, so forcibly presented the reasons for Nova Scotia's participation in this world's fair, that it was decided to proceed, although the general reorganization of the school system during the year would make the task specially difficult. An appeal to the educational constituency of the province was made through the August JOURNAL OF EDUCATION, and in other papers. Later, a circular outlining in detail a method of procedure and inviting all educational institutions to indicate their existence by contributing a representation of their character and work, was issued to inspectors and others for distribution. The result of this effort properly belongs to my next report. The exhibit will no doubt reflect the educational energy of the different schools, inspectorates, and public institutions of the province; and the official catalogue will preserve the record for comparisons in the future as well as in the present.

APPENDICES.

To make this Report cover as far as desirable the whole field of education throughout the Province, I have appended among many other papers a general view of each one of our Degree conferring institutions. Although the Universities receive no public money, they are intimately interested in and connected with the Public School system. Their acknowledgment of the Junior Leaving "Pass" of the High Schools constitutes a virtual, though partial, affiliation of the two. It seemed fitting, then, that a glimpse of this cope-stone of the educational structure should be given in a Provincial Report.

The Appendices, some of which this year are more voluminous than can be expected hereafter, are classified as follows:

A. Normal School.

B. Inspectors.

C. Halifax schools.

D. Schools for Deaf and Dumb, and the Blind.

E. Other institutions receiving public money or other consider-
ations from the Government, namely: —The Provincial School of
Agriculture, The Halifax Medical College, The Victoria School of
Art and Design, The Summer School of Science, The Kindergartens,
Manual Training, and The Educational Conventions of the year.

F. Universities and degree conferring colleges receiving no
public money from the Provincial treasury.

For the benefit of those who are unacquainted with our educational work, it may not be inappropriate at this time and place to
conclude with a brief conspectus of The Public Free School System
and other Educational Institutions of the Province.

The Public Free School system of Nova Scotia provides for the
free education of every inhabitant of the province, from the age of
five years and upwards, in a prescribed course of study extending
from the Kindergarten or Primary grade of the common schools to
the University or the end of the High School course.   Out of a total
population of 450,000 of all ages, 102,586 pupils were enrolled during the last year.

The common school course consists of eight grades representing a
year's work each for the average pupil who may complete the course
in his fourteenth year. The high school course consists of four grades
additional, enabling the more clever pupils, who have lost no time,
to graduate in their eighteenth or nineteenth year.   The highest
grade is practically a post-graduate course and will generally require
two years.   The prescribed course is here presented, as published in
the Teacher's Register. (The numbers of the paragraphs under
" General Directions" refer to certain columns in the statistical page
of the Register.)

In schools (in country sections, for instance) where several or all
these grades have to be taught in a small school by one teacher, the
order of studies is still indicated by this course ; but the time for
class work in each subject must be correspondingly contracted as
compared with a fully graded school.   In many subjects also the
work of several grades may be taken up in class simultaneously,
under these circumstances, such for instance as callisthenics, music,
hygiene and temperance, moral and patriotic duties, lessons on
nature, etc., etc.   Courses of study and time tables based on this
course but contracted to suit variously graded schools, are also prepared for the guidance of teachers.

COURSE OF STUDY FOR COMMON SCHOOLS.

GENERAL DIRECTIONS.

65. *Callisthenics and Military Drill.*—As often as found expedient; but "physical exercises" should be given once in the middle of every session over one hour in length, and in the lower grades more frequently than in the higher. Recommended, "*Physical Drill,*" (T. C. Allen & Co., Halifax), for the Common and High Schools.

66. *Vocal Music.*—Every pupil (excepting of course those known to be organically defective as respects music), should be able to pass an examination in vocal music, before promotion to a higher grade. For the present the following minimum is prescribed for each grade. At least one simple song with its Tonic Sol-fa notation for Grade I. An additional melody and its notation for each succeeding grade, with a correspondingly increased general knowledge of music. Vocal music may be combined with some forms of "physical exercises" as in marching and light movements. Recommended, "*National and Vacation Songs,*" (Grafton & Sons, Montreal), for Common and High Schools. Teachers musically defective may comply with the law by having these lessons given by any one qualified.

67. *Hygiene and Temperance.*—Orally in all grades, and as incidents or occasions may suggest. Text Book for pupils' use as follows: Grades V and VI, Health Reader No. 1. Grades VII and VIII, Health Reader No. 2.

68.—*Moral and Patriotic Duties.*—As enjoined by the School Law and when found most convenient and effective.

69.—*Lessons on Nature.*—The observation, examination and study of the common and more important natural objects and laws of nature as they are exemplified within the range of the School Section or of the pupils' observations. Under this head pupils should not be required to memorize notes or facts which they have not at least to some extent actually observed or verified for themselves.

70. *Spelling and Dictation.*—It should be strictly insisted upon that, from the very commencement in the first grade, the pupil should spell every word read in lessons, and common words of similar difficulty used in his conversation. Writing words in the lower grades. Transcription and dictation in the higher grades should be utilized more and more as facility in writing increases.

71.—*Reading and Elocution.*—1. Pupils must be enabled to clearly understand the portion to be read, then to read it with proper expression. 2. Faults of enunciation, pronunciation, etc., of tone, of posture and manner, etc., must be carefully noted and corrected. 3. Choice passages should be memorized occasionally for recitation with the proper expression. Ten lines per year at least for Grade I, twenty lines at least for Grade II, and a similar increase for each succeeding grade, is prescribed. Reading should be taught at first, partly at least, by word building from the phonic elements, occasional drills of this kind being continued in all the grades to obtain clear enunciation.

72. *English.*—In all grades practice should constantly be given in expressing the substance of stories, lessons, or observations, orally in correct language, and in the higher grades in writing also.   Discussion of subject matter of lesson.   Attention to the use of capitals, punctuation marks, paragraphing, etc., should be introduced gradually and regularly, so that at the end of the common school course,. language in correct form can be fluently used in description or business letters, orally and in writing.   The practical rather than the theoretical knowledge of English is what is specially required in the common school, and a large proportion of the school time should be .given to it.   Pupils should be continually exercised in finding synonyms or substituting "their own made meanings" for difficult words in their reading lessons, instead of memorizing definitions often given at head of lesson.

73. *Writing.*—Styles most easy to read should be cultivated. Simple, vertical writing is generally preferable to the sloping styles. No exercise in writing should be accepted by the teacher from the pupil unless its form shows evidence of care.   Should begin in the first grade with letters formed from the simpler elements properly classified, and taught in the order of difficulty.

77. *Drawing.*—Langdon S. Thompson's " Manual Training, No. 1," is recommended to the teacher as covering to some extent the *Drawing* and *Lessons on Nature* as they may be taught to pupils of the first five or six grades.   With Thompson's Primary Freehand Manual, in addition, the teacher will have a sufficient guide for the work in drawing up to Grade VII for the present.   The " American Drawing Cards," *first* and *second* series, may also be advantageously used to this stage.   Drawing of objects studied under the head of Nature Lessons to be constantly practised, and carried on even in the High School.

78. *Arithmetic.*—It is of the highest importance to secure the habit of obtaining accurate answers at the *first* attempt.   Every " slip " in mental or written arithmetical work is not only unnecessary, but is a positive education in a habit which will tend to render useless the most strenuous efforts afterwards to become accurate or even to make satisfactory progress in mathematics.   Accuracy is of supreme importance from the first.   Rapidity may then be neglected to look after itself.   In the first four grades the teacher will have to prepare a great number of exercises of a nature not specially arranged for in the present prescribed text book, so that the pupils may be accurate and rapid in their operations up to the limit prescribed.

75 and 76. *Geography and History.*—The verbal memorizing of these lessons at home by the pupil is for the most part injurious to the character of the memory and useless as practical knowledge. For in spite of all cautions and instructions to the contrary, most pupils when left to themselves mentally associate the facts memorized with the wording, the paragraph and the page of a book, instead of with the proper locus in the map, or with the proper system of related facts. These lessons should therefore be prepared under the careful and philosophic direction of the teacher in the schoolroom, at least until the pupils are trained how to study aright. The home work would then be only the review and perfecting of the lesson by the pupils in the proper manner by reference to the several items in the text. Local or current events, historical, economic or scientific, should be skilfully used to interpret the remote in time and place.

90. *Manual Training.*—(Optional). This may often be introduced as an alterative or recreation, and without therefore materially increasing the real labor of the pupil. Clay modeling, needle-work, wood-work, etc., as may be most appropriate or expedient, may be introduced with the consent of the Trustees. Teachers should at all times encourage the pupils in the production of any specimens of home-made handiwork or apparatus, in scientific experiments at home, and in the formation of collections of plants, minerals, and other natural productions of their own part of the country.

SPECIAL DIRECTIONS.

GRADE I.

Reading.—Primer with Wall Cards or Blackboard work.

Language.—Story-telling by pupil. Writing easy script letters, words and sentences.

Writing and Drawing.—Writing on slate, paper or blackboard. Drawing of easy, interesting figures.

Arithmetic.—All fundamental arithmetical operations with numbers, the results of which do not exceed 20, to be done with concrete and abstract numbers, accurately and rapidly.

Lessons on Nature.—Power of accurate observation developed by exercising each of the senses on simple or appropriate objects. Estimation of direction, distance, magnitude, weight, &c., begun. Common colors, simple regular solids, surfaces and lines. Simple observations on a few common minerals, stones, plants and animals.

GRADE II.

Reading.—Reader No. 1.

Language.—As in Grade I., but more advanced.

Writing and Drawing.—As in Grade 1, but more advanced. Angles, triangles, squares, rectangles, plan of platform and of school room.

Arithmetic.—Numbers up to 100 on the same plan as in Grade I.

Lessons on Nature.—As in Grade I., but more extended.

GRADE III.

Reading.—Reader No. 2.

Language.—As in II., but more advanced. Subject and predicate. Nouns and verbs.

Writing and Drawing.—Script letters on slate and in copy book; Freehand outlines on slate, blackboard, &c. Common geometrical lines and figures with their names. Map of school grounds and surroundings.

Arithmetic.—Number to 1000 as in previous grades, divisors not to exceed 12. Dollars and cents. Long Measure and Avoirdupois Weight, with reduction exercises.

Lessons on Nature.—Geography of neighborhood, use of local or county maps. Estimation of distance, measures, weights, &c., continued. Color. Study of, say, three or four each of common metals, stones, earths, flowers, shrubs, trees, insects, birds and mammals.

GRADE IV.

Reading.—Reader No. 3.

Language.—Oral statements of matter of lessons, observations, &c. Written sentences with punctuation, &c. Modifiers of subject and predicate, of noun and verb.

Writing and Drawing.—Copy Book. Primary Freehand Series No. 1., and Cards, &c.

Geography.—Oral lessons on the seasons as in pages VII. to X. of Elementary Geography, with the general geography of the Province begun on the school map.

Arithmetic.—Numeration and notation extended. More difficult exercises in fundamental rules and reduction. Common tables of weights, measures, etc., idea of fractions developed. Mental Arithmetic drill increasing.

Lessons on Nature.—As in grade III., but extended so as to include as many more new objects of each kind.

GRADE V.

Reading.—Reader No. 4, Part I.

Language.—As in Grade IV. and General Directions. All parts of speech and of sentence with inflections of noun, adjective and pronoun, orally. Composition practice increasing.

Writing and Drawing.—Copy Book. Freehand Drawing Series No. II., and Cards, etc.

Geography and History.—Ideas of latitude and longitude, etc., developed. Oral geography of Nova Scotia on map in fuller detail. General geography of Provinces of Canada and of the Continent, as on the Hemisphere maps. Oral lessons on leading incidents of Nova Scotian History.

Arithmetic.—As in first three and one half chapters of Kirkland and Scott's Arithmetic with reasonable rapidity.

Lessons on Nature.—From mineral and rock to soil, as shown in neighborhood, and, say, five or six each of the common plants, trees, insects, other invertebrates, fish, reptiles, birds, mammals, and natural phenomena, such as ventilation, evaporation, freezing, closely examined. Health Reader, No. I. begun.

GRADE VI.

Reading.—Reader No. 4. completed.

Language.—As in Grade V. extended. Formal compositions (simple essays) twice each month. Paradigm of regular verb. Simple parsing and analysis begun. More important rules of Syntax applied. Short descriptive sketches and letters. All from oral instruction.

Writing and Drawing.—Copy Book. Drawing No. 3, and Cards, etc. Increasing practice in representing common objects in outline.

Geography.—Elementary Geography text, to end of Canada. Thorough drill in outline of Hemisphere maps.

History.—British American History; text, chapters 3, 5, 10, 11, 12, 13, (in part) and 14.

Arithmetic.—As in chapters 4 to 6, Kirkland and Scott, (omitting circulating decimals), with continual review and mental exercises.

Lessons on Nature.—As in Grade V., but extended, say to at least nine or ten objects of each class specified. Distribution and values of all natural products of the Province. Health Reader No. 1. completed.

GRADE VII.

Reading.—Reader No. 5. begun. Character of metre and figures of speech begun to be observed.

Grammar.—Leading principles of Etymology (large type generally), with paradigms as in prescribed text, and exercises, with related rules of Syntax. Parsing and analysis to complex sentences.

Composition.—Written abstracts of oral or reading lessons. Simple discription, narrative and business forms. Punctuation and paragraphing.

Writing and Drawing.—Copy book. Drawing No. 4, and Cards, &c. Plotting of lines, triangles, rectangles, &c., according to scale. Simple object drawing extended.

Geography.—Elementary Geography to end of Europe, with thorough map drill.

History.—British American History completed.

Arithmetic.—As in Kirkland and Scott to end of chapter 7, with corresponding mental exercises.

Lessons on Nature.—As in Grade VI., and with the study of specimens illustrating the stones, minerals, etc. ; each class, sub-class and division of plants ; and each class of animals found in the locality. All common and easily observed physical phenomena. The Introductory Science Primer, and Health Reader No. 2 begun.

GRADE VIII.

Reading.—No. 5 completed. Elements of prosody and plain figures of speech, as illustrated in readings, to be observed and studied.

Spelling.—Prescribed Speller in addition to general directions.

Grammar.—Including rules of Syntax, (omitting *notes* and more difficult matter in medium print). Parsing. Analysis of simple and easy complex sentences. Correction of false Syntax.

Composition.—As in Grade VII. extended. Pupils at this stage should be able to express themselves fluently and with fair accuracy in writing, for all ordinary business purposes.

Writing and Drawing.—Copy Book. Thompson's Drawing, Model and Object Series, No. 1. Construction of angles and simple geometrical figures to scale and their measurement.

Geography.—Elementary Geography completed and reviewed with latest corrections and map drill.

History.—As in "Brief History of England," with review of British American History.

Arithmetic.—As in Kirkland and Scott.

Algebra.—Fundamental rules, with special drill on the evaluation of algebraic expressions.

Book-keeping.—A simple set.

Lessons on Nature.—As in Grade VII., extended to bear on Agriculture, Horticulture and any local industry of the School Section. Oral lessons from Science Primers—especially the Chemistry Primer. Health Reader No. 2, completed.

HIGH SCHOOL CURRICULUM.

The subjects, number and value of the papers for the different High School examinations, and the general scope of examination questions, are indicated in the prescribed curriculum which follows. Examination questions may demand description by drawing as well as by writing in all grades.

GRADE IX. or D.

1. ENGLISH LANGUAGE—100 : (a) 6th Reader, Part I., (or an author prescribed from year to year), with critical study, word analysis, prosody and recitations ; (b) Text-book on English Composition, with essays, abstracts and general correspondence.

2. ENGLISH GRAMMAR—100 : Text-book (excepting "notes," and "appendix") with easy exercises in parsing and analysis.

3. LATIN—100 : As in *Collar and Daniell,* to end of Chapter LIII., or any equivalent grammar with very easy translation and composition exercises. [To secure uniformity in pronunciation the *Roman* (or Phonetic) pronunciation of Latin is recommended to be used in all grades.]

4. FRENCH—100 : As in *French Principia,* Part I., or any equivalent with easy translation and composition exercises.

5. HISTORY AND GEOGRAPHY — 100 : (a) Text-book of British History up to the House of Tudor, and review of British American History. (b) Geography of North America and Europe as in Text-book.

6. SCIENCE—100 : (a=30) Physics as in *Balfour Stewart's Primer.* (b=70) Botany as in *Gray's How Plants Grow,* substituting for the details of "Flora," Part II., common or prescribed native plants. Drawing of parts of plants.

7. DRAWING AND BOOK-KEEPING—100: (a=20) Construction of geometrical figures and solution of easy mensuration and trigonometrical problems by mathematical instruments. (b=30) Freehand drawing as in Nos. 5 and 6, and "Model and Object drawing," No. 2, prescribed Text-books. (c=50) Commercial forms and writing with Single Entry Book-keeping problems.

8. ARITHMETIC—100: As in *Hamblin Smith* to end of section 21, (with a practical knowledge of the metric system, which will be required in all grades.)

9. ALGEBRA—100: As in *Todhunter* to end of fractions.

10. GEOMETRY—100: Euclid I., with very easy exercises.

NOTE.—Latin and French are optional; all others imperative. The minimum aggregate for a "pass" is 400, with no subject below 25.

GRADE X. or C.

1. ENGLISH LANGUAGE—100: (a) 6th Reader, Part II. (or an author prescribed from year to year), with critical study, &c., as in previous grade but more advanced: (b) Advanced Text-book of English Composition with practical work. [1893 (a) 6th Reader, Part II., and *Evangeline.*]

2. ENGLISH GRAMMAR—100: (a) Text-book (excepting "appendix"), completed with exercises in parsing and analysis.

3. LATIN—100: As in *Collar and Daniell*, complete, and "*Cæsar's Invasion of Britain*," by Welsh and Duffield, (MacMillan & Co., London).

4. GREEK—100: As in *Frost's Greek Primer* (Allyn & Bacon, Boston) to end of Part III., or *Initia Græca*, Part I.

5. FRENCH—100: As in *French Principia*, Parts I. and II. or any equivalent.

6. GERMAN—100: As in *German Principia*, Part I. or any equivalent.

7. HISTORY AND GEOGRAPHY—100:—(a) Text-Book of British History from House of Tudor to present time. (b) Text-book of Geography, excepting North America and Europe.

8. SCIENCE—100: (a=70) Chemistry as in *Williams.* (b=30) Mineralogy as in *Crosby's Common Rocks,* or Agricultural Chemistry as in *Tanner.*

9. DRAWING AND BOOK-KEEPING—100: (a) Mathematical drawing as in previous grade continued with prescribed Text-books Nos.

7 and 8, and Model and Object drawing No. 3.   (b) Book-keeping—
Double Entry forms and problems.

10.   ARITHMETIC—100 : Text-book completed without appendix.

11.   ALGEBRA—100 : As in *Todhunter* to end of simple equations,
including involution and evolution.

12.   GEOMETRY—100 : Text book with exercises to Prop. 20,
Book III.

NOTE.—Latin, Greek, French and German optional ; all others
imperative.   The minimum aggregate for a pass, 400, with no subject below 25.

GRADE XI or B.

1.   ENGLISH LITERATURE—100 : (a) Prose authors prescribed
from year to year, with critical study.   (b) Poetical authors prescribed as above.   [1893, (a) Macaulay's *Warren Hastings*.   (b)
Shakespeare's *Hamlet*.]

2.   ENGLISH GRAMMAR—100 : (a) History of English Language
and Text-book completed with difficult exercises.   (b) History of
English Literature; selected portions from *Stopford Brooke's Primer*.
(Spenser, Shakespeare, Bacon and Milton, with Chapters VI, VII
and VIII.)

3.   LATIN—100 : Grammar and easy composition partly based on
prose author read.

4.   LATIN—100 : (a) *Cæsar*, one book ; (b) *Virgil*, one book, as
prescribed from year to year, with grammatical and critical questions.
[1893, (a) *De Bell, Gal.*, Book V.   (b) *Æneid*, Book III.]

5.   GREEK—100 : Grammar and easy composition based partly
on author read.

6.   GREEK—100 : *Xenophon*, one book as prescribed from year
to year with grammatical and critical questions.   [1893, (a) *Anabasis*, Book I.]

7.   FRENCH—100 : *Brachet's Public School Elementary French
Grammar*, or an equivalent, and composition with author prescribed
from year to year.   (1893, Souvestre's *Un Philosophe sous les toits*.)

8.   GERMAN—100 : *German Principia* Parts I and II, or an
equivalent.

9.   HISTORY AND GEOGRAPHY—100 : General History and Geography as in *Swinton*.

10. PHYSIOLOGY—100 : As in prescribed text, *Martin's " The Human Body and the Effects of Narcotics."*

11. PHYSICS—100 : As in *Gage's Introduction* to Physical Science.

12. PRACTICAL MATHEMATICS—100 : As in *Eaton.*

13. ALGEBRA AND ARITHMETIC—100 : As in *Todhunter's* Algebra and *Hamblin Smith's* Arithmetic.

14. GEOMETRY—100 : Euclid I to IV with exercises ; definitions and algebraic demonstrations of Euclid V ; and Euclid VI (text).

NOTE.—Latin, Greek. French and German optional ; all others imperative. The minimum aggregate for a pass, 400, with no subject below 25. The examination on this syllabus may also be known as the Junior Leaving Examination of the High School.

GRADE XII or A.

The examination on this syllabus may be known as the Senior Leaving Examination of the High School. This portion of the course of study may be profitably undertaken in the lines best adapted to the staff of instructors or the demands of students in the larger Higher Schools or County Academies. There is in this grade a bifurcation of the course into a classical side and a scientific side, with minor options leading to the certificates of " A " (classical) and " A " (scientific) respectively.

(A.) IMPERATIVE FOR BOTH SIDES.

1. ENGLISH LANGUAGE—100 : As in *Lounsbury's English Language*, with prescribed authors.   (1893, Scott's *Ivanhoe.)*

2. ENGLISH LITERATURE—100 : *Stopford Brooke's Primer*, with prescribed authors.   (1893, Tennyson's *Princess.*)

3 BRITISH HISTORY—100 : As in *Green's Short History of the English People*, with the Canadian Constitution.

4. PSYCHOLOGY—100 : As in James' Text Book of Psychology (MacMillan & Co., London), or Maher's (Stoneyhurst Series.)

5. SANITARY SCIENCE—100 : As in the Ontario Manual of Hygiene.

(B.) IMPERATIVE FOR CLASSICAL SIDE, (Subjects for 1893.)

1. LATIN GRAMMAR AND COMPOSITION—100 : Grammar as in *Allen and Greenough*, and Composition as in *Bradley's Arnold* or equivalents.

2. CÆSAR—100 : *De Bell Gal.*, Books V and VI.

3. CICERO AND TACITUS—100 : (a) Cicero.—*Pro Lege Manilia.* (b) Tacitus—*Historia,* Book I to end of Chapter 45.

4. VIRGIL—100 : *Æneid,* Book III.

5. HORACE—100 : *Odes,* Book IV.

6. ROMAN HIST. AND GEOG.—100 : As in *Liddell's.*

7. GREEK GRAMMAR AND COMPOSITION—100 : Grammar as in *Goodwin,* and Composition as in *Fletcher & Nicholson,* or equivalents.

8. XENOPHON—100 : *Anabasis,* Books II and III.

9. DEMOSTHENES—100 : *De Corona,* to end of 220th paragraph.

10. EURIPIDES—100: *Alcestis.*

11. GRECIAN HIST. AND GEOG.—100 : As in *Smith's.*

(C.) IMPERATIVE FOR SCIENTIFIC SIDE.

1. PHYSICS—100 : As in Wormell's *Natural Philosophy.*

2. CHEMISTRY—100 : As in Wilson's *Inorganic Chemistry.*

3. BOTANY—100: As in *The Essentials of Botany* by Bessey (Henry Holt & Co., New York), with a practical knowledge of representative species of Nova Scotian flora.

4. ZOOLOGY—100: As in *Dawson's Hand-Book,* with dissection of Nova Scotian species, as in *Colton's Practical Zoology.*

5. GEOLOGY—100: As in Sir William Dawson's *Hand-Book of Canadian Geology* (excepting the details relating to other Provinces from page 167 to 235.)

6. ASTRONOMY—100: As in *Young's Elements of Astronomy.*

7. NAVIGATION—100 : As in *Norie's Epitome.*

8. TRIGONOMETRY—100 : *Lock's Elementary Trigonometry.*

9. ALGEBRA—100: As in Hall & Knight's *Higher Algebra,* (MacMillan & Co., London), to end of Chap. XXVI, or any equivalent.

10. GEOMETRY—100 : Including *Euclid VI, XI and XII,* as in *Hamblin Smith* with exercises.

(D.) OPTIONAL FOR BOTH SIDES.

1. FRENCH GRAMMAR AND COMPOSITION—100.

2. FRENCH AUTHORS—100 : (1893, Voltaire, *Charles XII,* Books I, II and III, and Racine's *Athalie.*)

3. GERMAN GRAMMAR AND COMPOSITION—100.

4. GERMAN AUTHORS—100 : (1893, Hauff's *Das Kalte Herz,* Heath & Co., Boston.)

To pass Grade A (scientific) a minimum aggregate of 1000 must be made on twenty papers, including all in groups (A) and (C) and any other *five* papers.

To pass Grade A (classical) a minimum aggregate of 1000 must be made on twenty papers, including all in groups (A) and (B) and any other *four* papers.

The old Grade A may be quoted as Grade A (classical.)

Those who obtain an A (scientfic) or A (classical) certificate will be allowed to pass an examination on all other papers of the full syllabus than those taken previously by them, and if successful will be granted the diploma " A (classical and scientific)." For the same diploma, former Grade A teachers must also take " Psychology " and " Sanitary Science ;" but their Grade A " Physics " or " Chemistry " or " Geometry " or " French " shall for this purpose be deemed the equivalents, respectively, of the papers (C) 1 or 2 or 10, or (D) 1.

Candidates for this grade of certificate who make the minimum passing aggregate but fail to pass on account of deficiency in one or more subjects, will be allowed a supplementary examination at a future terminal examination on all the subjects on which they made less than 50 per cent ; and if 50 per cent. of the maximum is made on each of such subjects the candidates shall be awarded an " A " certificate.

[Changes in Authors, etc., from year to year, announced in the JOURNAL OF EDUCATION, published semi-annually.]

COMMON SCHOOL LEAVING, OR COUNTY ACADEMY ENTRANCE EXAMINATION.

At the end of each school year, during the first week in July, a public written examination lasting two days, is held at each county academy (which is the high school in each county receiving a special Provincial grant of money for the free education of all in the county who are qualified to enter). The examination questions are sent out from the Education Department, and cover specially the work of the highest grade of the common schools. The examinations are held simultaneously in each county throughout the Province under strict and uniform conditions. The candidates' papers are examined by the principal of each academy and his staff, according to a prescribed plan. The successful candidates are entitled to Provincial certificates signed by the principals of the academies, which certificates will admit them without the payment of any fee into their respective county academies.

PROVINCIAL HIGH SCHOOL EXAMINATIONS.

During the same week all students of high school grade, whether studying in the academies or other high schools, are allowed to present themselves without fee for examination at one of the thirty Provincial stations, on any one of the four high school grades. The examination papers are sent out from the Education Department, and the candidates' papers are examined by one and the same Board of Examiners.

Provincial certificates of the *first, second, third* and *last* year of the high school, known also as Grades D, C, B, and A, respectively, are awarded on the report of the examiners. These certificates indicate definite grades of scholarship and are accepted as such for the non-professional qualifications of the various classes of teachers, for matriculation into the universities and technical colleges. The high school system is virtually a Provincial university of high school grade, and every academy and high school an affiliated college, the diplomas being granted on the report of the Provincial Board of Examiners. All teachers for the public schools must obtain a high school certificate of one of these grades before applying for a license to teach.

TEACHERS.

There are four classes of teachers whose qualifications are the high school certificates of Grade A, B, C and D respectively, with the corresponding Normal School training.

1. *Class A*, (which may be either " A, Classical " or " A, Scientific," according to the high school certificate). Teachers of this class contribute to the qualifications of county academies for obtaining the Provincial or academic grants when employed in them. When employed in other high school, they are entitled to a Provincial grant approximating $220, $180 or $120 per annum, in addition to salary from their school trustees according to the class of school.

2. *Class B*, whose Provincial grant as above approximates $120 per annum.

3. *Class C*, whose Provincial Grant approximates $90, and

4. *Class D*, whose Provincial grant approximates $60 per annum.

Teachers who have not the prescribed Normal School classification, but who have passed the Provincial examinations on School Law and Management, Teaching, Hygiene and Temperance, can obtain a class of license one grade lower than the corresponding Normal School classification would give. This examination is called the " Minimum Professional Qualification Examination," and with a grade D, will qualify only for a class D, (Provisional), good for one year. Teachers are also subject to strict conditions of character and age.

PROVINCIAL GRANTS TO TEACHERS.

These grants were originally fixed at the figures given above, until their total rose gradually to $167,500 annually. Then by Act of Legislature this sum was fixed as an annual total, and the grants to the various classes of teachers were directed to be paid out of it in the same *ratio* as before. The advance in the number and rank of teachers tends, therefore, to a reduction of the original amount to each class.

COUNTY ACADEMY GRANTS.

Classified by the amounts of the annual grants from the Provincial Treasury, there are four grades of county academies.

$500. *One* "Class A" teacher, a minimum average of *fifteen* regularly qualified high school pupils, with appropriate buildings, apparatus and salary.

$1000. *Two* Class A teachers, a minimum average of *forty*, and the other requirements in the same proportion as above.

$1500. *Three* Class A teachers, and a minimum average of *eighty*, &c.

$1720. *Four* or more Class A teachers, and a minimum average of *one hundred and twenty*, &c.

THE SCHOOL SECTION

is the smallest territorial division of the Province, averaging about four miles in diameter, with the school house near the centre. There are 1905 at present. Their boundaries are determined by the Board of School Commissioners, the formation of new sections requiring the ratification of the Council of Public Instruction.

THE BOARD OF SCHOOL COMMISSIONERS

is appointed by the Provincial Government, to adjudicate on matters specially connected with school sections, over a district on an average perhaps equal to half a county.

THE BOARD OF THREE TRUSTEES

is the executive body of the school section. Each year one of the trustees retires at the annual meeting of the ratepayers of the section and a new trustee is elected. The Board of Trustees, through its Secretary, collects and disburses the money voted at the annual meeting to be assessed on the section, engages the teacher, takes charge of the school property, etc. In towns which are incorporated, a committee of three from the Town Council, with three commissioners appointed by the Provincial Government, have the power of this Board. In the city of Halifax, twice as many, respectively.

THE ANNUAL MEETING

of the school section is held on the last Monday of June. It is then the Board of Trustees reports its transactions for the year to the ratepayers, and brings down an estimate of the amount of money required to be raised by assessment for the ensuing year. It is then the new trustee is elected, and the money to be assessed on the section is voted.

THE SCHOOL FUNDS

are not dependent on the sectional assessment alone. In the county assessment, an amount equal to thirty cents per head of the population is levied to form a fund called the county school fund. At the end of the year, when the section returns are approved, on the order of the Superintendent, twenty-five dollars are paid out of this fund to the Board of Trustees of each section for each teacher engaged, and the balance of the fund is divided between the sections in proportion to the total days' attendance made in each school. The trustees, then, obtain money from the sectional assessment and the county fund. The teacher in addition to the salary paid from the funds of the trustees receives a grant, already referred to, from the Provincial Treasury in proportion to the class of license held. Assessment last year on sections for support of schools, over $313,000; for building and repairs, about $97,000. Total assessment on sections, $410,000. Received from county fund, over $120,-000. Total raised by assessment, over $530,000.

THE SCHOOL YEAR

begins on the 1st of August, and consists of a maximum of forty-four teaching weeks, commencing towards the end of August, six weeks after the closing of the schools at the end of the first week in July previous. There are two weeks of vacation at Christmas, and certain other days throughout the year are holidays.

THE ATTENDANCE

at school is stimulated by the provision making the major portion of the county fund payable in proportion to the attendance. There is also a local option law, by which a school section at its annual meeting may make attendance compulsory within certain limits. The City of Halifax, which has several minor modifications of the general law, has a specially elaborate and effective law for securing at least a common school education for every child within its jurisdiction.

THE INSPECTION

of the school is performed by a staff of ten inspectors, most of whom include two counties within their inspectorates, approximating two hundred schools and teachers. They inspect the schools, direct teachers and trustees when necessary, and send monthly reports, &c., to the Superintendent of Education. They receive and tabulate teachers' returns for the Education Office, and pay the Provincial grants within their districts according to pay lists transmitted to them. They are also *ex officio* secretaries of the Boards of Commissioners within their districts.

THE COUNCIL OF PUBLIC INSTRUCTION

is the head of the Educational System, and consists of the Executive of the Provincial Government with the Superintendent of Education (appointed by the Governor-in-Council,) as Secretary. The Council has very extensive powers, and its regulations, although under the statutes, are equally as voluminous and important.

It has power to regulate the Normal School, inspection, classification and licensing of teachers, meetings of commissioners, time of teaching, books and apparatus, registers, county academies, Provincial examinations of high schools, to determine cases of appeal; etc.

THE SUPERINTENDENT OF EDUCATION

in addition to the executive duties implied in the secretaryship of the Council of Public Instruction, has general supervision and direction of the inspectors, the Normal School, county academies, and of public education in general.

SPECIAL INSTITUTIONS

(Forming part of the Public Free School System.)

THE PROVINCIAL NORMAL SCHOOL at Truro, for the purpose of training teachers for the public schools. No tuition fees. Instruction brought to the door of every candidate teacher by the regulation ordering the payment of travelling expenses to and from the Institution. Staff of six regular instructors, with model school of two departments and a kindergarten with their respective teachers.

THE PROVINCIAL SCHOOL OF AGRICULTURE at Truro, with model farm, partly affiliated to Normal School for special subjects. Teachers with "agricultural" diplomas receive a special Provincial grant.

THE INSTITUTION FOR THE DEAF AND DUMB at Halifax, where extensive provision is made for the free education of the Deaf and Dumb.

THE SCHOOL FOR THE BLIND at Halifax where the fullest provision is made for the free education of the Blind.

MINING SCHOOLS at the principal coal mining centres, for the preparation of overmen, &c., for the mines.

GOVERNMENT NIGHT SCHOOLS, for the benefit of those at industrial centres needing elementary education who cannot avail themselves of the free day schools.

SPECIAL INSTITUTIONS

(Aided by Provincial Grants of Money to some extent.)

THE VICTORIA SCHOOL OF ART AND DESIGN, at Halifax.

THE HALIFAX MEDICAL COLLEGE, at Halifax.

THE SUMMER SCHOOL OF SCIENCE for the Atlantic Provinces of Canada. A peripatetic institution, designed and utilized for advancing the scientific and literary culture of teachers during the holiday season.

UNIVERSITIES AND DEGREE-CONFERRING COLLEGES

(Not receiving any pnblic Provincial funds.)

The University of Dalhousie College at Halifax.

The University of Kings' College at Windsor.

The University of Acadia College at Wolfville.

St. Francis Xavier College at Antigonish.

The Presbyterian College at Pine Hill, Halifax.

St. Anne's College at Church Point, Digby.

In addition to these there are several ladies' colleges, convents, seminaries, and commercial colleges, &c., which are independent of Government grants and control. These, I have had occasion to know, are doing valuable educational work; and are not only useful in supplying a demand, but in sometimes throwing light on problems in our public free school system.

I have the honor to be,

Your Honor's obedient servant,

A. H. MACKAY,

Superintendent of Education.

PART II.

STATISTICAL TABLES.

PUBLIC SCHOOLS, COUNTY ACADEMIES, AND SPECIAL
INSTITUTIONS.

TABLE I.—PRELIMINARY.

County	No. of Sections	Winter Term ended April 30, 1892 — No. of Sections having no Sch'l this Term	No. of Schools in session	No. of Teachers and Licensed Assistants	No. of Teachers holding Normal Sch'l Diplomas	Pupils Registered	Summer Term ended October 31, 1892 — No. of Sections having no Sch'l this Term	No. of Schools in session	No. of Teachers and Licensed Assistants	No. of Teachers holding Normal Sch'l Diplomas	No. of Registered Pupils	No. of Pupils registered, not on Register of previous Term	Year ended Oct. 31, 1892 — No. of Sections having no Sch'l during year	Total No. of different pupils during year	Proportion of population (Census of 1891) at Sch'l during year
Annapolis	105	15	107	108	25	3710	6	116	116	25	3796	891	5	4601	1 in 4.2
Antigonish	81	10	90	98	6	835	1	96	97	5	3179	705	1	3740	1 " 4.3
Cape Breton	132	27	149	149	19	5875	16	160	160	22	6181	1332	12	7207	1 " 4.7
Colchester	122	18	133	188	57	661	15	146	161	60	5490	1465	30	6196	1 " 4.2
Cumberland	157	31	166	166	59	6720	17	180	183	69	7487	1666	6	8388	1 " 4.1
Digby	90	15	91	92	17	3694	5	101	103	18	4128	1140	2	4834	1 " 4.1
Guysboro	88	15	80	81	6	3154	5	92	92	6	8298	893	3	1047	1 " 4.2
Halifax (By.)	1														
" County	131	28	123	123	82	6445	11	127	127	82	6894	1105	6	7550	1 " 5.8
Hants	104	11	130	134	33	5246	5	144	159	34	5896	1446	6	6692	1 " 4.9
Inverness	104	9	114	116	28	1265	9	121	124	34	4570	1106	3	5371	1 " 4.1
Kings	175	9	166	176	8	5212	7	169	188	7	5881	1284	3	6496	1 " 4.
Lunenburg	104	13	114	120	28	4291	19	117	123	21	4169	1054	2	5345	1 " 4.2
Pictou	145	10	101	162	21	6364	4	155	156	21	5837	1108	3	7472	1 " 4.1
Queens	129	10	162	164	25	6152	7	170	178	25	6555	1348	3	7508	1 " 4.6
Richmond	46	6	54	54	8	1937	5	58	58	8	1831	256	4	2198	1 " 4.6
Shelburne	70	16	63	63	5	2361	6	74	74	4	2737	725	8	3086	1 " 4.6
Victoria	67	7	77	78	3	3020	6	78	78	2	3008	660	8	3680	1 " 4.
Yarmouth	74	22	72	73	2	2317	14	80	82	5	2142	540	6	2967	1 " 4.3
	74	10	106	106	19	4206	9	102	103	21	4130	805	3	5101	1 " 4.3
Total, 1892	1905	267	2158	2196	396	82965	151	2281	2340	419	87189	8021	73	102586	1 " 4.3
" 1891	1908	293	2120	2158	407	81304	175	2236	2300	424	85792	8220	87	101724	1 " 4.8
Increase		26	38	38		1661		45	40		1397			862	
Decrease	3				11		24			5		799	14		

TABLE II.—PUBLIC SCHOOLS: TEACHERS EMPLOYED.

County	Winter Term — Male Teachers				Winter Term — Female Teachers				Winter Term — Total			Summer Term — Male Teachers				Summer Term — Female Teachers				Summer Term — Total			No. of Licensed Assistants — Winter		No. of Licensed Assistants — Summer	
	A Acad.	B Cl. I	C Cl. II	D Cl. III	A Acad.	B Cl. I	C Cl. II	D Cl. III	Males	Females	Both	A Acad.	B Cl. I	C Cl. II	D Cl. III	A Acad.	B Cl. I	C Cl. II	D Cl. III	Male	Females	B'th	M	F	M	F
Annapolis	2	14	13	3		8	38	29	32	75	107	2	11	9	2		10	51	31	24	92	116				
Antigonish	2	5	30	8		3	24	28	35	55	90	1	4	27	10		3	23	38	42	54	96		1		
Cape Breton	4	20	20	29		8	37	38	66	83	149	4	19	24	24		9	42	38	71	89	160				
Colchester	2	4	10	3		11	67	41	19	119	138	2	6	6	3		17	67	59	18	133	151				
Cumberland	2	6	11	2		10	78	57	21	145	166	2	8	9	8		10	87	64	22	161	183				
Digby	2	11	4	6		7	22	40	22	68	91	1	9	4	3		7	29	43	22	79	101			2	
Guysboro'	3	4	5	2		5	21	43	12	69	81		5	4			4	30	48	10	82	62				
Halifax Co.	5	2	6	2		6	68	48	11	122	133	4	11	7	3		9	74	52	16	135	151				
" City	1	10			1	35		4	15	108	123	2	8	5		1	35	72	4	15	112	127				
Hants	1	8	8	4		14	59	20	22	98	116	3	15	55	46		17	64	24	19	105	124	5	4	6	6
Inverness	9	16	35	4		1	90	49	97	70	167	2	10	3	2			23	56	90	70	178		3		
Kings	8	15	11	4		8	61	26	32	86	117	1	10	9	2		11	57	78	18	104	122		1	1	1
Lunenburg	2	6	5	4		4	64	77	16	145	161	9	15	13	8		3	63	73	11	144	155				
Pictou	8	12	18			12	67	43	43	122	164	2	2	15			11	84	40	43	136	176				
Queens	2	6	6	1		2	26	16	10	44	54	1	10	7	1			28	15	39	47	53				
Richmond	2	7	10	1			18	16	29	81	63	2	4	7	1			17	18	14	85	74				
Shelburne	1	2	11	1		3	30	25	20	57	77		6	13	25		4	34	26	14	64	78	1	1		
Victoria	2	6	7	28			10	21	42	31	73	1	10	8	2			8	29	45	37	82				
Yarmouth	1	10	10	1		10	44	28	23	83	106	2	13			1	13	43	29	17	85	102	1	1		1
Total 1892	45	161	210	151	2	147	812	648	567	1609	2176	43	160	194	153	8	167	896	707	550	1773	2323	8	12	5	12
" 1891	44	170	203	155	2	154	816	596	572	1568	2140	44	161	199	157	2	144	870	708	561	1719	2290	7	11	7	13
Increase	1		7					52		41	36						23	26			54	48	1	1		
Decrease		9		4		7	4		5			1	1	5					4	11					2	1

TABLE III.—PUBLIC SCHOOLS: PERIOD OF SERVICE &c., OF TEACHERS.

County	Engaged same section as previous Term — Winter	Engaged same section — Summer	Removed to a new Section — Winter	Removed — Summer	New Teachers — Winter	New Teachers — Summer	Not more than 3 yrs in Service — Winter	Not more than 3 yrs — Summer	Male A&B 1st term	Male 2nd term	Male >½≤1 yr	Male >1≤3 yr	Male >3≤5 yr	Male >5≤7 yr	Male >7 yr	Female A,B,C 1st term	Female 2nd term	Female >½≤1 yr	Female >1≤3 yr	Female >3≤5 yr	Female >5≤7 yr	Female >7 yr
Annapolis	57	66	37	47	13	3	50	46									5	9	9	12	10	15
Antigonish	31	66	41	28	18	2	48	52									2	7	9	5	3	7
Cape Breton	102	123	39	34	8	3	49	50									3	6	13	11	10	18
Colchester	68	91	56	54	14	8	56	53									5	5	17	20	15	24
Cumberland	79	95	64	79	23	9	88	66									4	10	8	17	25	20
Digby	49	60	35	31	7	10	84	43									8	5	3	12	2	8
Guysboro	36	43	36	37	9	12	34	32									2	8		4	9	12
Halifax Co.	73	88	46	68	14	5	51	41										7	8	25	13	15
" City	118	123			5	4	15	6									3	5	7	17	13	59
Hants	50	63	34	46	32	15	61	50									8	9	2	24	14	16
Inverness	46	57	101	98	20	23	68	87										2	9	5	4	6
Kings	36	69	52	40	29	18	55	59									5	14	9	14	6	18
Lunenburg	97	104	40	43	24	13	65	71									6	15	19	10	13	13
Pictou	81	115	57	85	26	8	91	88									9	10	5	25	12	19
Queens	23	28	21	25	10	8	22	30									2	7	1	5	4	9
Richmond	40	45	19	27	4	2	6	28									3	4	9	4	2	5
Shelburne	87	51	30	28	10	1	39	40									2	8	1	4	5	10
Victoria	81	84	38	41	9	7	29	42										1		3		1
Yarmouth	68	73	34	25	14	4	47	35									3	7	6	11	6	22
Total 1892	1112	1394	775	796	289	133	924	932	6	12	23	16	37	17	93	31	65	134	140	226	173	297
" 1891	1094	1328	775	751	271	203	942	949	3	8	26	29	27	22	90	44	79	126	135	225	149	258
Increase	18	67		45	18				3	4			10		3			8	5	1	24	39
Decrease						70	18	17			3	13		5		13	14					

TABLE IV.—PUBLIC SCHOOLS : ATTENDANCE—WINTER TERM.

County	No. of Pupils registered at School this Term	Proportion of population at School this Term	No. Children 5-15 years of age in Sections not at School this Term	No. of pupils under 5 years of age	No. of Pupils from 5 to 15 years of age	No. of Pupils over 15 years of age	No. of Boys	No. of Girls	Grand Total Days' attendance made by all the Pupils	No. daily present at School on an average for time in Session	No. daily present at School on an average for full Term	No. daily present on average for time in Sess'n per 100 registered	No. daily present on average for full Term per 100 registered
Annapolis	30	1 in 5.2	599	10	3259	41	87	1673	247057	2243.5	2148.8	60.5	57.8
Antigonish	65	1 " 5.3	233	10	2672	33	105	1330	191046	1693.5	7590.7	55.8	52.4
Cape Breton	85	1 " 5.8	269	13	5489	43	80	2615	388290	3522.6	8396.	59.9	57.8
Colchester	91	1 " 5.4	511	7	4545	86	88	2318	346220	3117.2	2989.	62.8	00.2
Cumberland	80	1 " 5.1	868	17	6177	37	86	3924	416381	3731.4	3559.	55.8	52.9
Digby	3694	1 " 5.3	780	9	3348	37	97	1697	243798	1251.1	2170.3	60.9	58.7
Guysboro	3154	1 " 5.4	382	5	2875	24	86	1338	197946	1823.8	1754.4	57.8	54.9
Halifax City	6445	1 " 6.	600	13	6079	33	89	3276	525794	4556.8	4556.8	70.	70.
" Co.	5246	1 " 6.2	824	18	5014	94	89	2457	344403	3188.	2850	59.8	54.3
Hants	4265	1 " 5.1	948	18	3862	90	96	2019	272428	2282.9	2282.9	56.5	55.5
Inverness	5212	1 " 4.9	749	10	4702	60	67	2155	814295	2659	2362	50.	45.
Kings	6364	1 " 5.2	849	4	3737	50	88	1923	275524	2610.8	2436	40.6	56.7
Lunenburg	6152	1 " 4.8	915	41	5906	47	86	3008	413608	3722	8535	58.4	55.5
Pictou	1937	1 " 5.6	884	8	5585	69	92	2980	424104	3759.2	3630.2	61.1	59
Queens	2361	1 " 5.4	250	1	1732	84	09	918	126645	1147	1082	59.2	56.
Richmond	3020	1 " 6.1	870	4	2210	47	86	1015	154078	1412	1387.8	59.8	58.7
Shelburne	2317	1 " 4.9	564	6	2766	28	63	1368	196336	1795.4	1718.7	59.4	56.9
Victoria	4206	1 " 5.8	257	17	2129	71	1177	1140	125160	1204	1121	51.	49
Yarmouth		1 " 5.2	1027	7	8785	414	2197	2009	292769	2706.8	2568	64.3	61
Total, 1892	82965	1 " 5.4	12633	223	75892	6920	44627	88338	5494836	49493.6	47192.6	59.6	56.8
" 1891	81304	1 " 5.4	13855	227	74171	6906	43528	37776	5271436	47874.7	46215.7	58.8	56.8
Increase	1661				1651	14	1099	562	223400	1618.9	916.9	.8	
Decrease			1292	4									

TABLE V.—PUBLIC SCHOOLS: ATTENDANCE—SUMMER TERM.

County	No. of Pupils registered at School this Term.	Proportion of population at School this Term.	No. children 5-15 years of age in Sections not having Schools at School this Term.	No. of pupils under 5 years of age.	No. of Pupils from 5 to 15 years of age.	No. of Pupils over 15 years of age.	No. of Boys.	No. of Girls.	Grand Total Days' attendance made by all the Pupils.	No. daily present at School on an average for time in Session.	No. daily present at School on an average for full Term.	No. daily present on an average for time in Sess'n per 100 registered.	No. daily present on an average for full Term per 100 registered.
Annapolis	3786	1 in 5.1	548	19	3548	219	1828	1968	2828	2321.6	2242.8	61.3	59.2
Antigonish	3179	1 " 5.	288	20	2905	254	1677	1502	4404	1668.8	1637.1	52.5	51.5
Cape Breton	6181	1 " 5.5	1082	35	5784	362	3335	2846	369099	3619.8	3390.	58.5	548
Colchester	5490	1 " 4.9	402	30	5229	231	2702	2788	3886	8370.6	3279.	61.1	89.5
Cumberland	7487	1 " 4.6	583	27	7143	317	3569	3918	431198	4227.4	3962.4	564	52.
Digby	4128	1 " 4.8	562	26	3926	177	1977	2151	247158	2853.9	2738.7	69.1	66.8
Guysboro	3288	1 " 5.2	526	29	3134	125	1668	1620	189597	1650.7	159.7	50.5	47.4
Halifax Co.	5886	1 " 5.5	783	81	5607	208	2909	987	3826	8653	3485.	62.	59.
" City	6684	1 " 5.6	600	18	6557	319	3389	3505	434253	4883	88.	70.	70.
Hants	4670	1 " 4.8	571	30	4309	231	2221	2349	276506	2742.9	2647.5	60.	579
Inverness	5881	1 " 4.4	759	48	5666	207	3252	829	8862	2772	2517	47.	42.
Kings	4119	1 " 5.3	647	21	836	212	1968	2201	6465	2490.4	2321.3	59.7	55.6
Lunenburg	5887	1 " 5.2	1012	75	5576	186	2827	3010	3647	3493	3328	58	57.
Pictou	6565	1 " 5.7	509	17	6187	401	3825	930	4617	4018.9	3687.1	61.3	56.2
Queens	1881	1 " 5.2	250	8	1707	116	884	937	12262	1146	1112.	62.5	60.7
Richmond	2737	1 " 5.2	320	20	2636	81	1465	1272	3091	12.7	1616.5	57.4	55.4
Shelburne	3008	1 " 4.9	479	11	2876	121	1479	1529	3181	1985	1910.	66.	63.
Victoria	2142	1 " 5.9	298	9	1946	187	1168	974	892	1238.	24.	58.	52.
Yarmouth	4130	1 " 5.3	846	12	3907	211	1977	2153	269974	2741.7	2581.4	66.3	62.5
Total, 1892	87189	1 " 5.1	11055	535	82429	4225	43630	43559	5240241	52456.8	499225	60.	57.2
" 1891	85792	1 " 5.1	11276	620	81306	3866	42655	43187	6104241	50819.6	48391.1	59.2	56.4
Increase	1397				1123	359	975	422		1637.2	1531.4	8	8
Decrease			211	85					136000				

TABLE VI.—PUBLIC SCHOOLS: WINTER TERM.

Common School Course. Number of Pupils receiving Instruction in the various Branches.

County	Health	Moral and Patriotic Duties	Temperance	Lessons on Nature I	II	III	IV	V	VI	VII	VIII	Singing By Theory	By Rote	Reading I	II	III	IV	V	VI	VII	VIII
Annapolis	2704	2750	2925	238	401	381	426	404	342	340	339	187	796	318	362	424	486	440	415	442	428
Antigonish	1251	1290	1079	266	325	324	294	276	214	184	154	455	442	861	426	452	459	395	339	277	142
Cape Breton	2595	2513	2302	508	519	423	556	357	308	442	275	840	1346	933	925	803	869	611	500	614	360
Colchester	3416	3386	3210	429	462	500	515	453	473	547	448	1458	2063	607	568	641	629	586	512	748	467
Cumberland	5212	4503	4665	870	1215	680	735	514	430	568	211	1903	2496	1048	922	790	1029	718	623	838	334
Digby	2654	2656	2311	445	404	375	384	421	320	256	161	247	966	618	498	514	480	484	390	353	240
Guysboro	1146	1004	782	242	174	200	227	261	133	111	71	39	294	520	394	435	421	463	357	315	103
Halifax Co	3245	3447	8324	674	526	864	337	268	210	174	110	1420	8268	824	796	684	669	696	668	586	168
" City	5665	5667	5295	1533	948	772	838	625	568	473	271	5131	3145	1463	948	772	859	655	584	511	294
Hants	1940	2291	1826	258	257	323	342	303	262	360	254	420	1842	445	479	493	541	528	443	610	439
Inverness	1854	1825	1734	344	869	287	306	276	188	48	58	62	395	791	739	789	655	771	452	328	155
Kings	1779	1840	1681	210	249	290	366	286	257	324	825	116	1771	841	409	518	477	448	504	597	643
Lunenburg	2854	1974	1299	387	404	479	508	483	530	344	188	453	3487	798	893	881	950	836	852	605	226
Pictou	4023	3886	3304	348	428	411	554	546	422	721	412	341	2625	676	745	551	745	746	618	1013	605
Queens	683	682	681	169	92	196	161	161	117	158	88	269	356	207	242	200	257	283	218	270	164
Richmond	968	1296	810	258	218	196	180	137	103	39	85	65	293	522	420	379	319	286	188	108	78
Shelburne	2188	1766	1973	283	354	295	409	389	270	306	189	245	733	338	403	340	440	390	316	368	280
Victoria	1152	1041	1051	259	209	171	173	113	133	62	51	69	303	459	306	320	269	288	274	150	34
Yarmouth	3200	2847	2713	704	519	508	491	398	375	334	241	139	2141	791	587	577	561	384	413	897	296
Total, 1892	47995	46244	42705	8390	8053	7060	7779	6541	5757	5786	3896	13832	29168	12069	11064	10568	11120	10004	8616	9129	5484
" 1891	45883	42737	40078	7493	7638	6875	7652	6686	5647	5796	3520	14446	23949	11434	10614	11052	11117	10141	8546	8818	5551
Increase	2112	3507	2627	897	515	185	127		110		376		5214	635	450		3		70	311	
Decrease								145		10		614				484		187			67

TABLE VI.—PUBLIC SCHOOLS: WINTER TERM—(Continued.)

Common School Course. Number of Pupils receiving Instruction in the various Branches.

COUNTY.	SPELLING.							LANGUAGE.						GRAMMAR.		COMPOSITION.	
	GRADE.							GRADE.						GRADE.		GRADE.	
	II.	III.	IV.	V.	VI.	VII.	VIII.	I.	II.	III.	IV.	V.	VI.	VII.	VIII.	VII.	VIII.
Annapolis	362	424	488	440	415	443	426	245	806	366	480	438	413	432	405	249	337
Antigonish	418	452	444	415	350	277	88	232	318	402	385	335	290	408	262	207	205
Cape Breton	925	808	869	611	500	614	360	609	652	708	865	635	504	626	876	441	827
Colchester	582	687	632	562	516	764	456	363	483	603	573	546	530	795	470	540	423
Cumberland	1076	907	1032	708	664	800	340	781	803	840	933	711	554	819	379	347	311
Digby	489	514	480	484	390	353	240	571	467	496	462	474	390	324	220	217	192
Guysboro	511	453	477	460	439	353	132	245	268	322	416	405	283	417	244	201	100
Halifax Co.	796	684	669	696	668	586	168	794	796	682	665	673	622	564	168	424	126
" City	948	772	859	655	634	511	294	1492	934	818	808	645	527	520	291	520	294
Hants	682	495	535	520	534	620	490	334	433	510	507	550	473	834	480	525	366
Inverness	776	787	855	556	454	825	174	462	504	421	400	271	122	812	811	379	393
Kings	643	427	460	507	557	599	565	216	350	361	440	448	441	916	453	438	491
Lunenburg	872	886	947	817	873	611	283	486	997	619	976	650	749	589	176	496	149
Pictou	957	544	749	747	595	1023	605	313	670	521	699	698	581	978	505	649	483
Queens	290	200	257	289	218	269	147	112	194	126	243	266	108	879	123	277	90
Richmond	420	379	819	286	188	108	78	297	212	332	319	282	193	105	72	62	57
Shelburne	405	340	440	390	316	303	280	256	353	326	425	889	338	337	272	222	157
Victoria	341	301	294	289	274	150	30	309	295	369	279	122	42	272	304	194	189
Yarmouth	587	577	561	334	413	397	295	630	485	550	511	406	370	447	327	367	269
Total 1892	11980	10632	11367	9916	8918	9171	5456	8747	9520	9370	10386	8944	7380	10724	6428	8814	4989
" 1891	11037	9900	10930	10081	8491	8386	5778	8735	8948	9142	10176	9124	6994	10587	6713	6505	4924
Increase	943	732	437		427	585		12	572	228	210		386	187		309	75
Decrease				265			320					180			285		

TABLE VI.—PUBLIC SCHOOLS : WINTER TERM—(Continued.)

Common School Course. Number of Pupils receiving Instruction in the various Branches.

COUNTY.	GEOGRAPHY. Grade.						HISTORY. Grade.				ARITHMETIC. Grade.								ALGEBRA. Grade.	GEOMETRY. Grade.
	III.	IV.	V.	VI.	VII.	VIII.	V.	VI.	VII.	VIII.	I.	II.	III.	IV.	V.	VI.	VII.	VIII.	VIII.	VIII.
Annapolis	222	376	433	412	441	417	314	361	427	404	296	362	424	488	440	415	443	428	282	218
Antigonish	254	390	391	871	254	160	302	308	307	197	286	283	434	470	388	313	287	177	243	103
Cape Breton	576	765	572	486	626	370	432	429	597	380	750	829	808	883	635	502	629	370	340	160
Colchester	481	487	577	502	780	493	443	429	740	507	494	537	646	613	589	601	804	472	406	265
Cumberland	440	649	637	650	781	408	492	584	773	395	1069	789	915	933	705	692	797	387	338	186
Digby	410	471	475	890	349	219	334	369	341	210	602	498	514	440	484	390	354	240	153	114
Guysboro	219	343	426	348	299	128	257	237	317	178	841	318	451	540	472	344	266	146	160	82
Halifax Co.	690	627	642	426	557	161	673	601	537	129	792	784	664	642	653	587	496	299	299	138
" City	771	789	643	525	520	294	629	563	481	294	1582	950	829	816	655	563	482	243	243	28
Hants	381	461	543	443	544	457	321	405	570	477	411	493	494	515	545	456	562	477	347	229
Inverness	706	647	557	344	204	110	699	516	299	102	714	785	873	646	512	342	188	104	749	152
Kings	237	366	394	546	529	676	166	486	509	667	310	402	400	469	541	517	576	630	414	312
Lunenburg	677	811	667	789	625	208	514	566	598	211	779	862	931	929	836	877	656	246	215	68
Pictou	421	617	726	613	996	599	542	507	931	593	594	631	536	745	748	613	1013	603	476	840
Queens	198	153	256	197	269	120	170	174	262	135	259	190	227	238	285	206	311	127	111	60
Richmond	269	278	260	191	269	75	191	163	85	70	407	420	369	319	987	188	106	56	29	16
Shelburne	241	405	383	307	352	270	211	306	339	264	347	405	389	442	384	319	370	276	205	190
Victoria	352	347	243	144	44	22	257	255	93	22	377	341	361	592	208	144	94	92	179	71
Yarmouth	455	524	387	413	369	317	246	386	576	314	795	583	575	550	395	417	386	310	299	149
Total, 1892	7895	9566	9212	8108	8626	5504	7193	7705	8487	5554	11155	10452	10785	11001	9752	8316	8820	5529	5476	2862
" 1891	7409	9139	9187	7639	8408	5335	6979	7110	8045	5527	10793	10537	10037	10666	9779	7955	8474	5452	4949	3114
Increase	486	427	35	469	218	169	214	595	542	27	362		748	335		361	346	77	527	
Decrease												85			27					252

TABLE VI.—PUBLIC SCHOOLS: WINTER TERM—*Continued.*

Common School Course. Number of Pupils receiving Instruction in the various Branches.

County.	Writing Grade I.	II.	III.	IV.	V.	VI.	VII.	VIII.	Industrial Drawing Grade I.	II.	III.	IV.	V.	VI.	VII.	VIII.	Book-Keep'g Grade VIII.	Latin Grade VIII.
Annapolis	284	360	424	488	430	415	443	426	237	274	822	362	354	298	311	217	349	21
Antigonish	270	382	454	472	384	318	271	136	80	82	106	106	132	60	85	35	131	9
Cape Breton	711	838	710	900	530	501	605	369	172	183	130	283	146	127	178	126	130	4
Colchester	477	547	640	604	587	528	770	447	300	879	442	420	357	352	478	204	496	21
Cumberland	1021	891	897	986	793	638	805	364	666	429	568	376	855	328	392	144	487	6
Digby	588	403	514	480	484	390	353	240	470	428	452	429	423	358	215	156	151	18
Guysboro'	497	381	398	544	412	390	266	117	89	77	130	162	184	126	94	52	182	3
Halifax Co.	768	726	701	666	610	520	530	169	664	526	410	331	316	224	121	114	96	1
" City	1431	935	769	871	640	584	511	294	1501	955	769	860	628	534	511	294	5	
Hants	351	445	485	561	542	410	628	416	251	236	275	310	848	285	411	269	878	32
Inverness	713	779	762	805	647	288	64	40	92	100	111	94	64	24	58	24	307	6
Kings	286	387	415	481	491	573	547	641	58	122	87	120	159	233	233	218	421	32
Lunenburg	783	822	889	926	850	845	616	233	836	365	485	442	440	431	308	131	182	21
Pictou	588	689	530	784	738	594	1009	600	176	290	268	425	445	323	425	295	368	17
Queens	187	198	212	242	302	251	234	126	131	102	74	142	89	103	58	30	115	
Richmond	394	408	871	325	287	184	106	75	74	68	60	36	15	14	9	5	27	4
Shelburne	296	385	351	140	388	310	362	282	200	271	227	307	208	189	170	96	230	3
Victoria	328	343	371	264	20	194	104	28	40	40	42	68	50	19	19	22	106	6
Yarmouth	757	566	568	533	394	416	359	286	440	438	344	430	292	423	258	152	262	2
Total, 1892	10635	10696	10481	11322	9539	8244	8573	6292	5977	5365	5240	5707	4944	4446	4335	2650	4823	201
" 1891	9878	10256	10088	10874	9703	8086	8259	5408	5678	5462	5344	5802	5419	4343	3889	2589	4236	194
Increase	757	340	393	448		158	314	111	299					103	446	61	87	7
Decrease					164					97	104	95	475					

TABLE VI.—PUBLIC SCHOOLS: WINTER TERM—*Continued.*

High School Course. Number of Pupils receiving Instruction in the various Branches.

County	English Language		English Literature	Geography			History			Arithmetic			Geometry			Algebra			Practical Mathematics
	Year I.	II.	III.	I.	II.	III.	I.	II.	III.	I.	II.	III.	I.	II.	III.	I.	II.	III.	III.
Annapolis	251	94	48	269	98	18	259	92	18	267	100	18	238	92	17	245	91	17	86
...nish	53	93	41	53	86	25	53	58	25	53	66	25	53	58	37	53	56	37	24
Cape Breton	173	50	26	172	51	31	172	51	31	172	51	31	160	49	31	155	49	81	18
Colchester	147	68	37	147	68	37	147	68	37	145	70	36	132	69	36	130	70	37	14
Cumberland	109	34	12	109	34	4	119	34	4	91	48	4	95	48	4	109	34	4	3
Digby	101	13	12	108	13	14	105	13	12	106	13	12	100	13	12	101	18	11	8
Guysboro	29	22	5	29	22	5	28	22	6	28	22	4	24	25	6	24	26	6	6
Halifax Co.	96	37	10	92	36	...	84	46	...	84	53	12	46	22	...	74	37	...	...
" City	190	110	22	190	110	22	190	110	22	190	110	22	153	110	59	153	110	59	3
Hants	105	28	15	209	27	8	202	29	8	202	35	8	184	82	12	185	35	8	59
...ness	16	6	22	8	18	33	17	9	33	45	7	8	18	39	5	20	41	45	18
Kings	255	490	560	259	67	27	258	48	25	270	49	27	238	47	29	249	48	25	4
Lunenburg	42	20	10	42	21	7	42	21	7	42	21	7	59	39	7	59	89	7	26
Pictou	170	126	129	189	133	109	189	132	109	189	138	71	130	115	110	159	115	110	11
Queens	39	80	5	39	30	5	39	30	5	39	80	5	35	30	5	39	30	5	66
Richmond	17	...	3	17	...	3	17	...	8	17	...	3	13	...	3	17	...	8	5
Shelburne	61	47	28	65	42	12	64	42	18	66	42	13	62	42	13	65	42	13	3
...ria	26	8	5	26	8	5	26	8	6	26	8	5	26	8	5	26	8	5	9
Yarmouth	94	75	86	80	24	21	72	49	29	98	55	26	93	54	28	93	56	33	2
																			27
Total, 1892	2063	1851	1071	2101	838	396	2083	862	392	2135	918	337	1874	890	419	1956	900	456	342
" 1891	1594	804	470	1679	842	374	1715	797	383	1633	828	334	1708	821	359	1704	830	354	389
Increase	469	547	601	422		12	368	65	59	502	90	8	166	69	60	252	70	102	
Decrease					4														3

TABLE VI.—PUBLIC SCHOOLS: WINTER TERM—Continued.

High School Course. Number of Pupils receiving Instruction in the various Branches.

County	Industrial Drawing		Book Keeping		Physics	Botany	Chemistry (Inorganic)	Chemistry (Agricultural)	Physiology	Geology	Latin			Greek			French			German
	I.	II.	I.	II.	I.	I.	II.	II.	III.	III.	I.	II.	III.	I.	II.	III.	I.	II.	III.	III.
Annapolis	76	14	187	78	97	70	61	23	35		58	28	5		6	4	4	8	4	
Antigonish	10	15	49	56	69	12	61	51	4		8	49	33	2	14	14	7	29	37	
Cape Breton	29		127	31	40	82	39	17	31		10	6	21	2	3	28	19	14	6	
Col	118	55	156	70	3	5	60	8	30		90	61	43		8			17	14	
Cum	63	9	91	34	30	8	62		41		65	21	8			3	18	11	4	
Digby	41	4	34	12	26	29	16	4	15	1	22	8	6	1	2		5		2	
Guysboro	78	16	22	22	31	4	27		5		10						18			
Halifax C'nty	139	125	106	37	145	40	70	2	55		178	63	44	1	15	26	11		30	
" City	24	2	207	26	60	51	27	37	18	11	60	5	5	5	3	4	8		3	68
Hants	37	1	54	43	10	78	34	18	24	3	40	7	4	4		2		4	28	
Inverness	14	21	224	61	90	92	24	7			40	5	7	1		6		15	1	
Kings	36		68	6	54	43	9		55		12	14	6		23	63	8	69	40	
Lunenburg	102	68	150	131	114	11	127				77	48	93		5	3	56			
Pictou			18	30	5	20	5		3		10	12	2							
Queens			17			5			12				5			4				
Richmond	27	1	60	35	15	49	22	17		6	20	17	5	5	8				4	
Shel			26	9		38	39				9		4							
Victoria	41	5	77	13	51	57	54				18	20	1	2		5	46	36	25	
Yarmouth																				
Total 1892	829	336	1745	683	800	632	727	187	341	21	737	364	295	21	86	162	190	200	193	68
" 1891	737	252	1412	670	913	618	592	174	284	21	689	405	293	19	81	185	213	220	123	55
Increase	92	84	333	4		19	185	18	57		38		2	2	5				70	18
Decrease					113							41				27	23	40		

TABLE VI.—PUBLIC SCHOOLS: SUMMER TERM.

Common School Course. Number of Pupils receiving Instruction in the various Branches.

County	Health	Moral and Patriotic Duties	Temperance	Lessons on Nature — Grade I	II	III	IV	V	VI	VII	VIII	Singing — By Theory	By rote	Reading — Grade I	II	III	IV	V	VI	VII	VIII
Annapolis	2773	2814	2785	544	359	384	424	359	335	309	249	129	661	631	423	444	456	897	388	376	826
Antigonish	1649	1646	1324	410	278	276	247	251	171	163	103	421	349	622	473	452	375	407	306	241	163
Cape Breton	2523	2380	2249	681	447	468	474	334	283	256	247	541	1469	1407	1008	780	790	616	468	412	389
Colchester	4001	3926	3762	770	643	545	622	551	486	494	334	1065	3214	931	737	615	738	619	519	613	411
Cumberland	5844	5424	4938	1570	1086	883	899	758	530	582	316	1013	2939	1715	1151	916	1003	834	570	626	296
Digby	3246	3141	2871	713	490	471	463	334	279	250	109	243	956	998	685	548	653	460	315	321	176
Guysboro	1628	1365	1360	377	278	225	364	237	155	141	87	186	246	761	440	388	458	390	282	225	164
Halifax Co.	3390	3389	3384	713	592	470	391	821	204	145	101	1610	3223	1018	1004	800	828	655	684	496	228
" City	6392	6175	6327	1950	888	762	899	593	653	466	319	5324	2848	1898	888	762	915	607	653	466	319
Hants	2851	2137	2005	532	351	364	453	401	387	863	244	403	1364	830	587	550	579	491	393	559	353
Inverness	1546	1225	938	492	327	307	268	222	134	99	71	7	275	681	679	576	469	477	357	157	142
Kings	1877	1998	1835	889	294	833	370	262	328	274	201	184	1836	597	559	461	482	409	449	433	382
Lunenburg	1945	2111	1821	561	399	489	445	420	376	241	189	311	3083	1166	786	827	813	744	581	427	212
Pictou	895	782	759	697	753	473	636	560	551	623	381	1076	2234	1117	923	614	773	722	693	759	453
Queens	1148	1147	919	250	170	139	158	164	166	118	69		502	302	232	210	242	221	249	176	101
Richmond	2151	1529	1831	440	208	236	204	170	87	67	18	164	196	877	439	414	318	209	174	132	79
Shelburne	906	754	687	439	346	310	397	325	207	228	147	268	665	577	430	356	418	351	265	256	215
Victoria	906	754	687	149	145	139	154	132	172	29	2	227	234	234	294	250	339	209	319	138	25
Yarmouth	3012	8015	2561	910	433	250	457	378	228	263	151	171	1694	1059	628	571	491	392	262	291	290
Total, 1892	51701	49523	47116	12517	8482	7623	8226	6803	6632	6102	3338	13338	27504	17436	12314	10569	10300	9210	7927	7099	4628
" 1891	47084	44592	41556	11498	8852	7754	7972	6452	5308	4877	3160	15613	30069	17799	12097	11255	11434	9691	7531	7628	4452
Increase	4993	4981	5560	1019			253	351	394	225	178				217						176
Decrease					420	231						2275	2585	363		686	404	481	396	629	

TABLE VI.—PUBLIC SCHOOLS: SUMMER TERM—Continued.

Common School Course. Number of Pupils receiving Instruction in the various Branches.

COUNTY.	SPELLING. Grade							LANGUAGE. Grade						GRAMMAR. Grade		COMPOSITION. Grade	
	II.	III.	IV.	V.	VI.	VII.	VIII.	I.	II.	III.	IV.	V.	VI.	VII.	VIII.	VII.	VIII.
Annapolis	423	444	456	397	388	376	326	556	374	419	447	396	400	358	815	230	271
Antigonish	498	440	354	383	853	242	200	422	311	339	369	382	257	374	263	196	176
Cape Breton	1006	780	790	616	1088	412	389	881	769	080	738	023	463	435	257	337	298
Colchester	690	682	702	650	535	613	406	600	662	611	730	607	597	597	439	485	401
Cumberland	125	920	889	880	563	633	318	1297	889	898	979	789	500	606	349	422	344
Digby	635	548	553	460	315	321	176	881	380	526	529	428	315	317	175	257	150
Guysboro	499	422	431	398	303	296	175	897	296	301	377	370	321	432	298	199	141
Halifax Co.	104	800	828	655	682	496	225	946	984	796	814	632	678	492	222	215	103
" City	888	762	915	607	653	463	319	1967	868	782	915	607	643	476	320	476	827
Hants	802	572	566	391	520	494	489	489	448	511	542	529	46	788	555	513	270
Kings	679	374	469	477	357	217	142	667	650	674	576	490	349	377	321	873	317
class	935	464	98	408	269	491	302	375	361	434	435	445	415	773	422	367	282
Lunenburg	747	817	824	772	380	422	211	638	641	131	760	669	500	446	178	344	166
Pictou	920	631	781	703	701	754	459	835	736	580	741	647	614	764	468	625	412
Queens	231	206	243	218	294	172	08	208	202	98	210	223	202	192	61	165	50
Richmond	145	410	322	299	164	127	78	464	348	359	296	307	160	132	81	120	64
Shelburne	430	366	413	351	285	256	215	387	358	322	439	344	255	280	218	164	159
Victoria	230	219	259	249	250	108	24	237	276	209	155	66	21	296	306	203	143
Yarmouth	028	571	491	392	262	291	200	882	526	558	496	898	278	291	221	236	218
Total, 1892	11812	10818	10784	9436	7872	7157	1767	13129	10209	9807	10568	8951	7364	8396	5454	5927	4292
" 1891	12785	10915	11015	9301	7435	7207	4522	12072	9949	9651	9640	8211	6289	9178	5219	5445	4003
Increase		297	231	135	437		245	1057	260	156	919	740	1075		235	482	289
Decrease	978					50								780			

TABLE VI.—PUBLIC SCHOOLS: SUMMER TERM—Continued.

Common School Course. Number of Pupils receiving Instruction in the various Branches.

COUNTY	GEOGRAPHY Grade III	IV	V	VI	VII	VIII	HISTORY Grade V	VI	VII	VIII	ARITHMETIC Grade I	II	III	IV	V	VI	VII	VIII	ALGEBRA Grade VIII	GEOMETRY Grade VIII
Annapolis	293	395	894	888	377	323	295	377	353	320	653	423	444	446	395	388	376	327	216	180
Antigonish	315	329	410	800	286	146	230	296	280	181	461	427	426	378	375	308	216	56	200	112
Cape Breton	617	661	595	456	432	377	514	386	411	373	1211	966	791	787	622	1461	434	367	857	224
Colchester	404	604	598	646	628	430	417	484	605	434	1638	688	680	692	618	573	602	412	398	247
Cumberland	442	777	783	684	626	396	608	556	601	403	1688	1140	939	936	840	815	319	857	325	253
Digby	386	488	860	343	323	170	297	329	315	175	960	636	548	553	410	245	319	176	148	92
Guysboro	237	314	314	262	324	177	251	260	280	205	588	417	888	415	392	245	289	140	184	74
Halifax Co.	780	728	651	646	424	201	623	643	437	210	967	994	786	710	643	624	391	212	198	150
" City	743	915	607	648	476	320	607	643	476	820	1957	848	782	915	607	643	476	320	276	12
Hants	318	456	468	465	513	339	316	401	538	348	816	816	524	576	474	422	571	325	280	189
Inverness	669	679	574	341	127	108	671	344	137	102	671	679	441	491	476	852	209	89	345	161
Kings	244	425	874	493	456	389	297	411	453	398	584	526	510	497	396	481	429	890	805	185
Lunenburg	539	670	612	501	459	164	609	378	379	165	1039	771	584	814	762	614	416	194	188	8
Pictou	402	735	699	569	776	470	554	625	738	467	998	890	584	746	71?	698	763	470	458	246
Queens	184	145	197	219	192	68	247	182	166	65	309	232	206	224	248	243	168	89	117	75
Richmond	291	274	288	168	182	79	286	140	131	89	879	407	413	317	308	272	132	79	52	48
Shelburne	300	407	361	259	245	223	261	253	254	215	1056	628	574	505	399	272	280	200	242	135
Victoria	311	321	244	144	32	19	268	32	180	20	303	314	229	277	227	157	52	19	191	91
Yarmouth	499	488	303	265	284	193	314	257	277	209	581	438	357	427	352	264	253	207	182	159
Total, 1892	8029	9800	9052	7692	7107	4680	7663	6997	6968	4694	15971	11970	10429	10706	9807	8744	6980	4515	4657	2780
" 1891	7469	9139	9187	7639	8408	5335	6979	7110	8045	5527	10798	10537	10037	666	979	7935	8474	5452	4949	3114
Increase	560	867	135	47			684				5178	1433	392	140	472	789				384
Decrease					1301	749		113	1077	833							1494	937	292	

TABLE VI.—PUBLIC SCHOOLS: SUMMER TERM—*Continued.*

Common School Course. Number of Pupils receiving Instruction in the various Branches.

COUNTY.	Writing								Industrial Drawing								Book-keep's.	Latin.
	I.	II.	III.	IV.	V.	VI.	VII.	VIII.	I.	II.	III.	IV.	V.	VI.	VII.	VIII.	Grade VIII.	Grade VIII.
Annapolis	607	416	444	458	397	387	373	350	422	288	325	364	327	304	294	225	138	19
Antigonish	461	279	411	364	322	309	266	131	126	100	99	88	71	87	64	89	126	8
Cape Breton	1178	973	788	788	618	467	415	382	312	262	218	268	210	194	170	189	168	5
Colchester	320	706	615	710	608	489	587	397	323	877	403	472	418	304	388	306	235	15
Cumberland	1509	1096	914	990	805	581	635	312	1011	681	583	542	465	377	399	219	212	15
Digby	913	637	562	553	460	315	819	176	761	549	511	497	375	286	293	132	89	2
Guysboro'	526	439	389	395	404	264	203	152	64	39	59	77	103	70	66	50	53	1
Halifax Co.	977	937	940	833	818	726	479	216	769	695	666	715	550	356	230	162	118	18
" City	1888	868	782	915	607	643	476	320	1967	868	782	915	607	643	476	320	75	
Hants	647	578	514	570	498	410	503	348	440	344	349	899	378	292	316	170	272	10
Inverness	672	679	574	482	471	355	208	71	134	151	129	133	84	71	42	43	278	17
Kings	508	540	439	485	405	482	442	383	160	196	224	232	219	286	251	167	138	8
Lunenburg	980	574	839	818	744	570	412	227	408	374	451	482	457	328	251	82	159	23
Pictou	851	868	599	778	714	694	755	464	556	469	313	398	304	810	406	249	256	
Queens	262	229	191	543	205	251	186	100	175	142	116	152	124	166	98	71	40	5
Richmond	606	423	413	324	311	168	132	82	121	34	22	31	28	8	6	3	33	14
Shelburne	494	390	355	425	353	261	255	209	285	253	224	260	188	157	109	97	108	
V'tria	331	296	314	310	292	194	67	19	49	31	25	86	28	27	25	19	101	
Yarmouth	1029	603	570	502	408	253	277	193	632	335	342	387	332	220	237	158	98	11
Total, 1892	14704	11521	10653	10923	9440	7819	6990	4514	8615	6138	5841	6444	5263	4426	4180	2651	2696	168
" 1891	14660	11667	11217	11151	9223	7276	7064	4195	8795	6654	5859	6272	5382	4216	3860	2223	2623	184
Increase	44				217	543		319				172		210	270	428	73	
Decrease		146	564	228			74		180	516	18		119					16

TABLE VI.—PUBLIC SCHOOLS: SUMMER TERM.—*Continued.*

High School Course. Number of Pupils receiving Instruction in the various Branches.

COUNTY.	English Language I.	English Language II.	English Literature III.	Geography I.	Geography II.	Geography III.	History I.	History II.	History III.	Arithmetic I.	Arithmetic II.	Arithmetic III.	Geometry I.	Geometry II.	Geometry III.	Algebra I.	Algebra II.	Algebra III.	Practical Mathematics III.
Annapolis	194	81	16	200	95	12	200	95	12	200	95	12	192	94	12	201	94	12	19
Antigonish	88	58	99	25	15	6	68	26	21	68	26	6	72	26	21	72	26	21	21
Cape Breton	134	61	9	134	61	9	134	61	9	134	61	9	134	61	9	134	61	9	8
Colchester	150	44	45	147	44	45	144	44	45	147	44	45	146	44	45	147	44	45	21
Cumberland	84	88	48	72	38	14	101	38	14	109	49	14	105	49	14	105	49	14	14
Digby	61	36	17	61	36	14	61	36	14	61	36	14	60	86	14	61	86	14	12
Guysboro	33	12	8	24	11	5	34	10	5	81	12	3	34	12	8	34	12		5
Halifax Co.	68	22	3	66	21		76	28		76	48	5	22	3		26	16		
" City	145	76	101	145	67	101	145	76	101	145	76	101	145	90	87	145	90	87	87
Hants	176	39	11	192	26	8	200	20	8	191	25	8	176	33	8	179	33	8	8
Inverness	45	27	27	5	55	16	45	37		42	37	33	45	31		12	23		36
Kings	181	66	46	194	65	33	194	65	33	193	65		192	64	35	181	65	81	35
Lunenburg	71	38	7	64	39	6	71	39	6	71	89	6	71	58	7	71	38	7	7
Pictou	168	141	94	168	171	85	168	172	86	168	172	86	159	172	85	168	172	85	46
Queens	32	28	11	82	29	8	32	29	8	82	29	8	32	29	8	32	29	8	6
Richmond	40	4	2	10	4	8	10	4	8	10	4	3	8	4	8	10	4		2
Shelburne	49	47	16	46	44	14	56	38	9	57	43	12	55	45	12	57	43	12	18
Victoria	40		40		40		30	10		19	19	3	20	16	3	16	21	3	3
Yarmouth	110	73	57	107	45	14	69	58	38	110	58	28	107	5?	28	110	58	28	34
Total, 1892	1839	885	652	1692	915	891	1841	886	412	1864	938	392	1765	902	394	1761	908	390	377
" 1891	1594	804	470	1679	842	374	1715	797	333	1683	828	334	1708	821	359	1704	880	354	339
Increase	245	81	182	13	73	17	126	89	79	231	110	58	57	81	35	57	78	36	38
Decrease																			

TABLE VI.—PUBLIC SCHOOLS: SUMMER TERM—Continued.

High School Course. Number of Pupils receiving Instruction in the various Branches.

COUNTY.	Industrial Drawing Yr. I	Industrial Drawing Yr. II	Book Keeping Yr. I	Book Keeping Yr. II	Physics Yr. I	Botany Yr. I	Chemistry (Inorganic) Yr. II	Chemistry (Agricultural) Yr. II	Physiology Yr. III	Geology Yr. III	Latin Yr. I	Latin Yr. II	Latin Yr. III	Greek Yr. I	Greek Yr. II	Greek Yr. III	French Yr. I	French Yr. II	French Yr. III	German Yr. III
Annapolis	91	33	169	75	77	190	45	44	21		47	34	5		4	5	1	12	4	
Antigonish	18	10	68	21	73	88	25	5	3		37	21	28	2	4	5	17	16	27	
Cape Breton	37	22	111	51		100	28	9	6		17	6	3				25	8	2	
Colchester	141	42	123	24	7	157	38	9	39		106	40	34	1	4	11		10	32	
Cumberland	34		72	59	7	65	36	5	36		73	28	14			4	1		16	
Digby	23	11	47	39	13	33	17	9	13	3	15	20	6		1	6		9	2	
Guysboro			22	13	9	36	10	1	1		9									
Halifax Co.	64	7	5			129			69											
" City	145	173	145	62	95	194	96	4	28	9	146	53	66	12	7	28	31	71	47	28
Hants	51	20	180	37	86	104	2	10	26		51	7	3	18	3	3	24	3	3	
Inverness	11		45	16	40	21		3		24		18		1	8		18			
Kings	40	4	116	48	29	149	30	19	31		49	25	26	1	21	4	1	7	9	
Lunenburg	29	17	71	38	26	71	15	15	1		12	16	2		3			10		
Pictou	116	72	143	106	24	149	73	19	38		63	64	57			31	65	88	28	
Queens	24	19	24	29		29	5	1			10	11	8				6			
Richmond			9	4		4			2	1			1	7	8		4			
Shelburne	18	1	48	35	16	62	35	10	16		21	8	4			3	7	8		
Victoria	39				19		21					6				6			2	
Yarmouth	74	15	33	16	49	97	59	7	12		13	24	17	2		3	47	49	24	4
Total, 1892	955	446	1360	644	520	1678	518	170	342	37	669	380	274	44	63	112	247	282	196	32
" 1891	682	203	1291	632	479	1534	584	243	321	83	672	440	230	29	105	121	266	234	117	45
Increase	323	243	69	12	41	144			21				44	15				48	79	
Decrease							16	73		46	3	60			42	9	19			13

TABLE VII.

PUBLIC SCHOOLS; RECORD OF VISITATION.

COUNTY.	WINTER TERM.			SUMMER TERM.		
	No. of visits by Trustees and Secretary.	By Inspector.	By other Visitors.	No. of visits by Trustees and Secretary.	By Inspector.	By other Visitors.
Annapolis	227	98	1369	172	66	1197
Antigonish	428	79	740	419	82	967
Cape Breton........	750	104	2398	680	114	1604
Colchester..........	235	63	1452	253	139	1767
Cumberland	509	142	2343	371	164	2203
Digby	216	87	1069	184	66	1190
Guysboro	267	59	1282	255	74	1460
Halifax County	368	124	1246	355	166	1390
" City	233	100	1010	101	30	625
Hants	253	112	1365	200	114	1527
Inverness	1219	92	2372	1053	98	2457
Kings	344	105	1456	195	108	1486
Lunenburg	504	105	2026	411	138	1946
Pictou	545	59	2675	379	156	2452
Queens	110	33	447	86	45	389
Richmond	354	61	921	356	63	1002
Shelburne	183	64	895	134	70	1131
Victoria............	408	62	934	465	3	1008
Yarmouth	232	103	1514	178	96	1527
Total 1892	7385	1652	27514	6247	1792	27328
" 1891	8007	1538	29240	6038	1432	25551
Increase	......	114	......	209	360	1777
Decrease	622	......	1726	......	......	......

TABLE VIII.—PUBLIC SCHOOLS: TIME IN SESSION.

COUNTY.	Winter Term							Summer Term						
	No. of Schools open this term.	No. in session less than 80 days during this term.	No. in session 80 days or upwards, but less than 100.	Total No. in session less than 100 days.	No. in session 100 days or upwards, but less than full term.	No. in session the full term.	Average No. of days all schools were in session.	No. of Schools open this term.	No. of Schools in session less than 80 days during this term.	No. in session 80 days or upwards, but less than 100.	Total No. in session less than 100 days.	No. in session 100 days or upwards, but less than full term.	No. in session the full term.	Average No. of days all schools were in session.
Annapolis	107	4	4	8	40	59	111.8	116	5	4	9	42	65	105.3
Antigonish	90	5	6	11	27	52	109.8	98	7	10	17	30	49	101.1
Cape Breton	149	2	9	11	54	84	112.8	160	14	14	28	46	86	102.1
Colchester	133	9	9	18	52	63	110.4	146	5	8	18	71	62	104.4
Cumberland	166	6	10	16	74	76	111.	190	20	16	36	82	69	102.2
Digby	91	2	4	6	35	50	112.8	101	6	3	9	29	63	104.6
Guysboro	80	1	5	6	37	37	112.2	92	4	14	18	22	52	102.5
Halifax County	130	5	12	17	58	56	108.	144	4	9	11	49	84	102.
" City	123		1	1		122	120.	127	3	6	9		118	94.
Hants	114	5	6	11	48	55	110.9	121	12	10	22	48	51	105.2
Inverness	166	3	8	11	58	97	101.	169	23	15	38	29	102	99.
Kings	114	4	17	21	51	42	109.5	117	7	21	28	53	36	101.6
Lunenburg	161	1	8	4	42	115	112.	155	2	5	7	37	111	107.
Pictou	162	6	5	11	63	89	112.8	170	10	15	25	85	60	102.4
Queens	54		1	1	80	23	115.	63				21	32	107.
Richmond	63	2	3	4	24	35	115.	74	3	3	6	19	49	105.5
Shelburne	77	2	3	5	54	18	112.	78	5	5	6	50	22	104.9
Victoria	72	2	3	8	27	37	110.	80	7	7	15	13	52	100.
Yarmouth	96	7	6	7	36	33	111.	102	8	13	16	62	24	102.7
Total, 1892	2158	66	111	177	839	1138	111.2	2281	135	178	313	788	1180	102.8
" 1891	2120	57	110	167	705	1248	112.1	2236	115	157	272	753	1211	103.3
Increase	38	9		10	134			45	20	21	41	35		
Decrease			1			113	.9						81	.5

TABLE IX.—COMPARATIVE STATEMENT OF EXPENDITURE OF GOVERNMENT GRANTS TO COMMON SCHOOLS AND OF SECTIONAL ASSESSMENT.

County	Population	GOVERNMENT GRANTS								Amount voted at last annual Meeting for school purposes, exclusive of building and repairs.	Amount voted for building and repairs.
		WINTER TERM.				SUMMER TERM.					
		No. of Schools in session.	No. of Pupils regis-tered.	Sum of Govern't Grants.	Cost to Govern't per pupil.	No. of Schools in session.	No. of Pu-pils regis-tered.	Sum of Govern't Grant.	Cost to Govern't per Pupil.		
Annapolis	19352	107	3710	$4349 10	$1 17	116	3786	$4754 62	1 26	$13492 00	$2412 00
Antigonish	16117	90	3035	3313 81	1 09	96	3179	3467 50	1 09	5502 40	602 00
Cape Breton	34223	149	5875	5769 14	98	160	6181	94 22	97	20390 00	5900
Colchester	27180	133	4961	4973 73	1 00	146	5490	5450 84	99	16840 14	3879 50
Cumberland	34529	161	0720	6173 17	92	180	7487	6614 97	88	19935 40	34170 80
Digby	19896	91	694	3414 44	92	101	4128	3993 37	89	12684 00	8250 00
Guysboro	17198	80	3154	2806 45	89	92	3288	3094 36	94	6917 38	1404 00
Halifax County	32965	130	946	4858 88	92	144	6896	5428 40	92	17227 00	2825 00
" City	8S556	128	6445	5485 48	85	127	6894	5565 88	81	77000 00	7000 00
Hants	22158	214	4265	4624 67	1 08	121	4570	4785 00	.1 04	16706 00	3292 00
Inverness	25781	166	5212	5821 82	1 11	169	5681	5710 43	97	8510 00	2339 00
Kings	22492	114	4991	4564 84	1 06	117	4169	4443 02	1 06	13910 00	1080 00
Lunenburg	31077	161	6364	5667 11	89	155	5837	5494 36	94	15803 00	2687 00
Pictou	3350	162	632	6347 40	1 08	170	6565	630 27	99	22727 00	1209 00
Queens	10610	54	1937	2113 32	1 09	53	1831	2106 82	1 15	6195 00	317 00
Richmond	14400	63	361	2368 71	1 00	74	2737	2934 34	1 07	4274 00	924 00
Shelburne	14956	77	3020	2991 12	95	78	3008	2912 74	97	9551 00	1628 00
Victoria	12390	72	2817	2361 74	1 01	80	2142	2523 90	1 18	4248 00	591 25
Yarmouth	22218	106	4206	4096 07	97	102	4130	3924 82	95	21727 00	17373 00
Total, 1892	450523	2158	82965	82000 00	98	2291	87189	85498 85	98	813229 32	96788 05
" 1891	440572	2120	81304	82000 00	1 00	2286	85792	85487 58	99	341655 75	51421 93
Increase	9951	38	1661		.02	45	1397	11 27	.01	29426 43	45366 12
Decrease											

TABLE X.—PUBLIC SCHOOL TEACHERS' YEARLY EXAMINATION, 1892.

STATIONS.	Male Candidates.	Female Candidates.	Total Candidates.	A. Candidates for Grade A.	A. Received Grade A.	A. Received Grade B.	A. Received Grade C.	A. Failed.	Male B. Candidates for Grade B.	Male B. Received Grade B.	Male B. Received Grade C.	Male B. Received Grade D.	Male B. Failed.	Female B. Candidates for Grade B.	Female B. Received Grade B.	Female B. Received Grade C.	Female B. Received Grade D.	Female B. Failed.	Male C. Candidates for Grade C.	Male C. Received Grade C.	Male C. Received Grade D.	Male C. Failed.
Amherst	8	49	57						10	1	1			5				2	5	5	8	4
Antigonish	24	49	73			2			2	1	1	3		1		3	1		7	8	3	1
Arichat	16	4	20						4	1				1			1		9	4	3	1
Baddeck	20	20	40						1	1		3		7		3	1		8	4	1	
Barrington	2	24	26																2	1		
Bridgetown	19	72	91						5					2					13	5	6	2
Cheticamp	20	19	39			2					1			15	2	7	2		4	4	2	
Clare	4	29	33			1			9	3	1	4		9	5	3	4		5	5	3	1
Digby	9	24	33			1	8		13	5	5	2	1	2	2				7	5	3	
Guysboro	4	18	22			1			2	2	3	1	1						6	7	5	2
Halifax	20	93	113						3	1	1			4	2	7	2	2	7	5	7	1
Kentville	25	57	82					1	10	2	4	2	1	15	6	6	2		9	3	1	2
Liverpool	12	41	53						7	1	5	1	1	7		6	2		5	2	1	1
Lunenburg	9	62	71			2					1								7	1	2	1
Margaree Forks	19	21	40						9	4	3	2		4	2	1			7	2	1	
New Glasgow	19	47	66			1								15	6				6	3	2	1
Normal School	10	57	73			1			9	4	3	2		7	6	1	2		5	3	1	3
Pictou	14	48	62						3	1	1	1		2					18	13	18	4
Port Hawkesbury	11	21	33				1		9	3	4	2	1	1		1			8	4	5	1
Port Hood	24	29	53			1			4	1	2	1		6		3	3	3	8	6	3	1
Shelburne	11	29	40											7		5	2		7	1	1	1
Sherbrooke	1	13	14											8	3	5	2		4	1	1	1
Sydney	37	39	76																			
Tatamagouche	8	33	41																			
Truro	7	84	91																			
Windsor	5	49	54																			
Yarmouth	5	40	45																			
Total, 1892	372	1059	1431	22	5	10	6	1	104	30	46	21	7	92	26	40	17	9	152	48	58	40
" 1891	374	960	1334	11	5	5	6	1	87	20	37	17	13	78	26	24	24	4	175	70	52	53
Increase		99	97	11		5			17	10	9	4		14		16		5			6	
Decrease	2												6				7		23	22	6	7

TABLE X.—(Continued). PUBLIC SCHOOL TEACHERS' YEARLY EXAMINATION, 1892.

Stations.	Female C. Candidates for Grade C.	Female C. Received Grade C.	Female C. Received Grade D.	Female C. Failed.	Male D. Candidates for Grade D.	Male D. Received Grade D.	Male D. Failed.	Female D. Candidates for Grade D.	Female D. Received Grade D.	Female D. Failed.	Total received Grade A.	Total received Grade B.	Total received Grade C.	Total received Grade D.	Total received Licenses.	No. received higher Grade than held before.	No. received same Grade as held before.	No. received lower Grade than held before.	New applicants received License.	No. received Grade applied for.	No. received lower Grade than applied for.	No. failed.
Amherst	34	9	8	17	2	4	9	15	4	13		1	9	11	21	3	8		15	12	9	25
Antigonish	19	7	6	6	13	4	9	25	4	21		3	12	17	32	7	11	2	14	17	15	41
Arichat		5		5	4	1	5	4	1	8		1	1	9	11	2	2	1	9	4	7	18
Baddeck		5	1	20	1			13	5	7			9	7	12	6	5	4	10	15	7	18
Barrington	14	14	22	2		1		18	2	15		4	7	13	21	8	5		10	16	6	22
Bridgetown	56		11	9	11	3	8	9	4	7			25	30	50	6	8	4	36	28	31	32
Chedcamp		2	4	4	4			7	2	5			1	6	7		5		3	4	6	22
Clare	9	1	4	17				9	2	7			6	10	11	1	1	1	10	7	4	14
Olaro	10	7	3	12	11	3	1	20	5	15			6	9	19	4	5		9	11	8	11
Digby	13	13	19	14	4	1		12	2	10			11	10	11	4			10	6	5	17
Guysboro	56	17	7	1				21	1	21		3	4	6	10				33	33	43	57
Halifax	43	18	14	11	1		8	13	5	16	3	7	31	35	78	30	18	5	33	57	36	17
Kentville	39	8	13	18	0		3	17	1	16		1	20	24	65	16	14	8	22	18	10	11
Liverpool	26	9	8	13	1			10	4	9	1	4	12	11	34	2	3	3	19	16	7	37
Lunenburg	34	17	16	14	9	3		21	5	14		7	23	23	35	13	9		30	16	34	11
Margaree Forks	35	18	3	1	4		3	17	4	14			21	19	36	19	9		24	8	13	13
New Glasgow	37	8	21	8	17		1	14	5	11		4	19	21	60	4	15	3	30	13	24	25
Normal School	34	9	2			4	16	12	3	12		7	8	8	38	2	12		34	14	22	16
Pictou	5	1	7	3	1			5	2	4			6	8	16	8	4	2	7	5	8	9
Port Hawkesbury	19	4	4	8			8	17	3	13		7	13	12	28	11	9	1	9	10	13	8
Port Hood	12	1	2	9				5	2	6		3	9	8	16	4	3	1	4	19	24	22
Shelburne	14	5	7	4	1	1		17	3	13			9	12	16	12	7	2	24	20	8	26
Sherbrooke	43	12	14	16	2	2	8	36	6	19		4	17	27	44	12	4	1	29	30	13	18
Sydney	24	13	11	10		1		18	10	13		3	15	34	55	12	5		26	14	15	38
Tatamagouche	57	6	14	6	3	2		14	6	9		4	17	35	53	9	6		16	33	20	21
Truro	30	10	11	6	2			12	3	9		4	14	12	30	7	6	1	17	17	12	16
Windsor																						
Yarmouth																						
Total, 1892	**600**	**190**	**213**	**187**	**96**	**19**	**77**	**376**	**109**	**273**	**5**	**66**	**330**	**430**	**831**	**175**	**180**	**20**	**447**	**420**	**411**	**600**
" 1891	**605**	**146**	**160**	**218**	**102**	**23**	**79**	**358**	**90**	**273**	**6**	**51**	**286**	**366**	**698**	**160**	**136**	**20**	**392**	**379**	**319**	**636**
Increase	63	35	53	26	6	4	2	22	22			15	44	74	133	25	44	9	55	41	92	26
Decrease																						

TABLE XI.

Special Government Aid to Poor Sections.

County.	Paid by Government over and above the ordinary Grants, towards Salaries of Teachers employed in Poor Sections.		Total.
	Winter Term.	Summer Term.	
Annapolis	$103 70	$158 57	$262 27
Antigonish	97 31	132 26	229 57
Cape Breton	90 52	110 33	200 85
Colchester...........	150 00	150 00	300 00
Cumberland	78 71	170 34	249 05
Digby	108 96	121 80	230 76
Guysboro	63 46	87 13	150 59
Halifax........	73 88	155 00	228 88
Hants	65 02	113 18	178 20
Inverness	81 74	102 25	183 99
Kings	117 35	143 18	260 53
Lunenburg	120 18	138 55	258 73
Pictou	75 12	90 86	165 98
Queens	98 51	98 74	196 98
Richmond...........	55 72	71 82	127 54
Shelburne...........	42 03	40 63	82 66
Victoria.............	80 47	82 11	162 58
Yarmouth	45 02	74 63	119 65
Total, 1892....	$1547 70	$2041 11	$3588 81
" 1891....	1610 07	1887 14	3497 21
Increase	....	153 97	91 60
Decrease	62 37	....	....

TABLE XII.

POOR SECTIONS—SPECIAL COUNTY AID.

MUNICIPALITIES.	Number of these Sections having Schools.		Amount of County Assessment paid to these Schools over and above ordinary allowance.		
	Winter Term.	Summer Term.	Winter Term.	Summer Term.	Total.
Annapolis, County of......	13	22	$79 17	$132 33	$211 50
Antigonish, "	14	19	98 26	121 81	220 07
Cape Breton, "	16	18	110 07	101 97	212 04
Colchester, "	19	24	105 89	139 38	245 27
Cumberland, "	15	24	105 52	144 79	250 31
Digby, District of	13	14	93 05	93 05	186 10
Clare, " ..:.....	3	6	25 41	34 83	60 24
Guysboro', "	3	7	23 70	46 56	70 26
St. Mary's, "	5	5	39 51	31 74	71 25
Halifax, County of........	12	20	85 94	134 63	220 57
Hants, District of East	7	12	45 95	65 17	111 12
" " West....	9	8	64 22	56 51	120 73
Inverness, County of......	13	13	79 21	79 47	158 68
Kings, "	18	25	120 43	164 73	285 16
Lunenburg and New Dublin.	10	14	69 17	92 54	161 71
Chester, District of	7	5	41 82	34 06	75 88
Pictou, County of	12	'16	70 91	102 76	173 67
Queens, "	13	13	83 80	92 93	176 73
Richmond, "	9	13	70 43	91 68	162 11
Shelburne, District of.....	3	2	15 97	14 43	30 40
Barrington, "	2	4	12 41	23 19	35 60
Victoria, County of	10	10	69 56	67 67	137 23
Yarmouth, District of	7	8	45 51	49 35	94 86
Argyle, "	6	6	46 48	40 85	87 33
Total, 1892....	239	308	1602 39	1956 43	3558 82
" 1891....	236	295	1601 48	1936 83	3538 31
Increase	3	13	.91	19 60	20 51
Decrease..........	......	......	....	......	......

TABLE XIII.

APPORTIONMENT OF COUNTY FUND TO TRUSTEES FOR WINTER TERM ENDED APRIL 30TH, 1892.

MUNICIPALITIES.	Grand total days' attendance made by all the Pupils.	On account of Teachers employed.	On account of average attendance of Pupils.	On account of Pupils attending School for the Blind.	On account of Pupils attending Institution for Deaf & Dumb, Halifax.	Total amount apportioned.	Amount per Pupil in attendance the Full Term.
Annapolis,	247057	$1313 63	$1618 35	$27 50	$120 00	$3089 48	$ 75
Antigonish	191046	1091 43	1617 57	....	....	2709 00	96
Cape Breton	388299	1888 31	2807 23	....	60 00	4705 54	83
Colchester	346720	1428 65	1695 05	75 00	210 00	3308 70	68
Cumberland	416331	2062 15	2962 04	75 00	120 00	5179 19	81
Digby	154896	735 68	961 67	44 37	53 25	1814 97	73
Clare	88902	414 73	684 70	30 68	36 75	1166 81	91
Guysboro	141795	681 78	1212 09	28 13	....	1922 00	99
St. Mary's	55151	330 34	409 29	9 37	....	48 00	82
Halifax County	344403	1610 25	2439 75	....	150 00	4000 00	1 04
Hants, East	120990	663 72	814 51	....	73 77	1552 00	78
" West	151438	614 92	958 85	....	76 23	1650 00	94
Inverness	314295	1995 18	1791 82	....	60 00	3847 00	67
Kings	276524	1398 60	2089 86	37 50	....	3525 96	86
Lunenburg and New Dublin.	358478	1698 06	2077 22	30 98	49 57	3850 83	67
Chester	55130	293 49	499 79	6 52	10 43	810 23	99
Pictou	424104	1996 67	2902 33	225 00	60 00	5184 00	79
Queens	126645	718 83	872 83	....	....	1591 66	77
Richmond	154078	794 90	1381 70	....	90 00	2266 60	1 02
Shelburne	102991	532 61	595 79	....	31 10	1159 50	67
Barrington	98345	407 63	640 92	....	28 90	1077 45	80
Victoria	125160	880 72	989 28	....	....	1870 00	83
Yarmouth	171567	760 17	931 97	....	34 81	1726 95	63
Argyle	121182	559 34	881 12	....	25 19	1465 65	84
Total...,......1892	4971042	$24586 79	$33744 73	$600 00	$1290 00	$60221 52	82
" 1891	4810954	24380 82	33011 06	525 00	1350 00	59266 88	84
Increase	160088	205 97	733 67	75 00	....	954 64	......
Decrease	....	....	....	......	60 00	....	02

TABLE XIV.

APPORTIONMENT OF COUNTY FUND TO TRUSTEES FOR SUMMER TERM ENDED OCTOBER 31, 1892.

MUNICIPALITIES.	Grand total days' attendance made by all the Pupils.	On account of Teachers employed.	On account of average attendance of Pupils.	On account of Pupils attending Halifax School for the Blind.	On account of Pupils attending Institution for Deaf and Dumb, Halifax.	Total amount apportioned.	Amount per Pupil in attendance the Full Term.
Annapolis	249028	$1465 96	$1534 21		$90 00	$6090 07	$0 68
Antigonish	174404	1199 70	1509 30			2709 00	91
Cape Breton	369099	1922 08	2705 56		60 00	4687 59	85
Colchester	352386	1623 49	1332 83	$112 50	240 00	3308 82	48
Cumberland	431198	2198 53	2793 59	37 50	150 00	5179 62	68
Digby	147530	784 95	954 46	22 18	53 25	1814 84	66
Clare	99623	468 38	626 37	15 32	36 75	1166 82	67
Guysboro'	139175	788 64	1105 23	28 13		1922 00	84
St. Mary's	60422	343 41	395 22	9 37		748 00	51
Halifax County	377626	1585 56	2364 44		150 00	4000 00	77
Hants, East	125153	719 76	758 47		73 77	1552 00	64
" West	151363	628 23	945 54		76 23	1650 00	57
Inverness	284562	1972 71	1776 79	37 50	60 00	3847 00	67
Kings	240485	1469 61	1639 53	112 50		3221 44	70
Lunenburg & New Dublin.	306331	1635 55	2111 10	30 96	74 35	3851 96	74
Chester	55416	328 90	439 87	6 52	15 65	810 44	85
Pictou	411617	2065 73	2870 77	187 50	60 00	5184 00	76
Queens	121262	711 96	861 28			1598 24	75
Richmond	163091	940 44	1239 38		90 00	2269 82	80
Shelburne	106064	543 40	569 45		46 65	1159 50	58
Barrington	97127	418 24	615 86		43 35	1077 45	69
Victoria	89072	962 37	907 73			1870 00	76
Yarmouth	150859	758 50	878 53	20 28	69 64	1726 95	68
Argyle	119115	505 20	892 87	17 32	50 36	1465 65	81
Total—1892	4805988	26061 05	31767 68	637 50	1440 00	59906 23	73
" 1891	4689631	25770 82	31403 64	600 00	1260 00	59034 46	75
Increase	117357	290 23	364 04	37 50	180 00	871 77	
Decrease							2

TABLE XV.—EXPENDITURE OF GOVERNMENT FUNDS : PUBLIC SCHOOLS, COUNTY ACADEMIES, &c.

County	Common Schools			County Academies for the year.	Total Assignable to Counties.	Other Services and Total Expenditure for Education.
	Public Teachers—Winter Term.	Public Teachers—Summer Term.	Total.			
Annapolis	4848 10	4754 62	9102 72	492 38	9595 10	Inspectors' Salaries ... $12550 00
Antigonish	3313 81	3467 50	6781 31	*500 00	7281 31	" Stationery, Postage, &c. ... 500 00
Cape Breton	5769 14	6004 22	11778 36	984 76	12758 12	Examination ... $15
Colchester	4973 73	5459 84	10433 57	1477 15	11910 72	Travelling Expenses—Normal School Pupils ... 758 55
Cumberland	6173 17	6614 97	12788 14	492 38	18280 52	Salaries ... 3800 00
Digby	3414 44	3093 37	7107 81	492 38	7600 19	Travelling Expenses—Superintendent ... 400 00
Guysboro	2806 46	3094 36	5900 81		6393 19	Office Expenses (Registers, Register Covers, Postage),
Halifax County	4858 88	5428 40	10287 28		10287 28	Expressage, Telegrams, Stationery, &c. ... 1265 19
" City	5485 48	5585 88	11071 36	1693 81	12765 17	Total ... 20269 29
Hants	4024 67	4785 00	9409 67	492 38	9902 05	Last Column ... 1 805 03
Inverness	5821 82	5710 42	11532 24	492 38	12024 62	Total for Public Schools, 1892 ... 200744 82
Kings	4564 84	4443 02	9007 86	784 76	9742 62	" " 1891 ... 200902 12
Lunenburg	5667 11	5494 36	11161 47	192 38	11653 85	Decrease ... $157 80
Pictou	6347 40	6580 27	12977 67	1698 81	14571 48	
Queens	2118 32	2106 82	4220 14		212 52	Total for Public Schools ... 200744 82
Richmond	2868 71	2934 34	5303 05	492 88	5303 05	" Institution for Deaf and Dumb ... 3090 00
Shelburne	2891 12	2942 74	5833 86	492 88	6828 24	" Halifax School for the Blind ... 1675 00
Victoria	2361 74	2623 90	4885 64	475 71	361 35	" Manual Training School ... 750 00
Yarmouth	4096 07	3924 82	8020 89	984 70	9005 65	Normal and Model Schools ... 6995 00
						School of Agriculture ... 1669 76
						Tenement Night Schools ... 1705 65
Total, 1892	82000 00	85498 85	167498 85	12976 18	9675 08	Total Expenditure, 1892 ... 216429 73
" 1891	82000 00	85487 58	167487 58	14123 38	1610 91	" " 1891 ... 218905 01
Increase		11 27	11 27	1147 16	1135 98	Increase ... 2524 72
Decrease						

TABLE XVI.—AVERAGE SALARY OF MALE TEACHERS FOR THE SCHOOL YEAR 1891-92.

From Rates paid during Term ended 30th April, 1892.

COUNTY.	ANNUAL AVERAGE SALARY OF MALE TEACHERS.								
	1ST CLASS—GRADES A AND B.			2ND CLASS—GRADE C.			3RD CLASS—GRADE D.		
	Provincial Grant.	From Section.	Total.	Provincial Grant.	From Section.	Total.	Provincial Grant.	From Section.	Total.
Annapolis	$112 08	$286 40	$398 48	$84 06	$210 37	$294 43	$56 04	$110 00	$166 04
Antigonish	112 08	255 50	367 58	84 06	129 90	213 96	56 04	96 00	152 04
Cape Breton	112 08	276 33	388 44	84 06	120 35	204 41	56 04	92 27	148 31
Colchester	112 08	558 13	670 21	84 06	171 50	255 56	56 04	60 00	116 04
Cumberland	112 08	470 80	582 88	84 06	187 66	271 72	56 04	260 00	316 04
Digby	112 08	297 97	409 35	84 06	275 00	359 06	56 04	181 66	237 70
Guysboro'	112 08	410 00	522 08	84 06	146 00	230 06	56 04	110 00	166 04
Halifax County	118 08	427 75	539 83	84 06	195 00	279 06	56 04	140 00	196 04
" City	112 08	805 78	917 86						
Hants	112 08	350 00	462 08	84 06	207 50	291 56	56 04	142 50	198 54
Inverness	112 08	180 00	292 08	84 06	92 00	176 06	56 04	60 00	116 04
Kings	112 08	357 76	469 84	84 06	202 60	286 66	56 04	121 22	177 26
Lunenburg	112 08	366 00	478 08	84 06	137 50	221 56	56 04	115 00	171 04
Pictou	119 08	543 00	655 08	84 06	120 00	244 06	56 01	106 00	162 04
Queens	112 08	360 00	472 04	84 06	165 00	249 06	56 04	109 00	165 04
Richmond	112 08	187 14	299 22	84 06	132 00	216 06	56 04	99 09	155 13
Shelburne	112 08	294 00	406 08	84 06	212 73	296 79	56 04	137 50	193 54
Victoria	112 08	306 00	418 08	84 06	128 00	212 06	56 04	92 00	148 04
Yarmouth	112 08	428 73	540 81	84 06	212 00	296 06	56 54	200 00	256 04
Total—1892	112 08	376 87	488 95	84 06	171 39	255 45	56 04	124 01	180 05
" 1891	112 08	336 51	448 59	84 06	176 51	260 57	56 04	129 89	185 93
Increase		40 36	40 36						
Decrease					5 12	5 12		5 88	5 88

TABLE XVI.—AVERAGE SALARY OF FEMALE TEACHERS FOR THE SCHOOL, YEAR 1891-92.

From Rates paid during Term ended April 30th, 1892.

ANNUAL AVERAGE SALARY OF FEMALE TEACHERS.

County.	1ST CLASS—GRADE B.			2ND CLASS—GRADE C.			3RD CLASS—GRADE D.		
	Provincial Grant.	From Section.	Total.	Provincial Grant.	From Section.	Total.	Provincial Grant.	From Section.	Total.
Annapolis	$112 08	$160 00	$272 08	$84 06	$130 95	$215 01	$56 04	$92 24	$148 28
Antigonish	112 08	122 00	234 08	84 06	120 62	204 60	56 04	88 50	144 54
Cape Breton	112 08	276 33	388 44	84 06	121 84	204 41	56 04	92 27	148 31
Colchester	112 08	193 80	305 88	84 06	148 73	232 79	56 04	91 03	147 07
Cumberland	112 08	161 11	273 19	84 06	140 25	224 31	56 04	102 32	158 36
Digby	112 08	125 56	237 64	84 06	117 73	201 79	56 04	109 75	165 79
Guysboro	112 08	174 80	286 88	84 06	140 10	224 16	56 04	100 00	156 04
Halifax County	112 08	200 50	312 58	84 06	168 00	252 06	56 04	98 50	159 54
" City	112 08	357 92	470 00	84 03	277 94	362 00	56 04	243 96	300 00
Hants	112 08	173 68	285 76	84 06	143 20	227 62	56 04	99 50	155 54
Inverness	112 08	140 00	252 08	84 06	82 02	166 06	56 04	58 00	114 04
Kings	112 08	202 00	314 08	84 06	138 20	222 28	56 04	98 76	154 80
Lunenburg	112 08	156 67	268 75	84 06	132 50	216 56	56 04	109 00	165 04
Pictou	112 08	200 50	312 58	84 06	134 50	218 56	56 04	90 00	154 04
Queens	112 08	166 84	278 42	84 06	130 00	214 06	56 04	112 50	168 54
Richmond				84 06	100 00	184 06	56 04	98 12	149 16
Shelburne	112 08	148 67	260 75	84 06	130 00	214 06	56 04	97 83	153 37
Victoria	112 08	140 00	252 08	84 06	134 00	218 06	56 04	45 00	101 04
Yarmouth	112 08	206 60	318 68	84 06	173 91	257 97	56 04	117 64	178 65
Total, 1892	112 08	188 69	295 77	84 06	140 18	224 24	56 04	102 39	156 43
" 1891	112 08	178 95	286 03	84 06	139 00	223 06	56 04	107 52	163 58
Increase		9 74	9 74		1 18	1 18			
Decrease								5 13	5 13

TABLE XVII.—GOVERNMENT NIGHT SCHOOLS.

County	Section	Teacher	Assistant	Pupils enrolled	Average attendance	No. of Sessions
Victoria	West Ingonish	J. M. Macritchie		84	22	50
"	Englishtown	C. C. McLean		29	15	45
Richmond	West Arichat	James Hynes		33	14	32
"	D'Escouse	Do.		89	14	27
Cumberland	Springhill—(1).	N. D. McTavish		54	23	37
"	(1).	Herbert Wood	Lou Ella Logan	32	11	38
"	(2).	Stiles Vance		51	21	43
Lunenburg	Joggins	Geo. W. Huggins		27	21	50
"	Bridgewater	C. E. Williams		34	18	42
"	Chester	Wm. A. McKay		98	48	49
Pictou	Albion Mines	Wm. Dunbar	J. W. Henderson	30	11	29
"	Trenton	A. S. NcKenzie		49	25	47
"	Westville	Alex. D. McDonald		108	53	27
Inverness	Beaton	Jas. R. Macdonald		29	10	30
"	Kingsville	Arch. D. McLellan		28	10	46
"	E S Margaree	Wm. Haggarty		52	30	46
Cape Breton	Sydney Mines		Jeremiah Sullivan			
"	Caledonia Mines	Stephen A. McDonald		33	10	36
"	Little Bras d'Or	Mark T. Collins		34	16	53
"	Mitchell	Jas. A. Mitchell		20	8	58
"	Reserve Mines	Jas. W. Bissett		52	28	50
"	Low Point	Murdoch Matheson		52	12	51
"	Little Glace Bay	A. M. O'Handley		42	8	38
"	North Sydney	John D. McNeil		31	15	51
"	Bateston	Mark Bates		45	29	40
"	Bridgeport	Wm. Young		43	22	54

TABLE XVIII.—COUNTY ACADEMIES.

Academy	Principal	No. of Teachers	No. of Assistants	No. of Departments	No. of Pupils enrolled during year	Average No. of Pupils daily present during year	Average No. of Pupils daily present during winter term	Average No. of Pupils daily present during summer term	No. of 1st year's Pupils	No. of 2nd year's Pupils	No. of 3rd year's Pupils	No. of Pupils belonging to Section	No. of Pupils belonging to Co, but outside of Section	No. of Pupils from outside of County	No. of Pupils under 15 years of age	No. of Pupils over 15 years of age	Average age of Pupils	No. of Males	No. of Females
Annapolis	W. M. McVicar, A M	1		1	43	52.5	50.7	24.3	89	9	6	33	11		16	28	15.4	18	24
Antigonish	Rev. D. A. Chisholm, D. D.	4	3	5	162	90.9	110.8	64.5	64	57	41	45	30	87	20	142	17.9	122	40
Cape Breton	E. T. MacKeen	21		2	81	43.0	52.6	34.7	57	27	17	44	22	15	17	64	19.	63	19
Colchester	W. R. Campbell, B. A.	4		4	203	115.2	123.	106.1	112	54	26	183	66	4	135	68	15.5	111	92
Cumberland	{ H. S. Freeman, H. A. / E. J. Lay }	1	1	1	84	40.	33.6	47.4	31	36	17	68	16		25	59	15.5	34	10
Digby	John F. Godfrey	1		1	34	17.8	17.5	18.2	8	13	13	27	6		11	23	16.	16	18
Guysboro	{ I. M. Longley, B. A. / Jas. J. Buchanan, B. A. }	2		1	46	18.	18.4	17.0	22	23	1	57	9		30	16	15.	20	26
Halifax	Howard Murray, B. A.	28		0	303	187.8	187.9	18.4	124	91	50 / 38	227	57	19	80	214	16.9	141	162
Hants	John A. Smith, B. A.	1	1	1	47	27.9	31.9	23.9	34	16	7	38	8	1	11	36	15.	20	27
Inverness	{ John E. Eaton, B. A. / D. S. McIntosh, B. A. }	1		1	51	20.	22.5	13.1	16	29	6	40	11		18	33	17.	58	25
Kings	Angus McLeod	2		2	81 / 58	43.3 / 31.	40.8 / 31.	46.9 / 31.2	33 / 33	26 / 17	21 / 8	64 / 43	16 / 14	1	40 / 19	35 / 39	15.8 / 16.	30 / 13	51 / 43
Lunenburg	R. McKitrick, B. A.	4		4	261	139.4	160.	114.6	86	76	71	128	84	49	60	196	16.9	186	125
Pictou	Robt. McLellan	1		1	52 / 48	30.7 / 27.2	30.7 / 29.9	30.7 / 23.6	23 / 18	10 / 22	59 / 10	30 / 40	21 / 7	1	5 / 19	47 / 20	16.6 / 16.	20 / 21	32 / 27
Queens	Nicholas Smith	1		1	40	22.8	27.	18.4	32	11	8	18	11		35	35	16.	29	30
Shelburne	C. Stanley Bruce																		
Victoria	{ M. R. Tuttle, B. A. / J. B. Johnson, M. A. }	2	2	2	94	66.	56.	43.	47	30	17	89	5		26	46	15.6	43	51
Yarmouth	A. Cameron																		
Total, 1892.		36	6	35	1696	952.6	994.3	852.6	739	557	400	1122	394	120	567	1129	16.1	962	854
" 1891.		33	4	35	1663	905.1	968.8	701.1	716	553	394	1097	382	124	568	1046	15.9	847	816
Increase		3	2		33	27.5	5.5	61.6	23	4	6	25	12	4	1	34	.2	15	18
Decrease																			

*Where double figures occur in connection with the Returns of these Institutions, the upper indicates the third year pupils; the lower the fourth.

TABLE XVIII.—COUNTY ACADEMIES.—Continued.

ACADEMY.	No. of Bound Volumes in Library.	No. of Globes.	No. of Wall Maps.	No. of Dictionaries and Gazetteers.	Cash Value of other Apparatus.	From Fees.	Provincial Grant.	From other Sources.	Salaries of Teachers.	Expended on Buildings.	Expended for Books and Apparatus.	Miscellaneous.
					LIBRARY AND APPARATUS	INCOME			EXPENDITURE			
Annapolis	2020	2	17	3	$75 00		$492 38	$425 62	$900 00		$18 00	$200 00
Antigonish	250	3	26	5	620 00		500 00	2820 00	2500 00	50 00	70 00	
Cape Breton	55	2	22	5	270 00		984 76	730 24	1600 00	100 00	15 00	400 00
Colchester	6	1	9	7	400 00		1477 16	2347 85	8175 00	50 00	200 00	
Cumberland		2	10	3			492 38	607 62	1100 00			
Digby	200	2	7	1	80 00		492 38	706 16	750 00		122 78	3:6 76
Guysboro	700	1	8	2	35 00		492 38	257 62	750 00			
Halifax		1	37	7	1200 00	157 33	1693 81	9096 76	6906 06	219 00	221 00	3601 84
Hants	2	9	13	2	100 00		492 38	451 62	900 00		44 00	75 00
Inverness		1	10	1	25 00		492 38	362 62	750 00	20 00	30 00	
Kings		2	11	3	150 00		734 76	880 24	1500 00	100 00	15 90	100 00
Lunenburg	150	2	20	4	200 00		492 38	857 62	1000 00	100 00	150 00	378 50
Pictou	1160	2	53	7	1500 00	270 00	1693 81	2010 83	3400 00	188 64	12 00	
Queens		3	20	2	40 00		492 38	257 62	750 00			
Shelburne	40	9	25	2	70 00		492 38	292 62	750 00	25 00	10 00	30 00
Victoria		2	7	3	30 00		475 71	814 39	725 00	12 00	28 00	
Yarmouth		2	24	7	300 00		984 76	1165 24	2100 00		50 00	
Total, 1892	4572	31	318	63	$5095 00	$427 33	$12976 18	$23104 07	$29056 06	$364 64	$980 78	$5106 10
" 1891	4871	28	312	59	4480 00	503 50	14123 33	21756 39	29176 75	1371 00	5770 50	5257 97
Increase		3	6	4	665 00			1347 68			403 28	
Decrease	201					76 17	1147 15		379 31	506 36		151 87

TABLE XVIII.—COUNTY ACADEMIES—Continued.

STUDIES OF PUPILS.

Academies.	English Language. Year. I	II	III	Composition. Year. I	II	III	English Literature. Year. I	II	III	Geography. Year. I	II	III	History. Year. I	II	III	Arithmetic. Year. I	II	III	Geometry. Year. I	II	III	Algebra. Year. I	II	III	Practical Mathematics. Year. I	II	III	Industrial Drawing. Year. I	II	III
Annapolis	29	9	4	29	9	4				29	9	4	29	9	4	29	9	4	29	9	4	29	9	4						
*Antigonish	64	57	29/12	64	57	29			29/12	64	57	18	64	57	18	64	57	29	62	57	29/10	64	57	29/10	29		25	25		
Cape Breton	37	27	17	37	27	17			17	37	27	17	37	27	17	37	27	17	37	27	17	37	27	17	17					
*Colchester	113	55	25/10	113	55	25/10	113	55	25/10	113	55	25/10	113	55	25/10	113	55	25/10	113	55	25/10	113	55	25/10	10		113	113	55	50/38
Cumberland	30	35	14	30	35	14	30	35	14	30	35	14	30	35	14	30	35	14	30	35	14	30	35	14	14		30	30	35	
Digby	8	13	13		17	8	8	13	13	8	13	13	8	13	13	8	13	13	8	13	13	8	13	13	13					
Guysboro	17	17	3	17		8			3	17	16	3	17	16	8	17		8	17	17	1	17	17		17		17	17	17	50/38
*Halifax	124	91	50/58	124	91	50/38	124	91	50	124	91	50/38	124	91	50/38	91	50/38		124	91	50/38	124	91	50/38	50/38		124	124	91	50/38
Hants	24	16	7	24	16	7	24			24	16	7	24	16	7	24	16	7	24	16	7	24	18	7	7		24	24	16	
Inverness	16	29	6	16	29					16	29	6	16	29	6	16	29	6	16	16	9	16	29	6	8					
Kings	33	26		33	26	22		22		33	26	22	33	33	22	33	26	22	33	26	22	33	26	22	21		33	33	26	22
Lunenburg	33	17		33	17					33	17	8	33	17	8	33	17	8	33	17	8	33	17	8	8					
*Picton	85	76	71/29	85	76	71/29	85	76	71/29	85	76	71/29	85	76	71/29	85	76	71/29	85	76	71/29	85	76	71/29	71		85	85	76	40
Queens	20	21	9			9			9	20	22	9	20	22	8	20	20	9	20	20	9	20	20	9	7					
Shelburne	18	22	8	18	14	8	18	2	8	18	22	8	22	18	8	18	22	18	18	22	18	18	22	18	8					
Victoria	32	11	6	32	11	5			5	32	11	6	32	11	6	32	11	6	32	11	6	32	11	6	2		32	32		
Yarmouth	47	30	17	47	30	11	46	30	17	44	20	17	1	26	13	47	39	17	47	29	13	47	30	17	20					
Total, 1892	730	552	365	702	532	364	448	369	394	727	542	358	684	546	361	730	551	394	728	550	400	730	551	384	317		483	111	341	151
" 1891	714	555	281	688	552	348	260	400	392	714	565	323	714	554	357	714	565	299	706	554	369	713	554	369	348		372	82	259	5
Increase	16		84	14		16	188		2	13		35			4	16			22		31	17		15	31		111			146
Decrease		3			20			31			13		30	8			4	5		4			8							

*See foot-note on page 33.

TABLE XVIII.—COUNTY ACADEMIES—*Continued.*

STUDIES OF PUPILS.

ACADEMY.	Book-keeping. Year. I	II	III	Physics. Year. I	II	III	Botany. Year. I	II	III	Chemistry (Inorganic). Year. I	II	III	Chemistry (Agricultural). Year. I	II	III	Physiol. Yr. II	III	Geol. &c. Yr.	Latin. Year. I	II	III	Greek. Year. I	II	III	French. Year. I	II	III	German. I	II	III	Mens'l Train'g.
Annapolis	29	9	4		1	4	29	8	4		6	4							29	8	4					9	4				
*Antigonish	50	55	5		50	29	50	50			45	25		30	25		8		43	47	25			2	35	27	26		12	
Cape Breton	14	19	8	24	22	17	10	17		22	17	17				17		7	5	12		2		7	6	8			
*Colchester	113	55				4	118	55	4	55	22	10			4	16	10		113	53	20					20	10		5	
Cumberland	30	35				14	20	30			13		30	16		69		4	30	35	14					2			14	
Digby	4	9		8			8	12			20	1				11			5	5	8			7						
Guysboro'	17	17	7	12	11		21					45				29								17						
*Halifax	124	6	7	104		13	109	6	7	32	6				1	14			124	85	44		20	17	75	40	22	54	52	52
Hants	24	16	12	24		36	24		6	16	7				7	7			20	4	4		8	18	5	4	3			
Inverness	16	29				7	16	29		20			16						8	19	6		1	8	5	5				
Kings	83	26	22	29		7	26	17		12	13			7		7				10	13			7	6	6	8			
Lunenburg	83	17		33			33			17	8		17	8					12	8	3	1			3	10		20		
*Pictou	85	76		68	68	40	59	74		68	68	40				108			49	49	68		12	20	30	34				
Queens	15	9	6			11	15	10			6	6			6				10	12	9		3	28						
Shelburne	18	22	8			6		22			8	8			8	8			7	6	1			3						
Victoria	26	11	1	19		1	26	11		11	6		26	11		1			8	4	6					6	5			
Yarmouth	45	9		26			28	13		17	12					2			10	8	7				24	8	1			
Total—1892	676	420	82	329	142	195	587	347	42	364	230		30	74	88	303	7		470	352	306	3	59	161	118	225	183	54	52	52
" 1891	581	437	97	476	186	186	541	348	19	313	231			59	122	263	54		396	356	287	2	98	149	155	222	115	73		
Increase	95					9	46		23				30	15		50			74		19	1		12		3	68			
Decrease		17	15	147	44			21		41	1				34		47			4			39		37			19		

* See foot note on page 35.

TABLE XIX.—SPECIAL INSTITUTIONS.

INSTITUTION.	PRINCIPAL.	INSTRUCTORS.			NUMBER OF PUPILS, THEIR AGE, ETC.														EXPENSES.	
		No. of Regular Teachers.	No. of Regular Assistants.	No. of Assistants engaged part of time for special branches.	Whole No. of Pupils enrolled during year.	Average No. of Pupils on roll.	Average No. of Pupils daily present.	No. of New Pupils for year.	No. of former Pupils 2nd year of attendance.	No. of former Pupils 3rd year of attendance.	No. of enrolled Pupils belonging to Municipality or Town.	No. belonging to County but outside of Municipality or Town.	No. from outside of Co.	No. from Nova Scotia.	No. from other Countries.	No. of Pupils under 15 years of age.	No. of Pupils 15 years of age and upwards.	Average age of Pupils.	Annual Tuition Fee—Advanced Pupils.	No. of weeks in session during year.
Institution for Deaf & Dumb	Jas. Fearson	6	5	2	72	63	68	12	19	41				54	18	45	17	12		42
School for the Blind	C. F. Fraser	5		6	53	46	46	13						22	31	25	28			40

TABLE XIX.—SPECIAL INSTITUTIONS—Continued

INSTITUTIONS.	NO. STUDYING THE LANGUAGES ENGLISH.					FINE ARTS.			MATHEMATICS.			Modern Geography.	HISTORY.			PRIZES.	
	Reading and Elocution.	Spelling.	Grammar and Analysis.	Composition.	Rhetoric.	Music.	Drawing.	Penmanship.	Arithmetic.	Algebra.	Geometry.		British.	Roman.	English Literature.	No. awarded during the year.	Value of Prizes awarded during year.
Institution for Deaf and Dumb	...	...	...	...	...	...	76	76	75	...	...	80	13	...	...	...	...
*School for the Blind	24	21	18	15	...	27	...	15	31	8	14	28	21	5	16	8	23

```
No. studying science................  4
Braille system of point writing......  55
Kindergarten.........................  12
Singing..............................  11
Reading and Writing Music............  20
Theory of Music......................  **
```

TABLE XIX.—SPECIAL INSTITUTIONS—Continued.

INSTITUTIONS.	ROOMS, &c.		LIBRARY AND APPARATUS.					INCOME.				EXPENDITURE.					
	No. of School Rooms and Class Rooms.	Style of Desks.	No. of Globes.	No. of good Wall Maps.	No. etc. Dictionaries and other Apparatus.	Estimated Cash Value of other Apparatus.	Estimated Cash Value of all Apparatus.	From Fees and Contributions.	From Rates and Invested Funds.	Provincial Grant.	Total.	Salaries of Instructors.	Average of Salaries.	Expended on Buildings and Repairs.	Expended for Books and Apparatus.	Miscellaneous.	Total.
Institution for Deaf and Dumb..	2	Dawson	2	38				$905	$3065	$5650	$9625	$3038		$267	$115	$6781	$10201
School for the Blind	9	Horseshoe	1	3	2												

TABLE XX.

SUMMARY OF GOVERNMENT GRANTS FOR EDUCATION.

1892.

Common Schools	167,498	85
Normal School	6,995	00
Institution for Deaf and Dumb	3,090	00
Halifax School for the Blind	1,575	00
Manual Training School	750	00
County Academies	12,976	18
Inspection	13,050	00
Expenses (office)	1,265	59
Salaries (office)	4,200	00
Examination	995	15
School of Agriculture	1,569	76
Travelling Expenses N. S. Pupils	758	55
Government Night Schools	1,705	65
	$216,429	**73**

PART III.

APPENDICES.

APPENDIX A.

REPORT OF THE NORMAL SCHOOL.

A. H. MacKay, Esq., B. A., B. Sc., LL. D.,

Sup't of Education, Halifax, N. S.

.Sir,—

I have the honor to submit my twenty-fourth annual report of the Provincial Normal School as follows :—

The session opened on Wednesday, November 4th, 1891, and closed on Thursday, July 7th, 1892.

The total number of students enrolled was one hundred and fourteen, of whom sixty-four attended throughout the whole session. The average attendance was twenty-eight weeks. Eighty-one students were awarded diplomas, twenty-one receiving a diploma of the first-class, and sixty a diploma of the second class.

The Governor General's medals were awarded as follows :—

Ella Rettie.....................Silver Medal.
Clara Willett....................   "   "
Naomi Borden..................Bronze Medal.
E. May Hunter.................   "   "
Lamont Givan.................   "   "

Prof. A. G. MacDonald, A. M., who had been appointed on the teaching staff of the Institution during the preceding year, entered upon his duties as instructor in Mathematics and Physics at the beginning of the session. His accurate scholarship, superior teaching ability, and sound judgment, render him a valuable acquisition to the Institution.

The past year marks the close of an epoch in the history of the Normal School. Its curriculum has hitherto embraced both academic and professional work. Until recently the double function was in a measure necessary, on account of the lack of facility in many parts of the Province for obtaining the scholarship required for the various grades of license.   Probably in no feature of educatioual work has Nova Scotia made such marked progress within the past few years as in the development of its high schools, so that ample opportunity is now afforded in every county for securing the scholarship demanded of our teachers.   I think, therefore, that the Counc.l of Public Instruction has very properly determined to eliminate much of the academic work from the Normal School curriculum, and restrict the Institution more closely to its legitimate function of a training school.   The friends of the Institution and of education, must hail this measure as a most important step in advance.   In taking leave of the old order of things, I have thought it not out of place to give a brief sketch of some of its leading features.

The Provincial Normal School probably owes its existence in so far as the inception of the idea is concerned, to Sir Wm. Dawson, the first incumbent of that office which you, sir, so worthily fill. He strongly urged on the government of the day, two measures for the betterment of the educational system of the Province,—a Normal School for the professional training of teachers, and Free Schools, supported in large measure by assessment.   His recommendation for a Normal School was adopted with little delay, but the idea of Free Schools was deemed too revolutionary, and it required another decade with careful nurture for development before it could be realized.

The Normal School was opened in November 1855.   The first building was of mean proportions and unimposing appearance. The total cost of land and structure was only about $6000.   But the day of small things was not to be despised, and the friends of educational progress recognized in the establishment of the Institution the beginning of a new and better era in the common school education of the Province.

Thirty-seven years have completed their circles since first the doors of the Normal School were open for the reception of students. During these years 4,630 students have been enrolled on its Register, making a yearly average of one hundred and twenty-five.   Taking into consideration that during these years attendance at Normal School was entirely at the option of those who were seeking for license to teach in our public schools, and that the graduates of the institution enjoyed no special privileges and received no consideration or recognition above others, this attendance shows a good degree of enterprise among the teachers, and of appreciation on their part of the merits of the school.   On the whole, I think our graduates have most creditably maintained the honor of the Institution and have borne an important part in promoting the efficiency of our schools, and in the uplifting of our educational ideal to a higher plane. Often, especially in the earlier years, their work was little appreciated. Their ignoring of the *a b c* as a necessary first step in reading, their object lessons, their new methods of teaching, their singing, marching, and other new-fangled notions, were too radical to suit the conservative fathers and mothers of the old school. Often they were able to secure toleration only by toning down and tempering their methods and tactics to the measure of forbearance or endurance which their patrons were disposed to exercise. After a useful period of service in the school room many of our graduates have exchanged their vocation for some other honorable pursuit. They may be found to-day among those who guide the affairs of State around our Council Board and in our Legislative Halls, or they hold high rank among our farmers, our clergy, our physicians, and our lawyers; many of them are in other and distant lands as missionaries of the Gospel, or while changing their country they still hold to the old business as teachers of the young. To one and all, wherever and however employed, the Normal School bears them kindly feeling and sends them cordial greeting.

For over thirteen years, from its opening until April 1869, Rev. Alexander Forrester, D. D., presided over the Institution. Possessing broad and advanced views as to the true character of education beyond the prevailing sentiment of his time, he gave effect to his noble thoughts by a fine presence, by grace of manner, and by an indefinable persuasive power. But perhaps his great source of power lay in his glowing enthusiasm and inspiring personality. He kindled a fire in the heart of many a student who carried a benign influence to the remotest corners of the land. Dr. Forrester had no holidays. His vacation was simply an exchange of the narrow confines of the class room for the wider field of the whole Province; he exchanged his class of pupil teachers for the parents and others whom he could call together at every important centre throughout the Province. The fruits of his labor came in the fullness of time when our free schools made the blessing of education available to every child in the Province.

There has been considerable development in the original equipment and staff of the Institution. The building now occupied is a stone and brick structure of fine appearance, as shown by the cut given in your report of this year. The Faculty has been increased from three regular instructors to twice that number. We have also a Model School of two different departments and a Kindergarten in the Normal School Building.

I have been looking backwards. What of the future? Without detracting from the merits of the work of the Normal School in the past, I feel assured that something better should be expected in the years to come. Improved conditions of working widen the possibilities, and cannot fail to secure higher achievement. The students will enter upon their professional work with the advantage of higher scholarship and the increased mental discipline which comes from the acquisition of that scholarship, and so they will be the better prepared for the comprehension of pedagogical principles and for the attainment of practical skill in teaching.

I am not prepared, however, to say that henceforth we should withhold all efforts to advance the scholarship of our students. By no means. The Institution will no longer be a mill to grind crude material into some approach to shapeliness and due proportion. But there will be need of careful attention to scholarship. Students will come to us, it is true, duly accredited from the Academy, and with their certificate of scholarship signed by government officials ; but these certificates will be based on a general average of qualifications, and they may be held by students of low attainments in some branches of the curriculum. That this is probable is shown by a " Summary of Marks " now before me obtained by a recent applicant for a license of Class C. The " Rectified Average " is 57.3, while the average on the three subjects Geography, History of British America, and British History is 25. It must be the duty of the Faculty to search out defects and strengthen what is weak.

Indeed I am inclined to think that our professional course should require students to review every subject of the Common School curriculum. Normal School students need to look at these subjects from the teacher's stand-point. As learners they may have traversed the whole field of a subject, but they have never analyzed the processes by which they acquired their knowledge, and they have forgotten the steps by which they reached their present position. Probably they never clearly apprehended the relation of these steps to each other. Standing in the clear light of present knowledge, they simply know what they know ; but do not know how they know. May it not be that profound knowledge may sometimes be a cause of failure in the art of teaching ? Through processes of thought the deeply learned student has travelled far away from concrete facts, and now regards his abstract generalizations as simple truths which every body should understand as well as he does. The very brilliancy of the light in which he stands may so blind him to his educational history that he does not see that path by which he felt his way in the dim light of the early morning. Hence the candidate for the teacher's office needs to review his knowledge for the purpose of discovering its historic development in his own mind, and to mark the successive steps by which he reached his present standpoint. His future work also requires that he study the educational values of the various subjects for purposes of mental discipline, and note how these values may vary according to the mode in which the subject is presented.

Then I think that the Normal School should aim to develop the love of study and to inspire its students with higher ideals. For these purposes I should feel inclined to emphasize the study of natural science and English literature, seeking in the one field to develop some degree of facility in laboratory work and original investigation, and in the other to develop a literary taste and broader views of human interests.

The well-equipped teacher needs to know something of everything and everything of something. The Normal School probably cannot give him this outfit. It ought to wake him up and stimulate him to keep his eyes open. Every school section has its individuality of character and needs special qualifications in its teacher, which can be acquired only on its own ground. The Normal School should give the teacher the Key of Knowledge by awakening his perceptions and making him responsive to his environment.

Respectfully submitted,

JOHN B. CALKIN.

Normal School, Truro, N. S., Dec. 31, 1892.

STUDENTS OF SESSION, 1891-'92.

AWARDED FIRST CLASS DIPLOMAS.

Bently, Janie............ Upper Stewiacke, ... Colchester.
Bordeu, George L....... Berwick, ... Kings.
Calnek, Matilda... ...... Granville Centre, ... Annapolis.
Freeman, Binney S. ...... Montague,.... .... Kings.
Morton, Howard A........ New Germany....·... Lunenburg.
Macaskill, John J......... Little Narrows ...... Victoria.
Macdonald, Wm H. ..... Truro, ... Colchester.
Morris, Sadie........... Walton, ... Hants.
McNeil, Emily E........ .... Gore, ... Hants.
Mullins, Jennie E....... Liverpool, ... Queens.
MacKenzie, Annie H..... New Glasgow........ Pictou.
Murray, Sadie A. .... New Glasgow, ... Pictou.
Rettie, Ella ... . Truro.... .... Colchester.
Shaw, Arthur M. .... Middleton, ... Annapolis.
Smith, Eva C ... . Salmon River, ... Halifax.
Schaffner, Gertrude ...... Truro, ... Colchester.
Sommerville, Jennie..... .. Truro, ... Colchester.
Stapleton, Wm .. .. Hartford, ... Cumberland.
Woodland, George H..... Wallace,......... ... Cumberland.
Webber, Eva A.... ...... Chester,... .... Lunenburg.
Willett, Clara E..... .... Tupperville, ... Annapolis.

AWARDED SECOND CLASS DIPLOMAS.

Anderson, Jennie .... Musquodoboit Harbor, Halifax.
Anthony, Bertha......... Kennetcook,......... Hants.
Bradshaw, Frank.... .... Nictaux, ... Annapolis.
Beattie, Robt. .... Amherst,........... Cumberland.
Borden, Naomi.... .... Port Williams, ... Kings.
Burris, Mary ... . Upper Musquodoboit, Halifax.
Black, Florence J. .... Amherst, ... Cumberland.
Boyle, Hugh C.......... Strathlorne, ... Inverness.
Cunningham, Wm. A..... Tatamagouche, ... Colchester.
Coleman, Edna F.... .... Lakeville, ... Kings.
Collie, Ezelia Alice.... .... Milton, ... Queens.
Carman, Laura F.... .... Bedford,.... .... Halifax.

Cook, Clara	Gay's River,	Colchester.
Creelman, Maud	Masstown,	Colchester.
Daniels, Teresa M.	Liverpool,	Queens.
Davidson, Milton D.	Aylesford,	Kings.
Davison, George W.	Woodville,	Hants.
Freeman, Kate K.	Milton,	Queens.
Givan, Lamont	Port Williams,	Kings.
Hopkins, Florence	Centre Rawdon.	Hants.
Hennigar, Edith	Canning,	Kings.
Hunter, E. May	Springhill,	Cumberland.
Hiltz, Ida J.	Chester,	Lunenburg.
Hiltz, Jessie L.	Chester,	Lunenburg.
Johnson, Hattie M.	Greenfield,	Colchester.
Keith, Ethel	Advocate Harbor,	Cumberland.
Kirkpatrick, Lottie B.	Aylesford,	Kings.
Lewis, Gertrude	Truro,	Colchester.
Lightbody, Maggie	Belmont,	Colchester.
McGillivray, Angus J.	Dunmaglas,	Antigonish.
McLeod, Bessie J.	New Lairg,	Pictou.
Miller, Alice L.	Folly Village,	Colchester.
McCully, Juliet	Truro,	Colchester.
McElhinney, Mary A.	Masstown,	Colchester.
Macdonald, Anna M.	N. E. Margaree,	Inverness.
Morehouse, Lottie G.	Centerville,	Digby.
Moffat, Clara L.	Little Bras' d'Or,	Cape Breton.
McNeill, Bessie J.	Berwick,	Kings.
Nicolson, Jennie	Gulf Shore,	Cumberland.
Oxley, Priscilla	Springhill,	Cumberland.
Patterson, Maggie	Tatamagouche,	Colchester.
Purdy, Annie M.	Springhill,	Cumberland.
Park, Libbie	Beaver Brook,	Colchester.
Payzant, Lucille E	Windsor Forks,	Hants.
Ross, M. Janetta	Piedmont,	Pictou.
Reid, Abbie J.	M. Musquodoboit,	Halifax.
Reid, Nancy A.	M. Musquodoboit,	Halifax.
Ross, Maggie	Cow Bay,	Cape Breton.
Stephens, Laura	Walton,	Hants.
Sutherland, Mary G.	Truro,	Colchester.
Smith, Daisy	Shinimicas,	Cumberland.
Schofield, Florence	Vesuvius,	Kings.
Smith, Edith	Walton,	Hants.
Taylor, Lillie Jane	Lower Onslow,	Colchester.
Tingley, Gussie M.	Amherst.	Cumberland.
Wilson, Florence B.	Windsor Junction,	Halifax.
Wilson, Edna H.	Truro,	Colchester.
Webber, Emily	Chester,	Lunenburg.
Webber, Bessie A	New Germany,	Lunenburg.
Zinck, Ella	Lunenburg,	Lunenburg.

AWARDED D. CERTIFICATE.

Armstrong, Mertie	Port Medway	Queens.
Blair, Carrie T	Truro	Colchester.
Grant, Stella	Hardwood Land	Hants.
Higgins, A. Alice	Central Onslow	Colchester.
Johnson, Addie C	E. Mountain	Colchester.
Lindsay, Cora M	Belmont	Colchester.
Lindsay, Lizzie B	Belmont	Colchester.
Pearson, Frances E	Truro	Colchester.
Sibley, Susan J. K	L. Meagher's Grant	Halifax.
Taylor, Georgie	Lower Onslow	Colchester.

GRADUATES OF FORMER YEARS.

Carty, Maggie E	Deep Brook	Annapolis.
Sinclair, Alice M	N. E. Lochaber	Antigonish.

COURSE UNCOMPLETED.

Bigney, Ada	Truro	Colchester.
Belfontain, Cecelia	West Chezzetcook	Halifax.
Blair, Edith	Onslow	Colchester.
Blanchard, Fred. A	Truro	Colchester.
Cruickshank, Libbie	Sunny Brae	Pictou.
Ferguson, Creighton	Hardwood Land	Hants.
Kempton, Enos	Milton	Queens.
Lyons, Mamie J	Onslow	Colchester.
Mack, Edward E	Mill Village	Queens.
McLean, M. Alena	Weston	Kings.
McKeen, Gussie	Melrose	Guysboro'.
McQuien, Mary S	Kewstone	Inverness.
McMillan, Christina	Whycocomah	Inverness.
McIntosh, Julia	Truro	Colchester.
McMullen, Teressa	Truro	Colchester.
Nelson, Blanche	Truro	Colchester.
Purdy Fanny	Wallace	Cumberland.
Reid, Maggie D	Greenfield	Colchester.
Rutherford, Maggie	M. Stewiacke	Colchester.
Taylor, Minnie	L. Onslow	Colchester.
Winchester, Maggie R	Joggin Bridge	Digby.

Total number enrolled 114
Number awarded First-Class Diplomas............ 21
   "   "   Second-Class " 60
   "   "   Third-Class Certificate........... 10
Former Graduates 2
Number whose course is not completed 21

NORMAL SCHOOL.

Year	No. of Teachers	Total number enrolled.	STUDENTS. Attendance full session of 35 weeks.	Attended six months' course.	Average time of attendance in weeks.	Received Diploma.	EXPENDITURE. Salaries of Teachers.	Salary of Janitor.	Cost of Fuel.	Contingencies,— Stationery, etc.	Total.
1891	5	101	55	32	29	61	$0 00	$0	$248 00	$317 38	$5465 38
1892	5	114	64	27	28	81	00	400	210 00	440 00	5850 00

MODEL SCHOOL.

Year	No. of Teachers	PUPILS. No. registered—Winter Term.	Average daily attendance—Winter Term.	No. registered—Summer Term.	Average daily attendance—Summer Term.	Total number different Pupils registered during year.	EXPENDITURE. Salaries of Teachers.	Amount received from Province.	Amount received from Town of Truro.	Total.
1891	2	108	90	109	86	128	$1100	$600	$500	$1100
1892	2	07	85	110	88	112	1050	550	500	1050

APPENDIX B.

REPORTS OF INSPECTORS OF SCHOOLS.

DISTRICT No. 1.—HALIFAX.

HINKLE CONDON, *Inspector.*

Sir,—

At the last meeting of the Board of Commissioners for the Western District, a petition was presented for the division of a section which has seldom made an average daily attendance of 30. The principal reason given by the petitioners was that some of the children were obliged to walk three miles to attend school.

The Board, recognizing the importance of following the Regulations of the Council of Public Instruction, viz., "That such bounds should always be determined upon as will enable the people of all the sections to educate their children in the most efficient and economical manner, which can be attained only by means of large school sections," refused to grant the petition.

The action is to be commended, for it is certainly better for children to walk 2 or 3 miles to a *good* school than to have an *inferior* one at their very door. But so strong is the prejudice in favour of a school near at hand that there is not a single instance in my experience of twenty-one years where the Commissioners have been asked to unite sections, although we have in this county *five* very weak and small ones which are so situated that they could be advantageously united to adjoining sections, thus enabling all the children within their bounds to attend a good school the year round. For example, we have two small sections where the one cannot average more than 8, even for the summer months, and the other gives for the "No. of children in the section from 5 to 15 years of age" as 24. If they were united we should have a school making an average of 25 or 30, and not a child would be compelled to walk more than 2½ miles. Another instance occurs where two school-houses are located within one hundred rods of each other. The "No. of children in these sections from 5 to 15 years of age" is 35, and the average of daily attendance 26. "The sever a Boards of Commissioners have power to unite two or more school sections into one school section, on a petition of a majority of the ratepayers of each section." If discretionary power could be vested in the several Boards of Commissioners, subject to the sanction of the Council of Public Instruction, some of our poor schools would become efficient and a considerable amount could be saved, not only in Halifax county, but, I am quite sure in other districts.

HOUSES ERECTED IN THE WESTERN DISTRICT.

East Dover, notwithstanding the hard times, caused by the failure of fish, during the past season, has now a large and convenient house capable of accommodating 60 pupils. This is in striking contrast with West Dover section where they have been allowed for all these years the use of a building which never was fit for a public school house and must be condemned. The African section near Hammond's Plains, by the aid of sixty dollars from the County Fund, will have ready for occupation by the 1st of April, a schoolhouse that will be a credit to the settlement.

Montague, wisely taking advantage of the gold boom, has also provided a thoroughly good house.

Chezzetcook, No. 65, has made extensive repairs, so that with the graded school-house in the Grand Desert section, No. 65½, this French Settlement has excellent school accommodation for 240 children. No. 65 has the finest and largest school grounds in the county.

The East Dover, Montague, Cow Bay and Chezzetcook houses are furnished with approved patent desks.

Lower Jeddore, West, in the Eastern District, has now a schoolhouse in keeping with this enterprising community.

Ecum Secum, situate 110 miles east of Halifax, has at last a suitable house, ready for November 1st.

Several of the poorest houses have been repaired. On the whole Halifax County has done well in providing school-houses and voting supplies for the support of schools; but in school apparatus all are not up to the standard.

SCHOOL WORK.

Dr. Philbrick, Superintendent of the Public Schools of Boston for twenty-eight years, in his last report says :—

" In the management of educational affairs the chief problem is to secure good teachers. All other parts of the business are of secondary importance. It is through the immediate agency of teachers that other educational provisions and appliances are put to use for the attainments of the desired ends. Hence the principal test of the merits of a school system is found in the character and qualifications of the teachers in its service."

Grant that the " teacher makes the school," and in no way can
we give a better idea of the improvement of our public schools than
by following the examinations of candidates for licenses from year
to year.   I have had as assistant examiner for several years, a gentleman who has been familiar with the examination work since the
inception of our Common School system.   During the July examinations of 1892, when upwards of one hundred candidates of all
grades, from D to A, were earnestly at work, losing not a minute of
time, he called my attention to the many points and incidents that
gave unmistakable evidence of improvement in those who are to
carry on that noble work of developing mind and upbuilding character, on the success of which the future prosperity of our country
mainly depends.   No thoughtful person could observe those young
people, so painstaking, so concentrated in their attention to the work
in hand, without seeing a proof of the value of our schools in the
past, and hope for their increasing excellence in the future.

The grades of the 133 teachers who taught the 5246 pupils for
the winter term, were as follows :

Grade A........ 1
 "   B........ 8
 "   C........ 74
       D........ 50

The 151 teachers, in charge of 5,896 pupils for the summer term,
were :

Grade A........ 1
 "   B........ 11
 "   C........ 81
       D........ 58

The *primary* teaching is greatly improved, and is especially to be
marked in those who have had Normal School training, since the
establishment of the model Kindergarten in Truro.

The teaching is less mechanical, more sympathetic, and therefore
better adapted to the infant mind and more calculated to arouse and
develop.

Reading is taught far more skillfully and by better methods, and
perhaps the status of a school cannot be more correctly estimated,
if only *one* branch could be taken, than by a reading lesson.   This
would apply to all grades, for the bright teacher can take the short
exercises of the Primer and by intelligent treatment give the child
a vivid sense of language, as the vehicle of thought and feeling.

British American History is taught in all of our schools, so that
a majority of those who are in the 6th and 7th grades have a correct
knowledge of the history of our country as given in Calkin's book.

Arithmetic is the subject in which our schools are comparatively strong.

Geography in several of the schools is admirably taught.

Temperance is receiving attention, which depends very much on the personal estimate of its importance by the teacher ; but as we have several teachers, who are ardent temperance advocates, much faithful instruction which has already borne good fruit has been given. While, of course, the teacher should know enough to give valuable oral lessons, it is desirable that some suitable text book should be in the hands of the pupils. This book should be accurate in statement, moderate in tone, and quite low in price, so that it may be within reach of our poorest sections.

The Tobacco Act, is a step in the right direction, and the provisions of this act and the laws against intemperance should be carefully explained to the children, so that a correct public opinion on the improper use of narcotic stimulants may be formed in the school-room, in order that it may become a seed bed of progress and moral reform. In Nov., 1892, Mr. Craig, Grade A, was appointed Principal of the Dartmouth schools, but at the end of the term he was chosen by the government to succeed Inspector Lay, in District No. 10.

Mr. Miller, also Grade A, is now Principal, and arrangements have been made for doing High School work in Dartmouth for the future.

The Kindergarten under Miss Hamilton is not only doing well itself, but is a source of influence in other departments.

City Schools. During the months of March and April I visited the most of these schools, but in September and October I denied myself this pleasure and took the time journeying from section to section, for the second time in the term, in order to advise with teachers in regard to the new regulations. I only wish that I could have reached every section of the county, more especially as the Journal of Education containing a copy of the new regulations, was unavoidably somewhat late in reaching the sections.

The work done in the city schools is improving from year to year in range and efficiency. The primary schools are admirable in method and spirit. The best of them are in line with the Kindergarten.

The High School is increasingly attractive to our bright pupils of the county schools. Bedford has been very fortunate in the pupils who have attended from time to time the High School examinations. Two of the five candidates who went through with the A examination at the Halifax station were from this section.

The Manual Training department is, as elsewhere, realizing the expectations of its advocates, and making converts of those who, at first, were not in favor of it.

Halifax is in the path of progress, and may be proud of her system which, although not of long standing, is thoroughly well organized, so that a child beginning in the kindergartens may pass through all the grades of most excellent common schools, take a thorough course in the high schools, and then, having taken a degree in Arts, may finish with special training in one of the professions.

I have the honor to be, yours respectfully,

H. CONDON.

To A. H. MacKay, Esq., B. A., B. Sc., LL. D.,
    Superintendent of Education.

DISTRICT No. 2.—LUNENBURG AND QUEENS.

H. H. MacIntosh, *Inspector.*

Sir,—

I beg to submit the following brief report on the Public Schools of Lunenburg and Queens for the year ended October 31st, 1892.

I am pleased to say that Educational affairs, in this district, have been working very smoothly and satisfactorily the past year. The Gold River difficulty has at last been settled, and instead of strife and contention we have now two fine new school houses, and a registered attendance of over one hundred pupils enjoying school privileges, from which they have been deprived for the last four years.

Two new sections have been organized during the year, Lower Woodstock and Gold River, South, making 191 sections in the district, 145 in Lunenburg County and 46 in Queens County. There is now, in the entire district, only one small settlement without school, viz., Upper Woodstock, and I hope to see a school-house built in this section next summer.

The following tables comparing the attendance of the present year with that of 1891, show a steady increase:

LUNENBURG COUNTY.

	WINTER TERM.		SUMMER TERM.		
	No. of Schools.	No. of Pupils registered.	No. of Schools.	No. Pupils registered.	Total number of Pupils during year.
1891.......	156'	6197	152	5755	7351
1892.......	161	6364	155	5837	7433
Increase..	5	167	3	82	82

QUEENS COUNTY.

1891.......	50	1875	56	1980	2364
1892.......	54	1937	53	1831	2286
Increase..	4	62			
Decrease..			3	149	78

LUNENBURG COUNTY.

1891. Grand total attendance, Winter term............ 415,462
1892.   "   "   "   413,608

Decrease....................................... 1,854

1891. Grand total attendance, Summer term.......... 352,782
1892.   "   "   "   362,747

Increase.... 9,965

Increase in grand total attendance 1892, over 1891........ 8,111

QUEENS COUNTY.

1891. Grand total attendance, winter term..............124,026
1892.   "   "   " 126,645
      Increase.................................. 2,619
1891. Grand total attendance, summer term..............126,482
1892.   "   "   " 121,262
      Decrease 5,220
      Decrease in grand total attendance, 1892, from that
        of 1891 2,601
      Increase in grand total attendance—*Lun.* and
        Queens, 1892, over 1891 5,510

TEACHERS EMPLOYED.

WINTER TERM.

	A	B	C	D
Lunenburg Co........	1	10	69	81
Queens "	2	4	32	16

SUMMER TERM.

	A	B	C	D
Lunenburg Co........	1	8	' 66	80
Queens "	2	6	30	15

SALARIES.

The average annual salaries of teachers, from all sources, are given below, principals of academies not included :—

		Lunenburg Co.	Queens Co.
Males, Grade	B.....................	$477.64	$471.64
"	C.....................	221.23	248.73
"	D.....................	170.82	164.82
Females, Grade	B..	$268.31	$277.98
"	C.....................	216.23	213.73
"	D.....................	164.82	158.32

Compared with last year, there is quite an increase in the salaries paid first class males—the others remain nearly the same.

Improvements.—Seven new school-houses have been built during the year, viz.: Garden Lots, Blue Rocks, Chester Basin, Gold River North, Gold River South, Lower Woodstock and North River. The two, first mentioned, are fine large buildings, thoroughly built, well lighted and ventilated, have separate entrances and lobbies, supplied with patent seats and desks and are, without exception, the best buildings of their class in the district.

The others are well suited to their respective sections and supply long felt wants. Extensive repairs have been made in a number of sections, and I am glad to notice that outbuildings are receiving more attention than formerly. Under this head may be mentioned Bridgewater, improvement to school grounds ; Fauxbourg, Upper Northfield, Fancy's, Greenfield, Pleasant River and Port Mouton, repairs to buildings.

Something is being done, from year to year, towards fencing and improving the school grounds in country sections but much yet remains to be done.

Apparatus.—While a few sections are still deficient in this respect, yet as a general rule, sufficient apparatus is at hand for the use of the efficient teacher. Scarcity of maps, particularly of the

Dominion and Maritime Provinces, was a great drawback; but within the last two years, this has been remedied to a great extent, so that now nearly every school is fairly well supplied.

Teachers.—We have had, during the past year, a large number of good teachers, a larger number of fair teachers and quite a number of poor ones. All, I think, have done the best they could. The failures were largely the result of lack of experience and practical training. More Normal School teachers have been employed in this district during 1892 than in any previous year, and I trust that the amended "Regulations regarding Licenses" will induce a great many more to obtain a Normal training. Teachers change less frequently than in former years, and there is no doubt that the one term system will lessen this evil still more.

Course of Study.—The course of study is being better understood and modified to suit circumstances, every year. When a teacher, at all capable, has been in the same school for a number of terms, we generally find that school well classified and up to the requirements of the course. The oral work does not receive full attention in our miscellaneous schools, yet good results are to be daily observed from what has been attempted.

School Subjects.—Reading is far from satisfactory. Not more than 10 per cent. of our miscellaneous schools have what I consider good reading, and in over 50 per cent. it is decidedly poor.

More interest is being taken in penmanship, and the improvement in the writing of pupils the past year has been marked.

Arithmetic, one of the most important branches, and one which takes up more time than any other in the course, was for a long time unsatisfactory. I spent considerable time trying to impress upon teachers the necessity of making the Arithmetic practical and of attaining to quickness and correctness in figures. The result has certainly been encouraging, and in this subject, at least, we may say good work has been done.

Grammar, Geography and History are taught to a greater or less extent in all the schools and with varying success. Teachers are gradually finding out that more *oral* instruction and less text-book give best results.

High Schools.—The Lunenburg and Liverpool Academies have had a prosperous year, and the candidates for licenses from these schools were more than ordinarily successful. All the departments of the common schools in connection with these institutions are under trained and experienced teachers, and do excellent work.

The Bridgewater and Mahone Bay schools are also in fine condition and increasing every year in efficiency and attendance. The

advanced department of the former does High School work exclusive-
ly, and that of the latter, 8th grade and 1st and 2nd year High
School work.   The Milton and Chester schools also do more or less
H. S. work.

Changes.—The amended regulations which came in force November 1st, were the subject of considerable discussion in the profession.
Nearly all our teachers strongly favor the annual term and we look
for good results from the same.   I have talked the High School
course over with all our H. S. teachers and the general impression
is that the work of the first and second years is rather heavy considering the age and attainments of pupils usually found entering
these years.   All are giving it a fair and earnest trial, knowing well,
that any modification found necessary to be made in the interests of
High Schools in general, will be made.   The date of the annual
school meeting, last Monday in June, is not well suited to our shore
sections, as nearly all the ratepayers are away on the fishing grounds
at that time.   The latter part of March or first of April would suit
such sections much better.   I am glad to see that the section of the
Act referred to anticipated such cases.

For reasons, known to you, I was only able to visit two-thirds of
the schools during the winter term.   All the graded schools were
carefully inspected, and as many of the miscellaneous as possible.
During the summer term, every miscellaneous school in the district
was reached, as well as a majority of the graded schools.   This could
not have been accomplished, had it not been for the exceptionally
fine weather of September and October.   The recent Regulation
changes will give more time for the work of inspection, render such
more easily accomplished and, I hope, be productive of better results.

Accompanying this report are " Notes of Inspection" and Statistical
Tables for the school year, which I trust you will find complete and
satisfactory.

Your obedient servant,

H. H. MacINTOSH.

To A. H. MacKay, Esq.,B. A., B. Sc., Ll. D.,
         Superintendent of Education.

DISTRICT No. 3.—YARMOUTH AND SHELBURNE.

James H. Munro, Inspector.

Sir,—
    The two counties which constitute my Inspectoral District are
Yarmouth and Shelburne, the former being in the western extremity
of the Province, and the latter, adjoining it, in the most southern.
The English inhabitants of Yarmouth are mainly the descendants of
New Englanders, who began to settle here in 1761, and of Loyalists

who arrived about the year 1785. Besides, there is a large French population, whose forefathers either evaded the expulsion of 1755, or succeeded, after years of exile, in returning to "Acadie." Doubtless, the main attraction for the early settlers was the advantageous position of the county for prosecuting the fisheries, and in these and other pursuits on the ocean, Yarmouth people have been eminently successful. Some years ago when wooden ships were in demand, they owned 153,000 tons of shipping, which averaged eight tons to each person living in the county.

As one might expect, the capital of the county, the town of Yarmouth, shows evidence of that enterprise and prosperity which have made it the second in size and population in the Province. There are here some very fine public buildings and many beautiful private residences in keeping with the modern improvements of streets and buildings lighted with electricity and electric street railway, an excellent water supply for domestic and fire purposes, and a complete equipment of steam fire engines and other appliances for saving property. By the completion of the Western railway system of Nova Scotia, its advantages have been greatly enhanced. From this point two splendid steel steamers, property of the Yarmouth S. S. Company, carry passengers and freight between Boston and Yarmouth, in seventeen hours, each way. Hebron, Port Maitland, Ohio, Carleton, Tusket and Arcadia, are thriving villages. The most important French settlements are the Wedge, Belleville and Pubnico. The inhabitants are principally engaged in fishing, farming, and commerce.

Judged by their names and characteristics, the first settlers of Western Shelburne were of the same stock as the English people of Yarmouth. Under far greater disadvantages on account of the rocky soil, they had to draw their living almost entirely from the ocean. At the present day, the houses and tidy surroundings are very suggestive of comfortable circumstances. There "the poor fisherman" is a misnomer. I need not add that churches and temperance societies are well sustained in the Municipality of Barrington.

Animated with a desire to remain under British rule, some thousands of Loyalists came to Eastern Shelburne, and built the town of Shelburne. For a time it flourished, protected by British troops. But either the people were unable to utilize the resources of the county, or the resources needed to support a city of 12,000 inhabitants were not there—in either case the city was almost forsaken, the people passing into other parts, some settling in Yarmouth county, though the larger number returned to the United States. When those who were left learned to adapt themselves to their environment, Shelburne became noted for the fine ships built in its shipyards. Situated at the head of a magnificent harbor, ten miles from the ocean, the town has a delightful temperature in mid-summer. When the railway connects Yarmouth and Shelburne our American neighbours will have direct access to this delightful retreat from the heat of their cities. Of the other localities Lockeport is the most important. Bordering on the sea its one dependence is the fisheries. It is a pretty little town, and affords evidence that its business has been managed to good advantage.

In the early years of a settlement the energies of the people are taxed to secure the bare necessaries of life, and little can be done towards providing the means of education. Indeed, we are credibly informed that fifty years after its first settlement there were only three public schools in the county of Yarmouth. In 1819 a Grammar School was established, which in 1830 was superseded by an Academy. These institutions were taught by scholarly men, and to them the navigators and business men of Yarmouth were largely indebted for their education. But in the rural parts, says the Rev. J. R. Campbell, the historian of the county, "there were neither school-houses, nor text-books nor masters." By the year 1848 great improvements had been effected, thirty-six school houses having. been erected where 1700 children were taught.

Early educational statistics for the county of Shelburne are few and defective. Proof is not wanting that there were good schools in the town shortly after its settlement. Those who can look back 35 years and recall the old inhabitants of that time, will not need to be told that many of them had enjoyed the advantages of good schools. The data at hand are briefly these : In 1826 the county was divided into school districts (or sections); in 1832 twenty-four schools were in operation ; in 1840 there were thirty working schools ; and at a later date the Legislature provided four Grammar Schools with special grants attached to them. In 1863, 12 per cent. of the population attended school some part of the year.

For the years 1865 and 1892, the former the year after the introduction of the Free School System, the following statistics are given :

			(Winter.)		(Summer.)	
Dates.	Counties.	Sections.	Schools.	Pupils.	Schools.	Pupils.
1865	Yarmouth ..	57	45	2023	43	1765
1892	"	74	106	4206	102	4130
1865	Shelburne ..	56	24	1004	47	1600
1892	"	67	77	3020	78	3008

No. of different pupils attending school in Yarmouth county in the year 1892 :—4940, or 1 in 4.3 of population ; in Shelburne county 3610, or 1 in 4.1 of population.

The figures for 1865 hardly make a fair showing. The strong

and in some cases the violent feeling against the free school act threw educational matters into confusion. On the other hand, there were years when the attendance was larger in Yarmouth county than in 1892.

Among other improvements resulting from the new system, may be mentioned well defined school sections traversed by good roads, few pupils having to travel two miles to the school, comfortable school houses, supplied with apparatus and good furniture, qualified teachers, and permanent schools.   No one would now question the right of every child " five years old and upwards " to participate in school privileges.

During the past five years the assessments for building and repairs were quite large, but the expenditure was absolutely necessary.

No. of buildings repaired........................   24
    "   "   "   and supplied with patent
              furniture.............   41
 " School-houses built   23
 " Apartments in same...............   34
 ", School-houses in course of construction..   2

The repairs were extensive, involving new floors, sheathed walls and ceiling, and comfortable out-buildings. The new school houses are a great improvement on those that preceded them ; some indeed may be called beautiful. There is a marked and growing sentiment in favor of attractive school-rooms. What is wanted now is more attention to the exterior of the older buildings, improved grounds and proper inclosures. Unless the grounds are protected, the labour of Arbor Day will be fruitless.

The new building at the south-end of Yarmouth town, which takes the place of the one which was destroyed by fire last spring, will soon be finished. It is large and substantial, containing eight apartments, and has superior apparatus for heating and ventilation. The air is kept constantly fresh, without reference to windows or doors, the whole body of air changed every few minutes.

Nothing will be left undone for comfort and efficiency. It will be occupied in February. With teachers who have had long experience and who are devoted to their calling, Lower Town school will excel its past good record. In Milton the old fashioned hot air arrangements have given place to the hot water apparatus. The teachers highly appreciate the change. This school consists of seven departments. In the sixth department the common school course is finished and the high school course in the seventh, from which pupils are prepared to matriculate into any provincial university. It is well known the average Yarmouth mind is not enamoured of colleges. It thinks more of schools whose main function is to drill in the three R's, than of institutions whose main purpose it thinks is to swell professions already crammed to repletion. With some such ideas, four pupils were sent from Milton high school to take the course of instruction at the school of technology in Worcester, Mass., where their attainments and ability have made an excellent impression. Their career will be watched with much interest. The Yarmouth Seminary was once the finest building of the kind in the Maritime Provinces. It led the way in improved school architecture, and inspired wealthier communities to rival it. In use nearly thirty years it commands admiration for its dignified appearance and beautiful grounds. Though spacious, its departments are overcrowded, and the necessity for additional accommodation is urgent.

It is gratifying to learn that arrangements are about concluded which will enable the School Commissioners to greatly improve and augment the education facilities here. Additional buildings of a superior character will be erected on the seminary lot. In the summer term 485 pupils were registered, and of these 75 attended the two academic departments which are taught by able and experienced teachers. In their hands the course of instruction is an efficient instrument of mental discipline. Your predecessor put on record his estimation of Principal Cameron's classes in English literature. In my opinion he is second to none in the province for extensive and accurate knowledge of the subject, and his method of teaching it embraces everything within its scope. Teachers will profit much by studying his "Notes on English" now being published in the Educational Review. With "the suggestions" in the November number the authors he names should be read with fresh interest and "scholarly enthusiasm."

In Shelburne ounty thetwo leading schools are the Academy, which contains five departments, and Lockeport School, four. The fifth department of the Academy is exclusively occupied in High School work.

Many young people come here from the rural sections to qualify as school teachers. Successive Principals have had a valuable helper in the acting trustee, Dr. Morton, to whose exertions for the good of the Institution the town owes much. The grading of the Lockeport school is as perfect as its circumstances will admit. In each department, the examination was very satisfactory. Prominent among the studies in the Principal's room are classics and mathematics, in which subjects the pupils will bear comparison with the best in my district. The building is large and comfortable, and amply provided with apparatus.

In Barrington there are eight graded schools. Those which sent the largest number of pupils to the examination for licenses to teach are : Upper Wood's Harbour, Passage, Head, and Hibbert's Brook. The status of Port La Tour school is not now equal to what it was a few years ago. I should remark that every section in this Municipality has a good school house, and that last term there was only one vacant.

The following tables will show the number of pupils in each county taking the advanced course, wholly or partly.

COUNTY OF YARMOUTH.

	English Literature.	English Language.	Geography.	History.	Arithmetic.	Geometry.	Algebra.	Mathematics.	Drawing.	Book keeping.	Physics.	Botany.	Chemistry.	Physiology.	Latin.	Greek.	French.	German.
Academy	75	75	61	30	75	75	75	8	....	49	....	43	18	2	21	2	50	...
Milton	34	26	25	41	41	41	41	17	....	....	41	....	28	....	17	1	41	4
Rural Schools (15)	74	17	27	80	80	74	80	9	40	48	8	54	20	10	16	2	20	...
Total........	183	118	113	151	196	190	196	34	40	97	49	97	66	12	54	5	111	4

COUNTY OF SHELBURNE.

	English Literature.	English Language.	Geography.	History.	Arithmetic.	Geometry.	Algebra.	Mathematics.	Drawing.	Book keeping.	Physics.	Botany.	Chemistry.	Physiology.	Latin.	Greek.	French.	German.
Academy	32	9	41	41	41	41	41	9	....	32	9	25	18	9	8	....	...	..
Lockeport	17	0	12	11	20	20	20	1	....	....	....	9	8	3	19	18	17	...
Rural Schools (15)	47	7	51	48	51	51	51	3	19	51	7	28	9	4	6	....	....	..
Total	96	16	104	100	112	112	112	13	19	83	16	62	35	16	33	18	17	..

Tables showing the number of pupils in the Grades vii and viii. preparatory to the High School Course.

COUNTY OF YARMOUTH.

		Nature Lessons.	Reading.	Dictation.	Grammar.	Composition.	Geography.	History.	Arithmetic.	Algebra.	Geometry.	Writing.	Drawing.	Book-keeping.	Latin.
Town Schools, Grade VII	....	62	77	77	77	62	77	77	77			77	62	....	....
" " "	VIII	36	46	46	46	36	46	46	46	85	25	46	44	20	....
Rural " "	VII	272	320	320	370	305	292	299	309			282	181	....	....
" " "	VIII	205	250	250	281	233	271	268	264	207	124	240	136	242	2

COUNTY OF SHELBURNE.

		Nature Lessons.	Reading.	Dictation.	Grammar.	Composition.	Geography.	History.	Arithmetic.	Algebra.	Geometry.	Writing.	Drawing.	Book-keeping.	Latin.
Town Schools, Grade VII..	....	36	36	36	36	23	36	36	36	....	....	36	....	....	...
" " "	VIII	27	39	39	39	....	39	39	39	39	12	39	....	....	12
Rural " "	VII	270	332	332	301	199	316	303	334	....	....	326	170	....	..
" " "	VIII	162	241	241	233	187	231	225	237	166	178	243	96	230	3

Besides these subjects, teachers give oral instruction in health, patriotic duties and temperance; and a few teachers give lessons in singing.

	Co. of Yarmouth.	Co. of Shelburne.
No. of pupils in Grade I....	791	347
" " II....	587	405
" " III....	577	340
" IV....	561	440
" V....	384	390
" VI....	413	316

In the county of Yarmouth there are twenty-six French schools, most of them taught by French teachers. As in nearly every section the little ones cannot speak English, the teachers are obliged to teach two languages. Still, I sometimes hear better reading in English, among French pupils, than in the corresponding grades of some English schools. No teachers are more asiduous in the discharge of their duties. The schools at Middle West Pubnico and Upper Eel Brook are taught by Sisters of Charity In the primary of the former, a visitor will be much pleased with the daily exercises. In the advanced, my attention was drawn to the youthfulness of the senior pupils. The same tendency is seen in other sections near the sea. The expansion of certain lines of business has made boys' help more profitable, and thus life-long interests are sacrificed for temporary gain. I should state that these pupils went from French Schools to Truro, to receive a Normal School training.

I do not think there ever was a time when the schools generally were doing better work. Instead of loading the memory with lessons, teachers address knowledge to the understanding, and make use of the imagination when narrating events or describing objects. This is obvious in history and geography classes. For several terms I gave much attention to arithmetic with the view of impressing the need of rapid and correct work in the lower grades, and of the exercise of the reasoning powers in the advanced grades. I was astonished to find that even in good schools pupils relied chiefly on forms for the solution of questions. In my last visit there was noticeable improvements. Blackboards are in use, not as ornamental fixtures, but for daily work. Neatness in all kinds of work is regarded as an important element of education, conducing to the formation of good habits and to future success. In language teachers aim to be correct, and to govern their temper under provocation. The age of unreasonable threats and rough manners is past. Instances of undue severity are very rare.

The revised course of study for High Schools and Academies has received universal approval. The annual examinations of pupils who have done High School work in any schools in the county under the same arrangements and by the same examiners, will be a striking exhibition of the unity and equality which obtain in our school system.

In this " transition year" a suggestion or two will be in order

1st. Adopt a regulation prohibiting teachers from using books when teaching classes.

2nd. To impress on teachers that they ought to be students' insert a question in the school returns, asking for the list of books and magazines read during the school year.

3rd. Consider the examination of no candidate for a school license final, whose writing is marked " bad," until he can produce specimens of good penmanship. An examination of some registers and school returns would justify this rule.

4th. Modify the Inspector's certificate so as to bar him from signing it when the ratepayers of a section, after sufficient notice, fail to provide what is necessary to the comfort and progress of the school. The County Fund need not necessarily be forfeited.

5th. Considering the number of children who do not attend school at all during the year, upwards of 1300 in District No. 3 in the summer term, enact a law making the financial losses accruing to sections on account of absence fall directly on those parents who neglect the education of their families.

Before I conclude I wish to acknowledge my indebtedness to Alexander Lawson, Esq., for publishing annually my report in his widely circulated newspaper—the " Yarmouth Herald." As it is read in every section, my suggestions, commendations and censures have reached the parties for whom they were mainly intended. The unanimity and promptness of ratepayers over so wide an area in adopting my recommendations are largely due to this favour.

With assurances of much respect,

I have the honor to remain,

Yours very sincerely,

JAMES H. MUNRO.

To A. H. MacKay, Esq., B. A., B. Sc., Ll. D.,

Superintendent af Education.

———

DISTRICT No. 4.—DIGBY AND ANNAPOLIS.

L. S. Morse, A. M., *Inspector.*

Sir,—

The following general report on the state of Common School education in inspectoral district No. 4, for the year ended Oct. 31st, 1892, is respectfully submitted. For more detailed information than that which is herein contained, I beg leave to refer you to the statistical Tables, Monthly Reports, and Notes of Inspection, covering the same period.

The Boards of School Commissioners at the annual meetings in May and June, formed three new school sections—two in the district of Annapolis East, and one in the district of Digby. The action of the Commissioners in this regard was sanctioned by the Council of Public Instruction in two only of these cases, as you are already aware. In consequence of the formation of these new sections there are now *one hundred and eighty-seven* school sections in this inspectoral district. With two or three exceptions, these sections are regularly organised under the law, and are maintaining schools in most cases during the entire year. In a few of those classified as "*poor sections*" schools are sustained part of the year only. These "poor sections" are comparatively few in number, and do not represent more than one twentieth of the population of this inspectoral district.

At the inception of the present school system in 1864, this inspectoral district was laid off into *one hundred and thirty-nine* school sections, *eighty-three* of which were in the county of Annapolis and *fifty-six* in the county of Digby. There are now *one hundred and six* school sections in the county of Annapolis and *eighty-one* in the county of Digby. This increase of *forty-eight* sections within a period of twenty-eight years, is an indication not only of an increase in population, but more particularly of the popularity of the present free school system and of the advancement of education among the people. The efficiency of the public schools in the same period has increased in a greater ratio. At the present time almost every inhabitant of this district is living within the bounds of a regularly organized school section—a fact which did not exist when free schools were established by law.

It is gratifying to be able to report a steady improvement in the school accommodation. With the exception of a very few old buildings erected previous to 1864, and a very few others which have become too small to accommodate the increasing population, the school-houses are creditable structures. The old buildings are being condemned as fast as circumstances will warrant, and are giving place to others more in accordance with present requirements. During the year extensive repairs have been made to a few school buildings, and some sections have provided the paragon school desks in place of the common desks formerly used. The paragon desk is superceding the common desk in most cases where new furniture is being procured.

In Bridgeport section, No. 24, in the district of Annapolis West, and in Hillsburgh section, No. 3, in the district of Digby, the school-houses have become too small to accommodate the increasing population. At present three teachers are employed in each section. The school-houses were originally intended for two teachers only, with an assistant if necessary. The class-rooms in each case, for a few terms past, have been used for primary departments. These rooms are not suitable for this purpose. As these sections are situated at the village of Bear River, and the two school-houses are within a short distance of each other, I have for several years been urging the advisability of having these two sections united. At the present time the public sentiment of this village is becoming more favorable to this idea, and it is hoped that an effort will soon be made to consummate the union. Any such movement will receive my hearty approval, inasmuch as for educational purposes this village should never have been divided. Under existing conditions a union of the two sections would effect a saving in the employment of one teacher, and would increase the efficiency of the schools as a result of a more thorough system of grading. The united section would be in a position to sustain a system of schools second to none in any town or village in this inspectoral district, and at a cost no greater than at present incurred.

It is desirable that more clearly defined regulations be made regarding apparatus for schools. Some articles now deemed essential by existing regulations have not been provided in many of the schools. The attention of trustees has been repeatedly called to the deficiency referred to, but in many cases tangible results have not followed the notification. More explicit powers should be given to Inspectors in this regard. Sections should be compelled to provide all essential apparatus to the satisfaction of the Inspector as one condition upon the fulfilment of which the County Grant would be paid ; or Inspectors should be empowered to provide the same and charge the cost against the County Grant. If such regulations were formulated and sanctioned by the Council of Public Instruction, or if existing regulations were made more explicit and definite, it would have a beneficial effect upon trustees, and would insure a better supply of necessary apparatus in sections where a deficiency now exists. Inspectors have a fair idea of the financial ability of sections, and they would exercise any power granted them with proper discretion.

Good work has been performed by the teachers as a class during the year. In a few instances only failure to attain success in the school-room has resulted from inexperience and want of Normal training. A few have been found lacking ability to maintain order and discipline, without which satisfactory work cannot be done. A great majority, however, have laboured with enthusiasm and have been cheered by seeing creditable progress, notwithstanding hindrances caused by irregularity in attendance of pupils, and in some cases by lack of sufficient apparatus.

About twenty per cent. of the teachers employed during the year received Normal training. In view of the recent changes in the law and in the Regulations of the Council of Public Instruction respecting the Provincial Normal School, the day is not far distant when this percentage will be largely increased. This cannot fail to exert a beneficial effect upon the schools. Under existing conditions a very large proportion of the teachers, not having received a Normal training, retire from the profession about as soon as they obtain by experience the necessary aptitude in imparting instruction.

But little improvement can be reported in the permanency of the engagements of teachers. In some of the towns and villages teachers retain their situations for years at a time, but in the country sections the rule is to change every year, and in many cases every six months. During the past year about fifty per cent. of the sections have changed teachers each term, while probably not more than twenty per cent. will retain the same teachers for the ensuing year. The one term per year system now being introduced by law will mitigate this evil, and, it is hoped, produce more satisfactory results in most sections.

In regard to daily attendance at school some improvement can be reported. According to the returns received, one thousand three hundred and seventy-nine children, between five and fifteen years of age, were not at school in sections having schools during the winter term. One thousand one hundred and ten children between the ages named were thus reported during the summer term. The percentage of enrolled pupils daily present was *sixty and seven-tenths* during the winter term, and *sixty-two and two-tenths* during the summer term. No less than *one thousand seven hundred and ninety-eight* pupils were enrolled during the summer term whose names were not on the registers of the winter term. The proportion of the population at school during some portion of the year was *one in every four and four-tenths*. It will thus be seen that a very large proportion of the children of the district have been attending school during some portion of the year. There is yet, however, much room for improvement. A few children of school-going age have not been at school, and some of those who were enrolled attended so irregularly as to become a source of perplexity and discouragement to teachers in maintaining a proper grading of their schools. While some irregularity in attendance will necessarily exist, it should be reduced to a minimum by the enactment and enforcement of a compulsory attendance law, since no other means have yet been devised to accomplish this object.

The course of study, which is followed more or less closely in all schools, has produced beneficial results. A uniformity in school work now exists which was unattainable previous to its adoption. The oral work prescribed, however, does not yet receive in many schools that attention which was intended. Irregularity in the attendance of pupils, the lack of Normal training on the part of some of the teachers, and in some cases the large miscellaneous schools, including many grades, prevent as much work on these lines as their importance demands. The increasing number of trained teachers, and improved methods of teaching, will, doubtless, soon secure for the oral work of the course of study a greater share of time and attention in all schools.

The returns have all come to hand with reasonable promptitude. A large proportion of them were carefully prepared. A few were found incorrect in some particulars, showing want of proper care in their preparation. A shorter and more simple form of return involving less work in its completion would be a boon to teachers and Inspectors.

There are twenty-five French sections in this district, for which thirty-three French-speaking teachers are required. A great difficulty has always existed in finding regularly licensed teachers for these schools. During the past year it was necessary to grant permissive licenses to thirteen persons for the purpose of supplying these schools with teachers—the regularly licensed French-speaking teachers falling short of the demand by that number. Four of these teachers were a valuable acquisition, inasmuch as they were Normal trained teachers from the Province of New Brunswick. A few of the remainder did good work, and some were found to be poorly qualified educationally. The facts, that the French schools are large, that both languages are taught, that most of the teachers are of the third class, and that the hindrances to progress are, therefore, greater than in English schools, render advancement slow, and consequently very few French pupils obtain sufficient knowledge to obtain a third-class license.

The Teachers' Association for the inspectoral district held its meetings at Digby on the 6th and 7th days of October. About ninety teachers were in attendance. 1 was unavoidably absent, but from the published reports of the meetings, the proceedings must have been interesting and instructive. The programme presented included papers and illustrative lessons on the following subjects:—

" Patriotism," by L. H. Morse, B. A.; " Literature in our Schools," by Miss Emma J. Bacon ; " Reading," by Miss Julia L. Kinney ; " Hygiene in our Schools," by Miss Helen A. Vidito ; An illustrative lesson on " Our Flag," by Miss Jessie S. Titus ; "Home preparation of Lessons," by Joseph A. Crowe ; and " Teaching Geography," by Joseph A. McCarthy. All the papers were said to have been of a high order of merit, and were followed by discussion. Mr. Crowe's paper on " The Home p e a a on of Lessons," was published in the local papers, and Mr. Morse's paper on " Patriotism," appeared in a much condensed form in the " Educational Review." The presence of Dr. MacKay, the Superintendent of Education, added interest to the occasion. As this was his first meeting with our Association, an address of welcome was tendered to him and suitably acknowledged. The public meeting in the evening was well attended, and Dr. MacKay, who was the principal speaker on the occasion, won golden opinions from all for his very interesting and instructive address.

The Academies at Annapolis Royal and Digby, have been in successful operation during the year, under Principals McVicar and Godfrey respectively. The attendance has been good compared with other years. The character of the work done has been creditable. The large amount of High School work done in the other schools of Annapolis county, especially at Bridgetown, Paradise and Lawrencetown, interferes with the attendance at the Annapolis Academy, yet, notwithstanding this, the attendance has been quite as large as that at the Digby Academy, which suffers much less from the competition of other schools.

With very few exceptions all schools were inspected during the winter term. In consequence of the large number of schools in session, and the short time allowed for the work of inspection

owing to the long summer vacation, and the great amount of office-
work at the opening of the Term, it has been found impossible for
years past to inspect all schools during the summer term. This
year a larger number than usual were not inspected owing to leave
of absence of three weeks which was kindly granted to me on
application.

The general aspect of educational affairs in this inspectoral district at the present time, is encouraging. Although each year's
progress may not be conspicuously apparent, yet it becomes very
noticeable by contrasting the present with the .period twenty-eight
years ago when free schools were established. Within that period
the number of school sections has been augmented by the formation
of *forty-eight* new sections, thereby placing schools within easy
access of almost every inhabitant of the district. The style of
school buildings and furniture, and the supply of apparatus,
have greatly improved. The school-houses at the present time
are creditable structures, well adapted for the purposes intended,
and exhibiting a marked contrast with those which they
have superceded. The general educational attainments of the
generation now entering upon the active pursuits of life are
far in advance of those which their fathers possessed. The rigid
examination which teachers are now required to pass is a guarantee
that they possess acquirements of no mean order, and that they are
much better qualified for their work than the great majority of their
predecessors. For every teacher under the old system who could
boast of Normal School training, there are scores at the present day
who possess this qualification in a higher degree. The circulation of
periodicals devoted to the improvement of teachers in their profession was almost unknown twenty-eight years ago. At the present
time more than one half of the teachers of this district are subscribers
for one or more of such standard educational papers as " The Education Review," " The American Teacher," or the " New England
Journal of Education." Uniform courses of study for Common and
High Schools, embracing the elements of the natural sciences in
addition to the ordinary branches of study, have been introduced.
The text-books now prescribed are far superior to those formerly
used. The comparatively recent formation of Teachers' Associations
under the sanction of the law for the promotion of the efficiency of
the teaching service, has been productive of much benefit, and has
been the means of establishing an *esprit de corps* which did not
formerly exist in the profession. These and other facts which might
be mentioned are indicative of steady educational development under our present system—a development of which we have reason to
be proud. There is still, however, room for improvement. Since
much progress has been made in the past we are justified in believing that coming years will mark still greater advancement.

Thanking you sincerely for courteous treatment received at your
hands during the past year,

I have the honor to remain, Sir,

Your obedient servant,

To A. H. MACKAY, Esq., B. A., B. Sc., LL.D.,   L. S. MORSE.

Superintendent of Education.

DISTRICT No. 5.—HANTS AND KINGS.

COLIN W. ROSCOE, A. M, *Inspector.*

SIR,—

The following report of the condition of the schools in the counties of Hants and Kings, for the year ended Oct. 31st., 1892, is respectfully submitted for your consideration.

The aim of this report shall be to deal more particularly with matters not included in the pamphlets of statistics, sent herewith, or in the monthly reports of inspectoral work forwarded from time to time.

SCHOOL COMMISSIONERS.

In the district of West Hants there has not been a meeting of the Board of School Commissioners for two years. This is accounted for in part, by the loss sustained by the Board in the deaths of several valued members ; and in part by disinclination to give time and attention to public matters without remuneration. The Board of East Hants has been able to hold its meetings annually, by transacting business when but *three* or *four* members were in attendance. Notices of these Board meetings were given through the Journal of Education, the local newspapers, and by post card to each commissioner. The list of " Poor Sections," for West Hants, as determined by the Board in May, 1890, has been used to the present time as the basis for apportioning the extra allowance from the County School Fund to such sections. This was somewhat irregular, but thought best, in the absence of a meeting to determine otherwise. There are two ways out of this difficulty. (1.) To appoint a sufficient number of commissioners, willing to attend to the business for the honor it affords, or the benefit of it to themselves and others. (2.) To constitute a Board of about ten members and pay them similarly to the Municipal Councillors. The latter, in my opinion, is the course the times are demanding. Five deaths of commissioners have occurred in West Hants, and two in East Hants, since appointments were made. Business of importance that has been laid over for the past two years makes it imperative either to have new appointments made or to provide some other way for transacting this business.

INSPECTORAL WORK.

During the year I have made four hundred and thirty-nine official visits to the schools under my charge. In many instances these have been shorter than I would desire, but from the multiplicity of duties to be discharged, this used up all my time. The schools in some sections closed before, or opened after, my tour of inspection to that part of my district and thus, in some cases, prevented me from making two visits during the year. The correspondence and office work has been increasing from year to year since my appointment to this date. I am pleased to think that recent changes in the length of the school term, in the form of returns and registers, and in the time of making them up, will secure quite as much information of value concerning the schools as in the past, and at much less expense of labor by the Inspectors. The constant need of vigilance, that teachers perform their work thoroughly and well, neglecting no part of it, that trustees keep their school houses and appointments abreast of the times, and that advancement be made all along the line, was never more urgent than at the present time.

SCHOOL TRUSTEES.

There are trustees who understand the trend of educational sentiment and have prepared to advance with it. The school to them is second to no other interest in the community, and by their influence they mold the sentiment of the section. Another class of trustees is found in too many sections, who pose as the men who can run the cheapest school for miles around. They give the teacher $2.995 less than she ever received before; they provide green wood and give exercise to the big boys in keeping the fires alive; they exercise somewhat the patience of the teacher at the same time; they put off till next term repairing the blackboards, furnishing erasers, providing new maps, wall cards, etc., etc. They run a *cheap* school. It is *so cheap* that what is expended is virtually lost. I refrain from naming these in this report; but hope they may recognize themselves and reform before I take the liberty to use their names. A third class, and we have a few of them, never is ready to do anything. They forget to give notice of the Annual School Meeting at the regular time. They are pressed to call a special meeting by requisition of the ratepayers. They provide a school when compelled to do so, to prevent paying a fine for neglect of duty. I am glad this class is small and the first class is on the increase.

WINTER TERM.

	No. Schools.	No. Teachers.	No. Pupils.	Attendance.
Hants	114	116	4265	272423
Kings.	114	117	4291	276524
Total......	228	233	8556	548967

SUMMER TERM.

	No. Schools.	No. Teachers.	No. Pupils.	Attendance.
Hants	121	124	4570	276506
Kings..........	117	122	4169	240485
Total......	238	246	8739	516991

TEACHERS—WINTER TERM.

GRADE.	A	B	C	D	Male.	Female.	Total.
Hants.	3	22	67	24	23	93	116
Kings	3	23	62	29	32	85	117
Total	6	45	129	53	55	178	233

SUMMER TERM.

Hants	2	25	69	28	19	105	124
Kings	2	21	61	38	18	104	122
Total	4	46	130	66	37	209	246

SCHOOLS.

The foregoing tables give, in brief, an outline of the schools for the year. I am pleased to say that the past year has been one of considerable growth and advancement along certain lines of school work. There are individual schools and sections not taking full advantage of the School System; but on the whole progress is being made, and in many sections it is of such a nature as to stimulate the surrounding school forces. The County Academy in Windsor is still in charge of Mr. J. A. Smith, a very painstaking and efficient principal and a good teacher. He is aided and sustained by a staff of teachers of acknowledged ability and worth. There is the utmost harmony between the teachers and the school commissioners. During the year $50 worth of individual chemical apparatus, for laboratory practice, has been provided, also some physical apparatus, besides maps and an atlas for the study of ancient and classical geography. It is the intention to supply an equal amount each year till a thoroughly equipped laboratory is secured. Regular instruction has been given in nearly all the grades below the Academy in the Tonic Sol Fa system of music. The results have been most satisfactory. From grade 7, nineteen pupils were examined, five of whom received the Elementary, and twelve, the Junior Certificate. Two from grade 5 received the Elementary Certificate. The pupils of grade 7, Miss Burgoyne, teacher, have made wonderful advancement in music for the past term. There were five matriculants from the Academy into the colleges :—one to Acadia, two to Kings, and two to Dalhousie. Four candidates obtained grade C licenses at the last examination of teachers. Windsor needs a new Academy building on a more modern plan than the present building. The present one is not large enough for the school, has no ventilation, is not heated by the best system, has no convenient room for laboratory or chemical work, and must soon give place to something better if the school is to sustain its present high standing, when compared with other similar schools. Kentville Academy has been pressing to the front for a number of years and the attendance has so increased as to warrant the employment of a second grade A teacher. This was done the past year, and there was associated with Mr. McLeod, Principal, Mr. C. L. Moore, and the grant secured on the two-teacher basis. The teachers associated with Mr. McLeod in charge of the common school departments have labored faithfully that their pupils might advance from grade to grade till they reached the Academy. In this preparatory work the pupils have been disciplined and trained in lines of mental culture suited to their years, and much work of a high order has been performed. From this school several received grades B and C, and some were matriculated into college. The grant of $1,000 given to this Academy brings with it the requirements of expenditure to put its buildings in condition and supply them with apparatus to meet the demands of a school of such pretentions. I feel assured that the School Commissioners are men who will endeavor to meet your wishes in respect to buildings and appliances as soon as their attention is called to the needs of the school.

The school of four departments in Berwick, under the principalship of Mr. L. D. Robinson, continues to grow in the confidence of the people, and deserves mention in this report as the banner school in the number of candidates sent up to the teachers' examination; and I am pretty sure that no similar school in the province can boast of so many successful in capturing Grade B licenses for the number of applicants as this school. From eight B candidates six were successful; three others took Grade C and five Grade D. I wish it understood that the teachers in the common school grades, connected with this school, are fully meeting my expectations in contributing towards the very efficient state of the school sustained in Berwick. The same teachers have been in the school for several years, except for short periods of rest. The esteem in which they are held is manifest in the increase of $100 in the salary of the principal and smaller amounts to the others.

Wolfville has also four departments, having added one the past year. The advanced department has had three different teachers during the year—one of these for two portions of the year. This breaking up of the year into four parts seemed unavoidable, so far as the trustees were concerned; but it was impossible to make much progress under this kind of treatment. The three subordinate departments have been prosecuting their work to the satisfaction of the section and myself. In the matter of school accommodation, Wolfville has taken a step in advance of its own previous record and in advance of any section in the two counties. A new school house is in course of erection which promises to be the finest in the district. Provision has been made to heat and ventilate the building by the Fuller and Warner system, one of the most improved and best systems in America. The sanitary arrangements connected with this are said to be about perfect. By this system the impure air is conducted from the room and replaced by pure heated air, at a uniform and right temperature, every 7 or 10 minutes. Thus the air will not deteriorate when the rooms are occupied. The pupils will be freed from lassitude and headaches and enabled to do their work under conditions of healthfulness and happiness. The air is led from the rooms to the vaults, and after drying up all excrement, escapes by the flues, leaving all parts of the building pure. In my opinion there is more need of improvement in this matter of ventilation than in any other connected with the schools.

Hantsport has five departments and is one of our best schools. Mr. Geo. J. Miller, who has been principal of the school for five years, resigned at mid-summer to take charge of the Dartmouth High School. He is a man eminently fitted for a position of this kind, and the school under him and his excellent assistants has sustained a high standing among our schools. Mr. Miller will be much missed by the teachers of this district and by myself. He always took a prominent part in our teachers' meetings and associations, and leaves behind him many warm friends. He is succeeded by Mr. Isaac Crombie, a graduate of Acadia College, and of the Normal School, and a man who has already won distinction as a teacher. I expect to see no abatement in the progress of the school under his management.

The school at Maitland is pressing ahead admirably. For the past year, Mr. C. W. Brown has labored most faithfully and successfully as its principal. As a result a fourth department has been started and a good beginning made in providing chemical and other apparatus for teaching science. Canning school still maintains its good state of efficiency under Mr. Geo. W. Coffin, Miss Burbidge, and Miss Challen.

The other graded schools of this district have two departments each and are located at Somerset, Waterville, Woodville, Harborville, Hants Border and Kingsport in King's county, and Falmouth, Avondale, Brooklyn, Burlington, Summerville, Cheverie, Brookville, Shubenacadie, South Maitland, Upper Selma, West Noel and Walton, in Hants county. There are twenty-five of these graded schools in the district, and these represent seventy departments, as follows: One contains ten departments; two, five, three, four; and nineteen two, each. While I cannot group them all together as regards the merit of their work, I may say in general terms, they are all pretty good schools, and of more than half of them that work of a superior character is done in them. The miscellaneous schools do not have all the poor teachers. They are conducted in many cases by a hard-worked painstaking class of teachers. Many of them try to do more than it is possible to overtake; but on the whole do very valuable work. Some poor teachers still cling to the schools. I hope, however, the number of this class will grow gradually less as the new regulations, encouraging attendance at the Normal School, come to be understood and enforced.

TEACHERS.

Fifty-one of the teachers in winter, and fifty-five in summer, held Normal School Diplomas.

Of the teachers employed, 55 were male, and 178 female, in winter; and 37 male, and 209 female, in summer.

Fifty-three teachers in winter and fifty in summer closed their schools without holding the required public examination. Of the teachers doing this, not more than half gave any reasonable excuse for this infringement of the law. This loose way of treating the plain requirements of the law will, under the new regulations, be punished by loss of grants or license or both—if the case merit it. There is a necessity, too, for a more strict adherence to the curriculum of studies, on the part of some teachers. The teacher who teaches a Government school and participates in the Government grants must be held to the Government regulations or be ruled out for non-fulfilment of the conditions upon which such grants are made. Teachers should feel that they have nothing whatever to do with the selection of studies for their pupils. They should ascertain to what grades their pupils belong and assign them the work prescribed for those grades. It is the experience of those who have made fair trial of it, that the course of study in its aim is very useful, and much more can be accomplished by following it than by not doing so.

NEW SCHOOL HOUSES.

Welsford, Elmsdale and South Uniacke have built new school houses during the year. The last named is in East Hants, and was recently organized into a Section. The discovery of gold attracted settlers, and there are now 30 children so situated that a school is a necessity. The people built a school house and started a school even before the Section was sanctioned. Should the mines continue to yield as at present there will be a large school here.

POOR'S FARM, WEST HANTS.

This farm, owned by the Municipality of West Hants, on which the poor are maintained, is situated in MacKay School Section, in Newport. The property is not assessable for schools, and there are living here 16 children of school age. Objections on various grounds are made to having these children attend the public school. The people here feel they have no right to provide a school for these children, coming from all parts of the municipality, and would regard it as a hardship to have such a class of children thrust upon their school to associate with their children. They object most decidedly to this. The managers of the institution have had a young woman employed during the summer to teach these children. This seems to be a special case and is reported to you at the suggestion of some of the Councillors, in the hope that some special means may be provided to aid in the education of these unfortunates. It needs no argument to prove that Provincial grants are intended to aid in such cases, and I respectfully ask for this your thoughtful consideration.

CORPORAL PUNISHMENTS.

Almost every term some teachers feel impelled in the discharge of duty to inflict corporal punishment to bring into order refractory pupils or check the disobedient. This is done rather than turn such pupils adrift to become ruined and a nuisance to society. When parents understand the aim and intent of the teacher to be the ultimate good of the pupil and the school, this is almost always sure to result from the punishment; but not infrequently the parents hasten to the nearest Justice of the Peace, secure a writ and drag the teacher before his court and the public, to be tried and compelled to pay a fine and costs for common assault. The case is dealt with exactly as in the case of one assaulting another on the highway. The fact that the teacher is in *loco parentis*, and has a legal right to punish, in the same manner as a wise parent would, to keep his children in submission and make them obedient, is lost sight of. Teachers *may* and sometimes *do* punish to excess, and should pay the penalty therefor; but the publicity given to cases of punishment where the teacher is legitimately discharging his duties, and the great injustice in treating such cases as common assault, compels me in the interests of fair play for the teacher to protest against this mode of trial. Often, had the teacher means to carry his case to the higher courts, he would win; but he is not able to do this and he drops it with the loss of fine and costs and the complete overthrow of his influence and authority in the school. I have described an actual case, without giving names, and for the purpose of calling attention, in a general way, to the gross injustice done to teachers and schools in these little magistrates' courts, and of suggesting a remedy.

In cases of what may be termed excessive punishment by teachers, I would suggest that upon complaint being filed with the trustees in a legal way, they shall choose one of their number, the aggrieved parties shall chose a second person, and in case of disagreement, these two, thus chosen, shall choose a third, who shall have power to settle the case, and their decision shall be final and binding upon the parties concerned.

In order that trustees and others shall not be called upon to deal with cases of too trivial a character, the aggrieved parties must first present a certificate from a M. D. to the effect that the punishment was excessive, before they (the trustees), shall feel bound to investigate the case.

The full number of pupils in attendance for any part of the year was 10,613.

The schools at Kentville, Wolfville, Hantsport and a few others, were taught music by the Tonic Sol-Fa system.

I have the honor to be, Sir,
Your obedient servant,
COLIN W. ROSCOE.

A. H. MacKay, Esq., B. A., B. Sc., LL. D.
Superintendent of Education.

DISTRICT No. 6.—ANTIGONISH AND GUYSBORO.

W. MacIsaac, B. A., *Inspector*.

SIR,—

I beg to submit the following report on the public schools and educational affairs of District No. 6, comprising the counties of Antigonish and Guysboro, for the year ended Oct. 31st, 1892. As the period since my appointment to the office of Inspector of Schools has been entirely too short to become thoroughly acquainted with the schools, teachers and other educational forces of the district, I venture to bespeak your kind indulgence if you find this, my first report, less full and exhaustive than might, under more favorable circumstances, be expected.

In Antigonish there were 90 schools in session during the winter term and 96 during the summer term. In Guysboro for the same terms, the numbers were respectively 80 and 92.

The number of pupils enrolled in Antigonish during the winter term was 3035, and during the summer term 3179. The corresponding number for Guysboro were 3154 and 3288.

The grand total attendance is as follows :

ANTIGONISH COUNTY.

Grand total attendance, Winter Term........ 191,046
        "   "   Summer "   174,404

GUYSBORO COUNTY.

Grand total attendance, Winter Term.................. 197,946
        "   "   Summer "   189,597

The grand total attendance for Antigonish during the year was 365,450,—an increase of 35,075 over that of the previous one ; Guysboro under this heading shows an increase of 33,090. This showing is all the more satisfactory in view of the fact that the total enrolment of the year just ended was less than that of its predecessor. The explanation for this rather interesting circumstance is mainly to be found in the greater prevalence of the dread La Grippe during the winter term of 1890-91.

Average annual salaries paid to the teachers including Government grants.

	MALES.			FEMALES.		
	A & B	C	D	A & B	C	D
Antigonish..	$367.58	$213.96	$152.04	$234.08	$204.68	$144.54
Guysboro' ..	522.08	230.06	166.04	286.88	224.16	156.04

The following table shows the number of teachers of each sex and of different grades in each county :

ANTIGONISH COUNTY.

	WINTER TERM.				TOTAL.	SUMMER TERM.				TOTAL.
	A	B	C	D		A	B	C	D	
Male	2	5	20	8	35	1	4	27	10	42
Female	—	3	24	28	55	—	3	23	28	54
Total of grades and sexes..					90					96

GUYSBORO' COUNTY.

	A	B	C	D		A	B	C	D	
Male	1	4	5	2	12	1	2	4	3	10
Female......	—	5	21	43	69	—	4	30	48	82
Total of grades and sexes..					81					92

In the matter of erecting and repairing school houses there is but little to report. The school house at Lower White Head, Guysboro county, was destroyed by fire in September last, but it is being replaced by another which will be ready for use at an early day. The fact, however, is not less unfortunate than singular that this is the second time, within a few years, this section had to make good a loss sustained through the same agency.

While the ideal school building is not by any means to be found in every section, it is but the truth to state that there is no section without one, and that our people, as a whole, show in this particular an activity and a taste that are highly encouraging.

It will be readily observed from the last table submitted, that the number of grade B teachers is comparatively small, and that consequently nearly all the schools are in the hands of grades C and D. The reason is not far to seek. The trustees, as a general rule, are content to engage the services of the cheapest teacher. The tendency on the part of our more capable and scholarly teachers to abandon the profession for more lucrative and permanent avocations is becoming more marked from year to year; nor is there much hope that it can be obviated except by making the teaching profession financially more attractive.

I am glad to be able to testify that the teachers of the district generally, are most punctual and painstaking in the discharge of their various duties ; and it is a matter for congratulation that the ardor and enthusiasm with which many of them enter upon their duties, are not measured by the parsimony of their employers.

During last winter the Academy in Guysboro was in charge of I. M. Longley, Esq., who taught there with much acceptance for seven or eight years. Owing to illness he was obliged to resign his position last spring, and was succeeded by Mr. Buchanan of Sydney.

The school commissioners of Antigonish sustained a serious loss last year in the sad death of the Rev. R. MacGillivray, of Arisaig, and also in the removal of many valued members of the Board from the district.

The resignation of my predecessor, Professor A. G. MacDonald, caused universal regret among his many friends in this inspectorate. For eight years he taught with distinguished success in the Mathematical Department of St. F. X. College, Antigonish, and in both capacities as Professor and Inspector, he accomplished much to advance and elevate the condition of education in Eastern Nova Scotia. In the higher sphere of Professor of Mathematics in the Normal School, the teachers of this Province are afforded an excellent opportunity to benefit by his ripe judgment and practical experience as an educationist.

In conclusion, permit me to congratulate you most cordially on your appointment to the high and honorable position of Chief Superintendent of Education of your native province ; and to thank you sincerely for much assistance and many official courtesies received at your hands during the year,

I have the honor to be, Sir,

Your obedient servant,

W. MacISAAC.

A. H. MacKay, Esq., B. A., B. Sc., LL. D.,
> *Superintendent of Education.*

CAPE BRETON AND RICHMOND.

M. J. T. MacNeil, B. A., *Inspector*.

Sir,—

I beg leave respectfully to submit my report on the schools of the district under my supervision for the year ended Oct. 31, 1892.

Several petitions for the establishment of new sections by the division or re-organization of existing ones came before both Boards of School Commissioners at the last annual, as well as at subsequent adjourned and special meetings, but the proposed changes not having been granted by the Boards, or failing, as in one case, to be sanctioned by the Council of Public Instruction, the number of sections remain the same as last year,—132 organized sections in Cape Breton county and 70 in Richmond. The Boards have found by experience that it is not wise to be too ready to grant sub divisions petitioned for, there being several instances in both counties of the injurious effects of the undue multiplication of sections. It is much easier to secure the division of a section than a re-union, after experience has shown the un-wisdom of the experiment, as the law, in the latter case, requires the signatures of a majority of the ratepayers of each section to a petition, and this is generally found very difficult, if not impossible to obtain. I am of opinion that the Boards should have larger powers than they now enjoy in this respect, or that the law could be so amended as to restore the original section to its former status if, after the lapse of a reasonable time, it be found that the newly formed section is unable to support a school or fails to make any effort to establish one. There are two cases in point in the county of Richmond. Section No. 64, Bear Island, originally a portion of Section No. 47, Gut of Canso, was established in 1874. It has never had a school, as far as I know, and certainly not since my incumbency. In 1887, a new section named Macpherson, No. 17½, was formed by the division of Section No. 17, Grand Digue, and the annexing of a portion of Bray, No. 49. In the new section, no practical steps have been taken from that day to this to build a school house or establish a school, and Bray section has been seriously crippled. Several attempts have been made by the more public-spirited ratepayers, those who take an interest in the schools, to have these sections restored to their original boundaries, but they proved abortive owing to the difficulty above pointed out. As the law stands, I see no other means of effecting the desired reunion than a special Act of Parliament. In the meantime, many children are left without the benefits of education. Besides the above, another attempt was made at the last meeting of the Richmond Board to unite two sections in which are now maintained very indifferent schools, Hureauville and Richmond Mines, and though the time is most opportune, the school houses of both having been condemned, the scheme failed for want of the necessary signatures.

In the county of Cape Breton, 12 sections had no schools in operation any part of the year, as compared with 9 the previous year, and in Richmond county only 4 sections were idle the whole year as compared with 7 the previous year. The attendance in both compares favourably with that of the previous year as shown in the following tables :

CAPE BRETON COUNTY.

	WINTER TERM.		SUMMER TERM.		
	No. of Schools.	No. of pupils enrolled.	No. of Schools.	No. of pupils enrolled.	Total Number of Pupils during Year.
1891	150	5771	164	6252	6926
1892	149	5875	160	6181	6954
Increase .	. . . .	104	. . . .	. . . .	28
Decrease .	1	. . . .	4	71	. . . .

RICHMOND COUNTY.

	WINTER TERM.		SUMMER TERM.		
	No. of Schools.	No. of Pupils Enrolled.	No. of Schools.	No. of Pupils Enrolled.	Total Number of Pupils during Year.
1891	61	2187	70	2552	2615
1892	63	2361	74	2737	2903
Increase .	2	74	4	185	288

CAPE BRETON COUNTY.

1891.	Grand total attendance, Winter Term............	368,796
1892.			....	388,299

Increase 29,493

1891.	Grand total attendance, Summer Term...........	363,906
1892.	||	369,099

Increase 5,183

RICHMOND COUNTY.

1891.	Grand total attendance, Winter Term.............	132,361
1892.	||	154,078

Increase 21,717

1891.	Grand total attendance, Summer Term.......... .	144,856
1892.	||	163,091

Increase 18,235

While the above tables show a slightly decreased number of schools in operation in one county, and an equally slight increase in the other, it will be noticed that the enrollment in both was actually larger, and the increase in the attendance was satisfactory, indicating of course greater regularity. The total number of pupils registered during the year was, in Cape Breton county 1 in 4.5 of the population, according to the census of 1881, or about the same proportion as the previous year; and in Richmond county, it was 1 in 5.2, as compared with 1 in 5.77. The larger number of towns and villages proportionally to the population in the former county doubtless accounts in part for the greater proportion of children attending school. Besides the incorporated towns of Sydney, North Sydney and Sydney Mines, having from 9 to 11 departments each, such mining centres as Little Glace Bay, Cow Bay, Bridgeport, Victoria Mines and Reserve and Lorway comprise no

less than 24 departments between them, ranging from 3 to 7 each.
Then there are Louisburg, Mainadieu and Gabarus with two departments each. Against this, the other county can show only two sections with more than two departments each, viz. : Arichat 5, and
Acadiaville 4; and three having 2 each, viz. : St. Peter's, D'Escousse
and Poulamond. There are, nevertheless, such large and thickly
populated settlements as L'Ardoise, River Bourgeois and Petit-de-
Grat, which are divided up into several distinct sections. There is,
however, the further fact that while the census of 1881 was required
to be used in the statistical tables for the year, the recent census
credits the county of Cape Breton with an increase of nearly 3,000
in population, while the county of Richmond suffered a diminution
of 722. By the last census. the proportion would stand 1 in 4.92
for the former, and 1 in 4.96 for the latter county.

The number of the different grades and sexes of teachers employed
differed but slightly from last year, as seen from the following
table :

CAPE BRETON COUNTY.

WINTER TERM.				TOTAL.	SUMMER TERM.				TOTAL.
1891. A	B	C	D		A	B	C	D	
Male...... 4	22	22	26	74	5	19	28	28	80
Female....—	6	40	30	76	—	7	39	38	84
				150					164
1892.									
Male...... 4	20	20	22	66	4	19	24	24	71
Female....—	8	37	38	83	—	9	42	38	89
				149					160

RICHMOND COUNTY.

1891.									
Male...... 1	7	12	10	30	1	9	15	13	38
Female....—	1	11	19	31	—	—	12	20	32
				61					70
1892.									
Male...... 1	7	10	11	29	1	10	17	11	39
Female....—	—	18	16	34	—	—	17	18	35
				63					74

A comparison of the average annual salaries received does not show any very material difference, or any regularity of increase or decrease, in the different grades, such differences as exist being mainly due to accidental causes rather than any definite principle.

	MALES.			FEMALES.		
	A & B	C	D	A & B	C	D
Cape Breton, 1891.	$397.45	$215.32	$169.69	$296.18	$229.64	$150.75
" 1892.	388.44	204.41	148.31	300.83	241.89	146.97
Richmond .. 1891.	273.56	228.80	162.92	192.85	164.64	143.00
" .. 1892.	299.22	216.06	155.13	......	184.06	149.16½

I regret to report that the Richmond County Academy at Arichat has ceased to exist as such, having failed, by a small fraction, to make the requisite average. This failure to maintain the small average of 15 shows (1) that the local requirements for academic work are not very extensive, and (2) that the school was not, to any considerable extent, serving the purposes for which county academies were established. If all the students of the county who have been and are attending academies in other parts of the Province had patronized the local institution, more than the required average would easily have been maintained. While, therefore, the loss both in prestige and in cash is regrettable, as far as the town of Arichat is concerned, it will not be materially felt by the rural sections of the county.

Sydney Academy, under Principal MacKeen and Vice-Principal Stewart, is maintaining its efficiency and usefulness, and is assuming more and more the character of an Island institution, as all the counties of Cape Breton send a fair quota of students to its halls. The number registered last winter term was 65, making an average daily attendance of 52.6; and in the summer term there were 46 registered and an average daily attendance of 34.7, making for the year an average of 43.65. The students of this Academy have, for several years past, been publishing a monthly paper under the title of "The Sydney Academy Record," which, while not so pretentious, perhaps, as journals issued from larger institutions, is still very creditable to the students, and is fulfilling a very useful mission by fostering among them a wholesame *esprit de corps* and that love for *Alma Mater* which is so well calculated to promote the future welfare of any institution of learning. The students therefore deserve credit for their efforts in maintaining their scholastic organ, and they deserve the encouragement and practical sympathy and support of the citizens of Sydney in particular, and of all who have the welfare of the Academy at heart. It were much to be desired that the same spirit was manifested among the teachers in support of their own professional organ, the *Educational Review*, whose clientele in this district is, I regret to say, very circumscribed.

The number of new school buildings erected in the course of the year is not large, but at least one creditable addition has been made to the gradually increasing number of our really good school houses. The town of North Sydney, finding its school accommodation inadequate, determined, during the year, upon replacing some of its old buildings by one good convenient modern school house, and accordingly, on the occasion of my last visit, I found five of the departments scattered around the town in temporary and more or less suitable quarters, and the building in which they had previously been accommodated torn down and being replaced by a large and imposing structure for eight departments, with all necessary adjuncts in the shape of ante-rooms, etc. A more extended description of this fine school house will, however, more properly belong to next year's report, as it was not expected to be ready for occupation till some time in the early part of the current school year. The new school house at West Louisburg was found occupied, and though not finished inside, was fairly comfortable, being high and well lighted. A suggestion of mine with regard to arrangement of windows, carried out even after the building was well advanced, remedied what would have been a grave defect ; and this leads me to wish that inspectors were furnished with official plans which trustees in country sections could be compelled to adopt.

In the county of Richmond, new buildings were found to have been erected and occupied at Cape Auguet, Sec. No. 51, and Intervale No. 32. Neither of these were finished interiorly, and one of them was simply *habitable* for summer time. The building at Intervale [(Framboise District) replaces one destroyed by fire in 1890, since which time there had been no school in the section. The school-house of Framboise, No. 46, which had been allowed to fall almost into decay from desuetude was, last spring, partially repaired, and school was resumed for the summer term, after an *interregnum* of several years. The above cases, not to speak of several instances of more or less extensive repairs and embellishments, constitute the bulk of the building operations of the year, but I expect to see more new buildings go up in the near future, as several school-houses have lately been condemned in both counties, and several other sections notified that a similar fate awaited theirs.

No less than three school-houses were destroyed last July by the forest fires which, owing to the great drought prevailing at that time, raged in different parts of Cape Breton county, viz: one at Lakeville, Section No. 8, near Sydney, another at Grand Mira North, No. 84, and a third at Brickyard, No. 129, near Albert Bridge. The first two were comparatively new, having been built only two or three years ago, previous to which the second section named had not enjoyed the privilege of a school for several years owing to a similar calamity. The third was in course of construction, the old house having been torn down to be rebuilt. None of these buildings, as far as I know, were insured, and all of the sections could ill afford the loss, and I fear it may be some years before it will be made good in some of them. Trustees and ratepayers should take a lesson and

keep their school property reasonably insured.   Hard, however, as
the above losses are upon the sections concerned, they are not to be
compared in hardship to that of Section No. 18, South Head, Cow
Bay district.   In last year's report, I had this to say about this very
section :—" At South Head (Cow Bay), a neat new building replaces
the one reported last year as having been destroyed by fire, and the
people of this section deserve great credit and special commendation
for their energy and public spirit in overcoming exceptional difficulties.   This is the second time within a few years that they have been
obliged to make good losses by fire, in the face of the disheartening
suspicion amounting to a moral certainty in the latter instance at
least, that incendiarism was the cause of the trouble, and that possibly
the same dastard hand is lurking in their midst ready to subject them
to a similar ordeal.   The new school-house was fairly well finished
(interiorly), furnished and equipped, and the school was doing excellent work under an intelligent and painstaking teacher."

Well, about the beginning of December (1891), on a Sunday
morning, this same school house was seen on fire.   By great exertions, the flames were subdued but not before the building was
badly damaged.   It had been insured for $100.   A claim was made
for $50, which was paid, but the insurance company cancelled the
policy.   Temporary repairs were effected and the school was re-
opened and continued till Christmas vacation, when it was once
more, in the words of my informant, " made neat and comfortable."
School was again resumed, and on the third day, at 7 o'clock in the
evening, the house was again seen in full blaze, and so fierce was the
fire, that before the people could get to it, it was beyond control.
The section was thus once more left without a school-house, without
a dollar of insurance, and with a small debt on the burnt building.
The friends of the school were well-nigh discouraged, (and no
wonder) but, nevertheless, they managed by special permission to
maintain their school for the remainder of the year in the only
available building, which was very small and unsuitable.   What
steps, if any, have of late been taken to rebuild, I have not been
informed, but this is certainly a case that calls for sympathy and
deserves special consideration.

I am pleased to be able to report that the long-standing difficulty
between the town of Sydney and the remnant of the adjoining section of Muggah's Creek. No. 2, has been at length definitely and
satisfactorily settled by the special legislation of last session, whereby that portion of the latter section lying outside the town limit shall
henceforth, for all school purposes, " be deemed and be part of the
town of Sydney."   The town School Board has since taken over the
section school-house, removed it to a convenient site, repaired and
furnished it, and opened an elementary department for that suburb.

The number of candidates applying last July for teachers' licenses
was, at Sydney Station, 76, and at Arichat, 20.   The following table
shows the different grades applied for and the results :

SYDNEY.

No. applying for Grade.	No. obtaining Grade.				Failed.	No. already holding licenses.
	A	B	C	D		
A.......... 1	....	....	....	....	1	
B.......... 9	....	3	4	2	......	
C..........40	....	....	9	19	12	C 7
D...........26	....	....	....	7	19	D 14
Total 76	....	3	13	28	32	21

ARICHAT.

B.......... 4	....	1	....	3	......	
C.......... 6	....	....	1	4	1	C 2
D..........10	....	....	....	2	8	5
Total 20	....	1	1	9	9	7

It will be observed that of the 44 candidates at the former station who succeeded in capturing a license of some grade, 21 were already licensed teachers, so that 23 obtained a license for the first time, being a little over 30 per cent. of the whole number of applicants. The number already holding licenses out of the 11 candidates who were successful at Arichat was 7, the result being 4 *new* teachers, or 20 per cent. of the whole number of candidates.

While in Beaver's Cove school section in the county of Cape Breton last April, there being no school in operation in the common or public school, I availed myself of the opportunity of spending a couple of hours with Prof. J. D. McKinnon in his Agricultural school. The main course of lectures for the season had been completed and most of the farmer students had dispersed, but there were still five in attendance receiving special lessons, some of them well advanced in years, and some from distant parts of the Island. These expressed themselves as highly pleased with the instructions received, and I was much interested in Mr. McKinnon's account of the working of the school and of the results already accomplished. Mr. McKinnon being himself a practical farmer and withal an excellent teacher, imbued with a rare amount of enthusiasm in his work, he cannot fail to be successful as a teacher of agriculture. Mr. McKinnon taught the section common school during the summer term, and at my visit, his juvenile pupils displayed rare proficiency in Botany and Entomology, while they were quite up to their several standards·in Language, Geography and Arithmetic.

The returns show that nearly one half the pupils registered at school were receiving the oral lessons prescribed by the Course of Study. A good many of the teachers are themselves deficient in the knowledge and training necessary to enable them successfully to impart these lessons. Many complain of the difficulty of procuring the books prescribed or recommended as aids in preparing them. It is a question whether trustees should not be obliged to supply such books for the teacher's use.

For several years, I have been endeavoring to impress upon many teachers—and not always the younger ones either—the necessity of beginning earlier than they had been in the habit of doing the teaching of Language and Geography. It was a matter of common occurrence to find only one class—the most advanced in the school—having any idea of either of these subjects, and then, in many instances, it was merely a matter of recitation from the text-book, with no attempt at the practical adaptation of the principles of Grammar especially. Reading and Arithmetic seemed to be absorbing the lion's share of attention. I am pleased to say, however, that the above subjects are now receiving a great deal more attention in the earlier grades and being more intelligently taught. The results obtained are very gratifying, and the old excuse that parents do not wish to have their children learn this or that branch is seldom if ever heard. A subject which is still very often poorly taught, where it is not altogether neglected is History. It is difficult, however, to expect more than simple recitation in the case of teachers whose reading is necessarily confined to their little text-book, whence, in many instances, was derived all their own store of knowledge on this subject, crammed up for the occasion of their examination. Under such circumstances, it is not surprising to find history being taught as *modern* that is rather "ancient" as our text-books in History as well as those in Geography are not quite up to date in some particulars.

It would be very desirable that some means could be found of training more of our teachers in the Tonic Sol-fa system of music with a view to its introduction into more of our schools. Where this admirable system is in use, notably in the departments of the North Sydney schools conducted by the Sisters of Charity, where it has been in vogue for some years, and in the auxiliary departments of Sydney Academy where it has been introduced as a result of Rev. Mr. Anderson's visit and instructions last year, the results obtained are marvellous. Children of the tenderest years grasp it with so much ease!

I would remark, in conclusion, that our teachers are, as a body, zealous and industrious, and that as "the teacher makes the school," so our schools are, on the whole, well looked after. There are a good many exceptions of course, but so there are in all things. I wish it to be inferred, however, that we are making progress both

material and intellectual—slowly perhaps, but surely and substantially.

Allow me to express my high appreciation of your prompt attention and uniform courtesy in our official intercourse.

I have the honor to be. Sir,

Your obedient servant,

M. J. T. MACNEIL.

A. H. MacKay, Esq., B. A., B. Sc., LL. D.

Superintendent of Education.

DISTRICT No. 8.—INVERNESS AND VICTORIA.

John Y. Gunn, *Inspector.*

Sir, —

As required by law, I hereby beg to submit the following report
upon the present condition of education within the district comprising the counties of Inverness and Victoria, together with a
synopsis of progress made during the school year ended on the 31st
Oct., 1892.

The catalogue of school sections has undergone no material
change within the past year, the number reported for 1891 having been 268, while for the present year the number is 269. The
recent addition was made at the rear of the Upper South West
River in North Inverness, and the locality is now known by the
name of Kiltarlity section, No. 53. Each of the subdistricts comprises about the same extent of territory, although the highway
mileage in South Inverness far exceeds that of either North Inverness or Victoria.

Ten new school houses have been built, 5 in S. Inverness ; 2 in
N. Inverness ; and 3 in Victoria ; and at the last annual meeting
the sum of $2920 was voted for additional accommodation.

At the annual meetings of the School Boards, the school houses of
3 sections in Inverness and 6 in Victoria ,were condemned as unfit
for school purposes, and as six months' notice was given in every
case, sufficient money was voted at the last meeting, either to erect
new buildings or to prepare the old ones to the satisfaction of the
accredited authorities.

Taking the whole year, the number of schools in session was
somewhat in excess of the corresponding terms of the previous year,
the total number in session during the winter of 1891 having been
229, but during the summer following the number increased to 247,

while during the past school year *nine* additional schools were opened, and the number in session in summer remained undisturbed as compared with the summer of 1891.

The number of children at school exceeded the attendance of the previous year—the enrolment of the winter and summer terms having been respectively 7529 and 8023 pupils in attendance at the public schools—while total annual enrolment in both counties was 9728—an average of 1 in 5.1 for the whole population of Inverness and of 1 in 4 for Victoria.

Per se, this is a fairly satisfactory exhibit. It is, however, a matter of regret that in the County of Inverness there should have been no fewer than *nine* vacant sections during the whole year; and in Victoria the number was at least nominally larger. Now as a matter of fact nearly every school section in the district has been officially visited during the past year, and wherever a vacancy was found to exist, an honest effort was put forth to fan the smouldering educational embers of the locality by assuring parties interested that in the event of a duly licensed teacher being unattainable, a permissive license could be issued in favor of any person of fair attainments whom the local school commissioner could conscientiously recommend. In a number of cases this proposal was accepted, and schools were accordingly established ; but the fact is still glaringly manifest that many of the people seem to have no conception whatever of the inestimable boon the school Act has placed within their reach. Education is placed in the same category as good health, pure air, and an abundance of food, all mercies of prime importance, but at the same time rarely, if ever, estimated at their true value.

During the winter term there were 176 teachers and assistants employed in Inverness and 73 in Victoria, and during the summer following the numbers increased to 188 in Inverness and 80 in Victoria.

The number of teachers with their grades of license employed both terms may be tabulated as follows:

In Inverness during the winter term there were—

2	Teachers of	Grade	A
15	"	"	B
48	"	"	C
102		"	D

In Victoria during the same term there were—

1	Teacher of	Grade	A
5	"	"	B
16	"	"	C
48			D

During the following summer term there was a gratifying increase both in the number of schools in session and in the number of teachers employed—in Inverness 3 teachers of Grade A having been engaged; 18 of Grade B; 58 of Grade C, and 87 of Grade D; while in Victoria there were seven additional schools as compared with the preceding winter term.

Considering the times and the long vacations allowed, together with the fact that schools are in session for a few hours only every day for five days in the week, the salaries of teachers are fair. Taking the allotments of the past winter as a basis of distribution, the rates paid in Inverness were, for Grades A and B, $292; C, $176, and D, $116.

In Victoria the rates were somewhat higher for the more advanced grades—teachers of Grades A and B having received an annual salary of $418, and teachers of Grade C, $212—while teachers of Grade D received only $101 for the year.

During the past winter term the Government paid the teachers of this district the following gross amounts :—

```
South Inverness ........................ $3210.67
North Inverness ........................  2611.15
Victoria  .............................  2309.05
                                        ---------
    Total............................. $8130.87
```

And at the close of the summer term each sub-district was paid as follows :—

```
South Inverness ........................ $3112.98
North Inverness ........................  2587.24
Victoria  .............................  2524.00
                                        ---------
    Total............................. $8224.22
```

Making in all an annual disbursement by the Government, $16355.10.

It appears to me that this money is partially misapplied The School Act was framed especially in the interests of the poor, while as a matter of fact the wealthy and middle classes profit to just as great an extent as the poor.

I consider when pupils pass beyond the Fourth Grade in the prescribed Common School Course of Study, they should pay reasonable fees, and funds so obtained might be applied for the purpose of supplementing the semi-annual Prov. Grant. Do I disapprove of Secondary Education? Not by any manner of means. But I say when pupils are taught Mathematics and the Latin and Greek Classics they should pay for the instruction received.

In visiting schools my attention has been more largely given to English Reading than to any other subject—simply because I consider it to be by far the most important branch taught in our pub-

lic schools.   This is admitted by all to be a most difficult branch to
acquire correctly.   Clearness of tone and correct expression seem to
be an natural inheritance to some, while others require the utmost
assiduity to render them even partially successful in conveying the
author's idea.   It is an error to think that if the pupil reads as he
speaks the end is accomplished.   It should be borne in mind that the
child needs even his habits of speech corrected.   The teacher must
be his guide, and from him must the majority of pupils learn whatever they are to know of correct reading.

The exercise as is well known is largely imitative.   The lessons
must be short and there must be a simultaneous drill every day,
with the teacher himself or one of the most advanced pupils to lead.
With careful supervision and constant practice even very young
children can be taught to read intelligently ; indeed, young children
are more apt to catch the teacher's exact intonation than those more
advanced in years.   The success or comparative failure of a school
as a whole can be fairly estimated by the general appearance made
by the classes in English reading.   An invariable exercise connected
with English Reading is oral spelling, a branch which has been attended with much success in nearly all the public schools.

Intimately allied with oral spelling is spelling by dictation of
paragraphs in the regular reading lessons and writing prescribed
extracts from either " The Spelling Book Superseded" or the dictation exercises in the " Fourth Reading Book."   Any exercise of this
description is attended with good results.   The pupils are taught
almost unconsciously correct spelling, the proper use of capitals,
punctuation, the correct application of words, and indirectly writing
and more or less English composition.

When engaged in the work of professional visitation I invariably
examine the copy books from first to last, and carefully note any
evidences of progress made during the course of the term.   Among
the teachers of the district we have some of the best penmen in the
Province, and, I honestly believe, some of the worst.   In this as in
everything else the law of heredity probably plays a part.   The
black board is not sufficiently utilized in illustrating the best models
of penmanship, correct position is not always insisted upon—and in
some cases at least the head lines are written by hand.   Now, when
there is a change of teacher from term to term, each having a style
of penmanship peculiar to himself or herself, the result obtained by
imitating different models is apt to be productive of a composite
character of caligraphy which is certainly not pleasing to the eye.
In the January edition of the " Educational Review" appears an interesting report upon " writing in the Halifax schools."   I endorse
every word said by Mr. Symons, the chairman of the School Board,
and particularly his reference to the evil effects resulting from the
pupils using short pencils.   I may add that the best time for writing
is the last half hour of the afternoon session, and that each exercise
should be carefully examined by the teacher and marked in pencil
1, 2, 3, to indicate *Good, Fair,* and *Bad.*

In no branch taught in the public schools of this district has there been more success then in arithmetic. The results obtained by the candidates who apply from year to year at the teachers' annual examination amply attest the accuracy of the statement. In this exercise although the memory has a duty to fulfil, the great object is to develop the reasoning powers and to give the children clear ideas and a complete understanding of the work performed. Whenever I pay a professional visit I always insist upon an examination from the very first page up to the exercises on hand.

The above constitutes what is called in Germany the "*bread* and *butter*" branches of education, and that great nation's aptness in nomenclature is as clearly evinced as the fact that they are universally admitted to be the best educated nation in Europe.

Do you not consider that there is a manifest anomaly in the educational history of this province? Much time and energy have been spent and an enormous amount of money has been expended on education during the past quarter of a century, while the only test of progress publicly provided is the annual examination of candidates for the teaching profession. And if the question be asked of any of the applicants if they intend to adopt the vocation of pedagogy for life,—not one in one hundred will reply in the affirmative. It is quite right for the Government to provide intellectual gymnasia to test the attainments of candidates for the teaching profession. But should there not be a subsidiary test provided to indicate one's success in such essential branches as English reading, Arithmetic and Writing. I am so much impressed with the absolute importance of an annual public examination on these lines that I am prepared at any time, in the event of the idea being carried out—to furnish the necessary funds to provide the Department of Education with a silver medal to be awarded annually to the person making the highest aggregate average at any examining station within this district —the syllabus of examination to embrace English reading and spelling, the elementary rules of arithmetic, including the commercial tables, and writing, including dictation. The tests to be neatness of papers, rapidity and especially accuracy.

In the ordinary course of events nine-tenths of the children now attending school will pass lives similiar to their fathers, and while I am prepared to admit there may be some village Hampden among the number, the great body of them will be farmers, fishermen miners or craftsmen. I am therefore anxious to stimulate their young minds to healthy effort to do well whatever their hand findeth to do wherever their lot may be cast.

The County Academy at Port Hood was for the past two years conducted by Mr. Eaton, a teacher of first-class attainments. After the holidays the principalship was transferred to Mr. D. S. McIntosh, a recent graduate of Dalhousie University, who has the distinction of having passed several years ago for grade B, being fourth on the published list of successful candidates, and at the last

July examination in the county of Halifax, he was the *third*
successful candidate for grade A in the whole Province. Mr.
McIntosh is evidently on the threshold of a career of brilliant
promise.

During the winter term the academy at Baddeck was in charge
of Mr. Tuttle, a graduate of Acadia College, who was succeeded in
May by Mr. J. B. Johnson. The school was officially visited early
in October, and was examined in Geometry, Latin and English
composition. During the term there were 18 pupils in the First
Year ; 12 in the Second ; and 5 in the Third. The general success
of the classes is amply evidenced in the fact that two of the pupils
passed their university matriculation with honour.

The attendance was uncommonly large during the summer term
and the talented principal had in consequence to work much harder,
than he bargained for. He was therefore compelled to resign, his
health having failed. I was very sorry indeed to see him drop his
classes when they were so thoroughly grounded in elementary
academical work.

The Indian school at the head of Whycocomagh Bay has met
with a severe loss in the death of Mr. John McEachern, who had
been in charge of the reservation school ever since its formation 18
years ago. Mr. McEachern was the oldest teacher in the county,
and was always distinguished for his integrity and uprightness.

In adddition to his prescribed professional duties he, like aged
Nestor of Homeric story, was the faithful counsellor and staunch
defender of his dusky wards in many a battle. Time and again did
unprincipled adventurers jump the line fence of the poor defenceless
Indians, but in every case they were compelled, in the law courts,
to vault back again. The settlement is now peaceful and contented,
and the school is in charge of a native Micmac, who can teach the
poor children the elements of an English education, and can at the
same time converse with them in the euphonious language of the
children of the forest.

Miss McEachern is still in charge of the Wagamatcook school in
the county of Victoria. When I visited the school in October I
found the enrolment of pupils large, but the average attendance
small, and this unsatisfactory condition of things will continue
while the *Bedouin* instincts of the time live and flourish. In both
settlements farming operations are carried on to some extent, and
each individual who has attained the years of maturity has a small
cottage of his own.

THE ANNUAL EXAMINATION OF TEACHERS.

The number of candidates who applied at the July examination
of teachers was uncommonly large and the amount received in fees
exceeded the receipts of any previous year in our educational
history.

The number of candidates at each of the stations of examination, together with the names of *three* candidates who made the highest averages are arranged in order of merit as follows:

PORT HOOD.

53 candidates—12 C's and 41 D's; 6 C's passed for the grade applied for and four of the number took D; while 2 failed entirely. Of the D applicants 4 passed and all the rest failed.

The highest averages were made by Theresa McDonald, Port Hood, Grade C, average 62.9; Alex. Campbell, Black River, Grade C, average 62.2; Stewart McDonald, Whycocomagh, Grade C, average 60.5.

PORT HAWKESBURY.

35 candidates—1 A, 2 B's, 12 C's, and 20 D's. The B's failed to obtain the grade applied for although one passed for grade C and the other for grade D. Of the candidates for grade C, 6 passed for grade applied for and 5 passed for grade D.

The highest averages were made by Hannah M. McLeod, West Bay, grade C, average 60.8; Luella Embree, Hawkesbury, grade C, average 58.9; Alex. McFadyen, Malagawatch, grade C, average 55.6.

MARGAREE FORKS.

40 candidates—2 B's, 9 C's and 29 D's. Of the B applicants only 1 passed—the other obtained a good C; of the 9 C candidates none succeeded to obtain the grade applied for, 6 of the number, however, passed for grade D. There were 26 candidates for grade D—only 2 of whom received the grade applied for, all the rest failed.

The highest averages were made by Ronald Beaton, Mabou, grade B, average 57.8; Ellen J. Coady, Margaree Forks, grade D, average 52.6; Moses W. Murphy, Egypt, grade D, average 51.2.

CHETICAMP.

32 candidates—12 C's and 20 D's. Of the candidates for grade C only one succeeded in obtaining the grade applied for—but 6 obtained license of grade D, and of the 20 D applicants only 3 succeeded.

The highest averages were made by Ephraim Chiasson, Cheticamp, grade D, average 52.9; Hubert AuCoin, Cheticamp, grade C, average 51.8; Michael Crispo, Cheticamp, grade D, average 50.05.

BADDECK.

40 candidates applied at this station—2 for grade B, 14 for grade C and 24 for grade D. Both B's failed although one obtained C and another D; of the C applicants 8 obtained the grade applied for, 5 passed for D and one failed entirely; of the applicants for grade D 6 succeeded and all the rest failed.

The highest averages were made by Bessie F. McRae, Baddeck, grade C, average 63.7 ; Mary A. McDonald, Nyanza, grade D, average 60.2 ; Agnes J. McLennan, Nyanza, grade C, average 58.8.

The averages made particularly at some of the examining stations were certainly not very complimentary to the quality of the *pabulum* furnished in some of the public schools. When a candidate fulfils the requirements of the syllabus merely with "the skin of his teeth" he has not much to be proud of.

It is fully admitted that in some of the public schools there is ample room for improvement—but it is cheering to think that there are others which give the casual or accredited visitor as much genuine pleasure as a visit to Niblo's or the Alhambra. From the school house door of one of the most mountainous sections in the district, one can see the home of a clergyman, of a college professor, of a member of the medical fraternity and of a senator of the Dominion parliament—all of whom received their early education within the unadorned walls of the little district school house.

A few miles further on is another school which has produced scores of teachers of all grades and two ecclesiastical students of exceedingly bright promise, one of whom several years ago won a silver cup awarded by the corporation of the town of Pictou to the student of the third year in the academy who should make the highest aggregate average in all the branches of his year at the regular terminal examination ; and in the month of September last the other won a senior scholarship in Dalhousie University, worth $200 dollars a year and of two year's continuance.

Can two country sections within a few miles of each other, in the whole province, furnish a better record than the above ?

During the year, two of our youngest school commissioners have been called to their long homes—Mr. Colin Chisholm and D. A. McLellan, Esq. Mr. Chisholm had taught school for several years and at the time of his death he was Government Land Surveyor for this county. His technical knowledge and experience in teaching were much valued at the regular sessions of the Board.

Mr. McLellan was a person of fine intellectual attainments and was famed for his splendid acquirements. He travelled extensively. principally on the Pacific coast and Mexico, where he met his death,

Allow me to close this report with an expression of gratitude to you for your continuous co-operation in advancing the educational interests of the district and for your rigid adherence to the requirements of the School Act.

Very respectfully submitted,

JOHN Y. GUNN.

A. H. MacKay, Esq., B. A., B. Sc., LL.D.,
Superintendent of Education.

DISTRICT No. 9.— PICTOU AND SOUTH COLCHESTER.

W. E. MACLELLAN, LL. B., *Inspector.*

SIR,—

The annual statistical tables already forwarded to your office contain nearly all the information of special interest or value concerning my inspectoral district during the past school year. In addition thereto I have but little to report.

As you are already aware I was prevented by continued ill-health from fully performing my usual allotment of work during the winter term. In summer I visited all the schools in my district, with the exception of Pictou Island, Big Island, Greenvale and Thorburn, all in the district of South Pictou, which I was compelled to leave, for lack of time.

With reference to individual sections I have to report the loss, by fire, of the school house of Southvale, section No. 51, South Colchester. The section is a weak one. Owing to this fact and to disagreements among ratepayers, no steps have as yet been taken towards the erection of a new building.

A new school house has been built and provisionally equipped at Big Woods, Section No. 66, South Pictou. This is an old section, but has never before owned a building. From time to time in the past school has been conducted in private houses. Of late years, owing to the refusal of the Board of School Commissioners to permit this practice to be longer continued, the section has been without school privileges. The new building is a neat and comfortable one, well suited to the requirements of the section. School was held in it for the summer term.

The new school house at East French River, Section No. 54, South Pictou, over the site for which, as you are aware, so much contention arose, has at last been occupied and all disputes concerning it are, for the time being at least, ended.

Very handsome new buildings at Lansdowne, North Pictou, and South Branch, Stewiacke, South Colchester, have been completed and occupied during the year. The school house at Faneuil Hall, North Pictou, has been thoroughly repaired and made as good as new.

The question of laying off a new section, between East River St. Mary's, and Rocky Mountain school sections, was again brought up at the last meeting of the board of commissioners for South Pictou, and a committee was once more appointed to consider and report on the matter. The persons interested in the erection of a new section have already put up a building intended for school purposes within the limits of the proposed section, and also within the present limits of Rocky Mountain section.

A petition was also before the South Colchester commissioners, praying for the division of Alma section, No. 38, into two sections. As the matter was not regularly brought up, it had to lie over for a year.

The tendency in the country would seem to be to increase rather than to decrease the number of sections as advised by the Council of Public Instruction. These proposed divisions need careful watching, as the cause of education is at present suffering from too many small and weak sections which, in many cases, might be advantageously and profitably united with others.

School work in my district has gone on smoothly and, on the whole, satisfactorily, comparatively speaking, throughout the year. Every organized section has had school during some portion of the year with the exception of Carribou Island, where there would seem to be a failure of pupils, or at least a failure on the part of the parents of such pupils as there might be, to send their children to school when one is provided.

I think I may safely report some improvement in the methods of teaching certain subjects, if not all. In language and geography the teaching is certainly better. The text-books are being handled more rationally ; and the word-stuffing process is less vigorously pursued. Reading, writing and arithmetic are, I believe, the least satisfactorily taught subjects laid down in the course of study. " Reading," in too many schools, consists in the mere saying of words apparently without much consideration or regard for their meaning either individually or collectively. " Writing" means, generally, from fifteen to twenty minutes daily with a copy-book. " Arithmetic," in the majority of cases, is " getting through" so many pages of the prescribed text-book. To remonstrances against the apparent neglect of these most important subjects, the reply is almost uniformly made that pupils have to be taken over certain ground, marked out in the course of study, and that no more time than is given can be afforded for the " three R's." The better training of teachers provided for under the new regulations will, no doubt before long, rectify to a large extent the faults at present complained of.

The recent alteration in the school year seems to have been received with general favour. I have heard but few complaints against it, except from those who are constitutionally opposed to change of any kind on account of the trouble likely to be occasioned in becoming adapted to it. How considerable that trouble has really been in the case of the new school year, has been deeply impressed on my mind by the magnitude of the correspondence with my office to which it has given rise. My time has been in greater part occupied for weeks in answering enquiries concerning various features of the new arrangement.

In conclusion I have to submit for your consideration the fact that it is the opinion of most, if not all, the members of the various boards of school commissioners in my inspectoral district, that some provision should be made to indemnify them for time expended and expense incurred in attending board meetings. In South Colchester it is becoming difficult to secure a quorum at the annual meetings. An allowance sufficient to cover expenses, deducted say from the County Fund, might serve to promote larger meetings of commissioners.

I have the honor to be, Sir,
Your obedient servant,
W. E. MacLELLAN.

A. H. MacKay, Esq., B. A., B. Sc., LL. D.,
  Superintendent of Education.

DISTRICT No. 10.—CUMBERLAND AND N. COLCHESTER.

Inglis C. Craig, Inspector.

Sir,—

An official relation extending over half a year as Inspector of schools for North Colchester and Cumberland, does not enable me to speak with the authority I desire in reference to their growth or present condition.

By great diligence I was enabled to visit 232 schools—164 in Cumberland and 68 in Colchester. A few schools were not inspected, due to the indisposition of teachers, or sections not having schools when I was in their locality.

There are in this district 218 sections, representing 274 schools. During the past term 251 of these have been in session, employing 256 teachers.

These teachers are thus classed :—

Grade A...... 2 Male.
 "   B......12   "   Grade B...... 17 Female.
 "   C......11   "   "   C......112   "
     D...... 6   "   "   D...... 96   "
            ——   ——
            31   225

Grand total days' attendance for the year, 1,164,068. Average attendance for school year, 5150 pupils.

Average salary for Males A and B, in District $527.48
   "   "   Females   B,   " 270.43
   "   "   Males   C,   " 250.39
  ..   ..   Females   C, ... 226.91
                   Males   D, ... 215.60
                   Females   D, ... 152.79

It may seem like a loss of time to compare the present educational standing of Cumberland with that of less than a generation ago, when our Free School system was in its infancy, but it will suffice to show with reference to reports of intervening years, that there has been continual progress. The school population is much greater ; the equipment of schools has much improved ; the professional qualifications of our teachers have been advanced, and their literary standing raised at least 50 per cent. In proof of this last statement—there was not a lady teacher eligible for a grade B license, where there are now many holding this certificate.

Going backwards to the earliest records I have in my possession, four years after the inception of the Common School system there were in Cumberland 121 schools compared with 200 at the present time. This same year there were 6352 children in the schools taught by 107 teachers receiving as recompense from the province $7,821, and from sections $12,662 or a total of $20,483. While this year the school population is over 8000 taught by 172 teachers receiving from the Provincial Treasury $13,788, nearly double the amount as then, and as sectional aid $23,102 or in all $36,800.

The partition of Colchester makes it impossible to compare its growth with other years; consequently any neglect of mention is not intentional but forced upon me for want of distinct data.

In the past quarter of a century great changes have taken place in what was then small graded systems. While certain rural sections have not shown any great increase in school attendance the growth of such centres as Amherst, Springhill, Parrsboro' and Acadia Mines has been almost phenomenal.

In 1873 Amherst Academy was a school of five departments, " of few pupils and mostly residents of the town," where now thirteen full rooms exist with two just beyond the town limits.

Springhill, passing from a miscellaneous state about this time into a graded system, has two fine school buildings of twelve rooms. Besides these there are two departments in session in an old school-house making fourteen in all. Finding in one of these last named rooms at the time of my inspection 110 pupils present and 164 enrolled, I invited the School Commissioners to an interview to ascertain if there was any probability of giving these little ones, packed in a room too small for half the number, more accommodation. I found the school authorities alive to the necessity of providing more room in the near future if the press on their numbers continues. Their case is singular. Within five years they have built two fine houses after the most modern plans and now it is apparent that another is needed. The registration of this system is 1,100 pupils taught by 14 teachers. Dartmouth with about the same number has twenty one. My past knowledge of the Springhill schools enables me to say that their educational growth has been equal to their numerical. This year one of its departments is asserting itself to be classed as a high school. I cannot refrain from saying a kind word in commendation of the late principal, Mr. McTavish, who was so conscientious in the performance of his duties.

Fifteen years ago Parrsboro High School had but two departments. Now it has seven, conducted by a most efficient staff. A congested attendance makes it imperative that another room be added at an early date. I trust that the people of this favored town will soon see the necessity of providing accommodation in keeping with their status among the schools of the province. By extending the bounds of their present school premises they could have the finest grounds in the county.

Acadia Mines, another school of rapid growth, is under the competent principalship of Lenfest Ruggles. It ranks easily as a High School. Like Parrsboro it is in need of a better house, but owing to the unstable state of business in the town, the commissioners did not deem it prudent to ask them to build.

Oxford, a manufacturing centre, has four departments. It is complimentary to Mr. Slade, the principal, that he maintains so efficient a school at the head of four rooms. Beside the Common Schoool course he does work in Grades IX and X. A most pleasing feature in his work is the perfection to which he brings the art of song. He teaches both systems, the staff notation and tonic sol-fa. His advanced pupils are able to transpose from one system to the other.

Great Village School is in charge of H. Gratz, B. A., (Dalhousie), and Pugwash has Horace L. Brittain, an under graduate of New Brunswick University. Both these schools have three departments and are doing High School work.

Joggins, Tatamagouche, Lorne Vale, Folly Village, Central Economy, Five Islands, Advocate, River Hebert, Port Greville, Wallace, are schools of two rooms. I have not marked these schools or teachers to flatter them. I care not to be understood as making invidious distinctions. There are many excellent teachers and good miscellaneous schools maintained at greater odds than those mentioned, but space forbids me to particularize further.

Building or renovating school rooms has been much in operation during the past year.

Amherst, at an expense of $35,000, has erected the finest building and most modern in equipments in the province. It is situated in the south of the town on a beautifully level tract, embracing two and one half acres, which cost $3200. The building is 130 feet long and 72 feet wide. A portico 66 x 7 feet on the front extends full height of the structure. It is three stories in height with basement entire size of superstructure. The material of which it is built is brick with brown stone trimmings, obtained in the neighboring quarries. There are fourteen very spacious school rooms besides laboratory and teachers' room. The assembly hall is 66 x 71 feet. Principal's room 38 x 42. Every precaution has been taken to make it as nearly perfect as possible in its heating and ventilating arrangements. The system used is Fuller and Warner's, which is supplanting all others in the large American schools. Some of the points of merit are that the foul air duct is on the same side of rooms as duct admitting warm air, thus necessitating a complete circuit of the fresh warm air before it reaches the point of egress, a flue. Every teacher has control of supply of warm and cold air from the desk. Any demand for more heat is indicated at the furnace. The "dry closets" in the basement have a distinct chimney or flue so that it is impossible for noxious odors to reach any of the school rooms, and their return to the basement is prohibited by a heater placed in direct line with the current of air entering the pit. All matter is dried or burned without removing, thus completely obviating any possibility of infection or contagion.

Oxford Junction, Shulee, Truemanville and Northport have renovated their buildings. Amherst Point has made extensive repairs and enlarged their school grounds.

New Truro Road, Harrison's Settlement and Bass River have erected new houses. The enterprise displayed by the last named section in face of so many misfortunes is commendable. Having lost by fire a comparatively new building last winter, they straightway erected another of two rooms on the same beautiful site.

Special Mention is due Pleasant Hills and Little Bass in Londonderry for the interest manifested in having their rooms and schoolgrounds improved.

There are at least six buildings that have served their time, and I trust that it will not need coercion to show the people their need. I may cite the Joggins as an example.

Many of our schools could be better, that is, the teachers. Heretofore the avenues to the teachers' ranks have not been sufficiently guarded, and much useless *talent* has gained admittance. Recent changes in licensing must inevitably bring a beneficial change.

The one term system is also welcome. Short terms and frequent changes of teachers have wrought more mischief than can be measured. Its worst result was a poor classification for which you could hold no one responsible, since every teacher disclaims all errors made in this way, and assigns them to his predecessor. F. W. George, M. A., an Inspector of schools for this county, 1868, anticipated this time, when he writes in one of his reports on the frequent changes, saying :—" The evil cannot be rooted out in a day ; but once when the popular mind has been convinced that it is an evil, the educational authorities can apply a remedy."

I must here record my indebtedness to Mr. Lay, my predecessor, for his kindness in initiating me into office. His good influence will long be felt in this district.

I herewith forward to you the statistical tables, teachers' returns, and notes of inspection.

I have the honor to be,

Your obedient servant,

INGLIS C. CRAIG.

To A. H. MacKay, B. A., B. Sc., LL. D.,
Superintendent of Education.

APPENDIX C.

Report of the Board of School Commissioners

OF THE

CITY OF HALIFAX,

YEAR ENDED, OCT. 31, 1892.

(I.)

CHAIRMAN'S REPORT.

OFFICE OF SCHOOL COMMISSIONERS,
HALIFAX, November, 1892.

To A. H. MACKAY, ESQ., B. A., B. SC., LL. D., F. R. S. C.,

Superintendent of Education.

SIR,—

Herewith I have the honor to submit the reports of the Supervisor of Schools and the Secretary of the Board, which contain fully all details in reference to the management of the County Academy and the Common Schools of the city of Halifax, together with the esti- · mated as well as the actual expenditure incurred by the Board in the maintainance of same during the past year.

Debentures to the amount of $134,000, bearing interest at the rate of 6 per cent. per annum, maturing in January, 1892, were paid by an issue of 4½ per cent. debentures for a like amount and for which the Board obtained par, thus making a great saving in our interest account.

During the year the following properties have been purchased by the Board, which they consider great acquisitions to the school properties, viz : A lot of land at the N. E. corner of the Albro street school property and another at the east side of the Compton avenue school property.

It has been deemed advisable to alter the manner of paying the teachers, and they are now paid in ten equal instalments in place of twelve as heretofore, thus saving the trouble of paying salaries during the vacations.

The compulsory school Act has been found to work well during the year and Policeman Webster holds as high a place in my estimation, as he did in that of my predecessor.

The Kindergarten and Manual training classes are still realities, I think I am safe in saying that they are permanencies ; already the former has branched out so that Kindergarten work is taught more or less in every primary department in the city schools.

I would here take the opportunity of manifesting my appreciation of the valuable assistance so freely accorded me by the several members of the Board, while filling the office of chairman, they at all times evincing a desire to further the best interests of our schools. I have much pleasure in adding my testimony to that of my predecessors as to the high qualifications of the Supervisor, Mr. Alex. McKay, and the Secretary, Mr. R. J. Wilson, for their very responsible offices.

I have the honor to be,

Your obedient servant,

WM. J. BUTLER.

(II.)

Report of the Supervisor of Halifax Public Schools,

FOR THE YEAR ENDED 31st OCTOBER,

1892.

To the Chairman and Members of the Board of School
Commissioners for the City of Halifax :

Gentlemen,—I beg to submit for your information concerning the
Public Schools under your management, (1) the statistical tables
required by law, together with some additional interesting facts, (2)
a report of the condition and progress of the schools as a whole, and
(3) certain recommendations which, if adopted, will greatly increase
their efficiency.

ABSTRACT OF TABLES FOR COMMON SCHOOLS.

WINTER TERM, 1891–'92.

Grade	Male Teachers		Female Teachers			Totals		No. of Departments.	No. holding Normal School diplomas.	No. without professional training.	No. of teaching days.	No. of pupils enrolled.	No. over 15 years of age.	No. under 15 years of age.	No. of Boys.	No. of Girls.	Grand total days' attendance.	Average daily present.	Average number of pupils for each teacher.	Percentage of attendance.
	Academic. A	Class I. B	Class I. B	Class II. C	Class III. D	Male.	Female.													
1892.	2	9	34	68	4	11	106 117	32	85	120	6211	188	6023	3069	3152	501518	4368	37	70
1891.	2	8	33	67	3	10	103 113	30	83	119	5734	147	5587	2825	2909	437085	3822	34	68
Increase..	....	1	1	1	1	1	3 4	2	2	1	477	41	436	234	243	64733	546	3	2
Decrease..	....																		

SUMMER TERM, 1892.

1892,	1	10	34	72	4	11	110 121	32	89	94	6649	146	6498	3276	3373	428985	4696	39	70
1891.	2	10	33	67	3	12	103 115	31	84	93	6483	178	6305	3147	3336	400630	4513	39	69
Increase...	..	..	1	5	1	..	7 6	1	5	1	166	..	188	129	37	28455	183	....	1
Decrease ..	1	..	..	..	..	1	..	..	..	..	..	32	..	..	..	..	..	..	..

Total number of different pupils enrolled for the year, 7,310.

Cost per pupil for 1891, $12.45; for 1892, $12,33; decrease per
pupil $0.12.

Let me call attention to a few of the leading facts shown by this abstract.

1.   There has been a large increase in the number of regular teachers employed.   At the close of the school year ending October 1891, we had 115 teachers.   There are now 121, besides, of course, those in the County Academy, making in all 127.

2.   Women are gradually monopolizing the teaching profession, having increased in the last ten years from 85 to 91 per cent of the whole number of teachers in the city.

Although not approving of the change, yet I must admit that it has been attended with satisfactory results in Halifax.   For example, no male principals could be found for the National or Bloomfield schools, at anything like the salaries paid there at present, that would do nearly as good work as the ladies now occupying those positions.   Indeed, it would be difficult at any price to find men who would do better in those particular schools.

Men are either going out of the profession or making it a stepping-stone to something more remunerative, because in the less important schools or grades, their salaries are inadequate to a tolerable existence in the social positions to which their culture entitles them.

3.   The number of teachers having a recognized professional training is very low, only 26 per cent.

This showing is perhaps worse than the reality, for there are 31 teachers belonging to the religious orders, who, though not so well trained in the theory of education as they would be in a Normal school, are more carefully taught the practice of teaching before taking charge of public schools.

4.   The number of enrolled pupils for the winter term of this year as compared with that of the preceding year, shows an increase of 477 ; the summer term an increase of 166.   The total number of different pupils registered for the year was 7,310, being an increase of 272.

The increase of the summer term is about normal.   The extraordinary increase of the winter term after the decrease of the preceding year, shows most clearly the repressive influence of the diphtheritic scourge of the winter of 1891.

5.   It will be noticed that the average number of pupils to each teacher has increased from 34 to 39.

6.   The regularity of attendance has considerably improved. This may be partly caused by the improved sanitary conditions of

the schools, but we know that it is also partly the result of greater stringency in the enforcement of the Compulsory School Law.

I have not known of a compulsory law having been enforced in any country with as little friction as in Halifax.

Some of the credit of this is due to the wise provisions of the law itself, but much more to its wise administration. The prosecution of the cases is conducted by Secretary Wilson, without mistakes and with the skill and ability of a lawyer. Truant-officer Webster also does his part admirably. His diligence in looking up truants, in encouraging parents to avoid the penalties of the law, and his shrewdness in obtaining pertinent information, are worthy of all praise.

7. The cost per pupil has been $12.33, or 12 cents per pupil less than it was last year. This is a smaller expenditure per pupil than that shown by any of the large cities of the Dominion except St. John, which has scarcely yet recovered from the disastrous effects of the fire of a few years ago.

SCHOOL ROOM ACCOMMODATIONS.

In this connection I have not much to report for the last year.

The cleansing, painting, and white-washing operations have given us class-rooms of which we need not be ashamed. In these respects they will compare favourably with those of any city. The blue-tinged ceilings and the light-green walls are found to have a pleasing effect and to be easy on the eyes.

The janitors for the most part do their work well.

Many of the teachers decorate the walls of their class-rooms with pretty pictures, the windows with flowers and the blackboards with artistic drawings. In several instances the platforms are covered with oil-cloth, at the teachers' expense, and the pupils provide dumb-bells, wands, &c., for calisthenics. The school board has furnished pretty cabinets which are well stored with books or natural history speciments useful for teaching purposes.

Several sets of the most improved desks have been furnished.

Except in providing libraries, which should be done in part by the Government and in part by the pupils, and in supplying simple apparatus for science lessons, there is not much more immediately required for the complete furnishing of the schools.

It is perhaps worthy of special mention that through the liberality of one of the ex-commissioners a small library has been started in connection with St. Mary's Boys' School. It will be enlarged by donations from the pupils and their friends, and will be of very great benefit to the pupils, supplying them with good literature and displacing the harmful sensational novels which are nowadays ruining so many children in every city.

I may be allowed here to make some remarks on some of the recommendations made in my last report.

1. *Ventilation.* Several teachers are giving more attention than formerly to ventilation. There is, however, much carelessness yet. I often visit school-rooms unprovided with any effective means for carrying off the used-up air; crowded with children, and yet with every door and window closed. At ,the very least such rooms should have ventilating boards provided for the windows, and it should be made absolutely imperative on the teacher to have windows or doors slightly open at all times when many children are present. In addition to this, at recess, at noon and at dismissing of school every window should be thrown wide open long enough to clear the room. Experts tells us that even when the foul air is being continually replaced by pure air, a space of 200 cubic feet should be allowed for every scholar. While many of our school-rooms have that much or more yet there are some with only 80 or 90 cubic feet per pupil and the air in that limited space is not continually changing. If school commissioners, parents and teachers had any adequate conception of the gain to the pupils in mental work, in health and comfort, and even in morality, these evils would soon be remedied. Like a piece of delicate machinery befouled with dust, the brain poisoned with the impurities arising from fifty pairs of active lungs, is not likely to transmit the best and purest thoughts of the soul.

It is estimated by competent authorities who have gathered the statistics that the lives of forty per cent. of the people living in our climate are shortened by the vitiated air of our dwelling houses, public halls and school rooms. To this we may add the dangers arising from the morbific germs of zymotic diseases so readily conveyed in the clothing of children from the diseased inmates of their homes and so easily finding lodgment in tissues weakened by want of a proper supply of oxygen. Surely pure air as well as a free education, is the birthright of every child.

2. A new school building to replace those now used for the National and Acadian schools. It is a disadvantage to have duplicate classes in these two small schools; whereas if they formed one school there would be but one grade to each teacher and therefore more efficient work. With better classification a greater number of pupils could be taught by the same teachers. A healthier locality, some play-ground and better class rooms are other important advantages that would be secured by the change. And why should it not be made without delay ? Surely the $350 now paid as rent for the National school building and the proceeds arising from the sale of the Acadian school would procure funds enough for a building in the central part of the city that would be a credit to the school

commissioners, an ornament to the city, and what concerns us most an attraction to the parents of this important locality.

3. Bloomfield school, with an average of 65 pupils for each teacher, notwithstanding its having an additional rented room, is greatly overcrowded. Either it should be enlarged or what for the present would relieve it, Compton avenue school building might be completed at an annual expense not to exceed the rental of the two extra rooms now used in connection with these schools. One argument in favor of adding to Bloomfield school building arises from the fact that it has such a large site.

4. There is a district bounded on the north by Richmond street, south by Wellington Barracks and west by Gottingen street, in which pupils under ten years of age find it difficult to get the school accommodations which they desire. Another storey added to the Protestant Orphanage school building or a single class-room at the south end of North Star street, would meet the demand, relieve Bloomfield school, and enable several children now kept at home in winter to attend school.

5. As some of my other recommendations of last year have been receiving more or less attention it is unnecessary that I should further refer to them here.

WORK OF THE SCHOOLS.

Besides having made numerous visits on business matters I have during the last year made over 540 *regular* visits to the school-rooms, mainly for the purpose of ascertaining how the various subjects were presented to the pupils and which subjects were neglected. For faithful drill along the lines of the course of study, for good order without undue severity and for neatness in their school-rooms, our teachers excel. They are striving to get all the light they can on all that affects their work,—they take educational papers, they attend teachers' meetings, and readily adopt any reasonable suggestions, and the most of them consult and work with their Principals.

Taken as a whole they illustrate in their conduct, the three essential qualities of good breeding ; viz., morality, self-control, and courtesy. They deserve and invariably receive the treatment due to ladies and gentlemen from those who can themselves be placed in either of these categories.

But notwithstanding these words of praise, it is probably my duty to point out a few things in which some of them are deserving of censure.

1. A few of our weakest, but also a few of our strongest teachers are occasionally late in reaching their class-rooms ; that is, they are not in their places twenty minutes before the opening of the school

in order to prepare for the day's work, to look after the classrooms, &c. An occasional carrying out of the rule requiring such teachers to register the time of their arrival at their rooms, will probably remove the fault.

2. The subjects of drawing and singing are not receiving the steady, intelligent and systematic attention which they should in all departments. A provision in the new regulations of the Council of Public Instruction, making drawing one of the subjects of examination for entrance into the academies, will do much to increase its importance in the opinions of Principals.

Drawing from the flat, about the only kind at present in the schools, may give the pupil some facility in the use of the pencil, but it does not educate in the idea of form; it does not teach the pupil to see the essential characteristics of things. Every teacher should herself practice and teach drawing and shading from the object, no matter what may be the grade of her class.

3. Not all of our teachers are dominated by the idea that the development of character is the grand object of the school; that next to that comes the development in the child of the power of independent thought. The acquiring of a certain amount of useful information is of course important, but it is of secondary importance. There are some of our teachers who do not deliberately plan their school exercises with an intelligent view as to their effect in stimulating this or that particular element of character, habits of industry and accuracy, love of truth, &c. They do not frame their questions with the express purpose of making their pupils think for themselves. They are too often satisfied if their pupils can give the correct words of the answer—delighted if he understands what he says, even though he may have arrived at that understanding without any effort of his own, but merely through the simplified explanations of his teacher.

As I said in a former report, we have teachers who are satisfied to be lesson-hearers, who cultivate a mechanical memory rather than thought. These criticisms suggest to us the importance, the nobility, and the exceeding difficulty of the teacher's vocation.

4. Teachers neglect to utilize the practical for the instrument of culture. The masticatory powers of a child are more normally and profitably developed by chewing nourishing food of the proper consistency than by chewing a rubber ball. The powers of the mind can be better developed by grapling with the problems of real life and with problems conveying useful information, than by artificial mental gymnastics such as we find in arithmetical puzzles and dead languages.

REMARKS ON PARTICULAR SCHOOLS.

Acadian—The attendance was small, yet it was 15 more than for the corresponding term of the preceding year. The inability to get the necessary text-books causes, in the opinion of the Principal, a loss of 25 per cent. of the pupils' school work. The teachers have made every reasonable effort to keep up the attendance.

Africville—The attendance and work of the pupils have greatly improved.

Albro street—This school has suffered somewhat from frequent changes of teachers. Of those schools doing only common school work it still competes with Morris street school for the first place.

Alexandra—This is now the largest school in the city, enrolling 750 pupils, or 100 more than ever before. Thirty per cent. of the whole number belong to the first grade, and six per cent. to the eighth grade. In most of the rooms the new ventilating system is working very satisfactorily.

Compton avenue—An experiment in teaching writing without copy books was successfully tried in this school for the last year. The principles of penmanship are explained on the blackboard and practised on blank paper or in exercise books. Great care is required of the pupils in all written exercises, with the result that no other school in the city can show as good work in this subject. This school has also the distinction of having made the highest percentage of attendance during the last term.

Lemarchant street school, with an average of 72 enrolled pupils to each teacher, will soon be requiring more school accommodation. The pupils have made very satisfactory progress during the past year.

Morris street school enrols only 14 per cent. of first grade pupils, and as high as 15 per cent. of eighth grade pupils. This school is further characterized by its faithfulness in carrying out all parts of the course of study. It has opportunities for doing this that many other schools have not.

National—The attendance at the National school has been pretty steadily declining for the last twelve years, being now only 57 per cent. of what it was in 1880. The teachers are very much hindered in their work by the inability of pupils to get the needful supply of books.

R. C. Orphanage—Here we have an enrolment of 108 pupils. The senior department, in charge of Sister Berchmans, is especially worthy of mention for the excellence of its school work.

Richmond—The attendance in this section of the city is better now than it has been at any time since 1881. The new Principal, Mr. Marshall, stands high both as regards scholarship and aptitude for teaching.

Russell street and St. Mary's boys' schools are both without pupils doing eighth grade work, owing to the regrettable fact that the children are withdrawn before they complete the course.

St. Patrick's girls' high school—In consequence of an effort on the part of the teachers to raise the standard of work in this school, the entrance of pupils has been somewhat restricted—the number enrolled being only 66. Of these, 27 are doing 1st year academic work ; 35 second year ; and 4 third year work.

Thirteen pupils of this school were successful at the teachers' examination last July, in obtaining licenses of various grades. Many of those who secure licenses, however, are not likely to succeed as teachers, or they have to wait many years before they receive appointments. For the purpose, therefore, of putting the young ladies in the way of earning a livelihood as soon as they leave school, the teachers purchased a typewriter for their use, and a large class is now receiving instruction in shorthand and typewriting.

Halifax Academy—The record of the academy for the last year is remarkably good. Five regular and special students attained the scholarship requisite for academic licenses as tested by the provincial examination for teachers. Two obtained 'B' licenses ; 9 obtained 'C' licenses on 'B' papers ; 5 obtained 'C' on 'C' papers; 10 obtained 'D' on 'C' papers, and one a 'D' on 'D' papers—in all 32 students of the academy obtained teachers' licenses. Quite a number passed the simple matriculation examination at Dalhousie College ; two of them taking second and third ranks respectively, at the competition scholarship examination. Another pupil, Mr. William Mackintosh, took fifth place at Cornell University against 900 competitors, winning a $400 scholarship.

This is a record of which Halifax is justly proud. With such opportunities the young men and women of this city can hold their own against all competitors from outside, and prosper in all departments of life for which such an education prepares them. If only the education of the academy could be diverted somewhat into industrial lines, it might be still better for the prosperity of the city. Countries that occupy the proudest position in the world's history owe their pre-eminence in every instance to education rather than to material resources.

Mr. Howard Murray, the new Principal of the academy, has by his skill in teaching and good management, his interest in the success of all his pupils individually, his self-sacrificing and continuous labors, and his urbane manners, already won a warm place in the affections of all his pupils and of their parents.

Mr. Morton, the new teacher of science and mathematics, has so far amply justified the recommendations and expectations of his friends.

The academic teaching staff is a as whole particularly strong. Why attach so much importance to our high schools and have them like the common schools, free and open to rich and poor alike ?

1.   Because society has become so complex that a high degree of intelligence is necessary to the proper performance of the duties of citizenship.

2.   Because knowledge like riches is an element of great power, and if both these elements were confined to the few, the freedom of many would be endangered.

3.   Because the thrift, energy and industrial success of a people are in proportion to the general diffusion of the higher knowledge.

4.   Because every voter should be able, not only to read, but to comprehend what he reads and to reason accurately, so as to be able to detect the sophistries by which unprincipled demagogues try to force themselves to the front in politics or society.

5.   Because a man should be able not only to write his name and do a little book-keeping, but he should be able to express his thoughts clearly and use his pen in the defence of his rights.

6.   Because more important than the ' Rule of Three ' is a knowledge of the principles of local and national government and a knowledge of social science.

" The simple fact is, that looked at from the standpoint of the greatest utility to the state, the work of the common schools, except as a foundation for that which is higher, is not as valuable as the work of the high schools and academies.   All processes have become so intricate, all relations so complex, that the man who knows only the three ' R's has, without mastering the situation, added elements of danger to it.

'A little learning is a dangerous thing,
'Drink deep, or taste not the Pierian spring.'

" The whole country, especially in its cities, is suffering from deficiency in broadly educated men.   Our political business and social life are involving deep questions relative to the welfare of the community which can never be solved by men who are but half-educated."

7.   Because in a democratic country like ours, all have the same natural rights and all must be allowed so far as possible to have an equal start in life.   For very good reasons a large proportion of the brightest and best intellects are found in the homes of those who cannot afford a special training to their children.   They value, therefore, very highly that inestimable boon " The Poor Man's College ;" the High School and the Academy.

NEW SCHOOL LAW.

It is proper that I should, without dwelling on them, call your attention to a few of the recent changes in the school law.

1. Hereafter the school year begins on the first of August. This makes it desirable that pupils entering school for the first time should do so immediately after summer holidays, or at the beginning of February. Parents should have notice of this fact, otherwise much inconvenience will be experienced in primary classes.

2. An Act to provide for the more thorough study of the effects of alcoholic drinks on the human system has been passed by the Legislature. Upon it being shown that any teacher has failed to carry out the provisions of this Act, the government grant due to the school board on account of such teacher may be withheld.

3. Grade B scholarship without professional qualifications entitles hereafter only to a C license, and so with the other grades. Thus the advantages of a Normal school training are emphasized.

4. Penmanship, drawing and spelling are henceforth to be elements in determining the pupil's right to enter the academy. These subjects will, as a consequence, receive more attention in the common schools hereafter.

5. In the High school curriculum Latin, Greek, and the memory-work of History and Geography do not count for as much as formerly, while the practical sciences count for more.

SCHOOL EXHIBITIONS.

As being connected with the history of our city schools for the past year, the school exhibition of industrial and hand work should be mentioned. All the schools but one took part, and covered 6500 square feet of surface with samples of the handiwork of the pupils. Specimens of writing, drawing, commercial forms, map-drawing, Kindergarten work, wood-work, etc., from all the pupils according to their grades, formed a sight well worth seeing. The teachers deserve credit for the patriotic spirit with which they entered into the project. It served the purpose of stimulating to better work in these subjects, and of showing the public that really good work was being done in the public schools.

PSYCHOLOGY.

Prominent among the professional subjects engaging the attention of our teachers during the last year was a valuable course of lectures on Psychology, by Professor Seth. They were heard by nearly all the teachers, most of whom received much good from them.

WRITING.

After holidays special attention was given in the Teachers' meetings to the best methods of teaching writing. The result may be summed up in the following conclusions at which the teachers arrived after careful investigation.

1. Instead of slates pupils should use exercise-books. They would be noiseless, the work would remain for inspection or reference, being permanent more care would be exercised, while the cost would not be much if any more than that of slates.

2. Pupils when writing should sit in the " right central position" both arms on the desk at an angle of 45 with the front of the desk, writing lines parellel to the front of the desk.

3. Vertical script is better than slant, being more legible, more easily learned, better adapted to secure the hygienic position. It is the most used in English schools, in nine-tenths of them, and in many schools on the continent. It is recommended by German experts.

4. In normally shaped hands pens should be held as recommended by Gage in his system of penmanship.

5. Pupils when writing should be required to be always in correct positions and to hold their penholders or pencils correctly. Writing exercises should not be so long as to become tiresome. Writing should be chiefly taught from the blackboard and by the use of exercise paper and movable headlines.

7. No haste to get through with much work should cause the teacher to tolerate any written exercise which is not in good form.

KINDERGARTEN.

I am happy to be able to report that the five candidates in training for Kindergartners passed successfully their examinations at the close of the first year's work. The successful candidates were:

Miss Elizabeth M. Mahoney, Grade B.
" Helen T. Moody,   " C.
" Henrietta DeWolfe,   " C.
" Beatrice M. Lawrence,   " C.

These are all now engaged at half the regular salary of their grade for one year according to agreement.

Miss Kate Fletcher, grade C, a special student, also passed the examination, heading the list. She is now teaching in Albro street school.

After holidays the training school opened with six students. Mrs. Harriman, the Director, has more than realized my most favourable expectations regarding her success. She has been of very great service to the primary teachers to whom she has given a series of "talks" on primary work.

MANUAL TRAINING.

On this subject I beg to submit the special report of the teacher, Lee Russell, B. Sc.:

ALEXANDER McKAY, *Supervisor*,

SIR.—

In order to equip the shop and to make plans for work, I came to Halifax about the middle of August, 1891. After consultation with your Committee it was decided to buy the first half dozen benches and some of the tools in Boston and the remainder in Halifax.

We were able to receive the first class of six pupils from the academy on September seventeenth, and from that time on there has been a steadily increasing attendance. It was soon found necessary to increase the capacity and six benches were built by Mr. Morris, and put in place November 19th.

January 12th, 1892, six more benches were ordered of Gordon & Keith. They were nearly as good as those had from Boston, and at a much less cost.

With this last addition we are able to take eighteen pupils at a time or three times the original number. At each increase there have been boys ready to fill the new places, and never has there been, except just previous to examination and grading times, so great a percentage of absences as in the regular schools.

There has been a total enrolment during the school year ending in July, of one hundred and sixty pupils. Of these there were one hundred and eight or sixty-seven per cent. still attending regularly at the close of school.

Of the fifty-two who dropped out, I know definitely that twenty-three have left school altogether. This leaves twenty-nine, or eighteen and one-tenth per cent. of the whole number enrolled about whom I have no definite information. Comparing this with like schools under similar conditions in the United States, the showing is greatly in our favor. In one large city over forty per cent. dropped out of the manual training school while still continuing to attend the regular schools.

The work done during the first year has been largely experimental, but always along certain definite and well considered lines. In establishing Manual training in a community, it is necessary first to study the pupils, to find out what skill they have naturally, what

are their tastes and what kind of work is best suited to their needs.
For instance, the Sweedish Sloyd is not, in my opinion adapted for
Halifax boys. It was carefully tried and found unsuitable. The
same is true of the so-called Russian System. The plan devised in
the spring of 1892, is a modification of the Russian System and for
a kind of 'working hypothesis' serves quite well. It is amended and
improved as experience shows desirable. In the present state of
the whole subject of Manual training, it is very undesirable to
adopt any hard and fast lines. The most that can be done is to
keep constantly in mind certain known principles of mental
development and to try to found the course on them.

Preliminary exercises in the use of the simpler tools are first
given. The use of the rule, try-square, marking-gauge and scratch-
awl, is thus taught. Then simple exercises in sawing are introduced,
When the pupil has acquired some skill and confidence, he is allowed
to make a small pencil box. This combines the exercises already
learned, introduces the new difficulty of assembling parts, makes
apparent the result of good or poor work, and gives the pupil a
tangible stimulating result. The same plan is followed with the
later and more difficult work.

It appears that this plan works well. The pupil takes an intelligent and increasing interest in his work, he learns principles without realizing that he is so doing, and applies these principles with a
very keen interest in the result. The tools and work are so brought
forward as to give the hand, eye and mind a progressive training.

Mechanical drawing is taught from the first. So far as is possible
the pupil makes a working drawing either from a model or from
dictation. With this before him, he works out the idea in wood. In
this as in the woodwork, principles are taught rather by their
application than in the abstract. When he can fully comprehend it,
the pupil is shown that a certain plan underlies all his work.

Considerable attention is paid to the encouragement of independent thinking. Smart pupils make their own designs, and if
approved, are allowed to work from them. Any invention is made
much of and the pupil making such inventions is allowed special
favors. One boy has made the patterns for a sixteen light dynamo
together with the base and tightening blocks. Much of the wood-
work was his own idea and he was given every facility for working
it out.

If it should be thought desirable to add pattern making and wood-
turning to the course, a larger shop would be needed. An important
addition might be made by the purchase of a few sets of carving
tools. Wood-carving may be made an excellent means of training
hand and eye. The sense of beauty of form, taste in ornament, and
the general artistic sense are all guided by it and stimulated. It is
a valuable auxiliary to the regular work.

Respectfully submitted.

LEE RUSSELL,
Teacher of Manual Training.

Halifax is entitled to the credit of having the first Manual Training department in connection with the public schools in the Dominion. As the subject is new I thought a full report desirable.

Although for the past few years the expenses of the schools for tuition have not increased in greater proportion than the number of pupils to be educated, yet at a time when the City Fathers are struggling with the problem of a heavy taxation, it is not opportune to suggest any improvement in our educational system that would involve any additional outlay. But there is one subject which does not come under that heading which I would like to introduce for your serious consideration.

THE SCHOOL SAVINGS BANK.

In Europe it is a fully recognized educational and economic institution. To manage it takes but fifteen minutes a week and no time is better spent. It is an incentive to industry and study. This teaching of thrift is usually introduced through the practical interest of school directors or bankers, who are quick to see the benefit it necessarily brings a community. Frequently, mostly in fact, the Savings Bank to have the school deposits in trust takes the expense of furnishing the teacher's roll-books, blanks, cards, envelopes and slips as adapted to the system. When a child's savings reach one dollar he is given a separate bank book by the bank and stands in the light of an adult depositor acting through the school facilities. When he has three dollars he is allowed an interest of three per cent. on his deposit. The boys and girls are thus taught how money grows with care. They are told from time to time the advantages of industry, thrift and business knowledge. By the interest thus aroused parents who never had a dollar ahead have started savings banks' accounts for themselves.

" The School Savings Bank is a relief measure for pauperism, a preventive of crime, a developing force of honesty, sobriety and peace."

All of which is respectfully submitted.

ALEXANDER McKAY,
Supervisor.

Halifax, November, 1892.

(III.)

REPORT ON MANUAL TRAINING.

By Lee Russell, Esq., B. Sc.

It seems to me desirable to give in this report a brief outline of the work I have seen and a more complete account of the deductions and generalizations I have been able to make. In Boston and vicinity there are two well worked systems of manual training.

The Swedish Sloyd has been somewhat modified to meet the demands of the community and as the so-called Sloyd is vigorously taught and defended by Mr. Gustaf Larsson and his followers. Its main principles are these : 1. All practice shall be had in making useful articles which become the property of the pupils. 2. The models shall be so arranged as to bring into practice fundamental principles in the proper order of progression from the easy to the more difficult. 3. All work shall be from drawings made by the pupils. 4. As great a variety of tools as can properly be introduced, shall be used. 5. The models shall combine a variety of curved with plane surfaces.

Another system in more common use than the Sloyd, is the so-called Russian system. It aims to give Manual training by exercises illustrating the various principles of carpentry and joinery.

At Springfield, Massachusetts, there is a well-equipped Manual Training department in connection with the high school. But before entering the high school, pupils are instructed in the common schools. While the girls are engaged in needlework, the boys have practice in woodwork. Wooden covers are provided for the desks and knives, try-squares, rules, marking-gauges and prepared wood are distributed. The work is an ingenious modification of Sloyd and as a preparation for later work, has some value. It is worthy of mention that during the high school course the pupil spends each afternoon in the workshop. It seems open to question if so much time should be spent in Manual training. In several districts in Boston entire schools of sixty boys, go with their teacher to the workshop. In such shops two or three teachers are employed.

Mr. Larsson's training class has been well attended and he has turned out some very capable women teachers. This phase of the problem seems especially interesting to this Province. In most cases two or more women teach under the direction of a man. They devise and decide upon the course of models together. The director also takes care of the tools and has general charge. This seems to be a very successful arrangement. There is no doubt that women can acquire skill in Manual Training exercises and are as well able to teach this as anything else. It should be noted that the graduates of Mr. Larsson's school who are teaching most successfully were experienced and accomplished teachers before they took up Sloyd, and further that they took it up from natural liking.

The most significant feature of the present Manual Training movement is this. It is to a greater degree than any other branch of education, undergoing a constant healthy change ; new points of excellence are continually being added and faults weeded out. Each teacher is engaged in the most valuable and inspiring work known to our civilization—Original Research. All, or nearly all, are working in the true scientific spirit. In the extremely few cases in which this was lacking the schools showed a marked inferiority. It seems to me to promise well, not only for the future of Manual Training, but also for the future of any school course into which it is introduced. The spirit which it fosters, among pupils and teachers alike, is that of independent investigation, and this must sooner or later be felt in the course of education and in the community at large.

A significant feature in and about Boston, is the influence the various teachers have on each other. The half dozen original and energetic men who are leaders, are all working along the same lines, and the next result seems likely to be a system of Manual Training combining the good points of the various existing courses and lacking the weak ones.

A visit to a State Normal School in Connecticut made me acquainted with a phase of Manual Training which is of great value. Here is a shop in which all the students of the school work—women as well as men. It has a very intimate connection with the professional work in Physics and Chemistry. The students make actual apparatus which they take out with them to their schools, and are thus able, independently of the usual costly equipment, to demonstrate many of the fundamental truths of nature.

Here is a feature which might well be introduced into this Province. There are few cities, but in the country schools manual training of this sort will lead the pupils in a new and profitable direction. It needs no workshop. If the teacher has been instructed she can lead the pupils to make at home experiments and investigations. Further, a teacher who has had this sort of training looks upon the ceaseless constructive activity of children from a new standpoint. She sees in their water-wheels and boats a new means by which she can gain their attention, and spontaneous attention is the secret of all good instruction. She no longer looks upon their knives as implements for defacing desks, but sees in · them tools for fashioning the young minds under her charge.

It is evident that belief in Manual Training is advancing rapidly. New schools are being started every year, old ones enlarged.   From the report of Superintendent Seaver it is plainly a success in Boston.   The conditions in this Province seem to me especially to call for Manual Training.   With its great natural resources, Nova Scotia is certain of a period of industrial development in the near future. A population already partially educated in this direction must help along this development.   At any rate a healthy public opinion will be fostered and the community prepared to welcome any advance. In addition to all this, is the important truth just now beginning to be realized, that a child whose mind alone is trained is but half educated.

Respectfully submitted,

LEE RUSSELL.

HALIFAX, March 1st, 1893.

APPENDIX D.

SPECIAL INSTITUTIONS.

(I.)

INSTITUTION FOR THE DEAF AND DUMB,

Gottingen Street, Halifax N. S.

Patron.—His Honor M. B. Daly, *Lieutenant-Governor of the Province of Nova Scotia, &c.*

DIRECTORS.

Hon. D. McNeil Parker, M. D., and M. L. C.

Hon Provincial Secretary.

Rev. President Forrest, D. D.

William Tobin, Esq., M. D.

J. F. Kenny, Esq.

Andrew MacKinlay, Esq.

Secretary.—Rev. President Forrest, D. D.

Treasurer.—Andrew MacKinlay, Esq.

Physicians.—Donald A. Campbell, M.D., Murdoch Chisholm, M.D.

Consulting Physician.—Andrew J. Cowie, M. D.

Dentist.—Dr. A. C. Cogswell.

Oculist.—Stephen Dodge, M. D.

OFFICERS AND TEACHERS.

Educational Department.

Principal.—JAMES FEARON.

ASSISTANT TEACHERS.

MISS JULIA R. BATEMAN.   S. H. LAWRENCE.
MISS A. M. MOSHER.   MISS C. FRAME.
A. R. DODDS.

Matron.—MISS M. GLADWIN.

Matron's Assistant.—MISS E. BRYMER.

INDUSTRIAL DEPARTMENT.

Carpentry and Gardening.—MICHAEL McQUILLAN.

Shoemaking.—MARTIN ABBOTT.

By the Act of the Provincial Legislature of April 19, 1884, any Nova Scotian deaf or deaf mute child of *sound mind*, between the ages of *eight* and *eighteen*, is entitled to free admission to this Institution on the order of the Warden of the Municipality to which the child's parents belong.

REPORT OF DIRECTORS.

The Directors of the Institution of the Deaf and Dumb present their 35th Annual Report. During the past year the work has made very satisfactory progress. In the school everything has been most encouraging. Mr. Fearon has already proved himself to be such a painstaking and successful Principal that the minds of the Directors are relieved from all anxiety with regard to the practical working of the school. He is ably assisted by a band of teachers who discharge their duties with conscientious faithfulness. During the past year the staff has been strengthened by the addition of Mr. A. R. Dodds, who came highly recommended by the Principal of the Margate Institution. His work in Halifax fully justifies the testimonials which he brought. A short visit to the school, during working hours, will satisfy anyone that the work of instruction is being most faithfully and successfully carried on. The report of the Principal will show to those who have not an opportunity of witnessing for themselves, what is being accomplished.

In the home life of the Institution everything has been satisfactory. Miss Gladwin and her assistants have carefully attended to the comfort of the pupils. The Directors would gladly welcome the close and careful inspection of the public, for they feel confident that a healthier and happier family is not to be found in the land.

The physicians, Drs. Campbell and Chisholm, have been most attentive, visiting the Institution regularly, and promptly responding whenever called for. The Directors express their hearty thanks to them for their services. Their thanks are also due to Dr. Dodge and Dr. Cogswell, who always cheerfully respond to any call for their professional services.

During the past year Mr. Fearon visited a number of places in Nova Scotia and Prince Edward Island. One of the results has been that a number of children have been sought out and brought to the Institution. Every year the Institution is becoming better known, and consequently the number of pupils is steadily increasing. The steady growth in numbers presses every year more and more upon the accommodation afforded by the institution, until it is now absolutely necessary that a new building should be secured. The Institution has been conducted with the strictest economy, but the Directors now feel that it would be wrong to delay the erection of a new building much longer. They are quite confident that the community will heartily respond to their appeal. They feel that the Institution has the confidence of the public, and that the liberality which has sustained them in the past will come to their aid in the special effort that will now require to be made. The progress already made has been most encouraging, but the Directors cannot rest satisfied till full provision is secured for the education of every deaf mute in the community capable of receiving instruction.

During the past year the following bequests have been received : From estate of late Sir Edward Kenny, $400 ; estate of late John P. Mott, $11,876.00 ; estate of late A. K. Doull, $1,479.47. It has been the custom of the Directors ever since the founding of the Institution to put all such amounts to capital account, and not to use them for working expenses. The accounts for the year are herewith presented. The balance is still on the wrong side.

In conclusion, the Directors would express their gratitude to God for his goodness during another year. With His blessing resting upon the Institution it shall lack nothing.

On behalf of the Directors,

JOHN FORREST,

Secretary.

PRINCIPAL'S REPORT.

To THE DIRECTORS OF THE INSTITUTION FOR THE DEAF AND DUMB:

Gentlemen,—With the beginning of another year, it becomes my duty to furnish you with a report of the progress of the work of the last twelve months.

THE TOTAL ATTENDANCE

for the year has been seventy-two ; viz., forty-six boys and twenty-six girls, of whom sixty belong to the Province of Nova Scotia, and

twelve to the other Provinces.   The following table gives in detail
the whole attendance :—

	Boys.	Girls.	Total.
Pupils of previous years still present....	31	20	51
Additions during 1892	8	3	12
Absentees expected to return..........	0	1	1
Left school during the year	6	2	8
Total attendance for 1892........	45	26	72

NEW PUPILS.

admitted during 1892 :

LOUISA PATTEN..........Grand Bank, Newfoundland.
JOB SQUIRES ....St. John's,   "
ISRAEL ALLEZ .... .Sandy Point,   "
MAGGIE MOSHER ....St. Croix, Hants Co., N. S.
WILLIE MASON ....Lunenburg, N. S.
ERNEST HILTZ ....Lockeport, Shelburne Co., N. S.
ALBERT SMITH .... .Yarmouth, N. S.
LOUIS LANDERS..........   "   "
WILLIAM NOILES ....Amherst, N. S.
AUSTIN KIZER ....Fisherman's Harbour, Guys. Co., N. S.
REGINALD COOLEN ....Upper Prospect, Halifax Co., N. S.
JOSEPHINE SWIM ....Shelburne Co.. N. S.

      The following has been re-admitted :
ELIZA SMITH.... ....Cape Island, Shelburne Co., N. S.

      The following have left school :
GEORGE MCKENZIE ......Halifax City.
ARCHIE MCFATRIDGE......   "   "
JOSEPH GERO............Truro, Colchester Co., N. S.
WILLIE HEULIN ....Bay St. George, Newfoundland.
ELIZA HEULIN ....   "   "   "
DANIEL CAMERON........Scotch Hill, Pictou Co., N, S.
GEORGE SMITH ... .Cape Island, N. S.
JESSIE NIXON ....Margaretville, Annapolis Co., N. S.

HEALTH REPORT.

   During the first part of the year the health of the pupils remained
good, and though numerous cases of diphtheria and scarlet fever
appeared in the neighborhood, as the epidemic seemed to be abating
high hopes were entertained that we should reach the end of the
session without interruption.   Our expectations, however, were disappointed towards the end of March by the appearance among the
pupils of what threatened to be a serious outbreak of scarlet fever.
Preparations were being made to remove the first two cases from the
Institution when it was discovered that six of the pupils were already
attacked.   Everything possible was done by way of isolation and

disinfection, but notwithstanding this every day added to the list of cases until no less then twenty-seven children were prostrated, and the Institution became 'pro tempore' a hospital. The services of two experienced nurses were called in, and the officers of the Institution rendered every possible assistance. Fortunately the epidemic was of a mild type, and towards the end of April all had recovered and were back in the school-room. The skilful treatment and constant attention of Dr. Geo. Campbell cannot be too highly spoken of. He may be said to have been at the beck and call of the Institution during the whole course of the sickness, paying two or three visits daily, sometimes at great inconvenience. I regret to have to record the death of one pupil during the year, that of Joseph Gero, a coloured boy belonging to Truro. At the end of the session in June last he went on his holidays apparently in good health, but during the summer months symtoms of the fatal disease developed, and he died at his home of rapid consumption on October 11th. He had been two years at school, was quiet and gentle in his disposition, and consequently a favourite with both teachers and pupils. In the domestic department Miss Gladwin, and her assistant, Miss Brymer, have exercised their usual care and efficiency.

SCHOOL-ROOM REPORT.

The work of the school-room has 'been progressing satisfactorily. It is nevertheless, I think, the experience of every earnest teacher that however excellent his results may be, he believes he should and could produce still better. So it is with us. Ability, zeal, and fidelity characterize our present teaching staff, but the difficulties under which the deaf acquire a knowledge of language are so great and the field of operation is so wide that after our best efforts have been brought forth so little has been done and so much remains to be accomplished that even the most enthusiastic are inclined at times to become discouraged. Appended is the original compositions of some of the pupils from one to six years at school, which show clearly that decided progress is being made. In considering the compositions I would ask you to remember that they are the work of children dealing with a foreign language, with the additional disadvantages of limited daily instruction and a slow means of communication.

ORAL TEACHING.

With respect to Oral Teaching, as much attention is being paid to it as is possible in our present circumstances. At the beginning of last session an oral class was formed and the entire time of a teacher bestowed upon it, but while very satisfactory results were obtained it was felt that those who had previously received some oral instruction, as well as the new pupils capable of being so taught, were being neglected in this respect. Consequently, this year I thought it wise to go back to our old practice and to give at least an hour's oral instruction to every pupil in the school-room adapted to this method of teaching. The best results cannot be expected under these condi-

tions, but there is the advantage of every pupil receiving equal
justice.   The tide of Oralism that swept over England seems now to
be ebbing, and in spite of the recommendations of the late Royal
Commission and the impossible claims of too sanguine oralists,
instruction on the manual system will most probably occupy a
prominent place in the future as it has done in the past.   Great
benefit, however, has resulted from the introduction of the oral
• method into England, and numbers of the deaf now enjoy the blessings
of speech and lip-reading more or less perfect; the latent energies of
teachers have been drawn out, and with respect to the method of
imparting language a light has burst over the country the dawn of
which otherwise would have been long delayed.   The late Mr. J.
Scott Hutton foresaw at the beginning of the controversy the good
results that would assuredly follow, and speaking at the conference
held in London in 1881, he says, " I believe that the cause of the
deaf owes a debt of gratitude to the advocates of the oral method,
whose zeal and devotion put to shame the apparent luke-warmness
and lethargy of those who profess to be following a more excellent
way.   As storms clear the air carrying off brooding vapours and
noxious exhalations, imparting freshness and vigour to every function
and energy of sentient being, so the healthy breath of free discussion
stirs and purifies the social atmosphere, clearing away the mists of
prejudice, indolence or error. quickening the pulse and invigorating
the life-blood of society.   Anything is better than cynical indifference,
indolent self-complacency or facile acquiescence in mere traditionalism
and routine."   Whatever may be the future of the education of the
deaf in England the present conditions cannot demonstrate the
possibilities of the oral system, or rather cannot determine the percentage of the deaf capable of being successfully educated by means
of this method.   Owing to the culpable neglect of government the
education of the deaf is still to a great extent dependent upon
charity, and consequently the prospects, salaries and social standing
of teachers are insufficient to draw into the field high talents, ability
and education such as are required to ensure success.   Less arduous
and more remunerative occupations can be had any day, and why
not choose them ?   I think I may safely say that nine out of ten of
the young men and women entering the profession in England, do
so more by accident than with any pre-conceived idea or fixed
determination of making it their life's work and of preparing themselves accordingly.   To America, where the conditions are unspeak-
ably more favourable than in England, most probably will fall the
honor in the near future of deciding the merits of the oral method
and of saying definitely what that system can do and what it fails
to accomplish.

EXTRA SUBJECTS.

Under Miss Bateman and Mr. Dodds a deep and growing interest
in drawing has been aroused and marked progress has been made.
Through the continued kindness of Mr. Geo. Harvey, the senior
pupils, as formerly, attend the Art School and receive the benefit of
his instruction.   Classes in Clay-modelling and Type-writing have
been started which promise to be very successful.

APPOINTMENT.

After more than five years of faithful service Mr. R. W. McDonald resigned his position as a teacher in the institution at the beginning of the year, and Mr. A. R. Dodds, an instructor in the Margate Asylum for the Deaf, England, was appointed his successor, entering on his duties in the commencement of the following September. Mr. Dodds has had experience in both the manual and oral systems of instruction, having taught for over seven years in three of the most important institutions in the mother-country. He has fully realized the high opinion I entertain of him, proving himself a most competent teacher, and displaying a deep interest in the welfare of the pupils both in and outside of the school-room.

DEPUTATION WORK IN NOVA SCOTIA AND PRINCE EDWARD ISLAND.

In the month of October last, at your suggestion, I made a tour, accompanied by three of the pupils, through part of Nova Scotia, for the purpose of making known more widely the existence of the Institution, and of drawing in deaf children of school age not yet receiving the benefits of the Institution. I am glad to report that my efforts in both directions were met with success. Eleven places were visited, namely:—Windsor, Wolfville, Kentville, Bridgetown, Annapolis, Yarmouth, Shelburne, Lockeport, Liverpool, Bridgewater, and Lunenburg. The meetings on the whole were well attended, and in some places a very deep interest was displayed, notably Wolfville, Bridgewater and Lunenburg. As a result of the trip five new pupils were enrolled and a knowledge of the Institution brought to the parents of others not yet of school-age. These encouraging results led to my visiting Prince Edward Island in the end of the same month, where I held meetings in Charlottetown, Summerside and Souris. The audiences were large, and the good work which the Institution is doing seems to be recognized and appreciated. On the return journey I visited Pictou, Westville, New Glasgow and Truro; addressing large audiences and explaining by means of the pupils the workings of the Institution. In the last mentioned place I discovered a deaf and dumb boy 8 or 9 years of age, and elicited a promise from his parents that he should be sent to the Institution early in the coming spring.

Our increased numbers, with the consequent limited in-door as well as out-door accommodation, induce me to bring before you as strongly as possible the necessity of

A NEW BUILDING.

We require a building with modern conveniences such as are supplied by similar institutions in the United States and in the Old Country—situated in the healthiest suburb of the city, and surrounded with ample grounds where the pupils may have the benefit of proper out-door exercise and recreation so essential to the health of all children, but especially so to that of the deaf and dumb. The

present I think is auspicious, for never was more interest manifested
ed in education generally, and certainly never more public sympathy felt on behalf of this Institution.   Hitherto the hand of Providence has led us, and He will not desert us in this our new and
noble undertaking.

Yours respectfully,

JAMES FEARON, <i>Principal.</i></div>

TREASURER'S ACCOUNT.

INSTITUTION FOR THE DEAF AND DUMB IN ACCOUNT WITH A.
MACKINLAY, TREASURER.

1892.   *Dr.*

Jan. 1. To balance........................$ 578 71
Dec. 31.   " Salaries 3038 16
            " House Expenses................   5017 37
            " Repairs, etc...................   267 98
            " School Supplies................   119 92
            " Insurance 107 50
            " Telephones 43 00
            " Interest on Advances..........   264 54
            " Deposit Receipts.............. 13356 00
            " Investments 6500 00
            " Sundries 719 63
                                             ────$30058 31

1892.   *Cr.*

Dec. 31. By cash from pupils..............$ 160 50
            "   Province of N. S..........   3120 00
            "   Municipalities of N. S. 2940 00
            "   Government of N'fld......   500 00
            "   Interest on Investments ...   3065 19
            "   Deposit Receipts.........   6000 00
            "   Bequests................ 13809 63
            "   Donations, etc 130 14
            "   Sundries................   45 91
            " Balance to debit............   286 94
                                             ────$30058 31

1893.
Jan. 2. To balance at debit $286 94

E. & O. E.   A. MACKINLAY,

Treasurer.

LIST OF BEQUESTS AND DONATIONS, 1892.

Widow's Mite......................................$	1 00
Discount	7 14
New Gairlock Church, Pictou......................	9 00
Truro Union Prayer Meeting Collection.............	31 50
Estate J. Naylor..................................	53 50
United Church, New Glasgow......................	70 50
Estate late Sir Edward Kenny.....................	400 00
" J. P. Mott.............................	11,876 66
'' A. K. Doull	1,479 47
Sharon Church, Stellarton........................	6 00
St. Andrew's Church, Truro......................	5 00

[The Annual Report published contains 24 pages.]

(2)
HALIFAX SCHOOL FOR THE BLIND.
Incorporated in the year 1867.

MANAGERS AND OFFICERS OF THE INSTITUTION.

BOARD OF MANAGERS FOR 1893.

JOHN DUFFUS.
W. C. SILVER.
W. H. NEAL.
JOHN Y. PAYZANT.
GEORGE MITCHELL.
HON. S. L. SHANNON.
H. H. FULLER.
JAMES C. MACKINTOSH.
JAIRUS HART.
WM. MILLER.

THOS. RITCHIE.
WM. ROBERTSON.
HON. W. S. FIELDING.
   Premier of Nova Scotia.
HON. A. G. BLAIR,
   Premier of New Brunswick.
HON. FREDERICK PETERS.
   Premier of P. E. Island.
HON. SIR W. V. WHITEWAY,
   Premier of Newfoundland.

President.—W. C. SILVER.
Vice-President.—JAMES C. MACKINTOSH.
Treasurer.—JOHN DUFFUS.
Secretary.—C. F. FRASER.

STANDING COMMITTEES.

Finance.

H. H. FULLER.
JOHN DUFFUS.
JAMES C. MACKINTOSH.
GEORGE MITCHELL.

Instruction.

W. C. SILVER.
JAIRUS HART.
THOS. RITCHIE.
WM. ROBERTSON.

Manufacture.

J. C. MACKINTOSH.
W. H. NEAL.
HON. S. L. SHANNON.
JAIRUS HART.

House.

W. C. SILVER.
JAIRUS HART.
J. Y. PAYZANT.
GEORGE MITCHELL.

OFFICERS.

Superintendent.—C. F. FRASER.
Teachers.—*Literary Department*—E. P. FLETCHER, B. A.
     "   "   MISS K. SUTCLIFFE.
     "   "   MISS C. M. BOWMAN.
Music.—A. M. CHISHOLM.
Music Reader.—MISS A. SHERATON.
Girls' Work Department.—MISS BELLA BOWMAN.
Tuning Instructor.—D. M. REID.
Trade Instructor.—DAVID A. BAIRD.
Gymnastics Instructor.—T. C. WOODWORTH.
Steward.—R. T. BLAIR.
Matron.—MRS. R. T. BLAIR.
Attending Physician.—DR. A. W. H. LINDSAY.
Ophthalmic Physician.—DR. S. DODGE.
Dental Surgeon.—DR. A. C. COGSWELL.

TWENTY-SECOND ANNUAL REPORT OF THE BOARD OF MANAGERS
FOR 1892.

The Board of Managers have much pleasure in submitting to the members of the Corporation and to those interested in the education of the Blind, the Twenty-Second Annual Report of the School, and in so doing they desire to acknowledge their gratitude to a kind Providence for the many blessings poured out upon their work.

During the year 1892 the principle of the free education of the Blind has been endorsed by the Provincial Legislature of New Brunswick, and a law has been enacted providing for the free education of the blind youth of that Province in this Institution. This recognition of the claims of those who are deprived of sight, to participate in the privileges of a free education has been a great source of satisfaction to your Board, and now that so much has been accomplished they look forward with confidence to a similiar recognition being made by the Provinces of Prince Edward Island and Newfoundland.

In order that the friends of the Blind may more fully comprehend the scope of the work in which we are engaged, we have thought it best to briefly outline the history of the School from its inception, more particularly as respects its government and the sources from whence its revenues are derived.

In the year 1867 Mr. Wm. Murdoch, a retired merchant and banker of Halifax, died in London, and by will bequeathed the sum of £5000 Nova Scotia currency, ($19,466.67) toward the endowment of our Asylum for the Blind in Halifax, upon condition that a building would be erected at a cost of not less than £3000.

Steps were immediately taken by the Hon. M. B. Almon and other prominent gentlemen of Halifax to procure an Act of Incorporation, and a strong committee was selected to canvass the city for subscriptions.

The Act of Incorporation of the Halifax School for the Blind was passed on May 7th, 1867, and the requisite sum for the erection of the building having been subscribed, His Excellency J. H. Francklyn, C. B., Administrator of the Government of Nova Scotia, on April 11th, 1868, issued a proclamation declaring the Act to be in operation, and the Corporation was thereby authorized to meet on April 27th, 1868, as a body corporate and elect a Board of Managers and other Officers.

The first regular meeting under the Act of Incorporation was held in the City Council Chamber on Monday, April 27th, His Worship

Mayor Tobin in the chair, when the following gentlemen were elected as the Board of Managers for the ensuing year :—

HON. M. B. ALMON,	J. S. McLEAN,
CHIEF JUSTICE YOUNG,	M. H. RICHEY,
DR. AVERY,	CRARLES MURDOCH,
JOHN TOBIN,	JOHN DUFFUS,
HIS WORSHIP MAYOR TOBIN,	S. A. WHITE,
W. C. SILVER,	W. H. NEAL.

The City of Halifax having agreed to transfer to the Corporation a certain portion of the South Common containing three acres, known as Carey's Lot, and an arrangement having been made with Mr. Carey, the lessee, to surrender his lease for the sum of $500, the proper deeds were executed and recorded, and thus the Corporation became possessed of the property on which the buildings now stand.

In the summer of 1868 Mr. H. Peters was awarded the contract for erecting a building, the plans and specifications of which were prepared by Mr. David Stirling, an architect of Halifax. The building was completed in the autumn of 1869, at a cost of $14,027.08.

During the year 1870 the outhouses were erected, the property fenced in, and a large sum of money expended upon the improvement of the grounds.

Including the grant of $2000 by the Provincial Legislature of Nova Scotia the total subscriptions up to this date amounted to $15,557.38.

According to the original constitution and by-laws any original subscriber to the fund contributiug $1 per annum or any person contributing $5 per annum towards the funds became a member of the Corporation.

By the Act of Incorporation the School was placed under the control of a Board of Managers, consisting of twelve members, who were elected annually by the members of the Corporation. The officers of the Board of Managers and the officials of the School were appointed by the Board. Some modifications of the constitution have taken place, which will be referred to later on ; but in the main the government of the institution remains as it was originally constituted, and it may be said that it has been found to work satisfactorily to all concerned, and in our judgment in the best interests of the education of the blind.

The School was opened with four pupils on the first of August, 1871, since which time the number has slowly but steadily increased. For information as to the course of instruction, the appliances that have been or are in use, and the general results of the training of the pupils, we refer all interested to the report of the Superintendent herewith subjoined.

In 1874 applications were received and accepted for the admission of pupils from the Provinces of New Brunswick and Prince Edward Island, and the Board of Managers of that year applied to the Governments of these Provinces to join with Nova Scotia in helping to maintain the Institution by annual appropriations towards its support. The Legislatures of the two Provinces named responded liberally to the request for assistance, and thus the School became Maritime Provincial in the extent of its usefulness.

In 1877 the growth of the School demanded an increase of accommodation, and through the liberality of the public a commodious building was erected. This building contained a fine gymnasium and workshop, both of which have been in constant use for the past fifteen years.

In 1881 the main building of the School was greatly improved by the addition of a hot water heating apparatus, which was put in at a cost of $2,400. In this same year the Board of Managers made an urgent appeal through the Superintendent, Mr. C. F. Fraser, to obtain for the Blind of this Province the privileges of a free education. For several years the question had been considered by the Government and the Legislature, but no definite action having been taken, the Board decided to obtain an expression of public opinion, and accordingly public meetings were organized in the principal towns, cities and villages throughout the Province, and the claims of those deprived of sight to the blessings of a free education were fully and fairly expressed. Strong resolutions favouring the movement were unanimously and enthusiastically adopted, and the Legislature was petitioned to grant to the Blind of the Province the same free educational privileges as those enjoyed by their brothers and sisters with sight.

In the year 1882 the "Act in relation to the education of the Blind" was adopted by the Provincial Legislature, by which this Institution was recognized as a special academy for those deprived of sight, and the Provincial Secretary, as representative of the Government, became, ex officio, a member of the Board of Managers. The full text of this Act, with its amendments, will be found in the appendix to this report.

In 1884 it was decided by a vote of the members of this Corporation to ask the Legislature to change the name of the Institution to one more in keeping with its educational character, and in accordance with this request an Act was passed changing the name of the Institution from the Halifax Asylum for the Blind to the Halifax School for the Blind.

In 1887 two pupils were received from the Province of Newfoundland, and in that year for the first time pupils from all the four Provinces, namely, Nova Scotia, New Brunswick, Prince Edward Island and Newfoundland, were in attendance at the School.

In 1890 the Act of Incorporation was amended, by which the Board of Managers was given power to extend its number by electing as an ex officio member the Premier or first Minister of any Province contributing towards the funds of the School.   Under this Act the Premiers of New Brunswick, Prince Edward Island and Newfoundland became members of the Board of Managers.

In this year the increased number of applications for the admission of pupils caused the Board of Managers to make a strong effort to secure additional accommodations, which resulted in the erection of a fine new wing to the main building at a cost of $15,954. The Provincial Legislature of Nova Scotia liberally appropriated $4,000 toward paying for the building, and this sum being supplemented by the bequests of the late J. P. Mott, Esq., and the late S. A. White, Esq., and being further augmented by the handsome subscriptions of the many friends of the Blind throughout the Maritime Provinces, the Board of Managers was gratified to find that but a small balance of debt had to be incurred, which has since gradually been reduced.

The plans and specifications of the new building were prepared by Mr. J. C. Dumaresq, and the contract was taken by Mr. S. A. Marshall, builder.

The wing was completed and occupied in May, 1891, since which time the school has steadily increased in the number of its pupils, there being upon the register at this date 46 pupils.

This brief record of twenty-one years of progressive work cannot fail to be interesting to the members of the Corporation and to the friends of the Blind.

The two characteristic features of the year just drawing to a close, are, so far as this School is concerned, (1) the adoption of an Act by the Provincial Legislature of New Brunswick making the education in this Institution free to the blind of that Province ; and (2) the inauguration of a systematic plan, whereby the names, ages and addresses of all blind children under twenty-one years of age can be obtained.   This information is to be secured through the agency of the public school teachers.   Several questions have been added respecting the blind and the deaf to those answered semi-annually by the 2200 teachers throughout the Province of N. S., and through these answers we hope to learn the whereabouts of many blind children who might otherwise be overlooked and allowed to grow up in darkness and ignorance.   The current revenue of the School is derived from three sources, as follows :—

First.—A per capita grant of $150 for each pupil in attendance. In Nova Scotia and New Brunswick one half of this amount is paid by the government of the Province and the remaining half by the municipality in which the pupil has a legal settlement.   In Prince Edward Island and Newfoundland the grants are paid annually from the Provincial Treasuries.

Second.—The interest upon investments.— The invested funds of the School have been derived from the bequests of benevolent and public-spirited men and women, and as the Treasurer's report will show, the interest upon these funds forms a considerable portion of the revenues of the School.

Third.—Subscriptions and Donations.—The subscriptions of the Corporation and the donations of other friends and organizations have been and are of great assistance in carrying forward the work, and had it not been for these contributions the pupils would have been deprived of many of the advantages they have enjoyed.

The several departments of the School are in thorough working order. The teachers have been faithful in their duties and have zealously worked to forward the interests of their pupils.

The positions of Steward and Matron of the School are occupied by Mr. and Mrs. R. T. Blair, who have for the past seventeen years done their best for the comfort of the pupils and for the economical management of the domestic department.

The Board of Managers is pleased to acknowledge the receipt of $400, kindly bequeathed to the School by the late Sir Edward Kenny; and they also gratefully acknowledge the receipt of an additional amount of $11,876.66 as one of the residuary legatees of the late J. P. Mott, Esq., of Dartmouth. These funds have been invested in good securities.

During the year two tried friends of the School have resigned their positions as members of the Board of Managers.

Ex-Governor Richey has been connected with the School from its inception, and for many years acted as Corresponding Secretary of the Board of Managers.

Mr. E. D. Meynell has for the past twelve years filled the responsible positions of Secretary of the Board of Managers and Treasurer of the School ; resigning these positions on account of his leaving the Province to spend the evening of his days among his friends in the Motherland.

Both of these gentlemen have done much to forward the interests of the Institution, and in accepting their resignations, the Board of Managers desires to express its regret that circumstances have necessitated their severing their connection with the Board.

In each and every recorded step in advance the Managers recognize the able and devoted hand of the Superintendent, C. F. Fraser, who came to the work richly endowed with combined ability and zeal, eminently fitting him for the varied and responsible duties appertaining to his office. His late appointment to the office of

Secretary opens an additional field of usefulness, which his untiring energy will certainly turn to the benefit of the Institution. The thanks of the Board of Managers are hereby tendered to Drs. Lindsay, Dodge, Kirkpatrick, and Cogswell for their kindly attention to the pupils. To H. B. Clarke, Lessee of the Academy of Music, and to the Orpheus club for tickets to entertainments. To a number of leading lecturers and musicians in Halifax for lectures and concerts given to pupils in the Assembly Hall of the School ; and to the railway, steamship and coach proprietors for privileges granted to our pupils.

All of which is respectfully submitted.

W. C. SILVER,

President.

SUPERINTENDENT'S REPORT.

To the President and Board of Managers of the School for the Blind :

GENTLEMEN,—

The table of attendance herewith submitted shows that 54 blind persons have been under instruction during the past year, 37 of whom were males and 17 females ; 7 of these have since graduated or left the School, and one has been removed by death, making the total attendance on Dec. 1st, 1892, 46 ; of whom 22 are from the Province of Nova Scotia, 17 from New Brunswick, 1 from Prince Edward Island and 6 from Newfoundland.

TABLE OF ATTENDANCE.

	Boys.	Girls.	Adults.	Total.
Registered Dec. 1st, 1891	28	11	0	39
Entered during the year	7	6	2	15
Graduated or remained at home	5	2	0	7
Died during the year	0	1	0	1
Registered December 1st, 1892	30	14	2	46

LITERARY DEPARTMENT.

The work of this department has been faithfully carried forward by the teaching staff.

The pupils have been industrious and the results have been satisfactory.

Owing to ill health Miss J. E. G. Roberts resigned her position as a teacher in March last, and the School was, in consequence, deprived of the services of a talented teacher, and the pupils of a kind and sympathetic friend. The position vacated by Miss Roberts has since been occupied by Miss Kate Sutcliffe, of Halifax, who has thrown into her work a large measure of earnestness and enthusiasm, and whose qualifications eminently fit her to achieve success in this special department of education. Mr. E. P. Fletcher and Miss C. Bowman, the other members of the literary staff, have been conscientious and painstaking in their work, and with Miss Sutcliffe they have won the esteem of the pupils, and well deserve the confidence placed in them.

In the education and training of the blind great advances have been made during the century, but still more remains to be accomplished. Many of those engaged in this work have been, and still are imbued with the idea that the methods of instructing the blind should follow closely upon those employed in teaching children with sight. This idea led Haüy, the French apostle of the blind, into many errors, which have been perpetuated by the instructors of the blind in all parts of the world, and indeed so deeply rooted is this prejudice in favor of making the methods employed in the education of the blind conform to the standards of those with sight, that scarce an advance has been made or an improvement generally adopted without having been met with strong opposition. In the public school the eye is the main avenue through which knowledge is gained, while in schools for the blind the sense of touch is one of the principal mediums for obtaining information. These senses of sight and touch are as distinctive as taste and smell, and hence those instructors of the blind who have adhered to the seeing standards, have blocked the wheels of progress and have hindered rather than advanced this special educational work.

It has been our endeavor to keep this School in the front rank of similar institutions, and that we have succeeded in doing this, is a fact that can readily be verified. The appliances used in the School have been selected with great care. Experience has taught us that merit alone is the true test of superiority, and our choice of apparatus has been made with the sole motive of securing for our pupils the most practical and the very best results. It was this motive which led us to abandon books embossed in the line letter, and to substitute for them books printed in Braille point characters. The line letter is well adapted to the eye, but it is too intricate for the sense of touch, while the Braille point letter offers many advantages beside that of increased tangibility.

For the past fifteen years the Braille system has been exclusively taught in this School, and it is worthy of note that it was only during the present year that the American conference of instructors of the Blind declared in favor of the point system as opposed to the line system. We have now in our circulating library 170 volumes printed or written in Braille characters, and the eagerness with which these books are read proves that the point print is more generally popular than experience has shown any print to have been in the past.

In the study of Arithmetic, especially with beginners, calculating boards are of great use. We have used side by side the Philadelphia, Boston and Taylor ciphering boards, and in our experience the superiority of the latter is beyond question. Aside from its cheapness and simplicity it has the advantage of economizing the time of the pupil, which is well worthy of consideration. In the Philadelphia board the ten Arabic signs are embossed upon ten sets of type, and much time is lost by the pupil in the selection and distribution of these. The same objection in a lesser degree applies to the Boston board, in which there are two distinct classes of type. The type in the Taylor board are square on one end, one of the edges is raised into a prominent ridge; on the other end there is a similar ridge divided in the middle by a deep notch. The holes in the board are star-shaped with eight angles. In these the type can be placed in eight different positions, and by reversing the type in eight more; this gives ten signs for the Arabic numerals and six for the ordinary Algebraic signs.

In the teaching of geography raised wall maps have been very generally used in the School, but here again experience has shown us that much better and more effective work can be accomplished by the use of individual class maps. Many of these have been in the Institution, but as they are now manufactured at a comparatively cheap rate by the British and Foreign Blind Association, our supply of class maps is principally drawn from that source.

The appliances used in point and pencil writing, in the study of geometry and in the kindergarten department are in our estimation the best that have yet been provided; and in the foregoing the School is kept well abreast of the times, and the educational advantages enjoyed by the pupils are probably greater in proportion to the expenditure than those of any similar Institution in America.

The following is a list of the classes now under instruction :—

Geography, I. II. and III. Division.
Physical Geography, II.   "
Reading, II. and III.   "
Spelling, II. and III.
Braille Writing, II. and III.   "
Pencil Writing, I, and II.   "
Grammar, I. and II.
Composition, I. and II.
Literature, I. and II.
British History, II. and III.   "
Natural History, I.   '
Arithmetic, I., II. and III.   "
Geometry, I. and II.
Theory of Music, I. and II.   "
Kindergarten. III,

MUSICAL DEPARTMENT.

The aim in this department is to qualify the pupils to become teachers of music and pianoforte tuners.

During the past year Stephen Harivel of Stellarton, N. S., and John A. Dunn of Advocate Harbor, N. S., have received their graduating diplomas, and gone forth from the School prepared to maintain themselves. The former was awarded a first-class certificate as a teacher of music, and the latter a first-class certificate as a pianoforte tuner. Both of these young men have been carefully and thoroughly taught, both of them have gone energetically to work, and they both feel confident that with industry success is assured.

The thorough work being done by Mr. A. M. Chisholm, our teacher of music, is evidenced throughout the musical department, as well in the pianoforte work of the pupils as in the School band and choir. Mr. D. M. Reid, instructor of pianoforte tuning, has likewise done good work in his own department.

In the study of music, the Braille musical notation is found of great advantage. In addition to the use of our library of Braille point music, the pupils are able to write out from dictation and to afterwards memorize any piece of vocal or instrumental music they may be learning; and this enables them to at any time refresh their memories by a reference to the tangible copy, the great advantage of such a system of notation is at once apparent.

A knowledge of how music is written for persons with sight is acquired by careful instruction on the part of the teacher, and by the study of the work containing the characterters used by the seeing, embossed in such a way that they can readily be distinguished by the touch.

In pianoforte tuning the pupils are taught to examine, adjust, take to pieces and put together the models of differents actions, and in this way they gain a knowledge of the differences in construction of pianos of many different makers.

WORK DEPARTMENT.

Many trades have been tried in this School with a view to ascertaining which gave to the blind workman the best results.

Brush, corn broom and mat making as occupations for the Blind, at least in this country, having been "tried and found wanting"; the chief reasons being that the Blind cannot work to advantage with second-class material, that the material used had to be imported in comparatively small quantities, and that the margin between the cost of material and the selling price of the finished product did not leave a living profit. In our experience willow basket making and the cane seating of chairs are the trades best adapted to the

Blind in the eastern portion of Canada, as they afford a fair livelihood to any industrious workman.   As a preparation for the
learning of these trades and for instruction in the tuning department, our youngest boys are trained according to the Sloyd system
to use all kinds of carpenter's tools; and the results proved the
advantages of technical training for the young.

Our workshops are in charge of Mr. D. A. Baird, who makes
every effort to advance his pupils.

Our girls' work department is in a flourishing condition, and
under the careful instruction of Miss Bella Bowman it has shown
steady improvement.   Many of our girls and some of our graduates
have found remunerative employment in the making of various
kinds of useful and fancy articles, and as the orders are continually
increasing we hope to give employment to many more of our deserving graduates and thus to materially assist them in providing for
themselves.

OUR GRADUATES.

Thus far our report has dealt with the every-day work of the
School, but in order to appreciate the results we must look beyond
the walls of the Institution and see what the graduates of the School
are doing.

A careful record of the pupils and graduates has been kept, of
which the following is a brief summary of the graduates now
living :—

28 per cent. are engaged in teaching music.
12   "   in conducting or taking part in concert companies.
 8   "   in piano forte tuning.
 8   "   in business.
 4   "   in manufacturing.
12   "   giving instruction in or working at trades.
 2   "   as agents.
 2   "   in farm work.
 2   "   in literary callings.
22   "   residing at home.

Of these latter a large proportion help in the household and partially maintain themselves by the work of their hands.

25 per cent. of the graduates are married and residing in comfor-
able homes.

HOME TEACHING.

There are two classes of blind persons to whom we desire to lend
a helping hand, and for whom much can be done.

First—There are those who are too young to enter the School;
and Second—those who lose their sight when they are too old to

take advantage of regular School training. The first of these we endeavor to reach by correspondence with the parents or guardians, by supplying them with copies of the "Mentor" and other publications dealing with the education of the Blind, by furnishing them with books printed in raised letters and helpful appliances, and by advising them as to the best manner of training little boys and girls who are without sight. For the adult Blind who are not graduates of the school, we desire to do much more in future than as yet we have been able to accomplish. There are many hundreds of middle aged and elderly blind persons living throughout the four Provinces who require assistance. Many of these persons are overwhelmed by the loss of sight, and the results of the weary monotony of their idle lives is pitiable in the extreme. To such, this Institution should be a beacon light of hope, and thank God it has been a direct blessing to many such. Many of those who lose their sight after they reach manhood or womanhood can with very little help be taught to read raised print, and be encouraged to resume the active duties of life. There are very few callings or occupations which a man or a woman with sight has followed successfully which the same man or woman without sight could not follow with equal success.

Vidal, the French sculptor, who died in Paris last summer, lost his sight shortly after he had completed the study of his art. and yet he continued to follow his profession for the remainder of his life. Instances are on record of professional and business men, farmers and mechanics, housekeepers and salesmen and women having continued to follow their customary pursuits in life after they have been deprived of sight.

For this class of our blind we are doing all that lies in our power, but we feel that this particular branch of our work should be taken up and carried forward by a home teaching association ; that an experienced agent and teacher should be employed, and that a systematic effort should be made to brighten the lives and lighten the burdens of those who, being overwhelmed by the loss of sight, are powerless to help themselves.

FREE EDUCATION.

During the session of the Legislature of New Brunswick I took a representative party of the School to Fredericton, and afterward visited St. John, Moncton and Sackville. Enthusiastic and largely attended meetings were held, and resolutions endorsing the action of the Government in making education free to the Blind of New Brunswick were unanimously adopted.

The New Brunswick Act respecting the education of the Blind was favorably received by the supporters of the Government as well as by the members of the Opposition, and the unanimity with which it passed reflects great credit upon the liberality, intelligence, and broad sense of justice of the gentlemen who in their representative capacity form the Legislature of New Brunswick. The youthful Blind of New Brunswick and Nova Scotia now receive education in this School as a right ; and ere long these privileges, which the Blind youth of Prince Edward Island and Newfoundland enjoy, but for which they are dependent upon annual appropriations, should be confirmed to them by the Acts of their respective Legislatures. When this is accomplished and education is free by Act of Parliament to every Blind child of the four Maritime Provinces, the friends of the Blind will have reason to feel thankful, the status of the Blind will be improved, and those who are engaged in the work will be able to devote their energies to other departments, one of which, respecting the adult Blind, has been referred to in this report.

Among the acknowledgments of contributions towards our building fund will be found the names of many gentlemen well known in New Brunswick, some of whom have subscribed $25.00 and upwards and these have become life members of the Corporation. It is earnestly to be hoped that leading gentlemen in all sections of the Maritime Provinces and Newfoundland will show their living interest in the work in which we are engaged by becoming members or life members of the Corporation, by employing and encouraging our graduates, and by doing what lies in their power to help forward as opportunity offers an educational and benevolent work ; the success of which must always depend largely upon the number and earnestness of its friends.

In closing this report I beg to acknowledge my appreciation of the cordial co-operation and support of the Board of Managers, and to express my hope that the same mutually friendly relations may long continue to exist.

All of which is respectfully submitted,

C. F. FRASER,

Superintendent.

SCHOOL FOR THE BLIND IN ACCOUNT WITH J. C. MACKINTOSH, TREASURER.

CURRENT ACCOUNT.

1891.   *Cr.*

Dec. 1. By Balance........ ....   66 52
1892.
Dec. 1.   " Interest and Dividends.......... 2294 02
           " Donation and Thanksgiving Con-
               tributions 89 20
           " Grant N. S. Gov. and Municipalities 3109 25
           " Grant N. B. Gov. and Municipalities 975 00
           " Grant P. E. I. Govt.............. 150 00
           "   "   Nfld.   " 900 00
           " Rebates, etc...................   10 73
                                              --------- 7528 20
           " Transfer from Investment Ac. 2299 67

                                                        $9894 39

1892.   *Dr.*

Dec. 1. To House Expenses, including Salaries
            to Steward, Matron and servants.. 5378 79
           " Salaries to Supt. and Teachers.... 2106 00
           " Repairs to Buildings...........   401 84
           " Grounds 111 09
           " Printing, Paper and Stationery.... 99 55
           " Musical Instruments............   185 80
           " Prizes 18 00
           " Board of Adult Pupils...........   100 00
           " School Supplies................   91 45
           " Discounts, etc.................   7 35
                                              --------- 8499 87
           " Extraordinary Repairs 1040 53
           " Balance carried forward.........   353 99

                                                        9894 39

         By Balance brought down $353 99

E. & O. E.

Halifax, N. S., Dec. 8th, '92·

Examined and found correct.

                    W. H. NEAL,   } AUDITORS.
                    GEO. MITCHELL   }

SCHOOL FOR THE BLIND IN ACCOUNT WITH J. C. MACKINTOSH,
TREASURER.

INVESTMENT ACCOUNT, 1892.

1892.   *Cr.*
Dec. 1. By Legacy J. P. Mott Estate 11876 66
          " Deposit Notes Cashed......... 4649 34
          " Loan Repaid 200 00
          " Legacy J. Naylor Estate....... 26 75
                                    ———— $16752 75

                          Dr.
          To Invested in City Debentures ... 14453 08
          " Transferred to Current Ac...... 2299 67
                                    ———— $16752 75

RECAPITULATION.

1891.   *Cr.*
Dec. 1. By Balance.....................   66 52
1892.
Dec. 1. " Revenue 7528 20
          " Investments realized.........   16752 75

                                            $24347 47

1892.   *Dr.*
Dec. 1. To Current Expenses 8499 87
          " Extraordinary Repairs 1040 53
          " Investments 14453 08
          " Balance Cash................   353 99
                                    ———— $24347 47

E. & O. E.

Halifax, N. S., Dec. 8th, 1892.

Examined and found correct.

                W. H. NEAL,   } AUDITORS.
                GEO. MITCHELL.   }

Annual Report has 48 pages.

APPENDIX E,

- MISCELLANEOUS INSTITUTIONS.

(1)

The Provincial School of Agriculture,

. TRURO, NOVA SCOTIA.

DR. MACKAY,
Superintendent of Education.

DEAR SIR :—

I have the honor to submit to you the following report, containing a Short History of the School, Course of Instruction, and an account of some of the equipments of the School.

I am, Sir, your obedient servant,
H. W. SMITH.

THE PROVINCIAL SCHOOL OF AGRICULTURE,
TRURO, N. S.

MARCH, 1, 1893.

HISTORY OF THE SCHOOL.

The School of Agriculture was established in 1885. Its object was threefold. First, to give further instruction to the Normal School students in the Natural Sciences; second, to provide a course in Agriculture and Agricultural Chemistry for teachers; third, to provide a course in Agriculture for farmers and farmers' sons. This instruction was given in a room in the basement of the Normal School building, which had been equipped for this purpose. In the fall of 1888, a farm was purchased. This farm contains 104 acres, of which 50 acres are cleared upland, 30 intervale for pasture; and 24 acres wood and brush. It is furnished with all the necessary farm implements, live stock, splendid Dairy House and a fine Piggery.

During the past season, the Government has built a building on the farm for the use of the School of Agriculture. The attendance, which numbered seven for the first year of the school, has steadily and gradually increased, numbering twenty-five, (25) the past year,

Students and graduates of this school are now located all over this province, from Cape Breton and Inverness at the east to Yarmouth county on the west. These students and graduates are farmers, and following farming, with but few exceptions. There are some who having completed their course here, are now attending higher institutions of learning, as McGill and Cornell Universities. The number of graduates of the school is no criterion of the attendance, since there is no inducement for a farmer to graduate, further than the honor of having done so. As a result, we have a number of young men who have completed their course, except writing their thesis and graduating. The number of graduates, however, is as follows:

Years.	Total.	As Teachers.	As Farmers.
1886	2	2	0
1887	3	2	1
1888	1	1	0
1889	3	1	2
1890	5	1	4
1891	5	2	3
1892	4	0	4

Five of the above teachers own farms in the Province.

COURSE OF INSTRUCTION.

This comprises a course of lectures on Agriculture, and practical farm work, and includes the following subjects: Soils, Plants, Animals, Atmosphere and Water, Manure, Buildings, Implements, Horticulture, Small and Large Fruits, Dairy and Apiary. Besides the Agriculture proper, the following major and minor sciences: Chemistry, Botany, Veterinary Science for major sciences: Entomology, Geology and Zoology for minor sciences.

The Chemistry includes Introductory, General and Organic Chemistry, Qualitative Analysis and Quantitative Analysis of Agricultural products. The Botany includes Structural Botany, Anatomy and Physiology of Plants, Algæ and Fungi, Agricultural and Systematic Botany, Gramineæ and Compositæ. The Veterinary Science includes Hygiene, the Anatomy and Physiology of the Domestic Animals, Histology, Materia Medica and Pathology.

It is the design by this course of study to give the student a thorough knowledge of those sciences which lie at the foundation of modern agriculture, and thus enable him to become acquainted with the reasons for the various operations he performs on the farm. In order, however, to teach any science or agriculture, it is necessary that the student learn to do by doing. That is, if he wishes to learn to plow he must actually perform that operation himself ; he cannot learn it by reading about it. In the same way, in learning a science, he must learn the substance, plant or animal as the case may be by handling it, examining it, and experimenting with it. He cannot do it by the mere perusal of a printed page. In order, however, for him to make this examination, and handling and experimenting, of the greatest profit to himself, it is not only essential that he have a teacher to direct him, but that he also have proper appliances with which to pursue his studies. With this view, the Government has so well equipped the New School Building, that it furnishes the very best facilities for these sciences.

THE EQUIPMENTS OF THE SCHOOL.

For a general description of the building, see my report to the Secretary for Agriculture.

There are two chemical laboratories, the first one, a room 20 x 40 feet, which is for Introductory Chemistry and Qualitative Analysis. There are twenty-two individual desks, fitted with drawers and cupboards, water supply and gasoline burner. There are also four hoods in this room, two near each end, one of each fitted with steam cups for boiling and evaporating solutions, and the other for working with dangerous and noxious gases. The other laboratory is for Quantitative Analysis. This room has attached to it a small room containing the balances and other delicate apparatus. In other respects it is fitted like the Introductory room, except that the desks are larger, being two by four (2 x 4) feet.

The Anatomical laboratory is fitted with a large table for dissection, as well as individual tables for the use of the students. In this room there is a steam boiler for boiling and preparing specimens.

The Biological and Botanical laboratory is a room 25 x 30 feet. It is provided with individual tables and chairs, also microscopes (Simple and compound), proper staining fluids and all necessary equipments for the study of Histology, Biology and Botany.

The Entomological laboratory is a room of the same size and similarly equipped as the Biological laboratory.

As I have already pointed out, in order to study the natural sciences effectively, it is necessary to have a well equipped laboratory.

In the same way in order to study agriculture, it is necessary to have a well equipped farm, as the farm should sustain the same relation to the study of agriculture, as the laboratory does to the study of a natural science. And as one cannot become a chemist without working in the laboratory, neither can he become a farmer without working on the farm. But it must be observed that the mere working in a chemical laboratory does not make a chemist. The work needs to be supervised and intelligently directed and this is equally true in regard to the farm.

The farm for the school is well equipped with all appliances requisite for teaching farming, It has a splendid collection of farm implements, costing nearly $1500, all necessary dairy appliances and live stock. In regard to the last, it has seemed to me better to use the same kind of stock as the farmers possess, than to purchase expensive and high bred stock, as our aim should be to teach the farmer first how to care for and improve what he has. He will then not be slow in taking advantage of any improvement in the different breeds. I would like to impress the fact, that in this institution the farm is a part of the school, and is conducted strictly for the benefit and instruction of the students. Besides this, of course we try to make it as beneficial, in the way of experiments, to the general farmer, as possible.

With these equipments, the school affords the very best facilities for the study of the natural sciences in relation to agriculture.

LOCAL AGRICULTURAL SCHOOLS.

There are five local agricultural schools now in operation in the Province. Two in Cape Breton, one in Antigonish, one in Pictou, and one in Annapolis county. These schools are doing very good work, but as I have pointed out before, they labor under the disadvantage of not being permanent.

I have also instructed the classes in the Normal School, in Chemistry, Botany and Physiology.

H. W. SMITH.

(2)

HALIFAX MEDICAL COLLEGE.

THE CORPORATION.

ALEX. P. REID, M. D.,　　　　H. McD. HENRY, LL. B.,
EDWARD FARRELL, M. D.,　　　D. A CAMPBELL, M. D.,
JOHN F. BLACK, M. D.,　　　　A. W. H. LINDSAY, M. D.,
JOHN SOMERS, M. D.,　　　　　ARTHUR MORROW, M. B.,
GEORGE L. SINCLAIR, M. D.,　　M. A. CURRY, M. D.

President :—DR. ALEX. P. REID.
Registrar :—DR. A. W. H. LINDSAY.

EXECUTIVE COMMITTEE.

DR. SOMERS,　　　DR. LINDSAY,　　　DR. MORROW.

TRUSTEES.

HON. DR. PARKER,　　PROF. J. G. MACGREGOR,
H. H. FULLER, ESQ.

THE FACULTY.

ALEX. P. REID. M. D. C. M. McGill ; L. R. C. S. Edin. : L. C. P. & S. Can.; *Emeritus Professor of Medicine and Professor of Medical Jurisprudence and Hygiene.*

WM. B. SLAYTER, M. D., Chic.; M. R. C. S. Eng.; L. R. C. P. Lon. ; F. O. S. Dub. ; *Emeritus Professor of Obstetrics and Gynecology.*

EDWARD FARRELL, M. D., Coll. Phs. and Surg., N. Y.; *Professor of Surgery and Clinical Surgery.*

JOHN SOMERS, M. D., Bell. Hosp. Med. Coll., N. Y.; *Professor of Medicine.*

JOHN F. BLACK, M. D., Coll. Phys. and Surg., N. Y.; *Professor of Surgery and Clinical Surgery.*

GEORGE L. SINCLAIR, M. D., Coll. Phys. and Surg., N. Y., M. D., Univ. Hal., Supt. N. S. Hospital for Insane ; *Professor of Nervous and Mental Diseases.*

DONALD A. CAMPBELL, M. D., C. M., Dal.; *Professor of Medicine, and Clinical Medicine.*

A. W. H. LINDSAY, M. D., C. M., Dal. ; M. B. C. M., Edin.; *Professor of Anatomy.*

ARTHUR MORROW, M. B., C. M., Edin.; *Professor of Physiology.*

F. W. GOODWIN, M. D. C. M., Hal. Med. Coll., *Professor of Materia Medica.*

M. A. CURRY, M. D., Univ. N. Y.; *Professor of Obstetrics and Gynecology.*

STEPHEN DODGE, M. D., Coll. Phys. and Surg., N. Y.; *Professor of Ophthalmology and Otology.*

MURDOCH CHISHOLM, M. D. C. M., McGill ; L. R. C. P. Lond. ; *Professor of Clinical Medicine and Therapeutics.*

NORMAN F. CUNNINGHAM, M. D., Bell Hosp. Med. Coll. ; *Adjunct Professor of Surgery.*

WILLIAM TOBIN, F. R. C. S. Ire. ; *Professor of Laryngology and Rhinology.*

DR. GEO. L. SINCLAIR, *Dean of Faculty.*
DR. A. W. H. LINDSAY, *Secretary.*

LECTURERS, ETC.

G. CARLETON JONES, M. D. C. M., Hal. Med. Col.; M. R. C. S., Eng. ; *Demonstrator of Anatomy and Lecturer on Diseases of Children.*

GEORGE M. CAMPBELL, M. D., Bell Hosp. Med. Coll.: *Demonstrator of Histology.*

W. D. FINN, M. D., Coll Phys. and Surg. N. Y.; *Demonstrator of Pathology.*

F. U. ANDERSON, L. R. C. S. and L. R. C. P. Ed. ; M. R. C. S. Eng.; *Assistant Demonstrator of Antomy.*

C. E. Puttner, Ph. M., *Instructor in Dispensing.*

W. A. P. TERNAN, L. R. C. P. and L. R. C. S., Ed.; L. F. P. Glas.; *Class Instructor Clinical Surgery.*

W. H. HATTIE, M. D. C. M. McGill; *Lecturer on Bacteriology.*

WALLACE McDONALD, B. A., *Lecturer Medical Jurisprudence.*

A. I. MADER, M. D. C. M. McGill; *Assistant Demonstrator of Anatomy.*

EXTRA MURAL LECTURER.

GEORGE LAWSON, Ph. D., etc., *Professor of Chemistry and Botany at Dalhousie College.*

G. P. SKELLY, *Janitor.*

The College building erected for the special purpose of medical teaching, is in every way fitted for the object in view. It is situated in an open, airy locality, in close proximity to the Victoria General Hospital and the New City Alms House. The lecture rooms, dissecting room, etc., are well lighted, warmed and ventilated, and are fitted with appliances for imparting knowledge in the different subjects of medical education.

Certificates of attendance on the various courses of lectures are accepted as qualifying candidates for examination before the licensing bodies of Great Britain and Ireland, and the Medical Schools and Universities in Canada and the United States.

Druggists' Assistants and Pharmacy students generally, will be interested to know that the College has revived the curriculum formerly established in Pharmacy, and by co-operation with the Pharmaceutical Society, all endeavours will be made to provide a course thoroughly satisfactory in this department.

FACULTY OF PHARMACY.

It having been decided to re-organize the curriculum in Pharmacy, arrangments have been made with the co-operation of the Nova Scotia Pharmaceutical Association by which in addition to the lectures and instruction in Chemistry, Practical Chemistry and Botany given as before in connection with the Medical Faculty, special courses of lectures and instruction will be given in Pharmacy by Mr. Avery F. Buckley, L. Ph., Materia Medica by Dr. Campbell, and Microscopy by Dr. Lindsay.

HOSPITALS, ETC.

Medical students are admitted to the Victoria General Hospital, the Lying-in and Hospital Wards of the city Alms House, and to the Halifax Visiting Dispensary, on complying with the regulations of these institutions.

The Hospital has lately been very much enlarged and improved, and now affords an extended field to students for the observation and study of all acute and serious forms of disease.

In the City Alms House, a large new building accommodating about 400 inmates, and in close proximity to the Hospital and College, will be found the more chronic and incurable forms of disease. In the Lying-in Wards students will also be afforded every facility for acquiring experience in practical obstetrics.

The Visiting Dispensary is open daily, and is largely attended by the same class of patients as ordinarily present themselves in the outpatient department of hospitals, or come before the practitioner in his daily routine of office practice. Here also special instruction will be given in diseases of the Eye and Ear by the Surgeon in charge of that department.

ACADEMIC YEAR.

The Academic Year consists of one session. The session of 1892–93 will begin on Monday, October 31st, 1892, and end on Monday, April 24th, 1893. In order to qualify for Degree Examinations, the Medical Academic Year must include attendance on at least two courses of 100 lectures each, or one such course and two of 50 each.

INSTRUCTION.

In each of the following subjects there shall be delivered a course of at least 100 lectures during the six months' session, viz., Anatomy, Physiology, Materia Medica and Therapeutics, Chemistry, Medicine, Surgery, Obstetrics and Diseases of Women and Children.

In Practical Anatomy the course shall be of the same duration as each of the last named, but instruction shall be given during at least two hours of each day.

In Botany, Medical Jurisprudence, Clinical Medicine, and Clinical Surgery, at least 50 lectures shall be delivered during the six months' course. In Practical Chemistry and in Pathology the courses shall consist of at least 50 lessons.

The course in Histology shall comprise at least 30 demonstrations.

Each lecture shall be of one hour's duration.

Every professor shall occasionally examine his class upon the subjects treated of in his preceding lectures, and every such examination shall be considered a lecture.

ORDINARY CURRICULUM FOR M. D., C. M. DEGREES.

The following order of Study for each year, while not compulsory is recommended as most suitable to the ordinary student.

1st YEAR.—Chemistry, Anatomy, Practical Anatomy, Physiology, Materia Medica, Botany, Histology.

(Pass in Botany and Histology.)

2ND YEAR.—Chemistry, Anatomy, Practical Anatomy, Physiology Materia Medica, Practical Chemistry, Dispensary.

(Pass Primary M. D. C. M. Exam.)

3RD YEAR.—Surgery, Medicine, Obstetrics, Medical Jurisprudence, Clinical Surgery, Clinical Medicine, Ophthalmology (or in 4th year), Hospital, Practical Obstetrics, Pathology.

(Pass in Medical Jurisprudence and Pathology.)

4TH YEAR.—Surgery, Medicine, Obstetrics, Clinical Medicine, Clinical Surgery, Practical Obstetrics, Hospital, Opthalmology.

(Pass final M. D. C. M., Exam.)

Calendar, 1892–3, has 31 pages.

(3)

Victoria School of Art and Design, Halifax.

(Incorporated 1888.)

————

DIRECTORS.

Ex-Efficio : { THE SUPERINTENDENT OF EDUCATION,
              THE MAYOR OF HALIFAX.

MR. MICHAEL DWYER,	MRS. H. H. FULLER,
MRS. HOLT W. CLERKE,	MRS. J. F. KENNY,
MR. J. C. MACKINTOSH,	MR. J. M. SMITH,
MR. JAMES DEMPSTER,	MR. E. P. ARCHBOLD,
MISS ELLA RITCHIE,	HON. SENATOR POWER,
DR. J. G. MACGREGOR,	MR. P. F. MARTIN,
MR. DONALD KEITH,	MR. ALEXANDER MCKAY.

————

President, DR. ALLISON,
Vice-President, HON. L. G. POWER,
Treasurer, J. M. SMITH,
Secretary, A. MCKAY,
Asst.-Secretary, MISS K. F. HILL.

————

TEACHING STAFF.

Head Master :

GEORGE HARVEY, A. R. C. A.

Assistant Teachers :

MECHANICAL DRAWING.   ARCHITECTURAL DRAWING.
P. T. LARKIN, *Engineer.*

Saturday Class . . . . MISS K. F. HILL.

To A. H. MacKay, Esq., B. A., B. Sc., LL. D..
Superintendent of Education.

SIR,

I have the honor to transmit to you on behalf of the Directors of the Victoria School of Art and Design, the following report of attendance, &c., together with the Treasurer's Report.

The School year consists of three Terms of ten weeks each.

CLASSES.

AFTERNOON CLASSES FROM 2.30 TO 4.30.

Monday, ... Modelling.
Tuesday, ... Junior Drawing.
Wednesday, ... Senior Drawing.
Thursday, ... Painting and Lecture* at 4.30.

MORNING CLASS FROM 10 TO 12.

Saturday, ... Children's Class.

EVENING CLASSES FROM 7.30 TO 9.30 OR FROM 8 TO 10.

Monday, ... Modelling, &c. .... Junior Mechanical Drawing.
Tuesday, ... Junior Drawing ...... Junior Architectural "
Wednesday, ... Senior Drawing ...... Senior Mechanical "
Thursday, ...   Senior Architectural "
Friday, ...   Junior Mechanical "

*These lectures are open to all members of the Art School.

The *afternoon classes* were attended by 26 students of whom 8 held honor scholarships by competition from the Academies.

The *Head Master's evening classes* numbered 28, of whom five were free and the rest paid half the regular fee.

The *Architectural Class* had 21 students and the *Mechanical Class* 26. Nearly all of these are apprentices and receive tuition free. They show great interest in their work, attend well and make good progress.

The *Children's Class* numbers 16.

Total number of students in the Art School 117, an increase of 11 over last year.

Respectfully submitted,

A. McKAY,
Secretary.

Halifax, Jan., 1893.

THE TREASURER, IN ACCOUNT WITH VICTORIA SCHOOL OF ART AND
DESIGN.

Endowment Fund.

    Amount from 1891.......................... $15,657 35

Current Account Receipts.

    School Fees, &c.................... 338 00
    Provincial Government grant....... 800 00
    Interest.......................... 517 13
    Membership fees...................   10 00
    City grant........................ 500 00   2,165 13

                                                 $17,822 48

Disbursements.

    Salaries.......................... 1355 01
    Rent..............................   200 00
    Fuel and light....................   145 70
    Printing, &c......................   12 75
    School supplies and sundries......   100 77
    Janitor...........................   112 50
    Exhibition expenses...............   38 08

                                        1964 81
    Balance, Sept., 1891.............   3633 46

                                        $5598 27

Town of Kentville bonds........ 5100 00
City of Halifax consols........ 4950 00
Deposit receipt, Bank N. S.... 2000 00
Open acc'nt, Bank N.S. and cash 174 21   12124 21 $17822 48

                                        J. M. SMITH.

    Halifax, 15th Sept., 1892.

(4)

Summer School of Science for the Atlantic Provinces of Canada.

The Summer School of Science held its sixth session in the city of St. John from August 1st to 13th, 1892. The dates laid down in the programme issued in December previous— July 4th, 16th—were not adhered to an account of the meeting of the Dominion Association which some of our instructors and officers had engaged to attend. This postponement had an unfavorable effect on the attendance, as, previous to the announcement of the change of date, many teachers had made their plans for vacation. Such gatherings to be fully attended should not only be subject to no change of date but should follow immediately on the closing of the Public Schools, so that teachers can attend before setting off on the promised trip or settling down in some quiet retreat to rest. The attendance, however, was considerably larger than on the previous year,—sixty students and about twenty instructors and officers being present. Work of an eminently practical and satisfactory character was done in all the departments, a statement for which the names of the instructors given below is a sufficient guarantee. The large classes which attended the lectures in Literature, Pedagogy and Psychology prove the wisdom of the executive in adding these subjects to the course of Study.

The officers for the year 1892 were:

PRESIDENT.

G. U. HAY, Ph. B. *Principal Victoria High School, St. John.*

VICE-PRESIDENTS.

PROF. MACDONALD, *Normal School, Truro.*
SUPERVISOR MCKAY, *Halifax.*

SECRETARY-TREASURER.

W. T. KENNEDY, *County Academy Halifax.*

LOCAL SECRETARY.

ENOCH THOMPSON, *Albert School, St. John.*

EXECUTIVE COMMITTEE.

THE PRESIDENT,	THE SECRETARY,
SUPERINTENDENT MACKAY,	INSPECTOR CARTER,
INSPECTOR LAY,	SECRETARY MARCH,
PRINCIPAL CAMERON,	PROF. BRITTAIN,

SUPERINTENDENT HAYS.

The instructors were:

ASTRONOMY.

PRINCIPAL CAMERON, *Yarmouth Academy.*

BOTANY.

{ G. U. HAY, Ph. B., *High School, St. John.*
{ NETTIE FORBES, B. A., *Yarmouth Academy.*

CHEMISTRY.

PROF. W. W. ANDREWS, *Mount Allison, Sackville.*

DIDACTICS.

PROF. FRANK H. EATON, *Boston.*

ELOCUTION.

MISS M. A. ALEXANDER, *St. John School of Music.*

ENGLISH LITERATURE.

PRINCIPAL A. CAMERON, *Yarmouth.*

GEOLOGY.

PROF. A. E. COLDWELL, *Acadia College, Wolfville.*

ASSOCIATE LECTURER, GEOLOGY.

G. F. MATTHEW, A. M., F. R. S. C., *St. John.*

HISTOLOGY AND MICROSCOPY.

E. J. LAY, ESQ., *Inspector of Schools, Amherst.*

MINERALOGY.

PROF. A. E. COLDWELL, *Acadia College.*

MUSIC (TONIC-SOL-FA).

MISS A. F. RYAN, *St. Mary's School, Halifax.*

PHYSICS.

E. MACKAY, B. A., *Principal of Schools, New Glasgow.*

PHYSIOLOGY.

ALBAN F. EMERY, M. D., *St John.*

PSYCHOLOGY.

J. B. HALL, Ph. D., *Normal School, Truro.*

ZOOLOGY.

PROF. J. BRITTAIN, *Normal School, Fredericton.*

The citizens of St. John received the school most hospitably, extending not only to the school *as such* but also to its individual members every kindness and attention. The City Council voted one hundred dollars for its entertainment, which was expended on a trip by steamer " May Queen" up the river as far as Hampton. Mayor Peters and the majority of the City Council, with leading citizens and other friends of science, accompanied the school, and the day spent on the river will long be remembered as one of pleasure and profit.

The first part of each day was given to class-room work, the afternoons to botanical and other excursions, and to visiting such places as Park's Cotton Factory, Owen's Art Gallery, etc., and of the evenings three were occupied with scientific lectures, one with a musical and literary entertainment under the auspices of the school, and one with a reception tendered by the genial and scholarly members of the Natural History Society.

Of the few who took written examinations at the close of the session, certificates in Botany were awarded to C. Stanley Bruce, of Shelburne Academy, and Evan J. Ross, of Albro street school, Halifax ; and in Zoology to Isabella J. Caie, Richibucto, Edith Darling, Nauwgiewauk, and Emma J. Bacon, Brighton, Digby county.

The students in attendance were :—

Maggie McNaughton .... St. John.
Annie Robb............................ "
Mrs. C. E. Hamilton.................... "
Phœbe Van Wart...... ·············
Catherine D. Martin..... ....
Mrs. Fisk............................ ...
John McKinnon........................
Hattie Howard........................
Jennie E. Dunlop... ....
M. C. Ellis..........................
Agnes Warner.................... .. ..
James D. Warner......................
W. L. Ellis..........................
J. H. Scammell ....
Rev. G. Steele ....
Sarah J. Parkin......................
M. J. Mowatt ..:.....................
James Barry..........................
Austin C. Stead ....
Maggie R. Gray ....
Jessie K. Sutherland .....:..........
Clara R. Fullerton ....
Grace Murphy.........................
Eleanor Robinson.....:...............
Edith M. McBeath.....................
Maggie Sharp.........................

Lydia E. Williams...................... St. John.
Mrs. Bowden............................   "
Catherine Barton.......................   "
H. M. Shaw.........•............... ......
Secretary March........................
Inspector Carter.......................   "
Ada Munro.........................,..... Yarmouth
Hannah Heustis........................   "
Beatrice Tooker.......................   "
Dora Tooker...........................
Isabel Webster......... ....
F. J. Stewart.........................
B. Balfour Brown......................
Albinus W. Horner.....................   "
Jane McLeod...........................Truro.
Josephine Upham......................   "
Annie Hislop ....   "
Lizzie M. Colquhoun ....Shelburne.
William Brodie.........................St. Andrews, N. B.
Inspector Smith........................Petitcodiac, N. B.
Elizabeth Stewart ....Dartmouth.
Evan J. Ross...........................Halifax.
I. M. Longley ....Paradise, N. S.
Dora E. Smith.........................Moncton, N. B.
Fannie E.'Holt ....Wolfville.
C. Stanley Bruce ....Shelburne.
Isabella J. Caie.......................Richibucto, N. B.
John Moser............ ....Hunter's Home, N. B.
Elspeth Charters ....Moncton.
Edith Darling ....Nauwigewauk, N. B.
Emma J. Bacon........................Brighton, Digby, N. S.
Agnes Bacon.......................... .   "   "
Annie A. McNeil ....North Range, Digby.
Edith Hennigar ....Canning, N. S.

The following is the financial statement for 1892 :

Balance from 1891 ....   6 46
Grant from Government of Nova Scotia 100 00
    "   "   New Brunswick................ 100 00
    "   City Council of St. John 100 00
Students' Fees 186 00
Advertising in Report................................ 28 00
Proceeds of Concert.................................. 14 75
Sale of Chemicals.....................................   1 15
Balance due Treasurer 10 31
                                                       ——————
                                                      546 67

Paid Officers and Instructors 315 00
Excursion by " May Queen" to Hampton......... 100 00
Printing and Advertising 26 82
Printing 1500 Copies of Report................. 30 00
Postage and Stationery........................ 18 69
Chemical and Zoological material 11 25
Expressage and Truckage...................... 7 90
Lighting Centennial Hall and attendance 23 00
Sundries as per statement..................... 14 01

$546 67

W. T. KENNEDY,
Secretary-Treasurer for 1893.

N. B.—The next meeting of the school is to be held in the buildings of Mount Allison University, Sackville, from July 5th to 21st,
1893. The ladies will lodge in the beautiful rooms of the Ladies'
College, and the gentlemen in the Collegiate Academy. All, however, will board at the same table.

Mount Allison University has been a leading educational centre
for half a century, and is therefore richly endowed with all the
educational equipments necessary to contribute success to the school.
The class-rooms, laboratories, museums, etc., are such as will greatly
facilitate the prosecution of scientific work.

The excursions will include Tantramar Marshes, the Ship Railway,
Fort Lawrence and the Joggins.

Practical instruction, valuable for the school-room, will be given
in arranging and mounting plants, insects, etc., and a sufficient
knowledge of taxidermy will be imparted to enable students to preserve birds or small animals for purposes of ornament or study.
Teachers and others can attend the session of the school with great
profit without any previous preparation in the subjects to be studied.

A programme of work to be done has been prepared and published
and will be mailed by the Secretary to any person sending for it.

W. T. K.

(5)

The Kindergartens.

The Kindergarten system has during the year been making very evident progress throughout the province. The great difficulty in the way is its expense, yet this is not such as will prevent its ultimate establishment in our greater centres of population—the towns and cities. Into the Primary schools everywhere, however, the Kindergarten method can to a great extent be adopted, even in our High Schools, especially in the teaching of the sciences.

The Halifax Public School Kindergarten, under Mrs. Harriman, has been specially useful in training Kindergarteners selected from the most promising young teachers of the city. Diplomas are granted them after due service and proficiency tested by a severe written examination. The Dartmouth Public School Kindergarten under Miss Hamilton has also been a success. The Truro Kindergarten under Mrs. Patterson is utilized also for the training of teachers attending the Normal School.

The following list of public Kindergartens in Nova Scotia showing their chronological and geographical distribution, has been grepared by Mrs. Harriman :—

TRURO (NORMAL SCHOOL) KINDERGARTEN.

Established in 1887 in connection with the Normal School, mainly through the efforts of the Frœbel Institute of Nova Scotia and its president, Mrs. Hinkle Condon.

Teachers, MISS WOODCOCK, 1887–89.
MISS TWITCHELL, 1889–90.
MRS. PATTERSON, 1890–93.

DARTMQUTH, PUBLIC KINDERGARTEN.

Teacher, MISS M. A. HAMILTON, 1889–93.

HALIFAX, PUBLIC KINDERGARTEN.

Director, SUSAN S. HARRIMAN, 1891–93.

TEACHERS GRADUATED IN 1892.

MISS HELEN MOODY.
MISS ETTIE DEWOLFE.
MISS LIZZIE MAHONEY.
MISS BEATRICE LAWRENCE.

KINDERGARTEN IN SCHOOL FOR BLIND.

Teacher, MISS KATE FLETCHER, 1893.

There have been several private Kindergartens for some years in Halifax, and in a few other towns in the province.

(6)

Report of a Visit to Manual Training Institutions in New England.

By LEE RUSSELL, B.SC., OF THE HALIFAX MANNAL TRAINING SCHOOL.

To DR. A. H. MACKAY,

Superintendent of Education, Halifax, N. S.

It seems to me desirable to give in this report a brief outline of the work I have seen and a more complete account of the deductions and generalizations I have been able to make.

I visited all the Manual Training Schools in Boston and vicinity, and had interviews with the school superintendents, principals and others interested in the subject. I also visited Worcester and Springfield. In the latter place I made a careful study of the very extensive and original system of Manual Training. In Connecticut, I saw the Normal School at Willimantic and had a long talk with Mr. Morrill, the Principal.

In the twelve days, so generously allowed me by the Board of School Commissioners, I visited fifteen schools.

In Boston and vicinity there are two well marked systems of Manual Training.

The Swedish Sloyd has been somewhat modified to meet the demands of the community, and as the so-called "Sloyd" it is vigorously taught and defended by Mr. Gustaf Larsson and his followers. Its main principles are these :—

1st. All practice shall be had in making useful articles which become the property of the pupil.

2nd. The models shall be so arranged as to bring into practice fundamental principles in the proper order of progression from the easy to the more difficult.

3rd. All work shall be from drawings made by the pupils.

4th. As great a variety of tools as can properly be introduced shall be used.

5th. The models shall combine a variety of curved with plane surfaces.

The application of these principles is shown in the schemes and reports subjoined.

Another system in more common use than the " Sloyd" is the so-called Russian system. It aims to give manual training by exercises illustrating the various principles of carpentry, joinery and iron work.

Besides these two, there are many modifications and combinations. Each teacher has a more or less original method and series of models.

At Springfield, Mass., there is a well equipped Manual Training Department in connection with the High School. But, before entering the High School, pupils are instructed in the common schools. While the girls are engaged in needle-work, the boys have practice in woodwork. Wooden covers are provided for the desks and knives, try-squares, rules, marking-gauges and prepared wood are distributed. The work is an ingenious modification of " Sloyd" and as a preparation for later work has perhaps some value. It is worthy of mention, that during the High School course the pupils spend each afternoon in the workshop. It seems open to question if so much time should be spent in manual training.

In several districts in Boston entire schools of sixty boys go with their teacher to the workshop. In such shops two or three teachers are employed. All teachers complain of having too many pupils at a time. It is generally conceded that twenty-four is as large a number as one person can well handle, and many put the limit at eighteen.

Mr. Larsson's training class has been well attended, and he has turned out some very capable women teachers. This phase of the problem seems especially interesting to this Province. In most cases two or more women teach under the direction of a man. They devise and decide upon the course of models together. The man also takes care of the tools and has general charge. This seems to be a very successful arrangement. There is no doubt that women can acquire skill in manual training exercises, and are as well able to teach this as anything else. It should be noted that the graduates of Mr. Larsson's school, who are teaching most successfully, were experienced and accomplished teachers before they took up " Sloyd," and further, that they took it up from natural liking.

The pamphlets and papers accompanying this report are extremely suggestive. They show the constant adaptation which is going on, and the marked changes recently made.

This brings me to the most significant feature of the present manual training. It is, to a greater degree than any other branch of education, undergoing a constant healthy change. New points of excellence are continually being added, and faults weeded out. Each teacher is engaged in the most valuable and inspiring work known to our civilization,—Original Research. All, or nearly all, are working in the true scientific spirit. In the extremely rare cases where this was lacking the schools showed a marked inferiority.

This seems to me to promise well, not only for the future of manual training, but also for the future of any school course into which it is introduced. The spirit which it fosters, among teachers and pupils alike, is that of independent investigation, and this must sooner or later be felt in the course of education, and in the community at large.

A significant feature in and about Boston is the influence the various teachers have on each other. The half dozen original and energetic men who are leaders, are all working along the same lines, and the net result seems likely to be a system of manual training combining the good points of the various existing courses, and lacking the weak ones.

A visit to a State Normal School in Connecticut made me acquainted with a phase of manual training which is of great value. Here is a shop in which all the pupils of the school work, women as well as men. It has a very intimate connection with the professional work in physics and chemistry. The pupils make actual apparatus which they take out with them to their schools and are thus able, independently of the usual costly equipment, to demonstrate many of the fundamental truths of nature. The course did not seem to be well graded as manual traning, but the fundamental idea is excellent. There were models illustrating the hydrostatic press, Newcomen's engine, and Watt's improvement on it, test-tube racks and holders, and other similar apparatus.

I also saw a lesson on the hydrostatic press, and the principle of specific gravity, given to pupils of ten years, which alone proved the value of the manual training in the Normal School.

Here is a feature which might well be introduced into this Province. Manual training of this sort will tend to lead the pupils in new and profitable directions. It needs no workshop. If the teacher has been instructed she can lead the pupils to make at home experiments and investigations. Further, a teacher who has had this sort of training looks upon the ceaseless constructive activity of children from a new standpoint. She sees in their water-wheels and boats a new means by which she can gain their attention, and spontaneous attention is the secret of all good instruction. She no longer looks upon their knives as implements for defacing desks, but sees in them tools for fashioning the young minds under her charge.

I subjoin a full syllabus of the course of study pursued at this Normal School, together with detailed statements of the work in physics and chemistry.

From what I can gather it seems tolerably certain that some modification of "Sloyd" will be adopted in New England. One great fault of the Russian system is that it requires a great degree of ability to make its series of exercises interesting. Pupils tire of making joints, and using up lumber without any obviously useful result. On the other hand, it is discouraging to them to attempt to make a useful article, and have it prove a useless failure. A proper combination of the two systems prevents wearisome repetition, disheartening failure, and at the same time keeps the attention and interest stimulated and active.

The extensive course pursued at the Worcester Polytechnic Institute, drawings of which accompany this report,* is a good illustration of this fact. The pupils are eighteen years old, but the illustration is as good as if they were but ten. After working a considerable time on joints the course is varied by making patterns in wood. From these, moulds are made and castings in type metal taken from the moulds. It will be noticed that many of the patterns are of useful things. Further, the pupils are taught the use of machinery, and a variety of useful articles made. In the course in iron work pursued at this institution the practise is all in making useful articles.

It is evident that belief in Manual Training is advancing rapidly. New schools are being started every year and old ones enlarged. From the report of Superintendent Seaver it is plainly a success in Boston. The conditions in this Province appear to me especially to call for manual training. With its great natural resources Nova Scotia is certain of a period of industrial development in the near future. A population already partially educated in this direction must help along this development. At any rate a healthy public opinion will be fostered, and the community be prepared to welcome any advance. In addition to all this is the important truth, just now beginning to be realized, that a child whose mind alone is trained is but half educated.

Respectfully submitted,

LEE RUSSELL.

Halifax, March 1st, 1893.

*Filed in the Education Office.

(7)

Dominion Educational Association.

FIRST CONVENTION, 1892.

[From THE EDUCATIONAL REVIEW, *August, 1892.]*

The most important educational event of the year was probably the conference of prominent educationists from every province of the Dominion, at Montreal, from the 5th to the 8th July.

The attendance, although not large, was fairly representative of every shade of educational thought in the Dominion. The able lectures, carefully prepared papers and free discussion, of those four days, must have had a beneficial effect in welding the diverse elements of our widely extended young nation, in restraining the intemperate zeal of the enthusiast, and in spurring onward the self-satisfied conservative. Where so much is seen, said and done, it would be impossible to give an account of all that would be interesting to our readers, but we will make notes on several of the leading topics possessing most value at the present stage of our educational progress.

MEETING OF WELCOME.

The addresses of welcome to the teachers by Sir William Dawson, Hon. Mr. Ouimet, Chancellor Heneker, Dr. Adams, Abbe Verreau and Presidents Lacroise and Arthy, were able and enthusiastic. The Act of Confederation left the provinces to grow apart in the separate management of their educational affairs. But it would be the special work of the Dominion Educational Association to bring together the various races, creeds and institutions, and, fusing their best elements, develop that educational and national unity which was needed so much in making us a great nation.

In response Hon. George W. Ross eloquently pleaded for unity, for a broader nationality, and for patriotism that would sweep away all sectionalism. A teacher's qualifications and diplomas should be recognized as of equal value in all the provinces. Text books should not be provincial. There should be but one text book on Canadian History.

Dr. Inch claimed that the Maritime provinces were the Grecian States of the Dominion, supplying men of brains for the larger provinces; for had they not given Sir William Dawson to McGill, Dr. Grant to Queens and Dr. Rand to McMaster?

Dr. MacKay humorously made out many claims of excellence for his native province—the first in the Dominion to receive the rays of the rising sun.   Thus reviving the interest of his audience he outlined several national reforms which could be inaugurated successfully only in such a large, representative and authoritative body as the Dominion Educational Association ; such reforms for instance as phonetic spelling and shorthand, metric measures, etc.

A conversazione at McGill University occupied the evening very profitably and pleasantly.   The repast was excellent, but better still were the witty speeches by Sir William, Dr. McVicar, Dr. Robbins and Hon. George W. Ross, and the inspection of the magnificent physical, chemical and mechanical laboratories, of the library, and of the Redpath Museum with its " pretty zoological specimens, both dead and animated."

It appears that the observatory of McGill is the only spot in the Dominion whose exact longitude has been determined.

High School Education.

A very considerable amount of prejudice still exists against high school and academic education.   It is, however, rapidly disappearing.   That it has not almost wholly disappeared is largely the fault of the high schools themselves.   Bound by the traditions of the past they have given undue prominence to classics, theoretical mathematics and the dry technicalities of grammar, geography and history.

When the higher education is made to bear more directly on the occupations of all classes, even colleges need not fear to ask for state aid.   They will be absolutely free—even to the extent of supplying free text-books and apparatus.

Dr. MacKay's paper on " The Free Scope and Function of the High School" showed that he is in the van as a progressive educationist.   It is necessary for the peace and prosperity of the state that the poor should have *free* opportunities for a liberal education. The obstacles opposed to their progress develop in many of them an energy that places them among the ruling classes.   The state must therefore see that they are properly educated if all the classes are to work out with good feeling the development of the social fabric.

The practical value of the experimental study of the laws of Nature can scarcely be overestimated.   The moral value of such a study is equally great ; for, said the Doctor, " I never knew a true student of nature fascinated by her operations, who was an immoral man." Nature says to all, " the soul that sinneth it shall die." Ought not the students of Nature to realize that truth most vividly.

Another good thought beautifully elaborated by Dr. MacKay was this: Science and Manual Training dignify and invest with a new interest common things and occupations. How rich the life of the intelligent, scientific farmer! If then the schools train for all phases of life, the professions will not be overcrowded, nor will our farmers be leaving the country or dying of ennui.

FRŒBEL.

The Kindergartners of the Association were so numerously and ably represented that they had the constitution amended so as to form themselves into a separate section, of which Miss Newcombe, of Hamilton, was elected President, and Mrs. Harriman, of Halifax, Vice-President.

The absence of Mrs. Hughes was much regretted. Miss Boulton gave an interesting " Morning Talk," Miss Hart, Inspector of Kindergartens for Ontario, read a well-prepared paper on the relationship of the Kindergarten to art.

Frœbel and many of his followers (perhaps including Miss Hart) veil their ideas in mystic phraseology incomprehensible to ordinary common sense. The paper contained many good things about the parallelism between race development and individual development, and about the benefits, spiritual and material, arising from the cultivation of the creative imagination through the plays and occupations of the Kindergarten ; but its value was somewhat lessened by its vague generalities.

What for instance can this mean ? " 'What is life ?" questioning the child. The gifts answer, ' Life is unity ;' thus shadowing the great fundamental truth that rules all life. Each gift hints a new phase of the great principle. Thus science and religion are born of art, both for race and child, and then we begin to build up an organic education holding it in its inseparable unity as the education of the body, mind and soul."

Mrs. Harriman's very able paper dealt with the most characteristic value of the Kindergarten in developing the child socially. We will in a future number give a synopsis.

SOME THOUGHTS FROM DR. WARFIELD'S PAPER.

1. The English language is the most important thing taught in our schools. The student should be a master of the art of expressing his thoughts in such a way as to convey his exact meaning, and so as to be at once understood.

2. There is no reason why an earlier preparation for the university may not be obtained, provided the preparation is made more definite and simple. Not so many subjects, but a more complete mastery of a few subjects is the training which the university must demand.

3. Head and hand should be trained together till all men know the dignity of labor.

4. True mental development involves the training, not of the memory, but of the creative imagination, and of the will.

IDEAL SCHOOL DISCIPLINE.

The secret of Principal Hay's success as a teacher is disclosed in these thoughts from his excellent paper :

" The means to secure the Ideal Discipline are : first, love and respect between teacher and pupil ; second, the pupil must be in sympathy with his environment. The teacher, in order to discipline others must first discipline himself. It is a slow process this build-ing up of character; and defeat and discouragement, those twin friends of ours, must be endured before any fruition of our hopes can be realized. The pupil must be placed in full sympathy with his environment. The chief factor is work, a working teacher and a working pupil. The teacher must set the example of an inspiring, helpful, interested worker. The spirit of such a worker is catching. It makes tasks easy. It is the lesson bearer with his system of cram and memorizing from the text book, who is the cause of all the out-cry throughout the country, that the children are burdened with too many studies, but the real teachers are not doing their work that way ; they are teaching their pupils to observe and think, and such tasks are too inspiring, too elevating, to be a burden."

The paper on the punishment of juvenile offenders, by Principal McKinnon, of the Victoria School of Toronto, was a fine commentary on these fundamental principles so well expressed by Mr. Hay. Mr. McKinnon's essay should be published in full in the local papers of every city in the Dominion.

ONTARIO MAGNATES.

Wednesday evening was taken up by Inspector Hughes and Hon. Geo. W. Ross, the two most prominent public school educationists of Ontario. Mr. Hughes took the position that the prosperity of the state would be promoted by making the highest as well as the low-est education free to the poorest child,—that, therefore, the state should support and wholly control education—even to the extent of preventing teachers not licensed by the state from teaching in private schools. He thought a system of morals and religion satisfactory to all denominations should and probably would be taught in all public schools. There all classes should grow up in unity, in respect for each other and in love for the country.

Hon. Mr. Ross dwelt on the importance of eclectically harmonizing our provincial educational systems. Good ! But we regretted to find an educationist from the country which has given " the high school as its contribution to the world's progress in education," advocating proficiency in the three R's as the extent to which he would go in free state education. We must remember, however, that Ontario is behind the Maritime Provinces in the matter of free high schools as well as in the professional qualifications of teachers.

If the Ontario high schools were less scholastic and administered more immediately to the educational and industrial necessities of the great majority of the people, the Minister of Education would soon discover that they should be free, as Inspector Hughes would have them.

In deprecating the evils of promotion examinations Mr. Ross will be supported by many of our ablest educationists.

That so many teachers leave the profession after an average service of seven years is not an unmixed evil. These ex-teachers form, in their various stations in society, a most sympathetic constituency to which the active teacher can appeal, and they send to the schools the most teachable pupils.

After all are not young teachers, educated and well-trained, nearer to young children, more tolerant. and genuinely sympathetic, than old teachers, and therefore more successful? We have found them often do better work.

LATIN PRONUNCIATION.

The following resolution, carried unanimously, settles a very vexed and important question :

"Resolved, That uniformity in Latin pronunciation is desirable and that it can be most easily and most practically introduced by the Roman method."

This resolution was the outcome of a paper by Dr. Eaton, of McGill College.

The Roman pronunciation seems to be the nearest to the original —therefore that in which the Latin language will best flourish. With five different systems in vogue there was certainly a great waste of energy, and often much annoyance.

The Roman system is adopted universally in the United States and is coming to the front in Canada.

ENGLISH LITERATURE.

Specially interesting among the papers read at the Association, was that by Wm. Houston, librarian to the Ontario Government. He condemned text books on English composition, the old methods of paraphrasing, and dependence on the translating of foreign tongues. Text books might be useful for teachers, paraphrasing was a sacrelegious destruction of art, and as for translation less of it would be needed if we did like the ancients, write our own thoughts in our own language. "We copy from the ancients because they have written their own original thoughts." To learn to write English the best way was to write it Let the pupil be shown his errors and be shown how to detect them, and then be required to re-write, avoiding these errors.

Here as elsewhere we learn to do by doing,—by original work, not mere copying. There should be drill in analysis and on the shades of meanings of words.

Nothing after religion does more to make life worth living than the study of the beautiful. Poetry is well adapted to the average mind. If you would appreciate the force of human beings read Shakespeare; if you would realize the insignificance of human learning read the commentaries.

PROFESSIONAL.

Principal Calkin of Truro has crystallized into fine form the best thoughts regarding Normal Schools. A sound academic education, and a reasonable probability of professional success should be pre-requisites of entrance upon a regular course which should include special training on the principles, history and practice of teaching, laboratory work, drawing, music and calisthenics, and a general review of academic subjects from their professional aspects.

The Normal School should inspire the students with higher ideals of scholarship, and make them responsive to their environments.

THE CENTRAL FIGURE.

About forty years ago an educational convention was held at Wolfville, N. S., so far as we know the first ever held in the Dominion. At that time Mr. Dawson, Superintendent of Education for Nova Scotia, presided. He was then young and full of energy, and inspired an enthusiasm which still remains with the survivors of that meeting.

At Montreal there was present one member of that first convention, Principal Calkin, of Truro. As in years gone by Dr. Dawson was to him as well as to others the central figure of the association, and still young and full of vigor and inspiration.

A prominent educationist from Ontario thanked us for an introduction to Sir William, and said : "To have seen Sir Wm. Dawson would have repaid me for coming to this association, but having conversed with him I return happy."

In closing the association Sir William urged his hearers to remember that the true aim of education was to form character. The education which makes the man is really and truly the only practical education. Teachers should not be discouraged if the pendulum of educational reform did not at any particular time swing in the direction of their peculiar notions; it would return, and in the meantime the hands of progress were moving steadily forward.

RESOLUTIONS.

Before the Association as a whole resolutions were adopted favoring :

(1) University extension; (2) the exclusion of high school work from universities; (3) a common standard of matriculation; (4) the delimitation of the common and high school courses of study; (5) more thorough school inspection; (6) a uniform nomenclature in the designation of schools and grades of study, and a unification of the courses of study in the various provinces; (7) a more stringent compulsory attendance law ; (8) the professional training of all teachers; (9) the general establishment of kindergartens ; (10) uniformity in the requirements for teachers' certificates and an interprovincial recognition of them ; (11) school exhibitions.

TEACHERS' ASSOCIATION, KINGS AND HANTS COUNTIES, 1891.

[From THE EDUCATIONAL REVIEW, *January, 1892.]*

This was held at Hantsport, N. S., on the 17th and 18th December. The attendance was large—80 teachers being enrolled.

Miss S. B. Ford of Canning, read a paper on " Patriotism." She strongly emphasized the duty of the teacher in inculcating a true love of country and showed the best ways in which this could be done,—chiefly by making pupils familiar with the noble deeds of our greatest patriots.

Miss C. Mumford of Hantsport, discussed " Literature *versus* Grammar." She would not place the text book on grammar in the hands of the pupil before he entered the academy or high school. Instead of grammatical exceptions. parsing, and abstract definitions, she would have the pupils read suitable selections from the best authors, and frequently write composition exercises until they had acquired an easy use of their mother tongue. From the discussion that followed it was evident that the great majority of teachers would place grammar with logic and rhetoric in the high school grades where it belongs.

H. D. Ruggles, barrister, of Windsor, showed the close relation subsisting between the schools and the statutes in educating to a respect for law. The more education advanced the less the necessity for law.

Mr. L. D. Robertson of Berwick, made known the methods by

which the school-room could be turned from a state of disorder to a state of happy industry;—school-room neat, comfortable, and well ventilated; programme definite, carried out by signals, varied by music and calisthenics; plenty of work and no whispering.

Mr. E. W. Sawyer, B. A., of Horton Academy, advocated the teaching of Latin by the method now adopted for French and German. The pupils are to converse about ordinary things and events until they have acquired a command of common words and the most useful idioms. Constant drill on forms was also recommended, even in advanced work.

Mr. J. J. McLean recommended that Friday afternoons be devoted to such practical subjects, as current news, the explanation of commercial phrases and forms, calculations in frequent use by artisans, recitations, etc. "Method in Geometry" was treated by Principal Oakes, of Wolfville. The conceptions of an angle, triangle, line and point should be made as plain as possible by referring to the concrete. The methods of Wormwell and Wentworth were thought superior, especially in the systematic way in which they proved the equality of triangles. Original exexcises should be worked as the pupils advanced. Mrs. Chute, of Berwick, presented a short paper on "Reading." A nature lesson was given by Miss Maggie Burton. She selected the Turtle for her subject and went somewhat into the classification of animals of that order.

Principal Smith of Windsor dealt with such "Odds and Ends," as, the best methods of keeping order in the halls, directing the amusements of the play ground, the teaching of thrift and economy, the building up of character by developing control of self in the pupil, thoroughness in work, etc.

In the evening the teachers and public were addressed by the new Superintendent of Education, who made a most favourable impression. Teachers are attracted to him by his broad and deep sympathies with them in their work and his unselfish efforts for the advancement of education.

He was introduced by Principal Miller, of Hantsport, who is a ready and fluent speaker as well as an able teacher.

Inspector Roscoe has always been very successful in arranging for profitable Institute meetings, but on this occasion he improved upon all his former efforts.

TEACHERS' ASSOCIATION, ANNAPOLIS AND DIGBY COUNTIES.

[*From* THE EDUCATIONAL REVIEW, *November, 1892.*]

The Teachers' Association for this district held its annual session in the hall of the Digby Academy on Thursday and Friday, the 6th and 7th of October. There were present about ninety teachers from the two counties. The following officers were elected : Vice-Presidents, A. D. Brown and A. H. Morse; Secretary-Treasurer, Lyman B. Denton ; Executive Committee, A. D. Brown, Miss Helen Vidito, Miss B. Rice, Miss Challen and Mr. Shields.

The preliminary business being concluded, the programme was taken up. A paper was read by Mr. L. H. Morse, of Bear River, on "Patriotism." This paper alluded to the lofty feelings awakened in the minds of those who read the writings of the great men of the past, and pointed out clearly that similar results would follow by studying the great men of our country. The writer referred to the duty of the teacher in pointing out the great natural resources of our country. In his opinion a patriotic spirit could be awakened by the study of the geography of our land, particularly her ports, rivers, lakes and mountains.

The first paper read during the afternoon session was by Miss Emma Bacon, "Literature in our Schools." The writer strongly urged the study of standard authors during the earlier stages of the pupil's course. The children from the homes of reading parents were far more intelligent than those from illiterate homes. She thought that great care should be taken in the selection of authors.

The next was a paper by Miss Kinney, "Reading in our Schools." She dealt with the various methods employed in teaching children to read, the importance of an intelligent understanding of the subject in order that good expression might follow. Fluency, distinctness and pronunciation were strongly emphasized.

Dr. MacKay, Superintendent of Education, being present, was introduced. Much interest was added to the meetings by his sympathetic and practical remarks.

Miss Helen Vidito then read a paper, "Hygiene in our Schools." After defining her subject she alluded to the unfavorable hygienic conditions in a majority of our school-rooms, the care which should be observed by the teacher in relation to the seating of pupils, cleanliness of furniture and surroundings in general.

It was then suggested that reports from different parts of the district relative to the condition of the school-rooms, play grounds and difficulties with which teachers had to contend, would be of interest. Quite a number of the lady teachers responded.

A very interesting public meeting was held in the evening. Short addresses were delivered by the President, Wm. McVicar, of the Annapolis Academy, Mr. Godfrey, of the Digby Academy, and Rev. Mr. Fisher. Principal Godfrey read an address of welcome to Dr. MacKay, to which the Superintendent made a very appropriate and touching response. In his general address he referred to the recent advances in the education of our province, explained many of the changes which are about to come into practice, and dwelt on matters of general interest to the teacher.

On Friday morning an illustrative lesson on "Our Flag" was taught by Miss Titus, of Digby. This was not only a model lesson, but very instructive to the members of the association.

Mr. Crowe, of Annapolis, then read a paper on "The Home Preparation of Lessons." He thought the teacher should discriminate between those possessing extraordinary ability and those who were not so highly favored. He was in sympathy with the plan of explaining the lesson to be prepared. The teacher should not confine himself too much to the text-book. Much more could be accomplished by securing the sympathy and co-operation of the parent than by independent effort.

The last paper read was by Mr. McCarty, on "Teaching Geography." He considered this subject received too little attention in many of our schools. Map drawing was an essential feature in connection with the teaching of geography. He proposed various plans for giving the pupil a definite knowledge of the geography of his country.

The papers were freely discussed by the following members of the association: Dr. MacKay, Wm. McVicar, John Godfrey, Alfred Morse, A. D. Brown, Mr. Shields, Miss Vidito, Miss Parker and others.

The association tendered its thanks to the Superintendent of Education for his presence, sympathy, and for the many practic suggestions during the different meetings.

This was considered one of the most interesting sessions held during the history of the association of the district, a marked interest being manifest throughout the entire proceedings

APPENDIX F.

Universities and Degree Conferring Colleges

---OF---

NOVA SCOTIA,

RECEIVING NO GRANTS OF PUBLIC MONEY FROM THE PROVINCIAL TREASURY.

THEIR NAMES, GOVERNORS, SENATES, FACULTIES, NUMBERS OF STUDENTS, LIBRARIES, MUSEUMS, GYMNASIUMS, AND LEADING HISTORICAL DATES, ABSTRACTED FROM THEIR RESPECTIVE CALENDARS, FOR THE ACADEMIC YEAR, 1892–93.

DALHOUSIE COLLEGE AND UNIVERSITY, HALIFAX.

BOARD OF GOVERNORS.

[Governors appointed and removable by the Governor-in-Council of the Province of Nova Scotia (See Act, 20th April, 1833).]

HON. SIR ADAMS G. ARCHIBALD, K. C. M. G., P. C., D. C. L., Q. C., *Chairman.*

HON. SIR CHARLES TUPPER, BART., K. C. M. G., C. B., M. D., LL. D.

HON. S. L. SHANNON, D. C. L., Q. C., Judge of Probate.

REV. JOHN MACMILLAN, M. A., B. D.

REV. PRESIDENT FORREST, D. D., D. C. L.

HON. ALFRED G. JONES, P. C.

JOHN DOULL, ESQ.

REV. ROBERT MURRAY.

WALLACE GRAHAM, ESQ., A. B., Judge of Supreme Court.

E. L. NEWCOMBE, ESQ., B. A., LL. B., Representative of the Alumni Association.

ADAM BURNS, ESQ.

A. H. MacKay, Esq., B.A., B.Sc., LL. D., F. R. S. C., Superintendent of Education.

His Worship the Mayor of Halifax, *ex-officio.*

D A. Campbell, Esq., M. D., Representative of the Alumni Association.

JAMES FORREST, M. A., *Treasurer.*
WILLIAM M. DOULL, *Secretary.*

SENATUS ACADEMICUS.

REV. JOHN FORREST, D. D.. D. C. L, *President.*

CHARLES MACDONALD, M. A.

JOHN JOHNSON, M. A.

GEORGE LAWSON, PH. D., LL. D., F. I. C., *Secretary.*

J. G. MacGREGOR, M. A., D. Sc.

RICHARD C. WELDON, M. A., PH. D., M. P.

JAMES LIECHTI, M. A.

BENJAMIN RUSSEL, A. M., Q. C.

JAMES SETH, M. A.

ARCHIBALD MacMECHAN, B. A.. PH. D.

ACADEMIC STAFF.

REV. PRESIDENT FORREST, D. D., D.C.L., F. S. Sc. L., *George Munro Professor of History and Political Economy.*

CHARLES MACDONALD. M. A. (Aberd.), *Professor of Mathematics.*

JOHN JOHNSON, M. A. (Dub.), *McLeod Professor of Classics.*

GEORGE LAWSON, PH. D., LL. D., F. I. C., F. R. S. C., *McLeod Professor of Chemistry and Mineralogy.*

JAMES LIECHTI, M. A. (Vind.), *McLeod Professor of Modern Languages.*

JAMES GORDON MACGREGOR, M. A. (Dal.), D.Sc. (Lond.), F.R.SS.E.& C., *George Munro Professor of Physics, and Lecturer on Applied Mechanics.*

RICHARD CHAPMAN WELDON, A. M. (Mt. All.), PH. D. (Yale), *George Munro Professor of Constitutional and International Law, and Lecturer on Crimes.*

BENJAMIN RUSSELL, A. M. (Mt. All.), *Professor of Contracts, and Lecturer on Bills and Notes, Sales and Equity.*

JAMES SETH, M. A. (Edin.), *George Munro Professor of Philosophy.*

ARCHIBALD MACMECHAN, B. A. (Toronto), PH. D. (J. H. U.), *George Munro Professor of English Language and Literature.*

C. SIDNEY HARRINGTON, Q. C., *Lecturer on Evidence, Partnership Agency, and Companies.*

JOHN SOMERS, M. D. (Bell. Hosp. Med. Coll., N. Y.), *Examiner in Medicine.*

GEORGE L. SINCLAIR, M. D., (Coll. P. and S., N. Y.), M. D. (Univ. Hal.) *Examiner in Anatomy and practical Anatomy.*

D. A. CAMPBELL, M. D., C. M. (Dal.), *Examiner in Materia Medica and Therapeutics, and Pathology.*

A. W. H. LINDSAY, B. A. (Dal.), M. D., C. M. (Dal.), M. B., C. M. (Edin.), *Examiner in Anatomy and Practical Anatomy.*

JOHN STEWART, M. B., C. M. (Edin.), *Examiner in Surgery.*

A. C. PAGE, M. D. (Harv.), President N. S. Medical Board, *Examiner in Obstetrics and Diseases of Women and Children.*

HON. D. McN. PARKER, M. D. (Edin.), L. R. C. S. (Edin.), *Examiner in Medicine.*

EDWARD FARRELL, M. D. (Coll. P. and S., N. Y.), *Examiner in Surgery.*

ANDREW J. COWIE, M. D. (Univ. Penn.), M. R. C. P. Lond., *Examiner in Clinical Medicine.*

JOHN F. BLACK, M. D. (Coll. P. and S., N. Y.), *Examiner in Clinical Surgery.*

ALEXANDER P. REID, M. D., C. M. (McGill), L R. C. S. (Edin.), L. C. P. and S. Can., *Examiner in Medical Jurisprudence.*

ARTHUR MORROW, M. B., C. M. (Edin.), *Examiner in Physiology and Histology.*

HOWARD MURRAY, B. A. (Lond.), *Lecturer on Classics.*

M. A. CURRY, M. D. (Univ. N. Y.), *Examiner in Obstetrics and Diseases of Women and Children.*

MURRAY McLAREN, M. D., *Examiner in Physiology and Histology.*

MARTIN MURPHY, D. SC. (Vind,) C. E., Provincial Government Engineer, *Lecturer on Civil Engineering.*

EDWIN GILPIN, Jr., A. M. (Vind.), LL. D. (Dal.) F. G. S., F. R. S. C., Inspector of Mines, *Lecturer on Mining.*

F. W. W. Doane, C. E., Halifax City Engineer, *Lecturer on Surveying.*

C. E. W. Dodwell, B. A., M. I. C. E., M. C. S. C. E., Resident Engineer Public Works of Canada, *Lecturer on Hydraulic Engineering*

Roderick McColl, C. E., (Roy. Mil. Coll.) Assistant Provincial Engineer, *Lecturer on Surveying and Civil Engineering.*

E. L. Newcombe, B. A. (Dal.), Ll. B. (Hal.), *Lecturer on Marine Insurance.*

Wm. B. Ross, Q. C., *Lecturer on Torts.*

George Ritchie, Ll. B. (Harv.), *Lecturer on Real Property.*

Wm. S. Muir, M. D., C. M. (Dal.), L. R. C. P. & S. (Edin.), *Examiner in Materia Medica and Therapeutics.*

H. McD. Henry, Q. C., *Examiner in Medical Jurisprudence.*

William Tobin, F. R. C. S. (Ireland), *Examiner in Ophthalamology, Otology, and Laryngology.*

Librarian : Professor Seth.

Curator of the Museum : Professor Lawson.

Instructor in Gymnastics : Sergeant Kelly.

Janitor : Archibald Dunlop.

FACULTY OF ARTS.

The President.

Charles Macdonald, M. A.

John Johnson, M. A.

George Lawson, Ph. D., LL. D.

James Liechti, M. A.

J. Gordon MacGregor, D. Sc.

James Seth, M. A.

Archibald MacMechan, Ph. D.

Secretary of the Faculty—Professor MacMechan.

Lecturer : H. Murray, B. A.

Past Graduate Student—for M. A....... 1
Fourth Year Under-Graduate Students—for B. A.......... 21
Third   "   "   "   "   21
Second   "   "   "   "   29
First   "   16
Fourth   B. L.......... 1
Second   "   1

    Total Under-Graduates, etc., (as above).......... 90
    General Students in Arts....'..... 63
    Special   "   "   115

    Total   "   Classes 268

FACULTY OF PURE AND APPLIED SCIENCE.

THE PRESIDENT *(ex officio.)*

CHARLES MACDONALD, M. A.

GEORGE LAWSON, Ph. D., LL. D.

JAMES LIECHTI, A. M.

J. GORDON MACGREGOR, D. Sc.

JAMES SETH, M. A.

ARCHIBALD MACMECHAN, B. A., Ph. D

MARTIN MURPHY, D. Sc., C. E.

EDWIN GILPIN, JR., A. M., LL. D., F. G. S

F. W. W. DOANE, C. E.

C. E. W. DODWELL, B. A., M. I. C. E.

RODERICK McCOLL, C. E.

Dean of the Faculty: PROF. MACGREGOR.

Fourth Year Undergraduate Students—for B. Sc............ 1
Third   "   "   "   3
First   "   "   "   3

    Total Undergraduates in Science (as above) 7
    General Students   "   5
    Special   "   "   15

    Total   27

FACULTY OF LAW.

THE PRESIDENT *(ex officio.)*

RICHARD C. WELDON, A. M., PH. D.

BENJAMIN RUSSELL, A. M., Q. C.

C. SYDNEY HARRINGTON, Q. C.

EDWARD L. NEWCOMBE, M. A., LL. B.

WILLIAM B. ROSS, Q. C.

GEORGE RITCHIE, LL. B.

Dean of Faculty—PROFESSOR WELDON.

Secretary of the Faculty—PROFESSOR RUSSELL.

Third year Under-graduate Students—for LL. B. 22
Second "   "   "   "   " 22
First "   "   "   "   " 8

Total Under-graduates in Law 52
General Students   "   15

Total   67

FACULTY OF MEDICINE.

THE PRESIDENT *(ex officio).*

GEORGE LAWSON, PH. D., LL. D.,

JOHN SOMERS, M. D.

GEORGE L. SINCLAIR, M. D.,

DONALD A. CAMPBELL, M. D. C. M.,

A. W. H. LINDSAY, M. D., C. M.,

JOHN STEWART, M. B. C. M.

A. C. PAGE, M. D.

DANIEL McNEIL PARKER, M. D.,

EDWARD FARRELL, M. D.,

ANDREW J. COWIE, M. D.,

JOHN F. BLACK, M. D.,

ALEXANDER P. REID, M. D.,

ARTHUR MORROW, M. B., C. M.,

MATTHEW A. CURRY, M. D.,

MURRAY MCLAREN, M. D.,

WM. S. MUIR, M. D.,

WM. TOBIN, F. R. C. S. Ire.,

HUGH McD. HENRY, Q. C.

Dean of the Faculty: PROF. LAWSON.

Secretary of the Faculty: DR. LINDSAY.

Fourth Year Undergraduate Students—for M. D., C. M					7
Third " " " "					6
Second " " " "					9
First					18
Total Undergraduates in Medicine					40
General Students " "					1
					41

THE UNIVERSITY LIBRARIES.

The General Library consists of nearly 4,000 volumes, selected to meet the wants especially of students of the Faculties of Arts and Science.

It contains the MACKENZIE COLLECTION of works on Mathematical and Physicial Science, which was presented to the College by the relatives of the late Professor J. J. Mackenzie; and the ROBERT MORROW COLLECTION of works on Northern Antiquities and Languages, presented by Mrs. Robert Morrow.

During the past year, 350 volumes have been added to the Library.

THE LAW LIBRARY.—Mr. A. H. R. Fraser, LL. B., has been appointed Librarian of the Law School. It is Mr. Fraser's wish to make the resources of the library available to the students. Those engaged in preparing for Moot Court cases especially are urged to advise with the Librarian, who will make them acquainted with the less accessible books in the Library. Much care is being taken to perfect the sets of Statutes. Since the end of the Session 1891–92 large additions of American Reports have been made.

The Library has a good set of English and Canadian Reports, and will be found to contain almost all the books which an under-graduate will have occasion to consult.

THE UNIVERSITY MUSEUM.

The Museum* consists chiefly of the THOMAS MCCULLOCH and the PATTERSON COLLECTIONS.

The THOMAS MCCULLOCH COLLECTION was presented to the University in 1844, by the Rev. William McCulloch, D. D., of Truro, with a fund of $1400 for extending the collection. It formed the museum of Prof. Thomas McCulloch, who occupied the Chair of Natural Philosophy from 1863 to 1865. It contains a large and valuable collection of birds, especially of native birds of the Maritime Provinces, many specimens of minerals, especially of Nova Scotian species, which are now being arranged systematically for convenience of study ; also rock specimens, an ample set of Carboniferous fossils, chiefly Nova Scotian, and a collection of European Cretaceous fossils, Indian implements, shells of recent Mollusca, native plants, &c. These collections were made in part by Rev. Thomas McCulloch. D. D., the first President of the College. The McCulloch collection of birds has recently been increased by additions paid for out of the McCulloch Museum Fund.

THE PATTERSON ARCHÆOLOGICAL COLLECTION.—This collection of Indian Antiquities was made by Rev. George Patterson, D. D., while engaged during a number of years in researches regarding the history and modes of life of the aborigines of Nova Scotia. The collection was presented by him to the College in 1889, on the condition that the Governors should make suitable " provision for the preservation and exhibition of the same, in such a manner as is usual in well-managed museums." It is kept as a separate collection. It contains 288 specimens, separately catalogued, and is arranged conveniently for reference. About 250 of the specimens have been obtained in Nova Scotia ; they represent the stone age of its aboriginal inhabitants, and form an almost complete representation of the articles usually found among the remains of the native races of North America. There are also a number of similar articles from the United States, Scotland, the West Indies, and especially the New Hebrides. The classified catalogue of the collection, which is arranged according to the method adopted in the description of the archæological collections of the Smithsonian Institution, contains full particulars of the localities where the several specimens were obtained.

Donations of DRIED PLANTS from the Pacific Islands and Australia,

---

*The Provincial Museum, in the new Provincial Building, Market Square, contains collections illustrating the Mineralogy, Geology and Zoology of the Province, and is open to the public daily ; it may be conveniently used by Students.

have been made by Rev. Hugh Robertson and Rev. Joseph Annand, M. A. New Hebrides ; and of Nova Scotian Plants by Mr. George G. Campbell, B. Sc., Truro.

A collection of CARBONIFEROUS FOSSILS, from the coal measures at Spring Hill, has been presented by Mr. Swift, of the Spring Hill Mines, Cumberland County.

THE GYMNASIUM.

The Gymnasium is provided with apparatus which was purchased by funds contributed for the most part by former students.

Instruction is furnished by a competent Gymnast.

The following are the general regulations for the use of the Gymnasium :—

(1.) All male students, graduates, and members of the Alumni Association shall, on paying the sessional fee, be entitled to the use of the Gymnasium.

(2.) Students shall be entitled to instruction in gymnastics without the payment of any additional fee.

(3.) Graduates and members of the Alumni Association shall be admitted to the classes, on payment of a fee of three dollars.

HISTORICAL.

Dalhousie College was founded by the Earl of Dalhousie in 1821, "for the education of youth in the higher branches of science and literature."

The original endowment was derived from funds collected at the port of Castine, in Maine, during its occupation in 1824 by Sir John C. Sherbrooke, then Lieutenant-Governor of Nova Scotia. These funds the British Government authorized the Earl of Dalhousie, Sir John's successor, to expend " in defraying the expenses of any improvement which it might seem expedient to undertake in the Province ;" and the Earl, believing that " a Seminary for the higher branches of education is much needed in Halifax—the seat of the Legislature—of the courts of justice—of the military and mercantile Society," decided upon " founding a College or Academy on the same plan and principle of that at Edinburgh," open to all occupations and sects of religion, restricted to such branches only as are applicable to our present state, and having the power to expand with the growth and improvement of our society."

The original Board of Governors consisted of the Governor-General of British North America, the Lieutenant-Governor of Nova Scotia, the Bishop, the Chief Justice and President of Council, the Provincial Treasurer and the Speaker of the House of Assembly.

After unsuccessful efforts on the part of both the British Government and the Board of Governors to effect a union with King's College, the only other then existing in the Province, this College went into operation in 1838, under the Presidency of the Rev. Thomas McCulloch, D. D., and with a staff of three Professors.

By an Act passed in 1841, University powers were conferred on the College, and the appointment of the Governors was vested in the Lieutenant-Governor and Council.

In 1856, the Arts departments of the Goreham College, Liverpool, N. S., was transferred to this College " with a view to the futherance of the establishment of a Provincial University," and an attempt was made to conduct the Institution as a University under the Act of 1841.

This union, however, came to an end in 1857.

In 1863, the College was re-organized under an Act of the Provincial Legislature.

Annual Calendar for 1892, without examination papers, 116 pages.

University of King's College, Windsor, N. S.

[Governors members of the Church of England (See Acts, 4th April, 1853, and 19th April, 1883).]

PATRON.

HIS GRACE THE ARCHBISHOP OF CANTERBURY.

BOARD OF GOVERNORS, 1892–93.

(Ex officio.)

THE RIGHT REV. THE LORD BISHOP OF NOVA SCOTIA.

Visitor and President of the Board.

THE MOST REV. JOHN MEDLEY, D. D., Lord Bishop of Fredericton and Metropolitan.

Members of the Board Elected by Incorporated Alumni:

N. W. WHITE, ESQ., Q. C.

W. C. SILVER, ESQ.

HON. L. E. BAKER, M. L. C.

REV. CANON BRIGSTOCKE, D. D.

REV. C. BOWMAN, D. D.

C. WILCOX, ESQ.

C. E. A. SIMONDS, ESQ. B. C. L.

J. Y. PAYZANT, ESQ.

REV. GEORGE HASLAM, M. A.

J. C. MOODY, ESQ. M. D.

HON. SENATOR ALMON, M. D.

CLARENCE H. DIMOCK, ESQ.

Elected by the Diocesan Synod of Nova Scotia:

REV. CANON PARTRIDGE, D. D.

H. Y. HIND, ESQ., M. A., D. C. L,

Elected by the Diocesan Synod of Fredericton:

REV. J. ROY CAMPBELL, B. D.

HON. JUDGE HANINGTON.

Treasurer.

J. Y. PAYZANT, ESQ.

Secretary.

R. J. WILSON, ESQ.

OFFICERS OF THE UNIVERSITY.

Chancellor :

VERY REV. EDWIN GILPIN, D. D., D. C. L., DEAN OF NOVA SCOTIA.

Vice-Chancellor.—(ex officio.)

THE REV. CHARLES EDWARD WILLETS, M. A., D. C. L., PRESIDENT OF KING'S COLLEGE.

Public Orator :

REV. FRANCIS PARTRIDGE, M. A., D. D., CANON OF ST. LUKE'S CATHEDRAL.

Registrar :

WILLIAM R. BUTLER, ESQ., M. ENG., PROFESSOR OF MATHEMATICS AND ENGINEERING, KING'S COLLEGE.

FACULTY.

President of the College.

REV. C. E. WILLETS, M. A., D. C. L.

Vice-President.

PROFESSOR VROOM, M. A., B. D.

Professor of Classics.

REV. C. E. WILLETS, M. A., D. C. L.

Fellow and Professor of Mathematics, Natural Philosophy, and Engineering.

W. R. BUTLER, ESQ., M. ENG.

Fellow and Professor of Chemistry, Geology, and Mining.

G. T. KENNEDY, ESQ., M. A., B. A. SC., D. SC., F. G. S.

Professor of English Literature, Economics, and History.

C. G. D. ROBERTS, ESQ., M. A., F. R. S. C.

Professor of Modern Languages.
H. LOTHAR BOBER, ESQ.

Professor of Divinity.
REV. F. W. VROOM. M. A., B. D.

Tutor in Science.

Bursar :
PROFESSOR BUTLER.

Librarian and Scientific Curator.
PROFESSOR KENNEDY.

FACULTY OF DIVINITY.

THE REV. THE PRESIDENT, (*ex officio.*)

Professor of Divinity :
REV. F. W. VROOM, M. A., B. D.

Lecturer in Canon Law and Ecclesiastical Polity :
THE REV. CANON PARTRIDGE, D. D.

Lecturer in Apologetics :
REV. J. HASLAM, M. A.

Lecturer in Old Testament Exegesis :
THE VEN. ARCHDEACON SMITH, D. D.

FACULTY OF CIVIL LAW.

THE REV. THE PRESIDENT, D. C. L. (*ex officio.*)
HON. MR. JUSTICE TOWNSHEND, B. C. L.
HON. S. L. SHANNON, D. C. L.

LAW SCHOOL.

(Opened, Oct. 1892, at St. John, *New Brunswick.*)

HISTORICAL.

King's College was founded A. D., 1789, by an Act of the Provincial Legislature, chiefly through the exertions of the Right Reverend Charles Inglis, D.D., first Bishop of Nova Scotia. For this foundation funds were granted by the Provincial Legislature, and subsequently by the British Government.

By the Royal Charter granted in 1802, all the privileges of a University were conferred on King's College, which thus became the first University of British origin established in Canada.

A Provincial Act incorporating the Governors of King's College and annulling the Act of 1789, was passed April 4th, 1853. It provides that the Royal Charter of Incorporation shall not be affected by it further than is necessary to give effect to its own enactments.

The Patron of the University is the Archbishop of Canterbury, to whose approval "all Statutes, Rules and Ordinances" of the Board of Governors are subject by resolution of the Board of Governors recorded in the Statutes of the University.

King's College is open to students of all denominations, and imposes no religious test either on entrance or on graduation in any faculty, excepting that of Divinity.

The University confers degrees in Arts, Divinity, Law, Engineering and Science. The School of Engineering was added in 1871.

Candidates for Matriculation may now be examined at distant centres, under special regulations, which will be found in the Calendar.

There are at present in the University five Schools to matriculated students. :

I.   The School of Arts.
II.   "   " Divinity.
III.   "   " Engineering.
IV.   "   " Science.
V.   "   " Civil Law.

THE UNIVERSITY LIBRARY.

The foundation of the Library is due to the efforts of the first Bishop of Nova Scotia, and may be placed in the year 1790. Several contributions in money had previously been received, but it was not till that year that efforts were made to obtain books.

The orignal fund at the disposal of the Governors was not more than £250 sterling, and was intrusted to Mr. Inglis (afterwards Bishop,) son of the Bishop, and a graduate of the University, who repaired to England in 1800, for the purpose of purchasing books. The names of Dr. Moore, Archbishop of Canterbury, Dr. Porteous, Bishop of Rochester; William Wiberforce, Sir S. Bernard Morland, John Eardly Wilmot, M. P., and others, thus became connected with the early history of the Library.

Munificent gifts from the University of Oxford continued to increase the value of the collection, which was further enriahed by gifts from various English gentlemen, and from others settled in Nova Scotia.

The room in the College building set apart for many years for a Library Hall, was completed in 1810 at the expense of Sir Thomas Strange and the Archbishop of Canterbury.

Subsequently valuable works were presented by Drs. Bayard and McCulloch, and by the Society for Promoting Christian Knowledge.

Among later benefactors may be mentioned Dr. Greswell of Worcester College, Oxford ; The Smithsonian Institute ; The British and Foreign Bible Society ; the Dean and Chapter of Westminster ; T. B. Akins, Esq., D. C. L ; The Society of Incorporated Alumni of King's College ; E. Binney, Esq.; C. Cogswell, Esq., M. D. ; The Dominion Government ; The Radical Bay Club; The Haliburton Club; The Secretary of the Interior, United States : American Institute of Mining Engineers; The Royal Society ; The Religious Tract Society ; The Rev. George McCawley, D. D.; The late Rev. Canon Hensley, D. D.; General Sir. W. F. Williams, K. C. B. ; The late Bishop of Nova Scotia ; The Right Rev. D. Rigaud, late Bishop of Antigua ; The Rev. George Morris ; The late Rev. G. W. Hodgson, M. A., and Her Majesty the Queen.

This large collection of books now numbering about 10,000 volumes, contained till the year 1870 in a single room in the College building, was then removed to the new hall specially built for the purpose and presented to the University by the Incorporated Alumni. It contains a large number of standard works of reference in Theology, which is by far the richest department in the Library, and a fair selection of the great Greek and Latin Classics.

In modern History and Belles-Lettres it is very poorly supplied.

It is also much to be desired that some well-wisher to the College would present some volumes of German Literature to the Library, which contain scarcely any German books.

In Science some recent standard works have from time to time been added, and next to Theology and Classics, this is the largest department. The languages of Modern Europe are not so well represented.

In spite of many blanks, the Library is one of the largest in the Province, and contains all the elements requisite for making it a thoroughly well appointed and efficient Reference Library.

There is no special Library Fund, except the fee from students, and the collection can only be increased by grants of money from the Governors, the occasional lapsing of the Welsford prize money, and the benefactions of friends of the University.

THE MUSEUM.

NATURAL HISTORY.

GEOLOGY AND MINERALOGY.

The Geological Specimens, many of which are very fine, illustrate the most prominent features of general Geology, but the majority have been collected in Nova Scotia, and are especially adapted to show the character of the Fossil Flora and Fauna of the Province. There are several collections, which may be discriminated as follows :—

1.   The W. B. Almon Collection presented over forty years ago by Mrs. W. B. Almon, of Halifax, contains, with many minerals and a few shells, a considerable number of rock specimens and a few fossils, chiefly from Scotland, collected by the late W. B. Almon, M.D.

2.   The Governors' Collection consists of coal fossils obtained in 1860, at the expense of the Governors of the College; these were collected by Professor How, with the valuable assistance of a party headed by Richard Brown, Sr., Esq., then agent at the Sydney Mines, who from long study was familiar with the district.   Many of the specimens are exceedingly fine, and some are of large size.

3.   The Alumni Collection consists of Silurian and Devonian Fossils, chiefly from Arisaig, N. S., collected, named and arranged stratigraphically by Dr. Honeyman; purchased and presented in 1861 by the Alumni of King's College.

4.   The Australian Collection consists of specimens obtained through Colonel Nelson, in 1863, from Sir William Dennison, then Governor of New South Wales, in exchange for Nova Scotian specimens from the College Cabinet, sent by Professor How.   It contains some beautiful fossils, and is arranged stratigraphically; its value is increased by an accompanying large detailed colored section made by the Government Examiner of Coal Fields under instructions from Sir William Dennison.

5. A collection of British Fossils, chiefly Silurian and Devonian, obtained through Dr. McCawley in exchange for Nova Scotian specimens sent by Professor How from the College Cabinet, in 1860 to Captain, now Sir James Anderson.

6. A collection from Europe, illustrating chiefly the nature of crystalline and sedimentary rocks, purchased by the Governors.

7. Several collections, some of which are unnamed, and single specimens, given and obtained by exchange at various times; of these it will suffice to name; Reptilian Tracks of great geological interest presented by the widow of their discoverer, the late Dr. Harding; valuable Fossils, chiefly carboniferous, presented by H. Poole, Esq.; Silurian Fossils from Arisaig, presented by H. Hill, Esq., Sheriff of Antigonish; Coal Plants from Cumberland County, presented by Rev. Mr. Townshend, Rector of Amherst; Cretaceous Fossils from England, presented by C. B. Bowman, Esq., and Dr. Honeyman; Silurian and Carboniferous Fossils of Nova Scotia, from Professor How; Rocks and Minerals from the Dominion 'Government; Devonian Corals of Ontario and Canadian Rocks from Professor Spencer.

The Mineralogical specimens represent the most important species of Minerals,—some of them are of great beauty. They consist of those in the collection of Zeolites collected at the expense of the Governors, and of various others obtained by gifts and exchange, as mentioned with regard to the geological department. Sir Rupert George; Rev. Dr. Robertson, Rector of Wilmot; H. Brown, Esq., Director of the Geological Survey of Victoria, formerly a distintinguished student in Science at this College; Rev. J. Ambrose; Rev. J. C. Cochran; C. B Bowman, Esq.; J. Bowman, Esq.; Rev. D. W. Pickett; Hon. W. Odell, and Professor How, have presented interesting specimens.

ZOOLOGY.

The Willis Collection consists of specimens fully illustrating Nova Scotia Mollusca, named, arranged, and presented by late J. R. Willis, Esq.; a collection from the U. S. Government.

The department is further illustrated by a collection of foreign shells, some interesting skulls and skins, and a limited number of preserved animals.

BOTANY.

The Cogswell Herbarium, bound in fine imperial folio volumes, contains a fine systematically arranged collection of Phœnogamous and Cryptogamous Plants of Great Britain, presented by Dr. Cogswell.

The Gossip Herbarium consists of a small number of Scottish Plants presented by Dr. Gossip.

The Willis Herbarium consists of Nova Scotia Algæ and Terrestial Plants, presented by late J. R. Willis, Esq.

The Strange Herbarium consists of a considerable number of East India Plants, presented in 1805, by Sir T. Strange.

The Ball Herbarium of Nova Scotia consisting of about 250 species, presented by Rev. E. H. Ball.

There are also a few woods, barks, leaves and fruit—from various sources—presented by C. B. Bowman, Esq., Hon. W. J. Almon, M. D., and other benefactors.

THE GENERAL COLLECTION.

The General Collection consists of various curiosities from different parts of the world, and a small but choice cabinet of coins. Other interesting curiosities are the beautiful Indian Pipe from Queen Charlotte's Island, the models of the leaning Tower and the Baptistry at Pisa, and the memorials of Gens. Williams and Inglis, which include the sword worn by the former throughout the siege of Kars, and that used by the latter during the defence of Lucknow. There is also a model of the Cawnpore Memorial Cross, formed of wood from the house in the courtyard of which the women and children were massacred.

The College possesses also a number of autographs of royal and distinguished personages ; one of Thomas Moore, the poet, inscribed in a copy of Lucian, presented by him on the occasion of his visit.

The Coins illustrate the Numismatics of Rome, and most of the countries of the modern world.

The different departments of the museum are arranged in twenty-four flat cases, supported by the balustrade surrounding the gallery, and five large table cases all glazed and provided with lock and key. The large specimens which could not be conveniently .placed in cases are arranged on shelves or distributed in different parts of the hall.

The friends of Science in Nova Scotia and elsewhere are respectfully requested to contribute specimens to the Museum of King's College. The steps which have been lately taken by the Governors to provide suitable cases for the arrangement and display of the contents of the Museum in the fine Hall erected at the expense of the Alumni, offer a guarantee that the liberality of donors will be carefully recognized and fully recorded.

A superb collection of Loyalist China, over three hundred pieces, arranged in three cases, was presented by Judge and Mrs. Weldon, on the 79th anniversary of the landing of the Loyalists in New Brunswick.

In the library, in addition to a number of Photographs, there are several large Oil Paintings—including those of the late Drs. McCawley and Cochran, Rev. Charles Porter, A. M., the late Dr. J. T. Twining, and of Paul Mascarene. There are also marble busts of General Williams, and of Cicero and Demosthenes.

It is particularly requested that donors will send their contributions of Books, Coins and Curiosities, addressed to the *Librarian*, and of Natural History specimens to the *Natural History Curator*, King's College Museum, Windsor, N. S., in order that the receipt may be duly acknowledged, and the donation recorded in the yearly Calendars as heretofore.

The Annual Calendar of 1892, contains 132 pages.

Acadia University, Wolfville, N. S.

GOVERNORS OF THE UNIVERSITY.

[Governors appointed by the Baptist Convention of the Maritime Province, (see Act, 19th May, 1891).]

REV. A. W. SAWYER, D. D., LL. D.,

President of the University, EX OFFICIO.

MEMBERS WHOSE TERM OF OFFICE EXPIRES IN 1892.

COLIN W. ROSCOE, M. A.,   EDWIN D. KING, M, A., Q. C.,
WLLIAM CUMMINGS, ESQ.,   *F. H. EATON, M. A.,
*HERBERT C. CREED, M. A.,   REV. A. COHOON, M. A.,
REV. S. B. KEMPTON, M. A.   WILLARD O. WRIGHT, B. A.

MEMBERS WHOSE TERM OF OFFICE EXPIRES IN 1895.

*B. H. EATON, M. A. Q. C.,   C. B. WHIDDEN, ESQ.,
WILLIAM C. BILL, ESQ.,   HON. A. F. RANDOLPH,
RUPERT G. HALEY, ESQ.,   *A. P. SHAND, ESQ.
GEORGE G. KING, M. P.,   *C. M. WOODWORTH, B. A.

MEMBERS WHOSE TERM OF OFFICE EXPIRES IN 1898.

*REV. T. A. HIGGINS, D. D.,   G. J. C. WHITE, B. A.,
*REV. J. W. MANNING, B. A.,   HARRIS H. CROSBY, ESQ.,
W. F. PARKER, B. A.,   H. H. CHUTE, ESQ., M. P. P.,
HON. J. W. JOHNSTONE, D. C. L., REV. E. M. SAUNDERS, D. D.

REV. S. B. KEMPTON, M. A., *Secretary.*

X. Z. CHIPMAN, ESQ., *Treasurer.*

EXECUTIVE COMMITTEE OF THE GOVERNORS.

A. W. SAWYER.   E. M. SAUNDERS.
B. H. EATON.   S. B. KEMPTON.
R. V. JONES.   C. W. ROSCOE.
I. B. OAKES.   D. F. HIGGINS,

Secretary.

*Nominated by the Associated Alumni.

COMMITTEE OF INVESTMENTS.

E. D. King, *Chairman.*
D. McN. Parker.
J. Desbrisay.

C. W. Roscoe.
J. P. Chipman.
X. Z. Chipman.

Treasurer.

SENATE OF THE UNIVERSITY.

Rev. A. W. Sawyer, D. D., LL. D., *Moderator.*
D. F. Higgins, Ph. D., *Vice-Moderator.*
L. E. Wortman, M. A., *Secretary.*
E. M. Keirstead, M. A., *Treasurer.*

The Professors of the University and Seminary, and Principals of Academy, ex officio.

Vacating Office in 1894.

Rev. S. McC. Black, M. A.
" F. D. Crawley, B. A.
" P. A. McEwen.
W. M. McVicar, B. A.
Rev. S. Welton, M. A.

Rev. G. O. Gates, M. A.
" J. E. Hopper, D. D.
E. W. Sawyer, B. A.
F. M. Shaw, B. A.

Vacating Office in 1897.

H. H. Bligh, M.A., Q.C.
J. S. Rogers, B.A., LL.B.
Rev. E. P. Coldwell, B.A.
C. H. McIntyre, B.A.
A. K. DeBlois, Ph. D.

J. B. Hall, Ph. D.
Hon. Judge J. P. Chipman, M.A.
H. T. Ross, LL.B.
S. W. Cummings, B.A.

Vacating Office in 1890.

Rev. W. H. Warren, M.A.
J. E. Parsons, B.A.
A. J. Pineo, B.A.
I. B. Oakes, M.A.
Rev. J. Bancroft, B.A.

A. DeW. Barss, M.D.
Rev. W. H. Robinson, B.A.
H. A. Lovitt, B.A.
Miss Alice Fitch, M.A.

THE FACULTY.

REV. A. W. SAWYER, D.D., LL.D., President,
Professor of Psychology and Metaphysics.

D. F. HIGGINS, M. A., Ph. D.,
Professor of Mathematics.

R. V. JONES, M.A., Ph. D.,
J. W. Barss Professor of the Greek and Latin Languages.

REV. E. M. KEIRSTEAD, M. A.,
PROFESSOR OF MORAL PHILOSOPHY AND EVIDENCES OF CHRISTIANITY.

A. E. COLDWELL, M. A.,
PROFESSOR OF CHEMISTRY AND GEOLOGY.

L. E. WORTMAN, M. A.
PROFESSOR OF FRENCH AND GERMAN.

J. F. TUFTS, M. A.,
MARK CURRY PROFESSOR OF HISTORY AND POLITICAL ECONOMY.

FRANK R. HALEY, M. A..
ALUMNI PROFESSOR OF PHYSICS AND ASTRONOMY.

*

PROFESSOR OF ENGLISH LANGUAGE AND LITERATURE.

H. N. SHAW, B. A.,
INSTRUCTOR IN ELOCUTION AND DIRECTOR OF GYMNASIUM.

A. DeW. BARSS, M. D.,
LECTURER ON PHYSIOLOGY AND HYGIENE.

EVERETT W. SAWYER, B. A.
INSTRUCTOR IN LATIN AND ENGLISH.

A. E. COLDWELL,
CURATOR OF MUSEUM.

L. E. WORTMAN,
LIBRARIAN.

Fourth year Under-graduate Students—for B.A.						25
Third "	"		"	" "		22
Second "	"		"	" "		26
First '			"	" "		33

Total Under-graduates in Arts	106
Special Students "	12
Total	118

The financial year of the University dates from the first of August.

The first session of the Academy and Seminary begins the first Wednesday in September. The first session of the Arts Department of the University opens on the last Wednesday in September.

In April of each year occurs an Elocutionary Recital, in which all the members of the Sophomore Class take part. A record is kept

* Temporary provision is made for the work of this department until the appointment of a Professor.

to indicate the excellence of the respective members of the class in this exercise.

The Junior Exhibition is held at the close of the first session, at which time orations prepared by members of the Class are delivered in a public assembly.

On the first Thursday in June the anniversary of the College is commemorated, at which time the ceremonies connected with the graduation of students and the conferring of degrees, are observed by the authorities of the University.

The College Library contains a valuable collection of books especially selected for the use of students. Books can be taken from the Library-room subject to proper regulations. The Library is also open five afternoons of the week, under the supervision of the Librarian, for convenience in consulting works of reference. The leading Canadian, American and English periodicals are kept in the Library for the use of the students.

The Library receives donations both of money and of books; additions are also made to it by means of the annual income of the DeWolfe Library Fund.

The Scientific Rooms are provided with sufficient apparatus for a wide range of experiments in Chemistry and Physics. Special provision is made for students in Practical Chemistry. Considerable material has also been collected to illustrate studies in the department of Biology. The Museum is well furnished with collections from various parts of the world illustrative of the departments of Geology, Mineralogy and Botany.

In addition to the assignments in Elocution, opportunity will be given for advanced study in this department. A course for four years is marked out, and students who successfully pass the required examinations will receive a diploma for the same.

Though none of the present courses of study includes Vocal Music, yet it is desirable that all students, as far as possible, should give some attention to this subject. Classes under the direction of the teacher of Elocution are formed for practice in singing, at such times as will not interfere with the regular appointments of class work.

A large and convenient campus gives abundant opportunities for Athletic Games in the spring and autumn. There is also on the University grounds a large and well-equipped Gymnasium. From the first of November to the first of April, the students have regular gymnastic drill under the Director of the Gymnasium. Experience has shown that this practice is highly conductive to the health of the students.

ACADIA COLLEGE was founded by the N. S. Education Society in 1838. In the following year application was made to the N. S. House of Assembly for a Charter of Incorporation with the title: "The Trustees, Governors and Fellows of the Queen's College." An Act creating such a corporation with the powers of a University was passed in 1840. At the next meeting of the Legislature, this Act was amended by changing the name to Acadia College.

In 1851 the power of appointing the Governors of the College was transferred from the N. S. Education Society to the Baptist Convention of the Maritime Provinces.

Annual Calendar, 1892, 51 pages. Later additions announce extensions of the curriculum.

St. Francis Xavier College and Academy, Antigonish, N. S.

BOARD OF GOVERNORS.

[Governors in communion with the Roman Catholic Church, (See Act, 10th March, 1882).]

HIS LORDSHIP THE BISHOP OF ANTIGONISH, Chairman *ex-officio*).

REV. JOHN SHAW, P. P.   WILLIAM GERRIOR, ESQ.

REV. N. MCNEIL, D. D.   C. F. MCISAAC, ESQ., M. L. C.

REV. D. A. CHISHOLM, D. D., Sec., Treas. Board of Governors.

TEACHING STAFF.

REV. A. CHISHOLM, D. D., Professor of Latin and Ethics.

REV. A. MACDONALD, D. D., Professor of Metaphysics, Latin and English.

REV. A. J. CHISHOLM, D. D., Professor of French and Mathematics.

REV. D. A. CHISHOLM, D. D., Professor of Greek.

REV. A. THOMPSON, D. D., Professor of Logic and Physics.

HUGH MCPHERSON, Professor of Chemistry.

COLLEGE OFFICIALS.

REV. D. A. CHISHOLM, D. D., Rector.

REV. A. THOMPSON, D. D., Vice-Rector.

REV. A. MCDONALD, D. D., Prefect of Studies.

Total Students in attendance, 136.

St. Francis Xavier's College was founded in 1854 by the Rt. Rev. Colin F. McKinnon, D. D., Bishop of Arichat, for the higher education of students aspiring to the priesthood and to the learned professions. In this respect it has fulfilled the hopes of the Rt. Rev. Founder, and has moreover been a chief factor in supplying teachers for the Counties of Antigonish, Inverness, Richmond and Cape Breton.

In 1866 the College received University powers by Act of the Legislature of Nova Scotia.

THE LIBRARY.

The library consists of about 2700 volumes. Over fifty years ago a student named John Ryan, of Halifax, died in the Propaganda College, Rome. In his will he bequeathed his property to the Church in Nova Scotia, and after the division into two dioceses, that of Arichat received its share of Ryan's bequest, part of which was a large library purchased in Rome. The present College Library is in great part made up of the Ryan collection, but both Bishop Mc-Kinnon and Bishop Cameron contributed from their own libraries many valuable works. The late Rev. Alexander McLeod, of Arisaig ; Rev. John V. MacDonell, St. Andrews ; Rev. John Quinan, of Main-a-dieu, and Rev. John McDougall, Red Islands, also bequeathed their libraries to the College. Formerly the library books were used principally for reference, but of late years they have been utilized in supplying good reading matter to students, and thus cultivating their acquaintance with past and contemporary English literature. A drawback is want of revenue, and donations are solicited.

Annual Calendar, 1892, 23 pages.

The Presbyterian College, Pine Hill, Halifax, N. S.

BOARD OF MANAGEMENT.

(Appointed by the General Assembly of the Presbyterian church in Canada.)

DR. BURNS, *Chairman.*
REV. T. SEDGEWICK, *Chairman.*
PRINCIPAL MCKNIGHT, D. D.,
DR. CURRIE,
DR. POLLOK,
DR. MCCULLOCH,
PRESIDENT FORREST, D. D.,
REV. ALLAN SIMPSON,
  " J. MCMILLAN, B. A.,
  " J. S. CARRUTHERS,
  " E. SCOTT, M. A.,
  " JAMEL MCLEAN,
  " E. D. MILLER, B. A.,

REV. L. G. MCNEILL, M. A.
  " NEIL MCKAY,
  " D. M. GORDON, B. D.,
  " T. STEWART, B. D.,
  " A. B. DICKIE,
  " H. H. MCPHERSON, M. A.,
  " G. A. LECK,
D C. FRASER, ESQ., M. P.,
R. BAXTER, ESQ.
R. MURRAY, ESQ.,
JAS. WALKER ESQ., M. D.,
ED. JACK, ESQ.,
HUGH MACKENZIE, ESQ.

SENATE.

PRINCIPAL MCKNIGHT, *Chairman.*
DR. CURRIE, *Clerk.*
  " POLLOK,
  " DR. BURNS,
  " MACRAE,
PRESIDENT FORREST, D. D.,
REV. P. M. MORRISON,
  " THOMAS CUMMING,
  " A. SIMPSON,

REV. H. H. MCPHERSON, M. A.
  " D. M. GORDON. B. D.,
  " G. BRUCE, B. A.,
  " R. LAING, M. A.,
  " T. FOWLER,
R. MURRAY.
PROF. MACDONALD, M. A.,
  " SETH, M. A.

COMMITTEE OF EXAMINERS.

REV. P. M. MORRISON, *Convener.*
  " A. SIMPSON,
  " H. H. MCPHERSON, M. A.,
  " T. CUMMING,

PRESIDENT FORREST, D. D.,
PROFESSOR MACDONALD, M. A.,
  " SETH, M. A.,

PROFESSORS:

THE REV. ALEXANDER McKNIGHT, D. D., *Principal and Professor of Theology.*

THE REV. JOHN CURRIE, D. D., *Professor of Hebrew and Biblical Literature.*

THE REV. ALLAN POLLOK, D. D., *Professor of Church History and Pastoral Theology.*

LECTURERS.

THE REV. ROBERT A. FALCONER, B. A. (Lond.), M. A. and B. D. (Edin.), *New Testament Introduction and Exegesis.*

THE REV. JAMES S. CARRUTHERS, *Instructor in Elocution.*

LIBRARY.

Contains over nine thousand volumes.

STUDENTS.

```
Senior year Undergraduates ..................   9
Middle   "          "         ..................   7
Junior   "          "         ..................  11
Partial Course ...........................   1
                                            ——
                          Total.... ....... 28
```

Calendar, with examination papers, 1892, 36 pages.

St. Anne's College, Church Point, Digby Co., N. S.

BOARD OF DIRECTORS.

[Directors in communion with the Roman Catholic Church. (See Act 30th April, 1892).]

REVEREND GUSTAVE BLANCHE,
" JOSEPH HAQUIN,
" FRANCOIS OZANNE,
" AIME MORRIS,
" PHILEAS F. BOURGEOIS, A. M.

(Calendar not yet published.)

This institution was founded in 1890, by Rev. Gustave Blanche and other religious of the congregation of the Eudist Fathers, whom the Most Reverend C. O'Brien, Archbishop of Halifax, called from France for that purpose.

The present building known as St. Anne's College is a commodious structure, four-story building, 110 x 50 feet, and thoroughly well equipped in all its departments.

The teaching embraces the Classical and Commercial courses, instruction in each being given through the medium of French and English.

In April, 1892, the institution was incorporated and chartered as a college by the Provincial Legislature, with power to grant Academic degrees on graduates in Arts and Sciences.

The Faculty is composed of eleven professors, this year. Three are teaching in the Latin and Greek Department, four in the English Commercial and Business course, and three in the French Department.

Sixty-five students are following the various classes.

Two of the professors have a Grade B and one a Grade C from the Provincial Normal School. Two are Bachelors of Arts from St. Francis Xavier College, Antigonish. One is a Master of Arts from Laval University. The professors from France have all graduated from colleges or universities where they completed their classical course.

Printed courses of study containing the more essential information required by intending students have been published.

ANNUAL REPORT

OF THE

SUPERINTENDENT OF EDUCATION

ON THE

BLIC SCHOOLS OF NOVA SCOTIA,

For the Year ended 31st July,

1893.

HALIFAX, N. S.:
OMMISSIONER OF PUBLIC WORKS AND MINES
QUEEN'S PRINTER.

PRINTING AND PUBLISHING CO., 59 & 60 GRANVILLE STREET.
1894.

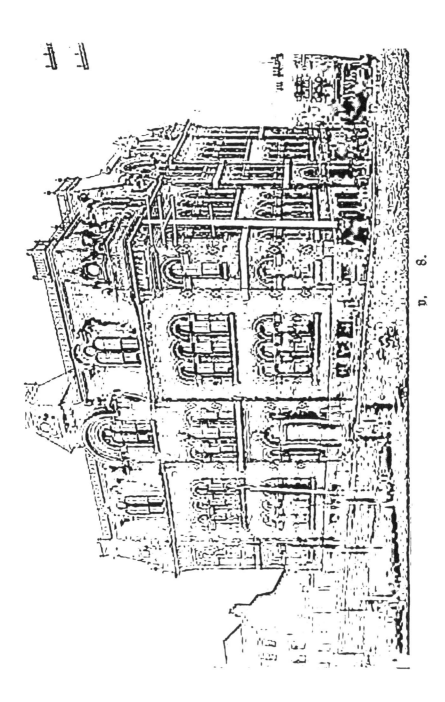

Fig. 8.

ANNUAL REPORT

OF THE

SUPERINTENDENT OF EDUCATION

ON THE

PUBLIC SCHOOLS OF NOVA SCOTIA,

For the Year ended 31st July,

1893.

HALIFAX, N. S.:
COMMISSIONER OF PUBLIC WORKS AND MINES,
QUEEN'S PRINTER,
1894.

EDUCATION OFFICE.

HALIFAX, January, 1894.

SIR,—

I have the honor to transmit herewith, to be laid before His Honor the Lieutenant-Governor, my report on the Public Schools of Nova Scotia, for the School year ended July 31, 1893.

I am, with respect,

Your obedient servant,

A. H. MacKAY,
Superintendent of Education·

To the HON. W. S. FIELDING, M. P. P.,
Provincial Secretary.

GENERAL CONTENTS.

PART III.—APPENDICES.

PART I.

GENERAL REPORT, 1893.

ANNUAL REPORT

ON THE

PUBLIC SCHOOLS OF NOVA SCOTIA,

1892-93.

To His Honor, Malachy Bowes Daly,
Lieutenant-Governor of Nova Scotia:

MAY IT PLEASE YOUR HONOR,—

I beg in accordance with the law, to submit my annual report on the Public Schools of the Province, for the School Year ended 31st July, 1893.

The amendments to the Education Laws which received your assent on the 30th day of April, 1892, have changed the date of the termination of the school year from the 31st of October to the 31st of July. The present school year is therefore a transition term, consisting necessarily of only the nine months between the 1st of November, 1892, and the 31st of July, 1893, forming but three-fourths of the normal school year, the first quarter of which (namely, August, September and October) is treated as missing.

From this cause alone it can be seen that comparison between the statistics of this and previous years can not be satisfactorily made in many cases.

Besides the anomaly referred to, there is also some considerable change in the statistical tables. The new information thus collected will not, of course, be available for the purpose of annual comparisons until, at least, the lapse of another year ; but, in the meantime, it will be found to be not only interesting but valuable.

For much detail that might otherwise appear in this annual report, I refer you to the two volumes of the Journal of Education issued semi-annually in April and October to the secretaries of the trustees of each school section in the Province and other educational officials, each volume containing over one hundred pages similiar to those of this report.

The most remarkable feature characteristic of the year is the absence of any serious friction in the carrying into effect of the

numerous changes incident to the amendments cited above, a state of
affairs testifying to a high degree of intelligence and executive tact
on the part of both teachers and trustees as a general rule, and to the
eminent energy and ability of the inspectoral staff.

The number of school sections has been diminished by one during
the year, indicating still a favorable drift of sentiment with respect to
the very important matter of the consolidation of small or weak school
sections. Such sections, more abundant in some quarters of the
province than in others, are the cause of unsatisfactory conditions
which give those interested in our educational improvement the
greatest anxiety and labor.

The attendance of pupils during the term does not equal three-
fourths of the attendance of the preceding normal year, which was an
exceptionally flourishing period with regard to attendance. It is,
however, greater than the corresponding attendance of the year ended
in 1891. But the fact that the number of pupils daily present on an
average was, for the two winter quarters of the present year, 49,590
as against only 49,493 of the previous year, seems to indicate that the
apparent falling off must have occurred in the last quarter, owing
probably to the fact that the new regulations brought on the mid-
summer vacation about the beginning of July instead of about the
middle of the month as formerly. This combined with the severity
of the winter specially referred to in at least one of the Inspector's
reports appended hereto, would lead me to say, that in respect of
attendance, the year should be ranked as a good one notwithstanding
the local difficulties affecting attendance in some districts.

In my last report I called attention to the extraordinary increase
in the money voted by the school sections for building and repairs—
an increase from a little over $51,000 to something over $96,000.
This year nearly the same sum, $95,687 09, has been voted for the
shorter term of three-quarters of a calendar year. Nothing can more
emphatically demonstrate the enthusiastic interest being developed
throughout the province in the matter of providing superior school-
room accommodation with special attention to improved methods of
warming and ventilation.

Last year I was glad to call your attention to a hopeful sign of
improvement in the status of the teaching profession. The average
salary of first-class male teachers increased forty dollars, and of first-
class female teachers, about ten dollars. I have now to report that
the advance of last year has not only been maintained in the said
classes of teachers, but has been still further advanced, not only in
respect of the first-class teachers, but in respect of the teachers of
every class of both sexes. As compared with three-fourths of their
respective average salaries of the previous year, classes A & B, males,
were better by $50.91 : C, males, by $13.68 ; D, males, by $17.13.
Classes A & B, females, by $23.46 ; C, females, by $10.79 ; D, females,
by $3.06. In other words, the average annual salaries of male
teachers of the first, second and third classes have increased over $67,

$18 and $22, respectively; and of female teachers, over $31, $14 and $4, respectively, during the year. This growing estimation in which the people hold efficient teachers accords well with their appreciation of improved school accommodation as illustrated in the preceding paragraph.

The following statistical abstract will give a general view of the more important details of the state of education during the year.

STATISTICAL ABSTRACT.

1.—SCHOOL SECTIONS.

Total number in Province	1904
" " " in 1892	1905
Decrease	1
No. of Sections without Schools	196

2.—NO. OF SCHOOLS, PUPILS, TEACHERS, &C.

Total No. Schools in operation	2252
No. of Schools in Session 50 days or under	37
No. over 50 days and up to 100	67
" 100 days and up to 150 days	219
" 150 days and under full term	913
No. full term (nine months) of 166 days	1016
Average No. of days all schools were in Session	152.7
No. of Teachers	2319
No. of Licensed Assistants	24
No. of Teachers holding Normal School Diploma	408
Total No. Registered Pupils	94899
Proportion of Population at School during year	1 in 4.7
No. of School Libraries	89
No. of School Scientific Collections	96

3.—CLASSIFICATION OF TEACHERS.

Academic.—(Class A. cl). Male Teachers	45
" (Class A. cl). Female Teachers	3
First Class.—(Class B). Male Teachers	169
" (Class B). Female Teachers	169
Second Class.—(Class C.)—Male Teachers	216
" (Class C.)—Female Teachers	898
Third Class.—(Class D).—Male Teachers	152
" (Class D.)—Female Teachers	667
Total No. Male Teachers	582
" Female Teachers	1737
No. Male Assistants	6
No. Female Assistants	18

4.—PERIOD OF SERVICE OF TEACHERS.

No. of New Teachers	288
No. of Old Teachers, but new to Section	910

No. of Teachers continued in same Section	1121
No. Teachers whose total service was one year or under..	325
No. over one year and up to two.....................	312
" two years and up to three	301
" three years and up to four	276
" four years and up to five	211
" five years and up to seven..................	295
" seven years and up to ten..................	220
" ten years and up to fifteen	199
" fifteen years and up to twenty..............	85
" twenty years	95

5.—ATTENDANCE OF PUPILS.

Total No. of pupils on register at end of second quarter..	78121
No. attended during second quarter	78121
Average daily attendance second quarter	49887.2
Per cent. attended during quarter daily present on an average.	63.8
Total No. of Pupils on Register at end of third quarter...	84239
No. attended during quarter	76928
Average daily attendance...........................	49292.9
Per cent. attended during quarter, daily present on an average	64.
New Pupils attended third quarter	6117
Enrolled Pupils who did not attend third quarter	7310
Total No. of Pupils on Register at end of fourth quarter.	94899
No. attended during quarter........................	77773
Average daily attendance.....	48991.4
Per cent. attended during quarter daily present on an average	62.9
New Pupils attended fourth quarter	9010
Enrolled pupils who did not attend fourth quarter	15475
Days taught *first* half year (one quarter)	119825.5
" *second* half year (two quarters)...........	228051.5
Total days' attendance *first* half year (one quarter)......	2800799.5
" " *second* half year (two quarters)....	4990577.5
No. of Pupils under *five* years of age (1st Aug. 1892)	1221
No. between *five* and *fifteen* years " "	85990
No. over *fifteen* years (1st Aug., 1892)	9688
Total Annual Enrolment ....:................	94899
No. of Boys	49775
" Girls	45124
Total days' attendance for year	7824166
Days' taught during year...........................	349020.5
Daily present on an average during year	50103.5
Average of quarterly percentages of attendance........	63.5
No. of Pupils who have attended 20 days or less........	10531
" " " " " over 20 and up to 50 days	19665
" " " " " " 50 " 100 "	26553
" " " " " " 100 " 150 "	30494
" " " " 150 days.........	7656

No. of Pupils belonging to Section 90959
  "   " from beyond limits of Section 3940
  " Deaf and Dumb not attending Institution in Halifax 70
  Blind   "   "   "   " 10

6.—VISITATION AND PRIZES.

No. of Visits by Trustees and Secretary 8011
  "   "   " Inspectors and other School Officials.... 2865
  "   "   " other Visitors........................ 26963
  " Parents and visitors at Public Examination 17312
  " Prizes awarded 1760
Value of Prizes awarded............................ $791.53

7.—SECTION STATISTICS.

Value of all School Property belonging to Sections.
    (Not including the City of Halifax)*........$ 1,032,890.42
Valuation of Property in Section according to last as-
    sessment roll 73,848,513.00
Total amount voted at last annual meeting for all School
    purposes.............................. 413,448.85
Amount voted for building and repairs.............. 95,687.09
  " of Teachers' Salaries paid during year by sec-
    tions, (not including Provincial Grants)...... 279,355.00
No. of Volumes in the School Libraries.............. 4183
  " Wall Maps, Charts and Globes................ 7108
Value of all Scientific Apparatus and Collections...... 6,577.65
Value of total Literary and Scientific equipment...... 28,728.36

8.—CLASSIFICATION OF PUPILS.

No. of Pupils in Kindergarten....................... 898
  "   "   " Grade I 17122
  "   "   "   " II 12515
  "   "   "   " III......................... 11653
  "   "   "   " IV 12283
  "   "   "   " V.......................... 10566
  "   "   "   " VI.......................... 9296
  "   "   "   " VII 9831
  "   "   "   " VIII 6361
  "   "   "   " IX 2506
  "   "   "   " X 1206
  "   "   "   " XI 497
  "   "   "   " XII 37
  "   " not " graded " (Errors) 127
Total pupils in Public Schools....................... 94899
No. ranked in the Teachers' Registers as of High School Grade. 4246
No. of these rec'd High School rank in the County Academies. 1397

---

* The City of Halifax owns School property estimated at $184,000
  "   "   " rents   "   "   "   "   " 94,000

9. Average of the time given by all the Teachers in the Province during the past year, in both the Common and High Schools departments, to the following groups of subjects in the course of study :

Subject.	Minutes Per week.	Minutes Per Day.	Percentage.
English Language	571	114	44.2
Arithmetic	264.4	53	20.4
Writing and Drawing	136.9	28	10.7
Geography and History	189.5	38	14.7
Object Lessons on Nature	32.5	7	2.3
Book-keeping	30	6	2.1
Hygiene and Temperance	22.8	5	1.7
Moral and Patriotic Duties	21.8	4	1.6
Vocal Music	15.2	3	1.2
Calisthenics and Military Drill	9.3	2	.7

(Were the departments giving more or less time to some of the High School subjects excluded in this averaging process, it would appear that in the 2000 Common Schools of the Province the proportion of time given to such subjects as Reading, Writing and Arithmetic is actually greater than the general average given above, while the proportion given to such as Book-keeping, Geography and History is actually less.)

10.—TOTAL EXPENDITURE FOR PUBLIC EDUCATION.

*Provincial Grants	$166,040.49
County Funds	89,623.36
Section Vote	413,448.85
Total	$669,112.70

Three-fourths of the corresponding figures for the previous year of twelve months are as follows:

Provincial grants	$162,322.30
County Funds	90,095.81
Section Assessments	307,513.03
Total	$559,931.14

Part II. of this report contains the Statistical tables in detail.

TABLE I.

Table I. shows among other things that in the following counties there were practically no schools which required a second teacher to

---

* The "Nine months term" includes all the grants payable in twelve months under the heads of Night Schools (in session during the winter only), travelling expenses of Normal School Students (payable in June) Provincial Examinations (held in July), &c., which partly accounts for the greater comparative expenditure this year.

complete the term begun by another teacher, namely Annapolis, Cape Breton, Digby, Richmond, Shelburne, Victoria and Yarmouth. The following counties had the numbers set opposite them as the excess of the number of teachers employed over the number of schools in session:

Antigonish	7
Colchester	14
Cumberland	5
Guysboro'	5
Halifax	2
Hants	9
Inverness	4
Kings	12
Lunenburg	3
Pictou	7
Queens	2
Total	70

This appears to indicate that in about 70 sections, there was a change of teacher during the year. This is not so bad as the previous year, when nearly 800 teachers changed sections within the year.

TABLES II. & III.

By the subtraction of the analysis of class A., B. & C., in table III. from the totals in table II., a "time-of-service" analysis of class D. teachers can be obtained.

TABLE IV.

By deducting the "total on Register" at the end of one quarter from that of the succeeding quarter the number of new pupils who entered school during the latter quarter may be found. Thus it appears that 6117 new pupils entered school during the third quarter and 9010 during the fourth quarter.

By deducting the "No. attended" each quarter from the number "on register" during the same quarter will be found the number of pupils who left school during the previous quarters. Thus it appears that 7310 left school during the second quarter, and 8165 during the third quarter.

The observation of this drift into and out of the schools during the four quarters of the year will be more instructive in future years, when the first quarter will not be missing as on the present occasion.

TABLE V.

It must not be assumed that the numbers given in the column "under five years of age" attended school while under five years of age. The ages recorded in the register are for the 1st of August—the first day of the school year. At the end of the school year each pupil is exactly one year older than the age inscribed when registered. The recording of the exact age of each pupil on a given day is deemed of importance for several objects, one of which is yet only prospective.

Attendance.—The following is a statement of the registration of pupils from 1866 to 1893 inclusive :—

Years.	No. of Pupils registered in Winter.	No. of Pupils registered in Summer.	No. different Pupils registered during the year.
1866	45131	56017	71059
1867	61818	70075	83048
1868	65983	72141	88707
1869	72756	75523	93732
1870	74321	76237	94496
1871	74759	77235	92858
1872	70780	76496	91637
1873	70320	78266	93759
1874	72645	79910	93510
1875	76349	81878	94029
1876	77593	82034	94162
1877	80788	83941	100710
1878	81523	84169	101538
1879	81640	84356	99094
1880	73978	78808	93700
1881	77468	80189	98148
1882	76888	81196	95912
1883	79091	81863	98307
1884	80041	84266	101069
1885	81472	86578	103288
1886	84570	86858	105410
1887	84217	86731	105137
1888	82486	86582	105231
1889	82371	86488	103688
1890	82794	88170	103597
1891	81304	85792	101724
1892	82965	87189	102586
1893	(Three-fourths of year.)		94899

TABLE VI.

Owing to the failure of the City of Halifax to report promptly the number of children within its bounds between the ages of 5 and 15, the sum total of these as estimated for the whole province could not be tabulated. The same remark applies to the next column, "number of these children who did not attend school during the year." Assuming that the number between 5 and 15 in Halifax is only a little over 7,000, we shall then have for the province over 92,000 children between these ages. Assuming the number of those not attending the public schools in the City to follow the same law o proportion as is found in the rest of the province, about 9,000 between

5 and 15 did not attend school during the past year. That will give
about 83,000 of this class as attending the public schools. But from
table V. about 86,000 were actually enrolled at school. Has the
census of the sections been taken carelessly? We c.n hardly think
many trustees would be found who would certify roughly guessed
figures to be solemn, statistical truth. This apparent discrepancy may
be due to the 3,000 and odd who are attending from outside the
section, as shown in another column of the table. But are there
9,000 who have not attended school at all? Nearly ten per cent. of
the children of school age! And of those who attended there are
over 10,000 who have been in school less than 20 days in the nine
months of this school term, and about 20,000 more who attended less
than 50 days. These are some of the facts which the new statistics
are discovering for us. When these figures are seen to refer to
children between the ages of 5 and 15, it will be readily understood
that the young people of our province are not yet all over-educated.
We have a general "compulsory attendance law" on the Statutes, but
it is practically useless. The burden of introducing the Act into the
section is left to local action. It would be better if the privilege of
exemption from the operation of such an Act should have been left to
local option. Then again, the present general Act is operative only
to a very partial extent, and then in such a manner as to throw a
certain amount of odium on those who attempt to enforce it.

Elaborate special legislation has been successfully introduced into
the school system of Halifax and later into Dartmouth. In Halifax,
children between the ages of 7 and 14, who are able to attend school,
must attend some school, private if not public, and the Supervisor is
required to inspect such private schools to see that the education given
attains at least a prescribed minimum. Even the employers of children
within the said age limits have been fined for thus encouraging them
to evade the law. In Dartmouth the effect of the special Act in one
term is thus shown by Principal Miller :

Registration, 1892, was .... 1074.
For same period 1893 was.................... 1200.

Percentage of attendance, 1892, was.............. 68
     "   "   1893, " 80

Average attendance, 1892, was 38
     "   "   1893, " 44

I am not yet ready to recommend so complicated a law for the whole
province as is found so beneficial in the sections named. Something
simpler may perhaps be found nearly as effective. Something which,
without being offensive, will always be fair, and which will always
act in proportion to the neglect of the school privileges provided.

TABLE VII.

In the City of Halifax, the estimated value of the school property
owned by the public school authorities is given in a note elsewhere as
$184,000 ; while the *rented* school property is put down at $96,000,

Adding in the former figure, we find the estimated value of property owned by school boards throughout the province to be $1,216,890.42. Adding in the rented property also, we have in Halifax, school property worth $280,000 ; and in the province, $1,312,890.42.

TABLE VIII.

The chief use of this table is not for its summary in this Report ; but for the purpose of allowing the Inspectors and other visitors of the schools to know the extent to which the teacher's time is absorbed in the various subjects of the course of study.

The difficulty found by many of the teachers in filling up this time-table illustrates the necessity of it. If the teacher himself cannot give a correct account of the manner in which he spends his school time, what idea can his trustees, his Inspector, or the Education department have of the matter ? The manner in which some of these time-tables have been filled in, shows, that if our teachers as a whole are improving, there are some in the ranks who should not be there. Unless we can have some method better than the ordinary written examination for estimating common sense and honesty, it will be necessary to have legislation compelling all teachers to pass the gauntlet of practical work in a Normal School, or to cut down the Provincial Grant one or more grades for evidence of carelessness, dishonesty or incapacity, as shown in the school work before the Inspector, or by the Register or Return.

Some of the returns suggest the suspicion, that the teacher having no confidence in the actual apportionment of his time, entered an ideal apportionment, such as would be thought to commend itself to the educational authorities above. At least such is the most charitable conclusion we can come to, when meeting with an apportionment of time which could not be tolerated under any conceivable conditions, and was certainly never carried out in effect. The plea of stupidity might save some of these cases from coming under the head of perjury, during the first term of its introduction. Inspectors cannot condone hereafter such looseness on the part of any teacher.

I arrange here in order of magnitude the average number of minutes given per week to each subject of the Common School curriculum in all the schools of the Province according to this table. But as a few of these schools are High School departments, and as many "miscellaneous" schools do a little High School work, we shall have this average affected in the direction of the High School studies. Book-keeping, History and Geography, to which more time is given in the High Schools, will therefore be a little larger than an average confined to Common School departments only. While on the other hand, the average time given to subjects not specially taken up in the High Schools will be less in this table than if based on the Common Schools alone. In the first column I give the maximum county average, then the minimum county average, then the average of all the counties (the provincial average), and lastly the percentage of time given to each subject.

Average number of minutes per week taken by teachers in the school-room during the year in the following Common School subjects:

	Max. Co. Average.	Min. Co. Average.	Prov. Average.	Per-centage.
Reading and Elocution	418.	86.9	311.9	24.1
Arithmetic	340.	28.	264.4	20.4
Spelling and Dictation	209.	67.6	151.0	11.7
English Comp., Gram., Lit., &c.	138.6	68.	108.1	8.4
Geography	149.	61.3	106.9	8.3
Writing	139.5	67.6	100.3	7.8
History	115.	47.4	82.6	6.4
Drawing	65.	15.7	36.9	2.9
Object Lessons on Nature	52.	21.	32.5	2.5
Book-keeping	74.1	13.	30.0	2.3
Hygiene and Temperance	32.	15.9	22.8	1.7
Moral and Patriotic Duties	34.	15.8	21.8	1.6
Vocal Music	52.	5.2	15.2	1.2
Calisthenics & Military Drill	45.	4.	9.3	.7

A glance over the table from which these figures are taken will arouse the suspicion that it is possible there are mistakes which should not be credited to the few blundering teachers referred to. I make these observations in the hope of securing accuracy in every individual return by next year as they have undoubtedly been in the overwhelming majority of cases this first year.

He is not fit to be a teacher who will yet come to the conclusion that the apportionment of time in his school for each of these subjects should be necessarily near that of the Provincial average. Some departments must give time to High School work.

Over 1600 of our schools are not required to do any appreciable work beyond the Common School grades. Some 500 more are required to spend a little time on more advanced work for a few pupils. About 100 more are required to provide for one or more classes of High School grade with some Common School classes. While there are at least over 50 schools or departments doing only High School work.

It must be remembered then, 1st, that the apportionment of time for each subject in these various schools must be very different; 2nd,—that the apportionment of time in even pure Common School must be as a general rule as diverse as the numbers and characters of the pupils attending them;—and 3rd,—even in the same school, and under the same teacher, the apportionment of time, may be required to change from year to year, to produce the best results.

The Education department does not require, does not suggest, that teachers should adopt any other division of time than that which the particular character of their schools demands from them in order to do their best work. The department wishes to know, however, what time each teacher has found best in his particular school. In other words, the Educational authorities want to know the facts, without which there can be no accurate knowledge of the state of Education.

TABLE IX.

A summary of this table has already been given in an earlier portion of this report. It must be remembered that this classification is the work of the teachers. It is approximate. With many teachers there will, no doubt, be a weakness in the direction of estimating their pupils at too high a grade. This tendency will soon be checked or measured in the case of High Schools generally and County Academies in particular, by the record of the Provincial Examination grades of Certificates held by their pupils. It is safe to estimate the *bona fide* pupils of High School grade at about three and a half per cent. Of these about two per cent. will be in Grade IX, about one per cent. in Grade X., and nearly one-half per cent in Grades XI. and XII.

TABLES X., XI., XII. & XIII.

As in the High School course of study options are allowed, it is necessary to have a yearly analysis of the number of students taking the various subjects, in order to measure the direction and rate of drift in the sentiment of our times with respect to the higher education.

TABLES XIV. & XV.

Some doubt as to whether the Academic grant should be classed as Provincial grant or as coming from the section, prevented the tabulation of these divisions in the case of class A teachers. The average total salaries are given, however. By the reduction of these tables and their comparison with the corresponding tables of last year, the general increase of salaries pointed out at the beginning of this report can be demonstrated.

TABLE XIX.

This table gives a full view of that specially subsidized class of High Schools denominated County Academies.

The dimensions of rooms, &c., are required to be given in the metrical system. To avoid decimal fractions the decimeter (a handbreath, nearly four inches), is used as the unit of measure. The reasons for using the metrical system in the Academic returns will be apparent later on to those who have not hitherto been paying attention to the subject.

TABLE XXI.

As the Provincial High School examination covers the ground of the late teachers' examinations, and as they are conducted on practically parallel lines, a few notes of comparison may be made.

Year.	Total Candidates.	Male Candidates.	Female Candidates.	A.	Received. B.	C.	D.	Failed.
1891...	1334	374	960	5	51	286	356	636
1892...	1431	372	1059	5	66	330	430	600
1893...	1506	505	1001	10	157	289	459	591

The examination proved comparatively more severe in the lower grades than in the higher. This was due chiefly, however, to the former neglect of the prescribed course of study, except so far as it was identical with the old syllabus of the teachers' examination. The remarkable success of a very great number of schools in the lower grades amply demonstrate the fairness of the examination questions. Next year all parts of the province, it is expected, will be more equally able to respond to a similar test.

On the whole, a larger number than usual came up to the examination, a larger number than usual was successful, and a less number than usual failed. That this should be the case at the first examination, after a rather radical change, evidently occurring earlier than expected by many, is very creditable to the teaching staff of the Province.

School Buildings.

While the increasing amounts voted at the annual meetings of the school sections for building and repairs, indicate general improvement in school premises, I have had the pleasure of seeing several buildings in process of construction during the year, which will, when completed, be superior to the best of the past in architectural design, sanitary conditions, and adaptation to the work to be done. The Amherst Academy and Public School Building is one of these. On a less expensive scale the Wolfville Public School is another. The New Glasgow High School will be another—probably unsurpassed in its adaptation to high school work. We must not, however, forget the pioneer movements, the inauguration of this period of architectural renaissance. Accordingly, we follow up the frontispiece view of the Provincial Normal School of last year, with one of the Halifax County Academy this year. Erected in 1878 as the Halifax Academy, it was and still is, one of the finest looking of our Public School buildings. In succeeding reports it is hoped the more notable of its successors will similarly figure in chronological order. At Bear River, on the border of Annapolis and Digby County, two good school sections re-formed themselves into one powerful section, and signalized the occasion by erecting a modern building, which a few years ago would do credit to our largest towns. Improved buildings, which I have not had the pleasure yet of personally inspecting, are also being erected in other sections of the Province.

The Provincial Normal School.

I refer you to the report of the Principal of this institution in Appendix A for fuller details. The attendance during the year was considerably increased over the preceding year. The work of the faculty was also greatly increased by the effort made to elastically accommodate the institution to the public needs during the strain of transition from the old to the new order. The programme outlined in my last report has been duly entered upon. Professor H. W. Smith has removed the apparatus of the old laboratory to the School of Agriculture, where it is supplemented by a finer equipment for biological and advanced chemical teaching than is to be found in most of our universities. For this work students will therefore attend the laboratories of the School of Agriculture. Professor Lee Russell, B. Sc., of the Worcester Polytechnic, Massachussets, after the successful inauguration of Manual Training in wood-work in connection with the Halifax Public Schools, was transferred to the Normal School, the City of Halifax henceforward assuming full responsibility for the support of its own Manual Training Department. The Laboratory has been refitted for the teaching of Practical Chemistry and Physics under Mr. Russell, while a neighboring room has been fitted up as a work shop, with twenty-four model benches and tools, also under his charge.

Teachers have therefore ample opportunities to *understand* all sides of human activity; and this understanding will give them, it is hoped, more power over themselves, more power with the young, and a power at the same time stimulating in industrial directions, while not less effective in the direction of language and art.

Our Provincial Normal School has now, as will be seen on reference to its calendar, a large and experienced staff representing all sides of our educational work. The student, having already passed his general scholarship examination before admission, can devote his time wholly to professional studies. In addition to the general and critical review of all the subjects taught in our public schools, method and the history and science of education, provision has been made for doubling the amount of the teaching exercise of candidates under the eyes of the professors. Two class-rooms have been added to the two Model school-rooms for teaching practice. In addition to these, there is also a kindergarten department. With this word, I await the result of our first year's work, which should give some sign of what may be expected in the future.

HYGIENE AND TEMPERANCE.

In obedience to the Act of the Legislature, graded text-books in Hygiene and Temperance have been prescribed for the schools:— "Health Readers," Nos. 1 and 2, for the common school, and Martin's "The Human Body and the Effects of Narcotics," for the high school grades. The law is being promptly observed so far as reported to me, as all law should be. If experience should show that the law is not in every respect perfect, then the law should be repealed or amended, but until so repealed or amended, it is the duty of all to have the law strictly enforced. Hitherto, however, not a single complaint has been filed against the action of the law or its administration. Teachers are examined on Hygiene and Temperance when competing for professional certificates; and the approximate average time devoted to teaching the subject in every school in the land, must be recorded in the register, and sworn to in the teacher's return.   \

VISITATION OF COUNTY ACADEMIES.

Owing to the work entailed by the changes made in the law, and to the shortness of the school year, County Academies, except those whose right to the Provincial grant might be doubtful, were not officially visited. The usual tabular statement of visitations, there-fore, do not appear in my report for the present year.

The classing of these institutions for the purpose of distributing their provincial grants in proper proportions, will be made much more uniform and thorough by the present system of Provincial Examination. The Superintendent will be spared the impossible task of examining individually and accurately, all the students of these institutions. The individual examination will be confined to those having "local grading" only, those having provincial certificates being exempt, except so far as is necessary to indicate the general efficiency of the school, its methods, discipline and character as a whole. In the tabulation of these results, the comparative number of students of provincial and of simple local grading will be reckoned a very important character.—all the more as there is an examination station with free admission in proximity to every County Academy in the province.   .   .

And lastly it will be observed that the buildings, grounds, appar-atus and general environment which might be tolerated at the commencement of our academic development should not necessarily be tolerated any longer. This will be seen to be only justice, when sections receiving no academic grants provide superior facilities for educational work, while some County Academies draw provincial funds for doing only local work, and even that under conditions neither pleasant nor comfortable to their pupils and teachers, nor creditable to the province.

THE HIGHER AND TECHNICAL INSTITUTIONS.

Although it has not been customary in the past, it may be found desirable in future, to have this report cover all the educational work directed by governmental departments or ai led by provincial funds, so that the "Education Report" may henceforth give a glimpse of all the educational work being done under the provincial auspices. It would then be more generally known that the public school system, so called, is not all of our provincial educational work. The object lessons on Nature in our Common Schools, and the elements of science and manual training in the High Schools, find an advanced and special development in the Provincial School of Agriculture, the Provincial School of Horticulture, the schools for Miners, and the Halifax Medi-cal College.

Further, it may sometime appear desirable to cap the whole by
giving an analysis of the work done by the Colleges and Universities
working under provincial charter. It might not be fair to ask institutions not receiving any financial aid to report any financial figures or
estimates. But it might be mutually agreeable and valuable to both
these institutions and the general public to have an annual statement
of the educational work done, in some convenient form showing the
number of students, distinguishing between undergraduates, general
and special students, indicating the numbers taking the various
courses, whether in arts, science, medicine, law, or theology, &c. Thus
the "Education Report" might from year to year very conveniently
contain for reference a summary of all the more important provincial
educational statistics.

It may be asked, why not compile such a summary from the
different calendars of these institutions?   The answer may be suggested by the thought, that each compiler of these calendars is
working on a line of his own, which does not necessarily run parallel
in every part with that of the others. An approximate analysis
taken nearly entirely from the calendars, or some other supplementary publication, is as follows:

	th Year.	3rd Year.	2nd Year.	1st Year.	Total.	GENERAL AND SPECIAL STUDENTS.
Arts	22.	25.	21.	25.	93	152
"	21	23.	30.	34.	108	2
" (?)..	?	?	?	?	18	..
Letters..	1	0	0	1	2	..
Science .	2	1	2	3	8	24
Medicine.	8	5	8	20	41	..
Law		22	10	13	45	15
Theology	9	6	8	12	35	..
	63	82	79	108	350	193

Two other institutions do not distinguish clearly between students
of university and of academic grades.

From these figures we may conclude that approximately, Nova
Scotian colleges and universities during the past year, were attended
by 350 undergraduates taking a regular three or four years' course,
and 200 general or special students. At least half of these 200 were
doing full college work; on which assumption 450 students have
been doing full work in the colleges and universities of our province
—that is one per thousand of our total population. One hundred
and fifty more may safely be estimated to have been pursuing their
studies at colleges and universities beyond the Province, the great
majority at institutions beyond the Atlantic Provinces of Canada.

In round numbers, more than one out of every five of our people
attended school during the year as pupils of common school grade,

less than one out of a hundred as pupils of high school grade, one out of a thousand as college students, and one out of three thousand as students abroad.

THE WORLD'S FAIR EXHIBIT.

The coincidence of the time for preparing this exhibit with the introduction of the numerous changes in our educational system, placed both the Education Department and the schools of the province at a very great disadvantage. In most schools the time for preparing work for the exhibition was the very time in which they were making an effort to adjust themselves to the new order of things. It was not surprising then, that the optional intimations and directions bearing on the Fair and published in the August *Journal of Education*, should be practically unnoticed among the number of imperatives in which the Amended Acts and Regulations abounded.

In December, the following circular (which is quoted to explain the list of exhibits in the Appendix) was issued.

CIRCULAR TO INSPECTORS AND TEACHERS OF PUBLIC SCHOOLS AND PRINCIPALS OF ALL EDUCATIONAL INSTITUTIONS IN NOVA SCOTIA.

I am directed to make arrangements by which Educational work of all kinds in Nova Scotia will be as fully represented as possible at the World's Fair which opens next April in Chicago.

In order that the exhibit may be a credit to our province, and perhaps a stimulus or aid to other countries, it is most desirable that all educational institutions, whether under government control or not, should lend a helping hand and show the best they have in every department. The effort, besides being of general utility, will not be without its direct reward. The pressure of new duties arising from recent educational changes, and the shortness of the time at our disposal, make it necessary, if this work is to be successful, that it should have your prompt and hearty co-operation.

The real products of our institutions Nova Scotia cannot any more than other countries exhibit. But as others represent their systems, so we may ours. The general historical and statistical views will be prepared by this department; and our schools, academies and colleges can show something as comparable with their real work as the exhibits from the institutions of other States can with theirs—enough to enable the comparative educationist to compare the development of our country with others.

The public school law, regulations and courses of study, university calendars and their curricula, will be illustrated by photographs of buildings, of rooms and apparatus, by printed examination papers, and by specimens of pupils' or students' work, etc., so arranged as to emphasize in outlines the educational status of the province.

GENERAL PLAN OF SELECTING SCHOOL WORK FOR THE EXHIBITION.

The teacher may give an exercise to the whole school on each of the subjects mentioned in the lists below (so far as they may be taught in the particular school).   Before the 18th of February the teacher should have selected the *three* best of each exercise and have them transmitted to the Inspector of Schools (or, if not a public school, to the principal of the institution, who will rank for such purposes as an Inspector).   The Inspectors will from these materials select a certain percentage, to be determined by correspondence, and have it forwarded before the end of February to the Education Department.   After further selection, if necessary, and final arrangement, it will be forwarded to Chicago.   In order to stimulate a school, the three names carrying off the honors in each particular exercise might be formally announced to the school or published in the local papers.   Those selected by the Inspector would in like manner win corresponding honors within the inspectorate, while exercises sent forward by the Education Department would win for their schools provincial distinction.

NAMING.

☞ At the bottom of every page exhibit, and on every exhibit, there must be written in a plain and beautiful hand, and in two lines, the following facts :—

(1st line.)   Name, age and grade of the pupil.
(2nd line.)   Names of school and county.

Thus : { JAMES B. SMITH, 11 years, Grade VI.
        { Kiltarlity School, Inverness County.

SIZE OF PAPER.

☞ Except for special maps, charts, drawings and paintings, &c., which should be larger, all exercises or page exhibits must be on paper about 8½ by 11 inches, ("letter paper size"—not "note paper"). For many, if not most exercises, it would be better unruled.   This uniformity of size is required for convenience of mounting on wall surface or on larger cards, or for binding into volumes as may be found most effective.

PHOTOGRAPHS.

☞ Photographs should be sent unmounted, with name and place on the back in some corner for identification.   At Halifax these will be mounted by a photographer on large cards, 22 x 28 inches, where photographs of parts of the same building or related buildings may be grouped according to the size of the photographs on the card, which will be under glass in frames hinged vertically to special holders.

SOME SPECIFICATIONS OF WHAT IS DESIRED.

CLASS I.—KINDERGARTEN WORK.

(The Kindergartens cf the Province are already working on the lines laid down for them by the Kindergarten Committee.)

CLASS II.—COMMON SCHOOL WORK.

1. *Writing:* Copy books of each Grade.

2. *Drawing: (a)* Any design on paper of the regular size (about 8½ by 11 inches.) In the lower Grades the small, simple designs of primary pupils should be in the centre of the page. For all Grades.

(b) A mathematical drawing for the higher Grades to test accuracy and neatness. The following exercise is given for all :—"Draw a square decimeter divided into square centimeters."

3. *Maps:* Of size in text books or multiples of the size, on 8½x11 inch (regular) paper, or multiples of the size where convenient.

4. *Accounts:* Page of accounts or of any Commercial Forms. For higher Grades.

5. *Arithmetic:* A problem stated with model solution. For all Grades.

6. *Grammar:* Sentence analysed and parsed in model form and on one (regular) page. For higher Grades.

7. *Composition:* Model letter on one page. For all Grades.

8. *Music:* A School Song in the Tonic Sol-Fa or staff notation. For all Grades.

9. *Nature Lessons:* Illustrated (by a drawing) presentation or explanation of any object, fact or experiment in lessons on Nature, on one page. For higher Grades.

10. *Manual Work!* Sewing, etc. Wood-work, etc., School Apparatus, home-made.

11. *Collections:* Cabinets or collections of specimens illustrating Nature Lessons in Common Schools—or photographs of them.

CLASS III.—HIGH SCHOOL WORK.

(In each Grade, viz.:—IX., X., XI. and XII, or such Grades as may be in any school.)

1. *Book-keeping:* Set of Books.

2. *Composition:* Model Business letter (one page.)

3. *Stenography:* Phonography, &c., (one page.)

4. *Drawing:* (*a*) Books or page of Freehand or Object Drawing, Industrial Design, &c.
(*b*) Mathematical Drawings.
(*c*) Maps or Charts.

5. *Mathematics:* Statement of problem with model solution all on one page, in (*a*) Trigonometry, (*b*) Navigation, (*c*) Geometry, (*d*) Algebra, (*e*) Arithmetic, (*f*) Any other Math. Subject in each Grade.

6. *English:* Page of work, Exercise or Examination paper, on some English subject, in each Grade.

7. *Foreign Languages:* Page of work in Latin, French, Greek and German in each Grade.

8. *Natural Science:* Page of Chart with an illustration presenting or explaining some fact, theory or experiment in (*a*) Botany, (*b*) Mineralogy or Geology, (*c*) Zoology, (*d*) Physiology, (*e*) Chemistry, (*f*) Physics, (*g*) Any other cognate subject.

9. *Music:* School Song in Tonic Sol-Fa or staff notation.

10. *Manual Training:* Woodwork, &c., Modelling in Clay, &c, Embossed Maps, &c. Apparatus made by students, &c.

11. *Collections:* Cabinets, Models and Specimens for the illustrations of Natural Science subjects as in 8, or photographs of the same.

12. *Typography:* (*a*) Printed examination papers, (*b*) Collection of catalogues of courses of study, (*c*) A collection of papers published by the students, if any.

CLASS IV.—SPECIAL PROVINCIAL INSTITUTIONS.

(These are asked to prepare exhibits on lines parallel to those laid down for the High Schools, but with special reference to their own curricula. Exhibits from these institutions will be sent from their Principals direct to the Education Office.)

1. The Provincial Normal School.

2. The Provincial School of Agriculture.

3. The Victoria School of Art and Design.

4. The Institution for Deaf and Dumb.

5. The School for the Blind,

CLASS V.—INSTITUTIONS NOT UNDER GOVERNMENT CONTROL.

1. The Universities, including (*a*) Arts, (*b*) Sciences, (*c*) Medicine, (*d*) Theology, (*e*) Law &c.

2. Ladies' Colleges, Convents and Seminaries.

3. Commercial Colleges.

4. Any other Educational Institution.

The following notes having special reference to *Class V.* may equally apply to the other classes in some cases.

The following exhibits are most essential : ·

1. Calendars for the past year, or better, for several years, when the set may be bound by the Education Department in a handsome volume for each institution.

2. Photographs or plans of buildings, laboratories, libraries, museums, apparatus, etc.

3. Special, novel or interesting apparatus or collections of any kind.

4. Specimens of work of every kind which can be exhibited, characteristic of the work of the institution. *Theology*: pages of Greek, Hebrew, Syriac, fac-simile of Ancient Codices, etc., etc. *Medicine*: Anatomical preparations, inventions. *School of Agriculture*: Collections of insects, rusts, etc., affecting agriculture. *Mining Schools*: Plans of mines, examination questions, etc., etc. Paintings, modellings, sculpture, music, needlework, etc., etc., from convents and ladies' seminaries. Type-writing, stenography, commercial forms, etc., etc., of commercial colleges. The peculiar books, apparatus and appliances for teaching the Deaf and Dumb and the Blind, with specimens of their work, etc.

5. Volumes of Students' publications, of all kinds.

☞ Exhibits will be carefully returned, free of expense, after the exhibition is over, to all who request it. The Education Department assumes the expense of transmission, final arrangement and installation of all exhibits sent to the Department.

* ☞ It is intended to publish a special report of the Nova Scotian Educational Exhibits in pamphlet form, which will at the same time serve as a Catalogue for general distribution, and show the institutions, schools represented, and the successful competitors in each kind of work.

---

* Owing to the unexpected loss of time caused by the transportation service of the World's Fair, and the backward state of the buildings, the Advisory Commissioner for Nova Scotia had to return as soon as the installation of the exhibit was completed, without waiting to compile and publish the proposed catalogue. In his report (Appendix E.) he therefore publishes a compilation of the lists descriptive of the material sent, which will serve the purpose of a record, as well as for the description of the exhibit. This explains the non-appearance of the catalogue in the pamphlet descriptive of the educational system and institutions of the province distributed at the Exposition.

Although the 18th of February is fixed as the limit of time, it is desirable that as much material as possible should be sent in earlier—say, during the month of January. Most of the work required can be prepared at short notice and in a few days, and should not be delayed. And it is hoped that a generous devotion to our educational interests will be shown by all educational institutions in preparing and forwarding the more valuable although not so easily obtainable exhibits.

I am, Your obedient servant,

A. H. MacKAY,

EDUCATION OFFICE,   *Superintendent of Education.*

Halifax, N. S., Dec. 12th. 1892.

Many sections of the country responded promptly and creditably to this appeal. To the energy of Inspectors as well as to the character of of the teachers, this result was no doubt due. From the well selected material sent to this department, it was not found necessary to make another selection, as on account of the reserve of very many sections of the province, the volume of material was not excessive. This allowed the sending on to Chicago, of *all* the material transmitted to Halifax. According to the general instructions issued under the authority of the Director of the Fair, the excess of material after the exhibition space was filled, was kept in drawers to replace every month or two exhibits becoming dusty and air-stained on the walls.

Your government was fortunate in securing as advisory commissioner, Alexander McKay, Esq., the Supervisor of the Public Schools in Halifax, to instal the Educational and Mineral exhibit at Chicago. After very considerable anxiety, trouble, and loss of valuable time, owing first to the railway blockade, and secondly to the unfinished state of the buildings when he arrived, the exhibit was finally installed in the most effective manner. Such has been the unanimous opinion expressed by the ablest judges, and such would I expect from a man who has had the most successful experience in the development of much of the best educational work in this province, and who has had also probably more extensive experience than any other in educational exhibitions. From the semi-official reports coming to this office, he has undoubtly made the best disposition of the material sent, for the credit and honor of the province.

For further details I refer you to Appendix E, where the full report of the Advisory Commissioner appears.

From Sydney to Yarmouth, the schools which took part in the competition have been, so far as reported by their teachers, beneficially stimulated. Some have spoken very enthusiastically of the unexpected benefit resulting from their efforts. On the other hand, the province has done its duty in taking its place among greater provinces and states ; and in doing its duty, I am glad to say, it has lost no prestige.

In conclusion, I refer you to the appendices among which will be found reports from Inspectors, &c., and from the institutions closely related to the public free school system of the province.

The more imperative duties of the Education Department during the year has entirely prohibited the mature consideration of several matters which might otherwise have been already determined. In the coming year there will be much to deliberate upon; but time is always bringing in new facts and experiences to contribute to the ensuring of right action.

I have the honor to be,

Your obedient servant,

A. H. MacKAY.
Superintendent of Education.

PART II.

STATISTICAL TABLES.

PUBLIC SCHOOLS, COUNTY ACADEMIES, &c.

TABLE I.—School Sections, &c. (General.)

Nova Scotia, Year (Nine Months) Ended July, 1893.

Counties	Total No. of School Sections.	No. of Sections without School any part of the year.	Total No. of Schools in Session during any part of year.	No. of Schools in Session 50 days or under.	Over 50 and up to 100 days.	Over 100 and up to 150 days.	Over 150 and under full term.	Full year of 168 days.	Average No. of days all schools were in Session.	No. of Teachers.	No. of Licensed Assistants.	No. of Teachers holding Normal School Diploma.	No. of pupils registered at School during year.	Proportion of Population (census of 1891) at School during year.	No. School Libraries.	No. School Scientific Collections.
Annapolis	106	14	110	1	5	7	56	41	155.2	110	0	25	4277	1 in 4.5		
Antigonish	81	6	89	1	2	11	49	26	155.2	96	1	2	3582	1 " 4.5	4	4
Cape Breton	131	19	161	2	1	21	53	84	157.	161		17	6848	1 " 5.	3	2
Colchester	122	6	146	2	2	14	77	51	129.2	160	2	68	5875	1 " 4.6	2	6
Cumberland	157	18	181	3	7	21	112	38	153.	186	1	75	8181	1 " 4.2	1	3
Digby	81	10	97	1	1	1	45	43	158.9	97	1	17	4501	1 " 4.4		2
Guysboro	88	14	85	1	1	24	26	33	149.9	90		2	3589	1 " 4.8		
Halifax Co	131	15	142	5	10	15	65	47	132.	144	1	23	6003	1 " 5.3	9	2
Halifax City	1		129		2	2		125	164.6	126		31	7133	1 " 5.4	2	
Hants	104	7	122	3	8	10	54	52	156.8	131		45	4948	1 " 4.3	19	50
Inverness	175	22	163	5	7	22	78	46	147.	157	11	7	5439	1 " 4.7	14	12
Kings	104	3	122	3	2	10	60	47	157.	134	3	23	5159	1 " 4.3	21	2
Lunenburg	143	8	171		6	11	72	82	157.5	174	1	28	7312	1 " 4.2	18	4
Pictou	128	5	167	1	5	5		156	160.	174	1	20	6971	1 " 5.	1	1
Queens	46	6	54		2	4	21	27	159.	96		5	1999	1 " 5.8	2	3
Richmond	70	9	70	4	3	13	19	31	147.2	70	1	5	2730	1 " 5.2		
Shelburne	67	8	77	1		5	46	25	160.	77		3	3374	1 " 4.4		
Victoria	94	26	68	3	4	9	30	22	146.	68		4	2221	1 " 5.5	1	2
Yarmouth	74	5	108	1	4	8	55	40	156.	108	1	18	4557	1 " 4.6	4	3
Total, 1893....	1904	196	2252	37	67	219	913	1016	152.7	2319	24	408	94899	1 " 4.7	89	96

TABLE II.—Teachers Employed (Classification and Analysis.)

Nova Scotia, Year (Nine Months) Ended July, 1893.

COUNTIES	MALE							FEMALE							TOTAL		
	A (cl. & sc.)	A (cl.)	A (sc.)	First-Class—B.	Second-Class—C.	Third-Class—D.	Third (Prov.)—D.	A (cl. & sc.)	A (cl.)	A (sc.)	First-Class—B.	Second-Class—C.	Third-Class—D.	Third (Prov.)—D.	Males.	Females.	Total.
Annapolis		3		14	12	2					10	40	30		30	80	110
Antigonish		4		5	21	14					2	23	27		44	52	96
Cape Breton		4		20	26	23					7	42	39		73	88	161
Colchester		3		7	9	1					18	72	51		19	141	160
Cumberland		3		8	9	2					10	93	61		22	164	186
Digby		1		10	4	6					6	25	45		21	76	97
Guysboro		1		4	5	4			1		4	32	40		14	76	90
Halifax Co.		1		3	7	2					7	76	48		13	131	144
" City		4		10	1			1			35	71	4		15	111	126
Hants		1		10	7	3					17	69	24		21	110	131
Inverness		3		16	33	44					1	20	40		96	61	157
King's		3		14	14	2					16	57	29		32	102	134
Lunenburg		3		6	5	3					4	68	86		16	158	174
Picton				13	14	8			1		11	83	38		41	133	174
Queens		3		3	4						3	28	16		9	47	56
Richmond				9	22	12						12	15		43	27	70
Shelburne		2		4	5	3					6	36	21		14	63	77
Victoria		3		1	13	17					1	12	22		33	35	68
Yarmouth		3		12	5	6			1		11	39	31		26	82	108
Total, 1893		45		169	216	152			3		169	898	667		582	1737	2319

TABLE II.—TEACHERS EMPLOYED (CLASSIFICATION AND ANALYSIS).—Continued.

Nova Scotia, Year (Nine Months) Ended July, 1893.

COUNTIES	Licensed Assistants — Males	Licensed Assistants — Females	New Teachers	Old Teachers, but new to Section	Teachers continued in same section as previous year	No. whose total service was one year or under	Over one and up to two years	Over two and up to three years	Over three and up to four years	Over four and up to five years	Over five and up to seven years	Over seven and up to ten years	Over ten and up to fifteen years	Over fifteen and up to twenty years	Over twenty years
Annapolis			20	43	42	22	14	10	13	11	9	7	9	8	7
Antigonish	1		10	32	54	10	21	18	14	4	7	11	5	2	9
Cape Breton		2	18	49	94	21	19	14	16	17	16	11	22	13	6
Colchester		1	16	82	62	34	17	15	25	25	19	15	5	2	12
Cumberland			34	84	68	39	21	44	19	15	23	10	7	5	3
Digby		1	16	31	50	17	12	13	11	9	8	9	12	3	3
Guysboro			7	34	49	14	14	14	11	9	11	8	4	2	3
Halifax Co.		1	10	58	76	10	15	19	29	14	16	16	14	6	8
" City			4	6	116	4	10	3	11	10	21	15	25	13	5
Hants		7	18	58	55	17	14	18	18	16	22	16	16	3	4
Inverness	4	2	9	89	59	9	18	18	19	16	25	19	13	6	11
Kings	1	1	25	62	47	30	19	16	8	7	20	11	13	7	8
Lunenburg		1	29	54	91	84	25	23	16	16	26	16	18	8	3
Pictou			30	68	76	83	40	18	15	12	20	12	18	5	2
Queens			10	17	29	11	10	12	7	2	4	5	2	1	6
Richmond		1	7	25	38	7	6	11	11	8	7	12	6	1	2
Shelburne			11	36	30	4	14	17	9	5	18	6	4		5
Victoria			3	37	28	3	10	8	14	6	11	8	5		4
Yarmouth		1	11	40	57	6	13	10	10	14	14	15	18	3	3
Total, 1893	6	18	288	910	1121	325	312	301	276	211	295	220	199	85	95

TABLE III.—Teachers Employed (Analysis of First and Second Classes.)
Nova Scotia, Year (Nine Months) Ended July, 1893.

COUNTIES.	Classes A & B.—Males.								Classes A & B.—Females.							
	Service one year or under.	Over one and up to three years.	Over three and up to five years.	Over five and up to seven years.	Over seven and up to ten years.	Over ten and up to fifteen years.	Over fifteen and up to twenty years.	Over twenty years.	Service one year or under.	Over one and up to three years.	Over three and up to five years.	Over five and up to seven years.	Over seven and up to ten years.	Over ten and up to fifteen years.	Over fifteen and up to twenty years.	Over twenty years.
Annapolis		2	4	1	1			5		3	2	2	1	1	1	
Antigonish		3	1	1	2	6	4	6		1	1	4	2	1		
Cape Breton	2		5	1		6	2	1	1	1	5	1	2	1		1
Colchester	1		2	4		1	2	1	3	2	3	1	2	2		
Cumberland		1	2	1			1			1	1	1				
Digby	1	5	1			2	1			2	1		1	1		
Guysboro			1		3	3	3	1	2	1	5	5	5	9		
Halifax Co.		1	3	2	3	5	3	4		2	7	2	1	1	2	
" City		1	4	3	1	5	1		3	6						
Hants		1					1	3	2	1	7	1	2	1		
Inverness	3	1	2	1		2	2	1	1	2	1	2	1	4		
Kings		1	3	1	1	2	1	4		1	2		1	1		
Lunenburg		1		1		1	1	2		3	1					
Pictou	3	6		1		1	1	3	1		4					
Queens		1		1			1			2						
Richmond			1	1	2	1	1	2		3	3	1	1	2	1	1
Shelburne	1	2	1	1		1	1									
Victoria			1	1		1	1	3		1	4		3			1
Yarmouth		2	3	1	2	3	1	2	3	1	3	3		2		
Total	10	33	36	24	16	35	26	34	11	35	44	23	24	24	4	7

TABLE III.—Teachers Employed, (Analysis of First and Second Classes).—(Continued).

Nova Scotia, Year (Nine Months) Ended July, 1893.

Class C.—Males.

Counties	Service one year or under.	Over one and up to three years.	Over three and up to five years.	Over five and up to seven years.	Over seven and up to ten years.	Over ten and up to fifteen years.	Over fifteen and up to twenty years.	Over twenty years.
Annapolis	5	2	1	1	—	—	2	—
Antigonish	—	8	4	—	1	2	1	2
Cape Breton	1	5	6	1	1	4	1	2
Colchester	1	1	5	3	1	1	1	—
Cumberland	1	3	1	1	1	1	1	—
Digby	—	—	3	1	1	—	—	—
Guysboro	1	3	—	—	—	—	1	1
Halifax Co.	1	1	1	1	—	2	—	—
Halifax City	3	4	—	—	4	—	3	3
Hants	1	8	5	4	1	—	1	1
Inverness	5	3	—	2	—	4	—	—
Kings	1	3	1	—	1	—	3	1
Lunenburg	2	7	2	1	—	—	—	1
Pictou	1	2	—	—	3	—	—	1
Queens	1	7	5	3	—	—	—	—
Richmond	—	1	—	1	3	—	—	1
Shelburne	1	1	5	1	—	3	1	1
Victoria	—	4	—	—	—	3	1	1
Yarmouth	—	—	—	—	—	—	—	1
Total, 1893	**25**	**63**	**39**	**20**	**17**	**20**	**16**	**16**

Class C.—Females.

Counties	Service one year or under.	Over one and up to three years.	Over three and up to five years.	Over five and up to seven years.	Over seven and up to ten years.	Over ten and up to fifteen years.	Over fifteen and up to twenty years.	Over twenty years.
Annapolis	8	10	8	3	4	5	1	1
Antigonish	1	9	4	4	—	3	—	2
Cape Breton	4	8	8	5	7	8	1	1
Colchester	10	13	20	13	10	3	1	2
Cumberland	14	35	16	14	3	7	3	1
Digby	2	5	7	4	2	1	2	2
Guysboro	1	11	6	5	3	1	—	2
Halifax Co.	4	14	18	15	8	8	4	3
Halifax City	6	5	11	13	9	13	10	8
Hants	2	17	18	14	8	4	3	1
Inverness	4	4	3	13	6	2	—	—
Kings	1	16	4	11	7	4	4	1
Lunenburg	8	16	14	14	8	5	3	1
Pictou	10	23	17	2	7	6	2	1
Queens	13	12	5	—	2	1	—	—
Richmond	6	3	1	5	4	1	—	2
Shelburne	1	13	7	3	3	3	1	2
Victoria	2	1	2	4	3	1	—	1
Yarmouth	2	7	7	5	6	7	3	2
Total, 1893	**99**	**222**	**176**	**147**	**100**	**83**	**38**	**33**

TABLE IV.—ATTENDANCE, (QUARTERS).
Nova Scotia, Year (Nine Months) Ended July, 1893.

COUNTIES.	SECOND QUARTER.				THIRD QUARTER.				FOURTH QUARTER.			
	Total on register at end of quarter.	No. attended during quarter.	Average daily attendance.	Per cent. of those attended during quarter or daily present on an average.	Total on register at end of quarter.	No. attended during quarter.	Average daily attendance.	Per cent. attended during quarter daily present on an average.	Total on register at end of quarter.	No. attended during quarter.	Average daily attendance.	Per cent. attended during quarter daily present on an average.
Annapolis	3613	3613	2355.	65.2	3846	3528	2205.2	62.5	4241	3477	2253.9	64.8
Antigonish	2684	2684	1553.1	57.8	3002	2765	1686.3	60.9	3483	2732	1617.6	59.2
Cape Breton	5521	5521	3306.	59.8	6059	5499	4381.	79.6	6823	5642	3272.9	58.
Colchester	4898	4898	3212.3	65.3	5232	4701	3024.1	64.2	5792	4926	3004.4	60.2
Cumberland	6451	6451	3964.7	61.4	7027	6248	3871.8	61.9	8131	6591	4086.5	61.2
Digby	3660	3660	2333.5	63.5	4059	3757	2267.8	60.1	4496	3754	2417.6	64.4
Guysboro	2700	2700	1657.7	61.4	3101	2873	1710.3	59.5	3357	2685	1568.2	58.4
Halifax County	5031	5001	3877.	67.1	5434	4946	3254.	65.7	6003	5164	3660.	70.8
" City	6335	6335	4574.4	71.	6448	6117	4195.6	68.	6830	6409	4682.4	73.
Hants	4033	4033	2557.	63.4	4387	3879	2448.6	64.9	4918	4147	2683.7	64.7
Inverness	4275	4275	2282.	53.	4807	4467	2558.	57.	5412	4796	2482.	51.7
Kings	4250	4250	2709.4	63.7	4444	3949	2463.3	62.4	5018	3799	2362.6	62.2
Lunenburg	6205	62C5	3982.4	64.2	6734	6239	3812.8	61.1	7153	5053	3450.8	61.
Pictou	5983	5983	3869.4	64.8	6271	5684	3689.5	63.8	6814	5888	3839.6	64.9
Queens	1727	1727	1166.9	67.5	1834	1657	1075.8	64.9	1940	1573	1053.2	66.6
Richmond	2179	2179	1376.4	63.1	2289	2042	1284.8	62.9	2625	2221	1226.9	55.2
Shelburne	2892	2892	1885.	65.1	3034	2846	1727.	60.6	3374	2699	1805.	66.8
Victoria	1624	1624	936.	57.6	1834	1647	1054.	64.	2118	1734	1007.	58.
Yarmouth	4060	4060	2799.	68.9	4446	4084	2618.	63.9	4720	3883	2567.	66.1
Total	78121	78121	49887.2	63.8	84238	78928	49292.9	64.	93248	77773	48991.4	62.9

TABLE V.—ATTENDANCE, (SEMI-ANNUAL AND ANNUAL.)

Nova Scotia, Year (Nine Months) Ended July, 1893.

COUNTIES.	Days taught first half year.	Days taught second half year.	Total days' attendance first half year.	Total days' attendance second half year.	Under 5 years of age.	Between 5 and 15 years.	Over 15 years.	Total annual enrolment.	Boys.	Girls.	Total days' attendance for year.	Days taught during year.	Daily present on an average during year.	Average or quarterly percentage of attendance.
Annapolis	5872.5	11206.	129939.	237308.	75	3726	476	4277	2229	2048	366645	17078.5	2806.4	64.2
Antigonish	4881	8975.	85592.	174763.	20	3109	403	3532	1937	1595	258355	18756	1535.6	59.1
Cape Breton	8547.5	16734.	185054.	348832.	79	6280	489	6848	3685	3163	533886	25281	3461.7	65.8
Colchester	7827.5	14952.5	182372.	310421.	53	5329	493	5875	3048	2827	502044	29771	3142.3	63.2
Cumberland	9250	18455.5	221684.5	414128.5	91	7405	635	8131	4195	3936	635763	27706	4022.8	61.4
Digby	5170	10242.5	128270.	247867.	77	4035	389	4501	2328	2173	376137	15412.5	2343.6	62.5
Guysboro	4073	8387	85852.	169181.	34	3293	262	3589	1947	1642	263644	19785	1736	59.6
Halifax County	7080	14080.	195736.	249508.	125	5646	232	6003	3459	2944	445244	21160	3707	67.9
Halifax City	7881	12757.	275907.	459920.	81	6754	298	7133	3572	3561	738270	20638	4573.7	70.6
Hants	6464	12668.	145204.	267615.	47	4482	419	4948	2567	2381	412810	19182	2630.2	64.3
Inverness	7564	14927	129779.	267557.	34	4845	560	5439	3011	2428	397336	22491	2555	53.9
Kings	6672.5	12485.5	152663.	255398.	48	4366	745	5159	2759	2400	408061	19158	2555.9	62.8
Lunenburg	9829.5	17587	223645.	385734.	187	6646	479	7812	3783	3529	609379	26916.5	3798.5	62.1
Picton	9352:	17295.5	217588.	387948.	42	6335	594	6971	3725	3246	617175	26712.5	3799.2	64.5
Queens	2929	5650.5	65584.	118168.	29	1775	195	1999	1000	999	178751	8579.5	1064.9	66.4
Richmond	3493	6813.	66379.	134002.	29	2548	153	2730	1504	1226	200462	10806	1857.7	60.4
Shelburne	4210.5	8080.5	99925.	191492.	55	3077	242	3374	1783	1591	291417	12292	1807	64.2
Victoria	3414	6764.	57623.	95012.	25	1998	198	2221	1141	1080	163331	9960	1017	59.9
Yarmouth	5844	10991.	154714.	270733.	90	4341	426	4857	2502	2355	425447	16035	2717	66.3
Total 1893	11982.5	228051.5	2800799.5	4990577.5	1221	85990	7688	94899	49775	45124	7824166	349020.5	50103.5	63.5

TABLE VI.—STATISTICS, (VARIOUS).

Nova Scotia, Year (Nine Months) Ended July, 1893.

COUNTIES.	20 days or less.	Over 20 and up to 50 days.	Over 50 and up to 100 days.	Over 100 and up to 150 days.	Over 150 days.	Belonging to this School Section.	From beyond limits of Section.	No. of children in the Section from 5 to 15 years of age.	No. of those who did not attend school at all during the year.	Deaf	Blind	No. of visits by Trustees and Secretary.	No. of visits by Inspector and other school officials.	No. of visits by other visitors.	No. of Parents and visitors at Public Examination.	No. of prizes awarded.	Value of Prizes awarded.
Annapolis	358	866	1275	1399	379	4106	171	4009	272	2		273	167	1831	604	47	$ 27.00
Antigonish	492	837	1101	981	171	3218	314	3180	234	3		461	113	982	398	114	25.50
Cape Breton	954	1424	2178	2123	169	6523	325	6754	672	9	3	886	246	1696	2019	142	142.50
Colchester	614	1197	1667	1859	538	5581	294	4671	288	2	2	396	153	1399	1040	147	54.35
Cumberland	1030	1893	2291	2842	575	7805	326	7761	533	3		548	214	1948	1088	62	34.85
Digby	408	908	1389	1450	346	4370	131	4569	494	2		296	118	1044	466	49	21.62
Guysboro	588	826	1020	971	184	3448	141	3550	386	2	1	350	77	1328	572	62	21.25
Halifax Co.	547	1271	1419	2160	606	5943	60	6546	900	5	1	409	299	1992	1850	227	71.45
" City	377	891	1512	3250	1103	7011	122					272	493	773	1111	44	14.60
Hants	548	1032	1366	1473	529	4763	185	4861	367	9		278	125	1344	1227	102	49.65
Inverness	843	1420	1581	1827	268	5003	436	4661	388	8		951	58	2388		24	11.45
Kings	612	1129	1507	1557	854	4875	284	4565	384	4		298	146	1450	1546	40	21.25
Lunenburg	855	1624	1974	2224	635	7152	160	7399	672	17	8	571	173	2335	1610	145	70.35
Pictou	640	1274	1969	2558	530	6613	358	7059	803	1		523	175	1720	949	279	93.40
Queens	195	365	538	643	258	1912	87	1965	208			145	53	553	655	28	10.55
Richmond	479	640	732	698	181	2568	162	2918	402	10		431	96	990	193	42	15.45
Shelburne	301	663	960	1169	281	3314	60	3329	254	2		248	180	991	807	88	44.76
Victoria	338	500	580	642	161	2019	202	2202	204	1		430	12	1145	150	85	16.35
Yarmouth	352	915	1494	1718	388	4735	122	4979	708	4		272	127	1604	1027	83	45.20
Total, 1893	10581	19665	26553	30494	7656	90959	3940	84978	8166	70	10	8011	2865	26963	17312	1760	$791.53

TABLE VII.—SECTION STATISTICS, (FINANCIAL).

Nova Scotia, Year (Nine Months) Ended July, 1893.

SECTION STATISTICS

COUNTIES.	Value of all School property, (ground, buildings, fixtures, &c.) belonging to the Section.	Valuation of property in Section according to last Assessment Roll.	Total amount voted at last annual meeting for all School purposes.	Portion voted for building and repairs.	Total amount of Teachers salaries paid during the year by Section, not including the Provincial Grant to Teachers.	No. of Volumes in library (if any), belonging to School.	No. of Wall Maps, Globes and Charts.	Estimated Value of all Scientific Apparatus and Collections.	Estimated value of total Literary and Scientific School Equipment.
Annapolis	$57,045 00	$4,408,246 00	$13,417 00	$2,872 50	$11,833 34	130	326	$188 00	$1,037 25
Antigonish	19,925 00	1,810,909 00	5,196 65	526 80	6,790 26	....	162	114 25	328 15
Cape Breton	56,321 00	2,925,965 00	21,765 50	8,152 00	18,494 50	286	283	391 00	1,501 05
Colchester	53,848 00	2,680,959 00	18,896 00	2,964 49	19,598 34	113	426	440 50	1,922 50
Cumberland	120,031 00	5,717,292 00	29,921 50	10,703 30	22,236 64	47	644	203 00	2,068 85
Digby	35,614 00	2,214,589 00	11,358 70	2,433 00	11,441 35	112	247	205 50	871 00
Guysboro	37,280 00	939,023 00	15,308 00	6,586 00	7,023 01	186	201	69 40	657 50
Halifax Co.	87,405 00	3,174,976 00	18,274 00	2,815 00	15,477 00	37	694	227 00	1,508 00
" City	......	20,470,985 00	101,500 00	7,000 00	36,034 36	1327	506	1320 00	3,114 00
Hants	67,527 42	4,584,718 00	17,103 50	2,940 00	13,023 82	70	493	146 00	1,455 11
Inverness	37,177 00	1,155,448 00	11,956 50	1,817 50		21	281	252 50	1,032 10
Kings	74,675 00	5,049,987 00	22,716 50	9,242 00	14,427 46	159	504	205 00	1,798 00
Lunenburg	74,357 00	4,326,817 00	19,694 50	2,303 50	25,411 50	161	464	258 00	1,905 75
Pictou	109,687 00	4,419,712 00	50,072 00	27,009 00	28,148 25	1196	618	1750 00	4,959 00
Queens	24,090 00	904,797 00	6,031 00	645 00	5,283 50	3	190	66 00	651 25
Richmond	12,340 00	717,963 00	6,807 00	983 00	5,604 67	120	137	21 50	651 60
Shelburne	46,710 00	1,419,535 00	10,168 00	2,151 00	8,101 00	80	356	183 00	1,107 00
Victoria	7,499 00	471,686 00	7,207 00	1,168 00	6,071 00	....	96	66 00	237 00
Yarmouth	111,414 00	6,603,906 00	26,066 00	3,875 00	19,240 00	185	480	521 00	1,923 25
Total, 1893	$1,032,890 42	$73,848,513 00	$413,448 85	$95,687 09	$279,355 00	4183	7108	$6,577 65	$28,728 36

TABLE VIII.—TIME TABLE.

Nova Scotia, Year (Nine Months) Ended July, 1893.

Average No. of Minutes per Week taken by Teacher during the Year in giving instruction in the various Groups of Subjects specified below. (For all schools in each County.)

Counties.	Calisthenics and Military Drill.	Vocal Music.	Hygiene and Temperance.	Moral and Patriotic Duties.	Object Lessons on Nature.	Spelling and Dictation.	Reading and Elocution.	English Composition, Gram., Lit.	Writing.	Book-keeping.	Geography.	History.	Drawing.	Arithmetic.
Annapolis	5.	12.	21.	34.	27.	144.	345.	125.	88.	27.	143.	115.	43.	287.
Antigonish	5.	7.	25.	20.	33.	127.	230.	121.	86.	29.	88.	84.	23.	178.
Cape Breton	5.3	14.4	16.	21.1	30.6	146.7	372.7	117.0	103.7	17.9	80.7	59.	20.6	308.2
Colchester	10.4	21.	26.6	20.5	24.1	166.	311.4	106.6	96.6	31.9	107.6	67.4	33.2	252.7
Cumberland	10.	25.	27.	17.	29.	163.	289.	103.	90.	30.	100.	80.	33.	280.
Digby	9.	9.	23.	30.	34.	165.	418.	85.	100.	21.	114.	73.	48.	316.
Guysboro	4.	14.	18.	16.	35.	145.	342.	98.	112.	24.	95.	78.	32.	28.
Halifax County	7.	9.	22.	23.	21.	196.	310.	98.	116.	13.	98.	96.	24.	340.
Halifax City	46.5	52.	27.	33.	52.	112.	250.	100.	121.	35.	86.	86.	65.	310.
Hants	11.4	17.9	20.6	20.2	31.6	155.8	335.4	138.6	91.3	36.8	135.1	102.8	53.	282.6
Inverness	5.	5.2	15.9	17.5	26.	94.6	272.2	112.1	139.5	74.1	79.7	74.8	15.7	287.3
Kings	6.6	10.2	16.2	15.8	30.6	144.9	278.7	123.4	88.1	37.4	131.9	99.5	40.9	263.4
Lunenburg	8.	27.	32.	18.	37.	209.	394.	99.	109.	24.	122.	80.	42.	318.
Pictou	7.3	12.6	21.1	21.8	27.7	169.5	377.9	117.2	101.8	31.3	113.3	85.6	33.2	282.7
Queens	7.	9.	32.	22.	38.	192.	300.	105.	102.	37.	149.	102.	43.	312.
Richmond	4.	10.3	21.6	18.8	41.2	128.5	386.8	120.3	110.5	29.5	85.6	70.5	22.7	305.7
Shelburne	4.	7.	25.	28.	35.	183.	319.	115.	96.	23.	135.	100.	44.	291.
Victoria	15.1	13.2	20.5	24.7	29.4	67.6	86.9	68.	67.6	29.3	61.8	47.4	35.7	87.5
Yarmouth	7.	13.	22.	25.	36.	150.	277.	101.	105.	20.	107.	70.	50.	293.
Total, 1893	9.3	15.2	22.8	21.8	32.5	151.	311.9	108.1	106.3	30.	106.9	82.6	36.9	264.4

TABLE VIII.—TIME TABLE—(Continued).

Nova Scotia, Year (Nine Months) Ended July, 1893.

AVERAGE No. OF MINUTES PER WEEK TAKEN BY TEACHER DURING THE YEAR IN GIVING INSTRUCTION IN THE VARIOUS GROUPS OF SUBJECTS SPECIFIED BELOW.

COUNTIES.	Mathematics, Practical.	Algebra.	No. of schools.	Geometry.	No. of schools.	Botany, Zoology, Geology, etc.	No. of schools.	Physiology.	No. of schools.	Physics.	No. of schools.	Chemistry.	No. of schools.	Latin.	No. of schools.	Greek.	No. of schools.	French.	No. of schools.	German.	No. of schools.	Manual Training.	No. of schools.
Annapolis	16.	120.		76.		30.		10.		20.		26.		15.		2.		2.					1
Antigonish	121.	188.	6	104.	40	64.	29	152.	11	101.	2	211.	6	950.	2	500.	2	233.	3			60.	2
Cape Breton	45.8	113.1	6	78.	70	36.3	46	31.4	23	42.7	7	46.3	11	1120.	11	150.	5	89.4	5			75.	
Colchester	88.1	56.7	10	53.4	80	29.6	73	26.2	72	34.5	19	75.7	19	131.8	9	77.3	6	270.	1				
Cumberland	38.	34.	14	60.		32..	60	28.	81	21.	22	41.	22	61.	14							40.	3
Digby	18.	98.		65.	8	25.	36	9.	24	19.	21	20.		8.	8	3.	3	25.	3	60.	1		
Guysboro		32.	2	94.		62.		37.		52.	7	49.	7									60.	1
Halifax County	29.	28.	4	26.	17	9.	10	8.	27	2.				33.	8	65.	3	144.	6	145.	4		41
" City	123.	86.	16	124.	67	41.	58	34.	57	50.	20	94.	9	250.	5	380.	7	30.	2	20.	1	83.	2
Hants	59.1	79.8	17	72.8		42.7		37.9		37.3	17	63.9	20	61.8	17	71.	7					22.5	
Inverness		112.2		71.1	79	44.4	77	48.8	51	67.	20	68.	20	83.3	16	43.2	3	52.	4			34.5	
Kings	61.5	88.	11	62.	70	47.	42	25.	30	43.	11	65.	11	46.	3								2
Lunenburg	54.	83.	7	71.6	93	29.8	84	31.9	58	37.	7	43.8	12	129.	15	285.	11						
Pictou	177.7	126.	2	82.	25	37.	24	63.	26	46.	3	69.	7	175.	1	150.	1	266.	2			30.	1
Queens	75.	99.7	6	17.7	35	59.6	23	28.	10	34.6	5	28.	5	75.	1			262.5	12	6.	1		
Richmond	80.6	75.	5	78.	44	30.	40	32.	30	60.	9	52.	9	75.	6	115.	6	70.	1			112.5	4
Shelburne	82.																						
Victoria		81.	6	74.	50	46.	37	39.	24	59.	15	52.	15	81.	12	55.	5	222.	24	117.	1		1
Yarmouth	86.																						
Total (1893)	72.1	85.3	112	70.8	678	39.1	634	37.7	1524	42.7	173	62.4	120	143.8	129	142.	61	138.8	61	69.6	8	57.5	57

TABLE IX.--CLASSIFICATION OF PUPILS.

Nova Scotia, Year (Nine Months) Ended July, 1893.

Counties	Kindergarten	\multicolumn{13}{c}{No. of Pupils in each Grade according to Provincial Course of Study.}													\multicolumn{4}{c}{Grades IX to XII.}				\multicolumn{2}{c}{Transfers.}	
		Grade I.	Grade II.	Grade III.	Grade IV.	Grade V.	Grade VI.	Grade VII.	Grade VIII.	Grade IX.	Grade X.	Grade XI.	Grade XII.	No. holding Provincial Certificates.	Total No. High School Pupils.	No. High School Pupils taking full course.	No. High School Pupils taking partial course.	No. of Pupils transferred out of sch'l.	No. of Pupils transferred into school.
Annapolis	18	577	434	421	511	454	402	563	435	274	153	35	15		462	265	197	16	16
Antigonish		595	398	437	426	420	351	373	225	745	56	24			112	102	10	28	30
Cape Breton		1870	1086	905	859	738	540	634	537	133	101	27			356	284	72		
Colchester	38	753	693	667	778	769	666	752	469	287	65	42			294	281	24	48	49
Cumberland	24	1731	1180	1052	1035	896	685	850	386	51	69	26	15		256	229	35	93	21
Digby		865	678	533	653	441	458	430	287	94	45	17			155	84	71	46	46
Guysboro	10	622	450	391	496	403	400	406	171	35	14	9			47	38	10	4	4
Halifax Co.	105	1052	889	845	964	744	718	410	212	159	1	1	11					111	101
Halifax City	419	1802	859	854	999	701	604	500	346	160	65	25			309	264	21	244	255
Hants	11	696	626	602	590	558	473	607	521	190	64	10			264	150	114	22	22
In ... ness	49	1137	763	769	713	688	472	441	265	348	140	8			51	26			
Kings	6	614	493	526	1562	622	508	717	628	111	42	37	9		488	335	183	9	9
... burg	70	1273	1001	1008	035	860	790	754	363	112	189	5						233	283
Pic ...	22	890	939	626	793	684	710	255	576	80		81			437	327	110	12	12
... eens		348	194	242	216	244	254	276	129	21	29	5						2	2
Richmond		724	416	430	365	240	193	923	128	12	12	1			12	6	6		
Shelburne		535	465	435	420	407	321	372	285	55	65	20			100	73	27	10	10
Victoria	126	342	289	325	237	252	365	166	57	28	27	20	1		4			9	12
Yarmouth		1196	662	586	631	507	386	402	366	111	51	43			202	167	35	136	134
Total, 1893.	898	17122	12515	11653	12383	10566	9296	9831	6361	2506	1206	497	37		3549	2601	921	1023	926

TABLE X.—ANALYSIS OF HIGH SCHOOL STUDIES, (GRADE IX OR D).

Nova Scotia, Year (Nine Months) Ended July, 1893.

COUNTIES.	English.	Latin.	French.	History.	Geography.	Botany.	Physics.	Drawing.	Book-keeping.	Arithmetic.	Algebra.	Geometry.	Manual Training.	Total No. High School Pupils.	No. Pupils taking full regular course.	No. taking partial or special course.
Annapolis	271	40	3	262	269	202	164	206	257	277	243	230	.....	277	131	146
Antigonish	69	43	41	69	69	68	68	68	58	69	69	69	.....	50	49	1
Cape Breton	226	6	24	224	224	177	118	194	213	218	220	218	.....	229	178	51
Colchester	154	123	.....	163	160	150	42	147	159	165	170	48	.....	181	161	20
Cumberland	129	46	.....	148	149	131	118	116	159	152	149	152	.....	160	139	21
Digby	94	14	.....	94	94	56	43	64	83	94	85	85	.....	94	28	66
Guysboro	18	13	.....	18	7	12	15	7	18	18	18	18	.....	18	18	.....
Halifax County	43	.....	26	36	36	38	38	38	39	41	37	37	.....	40	34	6
" City	166	155	15	160	160	152	160	168	160	160	160	160	49	160	151	9
Hants	179	45	18	174	179	97	126	113	166	158	171	164	.....	190	88	102
Inverness	95	13	1	40	40	92	56	29	99	77	98	94	.....	68	27	31
Kings	276	81	.....	266	277	139	130	153	223	281	241	234	.....	285	160	125
Lunenburg	100	17	58	93	93	84	76	62	94	100	90	85	.....	100	74	26
Picton	168	56	.....	167	169	138	125	128	154	168	114	106	.....	160	115	45
Queens	35	2	3	34	34	30	30	31	34	34	34	28	.....	35	29	6
Richmond	4	2	.....	12	12	10	3	1	12	12	12	12	.....	12	6	6
Shelburne	44	28	6	47	47	47	38	45	48	48	47	47	.....	48	40	8
Victoria	63	22	.....	6	12	62	59	20	47	37	45	61	.....	10	4	6
Yarmouth	109	16	51	110	109	72	73	100	77	110	110	108	.....	110	87	23
Total (1893)	2238	722	246	2123	2140	1757	1482	1682	2110	2219	2113	1956	49	2217	1519	698

TABLE XI.—ANALYSIS OF HIGH SCHOOL STUDIES, (GRADE X OR C).

Nova Scotia, Year (Nine Months) Ended July, 1893.

Counties.	English.	Latin.	Greek.	French.	German.	History.	Geography.	Chemistry.	Drawing.	Book-keeping.	Arithmetic.	Algebra.	Geometry.	Manual Training.	No. holding Prov. High School Certificates.	Total No. High School Pupils.	No. Pupils taking full regular course.	No. taking partial or special course.
Annapolis	149	54	1	12		147	147	126	119	140	151	144	142			151	111	40
Antigonish	81	58	4	54		80	80	89	78	78	78	78	78			61	61	
Cape Breton	93	14	4	23		93	93	70	88	100	100	93	93			100	91	9
Colchester	58	51	7	36		63	63	48	45	66	64	64	59			58	53	5
Cumberland	61	35				64	64	52	52	63	64	64				64	63	1
Digby	44	9	1	6		44	44	44	44	43	44	44	44			44	39	5
Guysborough	19			20		20	20	20	19	23	23	19	19			19	19	4
Halifax Co.	3	8	13	35	15	3	3	3	8	3	3	3	3	14		3	3	21
" City	64	37	2		6	63	63	60	61	63	63	63	63			65	44	8
Hants	57	29				59	59	56	56	59	58	58	58			60	52	
Inverness				16														50
Kings	143	37	2			138	138	89	117	123	141	124	124			141	91	2
Lunenburg	41	6	6	68		41	41	41	41	41	41	41	41			48	41	31
Picton	188	69	2			188	188	176	172	184	188	135	153			188	157	4
Queens	34	14		8		32	32	31	30	34	34	34	35			34	30	
Richmond			10															
Shelburne	55	17		29		54	57	36	37	56	57	53	53			57	30	27
Victoria																		
Yarmouth	50	16				50	50	43	46	44	50	50	50			50	41	9
Total	1140	444	52	307	21	1139	1142	984	1008	1120	1160	1078	996	14		1142	926	216

TABLE XII.—ANALYSIS OF HIGH SCHOOL STUDIES, (GRADE XI OR B).

Nova Scotia, Year (Nine Months) Ended July, 1893.

Counties	English	Latin	Greek	French	German	History	Physics	Algebra	Geometry	Prac. Mathematics	Physiology	Manual Training	No. holding Prov. High School Certificates	Total No. High School Pupils	No. Pupils taking full regular course	No. taking partial or special course
Annapolis	34	11	6	1		34	34	34	34	34	28			34	23	11
Antigonish	30	27		29		28	42	31	31	32				28	28	
Cape Breton	27	10	9	10		24	12	24	24	14	10			27	15	12
Colchester	47	36	4	19		42	39	41	46	46	37			47	41	6
Cumberland	21	19				21	21	21	21	21	21			21	21	
Digby	17	18		4		17	17	17	17	16	17			17	16	1
Guysboro	8			6		8	8	8	8	8				8	7	1
Halifax Co					18						7					
" City	94	57	29	54	5	94	85	95	94	85	6	6		95	94	
Hants	9		2			9	9	9	9	9				9	8	1
Inverness	35	18				36	35	37	35	32	9			37	37	1
Kings	5	1	7			5	5	5	5	5	5			5	5	
Lunenburg	80	54		40		78	80	55	55	54	55			81	55	
Pictou	5	5	21			5	5	5	5	5				5	5	26
Queens			1													
Richmond				5												
Shelburne	12	6	5			12	12	12	12	12				12	12	
Victoria																
Yarmouth	44	10	4	26	4	41	38	41	41	40	29			43	40	3
Total, 1893	468	272	88	194	27	454	442	435	437	413	219	6		469	407	62

TABLE XIII.—ANALYSIS OF HIGH SCHOOL STUDIES, (GRADE XII OR A.)

Nova Scotia, Year (Nine Months) Ended July, 1893.

COUNTIES.	English.	Latin.	Greek.	French.	German.	History.	Botany.	Physics.	Chemistry.	Algebra.	Geometry.	Psychology.	San. Science.	Zoology.	Geology.	Astronomy.	Navigation.	Trigonometry.	Manual Training.	No. holding Prov. High School Certificates.	Total No. High School Pupils.	No. of pupils taking full regular course.	No. taking partial or special course.
Annapolis																							
Antigonish	15	13	7	12		4				12	12	15	4				4	4			15	15	
Cape Breton																							
Col																							
Cumberland																							
Digby																							
Guysboro																							
Halifax Co.		1																					
" City	11	9	5		3	11	6	11	10	7	11	11	11	6	6	6	5	11			11	11	
Hants																							
Inverness																							
Kings		6	5						2	8	8							8			8		8
Lunenburg																							
Pictou	12															•							
Queens																							
Richmond	1	1	1	1				1	1	1	1	1	1					1			1	1	
Shelburne																							
Victoria																							1
Yarmouth	1	1	1	1																	1		1
Total, 1893	40	30	18	16	3	15	6	12	13	29	33	27	16	6	6	6	9	24			37	27	10

TABLE XIV.—AVERAGE SALARY OF MALE TEACHERS.

Nova Scotia, School Year (Nine Months) Ended July, 1893.

COUNTIES.	CLASS A—(MALE).			CLASS B—(MALE).			CLASS C—(MALE).			CLASS D—(MALE).		
	Provin'l Grant.	From Section.	Total.	Provin'l Grant.	From Section.	Total.	Provin'l Grant.	From Section.	Total.	Provin'l Grant.	From Section.	Total.
Annapolis			$588 75	$83 19	$299 89	$385 08	$62 39	$156 67	$219 06	$41 59	$103 90	$145 49
Antigonish			690 00	83 19	249 25	332 44	62 39	110 06	172 45	41 59	86 61	128 00
Cape Breton			687 19	83 19	248 05	331 24	62 39	109 98	172 37	41 59	75 06	116 65
Colchester			734 24	83 19	362 70	445 89	62 39	128 73	191 12			
Cumberland			664 99	83 19	340 00	423 19	62 39	107 14	169 53	41 59	177 50	219 09
Digby			562 50	83 19	254 48	337 67	62 39	228 30	290 69	41 59	205 19	246 78
Guysboro			675 00	83 19	302 34	385 53	62 39	115 00	177 39	41 59	65 63	107 22
Halifax Co.			825 00	83 19	296 00	379 19	62 39	198 00	260 39	41 59	162 50	204 09
" City			1082 0)	83 19	468 00	551 39						
Hants			750 00	83 19	224 20	307 39	62 39	183 00	245 39	41 59	106 67	148 26
Inverness												
Kings			695 00	83 19	243 50	326 69	62 39	150 35	262 74	41 59	115 53	157 09
Lunenburg			750 00	83 19	247 58	330 77	62 39	106 00	168 39	41 59	99 70	140 59
Pictou			700 50	83 19	223 01	306 20	62 39	94 44	156 83	41 59	58 04	99 63
Queens			514 44	83 19	200 00	283 19	62 39	138 75	201 14			
Richmond				83 19	146 72	229 91	62 39	103 67	166 06	41 59	77 55	119 34
Shelburne			458 19	83 19	176 25	259 44	62 39	160 00	222 39	41 59	130 00	171 59
Victoria			560 00	83 19	180 00	263 19	62 39	108 00	170 39	41 59	77 00	118 59
Yarmouth			691 69	83 19	305 67	388 56	62 39	231 00	293 39	41 59	118 33	159 92
Average, 1893			$675 85	$83 19	$264 86	$348 05	$62 39	$142 88	$205 27	$41 59	$110 58	$152 17

TABLE XV.—AVERAGE SALARY OF FEMALE TEACHERS.

Nova Scotia, School Year (Nine Months) Ended July, 1893.

Counties.	Class A—(Female).			Class B—(Female).			Class C—(Female).			Class D—(Female).		
	Provin'l Grant.	From Section.	Total.	Provin'l Grant.	From Section.	Total.	Provin'l Grant.	From Section.	Total.	Provin'l Grant.	From Section.	Total.
Annapolis				$83 19	$139 67	$222 86	$ 62 39	$ 94 21	$156 60	$41 59	$74 51	$116 10
Antigonish				83 19	124 89	208 08	62 39	103 68	166 07	41 59	75 62	117 21
Cape Breton				83 19	149 64	232 83	62 39	138 07	200 46	41 59	68 45	110 04
Colchester				83 19	137 10	220 29	62 39	102 89	165 28	41 59	64 06	105 65
Cumberland				83 19	166 00	249 10	62 39	115 81	178 20	41 59	81 41	123 00
Digby				83 19	143 21	226 40	62 39	92 73	155 12	41 59	90 15	131 74
Guysboro				83 19	162 50	245 69	62 39	120 17	182 56	41 59	79 73	121 32
Halifax Co				83 19	168 00	251 10	62 39	153 00	215 39	41 59	90 50	132 09
" City			600 00	83 19	275 25	358 44	62 39	262 50	324 89	41 59	171 75	213 34
Hants				83 19	138 82	222 02	62 39	111 50	172 89	41 59	81 56	123 15
Inverness										41 59	75 55	117 14
Kings				83 19	152 37	235 56	62 39	112 95	176 34	41 59	77 78	119 37
Lunenburg				83 19	132 50	215 69	62 39	101 25	163 64	41 59	57 17	98 76
Pictou			528 97	83 19	123 07	206 26	62 39	82 63	145 02	41 59	71 53	113 12
Queens				83 19	127 50	210 60	62 39	92 96	155 35	41 59	69 70	111 29
Richmond							62 39	68 75	131 14	41 59	71 38	112 97
Shelburne				83 19	126 83	210 02	62 39	102 03	164 42	41 59	71 38	112 97
Victoria				83 19	185 00	268 19	62 39	94 00	156 39	41 59	56 43	98 02
Yarmouth				83 19	207 27	290 46	62 39	148 46	210 80	41 59	87 97	129 56
Average, 1893			$564 49	$83 19	$156 45	$239 64	$ 62 39	$116 58	$178 97	$41 59	$80 29	$121 88

TABLE XVI.

APPORTIONMENT OF COUNTY FUND TO TRUSTEES FOR YEAR ENDED JULY, 1893.

MUNICIPALITIES.	Grand total days' attendance made by all the Pupils.	On account of Teachers employed.	On account of average attendance of Pupils.	On account of Pupils attending Halifax School for Blind.	On account of Pupils at the Deaf and Dumb Institution, Halifax.	Total amount appropriated.	Amt per Pupil in attendance the Full Term.
Annapolis	366645	$2001 27	$2217 79	$......	$135 00	$4354 06	$1 01
Antigonish	258355	1637 57	1988 74	....	....	3626 83	1 24
Cape Breton	533886	2639 67	3955 55	....	135 00	7030 32	1 21
Colchester	502044	2330 48	2043 99	168 75	360 00	4963 22	0 83
Cumberland	635763	3245 94	4197 11	56 25	270 00	7769 30	1 07
Digby	328043	1123 19	1412 05	33 28	79 88	2648 40	1 10
Clare	148094	675 76	1074 05	22 97	55 12	1827 90	1 10
Guysboro	202166	1086 64	1739 45	42 20	33 76	2902 05	1 37
St. Mary's	61478	393 03	548 51	14 05	11 24	966 83	1 39
Halifax Co	445234	2149 56	3790 45	....	225 00	6165 00	1 39
Hants, East.	182716	1100 16	1095 06	....	132 78	2328 00	0 97
" West	230163	961 83	1330 21	....	137 22	2429 26	1 21
Inverness	397336	2609 36	3014 89	56 25	90 00	5776 14	1 26
Kings	408064	2322 61	2569 19	168 75	....	5060 55	1 01
Lunenburg	1101429	2557 39	3060 75	46 47	111 53	5776 14	0 99
Chester	104950	589 18	593 58	9 78	23 47	1216 01	0 90
Pictou	617175	3099 86	4349 89	281 25	45 00	7776 00	1 15
Queens	178751	1030 44	1357 76	....	....	2388 20	1 23
Richmond	200462	1295 65	2062 04	....	135 00	3492 69	1 67
Shelburne	150909	838 64	312 94	....	93 30	1744 88	0 99
Barrington	140508	760 34	826 51	....	86 70	1673 55	1 08
Victoria	163331	1194 63	1610 37	....	....	2805 00	1 62
Yarmouth	243741	1286 94	1476 04	32 63	104 41	2900 02	1 09
Argyle	181706	926 08	1073 96	23 62	75 59	2099 25	1 07
Total—1893	7085436	$38126 23	$48200 88	$956 25	$2240 00	$89623 36	$1 16

TABLE XVII.

SPECIAL GOVERNMENT AID TO POOR SECTIONS.

COUNTIES.	Paid by Government over and above the ordinary Grants, towards Salaries of Teachers employed in Poor Sections.		TOTAL.
	First half year.	Second half year.	
Annapolis	$ 56 09	$ 108 69	$ 164 88
Antigonish.............	40 45	93 80	134 25
Cape Breton	48 65	102 33	150 98
Colchester	80 54	144 46	225 00
Cumberland...........	69 96	145 43	215 39
Digby................	41 08	79 17	120 25
Guysboro.............	39 04	89 41	128 45
Halifax Co	55 32	102 99	158 31
Hants................	46 08	90 05	136 13
Inverness.............	60 16	125 49	185 65
Kings................	72 79	138 45	211 24
Lunenburg............	83 96	141 04	225 00
Pictou	43 16	78 92	122 08
Queens..............	43 66	83 61	127 27
Richmond	17 17	49 16	66 33
Shelburne	9 67	17 80	27 47
Victoria	40 66	114 03	154 69
Yarmouth	43 66	84 56	128 22
Total, 1893	$892 10	$1789 49	$2681 59

TABLE XVIII.

POOR SECTIONS—SPECIAL COUNTY AID.

MUNICIPALITIES.	Number of these Sections having Schools.	Amount of County Assessment paid to these Schools over and above ordinary allowance.
Annapolis, County of	18	$ 139 37
Antigonish, ...	14	129 10
Cape Breton, ...	18	156 15
Colchester, ...	24	191 38
Cumberland, ...	22	185 99
Digby, District of	12	108 70
Clare, ...	2	30 12
Guysboro, ...	8	68 38
St. Mary's, ...	4	31 37
Halifax, County of	16	145 03
Hants, District of, East......	10	81 00
West	10	100 65
Inverness, County of........	16	153 23
Kings, ...	25	223 99
Lunenburg and West Dublin.	16	130 71
Chester, District of	7	64 88
Pictou, County of ...:......	13	125 14
Queens, ...	11	99 29
Richmond	13	118 72
Shelburne, District of.......	2	15 84
Barrington, ...	4	34 18
Victoria, County of....... ..	12	124 00
Yarmouth, District of	8	67 17
Argyle, ...	5	48 66
Total, 1893	290	$2573 15

TABLE XIX.—COUNTY ACADEMIES.

Academy.	Instructors.	Class of License.	Annual Salary (nine mts.)	Department, or subjects taught, (subjects may be given briefly by Nos. from 65 to 90, as in following table).	Hours per day.
Annapolis	W. M. McVicar, A. M	A. cl.	$ 675 00	All subjects.	5¼
Antigonish	Rev. Daniel A. Chisholm, D. D	R.	375 00	Nos. 76, 87, 88.	2
	Rev. Alex. Chisholm, D. D	A. cl.		" 86, 72.	5
	Rev. Alx. Thompson, D. D	A. cl.	1687 50	" 82, 83, 84, 83.	5
	Rev. Angus Chisholm, D. D	A. cl.		" 70, 71, 72, 74, 75, 76, 78, 80, 81, 88.	5
	C. P. Chisholm	A. cl.			
	Daniel MacNeil	B.	225 00	" 74, 75, 76, 77, 91.	4
Cape Breton	E. T. McKeen	A. cl.	675 00	" 67, 68, 70, 71, 72, 75, 76, 83, 86.	5
	Frank J. Stewart, B. A	A. cl.	525 00	" 74, 77, 78, 79, 80, 81, 82, 84, 85, 87, 88.	5
Colchester	W. R. Campbell, B. A	A. cl.	787 50	" 82, 85, 86, 87.	4¾
	Jas. Little	B.	731 25	" 78, 80, 81, 94.	4¾
	Josephine Upham	B.	875 00	" 65, 71, 74, 77, 83, 88.	4¾
	G. A. Cogswell, B. A	A. cl.	525 00	" 72, 73, 75, 76, 79.	4¾
Cumberland	E. J. Lay	A. cl.	960 00	" 72, 74, 76, 78, 79, 80, 81, 82, 83, 86, 88.	4¾
	A. S. Ford	B.	393 75	" 66, 71, 72, 74, 75, 77, 80, 81, 84, 85.	4¾
Digby	John F. Godfrey	A. cl.	562 50	" 71 to 89.	5
Guysboro	E. R. Smith, B. A	A. cl.	562 50	All subjects.	5

County	Teacher	Class	Salary	Subjects	
Halifax	Howard Murray, B. A	A. cl.	1350 00	Nos. 86, 87.	4
	Kate Mackintosh	A. cl.	600 00	" 67, 71, 72, 75, 76, 83, 68, 70.	4
	Silvanna A. Morton, B. A	A. cl.	825 00	" 74, 77, 78, 79, 80, 81, 82, 84.	4
	Wm. T. Kennedy	A. cl.	937 50	" 72, 75, 76, 77, 81, 82, 85, 86.	4
	Florenc. A. Peters	B.	525 00	" 72, 74, 78, 80, 82, 84.	4
	Jean V. P.otton	......	300 00	" 88.	4
	Gunther Von der Gr*ben	......	187 50	" 89.	1½
	K. Hill, J. Lear, E. Smith	......	187 50	" 77.	4
	Lee Russell, B. Sc	......	750 00	" 90.	
Hants	John A. Smith, B. A	A. cl.	750 00	" 72 to 89.	5
Inverness	D. S. McIntosh, B. A	A. cl.	562 50	All subjects.	5¾
Kings	Angus McLeod	A. cl.	750 00	Nos. 67, 68, 72, 74, 76, 78, 79, 80, 81, 83, 86, 98.	5
	C. B. Robin son, B. A	A. cl.	640 00	" 71, 72, 75, 76, 77, 82, 84, 85, 86, 87.	5
Lunenburg	Burgess M. Kittrick, B. A	A. cl.	750 00	All subjects.	5
Pictou	Robt. McLellan	A. cl.	900 00	Nos. 86, 87, 88.	4
	Clarence L. Moore, B. A	A. cl.	525 00	" 78, 81, 82, 84, 85.	4
	A. C. L. Oliver, B. A	A. cl.	562 50	" 71, 72, 76.	4
	A. O. McRae, B. A	A. cl.	562 50	" 74, 75, 77, 78, 80, 83.	4
Queens	Nicholas Smith	A. cl.	562 50	All subjects.	5
Shelburne	C. Stanley Bruce	A. cl.	562 50	" "	5
Victoria	J. B. Johnson, B. A	A. cl.	} 562 50	" "	5
	C. F. Hall, M. A	A. cl.			
Yarmouth	A. Cameron	A. cl.	900 00	Nos. 72, 75, 76, 78, 79, 84, 85, 87.	5
	A. Forbes, B. A	A. cl.	675 00	" 72, 74, 76, 77, 78, 80, 81, 82, 83, 86.	5
	Paul Kunzer	......	450 00	" 88.	1⅛
	J. M. G. Webster	B.	} 45 00	" 72, 75, 76.	1
	Beatrice Tooker	B.			

TABLE XIX.—COUNTY ACADEMIES, (Continued.)

Counties.	Second Quarter.				Third Quarter.				Fourth Quarter.				Half Year.			
	Total pupils on Register at end of quarter. 19	No. attended during quarter. 20	Average daily attendance. 21	Per cent. of those attended during quarter daily present on an aver-age. 22	Total pupils on Register at end of quarter. 23	No. attended during quarter. 24	Average daily attendance. 25	Per cent. attended during quarter daily present on an average. 26	Total pupils on Register at end of quarter. 27	No. attended during quarter. 28	Average daily attendance. 29	Per cent. attended during quarter daily present on an average. 30	Days open first half year. 31	Days open second half year. 32	Total days' attendance first half year. 33	Total days' attend-ance second half year. 34
Annapolis	49	43	32.	74.4	43	41	30.7	74.9	44	33	27.	81.8	58.	103.	1855.	2979.5
Antigonish	140	140	97.	74.1	148	139	112.2	86.3	158	114	80.6	73.2	42.	95.5	4387.5	9252.5
Cape Breton	50	50	42.	84.	54	50	41.8	83.6	72	58	44.4	76.5	58.	102.	2441.	4385.
Colchester	175	175	129.2	73.9	180	162	119.8	72.2	183	130	97.	74.6	57.	103.	7366.	11219.5
Cumberland	71	71	53.6	75.5	75	62	46.	74.3	76	55	38.9	70.8	58.	103.	3115.5	4397.
Digby	37	37	27.4	74.	38	38	31.8	83.	38	34	27.2	80.2	58.	101.	1362.	2953.
Guysboro	33	33	23.5	71.2	35	34	25.8	75.9	36	31	21.	67.7	58.	108.		2527.5
Halifax	246	246	211.	85.8	252	237	193.	81.4	253	214	188.8	87.9	61.	101.	12886.	19257.
Inverness	35	35	28.2	80.	35	32	21.6	80.	35	32	20.8	65.	58.	103.	1530.5	2405.
Hants	25	25	18.3	73.2	25	25	21.6	86.4	25	25	19.	76.	58.	103.	1061.	2095.
Kings	73	73	58.4	80.	73	65	51.4	79.	74	56	46.8	83.4	58.	103.	3389.5	5065.5
Lunenburg	42	42	36.1	85.9	42	42	36.8	87.6	43	39	32.4	83.	58.	99.	2072.	3442.
Pictou	197	197	144.2	78.2	202	181	138.6	81.2	202	145	100.1	74.	58.	108.	8949.	13079.
Queens	29	29	25.5	91.1	27	27	25.2	93.	27	21	21.9	81.1	58.	108.	1434.	2554.
Shelburne	37	37	27.1	73.2	40	27	24.5	66.2	42	30	18.3	43.6	57.	101.	1546.	2186.
Victoria	34	34	28.8	67.	37	34	23.4	63.3	37	29	17.7	47.8	51.	103.		2130.5
Yarmouth	57	57	47.	82.5	59	60	40.8	81.6	60	45	38.8	86.2	57.	102.	1165.	3901.
Total, ...1893	1324	1324	1039.3	78.4	1365	1256	989.	78.8	1395	1091	839.9	77.	56.6	102.7	58741.	93829.

TABLE XIX.—COUNTY ACADEMIES, (Continued).

ACADEMY.	WHOLE YEAR (NINE MONTHS).									No. ON REGISTER WHOSE ATTENDANCE DURING THE YEAR WAS					No. OF PUPILS ON REGISTER.		
	Between 5 and 15 years. 36	Over 15 years. 37	Total annual enrolment. 38	Boys. 39	Girls. 40	Total days' attendance for year. 41	Days taught during year. 42	Daily present on an average during year. 43	Average of quarterly percentages of attendance. 44	30 days or less. 45	Over 30 and up to 50 days. 46	Over 50 and up to 100 days. 47	Over 100 and up to 150 days. 48	Over 150 and up to 185 days. 49	Belonging to this School Section. 51	From beyond limits of Section, but within the County. 52	From beyond limits of the County. 53
Annapolis	13	30	43	18	25	4834.5	161.	29.9	77.8		5	10	21	7	31	9	8
Antigonish	26	124	150	110	40	13640.	187.5	99.2	77.8	7	18	41	84		71	43	36
Cape Breton	22	50	72	48	24	6826.	160.	47.2	81.3	2	18	18	19	15	42	13	17
Colchester	84	98	182	74	108	18586.5	161.	116.2	73.6	7	21	47	83	24	121	52	9
Cumberland	20	56	76	27	49	7512.	161.	46.6	73.5	7	9	13	36	11	50	26	
Digby	8	30	38	20	18	4538.5	159.	28.5	79.6		2	7	23	6	25	11	2
Guysboro	14	22	36	15	21	3889.5	166.	23.4	71.6	1		6	24		30	6	
Halifax	111	142	253	124	129	32143.	162.	198.4	85.2	3	21	23	120	86	179	52	22
Hants	14	21	35	13	22	3935.5	161.	24.4	75.	2	4	3	23	3	28	6	1
Inverness	15	10	25	15	10	3156.	161.	19.6	75.5			2	21	2	19	6	
Kings	34	40	74	27	47	8455.	161.	52.5	78.8	2	9	14	34	15	56	17	1
Lunenburg	20	28	43	10	33	5514.	157.	35.1	80.2		2	7	16	18	35	8	
Pictou	76	126	202	103	99	22028.	166.	132.7	85.7	8	20	48	103	23	104	66	32
Queens	5	24	29	14	15	3988.5	166.	24.5	77.4		1	4	5	19	16	12	1
Shelburne	18	24	42	18	24	3733.	168.	23.6	88.	3	6	14	20		39	8	
Victoria	17	20	37	24	13	3294.	154.	21.4	59.4	3	5	15	14		30	7	
Yarmouth	21	39	60	22	38	6487.	149.	42.4	83.3	3	8	12	23	14	54	5	1
Total, 1893......	518	879	1397	682	715	152,561.	169.4	960.8	78.	47	153	284	669	244	980	342	125

TABLE XIX.—COUNTY ACADEMIES, (Continued.)

AVERAGE NO. OF MINUTES PER WEEK TAKEN BY TEACHER DURING THE YEAR IN GIVING INSTRUCTION IN THE VARIOUS GROUPS OF SUBJECTS SPECIFIED BELOW.

ACADEMY.	65 Calisthenics and Military Drill.	66 Vocal Music.	67 Hygiene and Temperance.	68 Moral and Patriotic Duties.	69 Object Lessons on Nature.	70 Spelling and Dictation.	71 Reading and Elocution.	72 Composition, Eng., Gram., Lit., &c.	73 Writing.	74 Book-keeping.	75 Geography.	76 History.	77 Drawing.	78 Arithmetic.	79 Practical Mathematics.	80 Algebra.	81 Geometry.	82 Botany, Zoology, Geology, &c.	83 Physiology Psychology.	84 Physics.	85 Chemistry.	86 Latin.	87 Greek.	88 French.	89 German.	90 Manual Training.
Annapolis	50	110	40	30			80	180		60	100	105	80	120	60	150	150	50	60	70	80	270	90			
Antigonish		110	40	40		75	75	1170		210	50	250	180	540	300	720	720	120	400	300	360	1650	500	300		
Cape Breton			25	30		30	50	245		50	70	140	40	280	90	180	180	40	40	90	40	450	150	100		
Colchester	45		45	45		240	240	420	90	135	300	420	270	440	180	380	460	180	135	225	180	645	210	270		
Cumberland		40	10	30	100	120		60	60	208	120	200	120	100	100	45	60	60	90	80		60	40	40		
Digby			10				40	40		10	120	130	15	140	90	180	160	60	90	90	80	60		40		
Guysboro	10	15	15	15		80	100	140		65	150	150	50	60	60	50	150	70	100	100	60	60		60		
Halifax	10	25	220			55	240	610	15	160	290	380	260	540	165	485	480	450	200	230	350	1345	990	480	480	1200
Hants			30	30		30	80	65		22	60	90	22	45	90	60	60	12	40	40	40	78	52	40	20	
Inverness			15	2			100	120	30	60	180	130	60	75	35	45	300	40	140	180	40	200	30			
Kings						10	140	600		50	120	210	60	80	60	180	300	92	60	120	140	180	60	120		
Lunenburg							60	150		20	160	150	40		180	150	150	140	150	140	60	100				
Pictou						15	180	480		120	80	480	100	360	125	570	610	60	60	60	540	540	300	360		
Queens			5	10		10	40	150		50	50	90	10	150	100	125	100	120	15	75	75	175	150			
Shelburne							40	230		100	50	90		140	100	60	140	10	55	80	80	75				
Victoria						220	220	245		25	170	140	90	260	115	170	140	10	60	60	90	30		360		
Yarmouth								525	150	180	170	245	180	255	180	360	480	160	180	290	150	180	70			
Total, 1893	6	11	26	14	6	39	93	315	20	89	135	199	93	217	113	230	274	98	98	131	115	357	155	128	29	70

TABLE XIX. COUNTY ACADEMIES.—(Continued.)

ANALYSIS OF HIGH SCHOOL STUDIES.

ACADEMY.	ENGLISH. Grade IX.	X.	XI.	XII.	Total.	LATIN. Grade IX.	X.	XI.	XII.	Total.	GREEK. Grade X.	XI.	XII.	Total.	FRENCH. Grade IX.	X.	XI.	XII.	Total.	GERMAN. Grade X.	XI.	XII.	Total.	HISTORY. Grade IX.	X.	XI.	XII.	Total.
Annapolis	16	14	13		43	5	11	4		20		4			34	48	25	12	119					16	14	13		43
Antigonish	14	61	60	15	148	37	47	25	13	122	4		7	11		14			22					46	61	24	4	135
Cape Breton	36	26	10		72	6	11	7		23	1	4		5	102	36	19		157					36	56	37		70
Colchester	102	43	37		182	101	42	34	7	177	7	7		14		6	3		8	7	18			102	43	29	11	188
Cumberland	30	30	20		76	10	18	10		47	1	2		3		6	3		66	6	5		13	30	35	8		76
Digby	7	18	8		38	6	5	3		13						3	1		6					12	18			31
Guysboro	116	96	78	11	251	115	30	60		206	13	33	6	46	16	20	38	3	296					116	45	78	11	250
Halifax	11	46	6		35	3	14	1		17	1	9		9	6	25			17					11	18	6		36
Hants	14	18	6		35	12	13	9		13	1	6		7		3	1		4					11	19	7		35
Inverness	36	10	1		55	15	10	9		48		6	6	12		13			15					11	19	20		74
Kings	29	18	20		74	12	6			18		15		15		15	15		75					36	73	41		41
Lunenburg	68	12	54	8	200	28	33	43	6	111	15	9	5	20	15	34	20							23	21			190
Pictou	59	76	21		29	15	14			19			1	1					58					30	18	5		4
Queens	18	10	5		42			1		15						18	18							1	8			57
Shelburne	25	8	4		37	3	6	1		11			1	1			18							25	8			58
Victoria	34	22	14		60	15	7	2																34	23			
Yarmouth																												
Total 1893	**581**	**463**	**309**	**34**	**1387**	**577**	**261**	**205**	**28**	**877**	**28**	**72**	**18**	**118**	**177**	**218**	**134**	**15**	**544**	**13**	**23**	**3**	**39**	**581**	**462**	**303**	**15**	**1361**

TABLE XIX.—COUNTY ACADEMIES.—(Continued).

ANALYSIS OF HIGH SCHOOL STUDIES.

ACADEMY.	GEOGRAPHY.				BOTANY.			PHYSICS.				CHEMISTRY.			DRAWING.				BOOK-KEEPING.		
	Grade IX.	Grade X.	Grade XI.	Total.	Grade IX.	Grade XII.	Total.	Grade IX.	Grade XI.	Grade XII.	Total.	Grade X.	Grade XII.	Total.	Grade IX.	Grade X.	Grade XI.	Total.	Grade IX.	Grade X.	Total.
Annapolis	16	14	13	43	16		16	16	13		29	14		14	16	14		30	16	14	30
Antigonish	46	61	24	131	90		90	46	28	12	86	61		61	46	61		107	46	61	107
Cape Breton	36	26		62	62		62	36	5		41	26		26	36	26		62	36	26	62
Colchester	102	43	37	182	102		102	102	37		139	43		43	102	43		145	102	43	145
Cumberland	30	26	20	76	30		30	30	20		50	26		26	30	26		56	30	26	56
Digby	12	18		30	12		12	12	8		20	18		18	12	18		30	12	18	30
Guysboro	7	20	7	34	7		7	7	7		14	20		20	7	19		26	7	22	29
Halifax	116	45	78	239	116	6	122	116	78	11	205	44	10	54	116	45	50	211	116	45	161
Hants	11	18	6	35	11		11	11	6		17	18		18	11	18		29	11	18	29
Inverness	14	10	1	25	14		14	14	1		15	10		10	14	10		24	14	11	25
Kings	36	18	20	74	36		36	36	20		56	18		18	36	18		54	36	18	54
Lunenburg	29	12		41	29		29	29			29	12		12	29	12		41	29	12	41
Pictou	59	79		138	59		59	59	54		113	79	2	81	59	79		138	59	79	138
Queens		24	5	29					5		5	24		24		15		15		24	24
Shelburne	18	18	6	42	18		18	18	6		24	9		9	18	9		27	18	18	36
Victoria	25	8		33	25		25	25	4		29	8		8	25	9		34	25	8	33
Yarmouth	24	22	14	60	16		16	24	11		35	20		20	24	22		46	24	22	46
Total, 1893...	581	462	231	1274	643	6	649	581	303	23	907	450	12	462	581	444	50	1075	581	465	1046

TABLE XIX.—COUNTY ACADEMIES. (Continued.)

ANALYSIS OF HIGH SCHOOL STUDIES.

ACADEMY.	ARITHMETIC Grade IX	Grade X	Grade XI	Total.	ALGEBRA Grade IX	Grade X	Grade XI	Grade XII	Total.	GEOMETRY Grade IX	Grade X	Grade XI	Grade XII	Total.	Practical Mathematics Grade XI	Physiology Grade XI	Psychology Grade XII	Sanitary Science Grade XII	Zoology Grade XII	Geology Grade XII	Astronomy Grade XII	Navigation Grade XII	Trigonometry Grade XII	Manual Training Grade X
Annapolis	16	14	13	43	16	14	13		43	16	14	13		43	13	13								
Antigonish	46	61	26	133	46	61	26	12	145	46	61	26	12	145	26	20	15	4		27		26	26	
Cape Breton	36	26	8	70	36	26	8		70	36	26	8		70	8	8								
Colchester	102	43	37	182	102	43	37		182	102	43	37		182	37	37								
Cumberland	30	26	20	76	30	26	20		76	30	26	20		76	20	20								
Digby	12	18		30	12	18	8		38	12	18	8		38	8	8								
Guysboro	7	22	7	36	7	19	7		33	7	19	7		33	7	7								
Halifax	116	45	78	239	116	45	79	7	247	116	45	78	11	250	78	78	11	11	6	6	6	5	11	39
Hants	11	18	6	35	11	18	6		35	11	18	6		35	6	6								
Inverness	14	10	1	25	14	10	1		25	14	10	1		25	1	1								
Kings	36	18	20	74	36	18	20		74	36	18	20		74	20	20								
Lunenburg	29	12		41	29	12			41	29	12			41										
Pictou	59	79	54	192	59	79	55	8	201	59	79	55	8	201	54	55							8	
Queens		24	5	29		24	5		29		24	5		29	5	5								
Shelburne	18	18	6	42	18	18	6		42	18	18	6		42	8	5								
Victoria	25	8	4	37	25	8	4		37	25	8	4		37	4	4								
Yarmouth	24	22	14	60	24	22	14		60	24	22	14		60	14	14								
Total, 1893	581	464	299	1344	581	461	309	27	1378	581	461	308	31	1381	309	302	26	15	6	33	6	31	45	39

TABLE XIX.—COUNTY ACADEMIES.—(Continued).

ACADEMY.	No. Holding Prov. Certificate or Teacher's License					Total No. High School Pupils.					No. H. Sch. Pupils Taking Full Regular Course.					No. Taking Partial or Special Course.				
	Grade IX.	Grade X.	Grade XI.	Grade XII.	Total.	Grade IX.	Grade X.	Grade XI.	Grade XII.	Total.	Grade IX.	Grade X.	Grade XI.	Grade XII.	Total.	Grade IX.	Grade X.	Grade XI.	Grade XII.	Total.
Annapolis			10		10	16	14	13		43	16	14	13		43					
Antigonish		20	6		26	46	61	28	15	150	44	61	26	9	140	2		2	6	10
Cape Breton		3	7		10	36	26	10		72	36	26	8		70			2		2
Colchester		2	2		4	102	43	37		182	101	43	35		179	1		2		3
Cumberland	1				1	30	26	20		76	30	26	20		76					
Digby		1	3		4	12	18	8		38	12	18	8		38					
Guysboro						7	22	7		36	7	19	7		33		3			3
Halifax		1	15	8	24	116	47	79	11	253	115	44	78	11	248	1	3	1		5
Hants		2			2	11	18	6		35	11	18	6		35					
Inverness			1		1	14	10	1		25	14	10	1		25					
Kings			6		6	36	18	20		74	36	18	20		74					
Lunenburg		1			1	31	12			43	29	12			41	2				2
Picton			24	3	27	56	79	55	9	199	56	79	55	8	198				1	1
Queens			3		3		24	5		29		24	4		28			1		1
Shelburne		1	6		7	18	18	6		42	18	9	6		33		9			9
Victoria			4		4	25	8	4		37	24	8	4		36	1				1
Yarmouth		1	2	1	4	24	22	14		60	24	22	12		58			2		2
Total, 1893	1	32	89	12	134	580	466	313	35	1394	573	451	303	28	1355	7	15	10	7	39

TABLE XIX.—COUNTY ACADEMIES, (Continued.)

ACADEMY	AVERAGE AGE OF TOTAL PUPILS IN EACH GRADE. (on first day of School Year.)				REVENUE.					EXPENDITURE.					
	Grade IX. Yrs.	X. Yrs.	XI. Yrs.	XII. Yrs.	Provincial Grant.	School Section Funds.	Fees.	Other Sources.	Total.	Salaries.	Apparatus.	Building and Repairs.	Fuel and Attendance.	Miscellaneous.	Total.
Annapolis	14.7	15.75	17.61		$375 00	$465 00			$840 00	$675 00		$300 00	$165 00		$840 00
Antigonish	14.88	18.18	28.53	21.06	1125 00	550 00	$50 00	$1112 50	2837 50	2287 50	$50 00		150 00	$50 00	2837 50
Cape Breton	14.83	19.95	18.33		750 00	775 00			1525 00	1200 00	15 00		160 00		1525 00
Colchester	14.75	15.25	15.83		1125 00	2403 75			3528 75	2418 75	60 00	500 00	500 00	50 00	3528 75
Cumberland	15.81	16.02	15.74		375 00	900 00		7132 37	8407 37	1293 75		6375 00	100 00	138 62	8407 37
Digby	15.5	16.5	17.25		375 00	590 75			965 75	562 50	160 00		240 00	3 25	965 75
Guysboro	13.94	15.32	16.26		375 06	237 50			612 50	562 50			50 00		612 50
Halifax	14.36	15.85	16.35	18.55	1290 00	3921 78	220 16	1005 56	6437 50	5662 50		152 52	455 54	166 94	6437 50
Hants	14.69	15.24	16.8		375 00	398 00			773 00	750 00	23 00				773 00
Inverness	14.81	15.71	15.84		375 00	261 50			636 50	562 50	5 00	4 00	55 00	10 00	636 00
Kings	14.71	15.65	16.92		750 00	722 50			1472 50	1890 00	6 00	1 50	75 00		1472 50
Lunenburg	15.02	16.16			875 00	770 00			1145 00	750 00	20 00	200 00	150 00	25 00	1145 00
Pictou	14.52	15.91	19.68	18.92	1290 00	2152 00	205 00		3647 00	2550 00	5 00	446 00	470 00	176 00	3647 00
Queens		16.09	17.58		875 00	617 50			992 50	562 50		400 00	30 00		592 50
Shelburne	13.9	15.93	19.14		875 00	202 01			577 01	562 50	14 57				577 01
Victoria	17.	17.08	15.5		375 00	234 50			609 50	562 50	4 00	15 00	88 00		609 50
Yarmouth	14.72	15.54	17.04		750 00	1370 00			2120 00	2070 00	50 00				2120 00
Total, 1893	14.88	16.17	17.46	19.51	$10830 00	$16571 79	$475 16	$9250 43	$37127 38	$24422 50	$412 57	$8044 52	$3628 54	$619 81	$37127 38

TABLE XIX.—COUNTY ACADEMIES (Continued.)

ACADEMIES	GROUND. Dimensions of Grounds in which building is situated. (Decimetres)	REGULAR TEACHING ROOMS. Number of	REGULAR TEACHING ROOMS. Average dimensions of. (Decimetres)	ASSEMBLY ROOM. Dimensions of (if there is a special room). (Decimetres)	LIBRARY. Dimensions of room (if there is a special one, or of cabinet, cases or shelving if no spec'l room). (Decimetres)	LIBRARY. No. of Volumes.	LIBRARY. Estimated Value of the Books.	MUSEUM OF NATURAL HISTORY, PHYSIOL., &c. Dimensions of room (if there is a special one, or of cabinet, cases or shelving if no spec'l room). (Decimetres)	MUSEUM. Estimated Value of Collections, Models, &c.	LABORATORY. (Chemical.) Dimensions of room (if there is a special one, or of cabinet, cases or shelving if no spec'l room). (Decimetres)	LABORATORY. Estimated Value of Apparatus, &c., kept here.
Annapolis	104x139	1	31x55x123	37x109x178	33x52x78	2030	$3000 00	33x52x78	$ 100 00	31x55x65	$550 00
Antigonish	160x160	5	33x64x96		42x40x40	275	350 00			33x78x104	150 00
Cape Breton	90x110	2	42x90x90	50x110x215	48x18x48	60	100 00			42x40x30	300 00
Colchester	100x143	4	55x90x110	30x182x242						48x48x48	300 00
Cumberland	909x1818	2	30x91x106	36x74x198						30x61x91	
Digby	351x455	1	36x90x90			170	50 00			20x10x25	10 00
Guysboro	528x72	1	116x82x100								
Halifax	157x140	6	42x83x97	52x106x160	42x40x55	700	800 00	9x7x94	200 00	42x40x6	200 00
Hants	850x590	1	40x79x99							40x46x41	50 00
Inverness	210x300	2	30x60x70							20x15x15	20 00
Kings	640x640	2	47x78x87			150	100 00		20 00		20 00
Lunenburg	365x780	1	42x88x88		42x24x79						50 00
Pictou	650x1150	1	45x85x97	42x05x213	42x55x73	1170	1000 00	42x55x72	1200 00	45x52x50	200 00
Queens	305x955	1	42x86x110			55	25 00	14x10x3	20 00	28x19x5	
Shelburne	732x732	1	48x109x115						25 00		30 00
Victoria	500x660	1	30x60x70						50 00	22x4x22	25 00
Yarmouth	640x1460	2	39x81x89		14x13x15			22x4x22		22x4x22	250 00
Total, 1893		37				4610	$5425 00		$1615 00		$2155 00

TABLE XIX.—COUNTY ACADEMIES. (Continued.)

ACADEMIES.	LABORATORY. (Physical) Dimensions of room (if any), or of cabi-net, cases or shelv-ing (if no special room), Decimetres.	LABORATORY. Estimated Value of Apparatus kept here.	GYMNASIUM OR PLAY-ROOM. Dimensions of room (if any), Decimetres.	GYMNASIUM OR PLAY-ROOM. Estimated Value of Apparatus.	GENERAL. No. of Wall Maps, Charts and Globes.	GENERAL. No of reference books, &c., for teachers' desks.	GENERAL. Estimated Value of the same.	TOTAL VALUE. Estimated Value of all collections, ap-paratus, &c., (not including fur-niture, &c.,) used for teaching pur-poses.
Annapolis		$		$	19	4	$ 75 00	$ 125 00
Antigonish		150 00			30	50	150 00	4000 00
Cape Breton			44x90x166		40	10	40 00	800 00
Col.					12	11	15 00	500 00
Cumberland				100 00	10			400 00
Digby		25 00			10	1	60 00	160 00
Guysboro	29x7x24	150 00			15	2	8 00	93 00
Halifax		25 00	32x83x95		38	8	120 00	1650 00
Hants					12	3	25 00	100 00
Iness					4	1	15 00	35 00
Kings		70 00			21	6	97 00	181 00
Lunenburg		100 00			20	25	130 00	400 00
Pictou	42x52x52	500 00			56	4	100 00	3000 00
Queens	42x40x40	40 00			22	14	85 00	125 00
Shelburne					25	3	18 00	175 00
Victoria					8	10	9 00	59 00
Yarmouth					30	10	100 00	400 00
Total, 1893		$1060 00		$100 00	372	164	$1037 00	$12203 00

TABLE XX.—GOVERNMENT NIGHT SCHOOLS.

COUNTY.	SECTION.	TEACHER.	ASSISTANT.	Pupils Enrolled.	Average Attendance.	No. of Sessions.
Cape Breton	Bridgeport	Wm. Young		28	18	48
"	North Sydney	John D. McNeil		29	16	48
"	Mitchell	Jas. A. Mitchell		24	16	50
"	Batestou	Mark Bates		27	13	22
"	Gowrie	Edgar Wood		39	18	27
"	Little Bras D'Or	D. McK. Gillis		27	22	51
"	Reserve and Lorway	Jas. Hynes		49	11	35
"	Sydney Mines	Wm. Haggaty	Jeremiah Sullivan	47	26	50
"	"	Murdock Matheson		50	17	51
"	Low Point	S. A. McDonald		25	9	22
"	Little Glace Bay	Michael Mullins		31	21	40
"	Big Lorraine	Duncan Matheson		40	21	30
"	Mainadieu	A. Q. Ross		39	20	17
Cumberland	Amherst	N. A. Osborne		26	9	11
"	Joggins	John T. Gillis		35	16	23
Guysboro	St. Francis Harbor	Alex. D. McDonald		62	36	54
Inverness	Little Judique	John A. McDonald		41	19	54
"	Red Ban's	Daniel Di'l		32	22	45
Luneuburg	Mill Cove	Geo. M. Huggins		26	19	51
"	Bridgewater	Bruce McDonald		61	36	38
Pictou	Thorburn	A. S. McKenzie		48	22	46
"	Westville	John G. McDougall		66	20	84
"	Albion Mines	Jas. R. McD.nald		86	15	44
Richmond	St. Louis	Colin C. McLean		27	19	50
Victoria	Englishtown	D. F. McKay		27	23	45
"	N Smokey					

TABLE XXI.—PROVINCIAL HIGH SCHOOL EXAMINATION, JULY, 1893.

Station	Male Candidates	Female Candidates	Total Candidates	Male A — Candidates for Grade A	Male A — Received Grade A	Male A — Received Grade B	Male A — Received Grade C	Female A — Candidates for Grade A	Female A — Received Grade A	Female A — Received Grade B	Male B — Candidates for Grade B	Male B — Received Grade B	Male B — Received Grade C	Male B — Received Grade D	Male B — Failed	Female B — Candidates for Grade B	Female B — Received Grade B	Female B — Received Grade C	Female B — Received Grade D	Female B — Failed
Amherst	19	38	57	1			1	1			8	8		3		8	1	5	1	1
Annapolis	6	15	21	3	2	1					3	2		1		7	5	2	2	
Antigonish	23	33	56	1	1						8	8				4	2			
Arichat	8	5	13	1																
Baddeck	13	15	28								2	2	1			2	2		1	
Barrington	4	8	12								1	1								
Bridgetown	40	49	89	1	1			4	1	3	9	8				7	3	4	1	
Cheticamp	4	3	7																	
Clare	2	14	16	3		1	1				1	1				3	3	2		3
Digby	23	43	65	1							6	2	3		1	6	16	11	3	3
Guysboro	8	24	32								2		1			35	10	5	1	5
Halifax	77	154	231								25	10	6	9	5	16	3	1		
Kentville	23	66	89								5	2	2	1	1	4		1		
Liverpool	6	22	28								1	1				2		1		
Lockeport	13	11	24				1				2	1			1			2		
Lunenburg	7	49	56								1	1	1			1	1	1		1
Margaree Forks	7	6	13								1	1	2							
New Glasgow	29	54	83	2	1						7	5				7	5	1	4	
Normal School	5	70	75	1	1		1				1	1	1			24	11	8		1
Parrsboro	1	16	17								1									
Pictou	38	61	99								2	3	2	1	1	6	3	3		1
Port Hawkesbury	6	11	17								1					4		4		1
Port Hood	23	19	42	2	1						2	1				2	1			
Shelburne	2	8	10								1		1			1	1			
Sherbrooke		1	1													1	1		1	
Sydney	22	27	49			4					1					3	3			
Tatamagouche	6	18	24																	
Truro	41	67	108	1							5	5	2			8	3	3		
Windsor	16	34	50	1							1	1	1			3	4	1		3
Yarmouth	35	60	95	2	2						16	9	5		1	15	9	4	1	5
Total, 1893	**505**	**1001**	**1506**	**17**	**9**	**4**	**4**	**4**	**1**	**3**	**117**	**67**	**26**	**9**	**15**	**167**	**83**	**55**	**14**	**15**

TABLE **XXI**.—PROVINCIAL HIGH SCHOOL EXAMINATIONS, JULY, 1893, (Continued).

STATIONS.	Male C. Candidates for Grade C.	Male C. Received Grade C.	Male C. Received Grade D.	Male C. Failed.	Female C. Candidates for Grade C.	Female C. Received Grade C.	Female C. Received Grade D.	Female C. Failed.	Male D. Candidates for Grade D.	Male D. Received Grade D.	Male D. Failed.	Female D. Candidates for Grade D.	Female D. Received Grade D.	Female D. Failed.	Total received Grade A.	Total received Grade B.	Total received Grade C.	Total received Grade D.	Total received Certificates.	No. received Grade applied for.	No. received lower Grade than applied for.	No. failed.
Amherst																						
Annapolis																						
Antigonish																						
Arichat																						
Baddeck																						
Barrington																						
Bridgetown																						
Cheticamp																						
Clare																						
Digby																						
Guysboro																						
Halifax																						
Kentville																						
Liverpool																						
Lockeport																						
Lunenburg																						
Margaree Forks																						
New Glasgow																						
Normal School																						
Parrsboro																						
Pictou																						
Port Hawkesbury																						
Port Hood																						
Shelburne																						
Sherbrooke																						
Sydney																						
Tatamagouche																						
Truro																						
Windsor																						
Yarmouth																						
Total, 1893	174	62	63	49	422	142	138	142	197	88	109	408	147	281	10	157	289	439	915	598	317	591

TABLE XXII.—EXPENDITURE OF GOVERNMENT FUNDS FOR PUBLIC SCHOOLS, COUNTY ACADEMIES, &c.

School Year (Nine Months) Ended July, 1893.

COUNTY.	COMMON SCHOOLS.					County Academies.	Total assignable to Counties.
	Population.	No. of Schools in session.	No. of Pupils registered.	Sum of Government Grants.	Cost to Government per pupil.		
Annapolis	19350	110	4277	6525 70	$1 52	$375 00	$ 6900 70
Antigonish	16114	89	3532	4837 87	1 37	**2102 15	6940 02
Cape Breton	34244	161	6848	9145 17	1 33	750 00	9895 17
Colchester	27160	146	5841	8186 02	1 40	1125 00	9811 02
Cumberland	34529	181	8181	9945 80	1 22	375 00	10320 80
Digby	19897	97	4501	5212 50	1 15	375 00	5587 50
Guysboro	17195	85	3589	4206 77	1 17	375 00	4581 77
Halifax Co.	32863	142	6003	7605 07	1 26	.....	7605 07
" City	38495	129	7113	8327 06	1 17	1290 00	9617 06
Hants	22052	122	4948	7204 10	1 45	375 00	7579 10
Inverness	25779	153	5439	7848 58	1 44	375 00	8223 58
Kings	22489	122	5159	7322 46	1 41	750 00	8072 46
Lunenburg	31075	171	7312	8782 46	1 20	375 00	9157 46
Picton	34541	167	6814	9836 64	1 44	1290 00	11126 64
Queens	10610	54	1999	3182 52	1 56	375 00	3507 52
Richmond	14399	70	2780	4640 06	1 31	.....	3640 06
Shelburne	14956	77	3374	4400 07	1 30	375 00	4775 07
Victoria	12432	68	2221	3231 34	1 45	375 00	3606 34
Yarmouth	22216	108	4857	6232 01	1 28	750 00	6982 01
Total, 1893	450896	2252	94738	125622 20	$1 32	$11807 15	$137429 85

OTHER SERVICES AND TOTAL EXPENDITURE FOR EDUCATION.

Inspectors' Salaries	$9212 50
" Stationery, Postage, &c	500 00
Examination	1337 02
Travelling Expenses—Normal School Pupils	1439 80
Salaries	2550 00
Travelling Expenses—Superintendent	300 00
Office Expenses (Registers, Register Covers, Postage), Expressage, Telegrams, Stationery, &c	1449 14
Total	$ 16788 46
Last Column	137429 85
Total for Public Schools, 1893	$154217 81
Institution for Deaf and Dumb	1530 00
Halifax School for the Blind	1237 50
Manual Training School	750 00
Normal and Model Schools	5750 00
School of Agriculture	1125 00
Government Night Schools	1430 18
Total Government Expenditure	$166040 49

* $977.15 of this amount was for the previous year.

TABLE XXIII.

SUMMARY OF GOVERNMENT GRANTS FOR EDUCATION,
FOR (NINE MONTHS) ENDED, JULY, 1893.

Common Schools	$ 125,622 20
Normal School	5,750 00
Institution for Deaf and Dumb	1,530 00
Halifax School for the Blind	1,237 50
Manual Training School	750 00
County Academies	11,807 15
Inspection	9,712 50
Expenses (office)	1,449 14
Salaries "	2,850 00
Examination	1,337 02
School of Agriculture	1,125 00
Travelling Expenses Normal School Pupils	1,439 80
Government Night Schools	1,430 18
	$ 166,040 49

PART III.

APPENDICES.

APPENDIX A.

REPORT OF THE NORMAL SCHOOL.

A. H. MacKay, Esq., Ll. D.,
      Superintendent of Education.

Sir,—

During the last session of the Normal School, which closed on June 29th, the number of students in attendance was one hundred and sixty-three. The various counties of the Province were represented as follows :

Colchester 32
Cumberland................21
Pictou 21
Halifax....................16
Hants 12
Lunenburg................10
Inverness..................9
Kings 8
Queens....................7
Annapolis. 5
Yarmouth:................4
Cape Breton..............4
Antigonish 4
Shelburne................3
Guysborough 3
Digby 1
Richmond.................1
Prince Edward Island.......1
Newfoundland.............1

At the time of enrolment one held license of class A, nineteen held class B, fifty-four class C, and thirty-six class D.

Six were College graduates—two of Acadia, two of St. Francis Xavier, and two of Dalhousie. Several others were undergraduates of these Colleges and Mt. Allison.

On the whole the session may be regarded as a successful one. The attendance was larger than it had been for several years ; the ability nd scholarship of the students were above the average; and the eneral health was good. Two very promising students were comelled to leave the institution on account of ill health, Mr. John Sturk of Canning, Kings county, and Miss Annie C. Archibald of Watervale, Pictou county, the latter dying a few weeks after her return home. Miss Archibald was a most amiable young woman and greatly endeared herself to both teachers and students.

As the outcome of our work fifty-nine students were graduated in the first rank, fifty-nine in the second rank, and thirty-six in the third rank. Two graduates of a former session were not advanced to higher standing, and seven not completing the course did not receive diplomas.

It had been announced that academic work, in so far as it relates to the preparation of students in the scholarship required for license of the different classes, would be discontinued. Many applicants for admission, not fully understanding the nature of the change, came with the expectation that the work would follow old lines with some of the classes; that is, imparting the scholarship required for higher classes of license as well as giving the more strictly professional training. Among these were several of great promise, young men and women of excellent ability and possessed of those moral qualities which are ever to be ranked among the highest and most essential qualifications of the teacher. To obviate any disappointment and inconvenience which might arise out of an abrupt transition from the old to the new order of things, we thought it advisable to admit these applicants and give them the combined course which they desired. This decision involved the division of the school into five classes:

1. The first class pursuing the professional course for a diploma of the First Rank.

2. The second class taking the combined academic and professional course for High School Certificate of First Grade and diploma of First Rank.

3. The third class pursuing professional course for diploma of Second Rank.

4. The fourth class taking a combined academic and professional course for High School Certificate of Second Grade and diploma of Third Rank.

5. The fifth class taking a combined academic and professional course for High School Certificate of Third Grade and diploma of Third Rank.

It will be readily understood that this wide field taxed pretty heavily the energies of the teaching staff; every one, however, accepted the conditions as matter of supreme duty and wrought with willing

The Governor General's medals were awarded as follows:

1. Silver Medal to Mr. Albert E. Brownrigg.
2.   "   "   Mr. Harry Irwin.
3. Bronze Medal to Miss Florence Crawford.
4.   "   "   Miss Ellen M. Skerry.
5.   "   "   Mr. Patrick A. McGarry.

While the leaders of educational thought and of educational work in all civilized countries are pretty well agreed that the highest measure of success in practical education is conditioned on the special training of teachers, yet occasionally the utility of Normal Schools is challenged and especially the propriety of making this training compulsory. It is said by some that our teachers remain so short a time in the work that the service rendered is not an equivalent for the expenditure of time and means involved in the training process. There is another way of looking at the matter. If those who assume the office of the teacher made teaching a life calling, or a business of several years' duration, they might by and by acquire a good degree of skill in the school of experience and thus in the later years of their service make some compensation for their blundering in the earlier periods. But if our schools are for the most part in the hands of beginners, the impression forces itself pretty strongly on the thoughtful mind that there is all the more need of some special training that these tyros may, during their brief tenure, have the benefit of the thinking and experience of others.

True, indeed, training is not everything. It is not claimed, and it should not be expected, that every trained teacher will prove a success in the school room. There are essential qualities which the Normal School cannot impart. One must have the proper stuff to work on in making teachers as in other things, or the results will be as disappointing as the traditional failure to manufacture the silk purse from unsuitable material. There must be the solid substratum of natural ability, scholarship, moral character and common sense; otherwise professional training amounts to very little.

Nor is skill in teaching the exclusive gift of the Normal School. Some may by a sort of instinct know what to do and how to do it; others may be capable of discovering the road to success in the school of experience. But I cannot help thinking that the born teachers and those who have the gift of becoming self-made teachers may be able to work with less expenditure of energy and with more economy of time and material after some study of the fundamental principles on which successful teaching depends, and a little guiding by those who have given long years to the work. Success in this department of human effort is governed by law and is dependent on rational principles as well as in most other kinds of business.

I have the honour to be,
Sir, yours with much respect,

JOHN B. CALKIN.

Normal School, Truro, N. S., Sept. 30th, 1893.

.

STUDENTS OF SESSION, 1892-'93.

AWARDED FIRST RANK DIPLOMAS.

Allen, Olga F	Dartmouth	Halifax Co.
Armstrong, Mertie	Port Medway	Queens.
Atwood, Alice J.	Clementsport	Annapolis.
Beattie, Frank H	Pictou	Pictou.
Bigney, Anna L	Wentworth	Cumberland.
Bigney, Annie M	Hantsport	Hants.
Bigney, Arthur O.	Mt. Denson	Hants.
Brooks, Ethel	Burlington	Hants.
Brownrigg, Albert E	Pictou	Pictou.
Campbell, Robert S	Tatamagouche	Colchester.
Carter, Bessie M	Canaan	Kings.
Christopher, Maude	Brookfield	Queens.
Clements, Annie M	Port Medway	Queens.
Church, Nina E	Bedford	Halifax.
Connolly, Edward	North Intervale	Guysboro.
Corbin, Maude E	Bedford	Halifax.
Cox, Jeannette	Upper Stewiacke	Colchester.
Creelman, William A	Truro	Colchester.
Culton, Sophia A	Springville	Pictou.
Cunningham, Wm	Tatamagouche	Colchester.
Davidson, Lucretia F.	Little Bass River	Colchester.
Dickson, Hattie	Onslow	Colchester.
Dickson, Julia	Oxford	Cumberland.
Fisher, L. Louise	Bridgetown	Annapolis.
Ford, Andrew S	Amherst	Cumberland.
Fraser, Hugh McL	Pictou	Pictou.
Gray, Wm. S	Hopewell	Pictou.
Gunn, Annie C	East River St. Mary's	Pictou.
Hardwick, Mary L	Annapolis	Annapolis.
Hebb, Bertha B	Bridgewater	Lunenburg.
Hemmeon, Morley D	Wolfville	Kings.
Hogg, Henry B	Yarmouth	Yarmouth.
Irwin, Harry	Shelburne	Shelburne.
Johnston, Isabel	Westville	Pictou.
Kaulback, Mary	Bridgewater	Lunenburg.
Mack, Edward E	Mill Village	Queens.
McGarry, Patrick A	Margaree	Inverness.
MacInnes, Lenora	Truro	Colchester.
MacGregor, Helen	Halifax	Halifax.
MacKenzie, Ellen M	Stellarton	Pictou.
MacLennan, Alexis	Cow Bay	{ Cape Breton.
MacNeill, Bessie	Berwick	Kings.

MacPhee, Margaret J..... South River .... Antigonish.
McPherson, Hugh........ Fraser's Mills .... Antigonish.
Martin, Oscar McN..... East Jordan .... Shelburne.
Messenger, Laura........ Tremont .... Kings.
Morton, Flora.......... New Germany .... Lunenburg.
Murphy, Jennie B ...... Shelburne .... Shelburne.
Murray, Sadie E......... New Glasgow .... Pictou.
Nichols, Edward H ..... Digby .... Digby.
Ross, Susie .... Canning .... Kings.
Skerry, Ellen M........ New Ross .... Lunenburg.
Smith, Pearl........... Chester .... Lunenburg.
Sullivan, Lillie J .... Guysboro' .... Guysboro'.
Tomkins, Morris........ Margaree............ Inverness.
Wallace, Flora B....... Avondale............ Hants.
Willett, Clara.......... Tupperville .... Annapolis.
Wilson, Blanche........ Truro .... Colchester.
Woodill, Arthur .... Sydney .... Cape Breton.

AWARDED SECOND RANK DIPLOMAS.

Barnes, Belinda .... Harbor Grace .... Newfoundland.
Barrett, Frederic E ..... Truro .... Colchester.
Boyd, Annie L .... Loch Lomond........ Richmond.
Brennan, Jessie J. C..... Lake George......... Kings.
Burris, Estella .... Lower Musquodoboit... Halifax.
Calder, Maud .... Truro .... Colchester.
Cameron, Lizzie M...... Piedmont Valley ..... Pictou.
Carter, Ida .... Amherst .... Cumberland.
Chisholm, Sarah J...... Salt Springs .... Antigonish.
Chisholm, Annie .... Great Village .... Colchester.
Crandall, Ella D........ Wolfville .... Kings.
Crawford, Florence ..... New Dublin .... Lunenburg.
Crowe, Clara........... Pleasant Hills........ Colchester.
Cumming, Mabel .... Westville .... Pictou.
Currie, Minnie .... West Dublin......... Lunenburg.
Davison, Geo. W....... Woodville .... Hants.
Doyle, Mary A .... Melford .... Inverness.
Freeman, Winnie... .... Pleasant River ...... Queens.
Frizzle, Wm. H........ Margaree .... Inverness.
Fulton, Susie D........ Folly Village .... Colchester.
Gammell, Nessie .... Upper Stewiacke...... Colchester.
Graham, Lois A .... Wentworth .... Cumberland.
Grant, Mary .... Middle Musquodoboit .. Halifax.
Grant, Jessie E. .... Springville .... Pictou.
Harris, Laura J........ Bear River .... Annapolis.
Henderson, Bella .... Henderson Settlement.. Cumberland.
Higgins, Roxie........ Middle Musquodoboit .. Halifax.

Johnson, Addie C........	East Mountain	Colchester.
Kaulbeck, Tena.........	Clifton ....,	Colchester.
Layton, Fannie L........	Middle Musquodoboit ..	Halifax.
LeBlanc, Emilie	Eel Brook	Yarmouth.
Lightbody, Maggie	Belmont	Colchester.
Lindsay, Lizzie..........	Belmont	Colchester.
Lynds, Laura E..........	DeBert	Colchester.
Lyons, Mamie I	Upper Onslow	Colchester.
MacCurdy, Tena	Clifton.............	Colchester.
MacDonald, Lizzie.......	Iron Ore	Pictou.
MacKay, Janet..........	Plymouth	Yarmouth.
MacKay, Mary F	Plymouth	Yarmouth.
MacLachlin, Ethel.......	Lunenburg	Lunenburg.
MacTavish, Jessie	Carriboo	Pictou.
MacGregor, Ellen........	Westville............	Pictou.
Miller, Stella............	Folly Village...	Colchester.
Moffatt, Annie M........	Little Bras d'Or.......	Cape Breton.
Moffatt, Mary E	Little Bras d'Or.......	Cape Breton.
Munro, Sadie E	Central Onslow	Colchester.
Murdock, Selina	West Gore............	Hants.
Murray, Christena S.....	North Earlton	Colchester.
Nelson, Blanche S	Truro	Colchester.
O'Brien, Helen..........	Noel.................	Hants.
Partridge, Ethel	Halifax	Halifax.
Roy, Bessie	Maitland	Hants.
Salter, Hattie M.	Scotch Village	Hants.
Shankel, Bolton	Hubbard's Cove	Halifax.
Simpson, Lydia W.	Springhill	Cumberland.
Sinclair, Maggie	Bridgeville	Pictou.
Sturk, John N..........	Canning	Kings.
Sutherland, Rose A	Goshen	Guysboro'.
Swift, Sara A.	Springhill	Cumberland.

AWARDED THIRD RANK DIPLOMAS.

Anderson, Tillie.........	Harbor Bouche........	Antigonish.
Annand, Laura..........	Gay's River Road......	Halifax.
Archibald, Mary Maud ..	Upper Musquodoboit...	Halifax.
Atkinson, Janie.........	Southampton	Cumberland.
Beaton, Katie ....:...	Mabou	Inverness.
Blair, Carrie T	Truro................	Colchester.
Caldwell, Hannah M.	New Germany	Lunenburg.
Carle, Bessie............	Truro................	Colchester.
Ervin, Anetta	Gay's River Road......	Halifax.
Goodwin, Bessie F	Lorneville	Cumberland.
Graham, Melissa	Upper Stewiacke	Colchester.
Hebb, Eugenie F	Kempt	Queens.

Henderson, Emma B . . . . . Henderson Settlement. . Cumberland.
Henderson, Eleanor J . . . . Henderson Settlement. . Cumberland.
Leslie, Lillie . . . . Spry Bay . . . . Halifax.
MacAloney, Maggie . . . . . . West Brook . . . . Cumberland.
Mayne, Minnie B . . . . Noel Shore . . . . Hants.
MacCloskey, Addie E . . . . Northport . . . . Cumberland.
Mahoney, Libbie . . . . Henderson Settlement. . Cumberland.
MacDaniel, Matthew G . . Margaree Forks . . . . Inverness.
McDonald, Sarah . . . . River Dennis . . . . Inverness.
MacDonald, Tena S . . . . . . Whitburn . . . . Pictou.
Mackay, Maggie B . . . . . . Waugh's River . . . . Colchester.
MacKay, Cassie . . . . McLellan's Mt . . . . Pictou.
MacKenzie, Maggie E . . . . Durham . . . . Pictou.
MacMaster, Maria C . . . . . . Creignish . . . . Inverness.
Minard, Clara V . . . . Brookfield . . . . Queens.
Mitchell, George S . . . . . . Linden . . . . Cumberland.
Munro, John A . . . . Pugwash . . . . Cumberland.
O'Regan, Mamie . . . . Parrsboro' . . . . Cumberland.
Patterson, Daisy E . . . . . . Linden . . . . Cumberland.
Redmond, James A . . . . . . Pugwash . . . . Cumberland.
Reid, Maggie D . . . . Union . . . . Colchester.
Smith, Elmer . . . . Pugwash . . . . Cumberland.
Wilson, Maggie N . . . . River John . . . . Pictou.
Wright, Lilah J . . . . Upper Nine Mile River. Pictou.

FORMER GRADUATES.

*Archibald, Annie C . . . . Watervale . . . . Pictou.
Hiltz, Jessie . . . . Chester . . . . Lunenburg.

COURSE UNCOMPLETED.

Bradley, John A . . . . Princeport . . . . Colchester.
Fulton, Sadie . . . . Folly Village . . . . Colchester.
Hubley, Winifred . . . . French Village . . . . Halifax.
Hunt, Henry J . . . . Mabou . . . . Inverness.
McKay, Thomas C . . . . . . Dartmouth . . . . Halifax.
Ross, Mary Sophia . . . . . . North Bedeque . . . . P. E. I.
Teck, Henry J . . . . Milford . . . . Hants.

*Deceased.

NORMAL SCHOOL.

Year.	No. of Teachers.	PUPILS.		EXPENDITURE.				
		Total number enrolled.	Received Diploma.	Salaries of Teachers.	Salary of Janitor.	Cost of Fuel.	Contingencies— Stationery, etc.	Total.
1893	6	163	154	$5400	$400	$219 47	$382 82	$6402 29
1892	5	114	81	4800	400	210 00	440 00	5850 00

MODEL SCHOOL.

Year.	No. of Teachers.	PUPILS.		EXPENDITURE.			
		Average daily attendance.	Total number different Pupils registered.	Salaries of Teachers.	Amount received from Province.	Amount received from Truro.	Total.
1893	2	87	119	$1100	$600	$500	$1100
1892	2	86	112	1050	550	500	1050

APPENDIX B.

REPORTS OF INSPECTORS OF SCHOOLS.

DISTRICT No. 1.—HALIFAX.

HINKLE CONDON, *Inspector.*

SIR,—

I respectfully submit the following as my twenty-second annual report on the public schools for Halifax District, No. 1.

The new regulations which came into operation on the 1st of November, 1892, introduced several important changes, so that the three quarters of eleven weeks each that ended on the 31st day of July, 1893, may fairly be considered as a period of trial and transition.

The changed date for holding the annual meetings from the last Monday in September to the last Monday in June caused some anxiety as to its effect on the amount to be voted by the ratepayers for the support of schools.   These apprehensions were not wholly unreasonable, when we remember that five-eighths of the sections in Halifax County are situated on or near the sea coast; and that many of the ratepayers are necessarily away from home in the months of June, July and August.   As you are aware one of the strongest objections against the change from the old two-term system to the present, was made on this ground that the last of September saw the fishermen's harvest pretty well gathered in, and the ratepayers would perhaps be better able and more willing to vote the necessary supplies for carrying on the school work of the section.

I received several letters assuring me that it would be useless to attempt to hold the annual meeting at the newly appointed date.   To each my answer was, " Put up your notices, hold your meeting, do your best, and report promptly."

I was requested to call a special annual meeting in three cases only

Furthermore, a careful examination of the minutes of the annual meetings discloses the fact that the amount voted in a majority of the sections for all school purposes fully came up to that of 1892.

At the annual meeting in St. James' section, No. 3, head of St. Margaret's Bay, some of the ratepayers were in favour of repairing their school-house while others were for building a new one. It was finally decided that, inasmuch as the site of the present building is very bad and cannot be improved, and moreover, as the total enrolment for 1893 was 84, and as the law requires for "any section having between 50 and 80 pupils, a house with comfortable sittings for the same, and a good class room for the assistant," a suitable house should be erected upon a site where sufficient room would also be afforded with land for a good play-ground. A few days after this decision, the house was in ashes. This makes the third school-house destroyed by fire in three adjoining sections, viz: No. 4, in Head Harbour section ; No. 3½, in East River, for which the incendiary is serving a three years' term in the penitentiary ; and now this one in No. 3. The house in the Partridge River, Preston section, was also burned in February last; but this was caused by the "ash barrel." John Shatford, Esq., warden of Halifax Municipality, at the last meeting of the Western Board, moved the following resolution: "That whereas, so many school-houses, in Halifax county and in the Province at large, have been destroyed by fire; therefore resolved, that in the opinion of this Board, a law should be enacted rendering it compulsory on trustees to keep the school property in their charge properly insured."

The South section, in Middle Musquodoboit, has erected a large and commodious house.

In no two years of my experience as Inspector, have as many school and out-houses been repaired and either painted or white-washed. I have called the attention of teachers and trustees to the following, as contained in the August and April Journals of Education: "If out-houses are not kept inoffensive, both as to odor and sight. the school buildings should be condemned until they are made safe both as regards the public health and morals. Both teacher and trustees should lose the public moneys while the buildings continue, according to the Inspector's opinion, unsightly or unsafe."

The number of schools in session during any part of the year (nine months) was 142, and the number of pupils registered, 6003. In 1892, (twelve months) 144 schools were in session and the number of pupils in attendance was 6692.

The Classes of the 144 teachers in charge were:

Class A 1
 " B............ 10
 " C............ 83
 " D............ 50

Males numbered 13, and females 131.

You will find in Table 8, that the average number of minutes per week, taken by teachers during the year, in giving instruction in the various subjects gives:

For reading................ 310 minutes.
  " arithmetic 330   "
  " spelling 196   ..
  " writing................ 116   ..
  " geography 98   ..
  " history 96   ..
  " grammar 98   ..

Reading, spelling, writing and arithmetic make a total of 952 minutes per week, and these together with grammar, geography, history and drawing give 1328, out of, say, a possible 1500, or about 22 hours a week out of 25.

The average salary from the sections for Class B, male teachers, is $296. For 1892, Classes A and B, $427. Up to the present year Classes A and B have been taken together, and Dartmouth has paid a salary of $1000 less the Provincial grant of $118. For 1893, Dartmouth pays to Principal Miller $1100, less the government money.

Hygiene and Temperance. I anticipate much good from the introduction and use of the "Health Readers," especially in the hands of earnest and competent teachers. Our schools are ready for them. The Temperance and Tobacco Acts did not come into operation any too soon.

I have in many of our schools recommended two short recesses in the forenoon and two in the afternoon. The windows are then thrown up and in this way good ventilation is secured. An authority says: "As a hygienic agency nothing can take the place of amusements. Recreation is *re*-creation. Study exhausts; play rests."

I am happy to say that our teachers as a body are steadily advancing in efficiency. Experience and application have enabled many, who commenced with but slender qualifications, to obtain higher Classes and become useful teachers.

"Good schools are the natural results of good teaching. They never come of good school-houses, or good courses of study, or good superintendence. All these external means are useful and necessary as conditions, but good teachers, guided by a true method of work, constitute the efficient causes of all good schools."

More than half of our schools responded to the invitation and prepared more or less work for the World's Fair. The best specimens were submitted to very competent judges and pronounced creditable to the teachers and pupils.

On the first of March it was my pleasing duty to attend the opening of a public school in the Indian settlement, about five miles from Dartmouth. The school-house was built by the Dominion Government, to which they have added a grant, thus far, at the rate of $150 per annum.

As this is the first and only school in Halifax County established for these " dusky sons of the forest," the opening proceedings which the parents of the children attended, gave me an opportunity to observe how keenly they appreciated the privilege this school will afford for the education of their children.

The school began with 12, but at the examination on the 10th of July there were 17 present; and it w.s pleasant to see how much had been accomplished in the short time of four months. I succeeded in getting a teacher who knew enough of kindergarten games and object lessons to interest the little ones and arouse their intelligence. My deep interest in this school has led me to visit it on four occasions and to aid the teacher by advice. The kindergarten occupations have been wonderfully developing and it has been a delightful surprise to see how readily they would build up forms, and how quickly and accurately they learned to count and calculate from objects. Justice compels me to ~ay that I have never seen parents who were more grateful to the teacher who has endeavoured to inculcate habits of neatness, cleanliness and good manners. The house is kept scrupulously clean and wholesome.

During the school year, I made 197 visits to the county schools and 103 to the city schools.

The Dartmouth schools, 21 in all, are under the able supervision of Principal Miller, assisted in the high school department by Miss Sara Findlay. Mr. Miller devotes about three hours of the day to teaching and the remaining time to the work of supervision.

City Schools. I have never visited the Halifax schools, with more perfect satisfaction than during the months of March and April of the present year. The steady improvements in the primary schools with regard to accommodation, teachers and classification in every respect during the last ten years, is remarkable and most encouraging. Writing on slates that would have done credit formerly to pupils of the third Grade is now to be seen in all the primary departments.

The city schools are now in a state of higher efficiency than at any previous period. They are conducted as a whole by a competent class of teachers who certainly discharge their important duties with energy, ability and fidelity.

The time for mere cramming or even for book teaching alone, and for lifeless routine in our schools is most certainly past.

Respectfully submitted,

H. CONDON.

To A. H. MacKay, Esq., Ll. D.,
      Superintendent of Education.

DISTRICT No. 2.—LUNENBURG AND QUEENS.

H. H. MacIntosh, *Inspector.*

Sir,—

I beg to submit the following report on the Public Schools of Inspectoral District No. 2. for year ended July 31st, 1893.

The number of sections remains the same as last year, 191, made up as follows:

District of Lunenburg and New Dublin ..... 116 sections.
   "   " Chester .... 29 "
   "   " South Queens................... 26 "
   "   " North " .... 20 "

There were 9 sections without school during the year, viz: 2 in Lunenburg and New Dublin, 1 in Chester, 4 in South Queens, and 2 in North Queens.

The year just closed cannot readily be compared, in regard to statistics, with previous years; suffice to say, that in grand total attendance there has been a marked increase over the corresponding part of the year 1892. The following table gives the number of schools in operation, number of pupils registered and attendance:

LUNENBURG COUNTY.

District.	No. of Schools.	Pupils Registered.	Grand Total Attendance.
Lunenburg & New Dublin	141	6002	504,163
Chester	30	1310	105,216
Total	171	7312	609,379

QUEENS COUNTY.

South Queens	36	1435	136,901
North "	18	564	41,850
Total	54	1999	178,751

In Lunenburg county the average attendance was 52 per cent. of the number registered, and in Queens county 55 per cent. The proportion of the population attending school in Lunenburg county was 1 in 4.25, and in Queens county, 1 in 5.3.

There were 230 teachers employed during the year, 174 in Lunenburg county and 56 in Queens, divided among the different Classes as follows:

	A	B	C	D
Lunenburg County...	2	10	73	89
Queens " ...	2	6	32	16

* Of these, 25 were males and 205 females, 28 being graduates of the Normal School.

On account of the recent changes, the past year was, in certain respects, one of considerable anxiety to many of our teachers, but at the same time was a very successful one, and the result of the year's work was most encouraging.

The meetings of the Boards of Commissioners were well attended with the exception of that of Chester, where a quorum could not be obtained. As the Board stands at present, it is difficult to get a quorum, some of the members having to come from fifteen to twenty miles to attend. The appointment of say three new commissioners in Chester town or vicinity would obviate the difficulty.

With a single exception, New Elm, all the schools on the mainland were visited and a number of them a second time. I was twice prevented from reaching New Elm on account of bad roads and stormy weather. In a number of instances, schools were not in session at the time of my visit to their neighbourhood, which necessitated my travelling over the same ground twice. Six out of nine island schools were visited; the other three were open during the winter months only and closed at the season of the year most suitable for visiting such. In some schools a day was spent, in others, a half-day, the average length of visit being from two to two and a half hours. This enabled me to make the work of inspection more thorough and satisfactory. Shorter visits would have given but little time for examining school work, as, in nearly every instance, more or less time had to be given to the explanation of registers, returns and new regulations.

Our school buildings, as a class, are improving from year to year. I say, as a class, for many are yet in a very unsatisfactory condition. Every year the worst of these are condemned and new ones take their places. Ten new school-houses have been built in Lunenburg county during the past three years and about fifteen thoroughly repaired within the same time, so that to-day there is a marked improvement in the general character of the buildings. The inside of many school-houses is much better than the outside and surroundings would seem to indicate, and if trustees would give a little attention to the exterior of the buildings, grounds, fences, &c., they would be surprised to see the improvement in appearance that can be made at a small cost.

The First Peninsula section has just completed and furnished with patent desks, a schoolhouse which easily takes a place among the best in the county.

The improvements to the Bridgewater school grounds have been completed, and they are now both an ornament and credit to the town.

The Trustees of Liverpool section have spent about $400 on the Academy.

Port Medway has repaired and improved buildings and surroundings.

Chester, Centreville, Pine Grove, Newburn and Hemfoid have effected much needed repairs to buildings.

A number of other sections have supplied patent seats and desks, painted buildings and enclosed grounds.

In justice to trustees, I must say that in nearly every instance they are ready to do what they can to benefit their school, and generally prompt in making suggested improvements. Several of our commissioners have also, in various ways during the past year, rendered valuable assistance.

I think our schools may be said to be fairly well supplied with necessary apparatus. In the way of maps, I endeavor to have placed in every section the Hemispheres, Dominion of Canada and Maritime Provinces. Calkin's Object Lessons, and text-books on health and temperance are in many schools. The largest graded schools, in addition to what is required for the common school departments, are suppplied with dictionaries, gazetteers, globes, and a few with chemical and physical apparatus.

Lunenburg Academy continues increasing in attendance and efficiency. This year the number enrolled was 664, an increase of 35 over last year. The number of High School pupils is also increasing every year, and their success at the Provincial Examination shows how thoroughly the work is being done. Principal McKittrick and the same staff of teachers continue in charge next year.

Liverpool Academy also made a splendid showing at the recent Provincial Examination and the general work of the whole institution was up to the usual high standard. Mr. Smith, principal for over fourteen years, retired at the close of the school year. He was one of the oldest and most successful members of the profession in the Province and as a classical teacher had few equals. During his principalship, the Academy enjoyed continuous success, and many of his former pupils are now occupying prominent positions in the professions both at home and abroad. He is succeeded by J. D. Sprague, Esq., for years preparatory teacher in the institution, a gentleman who has few peers in the profession and one to whom Liverpool Academy owes much.

H. B. Hogg, Esq., Class A, succeeds G. M. Huggins, Esq., as principal of the Bridgewater schools.

Principals Quinlan and Williams remain in Mahone Bay and Chester respectively. Both these schools do High School work and their candidates invariably do well at examination.

Although quite a number of the miscellaneous schools are still in the hands of inferior teachers, yet far the greater number are improving in character of work.

The greater part of the time is spent on the three R's and geography, grammar and history. In the teaching of these subjects, I am pleased to see that there is a growing tendency to make the work as practical as possible. A much better use of the text-book is made than formerly, and in the lower grades especially, nearly all the lessons are taught orally. The subject of temperance was taken up very generally throughout the district in the way of oral lessons from Richardson's text, so that the Health Readers will come on naturally, as a continuation of what has already been begun in this line.

The change from a semi-annual to an annual term, was received with general favour throughout the district, and has already commended itself to Trustees and Teachers. From the past year's experience, we find that trustees are now more particular about the kind of teacher they engage since the contract is for a year instead of six months, and having secured a good one are very loth to risk a change. Better work is also done by having the same teacher in charge for an unbroken term of a year. The summer vacation, coming at the close of the school year, is a great improvement, except that it robs the Inspectors of their holidays. The annual term is also decidedly favourable to the work of inspection. Besides, it bears hard on no section however small or weak, as the law provides for shorter terms for those sections unable to maintain a school throughout the whole year.

The system of Provincial Examinations is, I may say, universally favored by our teachers and has already proved quite an incentive, especially to our High Schools — pupils now not being debarred by age from asserting their scholarship.

About 85 candidates presented themselves at the two examining stations in this district, nearly two-thirds of them being pupils of the County Academies and High Schools, and I am proud to be able to state that compared with the rest of the Province they have made an excellent showing. Twenty-seven of the candidates also wrote for professional certificates — a large percentage of them being successful.

Our High Schools are now confining themselves exclusively to scholarship — professional work not being attempted. The result of this will necessarily increase the attendance from these counties at the Normal School.

The new register was a source of trouble to many teachers at first. They had not studied the directions and explanations and of course blundered sadly. Some misconstrued the directions and made what would seem almost impossible mistakes. These errors were pointed out at the time of inspection and teachers given to understand that the register must be kept and completed, exactly in accordance with the directions laid down therein. When the returns came to hand they were much more satisfactory than anticipated. I think this was largely due to the note in the register requiring every column to be filled in. Very few had to be sent back for completion or correction. As a consequence, the statistical tables lately forwarded you are more reliable than those of former years.

Trustees are required by law to file a copy of the minutes of the annual meeting with the inspector, within one week of the date of the same. Their attention has also been called to this regulation in the Journal of Education and the local papers. About 90 per cent. of the trustees in this district attend to the matter promptly; the others have be to personally reminded at the time of the distribution of County Fund.

In every instance, the teachers complied with the new regulation requiring them to give notice of the opening of school.

My correspondence for the past year would not have been nearly so great had all teachers made themselves acquainted with the contents of the Journal of Education. I had to answer scores of letters asking for information that was fully and clearly laid down in the Journal. We hope for an improvement in this respect next year.

The estimated value of school-buildings and grounds in the district is given at $98,445, and the value of school apparatus $2556—making the average value of school buildings $491 and average value of apparatus, $14 per school.

AVERAGE SALARIES, THREE-FOURTHS OF A YEAR.

		B	C	D
Lunenburg and New Dublin,	male...	$330.79	$167.39	$140.59
" " "	female .	215.69	164.39	121.23
Chester,	male...	330.69	162.39	......
"	female		159.61	114.96
South Queens,	male...	270.69	212.39	......
" "	female .	210.69	154.27	106.24
North Queens,	male...	308.19	167.39	......
" "	female		155.35	113.12

All required details are furnished in the abstracts already forwarded.

Your obedient servant,

H. H. MacINTOSH.

To A. H. MacKay, Esq., LL. D.
Superintendent of Education.

DISTRICT No. 3.—YARMOUTH AND SHELBURNE.

JAMES H. MUNRO, *Inspector*.

SIR,—

The recent changes will be fruitful of important results. They have been been effected so gradually that rate payers are learning to adapt themselves to them without inconvenience. There is a very general concensus of opinion that a year of one term will promote best the interests of education. The only objection offered—" What if we get a poor teacher?"—shows that trustees feel a deeper responsibility in regard to the fitness of the person whom they may engage. But even this risk will be lessened by the regulation which virtually compels teachers to make special preparation for their vocation at a Normal School. No enterprising teacher with an academic certificate will be satisfied with a license a grade lower.

Notwithstanding the misconstructions incident to a period of transition, the usual number of schools was in operation: in Yarmouth county, 108; in Shelburne, 77. In Yarmouth, a few which were miscellaneous schools have now two departments, namely: Lower East Pubnico, Upper East Pubnico, and Lower West Pubnico. On the other hand, in two which were graded the primary departments have been closed. The large attendance at Pembroke, Tusket Hill, and Sluice Point would warrant accommodations for two departments each.

I believe teachers in most instances feel responsible for the figures they enter when reporting the number of schoolable children that do not attend school at all during the year. These, I am happy to say, are conspicuous for their reduced number, more particularly in Shelburne county. The showing for Yarmouth county must ever be bad, so long as no special effort is made to educate the three hundred vagrants in the town of Yarmouth. It is true there is no accommodation for them; but what is a free school system for, if not to provide education for those who are too poor and neglectful to educate themselves? Judged by the past history of this town, the rate payers are willing to bear the burdens incident to the education of this class, and they would co-operate in procuring legislation to compel attendance at school. By all means let an effort be made for the benefit of these unfortunate children.

Two new school-houses were built and are now occupied for the first time. That at Forbes' Point deserves special notice. Of their own voluntary action, the rate payers purchased a new site with a lot capable of being made a fine play-ground, and erected a building, modern in its finish, and suitable as regards its appointments to the needs of the section. With an economical forethought, too rarely exercised, they assessed themselves in advance, and when the new building was ready for use, there was not one dollar of debt on it. And this by a people whose assessable property is estimated at seven thousand five hundred dollars! Truly, "where there is a will there is a way." In this district much confusion and mistrust have arisen by allowing debts to become old. In one section the people woke up to the fact that there was a heavy claim against them on receiving notice that the school-house was condemned. In another, rate payers refused to act as trustees, because the finances, dating back to the building of the school-house, had become an inextricable tangle. The example of the good people of Forbes' Point is a valuable object lesson, and should shame chronic croakers. I have referred to West Green Harbour. It is very strange to see in these days a new school-house close up to the public road, and without the vestige of a playground.

School repairs have been made in comparatively few sections. A year ago, recommendations of the Boards of Commissioners were forwarded to trustees, but being only "recommendations" little was done. Since then more energetic measures have been adopted, with the result that several school houses will soon be repaired and provided with modern furniture.

The School Commissioners have had their attention drawn lately to "the poor sections." It is felt that, in some instances at least, the law is too kind to them. In one place a rate payer whose tax used to be ten cents per annum was roused to "wrath unspeakable" when he had to pay fifteen. As the school tax was merely nominal, except to a limited few, the Commissioners removed Comeau's Hill from "the poor list," as also East Quinan, and Surrette's Island. All the sections receiving the special grants have been warned "that unless their school-rooms and furniture are kept good and comfortable, and such a supply of apparatus as is required by the C. P. I. provided, and a good percentage of attendance made, the extra grants will not be paid." While the fault of irregular attendance is seen in several of these sections, there is no place where it is so glaring as in Norwood (Lake George). With the youngest, most inexperienced, most timid, and certainly the cheapest teacher they can get, the trustees will excuse themselves—" how can you complain of poor attendance when the teacher is so poor?" I have been informed that there is a family here of several children of school age whose united attendance in a term would not equal the days the school was open.

I cannot boast of the efforts of rate payers to carry out my ideas of painting, fencing, levelling, &c. A few sections like Arcadia and Argyle Harbour have made a beginning, but the movement is not general. Rate payers should know that this is "a policy" which is backed by every Board of Commissioners in the district, and as it was recommended by the Council of Public Instruction nearly thirty years ago, it is time it had taken tangible shape. As a means to protect the school house, nothing is more effective than an attractive exterior, pleasant grounds, and neat paling.

I regret to say that too many of our school-houses have been built and repaired without reference to ventilation. Consequently the necessity was never more pressing that every school-room should be provided with convenient ventilators. Indeed, I hesitate not to say, that this is so important a matter as to call for prompt legislation. No school-room should be pronounced safe which has not board ventilators, or an equivalent, in two windows at least.

During the year the usual amount of work has been done, the good teachers doing their work better, the poor teachers doing it the same or more mechanically. In, nearly all cases the course of study is closely followed in spirit, if not always in the letter. In two or three schools I noticed a deviation—pupils in the fourth grade geography using a book. That is what the lazy teacher dearly loves. The mischief of such "teaching" is seen in the result—the study of geography is a memory exercise only, the map is without meaning, and the progress a mere turning of the leaves without benefit. One need have no difficulty in picking out pupils in advanced grades, who got their early lessons in that way. They will indicate the direction of the current of a river by pointing to its mouth and tracing it to its source, and not manifest surprise when properly informed. As they were never taught to associate the employments of the people with the resources and needs of the country, they can give no intelligent reason for the pursuits and habits of the people. Facts, isolated facts, make their whole stock of knowledge which often passes for education. The temptation to take such liberty with the Course would not exist, if it were authoritatively declared that no teacher should use books when engaged with classes.

It would have gratified me to have seen a deeper interest taken in the circulars sent from the Education Office, inviting the schools to prepare specimens of their work for the World's Fair. In Yarmouth county sixteen schools contributed, by far the largest number coming from schools in the town. Four French schools, Lower East Pubnico, Middle Wedge, and the Sisters' school at West Pubnico, and Eel Brook, furnished a large and varied assortment, and the Convent, situated in the latter section, very pretty exhibits in the kindergarten line. The teachers in Barrington municipality, could not have been more irresponsive had the circulars been written in an unknown tongue, and little better mention is due to those in Eastern Shelburne, for the only acknowledgment came from the school at Jordan Falls, which sent a general show of every day exercises, and from Lockeport, which favoured me with two photographic views of the local High School. Even that much was not received from the Shelburne Academy. In this connection I wish to suggest that when the schools are invited to furnish exhibits of their work, they should be provided with material by the Department. In no other way can country schools, at least, be able to show to advantage what they can do on the occasion referred to. Weeks were lost while waiting for the stationery that was needed.

An original feature of the new register, is the table for the entry of the number of minutes per week devoted by the teacher to each subject taught. Everyone will admit the utility of this table; but I would humbly submit that it ought to be preceded by a positive mandate for teachers to have a time-table in the school room, subject to the review of the Inspector of schools. The public would then have a guarantee of the actual application of the time as entered in the register. That some entries were thoughtless calculations I have ample proof, as the sum of the minutes was in excess of *seven* school days, and in other instances it was less than *three* days.

The Provincial examination of High School pupils in Yarmouth county was a great success. Nearly one hundred pupils presented themselves, and of these about three-fourths came from the Academy and Milton High School. The rest were mainly from Hebron, Maitland, Ohio and Tusket. No official statement of results has been received, but as far as I can learn a good proportion of candidates has made satisfactory averages. The late discussion about the course of study gives an interest to the element of age. The following are the ages of the youngest successful candidates in the D, C and B Grades :

> Grade D......12 years and 7 months.
>   "   C......14   "   " 3   "
>   "   B......15   "   " 8   "

Others succeeded who were only a few months the seniors of these.

Our local educationists are of one opinion in regard to the tests— they were easy enough to be passed by those who were sufficiently drilled in the subjects, and difficult enough to discourage reliance on superficial preparation. In a well appointed school, they maintain the course can be completed without undue pressure. These remarks are limited to the practical experience in D, C, and B grades. Next year Grade A will be on trial.

At Lockeport Station there were 22 candidates, and at Shelburne and Barrington a smaller number.

On reviewing the work of the year, I can see progress, and indications of a healthful interest in the public schools. Changes discretely made do much good: they excite a fresh interest, and mark a new starting point toward greater endeavour. Though they may seem simple enough when they have taken shape, every intelligent man knows that their elaboration required protracted thinking, sound judgment, and a familiar acquaintance with the educational systems of other countries. I trust you may enjoy the happiness of seeing great and lasting good resulting therefrom.

With assurances of profound respect,

I have the honor to remain,

Yours very sincerely,

JAMES H. MUNRO.

To A. H. MACKAY, ESQ., LL. D.,
      Superintendent of Education.

DISTRICT No. 4.—DIGBY AND ANNAPOLIS.

L. S. MORSE, A. M., *Inspector.*

SIR,—

In addition to the monthly reports, notes of inspection, and statistical tables already in your hands, the following general report for the school year ended on July 31st, 1893, is hereby submitted :

In consequence of the incorporation of the towns of Digby and Annapolis the established boundaries of the two sections at those places were disturbed. By the Town's Incorporation Act, incorporated towns form school sections of themselves, and in the two cases above named the limits of the towns do not correspond with the boundaries of those sections as they existed previously. Comparatively large and populous districts were thus thrown beyond the limits of said sections. An effort was made last winter to get special Acts passed by the Legislature of the Province to join those districts to the said towns for school purposes, but in both cases the attempt failed in consequence of opposition manifested by the rate-payers. In the case of Digby, the question was referred to the Board of School Commissioners for that district to recommend union with the Town of Digby or not as the Board in its wisdom might determine. At the meeting of the said Board, in May last, the Commissioners adjudicated upon the matter. A portion of the excluded district petitioned to be annexed to Hillgrove, Section No. 6, and another portion, north of the Racquette, asked to be formed into a new section. The Commissioners, by a majority vote, granted the prayer of these last named petitioners and formed a new section north of the Racquette, subject to the approval of the Council of Public Instruction. They also, by a unanimous vote, recommended that the limits of the town of Digby be extended so as to include for school purposes all the territory formerly included in Digby, Section No. 28, except that portion lying north of the Racquette; and in case the Council of Public Instruction should not sanction the formation of said new section, the Board also unanimously recommended that that portion of the original section, No. 28, lying north of the Racquette be also annexed to the town of Digby for school purposes. The Council of Public Instruction, as you are aware, did not sanction the formation of the said new section, and consequently it is expected that a special Act, necessary to extend this section to its original boundaries, will be passed during the coming winter.

In the case of Annapolis, Section No. 19, the Board of School Commissioners for that district was petitioned in May last to form the excluded portion of that section beyond the present town limits into a section by itself. No action was taken by the Board at that time in consequence of an informality in the application. A special meeting of the Board has since been called to adjudicate upon this matter so far as it has power, but at this writing a final decision has not been reached. Part of the rate-payers in this district wish to unite with the town for school purposes, and the other part wish the formation of a new section. The result in this case is yet unknown. It is hoped, however, that the Board of Commissioners, at the special meeting referred to, will take such action as will be satisfactory to those most deeply interested.

Reference has been made in former reports to the desirability of uniting Hillsburg, Section No. 3, in the district of Digby, and Bridge-port, Section No. 24, in the district of Annapolis west. This union had been recommended for years past, and the idea has been agitated and discussed in both sections until at last a majority of the rate-payers were lead to favour the project. At a public meeting of the rate-payers of both sections terms of union were amicably arranged, and the Boards of Commissioners of both districts were petitioned to unite the sections. As no opposition was offered, the said Boards, in May last, unanimously ordered the union of the said sections, which was finally accomplished by operation of the law on the date of the annual meeting in June. New school grounds have been selected and and approved, and a fine new school house will be erected during the ensuing year. The united section will be known as Bear River Section, No. 24, in the district of Annapolis West—the site for the new school-house having been located in Annapolis County.

Six sections in this Inspectoral District are not organized, and do not maintain schools in consequence of sparsity of inhabitants and general proverty. A few children from these sections obtain school privileges in adjoining sections. A few of the very weak sections other than those above mentioned cannot maintain school continually. By order of the various Boards of Commissioners, the sections classed as "*poor*" and therefore entitled to extra financial aid from the municipalities and government numbered *fifty*, of which *seventeen* had no schools during the year. *Twenty-seven* of these "poor sections" are in Annapolis county, and *twenty-three* in Digby. It has been the aim of the various Boards of Commissioners to reduce the number of "poor sections" as much as justice would permit, and in doing this no sections have been placed on the list which could reasonably be expected to maintain schools without extra aid. In this, as in all other respects, the Commissioners have discharged their duties faithfully and conscientiously.

A gradual improvement in school buildings and furniture can be reported. A new school-house has been built and furnished in South Range, East Section. Victory section has a new house in process of erection. At Paradise a fine new house of modern style for a graded school of two departments will be ready for occupation shortly after the beginning of the ensuing year. Extensive repairs have been made on the school-houses in Mount Hanley, Havelock, Springfield, Chesley and Milford sections. In other cases repairs of a less durable nature have been effected. When new furniture is required most sections provide the paragon desk, thereby securing greater comfort for the pupils, more elegance in the appearance of the school room, and greater durability.

No increase in quantity of apparatus provided can be reported. A few of the leading schools are fairly well equipped, but in most cases an insufficient supply has been provided. It is oftentimes difficult to induce trustees to procure any more than the most absolutely essential articles. Sections should be compelled to furnish a more liberal supply of apparatus, and in order to accomplish this object it would be well to clothe Inspectors with more clearly defined powers in this regard. Existing regulations on this point are not sufficiently definite.

Most schools have been found in a fairly satisfactory condition so far as the work of teachers and pupils were concerned. Some were superior in these respects, while a few were decidedly poor. My notes of inspection for the year deal with each school separately, and may be consulted if more definite information be required. Many of the teachers have been earnest and enthusiastic in their work, but their efforts have been partially neutralized in some cases by want of apparatus, by irregularity in the attendance of pupils, and by indifference and apathy on the part of Trustees and parents.

About twenty per cent. of the teachers employed during the year hold Normal School diplomas. The change in the mode of obtaining licenses and in the work of the Normal School will probably soon increase this percentage, and thereby ensure more thorough work being done in the schools. Under conditions recently existing a large proportion of the teachers who have not received a normal training, leave the profession about as soon as they gain by experience that aptitude in imparting instruction and in school management which is necessary to insure success.

At the Provincial Examination in July, two hundred and ten candidates made application to be examined at the various stations in this District for Certificates of Scholarship, of which number *fifty-six* only took the *minimum professional qualification* examination. Judging from experience it is probable that not more than fifty per cent. of the latter class will succeed in obtaining a license to teach. As those who take the minimum professional qualification examination instead of a course of professional training must under present regulations be content with a license one class lower than their Certificate of Scholarship would otherwise entitle them to receive, it may be assumed that largely increased numbers from this District will be induced to obtain licenses after taking a course of professional training at the Provincial Normal School. Unless this be the case the supply of teachers will soon fall short of the demand.

There are about *thirty* schools in the Municipality of Clare for which French speaking teachers must be employed. Regularly licensed teachers cannot be found for all of these schools. To meet this demand about one dozen permissive licenses must be issued each year. Great difficulty is experienced by French candidates in successfully passing the Provincial examination. This may be accounted for in some measure by the difficulty experienced by these candidates in passing an examination in the English language, but probably it is very largely attributable to the very elementary character of the French schools. The large attendance at these schools, and the fact that both languages are concurrently taught, necessarily hinder progress. A very large proportion of the pupils are to be found in the elementary grades and very little work is done beyond that. French candidates who prepare for examination in these schools must necessarily fail owing to lack of mental training. Most of those who succeed have received their training in the schools at Port Acadie and Meteghan taught by the Sisters of Charity.

The registered attendance at the schools was fairly satisfactory. In this district the number of children between five and fifteen years of age, reported in sections having schools, was 8578. Of this number 766 did not attend school. The whole registered attendance of pupils was 8803. This number includes those in attendance upwards of fifteen years of age. The percentage of enrolled pupils daily present during the year was 63.4—a slight increase over the preceding year. It is evident that there is yet much room for improvement. Perhaps there is nothing more discouraging to the teachers than irregularity in attendance. It interferes with the progress of the school, causes needless repetition of class-work, and prevents proper classification. This evil must necessarily exist to some extent, but it is hoped that some means will be devised to reduce it to a minimum.

The course of study has produced beneficial results. A uniformity of school work now exists which was formerly unattainable. The main studies of the course are receiving due attention. The chief difficulty experienced by some teachers consist in a supposed inability on their part to teach drawing and to give the prescribed oral lessons on health, temperance and nature. The lack of previous training in methods of oral instruction causes some to shirk this work as far as possible. The use of the books on health and temperance recently prescribed will help to remove this difficulty. The gradually increasing number of trained teachers will also tend to more general and systematic instruction in the rudiments of natural science.

With one or two exceptions the returns came to hand within the time prescribed. Most of them were carefully prepared. A few were unfinished and were returned for completion. The form of the return being new caused difficulty in some cases, especially that part requiring the average number of minutes per week devoted to the different subjects required to be taught. Some teachers were found bold enough to question the expediency or necessity of giving such information, as at best it can only be approximately correct. It is hoped, however, that it will cause time to be given to all the subjects of the course of study, some of which might otherwise receive scant attention at the hands of inexperienced teachers.

The County Academy at Annapolis was taught by Principal McVicar, a teacher of scholarly attainments and much experience. The attendance was large. Excellent work was done in all classes, and several of the students made an excellent record at the Provincial examination in July. Principal McVicar commands the confidence and respect of his students and of the whole community. This Academy has lagely increased in efficiency since he took charge. In consequence of the large amount of high school work efficiently done at the other graded schools of the County, this Academy has much competition, and owes its present state of efficiency very largely to its talented Principal.

At Digby the County Academy was presided over by Principal Godfrey, a teacher of much experience. The attendance was as large as usual, and fair work was done. This academy does not suffer materially from competition with other schools in the County, and as a consequence a fair proportion of its students were drawn from other sections. A considerable number of the students attended the Provincial examination in July, some of whom made a creditable record. Principal Godfrey's term of service expired at the end of the year. In consequence of the very small number of pupils from the Preparatory Department who succeeded in passing the entrance examination in July, the attendance next year will be materially affected.

With two or three exceptions, all schools were inspected during the year. These exceptions occurred because the schools closed previous to my tour of inspection in their vicinity. This being a transition year of nine months only, but one official visit was made to each school. The large increase in correspondence caused by this change in the law and regulations, and the work connected with the Educational Exhibit for the World's Fair, collected from this district, prevented more frequent visits of inspection. The work of correspondence has become a serious tax upon an Inspector's time and patience.

The one term system has been so recently inaugurated that its benefits or disadvantages will become more apparent after further experience. One year's trial, however, has clearly shown that both Superintendent of Education and Inspectors are most busily engaged in office work at the time when teachers are enjoying a well earned vacation.

In closing, permit me to suggest that the issue of a new Manual of the School Law and Regulations has become a necessity. The changes recently made have been so radical that the Manual issued in 1888 is almost valueless. It is hoped that this suggestion will commend itself to your judgment, and that something practical in this line will be the result.

With due appreciation of your courtesy in our official intercourse,

I have the honour to be,
Sir, your obedient servant,

L. S. MORSE.

To A. H. MacKay, Esq., LL. D.,
Superintendent of Education.

DISTRICT No. 5—HANTS AND KINGS.

COLIN W. ROSCOE, A. M., *Inspector.*

SIR,—

I beg leave respectfully to submit the following report of the condition of the schools in Inspectoral District, No. 5, for the "provisional year," ended July 7th, 1893:

All sections were not prepared at the beginning of the year to open schools. Some could not secure the teacher they desired, some preferred, and could engage a male teacher for the winter and a female for the summer, which could not engage a teacher for the full term, some had school for a term shorter than the year, some "poor sections" chose a short term, and a few could not get teachers and had to be satisfied with a three months' school. These cases were met and disposed of as follows:

White Waters, Kings County, and Mills, Lakelands, North Beaver Bank and East Uniacke, Hants County,—"poor sections"—had school for three months only. Most of these preferred a longer term but could not secure teachers. West Halls Harbor in Kings, and Cambridge in Hants, were allowed to have school three months; because it seemed impossible to get teachers before spring. Blue Mountain and Lake George in Kings, chose six months terms, and Australia eight months. These were "poor sections," and had the right, under law, to have school less than a year. Birch Brook, Hants, had a six months' school with my consent. Black River, Greenfield, Ormsby Road, Kings, and Newport and Douglas, Tenecape, Rhines' Creek, and Mill Village, Hants, did not have school quite all the term because they could not engage teachers to begin November 1st. Brookville, Hants, had a teacher for the primary deparment for about 3½ months. This seemed best for the school and I consented to the arrangement. The following had school for the full term or nearly so, but under two teachers, each: Piedmont, Long Point, Kingsport (advanced), Church St., Canaan, South Berwick Woodside, Prospect, Somerset (primary), Centreville Islands and Waterville (advanced), in Kings; and Martock, Hantsport (advanced primary), Maitland (primary and intermediate), and Manganese Mines in Hants. Cheverie and Noel had three different teachers each in their advanced departments. A few of these had my consent to have a male teacher in winter and a female in summer, and one had my consent to put a male of the same grade in to finish the term. While I regarded these changes as not being beneficial to the schools in all cases, the circumstances seemed to point to this as the best, and so I consented. Most of the other changes occurred, however, either from illness of the teacher, from offers of marriage or from inability to teach and manage the school after a trial of it. The two cases of three teachers to a school seemed unavoidable, unless the trustees closed the schools. Thus it will be seen that there were eight three months' schools, three six months' ones, and six others for nearly the

full term, and nineteen for the full term, or nearly so, with a change
of teachers. There were two hundred and forty-four schools in
session during the year—less the thirty-six referred to above—leaving
two hundred and eight, in which the teachers were continued
throughout the term. While so many changes in teachers were to be
regretted, it was deemed desirable to be as liberal in the interpretation of the law as possible until teachers and trustees became
acquainted with it. Now, however, since it has been commented on
so extensively through the Journal of Education and the newspapers,
there cannot be the same latitude given; and teachers and trustees
will be ready for a stricter interpretation.

For information in brief, I refer you to the following tables, and
for complete statistics, to the tabulated statement sent herewith :

SCHOOLS.

	No. Schools.	Teachers.	Pupils.	Attendance.
Hants	122	131	4,948	412,819
Kings	122	134	5,159	408,061
Total	244	265	10,107	820,880

TEACHERS.

	Classes A	B	C	D	Male.	Female.	Total.
Hants	1	27	76	27	21	110	131
Kings	2	30	71	31	32	102	134
Total	3	57	147	57	53	212	265

The sections having no school for the year were Randville, East
Pereaux Mt., and Kellyville in Kings; and Pembroke, Stillwater,
Renfrew, Georgefield, Greenfield, Glencoe and Rawdon Gold Mines, in
Hants. Randville still sends to Canning, depriving no one of school
privileges, so far as I can learn, and thus making a school in the section
unnecessary. East Pereaux Mt. and Kellyville are weak sections, and
have a small number of children. They did not succeed in getting
teachers, but have arranged for schools next year. Renfrew and
Rawdon Gold Mines are almost abandoned on account of the failure
of the mines. Schools cannot be expected here till the mining interest
revives. Georgefield and Greenfield are small and not at all strong,
but have done themselves discredit by closing their schools. Glencoe
has become so depopulated that I fear the school will have to be given
up till there are more people or children. Stillwater is another small
section, which on account of the removal of some families was prevented
from having school. There is not much prospect of a school here for
next year. Pembroke failed in getting a teacher but has secured one
for the year 1893-94.

The schools have been maintained with a good degree of regularity
and efficiency. The subjects taught previous to the new requirements—

which may be regarded as standard subjects—have been carefully taught, and substantial progress has been made therein. A greater attempt, than usual has been made to teach calisthenics, vocal music, moral and patriotic duties, and the lessons on nature, and in some cases the results have been all I could desire. The majority of the teachers, failed or nearly so, in this kind of work. Most of them do what they call oral work ; but it consists chiefly in repeating what they have memorized from a text-book for their pupils to learn. This seems to me worse than neglecting it altogether. I see no way out of this difficulty but by establishing summer Normal Schools in each county for the training of teachers during the vacation. To be of service this work need be very plain and elementary for a large number of teachers. The necessity for *Normal* training was never more apparent than at the present time. The step to make attendance at a Normal School compulsory must soon be taken. I would say, let it be taken at once.

The County Academies have maintained an efficient standing during the year and contributed very largely to the number of candidates for examination for High School Certificates. Kentville sent 49, or more than half of those examined at Kentville station, and Windsor sent about one-third of the candidates at that station. I have not received the results of the examination, but presume these candidates compare favorably with others in the Province. The examination, if made compulsory would save the principals of academies much labor and prove a good test of the character of the work done in the various schools. It seems to me if this were made the only grading examination for all above Grade VIII, it would stimulate teachers and pupils not to overlook the importance of any subject in the course of study ; and make the work uniform to a degree not now attained. Kentville has purchased a large addition to its school grounds and by laying out the grounds and setting out ornamental trees and shrubs, and properly cultivating them, can have as fine school premises as can be found. Windsor has a good site and grounds for fine school buildings. I hope the time is not far distant when the town may arise and build a house creditable alike to the ability and to the intelligence of the people. Hantsport sustains five departments and has made provision to improve its school buildings during the present year. The school here is good. Maitland opened a fourth department. Berwick and Wolfville are the other two schools having four departments each. These three schools maintain an excellent standing. Wolfville will enter the new school house at the beginning of next term. The house provides six rooms all finished. Four are furnished for immediate use. The cost of the house was about $8000.00 and it is in all respects up to date in its plan and finish. The Fuller and Warner system of heating and ventilation has been put in at a large expense, and appears to possess all the good qualities claimed for it. Connected with this are dry air closets in the basement. Messrs. Robb & Son of Amherst put in the furnaces and apparatus connected therewith and guaranteed their successful operation. I have no doubt that the expense incurred in this way will prove to be one of the best investments ever made by this town. Should it come up to my expectations, I shall feel it my

duty to give particular attention to improvements in the ventilation
of all school buildings in my district, and shall advocate this system
whenever new houses are built and the sections can afford the expense.
Wolfville is the first and only school in this district that has adopted
this system.   Noel and Elmsdale use hot-air furnaces for heating ; and
the former has registers for the escape of foul air.

Canning is the only school of three departments in my two
counties.   There are twenty-one schools maintaining two departments each.   Thus in the counties of Kings and Hants there are,
including   the   County   Academies,   twenty-seven   graded   schools
representing seventy-six departments, 2965 pupils, and requiring 76
teachers.   The graded schools represent nearly one-third of the whole
schools and pupils of the district.   By vote of the Commissioners of
West Hants, St. Croix, and Three Mile Plain sections are required to
grade their schools, so that next year there will be at least 80 departments to report.   The number of the different grades to be found in
almost all the miscellaneous schools, and the variety of the subjects to
be taught make the grading of schools imperative. as soon as the
number of children and the ability of the section will admit of it.
And there can be no question as to the superiority of the graded, as
compared with the miscellaneous school.   Did space permit I might
report many superior miscellaneous schools, as wholes, and particularize the points of excellence in others ; but I must content myself
by saying, that, regarding the financial standing of the sections and
all other circumstances affecting the schools, I am pleased to be able
to report a fair degree of progress for the year.

SCHOOL COMMISSIONERS.

The appointment of new Commissioners came at a time when new
recruits were much needed, and I am of opinion, those appointed are
men of the right stamp and will prove a valuable acquisition to the
Boards.   One duty of the School Commissioners is to declare, upon
the Inspector's report or other reliable information, the shool house or
houses or buildings used as such, or the appurtenances thereof, unfit
for school purposes.   Such action greatly aids officials in keeping
school sections some where near the requirements of the law in these
respects.   It is necessary to have regard to the ability of the sections
in all cases ; but it is quite as necessary to impress them with the fact
that any kind of buildings and appurtenances cannot be tolerated.
At the last meetings of the Boards, in each of the districts, houses
were declared unfit for use and trustees informed what was expected
of them that their sections may continue to participate in the grants.
In many cases it was found necessary to notify sections to refurnish
their houses with better furniture.   The old seat, made by placing
two boards at right angles to each other, has had its day, and we are
endeavouring to have them replaced, as fast as possible, with
improved seats and desks of the best kind.   As a first step, the
Boards instruct their Secretary to write trustees and call attention to
what is needed to be done.   When this is not heeded, the trustees are
told plainly what they must do or lose Provincial grants.   In the

matters of furnishing, supplying maps and other school requisites, much still remains to be done before I can report a satisfactroy state of things.

BUILDINGS.

The pressure of hard times prevents the advancement desirable in school-houses and premises. Many houses must soon be renovated, repaired thoroughly, and reseated. Good, comfortable furniture can now be purchased at reasonable prices; and I believe the sentiment is growing in many sections that the best is not too good for the schools. As a school official, I feel impelled by a sense of duty, to press trustees to make improvements along this line.

During the year, Welsford, Upper Pereaux, Wolfville and Elmsdale have built new school-houses. These are all provided with patent seats and desks and are a decided improvement upon houses built even five years ago. Weston, Brooklyn (Aylesford), Brooklyn (Cornwallis), Sheffield's Mills, Mount Denson, and Avondale have made considerable repairs, reseated their houses with approved seats and desks, and thus, I am able to report, are advanced in this direction. St Marys, W. Black Rock and Upper Nine Mile River are required, by the Commissioners, to build new houses; and Kingsport, Three Mile Plain, St. Croix and Cheverie to enlarge and repair so as to meet the requirements of the law. The new house in Upper Pereaux is to replace the one destroyed by fire last winter. It was insured and thus the loss was not so great as it otherwise would have been.

SCHOOL INSPECTION.

I made two hundred and seventy-one official, and several non-official visits to the schools during the term. Many of these visits were longer than I was accustomed to make in the past. It was found necessary to spend considerable time in explaining the changes made in the registers and return blanks. I invariably instructed teachers to complete their registers and sign them, *themselves,* and have them signed by the Secretary of Trusrees before making out their returns. This instruction, in addition to your concise and clear notes in the April Journal of Education, led me to expect perfect returns. But nearly one-half of the whole number had blunders in them. These were found in the quarterly and general averages and and percentages, in the number of, minutes per week reported for the various groups of subjects—the sum of these varied from 200 to 2000—in the number of pupils in the various grades, the sum of which did not agree with the number enrolled, and in the sum of the attendance for the two half years not agreeing with the total attendance for the year. The number of days lost was frequently given wrong. I have fault too to find, in that all the questions requiring answers were not answered. It appeared that teachers and trustees answered or not, according to their estimate of the value of the answers to themselves. Frequently I was compelled to write for an answer to a single question—left out because some one did not think it of any consequence or from carelessness. It seems to me the rules in the back of the Register are too plain to need a word of explanation for the teacher of the lowest grade. I regard these blunders, therefore, as the result of simple carelessness. I would suggest as a remedy for this either to withhold grants for six months, or impose a fine for each error, or publish the names of all who send correct and complete returns, with the understanding that all whose names do not appear on the list have not sent in acceptable returns.

REGISTERS.

I have already informed teachers that the past term's registers will be called up, and that all cases of incorrect or incomplete ones will be reported. To this end I purpose to notify schools of my next visit and ask for registers, agreements, licenses and all papers affording information concerning the school in all its respects. The register is printed on brittle paper, is to big for the old covers in use, and in consequence is crumpled on its edges and torn to an extent very undesirable in a document the trustees are required to preserve. This can be remedied by the use of a tougher paper, by making it a half inch narrower or providing covers to protect it as is now being gradually done.

WORLD'S FAIR.

The teachers and pupils of this district interested themselves to send some of their best work to me, from which to select for the World's Fair. From the large amount sent, I made selections of the best, as you instructed, and forwarded it to you. Those upon whom the labor came feel somewhat disappointed that so little of it was considered good enough for a place in the Nova Scotia exhibit, and teachers from here, who have visited the World's Fair, are of opinion that the specimens sent are far from our best, and do not fairly represent us. Of course the stimulus given to the schools in the preparation of the work, and the publication of the names of those whose work was forwarded to Halifax, had their beneficial effects at the time; but to be regarded as failing in the principal lines of work, as compared with others, was not expected; and then to be informed that the best of it went no further than Halifax, or does not appear as part of the exhibit, cannot fail to have its effect upon the schools, should anything of the kind be required in future.

SUMMER SCHOOLS, INSTITUTES, &C.

If there could be a Summer Normal School or Teachers' Institute established in each district or county, for four weeks, during each year, for the purpose of training young teachers, and old ones too, when they need it, in new methods; instructing them in the new subjects introduced into the course of study, and stimulating them to make more of their time in the school-room and do better work, it would prove of great advantage to the schools. One Normal School may train 150 teachers each year; but these are not enough to supply half the vacancies from ordinary causes. The time lost by not knowing how to teach is making our schools too expensive for the progress made. Of the 265 teachers employed in Hants and Kings 68 only, hold Normal School diplomas. If the Normal School is what is claimed for it, then it goes without showing that all teachers should, in some way, be put in possession of Normal training.

STATISTICS.

I have sought to prepare correct statistics of the school work for the past term; but from the errors found in returns—which at much pains, and by correspondence, I sought to correct—I dare not say that I think they will do more than approximate the truth. I believe the way I have treated the matter of incorrect returns and the plan I have determined to follow for the next year will enable me in my next report to speak with more assurance of the corrections of the statistics to be submitted. I have begun on this line and shall not feel like discontinuing till the result is to my satisfaction.

Allow me to conclude this report by sending you the names, addresses and ages of the young persons, who have not attended school and who are deaf and dumb.

I have the honor to be, Sir,

Your obedient servant,

COLIN W. ROSCOE.

A. H. MACKAY, ESQ., LL. D.,
Superintendent of Education.

DISTRICT No. 6.—ANTIGONISH AND GUYSBORO.

W. MACISAAC, B. A., *Inspector.*

SIR,—

The following report on the schools of District No. 6 for the year ended July, 1893, is respectfully submitted:

The total number of schools in operation in Antigonish was 89, and in Guysboro 85.

There were six sections without school in Antigonish during some portion of the year, and fourteen in Guysboro.

The total annual enrolment in Antigonish was 3532. The corresponding number in Guysboro was 3589.

Grand total of attendance: Antigonish, 258,355; Guysboro, 263,644.

It will be seen by reducing the grand total of both to the same basis, that the attendance for the past year, which was only three-fourths of the ordinary one, was less than that of the preceding.

By increasing the grand total of attendance in Antigonish by one-third we have 344,473 as compared with 365,450 for last year.

Similarly, the grand total for Guysboro for this year is less than that of the previous one by 36,018. The cause of the decrease was the unusual severity of the season during the months of January, February and March.

Average annual salaries paid to the teachers including Government grants are as follows:—

	MALES.			FEMALES.		
	B	C	D	B	C	D
Antigonish..	$440.71	$228.03	$169.66	$274.90	$219.52	$154.21
Guysboro ...	538.37	244.85	147.51	325.04	241.50	960.41

Number of teachers employed of different classes and sexes :

ANTIGONISH COUNTY.

	A	B	C	D
Male..........	1	5	21	14
Female		2	23	27
Totals....	A 1	B 7	C 44	D 41

GUYSBORO COUNTY.

	A	B	C	D
Male..........	1	4	5	4
Female		4	32	40
Totals....	A 1	B 8	C 37	D 44

A new school house has been erected at White Head ; and a large and commodious department has been added to the Canso school, which will afford this flourishing section sufficient educational facilities in future.

The school house at Dover, Guysboro county, was destroyed by fire in July. It appears strange that such a serious misfortune should happen at that season of the year, when, as I am credibly informed the locality was free from bush-fires.

At the meeting of the School Board at Guysboro in May, a new school section was established at Yankee Cove. The children of this sparsely-settled district have been in the past deprived of the benefits of a common school education ; and the Commissioners of Guysboro with commendable public spirit determined that such a state of affairs shall no longer continue.

During my tour of inspection I found the teachers in general, energetic and attentive to duty. There is much truth in the trite saying that the teacher makes the school. But the efforts of the best and most skilful teachers often fail unless generously seconded by those of parents and trustees, which unfortunately in many instances is not the case.

School work is in many of our schools, particularly the rural ones, conducted by teachers of the lower grades, needlessly monotonous to the pupils. Though many of these teachers do creditable work in giving oral lessons on various natural objects, there is a large number who do not attempt this interesting part of school work from sheer diffidence, and because they did not make a special study of nature lessons in the school in which they were trained themselves. Indeed, the elements of a great many of the natural sciences by a little private study on the part of the teachers, could easily be taught in our most elementary schools. Besides the educational advantage which would result from work of this kind, it would remove much of the tedium that makes school life so unattractive to children. Classes might be taught to distinguish the principal organs of plants and flowers; to name and recognize the various forest trees of the locality or neighbourhood, the different materials of their own clothing, as cotton, wool, flax or silk, and the principal varieties of animate life from the insect tribes to the large domestic quadrupeds. The geography of the school vicinity, of hill, dale and brook, as well as the leading figures of geometry, as squares, triangles, circles, cubes, spheres and cylinders, might also be made from time to time the subject of inspiring oral lessons. The simplest mechanical laws, steam and electricity, in an elementary way, might also receive some attention. The importance of cultivating in the youth a taste for studies of this kind cannot easily be overestimated.

The Academy in Guysboro has been under the efficient charge of E. B. Smith, Esq., B. A., during the year.

The Antigonish Academy opened in September last under most favorable auspices. In addition to its usual staff of excellent professors, the services of the Rev. Angus J. Chisholm, B. A., D. D., were secured to teach Higher Mathematics, English and French. Early in November this brilliant and accomplished scholar fell a victim to typhoid fever, and died at the end of the month. His death, in the prime of life, was not only a loss to the institution, but a loss to the community and the country at large. In him, with a mind truly majestic, were combined all the best and highest qualities of the true man and the good christian. The beauty of his character and chivalrous benevolence left impressions deeper, more enduring and tangible than mere " footprints in the sands of time."

The best criterion of the high order of work done in Antigonish Academy is the success of its candidates at the Antigonish Station at the Provincial High School Examination in July. Three of its students succeeded by respectable aggregates in obtaining Grade A (classical) scholarships. The success of those of its students who applied for grades B, C and D is highly gratifying.

Permit me in conclusion to express my sincere gratitude to you for uniform courtesies in our official relations.

I have the honor to be, Sir,
Your obedient servant,
W. MacISAAC.

A. H. MacKay, Esq., Ll. D.
Superintendent of Education.

DISTRICT No. 7.—CAPE BRETON AND RICHMOND.

M. J. T. MACNEIL, B. A., *Inspector.*

SIR,—

I beg leave to submit the following report on the schools of my inspectoral district for the nine months' term, ended July 31st.

At the meeting of the Board of School Commissioners for the county of Cape Breton in May last, School Section, No. 76, Gabarus, was divided into two distinct sections. This division has since been confirmed by the Council of Public Instruction, and thus a difficulty of long standing, referred to in previous reports, has been finally and definitely disposed of. Thus also has the number of sections in the county been increased by one, but as the change only came into effect at the commencement of the current school year, the number of sections taken into account for this report will be the same as hereto-fore, 132. The number in the county of Richmond remains unchanged—70. Two petitions for division were presented to the Board, one of which was rejected and the other granted, but the C. P. I. declined to sanction the proposed division.

The number of sections having no schools in session any part of the term was, in Cape Breton County 19, and in Richmond 9. These numbers are unusually large, but they are the result of exceptional circumstances. It will be remembered that this was a transition term inaugurating several changes in our educational system, one of which renders illegal the engagement of teachers for a period less than one year, " except by express authority from the inspector under special circumstances." Obviously this enactment applies to contracts entered into at the commencement of the yearly term, and does not contemplate that sections failing to secure teachers at that period shall remain vacant for the remainder thereof. It seems, however, that in several instances that have come to my knowledge, the latter interpretation was put upon it, while the saving permissive clause was entirely lost sight of or overshadowed by the direct prohibition. The same causes—the change of terms and annual engagements—rendered unavailable the usual recruits from the colleges and academies in the spring.

It would be difficult, if not impossible, to make comparative statements between this nine-months' term and the previous year of two semi-annual terms. I shall therefore only extract from the tables a few of the more important items in connection with the work of the term under consideration.

The number, class and sex of the teachers employed in the 111 sections having school in Cape Breton County and the 61 in Richmond were as follows:

	MALE.				FEMALE.			TOTAL.		
	A.	B.	C.	D.	B.	C.	D.	M.	F.	Total.
Cape Breton..	4	20	26	23	7	42	39	73	88	161
Richmomd	—	9	22	12	—	12	15	43	27	70

Of those in the former county, 18 were teachers employed for the first time, and in the latter, 7, making 25 new teachers in the district. Many other more or less interesting details of the classification and analysis of teachers as to period of service, etc., will be found in the accompanying tables.

The number of pupils registered at school in Cape Breton County was 6848, (3685 boys and 3163 girls) being exactly one in 5 of the population, making an average daily attendance of 3461.7 and an aggregate days' attendance for the term of 533,886. The number of children between the ages of 5 and 15 in the different school sections of the county is returned as 6754, and of those who did not attend school at all during the term as 672 or very nearly 10 per cent. The number enrolled in Richmond County was 2730—1504 boys and 1226 girls—one in 5.2 of the population, making an average daily attendance of 1359.7 and a grand total of 200,464. The number in this county between the ages of 5 and 15 is placed at 2,918, and those of them who did not attend school at 402 or 13.7 per cent. There certainly seems to be something wrong about this state of affairs, but I must say that I would not by any means vouch for the correctness of the figures in this particular item. I have found it very difficult to procure correct returns under this head. After having taken what were looked upon as extreme measures, even to withholding the warrants for payment of the County Fund, to compel the correction of returns, I have reason to believe that the figures sent in were mere guesses, the returns themselves bearing evidence of the fact on their faces in the non-agreement of the total reported in section with the sum of those registered at school and the absentees. Trustees in large sections assert that they have no means of procuring the correct figures without a great deal of trouble which they seem to look upon as the duty of nobody in particular and which, therefore, no one is willing to assume, forgetting that their secretary could, with very little trouble, take this miniature census when collecting the sectional school rates.

While on the subject of returns, I may state that I have been greatly perplexed and retarded in my work of compiling the statistics by the inaccuracy and incompleteness of many of them. A great many had to be referred back for correction (some, indeed, a second time!) after the first cursory glance or after having been used for the primary purposes of government grant and county fund distribution sheets. With an almost entirely new form of return some mistakes and omissions were to be expected, but I was not prepared for such an amount of blundering and inconsistency. The returns, though largely corrected, will still in a great measure bear me out in this statement when they reach your office. There is as much to complain of for the sins of omission as for those of commission. There is far too much laxity in this matter of school returns—documents, the correctness and completeness of which have to be attested under oath by teacher and solemnly certified by trustees. Do representative men elected to fill the serious and responsible position of trustees of public schools mean nothing when they append their names to a declaration like this: " We certify *   *   *   *   *   that we have faithfully sought to procure accurate answers, which are recorded in the register to *every enquiry* found in this return, and we further certify that this return is, *to the best of our knowledge and belief correct in every particular*?" And yet I found in a certain school several days before the close of the term a *blank form* of return certified as above over the signatures of the three trustees! Needless to say that that blank form never served its intended purpose, but the incident goes to show how readily some people can be got to certify to anything or *nothing*; while the many columns in the returns found unfilled and questions left unanswered would seem to indicate a wide-spread conviction that a considerable portion of the forms is gotten up for the sole purpose of giving employment to the printer. One would certainly have thought that the directions and injunctions laid down in the April edition of the Journal of Education were sufficient to ensure, as nearly as possible, absolute perfection or at least a conscientious endeavour to procure the information asked for; but the futility of the expectation was painfully brought home to me, as already stated, in the compilation of my annual returns. In the columns, for instance, requiring " the average number of minutes per week taken by teacher during the year in giving instruction in the various groups of subjects specified below," how many of the figures given are absurd ! It would be wearisome to go into details. Again in the matter of the "Analysis of High School Studies" I am certain that many teachers have not done justice to their schools, for I have personal knowledge of some wherein I examined classes in High School subjects, the returns from which contain no records of pupils in those grades. This neglect accounts for the County of Richmond getting credit for only 12 High School pupils—see Tables IX and X. The omissions referred to were, however, noticed too late to have them supplied.

The new school building at North Sydney was occupied after the Christmas holidays. It contains eight large rooms with spacious halls and all necessary ante-rooms, and closets, is thoroughly heated by hot water and well and completely furnished. It is the largest and finest public school building in Cape Breton and is a credit to the enterprising town that erected it.

An additional department was opened in Gowrie Section (Cow Bay) on the 30th January, making the sixth in that thriving section. The building erected for its accommodation is situated some distance outside the village, near the workings, and is rather a neat building, but poorly planned for a modern school-house.

South Head, to whose misfortunes reference was made in my two last reports, with indomitable pluck replaced its many burnt school-houses by still another new one, and was enabled to open school the latter part of the term—April 17th. A new school-house, to replace the one destroyed by forrest fires in the summer of 1892, was being erected at Lakevale, near Sydney, and would be ready for occupation for the beginning of the current term.

The county of Richmond has not much to show in the matter of buildings. The school-house of Rockdale was neatly finished inside and now makes one of the neatest and most comfortable in the rural sections of the county.

None of the several school-buildings condemned last year have as yet been replaced, the trustees in each case having obtained an extension of time, on account of sectional difficulties of different kinds. The school-house and site, at Poirrierville (Lower D'Escousse), were condemned at the last meeting of the Board. Two school-houses were destroyed by fire—the one at Loch Lomond, section No. 35, on the night of the 18th November, and that at Bray, section No. 49, on the night of December 23rd, the origin or cause of fire in both cases being unknown.

Trout Brook, in Cape Breton county, also had the misfortune of losing its school house by the disastrous forest fires of last summer, this being the second time within a few years.

All the schools in the district were visited once during the term with the exception of a very few which, for unavoidable reasons, could not be reached but at the sacrifice of a great deal of time. Only a few could be visited a second time. As you are aware, the recent changes entailed upon Inspectors, during the past term, a great deal of unusual work in the way of correspondence—answering questions, circulating new forms, distributing World's Fair circulars, etc. In addition to this the lateness of the publication of the Journal of Education caused a great many sections to omit calling their annual meetings at the proper time, thereby necessitating an application to the inspector under the law, to appoint a day for a special annual meeting.

I attended meetings, either by appointment or by request, in the following sections having no schools in operation, with the results named: November 9th, at Beaver's Cove, a public meeting of rate-payers to assist in putting the section on a proper legal footing with a view to enabling the trustees to engage a teacher. School was opened on the 14th of the same month. November 25th, met the trustees of L'Ardoise, section No. 28, to provide a class-room and an assistant. Class room was prepared and opened on November 28th. November 26th, met trustees of Grand River to determine upon a site for a new school-house. A site was chosen and sanctioned then and there. November 26, attended a meeting of rate-payers of Loch Lomond, No. 35, after the burning of the school-house in order to take measures, if possible, for continuing the school in temporary quarters, and to provide for a new building. Nothing was effected, owing to a difficulty as to disputed boundaries and other causes of disagreement. April 12th, met Secretary of Trustees of Petit-de-Grat, section No. 8, to determine site of projected new school-house, size and plan of building, &c., all of which was satisfactorily arranged. Several other vacant sections were visited in the course of my regular tours of inspection, without previous notice or appointment, and without, to my knowledge, any immediate or determinate results.

At the Sydney Academy, there were registered during the term 72 pupils, 70 of whom are reported as following the full regular course of studies, and the remaining two only a partial or special course; 42 belonged to the town, and 30 were from beyond its limits, every county of the Island being well represented. The average daily attendance made during the term was 42.7. The number pursuing the different grades of the course was as follows: Grade IX, 36; Grade X, 26; Grade XI, 10. Some $20 cash and other prizes were distributed, aggregating in value $105. The Academy continues under the efficient management of Principal MacKeen, with Vice-Principal Stewart. Besides the usual staff in the common school departments, which remains unchanged, three departments conducted by the Sisters of the Congregation de Notre Dame, have been taken over under engagement with the School Board, making now, with the "Creek School"—a primary sub-urban department—ten departments under the control of the town commissioners.

The following are the sections of from two to ten departments, with the number of pupils pursuing more or less closely the High School course. I place them in the order of attendance of such pupils: Sydney Mines 50, Little Glace Bay 40, Bridgeport 39, North Sydney 33, Gowrie 27, Louisburg 9, Low Point, Block House and Mainadieu each 5, and Reserve and Lorway 0. Two departments were in operation in Gabarus, but they cannot be said to have constituted, strictly speaking, a graded school. In all these schools good live teachers are generally employed, and excellent work is being done, as well as in many of the miscellaneous schools throughout the district, and it is not too much to say that we are making (perhaps slow) but sure progress along the line.

With thanks for your unvarying kind attention and courtesy,

I have the honor to be, Sir,

your obedient servant,

M. J. T. MACNEIL.

A. H. MacKay, Esq., Ll. D.

Superintendent of Education.

DISTRICT No. 8.—INVERNESS AND VICTORIA.

John Y. Gunn, *Inspector.*

Sir,—

I beg respectfully to submit the following condensed report relating to the present condition and progress of education within the counties of Inverness and Victoria during the nine months ended, July, 1893.

It may be necessary to state at the outset that changes recently introduced in the prescribed regulations for the government and maintenance of the public schools throughout the province, have very largely increased the clerical duties of this office—thus materially hampering the regular duties of school inspection. The School Act, in its amended form, is now, however, in the hands of every board of trustees within the District. It is therefore to be hoped explanations relating to school registers, length of term, dates of teachers' pay days, together with varied intricacies relating to the public examinations, are by this time fairly well understood by all partiesc oncerned, and that hereafter the legitimate functions of accredited visitors may not be seriously impeded.

Within the present quarter of a century, this district has improved immensely both materially and educationally. The country was then covered with the virgin forest, and in the fierce struggle for existence with which the early settlers had to contend, aesthetics were sacrificed to utility, but increased comfort and improved social relations, together with the magical influence exercised by the establishment of " Arbor Day " in connection with the public schools, has gradually evolved a marvellous change. Then a·tree was regarded as a deformity to be plucked out and destroyed—now nearly every homestead is decorated with ornamental trees, and even along the lanes and highways an occasional evergreen graces the beauty of the landscape.

In 1864 free schools were established by Act of Parliament throughout the province. Messrs. James McDonnell, of Port Hood, and Angus McIver, of Little Narrows, were appointed School Inspectors for the Counties of Inverness and Victoria respectively. By these gentlemen, in conjunction with the local land surveyers and school commissioners, each county was sub-divided into district school sections, and the boundaries of each sectionengrossed in the commissioners' record books. In Victoria the County Academy was established at Baddeck, and in Inverness schools of advanced character were founded at Port Hastings and Port Hood, in South Inverness and at B. C. Marsh and Margaree Forks in the north.

Under the new law superior schools were established in both counties. Schools so distinguished were required by the regulations to be of a high order ; the building, furniture and apparatus to be first class and the teacher of high rank in his profession. The competing schools were specially inspected and full notes sent to the Education Office—the final arbitrament being relegated to that tribunal. The grant was unquestionably a potent stimulus to high effort on the part of both teacher and trustees.

In 1870 the grant was withdrawn, but the impulse imparted through this extra agency is felt in the localities to which the grant was awarded unto this day.

For several years the Academy grant in Inverness was distributed by the school boards to assist indigent school sections in building and equipping their school houses with improved furniture and apparatus. But, by a Minute of Council dated April, 1877, the Academy grant was withdrawn, to be given thereafter as a *bonus* to four advanced schools in the county. This was the origin of the Inverness Select School Grant. The county, however, comprises *two* sub-districts and the selection of advanced schools, fulfilling the conditions imposed under the Act, involved the local educational authorities in a succession of vexatious broils. A special meeting was called in March, 1879, and soon afterwards, by a Minute of Council each board was allowed the privilege of selecting *four* special schools, each to receive an equal allotment of the grant.

Sometime after, the Act was annulled and the County Academy for Inverness was established at Port Hawkesbury.

Here and now I beg to express my obligations to Messrs. A. & W. Mackinlay, booksellers and stationers, Halifax, for their thoughtful generosity in furnishing, on several occasions, boxes of books and other school requisites for gratuitous distribution to poor children in indigent school sections; to Dr. Selwyn and Hugh Fletcher, Esq., of the Geological Survey, for a valuable cabinet of rocks and minerals of the Dominion ; to the gentlemen comprising the school boards, for their punctual attendance at the regular annual meetings; and to W. W. Williams, Esq.. for inserting copies of the minutes of the school boards in the "*Hawkesbury Bulletin.*" ·

Within the district there are institutions of a private or special character—the public educational appliances being solely confined to the County Academies of Port Hood and Baddeck, and to the High School at Port Hawkesbury, together with the miscellaneous and graded schools distributed through the hamlets and most thickly settled localities generally.

The *Port Hood* Academy comprises *two* separate buildings, *one* at the southern end of the village and the other at the west. The main building consists of *two* departments—the *academic* and *intermediate*. The Convent School, which is affiliated with the Academy and is intended exclusively for girls, has also *two*—the preparatory and elementary. Artistically, the main building of the Port Hood Academy does not reflect much credit upon the large and moderately wealthy county of Inverness. The style is neither Doric nor Ionic, Corinthian nor Composite. The rooms are, however, large, and the appliances for heating and ventilation, ample. The Convent School had at one time been the residence of a gentleman in the village, and all the departments are well finished and furnished with imported desks and chairs.

The County Academy at Baddeck is a plain, unadorned public building, consisting of *four* rooms,—*two*, the *advanced* and the *elementary* on the lower flat, and *two*, the *preparatory* and *intermediate* in the storey above. All the rooms are well finished and supplied with improved furniture throughout. The academy is also furnished with a Globe and Gazetteer, together with a fine cabinet of geological specimens of local rocks and curios from heathen lands. The site is poor—being several feet lower than the street in front.

Hawkesbury is the only village within the district invested with civic dignity. Ever since the inauguration of the existing school system the trustees insisted upon having the best teachers available. The rate-payers always voted a handsome sum for school support. The present building has been in use for over a quarter of a century, but it has been lately renovated.

The institution now consists of *four* departments, the *high school* and *preparatory* on the same flat, and *primary* and *intermediate* in the storey below.

For many years the high school was awarded the Academy Grant. But Port Hood being the capital of the county it was transferred thither, *ten* or *eleven* years ago. Since then the teacher of the advanced department has been accorded an additional allowance from the provincial treasury, as provided in Regulation 16.

Port Hastings has *two* departments for the present. Both are in charge of Normal School graduates of high standing.

Mabou has *two* district buildings—*one* for both sexes in charge of a teacher of Class B—the other being the neighbouring Convent, consists of *three* departments—the *preparatory* and *intermediate* exclusively for girls on one flat and the primary for boys in the storey below. Both buildings are thoroughly finished and furnished with imported Dawson seats and desks.

The graded school at Whycocomagh consists of *two* departments—the *advanced* having been in charge of a Normal School graduate of the first Class and the *elementary* of an experienced teacher of Class C. The building is old and more or less delapidated. But improved accommodation is contemplated.

At Belle Cote the building is well finished and furnished with all the ordinary school requisites. Here the children are largely French and the elementary department is always in charge of a person who can speak and read that language.

At Grand Etang *two* of the departments in the convent school has been lately closed, and all the school going children of the section are now crowded into *one* school with *one* teacher and *one* or *two* assistants. This is a matter of regret to every friend of educational progress within the section.

Miscellaneous Schools of high character are also established in the wealthiest localities, in each sub-district. The names of each section may be of some interest for the purposes of comparison :—

SOUTH INVERNESS.

Hillsboro, No. 27,
West Bay, "   40½,
Little Harbor, " 44,
Brook Village, " 34,

NORTH INVERNESS.

Margaree Chapel, No. 8,
Margaree Forks,   "   9,
Margaree Harbor, " 31,
Broad Cove Marsh, " 34,
Brook, No. 34½,

VICTORIA.

Englishtown, No. 50,
East Ingonish, " 64,
New Haven, " 73,
South Ridge, " 86,

and a number of others which is not necessary to specialize.

The necessary funds for the support of the public schools are derived from the following sources—The Provincial Treasury, the County fund, and local assessment. The Provincial grant is paid semi-annually directly to the teachers—the first instalment in February and the second in August. The County fund is apportioned annually, and the trustees of each section are furnished with warrants for their money upon the County Treasury. The balance of the sum voted at the annual meeting is levied upon the section without any unnecessary delay—and the trustees are then in a position to discharge their obligations to the teacher.

During the past year of nine months, teachers of Class A in the County of Inverness were paid at the rate of $695; B's, $265; C's $220 and D's $185. Female teachers as a rule received rates somewhat lower. In Victoria the A teachers employed in the Academy were paid but $560 for the *nine* months; B's, $262; C's $230 and D's $185, while female teachers were paid a shade higher in all the Classes.

Number of teachers employed during the past *nine* months in both Counties may be tabulated as follows :—

Term ended February 3rd, 189?.

VICTORIA.—No. Teachers Class A 1
  "   "   "   " B 2
  "   "   "   " C 22
  "   "   "   " D 34

INVERNESS (South).—No. Teachers Class A 3
  "   "   "   "   " B 5
  "   "   "   "   " C 29
                                     " D 36

INVERNESS (North).—No. Teachers Class A 0
  "   "   "   "   " B 9
  "   "   "   "   " C 16
                            "   " D 38
                     Assistants 9

Term ended 7th July, 1893.

VICTORIA.—No. Teachers Class A 2
  "   "   "   " B 2
  "   "   "   " C 25
  "   "   "   " D 40

INVERNESS (South).—No. Teachers Class A...... 3
    "   "   "   "   " B...... 8
    "   "   "   "   " C......31
           "   "   "   " D......48

INVERNESS (North).—No. Teachers Class A...... 0
    "   "   "   "   " B...... 9
    "   "   "   "   " C......22
                   "   " D......36
                  Assistants............11

The County Academies. Mr. Hall who was in charge of the Baddeck Academy during the first quarter was succeeded by Mr. Johnson, who, after a few weeks' service, was forced to retire on account of ill-health. Mr. T. C. McKay now holds the fort. Mr. McKay has the distinction of being the youngest A graduate in the Province, and if heredity counts, he should be a paragon of unobtrusive honesty and indefatigable application.

The trustees of the Port Hood Academy have indicated their appreciation of Mr. McIntosh's signal success, both as an instructor and citizen, by re-engaging him for the current year at an advance of salary.

The Indian School at Whycocomagh has been, during the past year, in charge of Mr. Victor Christmas, a native Micmac, of Class D. This school was officially visited early in June. The registration was fairly good, but the attendance small, the average up to date being only 8. I was assured the number of children present was not a fair representation of the ordinary attendance. Thechildren were examined in English reading and spelling, including dictation, together with arithmetic, including the multiplication and simple commercial tables. The building is large and comfortable, well finished, and sufficiently furnished with benches, blackboards and maps.

Miss McEachern, who is a duly licensed teacher of Class C, is in charge of the Wagamatcook school, where she has been employed for many years. Her ignorance of the vernacular language places her of course at a disadvantage, but her long experience and her untiring patience and cheerfulness in contending with a host of difficulties renders her a most valuable public servant. The school-house is a fine, well finished building. The furniture, although of the long seat pattern, is good of its kind—there is sufficient black surface for ordinary service—together with maps of the Maritime Provinces and Dominion of Canada.

The school houses in both sections are intended for public worship on Sunday, and as will be readily understood, the seating accommodation has been constructed with a view more to the convenience of adults than of school going children.

From the foregoing synopsis it will be observed that the educational appliances provided within the district, are quite ample to meet the reasonable requirements of the resident young and rising generation— miscellaneous schools in the rural settlements, graded schools in the villages, and academies in the country towns—together with the Indian schools located at the Indian Reservations of Inverness and Victoria.

The course of study prescribed by law is used in all the public schools, and in cases where for various reasons its provisions cannot be strictly carried out, it is utilized as a general guide for the proper arrangement and orderly sequence of studies and a basis of classification. As is well known, its primary aim is to improve the education imparted to the children, not so much with a view to make all schools alike by impressing on their operation a mechanical uniformity as to make each school more effective by giving to its work a definite and continuous character.

That the regular annual high school examinations are now unified with the course of study in the public schools, furnishes an additional reason for its virtual adoption in all the public schools.

The Provincial High School examination was conducted as usual at the following stations:

PORT HOOD.

Deputy Examiner, the Inspector, assisted by D. F. McLean, Esq.

No. candidates, 46—one B, 15 C's and 30 D's. 13 of the applicants were successful, the rest failed. The highest averages were made by P. S. Smith, 454 B; Malcolm McPhail, 445 C; William McDonald, 419 D.

BADDECK.

Ewen McAskill, Esq., Deputy Examiner.

No. candidates, 33—1 A, 4 B's, 4 C's and 24 D's. 15 were successful, the rest failed. The highest averages were made by J. M. Macritchie, 1258 A; Tena McLean, 544 B; John J. McAskill, 521 B.

PORT HAWKESBURY.

Dr. P. A. McDonald, Deputy Examiner.

No. candidates, 19—4 B's, 8 C's and 7 D's. 13 were successful, the rest failed. The Highest averages wore made by John Archy McLellan, 515 C; Joseph D. Matheson, 430 B; Lizzie J. Reeves, 411 B.

MARGAREE FORKS.

Dougald Campbell, Esq., Deputy Examiner.

No. candidates, 13—1 B, 1 C and 11 D's. 3 were successful and 10 failed. The successful candidates were P. A. McGarry, 310 B; Amy L. Ross, 314 C; Sarah L. Doyle, 423 D.

CHETICAMP.

Dr. Fiset, Deputy Examiner.

No. candidates, 8—3 C's and 5 D's. 3 were successful and 5 failed. The successful were Michael Crispo, 453 C; Dan Buckles, 477 D ; Mary S. LeBlanc, 402 D.

On Saturday, the 8th of July, the Minimum Professional Quali- fication Examination was held at the same stations.

PORT HOOD.

No. candidates, 20—successful, 11 ; failures, 9.   The three making the highest averages being :

> William McQuarrie, 134.   Third rank.
> Kate A. Kennedy, 133.   "   "
> John D. Murray, 124.

BADDECK.

No. candidates, 13—successful, 11 ; failures, 2.   The three making the highest were :

> Duncan McAskill, 134.   Third rank.
> John McIver, 128.   "   "
> Murdo McIver, 126.

PORT HAWKESBURY.

No. candidates, 8—successful, 6, failures, 2.   The three making the highest averages were :

> Annie McDonald, 158.   Second rank.
> John A. McLellan, 153.   "   "
> Hector McDonald, 147.   Third rank.

MARGAREE FORKS.

No. candidates, 9—successful, 4 ; failures, 5.   The three making the highest averages were :

> Michael E. Coady, 119.   Third rank.
> Mary J. Cameron, 113.   "   "
> Peter Coady, 106.

CHETICAMP.

No. candidates, 4—successful, 3 ; failed, 1.   The names of the successful :

> Dan Buckles, 127.
> Lucy Arseneaux, 126.
> Mary S. LeBlanc, 106.

In connection with the general results of the public examination, it may not be amiss to append the results of the examinations as far as the county academies and high school at Hawkesbury are concerned :

PORT HOOD.

22 candidates—1 B successful. 10 C's—1 successful in obtaining grade applied for and 3 obtained Grade D.

Minimum Professional Examination. 7 candidates—2 obtaining third rank certificates.

BADDECK.

12 candidates—of these 3 went up for B, 3 for C, and 6 for D. 3 obtained B and 5 D. This last includes 2 who failed to obtain C but who obtained D.

HIGH SCHOOL, HAWKESBURY.

11 candidates—4 B's and 7 C's—2 B's successful, and 3 C's in obtaining the grade applied for. 2 of the B candidates obtained C, and 4 of the C's obtained D.

The rather limited number who passed at the July examination has necessitated the employment of teachers with only permissive authority. I am exceedingly sorry that such should be the case. I am, however, quite satisfied that many to whom this privilege has been accorded are fully as capable as some teachers who are regularly licensed. The system, however, is bad.

With respect to our educational standing during the past year, I beg to assure you that we were well provided for. The fact that six teachers of Class A were employed, abundantly verifies this statement.

So far as general results are concerned, I may say that I am myself a disciple of Herbert Spencer. Every one has a hobby. Mine is the three R's. A high school education is admirably adapted for the *'oi ologoi* of the community, but for the *'oi polloi*, something of a more practical character would be more serviceable. I believe (1) every child in the county should receive such an education as will fit him for that rank and position in life to which he is adapted ; (2), our schools should give every child that kind and degree of training which his abilities and environments demand ; and (3), training required should recognize the triune nature of the child, viz: his physical, intellectual, and moral nature. Physically, he should be trained to the performance of such physical labour as may be required of him when he assumes the *toga virilis*. Intellectually, his natural inclination should be consulted and his studies adapted to the natural trend of his mind, and morally, his individual accountability for every thought, word and action should be constantly impressed upon him.

Every youth in the land should be taught how to harness a horse and drive a carriage, how to row and manage a boat, how to swim and resuscitate a person apparently drowned, and how to conduct himself generally in any emergency.

I beg to congratulate you upon your success in raising the standard of the teaching profession throughout the Province, and in engrafting the syllabus of examination upon the lines of the prescribed course of study. Had this policy been adopted years ago, there would not have been so many failures at the recent examination of teachers within this district. It was also a happy thought to have the age limit of the candidates for classification in scholarship annulled and to have the limitation of fees confined to candidates for the Minimum Professional Qualification Examination.

Early in July two of our most promising teachers were called to their long homes—James D. Gillis and John L. McKinnon. Mr. Gillis in addition to his regular professional duties was one of the Government Land Surveyors for a number of years. Mr. McKinnon was a student of high promise. Both taught in the section in which I reside, and I knew them intimately. I never knew young men who were actuated with higher conceptions of rectitude or moral purity.

In conclusion allow me to express my high regard for you personally and professionally, and to thank you most sincerely for your courtesy and forbearance during my official intercourse with you in the education office.

I am dear Sir,

Very truly yours,

J. Y. GUNN.

To A. H. MacKay, Esq., LL. D.
      Superintendent of Education.

———

DISTRICT No. 9.—PICTOU AND SOUTH COLCHESTER.

W. E. Maclellan, Ll. B., *Inspector.*

Sir,—

I beg leave to submit the annual report of my inspectorate for the year ending July 31st, 1893.

During the said year or nine months term, 167 schools were in operation in the county of Pictou and 75 in the district of South Colchester.

In Pictou county five sections, namely: Mount Adam, Green's Valley, McIntosh Mills, Fraser's Mountains and Carriboo Island, were without school throughout the period mentioned. The three first named are weak sections with but few pupils; and in the past have usually only maintained school in the summer term. Hereafter they will probably adapt themselves to the new order of things, and keep their schools open, as heretofore, for a considerable portion of the year. Fraser's Mountain is permanently disorganized and might as well be struck off the list of South Pictou sections. It has had no school for years, its pupils being within easy reach of other schools. Carriboo Island has been without school since 1889. There are very few children of school age in the section. The last term in which its school was open the average attendance was between two and three.

In South Colchester four sections were without school, namely:— Kemptown, Springmont, Green's Creek and Southvale. The two former have long been disorganized, mainly from lack of school children. Southvale had its school house burnt over a year ago and has not yet re-built. A good many of its children are attending Meadowvale school. It would be better for both if these two sections could be united. Green's Creek is a weak section, but much more able than it would seem to be willing to maintain school.

The new and lengthened school term has operated to the disadvantage of a number of poorer sections, which have heretofore been in the habit of maintaining school only in summer. In several cases in my district such sections have buildings fit only for occupation during the warmer weather, no provision having been made for winter work, because, owing to scattered settlement, there would be no attendance of pupils at that season. Such sections have experienced, and are likely to experience, considerable difficulty in finding teachers willing to engage for the three first and three last months of the new school year.

During the year two school houses have been built. The Camden, South Colchester, building was destroyed towards the end of the first quarter, the East French River, South Pictou, building at the close of the third quarter. The fire in the latter case was undoubtedly of incendiary origin. You are aware of the dispute concerning the school house site which has been going on for years at French River. You are also aware of the settlement effected last winter and the agreement entered into between the parties, to the effect that the late school house should be accepted and used for school purposes "so long as fit for occupation." Although only a year old, it has been effectually unfitted for occupation by means of petroleum and matches.

Both the Camden and French River registers were destroyed with the buildings; so the statistics furnished by these sections are mainly estimated.

Another unfortunate event of the year in my district was the loss, by drowning, of Mr. James McGregor, teacher at Big Island,

Merigomish. As no one was with Mr. McGregor at the time of his falling into the water, and as his body was not recovered for several months, a doubt of his death was entertained for a time by his family and friends; consequently no teacher was engaged by the section to complete the school term. The return from Big Island is therefore unattested; but inasmuch as it was made out at my request by Mr. Fred. W. Mitchell, a Class B teacher employed at Merigomish, I have no doubt of its strict accuracy.

At the annual meeting of the Board of School Commissioners for South Pictou, in May last, a new section was laid off at Ferrona and Eureka in the county of Pictou. The action of the Board was subsequently ratified by the Council of Public Instruction and the section duly established. It has since been organized, and is now preparing to erect a substantial school-house with rooms for the two departments, which will be required as soon as they can be provided.

Hopewell Section has been somewhat weakened through the estblishment of the new section at Ferrona; and Riverton has been left with a mere handful of pupils. It is to be regretted that the latter section was not at once divided up among adjoining sections. Upper Hopewell, also, might well have been dismembered in favour of Hopewell and Lorne.

Camden has about completed a new building to replace the burnt one. This is the only new school-house erected in my district since the date of my last report. A number of sections, however, have arranged to thoroughly repair and re-furnish their buildings during the summer holidays, having the work completed in time for the re-opening of school at the beginning of the new year.

In addition to the new school-house to be put up at Ferrona, New Glasgow has voted $25,000 for the erection of a new high school building, which, when completed, will probably be one of the handsomest of its kind in the Province. Westville, also, is preparing to put up a new two-roomed building to accommodate its ever increasing school population.

A petition for the establishment of a new school section at East River, St. Mary's, was again presented to the Board of School Commissioners for South Pictou at its last annual meeting, and was once more negatived.

Alma School Section, in the district of South Colchester, appeared a second time before the annual meeting of Commissioners at Truro with a petition for the division of the section into two parts. The petitioners having failed, as on a former occasion, to give legal notice in the section of their intended application, the Board was unable to consider the matter. It is probable that the petition will again be brought forward, although the whole section has only an annual enrollment of 54 and a total valuation of $19,740. One of the proposed new sections would have some twenty pupils in all, and a valuation of six or seven thousand dollars. The inclination of the people seems to be to increase rather than to lessen the number of schools. Alma Section is badly in need of a new school-house; but the building of it is being delayed as long as possible in the hope that the privilege may be obtained of putting up two instead of one.

During the year I have visited all the school sections in my district, with the exception of Pictou Island, and inspected all the schools open at the time of my rounds. School work has been proceeding along the usual lines. I think I can note some improvement in the methods of teaching geography and language. Arithmetic is a poorly taught subject in many schools. The great defect in the schools generally is the too slavish adherence to text books. Many teachers seem to think that their sole function is to listen to home-prepared " recitations." The directions given in the new registers ought to do much to correct this most harmful idea, if only teachers can be induced to study and practise them. But a great deal of time would seem to be required to effect any material change in traditional methods of teaching. I believe that if the Educational Department were to issue a brief manual to teachers, containing simple and precise directions as to the way in which the various subjects in the prescribed course of study should be taught, improvement might be effected in a comparatively short time. The official character of such a publication would secure for it prompt and careful attention, and it would provide inspectors with a means of enforcing their directions.

The statistical tables herewith furnished you will afford detailed information concerning educational work in my inspectoral district. I am sorry to be forced to say that the returns from which these tables have been compiled are by far the worst that have ever been sent me. The new forms of return would seem to have overturned the reason of not a few of those who undertook to fill them out. That at least would be a charitable assumption since affidavits were duly made to the correctness of a good many which displayed unmistakable marks of worse than ordinary carelessness. I had to send a number back to be re-written, still more should have gone, and would, but for the difficulty of finding teachers when once their engagement in a section has terminated. One teacher, the holder of a Class C license, gravely asserted that the school over which she presided had " $534\frac{1}{2}$ " pupils " on register at end of first quarter," that her average daily attendance out of that number was " 9.7 " and that the per centage of attendance during the quarter was " 46.8." She further alleged that she had " 728 " on register at end of second quarter and " 671 " at end of third quarter. Then to clear up these little complications she went on to state that the "number of children in the section from 5 to 15 years of age" was "7," and that the " number of those who had not attended school at all during the year " was " 7." The whole of this return was of a piece with the foregoing quotations. It is unnessary to say that none of the others came quite up to this standard of absurdity, but some were not far behind.

The "estimates" of the value of school property, &c., you will find very far from even approximate correctness in many cases.

The "time table" is in large part mere guess work—the guessing frequently of the wildest character. Teachers, generally, complain seriously of this table, alleging that they cannot conscientiously apportion their time in the minute and exact manner required. In miscellaneous schools, particularly, the oral subjects, and not a few others, are taught just as occasion arises, and often in connection with other subjects. It is then difficult in the extreme, if not impossible to give anything approaching an accurate account of the time devoted to them. In miscellaneous schools, too, the teacher is frequently occupied with two classes in different subjects at the same time. Then there is the further element of the uncertainty in the varying size of classes from day to day and quarter to quarter. Such are some of the objections of honest and capable teachers to the time table of the return.

The one year term is, I believe, affording general satisfaction. The prevention of the former system of half yearly changes of teachers, prevailing in so many sections, cannot but prove highly beneficial. An improvement seems to have been effected already in the matter of regularity of school attendance on the part of pupils. Formerly the attendance began to fall off rapidly towards the end of each term as well as at the approach of the summer holidays. The autumn break up of the schools will certainly be prevented to a large extent for the future. Many of the larger pupils will yet, as a matter of course, in the country districts, leave school about the first of April; but as younger pupils will then be beginning to come in, the schools will not wear their former deserted and disheartening appearance at that season.

The only complaint I have heard respecting the new school year in the country districts is its too great length. The children grow weary of so long a period of steady attendance, and manifest an almost irresistible inclination to withdraw from school towards the end of the year. I found a number of schools almost deserted in July last, and one or two closed entirely for want of pupils. Many parents maintain that their children should have a longer period out of the year for home work and home training. I believe it would be found, were a nine months' term made optional, that a large majority of sections would avail themselves of it.

The question of payment for School Commissioners came up again at the annual meeting of the Boards of South Pictou and South Colchester. It is the opinion of both Boards, that an allowance of at least two dollars per day should be made to members in actual attendance at the meetings of the Boards, or when engaged in special committee work—this sum to be deducted from the County Fund. If a regulation giving effect to this suggestion were to be enacted it would no doubt have its effect of increasing the attendance at Commissioners' meetings—something much to be desired. I have been requested to lay this matter before you for the consideration of the Council of Public Instruction.

I have the honour to be

Your obedient servant,

W. E. MACLELLAN.

A. H. MacKay, Esq., Ll. D.,
Superintendent of Education.

DISTRICT No. 10.—CUMBERLAND AND N. COLCHESTER.

Inglis C. Craig, *Inspector.*

Sir,—

This district is under the general supervision of four boards of Commissioners, representing Cumberland (proper), Parrsboro, Sterling, and West Colchester.

The following information relative to each of the four districts is gathered from the statistical tables forwarded herewith:

Commissioners' District.	No. of Com.	Chairman of Board.	Sections.	Teachers.	Pupils Enrolled.	Provincial Grant.	County and Sectional Aid.	Cost of maintenance of each Pupil at School.
Cumberland.......	14	Rev. V. E. Harris.......	127	151	6688	$8125 62	$30757 10	5.81
Parrsboro...........	10	Rev. Simon Gibbons.	30	30	1443	1805 93	6598 11	5.82
Sterling..............	11	J. Millar, Esq...........	30	30	·1077	1652 14	3635 75	4.90
West Colchester..	7	J. C. Crowe, Esq......	31	53	1753	2335 86	7256 89	5.47

The entire cost of educating 10,961 pupils for the school year of nine months was $62,167.40 or $5.67 per pupil, or at the rate of $7.56 for a full school year.

There are 7 graded schools in Cumberland; 5 in Parrsboro; 1 in Sterling and 6 in West Colchester. Of these, Springhill, Parrsboro and Acadia Mines are the largest. The former two enjoyed the High School grant during the past year. W. W. Torey, Principal at Springhill, established his claim by passing at the government examination in July, the number of pupils required by the department. This endorsement of my recommendation gives me pleasure.

Thirty-eight per cent. of the teachers of this district are graduates of the Normal School, and 18 per cent. are in the public service for the first time.

Five and one half per cent. of the entire enrolment are classed as high school pupils.

I have made these notes relative to the condition of houses, apparatus and school grounds.

CUMBERLAND PROPER.

Stake Road, No. 4.—This section has a very poor house. The trustees give the Board assurance that it will be replaced by another one at an early date.

Six Mile Road, No. 9.—The school house here was in a wretched condition. At the suggestion of the Commissioners it has been completely remodelled.

The school rooms in Middleboro No. 11, Mapleton 63; Pugwash River East 23; Wallace Bay 10; Lower Wentworth 12, and Joggin Mines 51, were condemned at the Board's regular meeting in May, as unfit for school purposes. In most instances where condemnation was a necessity the sections were only awaiting the will of the School Board, and have very promptly taken steps to build anew. From the minutes of a special meeting held at the Joggins, I learn that $3000 has been voted to build a house of four departments.

Wallace 8.—The advanced department has been reseated with modern furniture.

Northport 36.—An extension was made to the school house here to accommodate the increased attendance more comfortably.

Amherst Academy.—This is now being occupied for the first time, and every parent feels that here his children cannot have a better home than in these elegantly furnished appartments. The heating and ventilating by the new system, Fuller and Warner's, are all that can be desired.

Principal Lay is indefatigable in making in every way the Academy worthy the peoples' sacrifice and pride. An elegant piano has been placed in the assembly hall, and has been paid for by his exertions. A series of exhibitions, concerts and lectures are contemplated early in the autumn as a means to raise funds for further furnishings and apparatus.

Nappan 44, has been the subject of much attention during the past year. The house was condemned in 1892, as well as the site. As soon as it was learned that a new house was to be built two seceding elements arose asking for the tripartite division of the section. Their petition was granted by the Commissioners, but not without strong and centralized opposition. The Council of Public Instruction not finding sufficient reason to endorse the Boards's recommendation deferred the ratification. Meanwhile at the regular annual meeting in June, the whole matter was amicably settled, and it is hoped that all opposition to a central and graded system will pass away. A beautiful site has been selected for the new house, which will have two departments.

In Oxford 79, and Springhill 108, a department has been added in each.

At Greenville 86, the attendance is so great that another department is needed at once.

Clifton 107. This section has taken first place among the rural sections in erecting the neatest, most thoroughly built and elegantly furnished room in this district. I commend it as a model to other sections of the county intending to build. Cost, furnished, $561. Property in section, $15,000.

Greenville Station 113. The house in this locality was destroyed by fire in February. Ashes had been left in a barrel near the entry, and in the absence of the teacher, set the house on fire. Another house at Truro Road, Sterling, was also burned. This is ascribed to an incendiary when the house was being moved to a more convenient site. It is to be regretted that the party or parties to the act should go unpunished. The province over, this is the common revenge for imaginary grievances relative to public school property. Undoubtedly, if a detective had been given this case, an example could have been made of a dangerous citizen.

In section 120, West Chester Valley, the generosity of Councillor Halliday will not be forgotten soon on account of the gift of $100 toward the liquidation of debt on the neat little school room recently built in this locality.

PARRSBORO' DISTRICT.

Many improvements have been projected for the comming year in this part of Cumberland. Parrsboro' Town has had several meetings for the puurpose of getting an opinion from the public relative to new and more modern school accommodation. Nothing tangible has yet been done.

Fox River 9. A new house is being built here as well as in Salem 16.

Cape D'or 13. This large miscellaneous school has been divided into two departments.

STERLING.

The division of Tarbet No. 9, was asked this Board and granted, but subsequently finding the procedure of applicants irregular the C. P. I. did not ratify the division.

The Falls 23. A new house is being built in this section on the opposite side of Waugh's River from the old house. This was the best site in the immediate locality. Much opposition arose in this section to the Commissioners' decision.

The School House at Mill Brook No. 10 has been condemned.

WEST COLCHESTER.

For the past two years it has been difficult in this district of Commissioners to get sufficient members of the board together to do the public business. There is immediate need of an increased membership to this board.

Portaupique 9. On the solicitation of the Board this section purchased a large area for a school ground and removed the school house to the rear of it.

Masstown 20. Here the trustees have, with very pleasing effect, re-modelled and painted the interior of their house.

At Folly, 22, the deaths of Misses Jean MacDonald and Mary Layton, two estimable teachers, was a great shock to this community. The sad coincidence of their demise within a few days of each other, after being associated in the same school was remarkable.

RETURNS.

I regret the carping tone that pervades my reports, but the compilation of the annual returns gives another opportunity to complain. The numerous blunders and untidy registers and returns mark the teacher. When forty per cent. of the returns have to be sent back for the correction of time table alone there is but one inference to be drawn : that these teachers have no methodical plans, no time set for any particular work, but allow one recitation or lesson to crowd upon another's heels until the weary day is over. I cannot but commend the time table of the annual return for it has discovered a serious defect in too many schools—a go-as-you-please-style. How many teachers give the proper time to each subject which its relative importance demands? Hereafter in this district I shall believe it is my duty to know.

I beg leave to make this suggestion in the plan of the Superintendent's sheets ; instead of returning the names of the trustees of each section let the name of the secretary be given in stead of or in addition to them. The names of the trustees are not any protection to the County Treasurer, as all the business of the section is done in the secretary's name. This change would save these county officers much unnecessary trouble and also protect them from imposture.

Your obedient servant,

INGLIS C. CRAIG,

To A. H. MacKay, Esq., Ll. D.,
        Superintendent of Education.

APPENDIX C.

Report of the Board of School Commissioners

OF THE

CITY OF HALIFAX,

YEAR ENDED, JULY 31st, 1893.

I.

CHAIRMAN'S REPORT.

OFFICE OF SCHOOL COMMISSIONERS,
HALIFAX, Oct., 1893.

A.. H. MacKay, Esq., Ll. D.,
    Superintendent of Education.

Sir,—

For the information of the Council of Public Instruction I have the honor to submit herewith the report of the Supervisor of Schools and the Secretary of the Board.

The members of the Board have been most assiduous in their duties, and have given strict attention to maintaining the efficiency of the schools without permitting any unavoidable increase of an expenditure already found burdensome, and have practised the utmost economy consistent with efficiency.

I am of the same opinion as my predecessors that too many subjects are taught in the Academy, pupils studying for professions might go to the colleges, but those intending to follow a commercial career would be more benefited by a course at a commercial college. In pursuance of the same principle the boy who intends to follow any mechanical pursuit will find himself placed at a disadvantage if he too long delay an acquaintance with its practical details.

The Supervisor and teachers are now at work improving the system of writing. In the near future, it is hoped our schools will produce better results than formerly.

The lease of St. Patrick's boys school having expired it has been re-leased on the agreement that the owners keep the building in repair. I trust that when other leases lapse the properties may be re-leased in the same way, and also that insurance be paid by the owners. I believe it will save friction, expedite the business of the Board meetings, and perpetuate friendship.

The Board has bought a lot of land in the north suburbs extending through from Young street to Kaye street, on which they are erecting a school house of eight departments so planned as to admit of enlargement when required. It is expected to be finished about the first of March, and will accommodate the children now attending the rented buildings on Campbell road and Gottingen street.

The attendance at Compton Avenue and Bloomfield Schools having outgrown their accommodation, the Board some time ago found it necessary to hire outside rooms. The attendance still increasing, the Board thought it advisable to complete Compton Avenue building as originally planned, making it an eight department school. It is now nearly completed, and the two rented rooms on Robie and Agricola streets can then be vacated.

' During the present year we have lost the services of Mrs. Harriman who for two years very ably conducted the Kindergarten department. She was called to a higher and more lucrative position in Rhode Island. One of her pupils, Miss Ackhurst, is now in charge and is doing satisfactory work.

The Board has also lost the services of Mr. Lee Russell in the Manual Training Department, and as you know, he has been appointed by the Provincial Government to inaugurate a similar work in connection with the Normal School at Truro. His work here is being carried on by Mr. N. H. Gardner, a practical man who received technical training from Mr. Russell.

During the past year the Board was called upon to lament the loss of one of its most faithful teachers, Miss Waddell, of Morris Street School, who died suddenly last Christmas. For many years she served the Board with success, and was a living example of the virtues which she strove to inculcate in her school. She was succeeded by Miss Moseley, who for several terms was regarded as one of the best teachers of Dartmouth.

The Secretary's books show that the expenditure for the 12 months ending, October, 1893, is about $4000 less than for the 12 months ending, October, 1892.

The Board is fortunate in having two such able officers as Mr. A. McKay, the Supervisor, and Mr. R. J. Wilson the Secretary, the latter of whom puts about fifteen months work in a year.

I have the honor to be,

Your obedient servant,

JNO. H. SYMONS,
Chairman.

II.

Report of the Supervisor of Halifax Public Schools,

FOR THE YEAR ENDED 31st JULY,

1893.

To the Chairman and Members of the Board of School Commissioners for the City of Halifax :

GENTLEMEN,—I have the honor to submit to you herewith statistical tables relating to the Halifax schools for the school period from November 1st, 1892, to July 31st, 1893.

On account of certain changes in the Provincial school law, this period covers only 34 weeks instead of 43 weeks as formerly. It will therefore be impossible to institute accurate comparisons with other years.

A few figures, however, will be of some interest. There were enrolled on the school registers for the period named 7,133 pupils. As the tables giving this result were compiled on a different principle from former tables, it would be difficult to say whether or not there has been the decrease that these figures seem to indicate. The grand total days' attendance was 738,270. Allowing for difference of teaching days it would have been 946,046, or 12,000 days less than last year.

The average of quarterly per centages is 70.6 ; the corresponding number for last year being a fraction less.

There having been 129 departments open, with a total of 7,133 pupils, it is manifest that each teacher had, on an average, 55 pupils enrolled. This is a large number for each teacher—a larger average number than other cities place in each department.

Each teacher in Portland, Maine, cares for 38 pupils; in Springfield, Mass., for 43 pupils; in Worcester and St. John, for 47 pupils; in Boston, for 50 pupils; but in Halifax each teacher has to educate 55 pupils on an average.

In the higher departments the principals seldom take so many; with their other duties and the number of subjects they have to teach in the higher grades, it is only by the closest attention to their work that they are enabled to hold their own in the severe competition which takes place every year for entrance into the High Schools.

If schools are well graded, the school rooms well furnished and adapted for the work, and the pupils well supplied with suitable text books, a good teacher can teach a large number of pupils satisfactorily. But when we have already so far exceeded other cities in this kind of economy we should be careful not to go too far for the sake of breaking the record.

Every pupil differs from every other pupil in some respects, and therefore every pupil requires some individual attention, which he cannot have if there are too many.

The tables show that there are 2,700 pupils who attended less than 100 days out of 167 teaching days since November 1st, 1892. This would seem to indicate that at least one-third of those attending school will fail to comply with the provisions of the compulsory school Act, which requires a minimum attendance of 120 days out of 215.

If we consider the loss implied by this want of regularity it will be seen to be very serious.

1. The irregular pupil is unable to get the benefit even of the days when he is present. The continuity of his studies is broken. On the day when he is absent he misses important explanations necessary to the clear understanding of the problems of the day when he is present. He loses interest in his work. And perhaps worse than all he develops unsystematic habits in all his business relations.

2. The punctual pupil also suffers loss. He gets into idle habits by being obliged to wait in his work for the teacher while repeating explanations which are necessary to carry along the irregular pupils. It is a large task to investigate the causes of so much irregularity, but it should be done if we are to get the benefit of the teaching done in the schools, and if the pupils are to hold the compulsory attendance law in due respect.

Our tables for this year show the number of minutes devoted each week to the various studies prescribed for the common and high school courses.

Here are the most important :

Arithmetic, 310 minutes per week ; reading, 250 ; writing, 121 ; spelling, 112 ; composition and grammar, 100 ; geography, 86 ; history, 86 ; object lessons, 52 ; music, 52 ; drawing, 65.

The judgment shown by the teachers in regard to the division of their time to the several subjects according to their relative importance will be approved by most educationists.

For arithmetic a full hour each day is certainly needed, at least until we can discover or act upon better methods of teaching it.

For reading, an hour each day is perhaps too little, but it must be remembered that in connection with the composition, geography, grammar, etc., there is a considerable amount of practice in reading. To the training of the hand for using the pen and pencil with facility there is devoted specially three hours each week, besides more than twice as much more time in the writing exercises, which, if carefully executed, are as good training as the special writing lessons.

From this statement it is plain that three hours out of every five are devoted solely to the three R's, while indirectly one of the remaining hours is likewise subsidiary to them.

The most ardent advocates of these fundamental branches can scarcely fail to be satisfied with this showing.

Manual training (including SEWING under the term), is reported from 41 departments as occupying about 83 minutes per week.

REVIEW OF THE LAST TEN YEARS.

In my former reports I devoted much attention to those educational principles which should guide us in the management of the schools, both as to the teachers' work, and the appliances which should be placed at his disposal.

It might be more profitable at this time to review the work of the past ten years—to take stock—to see what progress you have made and in what direction. Then you will be better able to shape your course for the future.

In the first place we naturally think of the teacher, who is the all-important factor in any system of education, for as the teacher, so is the school. We find, then, that during the ten years we have in review there have been many changes in the teaching staff. Of the 101 teachers employed in 1883, fifty-three have left us, some deceased, some married and some employed in more remunerative occupations; several of them were among our most faithful teachers and we will not soon forget their valuable work. But it is gratifying to know that the great majority of the best teachers of ten years ago are still with us and still at their best.

Besides the changes occasioned by the retirement of the 53 teachers above referred to, there have been many other changes of teachers appointed since that date—the most of these changes arising from the fact that aspiring young men have been making teaching a stepping stone to the other professions.

Of those appointed since 1883, I find that 26 rank as superior. Seven of them have since retired. There have been on the average about ten appointments each year, and so far as my knowledge goes, they have been remarkably free from nepotism or favoritism, the appointments being made simply on merit.

We might, perhaps, have had somewhat better teachers if we had in most cases selected the best from the whole province instead of from the City of Halifax. But if we had done so we would have deprived the girls of our schools of an important inspiration to work. Many of our most advanced pupils are now striving to become worthy of positions as teachers, and this desire acts as a wholesome stimulus to good work, especially in the higher departments.

Besides, our own girls living in their own homes, can afford to work at a smaller salary, and thus the cost of the schools is kept down. Many of the best country teachers refuse to accept the salaries we offer, as their expenses in the country are so much less than they would be in the city.

One thing our teachers lack, and that is professional training. By professional training I do not mean courses of lectures on the science, art and history of pedagogy, but an apprenticeship at teaching, conducted under intelligent supervision—such an apprenticeship as a doctor, lawyer or machinist must serve before he enters into the independent practice of his profession.

The experience of other cities would serve to show that it is inexpedient to ask city graduates of the Academy to leave their homes to prepare for their work as teachers. It is found that the most useful professional training is that secured by practice in the best city schools, supplemented by the timely suggestions of superior teachers, and such knowledge of theory as can be obtained from educational conferences and a judicious course of reading.

Since 1884 such training schools and classes have been established in 25 towns of Massachusetts.

An admirable system of the same kind has been connected with the Normal School in Boston.

Canadian cities are moving in this direction. London, Ont., is endeavoring to organize such a school. We could conduct professional training classes without any additional expense.

SCHOOL ACCOMMODATION.

In 1881 the average school of this city was very imperfect, badly ventilated, lighted and seated, untidy, with defective playgrounds and latrines,—anything in fact but a credit to our school system. Compare, for example, the two cap-rooms in Morris street school, in which 120 children were hived, with the beautiful class rooms to which they gave place; the low ceilings and circumscribed rooms which afforded shelter to the girls of St. Mary's and St. Patrick's, with the commodious buildings in which they now assemble; the barn-like structures in which the children and teachers of the northwest parts of the city used to shiver throughout the long winter, with the comfortable quarters which all but a few of them now occupy. Consider the splendid building which has replaced the Tabernacle school, and the improvements made in the internal structure of the Albro street school, the extension and adornment of the playgrounds, the introduction of improved furniture into a majority of classrooms, and you will be astonished at the transformation effected in ten years; pleased when you know that your predecessors as well as yourselves in making these changes were influenced by considerations of economy in administering the school funds, as well as by considerations of humanity to the children placed under your charge; proud when you reflect that Halifax now stands behind no part of the province in respect of its school accommodation.

SYSTEMATIC DEVELOPMENT.

As stated in another part of this report, the teacher is looked upon as the all-important factor in our school system.

If the schools are to be improved it must be done by increasing the knowledge, skill and enthusiasm of the teachers. An ESPRIT DE CORPS must be created among them, similar to that which exists among the members of other professions. This can best be done by holding teachers' meetings for the discussion of educational questions, by the formation of teachers' classes for the study of special subjects, by attendance at educational conventions and Summer schools, the study of educational literature, and by seeing the methods used by successful teachers in the arrangement of their classes.

By a resolution of the Board in 1884, I was instructed to organize teachers' meetings for the discussion of educational questions, for the observation of improved methods of teaching and for the formation of a professional library. It was made a part of each teachers' duty to be present at such meetings. The first meeting was held on the 3rd of July, 1884, the Chairman of the Board presiding. As a result of such general meetings, and of special meetings of teachers, with their principals, their various duties were defined, time tables were drawn up, and more uniformity was secured.   •

In 1885 nearly all the teachers took a course of lessons in freehand model and object drawing and perspective from Mr. James of the Academy.

In the same year Halifax Academy was reorganized on its present basis with free admission to all qualified pupils, and it received thereafter the maximum government grant of $1,720 annually.

In 1886, the teachers, at their meetings, took up the systematic study of Locke's Thoughts on Education, followed by Spencer's Education, and Sully's Psychology.

Aided by subscriptions from Commissioners Roche, Sweet, Blackadar and Woodill, they started a professional library, which has supplied to them valuable reading in the line of their work.

For 1887, we have to record our first efforts to found school libraries. The movement began in Summer street and St. Patrick's schools, followed by the Academy, which raised $400. Other schools followed the example, so that now we have 19 school libraries, some of them of course rather small.

The teachers' meetings were well sustained. The late Dr. Honeyman lectured on local Geology, Dr. Lawson on Botany, and Mr. Bowman and others on Mineralogy. Similar lectures were given in other years by Mr. Kennedy in Chemistry, and by Miss Creighton in Botany.

At the first session of the Summer School of Science held at Wolfville, Halifax teachers numbered 25 per cent. of the whole attendance. At other sessions we did even better than that.

In 1888, the Board engaged Sergt.-Major Bailey to draw up a system of calisthenic drill suited to our schools, and to instruct our teachers in the use of it.

The most notable of our educational conventions took place this year. We were privileged to meet Dr. Fitch, of London, Sir Wm. Dawson and Dr. Parker, world-renowned educationists. Halifax was always well represented at such meetings.

In our professional development, the year 1889 is characterized by the introduction of Tonic Sol-fa in our schools. It was subsequently prescribed for the schools of the whole province. Seventy teachers received instruction in this subject from Revd. J. Anderson, A.M., and Miss A. F. Ryan.

But I would weary you by relating all that the teachers did, and are doing, toward their own self-improvement—how they took lessons on elocution from Miss McGarry, lessons in drawing at the Art School, lessons in modern languages, lessons in zoology from Dr. MacKay, lessons in child culture from Mrs. Harriman, manual training lessons from Prof. Russell—all for the sake of coming up to your idea of what a good teacher should be, so that they could successfully pursue in their schools all the branches demanded by the prescribed course of study and the progressive spirit of the times. As I stated in my report for 1888, referring to their attendance at the Summer School of Science, " we find them voluntarily giving up a large part of their holidays, studying faithfully in advance and during the sessions, incurring, besides, large expense for fees, travelling, board and books—all for the benefit of the pupils."

KINDERGARTEN.

A review of this kind would be incomplete without some reference to certain other reforms which were pursued to a successful issue. Recognizing that development of the spontaneous and pleasureable self-activity of the child is the correct way of beginning his education, you established, two years ago, a Kindergarten Training Department, and placed at the head of it a lady of large culture and special qualifications for the work. You have now several teachers who have been trained under her, and who, having been selected with special reference to their fitness for that kind of work, will probably develop superior skill. We hope that they are just inaugurating the time when all teachers of every grade will be animated by Kindergarten *principles*,—though some Kindergarten *practices* may fall into desuetude.

MANUAL TRAINING.

I will also refer to the Manual Training School—an institution which, first started in Halifax as an experiment, under special encouragemt from the government, has been engrafted on the Normal School system.

In continuing the Manual Training School as a part of our school system, you enter a protest against that education which does all for the boy looking towards a profession, but which largely ignores that training which begets a healthy love of labor and developes the preceptive, inventive and executive faculties. We do right in training the hand and the eye as well as the brain, for assuredly nine-tenths of our pupils will have to live by some form of manual labor.

COMPULSORY EDUCATION.

Among the many improvements introduced during the last ten years, perhaps few are so important as the Compulsory Education Act, in the enactment of which you express your belief that prevention is better than cure—that a Christian education such as is given in all our schools is a preventive of crime and a protection, more effective, humane and economical than prison bars or policemen. You have, in my opinion, the best law for securing adequate school attendance that exists in any English-speaking country. A somewhat more stringent application of its provisions would secure better results.

IMPROVED WORK.

No person will be disposed to dispute the existence of the educational activity which I have just described. But some may ask to be shown the fruits—the superior scholarship—the improved morals—the better physical development—the greater preparation for life's work. These can all be shown, but perhaps I am not the proper person to do so. I cannot fail to be prejudiced. I will therefore only refer to a very few facts, and then let others speak.

The almost universal testimony of the teachers is that their scholars are much more easily governed than formerly—the pupils are more amenable to authority—more civilized. Finding the public schools improved in moral and sanitary conditions, an increasing number of our most aristocratic families are sending their children to them and are expressing satisfaction at the results.

Employers of labor tell us that a well-educated boy from the public schools, though awkward at first in details, yet is so well grounded in principles and so quick in apprehension that he masters his business in half the time required by the boy of untrained mind.

But not to be unmindful of the precept : " let another praise thee, and not thine own lips," we will take the verdict upon our work from twelve competent and impartial men—the Provincial Board of Examiners.

At the last provincial examination there were 231 candidates from Halifax, of whom 73 per cent. received grades.   From all the rest of the province there were 1275 candidates of whom 59 per cent. were successful.

Notwithstanding the large number in Halifax who attend private schools or go abroad for an education, our public schools furnish between one-fifth and one-sixth of the whole number of certificates taken in the province.

Only a few years ago we stood far behind Pictou in all that relates to education.   Now we are ahead of Pictou, Annapolis and Lunenburg combined.   Halifax shows up with 4 grade A's, 30 grade B's, 41 grade C's and 84 grade D's.   It must have been a satisfaction to you to have read in the Acadian Recorder of the 24th, such a long list of successful Halifax boys and girls.

COST OF THE SCHOOLS.

But now admitting what cannot well be denied, that the schools are showing good results, some one will ask : But has the cost not increased enormously ?   Emphatically, no.

On general principles it would be surprising if it had.   All the School Boards have been composed of hard-headed, practical business men, decidedly conservative in their educational policy, if not in their politics, and accustomed to act only from good motives, for good reasons and after careful thought ; while at the same time they were themselves large taxpayers, and before assuming their positions, were abundantly admonished to be economical where economy was possible. But let this question be settled by figures.

COMMON SCHOOLS.

To compare one year with another would be unfair, as exceptional circumstances may affect the results.   But I will take the average of years 1882-83 and compare it with the average of the years 1891 and 1892 (the last years for which the accounts are published) and make allowance for the reduction of ten per cent. in salaries at the former dates :

Average cost of common schools for 1882-83..............$69,832
Average cost of common schools for 1891-92.............. 88,762
    Increase, 27 per cent.

Average number of pupils for 1882-83 5,334
   "   "   "   " 1891-92 7,174
  Increase of enrolled pupils, 34 and one-half per cent.

Therefore the cost has increased 7 and one-half per cent. less than the number of enrolled pupils.

Average teachers' salary for 1882-83 .... $42,835
   "   "   salaries for 1891-92 49,656
  Increase of total salaries, 16 per cent.

But the number of registered pupils increased 34 and a half per cent., therefore the number of registered pupils increased $18\frac{1}{2}$ per cent. more than the aggregate of the teachers' salaries.

From these two comparions it is evident that the expenditure for the common schools did not increase nearly as fast as the number of pupils.

The average cost per pupil in 1882 was $13.28; ten years afterwards it was only $12.29, about one dollar per pupil less. That is on 7310 pupils there is a saving of about $7,000 a year.

HIGH SCHOOL EXPENDITURE.

Average city assessment for Academy in 1882-83 .... $5,493
Average city assessment for Academy in 1891-92 8,803
  Increase, 60 per cent.
Average number of pupils enrolled 1882-83 114
Average number of pupils enrolled 1891-92 249
  Increase, 118 per cent.

That is, while the expenditure for the Academy increased 60 per cent. the number of pupils increased 118 per cent.

Average cost per pupil 1882-83 .... $48
   "   "   " 1891-92 35
  A saving on each pupil of $13.

The increase in the number of Academic pupils has been very great but as you have seen the improvement in their scholastic status has been still greater.

Besides the direct benefit of the Academy, it affords the most powerful stimulus to the senior grades of the common schools. Many a pupil's last year in the common schools would be largely wasted in idleness were it not that he is stimulated with the desire to graduate into the Academy.

Ten years ago the ratepayer, seeking academic education for his child, had to pay his share of $48 for every pupil in the Academy, besides a fee of $20 for his own, unless he was so fortunate as to secure a scholarship.

Now vastly improved academic advantages are free to all qualified pupils, and the ratepayers are taxed $13 per pupil less on account of the Academy. The government now takes its full share in the support of our higher education. All this argues wisdom and far-sighted economy.

Let us look at this matter of expenditure from one other point of view.

Estimated for assessment in 1883...... ....$64,820
 "   "   " 1893....................... 85,000

An increase of 30 per cent., or 42 per cent. less than the increase of registered pupils. But this increase for the last ten years includes not only provision for the natural increase of pupils, but also greatly improved accommodation. Six large new schoolhouses, with 43 departments, and much additional playground, and also extensive repairs, and yet there has not been the increase of expenditure which the actual increase of pupils would seem to make necessary.

Ex-Chairman Blackadar has put this matter very clearly in his report. He says: "Contrary to general impression, the cost of school instruction in Halifax is the reverse of oppressive, as can be easily shown." He then points out how that a tax of $3.00 secures to the average ratepayer free tuition for one, two or three or even half a dozen children, besides free copy-books, pencils, pens, chalk and stationery for some branches of study, and then adds: "The same proportion will hold in the case of larger assessments; it will be seen that by no means a heavy burden falls, at all events, upon the greater portion of the community, and who contribute most largely to the school registers."

I might give striking instances of the economy of the School Board where by wise planning they save hundreds of dollars without any loss of efficiency. As for example, in the establishment of the Kindergarten, which for the first year was actually a source of revenue.

I might show that Halifax spends less per pupil than any other Canadian city of the same size, except St. John, which has not yet recovered from the effects of a disastrous fire. But I will not tire you.

I will close by referring to two recommendations in a former report—the first regarding school savings banks, which are easily managed, and pay for themselves; the second implies a difficult but important problem—the management of truants who are not criminals, yet are beyond the control of parents and teachers.

All of which is respectfully submitted.

                              ALEXANDER McKAY,
Halifax, August, 1893.   .   *Supervisor of Schools.*

APPENDIX D.

SPECIAL INSTITUTIONS.

(I.)

HALIFAX INSTITUTION FOR THE DEAF AND DUMB.

Principal, J. Fearon, Esq. Other teachers, Miss J. Bateman, Mr. S. H. Lawrence, Miss M. Mosher, Miss E. Mahoney and Mr. A. G. Forbes.

Language is the main subject of instruction, the other subjects being subordinate to it.

The whole number of pupils for the year was 63, of whom 7 were in attendance for the first year. Boys 35, Girls 28. Under 15 years of age 52; fifteen years of age, 11. Average age of all, 12 years. From Nova Scotia 54; from other provinces 9. No. of weeks in session annually 42. Dimensions of ground lot, about one and a half acres. Estimated value of grounds and building, $10,000. Government grant $1530; County fund grant $2340.

(II.)

HALIFAX SCHOOL FOR THE BLIND.

Superintendent, C. F. Fraser, Esq.

Teachers, Miss Kate Fletcher (Arithmetic, Algebra, Geography with Maps, Mathematical Geography, Reading Braille Point Characters, Spelling, Pencil writing, Six classes in Kindergarten work, Kindergarten music); Miss C. R. Frame (Reading Braille Point Characters, Geography with maps, Canadian, British and Ancient History, English Grammar, English Composition, English Literature); Mr. S. R. Hussy (Arithmetic, Geometry, Spelling Braille Point Writing, Braille Music Writing, Geography with maps and globe, Private instruction of William Hulan who is deaf, dumb and blind). Mr. A. M. Chisholm (Pianoforte, Singing class, Band and Cabinet Organ); Mr. D. M. Bird, (Piano-forte tuning); Mr. D. A. Baird, (Basket Making, Chair-Seating), Miss Bella Bowman, (Sewing, Knitting, Fancy work and the use of the sewing machine); Sergeant-Major Kelly (Calisthenics for girls and Gymnastics for boys).

Note.—The teachers are assigned classes in the first, second and third divisions, the purpose being to have each teacher give instruction in that which he or she is best qualified to teach.

The whole number of pupils during the year was 47 of whom 7 were in their first year of attendance, 14 in their second, and 12 in their third year. Boys 34; girls 13. Number from Nova Scotia 24; from other provinces 23. School in session 40 weeks annually.

The number of pupils taking each separate subject in the course of study is as follows: Arithmetic 45, Algebra 8, Geometry 9, Spelling 45, Reading 29, Writing Braille 26, Pencil writing 9, Music writing 20, Geography 39, History 32, Grammar 23, Composition 21, Literature 21, Kindergarten 15, Kindergarten music 15, Pianoforte 29, Cabinet Organ 5, Singing class 9, Band 15, Pianoforte-tuning 6, Basket-making 4, Chair-seating 9, Sewing 13, Knitting 11, Fancy work 9, Sewing-machine 3.

Estimated value of grounds and buildings $60,000. Dimensions of grounds 552 x 250 feet, of building 126 x 56 feet, containing 9 school or class room, 19 dormitories and 22 other rooms. The Library contains 250 volumes valued at $750. Estimated value of apparatus $600.

Government grant $1237.50; County fund grant $956.25.

(III.)

Victoria School of Art and Design, Halifax.

(Incorporated 1888.)

DIRECTORS.—1892-93.

Ex-Officio : { THE SUPERINTENDENT OF EDUCATION,
{ THE MAYOR OF HALIFAX.

MRS. J. F. KENNY,	MISS E. RITCHIE,
MRS. M. B. DALY,	MISS H. ALLISON,
MRS. H. H. FULLER,	MR. J. M. SMITH,
MR. J. C. MACKINTOSH,	MR. JAMES DEMPSTER,
MR. E. P. ARCHBOLD,	HON. SENATOR POWER,
MR. D. HEALEY,	DR. J. G. MACGREGOR,
MR. D. KEITH, ————	MR. M. DWYER.
MR. ALEXANDER MACKAY,	

Auditors.

MR. J. M. DEWOLFE,
MR. R. J. WILSON.

President, MAYOR KEEFE,
Vice-President, HON. L. G. POWER,
Treasurer, J. M. SMITH,
Secretary, A. MCKAY.

TEACHING STAFF.

Head Master :

GEORGE HARVEY, A. R. C. A.

Assistant Teachers :

Mechanical Drawing ....J. T. LARKIN, *Engineer.*
Architectural Drawing....... " "
Saturday Class...........MISS K. F. Hill.

TREASURER'S REPORT.

The Treasurer, in Account with Victoria School of Art and Design.

Endowment Fund.
   Amount from 1892 .... $ 7,702 40

Building Fund.
   Amount from 1892 .... $ 7,954 95
   Transferred from Interest account 45 05
                                    8,000 00

Current Account Receipts.
   School Fees, &c .... $ 289 97
   Local Government Grant 800 00
   City Grant 500 00
   Membership Fees 30 00
   Interest, $569.94; less to Building Fund,
      $45.05 .... 524 89
   Sundries 1 61
                              2,146 47

                                   $17,848 87

Disbursements.
   Salaries .... $ 1,366 98
   Rent 200 00
   Fuel and Light 105 05
   Printing, &c 10 00
   School Supplies and Sundries 38 23
   Janitress 112 50
   Chicago Exhibition 7 50
   Furniture and Repairs 101 87

                     $ 1,942 13
   Balance, September, 1892 .... 3,433 14

                     $ 5,395 27

Town of Kentville Bonds $5,100 00
City of Halifax Consols 4,950 00
Deposit Receipts, Bank of N. S... 2,200 00
Open Account,   "   " .. 223 60
                     $12,473 60
                                $17,848 87

                           JOHN M. SMITH,
Halifax, 23rd Sept., 1893.   *Treasurer.*

Examined and found correct, R. J. Wilson, *Auditor.*

SECRETARY'S REPORT.

To the Directors of the Victoria School of Art and Design·

Ladies and Gentlemen :

For your information I beg to present the following Report of the work of the Victoria School of Art and Design for the year ending June 1893.

The classes were opened on the 17th of October, 1892, and closed on June of this year.

TABULAR STATEMENT OF ATTENDANCE, &c.

Class.	Teacher.	Subject.	No. enrolled.
Children's,	Miss K. F. Hill,	Freehand and Object Drawing.	16
Mechanical,	Mr. J. T. Larkin,	Mechanical Drawing. (Practical Geometry, Copying, Draughting).	26
Architectural.		Architectural Drawing.	21
Evening.	Geo. Harvey,	Modelling, Freehand and Object Drawing.	38
Afternoon,	Geo. Harvey,	Modelling, Painting, Freehand and Object Drawing.	33
Deaf and Dumb.	Geo. Harvey,	Freehand and Object Drawing and Modelling.	21

In all there were enrolled 155 students of whom 8 held free scholarships won by competition from the Academies and High Schools. There were 48 free students, most of whom were apprentices. A class of 21 from the Institution for the Deaf and Dumb also received free instruction for the year.

Mr. Harvey, who had been the Head Master of the School since it first opened in 1887, sent in his resignation, which was accepted with much regret on the 13th January.

He was succeeded on the 11th March, by Mr. O. Dodge, of the Art Student's League of New York. Mr. Dodge has been very successful in his management of the school.

Miss Hill obtained leave of absence at the end of the first Term in order to prosecute her studies in New York and Paris. Her work was carried on very satisfactorily until the end of the year, by Miss M. Graham, formerly a student of the school.

It will be gratifying to the directors to learn that students of this school are beginning to obtain good positions, as the result of their training here. As an example, Mr. Lewis Smith has been placed in charge of the Art Department of the Halifax Ladies College. He succeeds Miss Vondy, and will be assisted by Miss Edith Smith and Miss Hill. These are all graduates of this Art School and reflect much credit on its teaching.

Mr. Wilson from the Mechanical Class has entered the Second Year of the Agricultural College at Lansing, and writes in the highest terms of the character of our work and of the advantage that it has been to him. We could multiply examples of this kind. They will serve to show our young people what they are losing by not availing themselves of the benefits of our school; so that hereafter we may expect a larger attendance and more earnest work.

Our courses in Art are accepted in Dalhousie College in part for the Degree of Bachelor of Science.

At the request of the Provincial Government, we sent an exhibit of our work to the World's Fair. It helped very materially to make the Nova Scotia Educational Exhibit a success.

Respectfully submitted,

A. McKAY,
Secretary.

Halifax, 19th September, 1893.

DIRECTORS AND OFFICERS.—1893-94.

Ex-Officio: { THE SUPERINTENDENT OF EDUCATION,
{ THE MAYOR OF HALIFAX.

MRS. J. F. KENNY,	MRS. LEONOWENS,
MRS. H. H. FULLER,	MISS E. RITCHIE,
MISS H. ALLISON,	MR. J. M. SMITH,
MR. J. C. MACKINTOSH,	MR. E. P. ARCHBOLD,
MR. GEO. HARVEY,	MR. D. KEITH,
MR. J. DEMPSTER,	HON. L. G. POWER,
DR. J. G. MACGREGOR,	MR. M. DWYER.
A. McKAY.	

President, MAYOR KEEFE,
Vice-President, A. H. MACKAY,
          Superintendent of Education.
Treasurer, MR. J. M. SMITH,
Secretary, A. McKAY.

Head Master:

OZIAS DODGE, ESQ., (Yale Un.)

APPENDIX E.

WORLD'S FAIR.

REPORT ON EDUCATIONAL EXHIBIT.

[Installed by A. McKay, Advisory Commissioner for Nova Scotia.]

To A. H. MacKay, Esq., Ll. D.,
Superintendent of Education.

Sir :—

I beg to submit to you for the information of the Council of Public Instruction the following account of the installation of the Educational Exhibits of Nova Scotia at the World's Fair, Chicago.

All the Educational Institutions of Nova Scotia were notified by you at an early date of the intention of the Nova Scotia Government to take part in the Exhibition. They seemed however to be so apathetic or so engrossed in their ordinary work that they did not readily respond. It was only after very great labor and personal effort on your part that several of them began to display an energy which they afterwards turned to good account in the production of a very considerable amount of excellent work.

By the 27th of March the greater part of the material had been collected. It was examined, partly classified, and exhibited in the Assembly Hall of the Halifax Academy.

It was then sent to Chicago at the expense of the Canadian Government.

I left Halifax on Tuesday the 11th of April, and submitted the plans for the Nova Scotia Educational Booth to the Canadian Architect on the 18th. After much delay and difficulty in securing workmen and material the booth was so far completed that I was able to begin to place the exhibits about the first week in May. The booth was not completed until the 20th. The exhibits were all in place on the 25th. About one-third of my time was devoted to the mineral exhibit sent by the Mines Department. The cost of the wood work of the booth was borne by the Dominion Government— the furnishing by the Government of Nova Scotia.

I must here acknowledge the urbanity of the Canadian Executive Commissioner, J. S. Larke, Esq., and of the Secretary, W. D. Dimock, Esq., but more particularly the valuable services of Wm. Morton, Superintendent of the Canadian Department of Liberal Arts, who was unremitting and successful in his efforts to harmonize all conflicting interests and make the exhibit a credit to Canada.

The space occupied by Nova Scotia is situated on the west side of the great gallery overlooking the Columbian aisle in the liberal arts and manufactures building. This is the largest building on the fair grounds—the largest building in the world—having a floor space, including galleries, of 44 acres. The Nova Scotia space is bounded on the north by that of Quebec, on the east by the great central hall, south by Russia, and west by the North West Territories and Canada general section. It is 28 feet long, 21 wide, walls and a central partition running lengthwise 13 feet high. On the east and west are arched doorways. On the ends of the central partition are groups of hinged frames, which show to great advantage a large quantity of school work under glass. The walls are covered on the exterior by blue cloth, on the interior with drab and terra cotta, and the tables with green, while overhead there is a covering of light pink cloth, which protects the booth from dust and softens the glare of sunlight which comes through the immense glass roof, 200 feet above. To protect the walls from any probable leak a strip of figured oil-cloth is laid horizontally on top of the walls and central partition.

The exterior walls show by enlarged photographs much of the finest scenery of the province. Nature studies by Miss Edith Smith of Halifax, show that there is some real artistic talent in the little province by the sea. A very pretty map by Arthur Drew, of Liverpool academy, and a selection of work from various schools give a hint of the nature of the work within the booth and invite the educationist to a further inspection.

Entering from the west and turning to the right the Normal and Model schools of Truro and the Truro academy occupy 300 square feet of surface. All the work shown here is good—maps, drawings, original designs, nature lessons illustrated, problems in mathematics and science, etc. Miss Ottie Smith, the Art Instructor in the Normal School, merits special praise for the work done by her students. The Kindergarten exercises, gotten up by Mrs. Patterson's little pupils, are superior and a credit to the province. The same may be said of the Kindergarten work from the classes taught by Mrs. Harriman, in Halifax, Miss Hamilton, in Dartmouth, and the New Glasgow Kinder-garten.

Following round the east wall there are shown specimens of excellent school work from the Institution of the Deaf and Dumb; apparatus and work from the School for the Blind. Then come samples of all classes of schoolwork from schools and academies all over the province. Prominent among them is a collection of pressed plants from Morris Street school, Halifax. Latin, Greek and ancient geography exercises from Antigonish Academy. Very neat work from Milton school, Yarmouth, and from Inspectoral district No. 4 and 5, and other places.

A large map showing the exact location of every school house in the province hangs on the north wall. From this map to the entrance the west wall is taken up with drawings, maps and manual training work from Halifax Academy. On one side of the middle portion is shown art work from the Church School for Girls at, Windsor, and from Acadia Seminary; on the other side mechanical and architectural drawing and oil paintings from the Victoria School of Art and Design, also some art work from the Halifax Ladies College.

In show cases on the tables are shown clay-modelling from the Kindergarten, and the Normal School, sewing, minerals from Halifax Academy and Mr. A. J. Pineo, chemical preparations and microscopic slides from Halifax Ladies College and a pretty hand painted placque from the Church School for Girls, Windsor. There are also several bound volumes of school exercise copy books, text books, etc.

The educational work from our province is very creditable. Its merits or defects are not obscured by gilt picture frames, showy labels, expensive cloth backgrounds, carved and polished woodwork and gaudy surroundings. The work stands upon its merits, and while not so attractive to the general passer-by as some other exhibits, it compares favorably with those of much wealthier states and has received the commendation of all educationists who have seen it.

All the articles sent to the Education Office for exhibition were sent to the World's Fair.

As many as possible were shown and a certain number reserved to replace such as might become injured by exposure. The following lists of exhibits are not complete on account of the neglect of some of the Inspectors in not forwarding complete catalogues of their selections and on account of the great amount of work and the shortness of the time.

All of which is respectfully submitted.

A. McKAY.

CATALOGUE OF SCHOOL MATERIAL

EXHIBITED BY THE

Education Department of Nova Scotia

AT THE

WORLD'S FAIR, CHICAGO, 1893.

CLASS I.

Halifax Kindergarten.—MRS. S. S. HARRIMAN.

Morning Talks.—1. Sheep.
2. Cow, "Our Friend Daisy."
3. Products of Nova Scotia.
Parquetry.—4. Our Pansy Garden.
5. Units of Border Work.
Cutting.—6. Prang's System.
7. Snow Crystals.
Sewing.—8. Original Designs.
Pricking.—9. Leaves and Vegetables.

Truro Kindergarten.—MRS. S. B. PATERSON.

Morning Talk.—1. Shoemaker.
Pricking.—2. Colored Pricking.
3.   "   "
4. Plain   "
Sewing.—5. Sewing on Felting.
6.   "   " Cards.
7.   "   "   "
Cutting.—8. Mosaic.
9.   "
10. Froebel System.

New Glasgow.—Miss Smith.

Sewing.—1. Miscellaneous.
2. Plant Life.

Dartmouth Kindergarten.—Miss M. A. Hamilton.

Morning Talks.—1. Columbus.
    2. Bees and Butterflies.
Drawing.—3. Heath System.
    4. Original design and Illustrated Story.
    5. Border Work.
    6. Object Drawing.
    7. Color Work.
Weaving.—8. Original Designs.
    9. Freehand.
    10. Forms of Life.
Parquetry.—11. Prismatic Colors.
    (*a.* Warm to Cold.)
    (*b.* Cold to Warm.)
    12. Symmetrical Designs and Forms of Life

DISTRICT No. 5.—C. W. Roscoe, M. A., *Inspector.*

CLASSES II. & III.

WRITING.—Grade IX.

George Farquhar, Union School, Hants.
Annie Chipman, Upper Church Street, Kings.
Harry Chipman, " " " "

BOOK-KEEPING.—Grade X.

Janet Wardrobe, Kentville Academy.
Mary W. McCarthy, " "

BOOK-KEEPING.—Grade IX.

Annie Chipman, Upper Church Street, Kings.
Harry Chipman, " " " "
H. Newton Pyke, " " " "

COMPOSITION.—Grade IX.

Laura Masters, Church Street, Kings.
Annie Chipman, Upper Church Street, Kings.
Jean Creelman, Maitland, Hants.
Ila Kempton, Wolfville,

WRITING.—Grade IX.

Mary E. Johnson, Wolfville.

FREEHAND DRAWING, ETC.—Grade IX.

George Scott, Upper Selma, Hants.
Bessie Putnam, "   "   "
Fred Monteith, Maitland, Hants.

MAPS.—Grade XI.

Clarence P. Smith, Windsor Academy.

MAPS.—Grade X.

M. Rena Thompson, Windsor Academy.
Bessie H. Wickwire, Kentville Academy.
Eleanor Newcombe,   "   "

MAPS.—Grade IX.

Flora Prevost, Wolfville, Kings.
Sarah E. Cox, Upper Canard, Kings.
Alfred Borden, Hantsport, Hants.

PRACTICAL MATHEMATICS.—Grade XI.

Roberta M. Blanchard, Kentville Academy.
Winifred Hensley, Windsor Academy.
Georgie Begg, Kentville Academy.

GEOMETRY.—Grade XI.

Florence Anslow, Windsor Academy.
Roberta M. Blanchard, Kentville Academy.
Alice M. Shaw, Kentville Academy.

GEOMETRY.—Grade X.

Rose Tobin, Town Plot, King's Co.
Jas. B. Woodworth, Windsor Academy.
Leonard D. Pineo, Maitland.

GEOMETRY.—Grade IX.

Annie Chipman, Upper Church St., Kings.
Bertha Allen, Upper Selma, Hants.
Hattie A. Parsons, Wolfville.
George Yeaton, Hantsport.

ALGEBRA.—Grade XI.

Robert M. Blanchard, Kentville Academy.
Georgie Begg,　　　　　"　　　"
W. E. Begg.　　　　　"　　　"

ALGEBRA.—Grade X.

Mary M. McArthy, Kentville.
Gertrude Urquhart, Maitland.
Leonard D. Rines,　　　"

ALGEBRA.—Grade IX.

Annie Chipman, Upper Church St.
Lottie R. Merry, Kentville.
James L. Kennikle, Upper Church St.

ARITHMETIC.—Grade XI.

Alice M. Shaw, Kentville.
W. A. Begg,　　　"

ARITHMETIC.—Grade X.

Alice G. Roy, Maitland.
Gertrude Urquhart, Maitland.
Frank Lyons, Kentville,
Ethel G. Arnold, Kentville.

ARITHMETIC.—Grade IX.

Leah Brown, Maitland.
Annie Chipman, Upper Church St.
Lottie R. Merry, Kentville.
Cassie M. Hayes, Wolfville.

GRAMMAR.—Grade X.

Alice G. Roy, Maitland.
Gertrude Urquhart, Maitland.
Leonard Rines,　　　"

GRAMMAR.—Grade IX.

Bertha Allen, Upper Selma.
Minnie McIntosh, Maitland.
Edgar D. Putnam,　　"

LATIN.

Annie Chipman, Upper Church Street.
Mabel L. Wortman, Wolfville.
Lena D. Burgess,　　"

COMMON SCHOOL WORK.

Copy Books.—Grade VIII.

Lavinia O. Burns, Windsor.
Edith Harvey, Union School.
Alina D. W. Pellow, Windsor.

GRADE VII.

A. Maude McKinnon, Windsor.
A. Winifred Smith,   "
Louis Shaw,   "

GRADE VI.

Ruth E. Daniels, Windsor.
J. Howard Streekland, Windsor.
Vinnie Hockie, Hantsport.

GRADE V.

Willie Chipman, Upper Church St.
Laurinda Brown, Wolfville.
Maggie Lowthers, Windsor.

GRADE IV.

Duncan Geldert, Windsor.
Beatrice Martin, Kentville.
Clarence Wood, Windsor.

GRADE III.

Mary Aker, Windsor.
Annie Muller, Windsor.
Evelyn Millet,   "

Drawing, Freehand, Original Design.—Grade VIII.

John W. Ryan, Kentville.
Annie B. LeCain, Kentville.

GRADE VII.

John Quigley, Kentville,
Louie C. Beckwith, Kentville,
Fannie Woolaver, Hantsport.

FREEHAND FROM MEMORY.—Grade VII.

Ralph Jones, Wolfville.

ORIGINAL DESIGNS.—Grade V.

Walter Lawson, Windsor.
Eva Borden,   "
Mabel Dickie, Hantsport.
Percy Kidson, Church St.

GRADE IV.

Arthur Nalder, Windsor.
Duncan Geldert,   "
Willie Cochrane, Hantsport.

GRADE VI.

Harry Margeson, Hantsport,
Ruth E. Daniels, Windsor.
Annie M. Della Torre, Windsor.
Percy Cook, Kentville.

GRADE III.

Evelyn Millett, Windsor.
Julia Cox,   "
Walter Geldert,   "

GRADE II.

Jean Smith, Windsor.
Blanche Smith, Windsor.
Lillie Carson.   "

MAPS.—Grade VIII.

Charles W. Roach, Windsor.
Willie Comstock, Church St.
Colin D. Wood, Kentville.

GRADE VII.

Wallace Hutchins, Wolfville.
Harold B. Kempton,   "
Fred O. Burgess, Windsor.
Frank L. Comstock, Church Street.
Annie McCabe, Hantsport.

GRADE VI.

Clara L. Roach, Windsor.
John H. Redding, Kentville.
Harry Margeson, Hantsport.

GRADE V.

Eva Borden, Windsor.
Walter Lawson, Windsor.
Edna Coalfleet, Hantsport.

ACCOUNTS.—Grade VIII.

Ella McKenzie, Maitland.
Maria Putnam　　　　"
Jack C. Jones, Wolfville.

GRADE VII.

Percy Spencer, Central Rawdon.

GRADE V.

Laurinda Brown, Wolfville.
Ralph Shaw, Wolfville.
Percy Kedston, Church St.

ALGEBRA.—Grade VIII.

Gertie V. Roscoe, Wolfville.
Jack C. Jones, Wolfville.
Lucy Lawrence, Upper Selma.

ARITHMETIC.—Grade VIII.

Alicia Healeo, Town Plot.
Hattie M. Masters, Church Street.
Gertie V. Roscoe, Wolfville.
Jack C. Jones, Wolfville.

GRADE VII.

Alice M. McKinnon, Windsor.
Annie Putnam, Upper Selma.
F. Winifred Smith, Windsor.

GRADE VI.

Blanche Douglas, Maitland.
Mabel Chipman, Kentville.
Alice Chase, Church St.

GRADE V.

Elizabeth Campbell, Central Rawdon.
Annie Northup,　　　　"　　　"
Charles Wier,　　　　"　　　"

GRADE III.

John Riley, Hantsport.
Maggie Carroll, "
Marian Shaw, "

GRADE II.

Cecil Borden, Windsor.
Victor Hughes, "
George Kilcup, "

GRAMMAR.—Grade VIII.

Minnie F. Burns, Windsor.
Lavinia O. Burns, "
Gertrude A. Chandler, "

GRADE VII.

Alice M. McKinnon, Windsor.
Fred. O. Burgess, "
Frank S. Burgess, "

COMPOSITION.—Grade VIII.

Hattie Masters, Church St.
Maggie Wardlow, " "
Jerry Northup, Centre Rawdon.

GRADE V.

Elizabeth Campbell, Centre Rawdon.
Charles Wier, " "
John Mason, " "

GRADE IV.

Eva Spencer, Centre Rawdon.
Adam D. Hall, Maitland.
Edith A. Leedham, Centre Rawdon.

GRADE II.

Jean Penten, Hantsport.
Horace Lyon, "
Edith Penten, "

PRINTING.—Grade I.

Hilda Hockin, Hantsport.
David Pulsiver, "
Hattie Faulkner, "

MUSIC.—Grade VIII.

Lavinia O. Burns, Windsor.
M. Ethel Christie,   ,,
Dorothy W. Smith,   ,,

GRADE V.

Laurinda Brown, Wolfville.
Hattie Eye,   ,,
Horace Jones

NATURE LESSONS.— Grade VII.

INSECTS.

Charles J. Seymour, Windsor.
Graham P. Morse,   ,,
Joseph F. Burns,   ,,

GRADE VI.—Quadrupeds.

Alice Reeves, Kentville.
Lillie Webster,   ,,
Maggie Tully,   ,,

LATIN.—Grade VIII.

Roland R. Sanford, Wolfville.
Jack C. Jones,   ,,

DISTRICT NO. 3.

JAMES H. MUNRO, ESQ., *Inspector.*

ST. ANN'S CONVENT.—6 Exhibits.

4 Figures stitched on paper.
2 Drawing.

PUBLIC SCHOOLS.

GRADE II.—3 Exhibits.

1 Industrial Drawing.
2 Arithmetic.

GRADE IV.—16 Exhibits.

3 Drawings.
3 Industrial Drawing.
5 Maps.
3 Arithmetic.
2 Fancy sewing on paper.

Grade IV.—16 Exhibits.

3 Industrial Drawings.
1 Wall Map.
3 Arithmetic.
3 Composition.
1 Knitting work.

Grade V.—13 Exhibits.

2 Drawings, Sketches.
5 Industrial Drawings.
3 Maps, pencilled.
3 Maps, painted.

Grade VI.—16 Exhibits.

1 Written Copy Book.
1 Decimeter, etc.
4 Industrial Drawing.
3 Maps.
1 Wall Map.
2 Arithmetic.
2 Grammar.
2 Composition.

Grade VII.—19 Exhibits.

2 Copy Books.
3 Drawings.
3 Industrial Drawings.
2 Maps, painted.
2 Maps, pencilled.
2 Business Forms.
2 Arithmetic.
2 Sewing.

Grade VIII.—32 Exhibits.

2 Writing.
3 Drawing, Sketches.
3 Industrial Drawing.
1 Decimeter.
3 Maps pencilled.
2 Maps painted.
4 Wall Maps.
3 Business Forms.
2 Book-keeping.
4 Arithmetic.
3 Analysis.
1 Grammar.
1 Composition.

GRADE IX.—16 Exhibits.

1 Analysis.
3 Arithmetic.
2 Business Letter.
3 Drawing, Freehand.
3 Geometry.
1 Algebra.
1 Centimeter.
2 Physiology.

GRADE X.—13 Exhibits.

1 Analysis.
1 Map.
4 Arithmetic.
4 Drawing.
2 Geometry.
1 Algebra.

GRADE XI.—8 Exhibits.

3 Arithmetic.
3 Geometry.
1 Algebra.
1 Trigonometry.

Photographs of Lockeport and Barrington school houses.

DISTRICT NO. 1.—HALIFAX COUNTY.

H. CONDON, ESQ., *Inspector.*

WRITTEN COPY BOOKS.—Grade VII.

Maude Seeton, Loressa E. Dunbrack,
Ida Seaton, Meagher's Grant.
Blanche Logan, Dufferin Mines.
Gregory Lapierre, Grand Desert.

GRADE VIII.

Seymour Ogilvie, Little River.
Janie Niforth, Cole Harbor.
Nellie McDonald, Fall River.

DRAWING.—Grade V.

George Murphy, West Chezzetcook.
Mary Cranford,   "   "

GRADE VI.

Jennie Taylor, Taylor School.
Amelie Bellefontaine, West Chezzetcook.
Mary   "   "   "

GRADE VII. ,

Susie E. Shultz, Sackville.
Katie M. Lindsay, Taylor School.
Rebecca F. Irwin,   "   "
Rebecca M. Erwin, Taylor School.
Clifford Peveril, Sackville.
Alex. Bellefontaine, West Chezzetcook.

GRADE VIII.

Sadie H. Erwin, Taylor School.
Mary Erwin,   "   "
Edna   ,   "   "
Morton L. Annand, "   "
Ella Browne, Little River.
Maggie Murphy, West Chezzetcook.

MAPS.—Grade V.

Harold Tremaine, Sackville.
Harvey Stewart, Fall River.

GRADE VI.

Jennie Murphy, West Chezzetcook.
Isabel Bellefontaine, "   "
Amelia   "   "   "

GRADE VII.

Sadie E. Schultz, Sackville.
Rose Murphy, West Chezzetcook.
Alex. Bellefontaine, West Chezzetcook.
Edwin F. Fulton, Sackville.
Clifford E. Peveril,   "
Duff Murray, Little River.

GRADE VIII.

Birdie Tremaine, Lower Sackville.
Arthur Tremaine,   "   "
Maggie Murphy, West Chezzetcook.
Ella Brown, Little River.
Nellie McDonald, Fall River.
Ettie Wilson,   "   "
Lucy Auld,   "   "
John McLean, Taylor School.

ARITHMETIC.—Grade VIII.

Etta Murray, Little River.
Maggie Calkin, Sackville School.
Sadie H. Erwin, Taylor School.
Henry Archibald, Greenwood.

GRADE V.

Janie McGunnigle, Henry School.

GRAMMAR.

Etta Brown, Little River.
Warren Ogilvie, Little River.
Carrie Taylor,   "   "

COMPOSITION.

Maude Auld, Fall River School.
Jennie M. Niforth, Cole Harbour.
Aggie M. Giles,   "   "

MUSIC.—Grade VII.

Rebecca F. Erwin, Taylor School.
Kate May Lindsay,   "   "
Sadie H. Erwin,   "   "

GEOMETRY.—Grade VIII.

Sadie H. Erwin, Taylor School.
Warren Ogilvie,   "   "

GRADE X.

Janie McGunnigle, Henry School.
Grace Burris,   "   "

ALGEBRA.—Grade X.

Janie McGunnigle, Henry School.

DISTRICT NO. 4.—ANNAPOLIS AND DIGBY.

L. S. MORSE, M. A. *Inspector.*

COMMON SCHOOLS.

WRITTEN COPY BOOKS.—Grade III.

Emelie Trahan, Mavillette School, Digby.
Isidore Saulnier,　　"　　"　　"
Mary H. Harris, Gesner School, Annapolis.

GRADE IV·

Edmond Deveau, Mavillette School, Digby.
Minnie McLean, Bridgetown School, Annapolis.

GRADE VI.

Ida Deveau, Mavillette School, Digby.
Una Cameron, Bridgetown School, Annapolis.

GRADE VII.

Willie Soulis, Bridgetown School, Annapolis.
Mary Dodge,　　"　　"　　"
Lea Deveau, Mavillette School, Digby.

FREEHAND DRAWING.—Grade II.

Lea Deveau, Mavillette School, Digby.

GRADE III.

Leonice Deveau, Mavillette School, Digby.

GRADE VI.

Bertha T. O'Connor, St. Mary's Convent.
Jessie Campbell,　　"　　"　　"

GRADE VII.

Mary Deveau, Mavillette School, Digby Co.
Lea T. Deveau,　　"　　"　　"　　"
Eveline Saulnier,　　"　　"

MATHEMATICAL DRAWINGS.—Grade VI.

Louis F. Deveau, Mavillette School, Digby Co.

GRADE VII.

Theresa Melancon. Church Point School, Digby Co.
Lea Deveau, Mavillette School, Digby Co.

GRADE VIII.

Zelie Saulnier, Church Point School, Digby Co.
Gertrude O'Conner, Church Point School, Digby Co.

MAPS.—Grade IV.

Rosie Deveau, Mavillette School, Digby Co.
Frank Dodge, Bridgetown   "   Annapolis Co.

GRADE V.

Eveline Deveau, Meteghan, Digby Co.
Mary R. LeBlanc,   "   "   "

GRADE VI.

Isidore Saulnier, Mavilette, Digby Co.
Jennie LeBlance, Weymouth Bridge, Digby Co.

GRADE VII.

Evangeline Saulnier, Church Point, Digby Co.
Theresa Melancon,   "   "   "   "
Edward G. Harvey, Clements West, Annapolis Co.

GRADE.

Josephine Melancon, Meteghan, Digby Co.
Charles Ray, Clements West, Digby Co.

ACCOUNTS.

GRADE VII.

Laurence Johns, Weymouth Bridge, Digby Co.
Alice M. Berry,   "   "   "   "
Eveline Saulnier, Church Point, Digby Co.

GRADE VIII.

Ella M. Marshall, Hainsville, Digby Co.

ARITHMETIC.

GRADE I.

Juliette Deveau, Mavillette, Digby Co.

GRADE II.

Emeline Trahan, Mavillette, Digby Co.

GRADE III.

Isabelle Saulnier, Mavillette, Digby Co.

GRADE VI.

Thos. F. Freeman, Weymouth Bridge, Digby.
Edmund Deveau, Mavillette   "
Louis F. Deveau,   "   "

GRADE VII.

Lea Deveau, Mavillette, Digby.
Evangeline Saulnier, Church Point, Digby.
Curtis H. Wilson, Hamesville, Digby.

GRADE VIII.

Edith T. Robinson, Digby.
Lottie M. Marshall, Hamesville, Digby.
Inez Price, Smith's Cove, Digby.

GRAMMAR.—Grade VI·

Evangeline Gaudet, Meteghan, Digby.
William Muise, Weymouth Bridge, Digby.
Grace Oakes,   "   "   "

GRADE VII.

Therese Melancon, Church Point, Digby.
Grace Doucette,   "   "   "
Eveline Saulnier,   "   "   "

GRADE VIII.

Celina Robicheau, Meteghan, Digby.
Josephine Melancon,   "   "
Alice F. Hunt, Hillgrove,   "

COMPOSITION.—Grade V.

Eva B. McNeill, North Range School, Digby Co.

GRADE VII.

Lea Deveau, Mavillette, Digby Co.

GRADE VIII.

Ena H. Nichols, Hillgrove, Digby Co.
A. F. Hunt, Hillgrove,   "   "
Susie P. Aymar,   "   "   "

MUSIC, TONIC SOL FA.—Grade VI.

Minnie McLean, Bridgetown, Annapolis Co.
Una Cameron,   "   "   "
Nellie Balcom,   "   "   "
Mary Melancon, Digby Co.

GRADE VII.

Willis Soulis, Bridgetown, Annapolis Co.
Lizzie Saunders,   "   "   "
Harry Bishop,   "   "   "

SEWING.—Grade V.

Nellie Comeau, Meteghan, Digby Co.
Mary Mountain,   "   "   "

HIGH SCHOOL WORK.

BOOK-KEEPING.—Grade IX.

Minnie Morse, Bridgetown, Annapolis Co.
A. Harold Crosskill, Bridgetown, Annapolis Co.
Loran Craig,   "   "   "

GRADE X.

Lucy E. Chesley, Chesley School, Annapolis Co.
Helen A. Munroe,   "   "   "   "

FREEHAND DRAWING.—Grade X.

Jennie L. Holdsword, Digby Academy.

MAPS.—Grade IX.

Annie M. Morse, Paradise, West Annapolis Co.
Carrie A. Morse,   "   "   "

GRADE X.

Egbert P. Morse, Paradise West, Annapolis Co.
Lindsay Dykeman, Digby Academy.

TRIGONOMETRY.—Grade XI.

Chas. R. Gates, Digby Academy.
Wm. T. Morse, "   "

GEOMETRY.—Grade IX.

Camillo G. Fisher, Digby Academy.
Mary A. Hunt,   "   "
Albert L. McDonald, Weymouth Bridge, Digby.

GRADE X.

K. L. Porter, Hillgrove School, Digby.
Blanche J. Bacon, Hillgrove School, Digby.

GRADE XI.

Laura Woodbury, Digby Academy.
G. Etta Stayling,   "   "

ALGEBRA.—Grade IX.

Alberta L. McDonald, Weymouth Bridge, Digby Co.
Emma Journeay,   "   "   "   "
Jessie M. Bell, North Range, Digby Co.

GRADE X.

K. L. Porter, Hillgrove, Digby Co.
Blanche J. Bacon, Hillgrove, Digby Co.

GRADE XI.

Chas. R. Gates, Digby Academy.
Laura Woodbury, Digby Academy.
Welton H. Robbin, "   "

ARITHMETIC.—Grade IX.

Alberta L. McDonald, Weymouth Bridge, Digby.
Helen M. Dahlgreen,   "   "   "
Emma Journeay,   "   "   "

GRADE X.

Jennie L. Holdsworth, Digby Academy.
Mamie Chaloner,   "   "
Samuel E. Woodman, Hillgrove, Digby.

ENGLISH.—Grade IX.

Edna E. Mackintosh, Smith's Cove, Digby.
Otto Cossett,   "   "   "

LATIN.—Grade IX.

Alberta L. McDonald, Weymouth Bridge, Digby.
Emma Journeay,   " " "
Helen M. Dahlgreen,   " " "

CHEMISTRY.—Grade X.

Mamie Chaloner, Digby Academy, Digby.
Jennie L. Holdsworth, Digby Academy, Digby.
Janet L. Warne,   " " "

PHYSICS.—Grade XI.

Welton H. Robbins, Digby Academy, Digby County.
G. Etta Stailing, " " " "

WOODWORK.—Grade IX.

A. E. Walker, Gesner School, Annapolis County.

DISTRICT, NO. 10.

I. C. CRAIG, ESQ., *Inspector.*

COMMON SCHOOLS.

WRITING.

Grade.	Name.	School.
V.	Nellie Howard	Spencer's Island.
	Cassie Cole	" "
	Grevena Morrison	" "
VI.	Stanly W. Spicer	" "
	Alice Betts	Acadia Mines.
	John McKinnon	" "
	James Evans	" "
VII.	George Miner	Spencer's Island.
	Maggie Hattie	Acadia Mines.
	Maggie Works	" "
	Nellie Dunlop	" "
VIII.	Helen W. Bigelow	Spencer's Island.
	Bessie Miner	Acadia Mines.
	Media Hiscox	" "
	Annie Adams	" "
	Frank Totten	"

DRAWING.

I.   Susie P. Ogilvie ....Parrsboro.
II.   Gordon A. McRae ..   "
III.   Frank Morris ......   "
IV.   Willie Weatherby ..Acadia Mines.
       Nellie Worrell .....Parrsboro.
V.   Jennie Blenkie ....Acadia Mines.
       Howard Verge .....Parrsboro.

MAPS.

VII.   Whitney Spicer.....Spencer's Island.
       Lilly Coleman..... Amherst.
       Mabel Cole ....   "
       Grace B. Embree....   "

COMMERCIAL ACCOUNTS.

VII.   Melissa Evans......Acadia Mines.
       Willie Dunlap......   "   "
VIII.   Lena Willing ......Amherst.
       Bell Campbell......   "
       Nina Sturk ....Acadia Mines.
       Mary Patriquin ....   "   "
       Clara Totten ......   "   "

ARITHMETHIC.

II.   Nettie J. McDougall..Parrsboro.
       Freda Tattrie.......Acadia Mines.
III.   Colin H. Craig.....Amherst.
       Elsie Swanson......   "
IV.   Helen Fowler ......   "
       Sadie Ferguson ....Acadia Mines.
V.   Lavinia Faber ......   "   "
VI.   Bella Ferguson .....   "   "
VII.   Willie Dunlop ......   "   "
       Mamie O'Brien .....Westchester Station.
       Avoria McLeod .....Parrsboro.
VIII.   Lottie E. Tate ......   "
       Avery O'Brien......Westchester Station.

ANALYSIS.

VII.   Mamie O'Brien .....Westchester Station.
VI.   Willie McDougall ...Parrsboro.

LETTERS, Composition.

II.   Evelyn M. Coates ...Parrsboro.
       Gordon A. McRae ...   "
       Edna J. McLeod ....   "

LETTERS, Composition.

IV.   Leonard Tattrie.....Acadia Mines.
      Mary B. Patriquin...   "   "
      Addie Buck........   "   "
V.   Minnie Beadshun ...Amherst.
VI.   Fred Douglas.......Acadia Mines.
      Bella Ferguson .....   "   "
      Jennie Howard .....   "   "
VII. Mabel Betts........   "   ..
      Lizzie Wilson ......   "   ..
      Maggie Works......   "   ..
      Clara Fulton ......   "   "
      Media Hiscox ....

HIGH SCHOOL WORK.

GEOMETRY.

IX.   Carrie Sproul ......Parrsboro.
      Rose E. Wetherby ..   "
      Sarah M. Brown.....   "
X.   Jessie M. Pierce ....   ..
      Mary E. Woodworth..   "
      Nellie Leitch ......   "
      Lorne Logan ......Amherst.
      Helen R. Pipes......   "
      Willie G. Pugsley ...   "
XI.   Bella Smith........Acadia Mines.
      John J. McKeen.....   "   "

COMMERCIAL FORMS.

X.   Lizzie Myers .... ..Acadia Mines.
      Lottie Daye .. ....   "   "
XI.   John McKean......   "   "
      Bella Smith........   ..

DRAWING.

IX.   Frank E. Forrest. ..Amherst.
      Eddie Dumphy .. ...Acadia Mines ;
      Edgar Ruggles......   "   "

BOTANICAL DRAWING.

IX.   Stanley McCulloch ..Acadia Mines.
      Myrtle Morrison ....   "   "
X.   Lizzie Myers ....   "   "

FREEHAND AND OBJECT DRAWING.

X.   Lizzie Myers .... Acadia Mines.
    Grace W. Clark ..... Amherst.
    Maggie Acorn ......   "
XI.   John J. McKeen .... Acadia Mines.

LATIN.

IX.   Gussie Holmes...... Parrsboro.
    Hattie McKay......   "
    Andrew Murphy ....   "
X.   Holly Leitch ....   "
    Joey Gillespie ......   "
    Mary E. Woodworth.   "

ALGEBRA.

IX.   Rose E. Hetherby ... Parrsboro.
    Sarah M. Brown ....   "
    Gussie Holmes......   "
    Mary Thomas ...... Acadia Mines.
    Laura Wilson ......   "   "
X.   Mary F. O'Mullin ... Parrsboro.
    Mary E. Woodworth.   "
XI.   Derritt E. Elderkin .. Amherst.
    Josie Strothard .....   "
    John McKean ...... Acadia Mines.

ARITHMETIC.

IX.   Hattie Daye........ Acadia Mines.
    Eddie Dumphy .....   "   "
    Everett H. Young ... Parrsboro.
    Sarah M. Brone .....   "
    Rose E. Hatherby ...   "
X.   Annie Farrell.......   "
    Holly Fritch ....   "
    Dennis Blake ....   "

DISTRICT NO. 9.

W. E. MacLellan, Esq., L.L.B., *Inspector*.

HIGH SCHOOL WORK.

DRAWING BOOKS.

IX.   Adam Bell .... New Glasgow High School.
X.   Isabella McKay .... " " " "

MAPS.

X.   Pauline Mitchell....River John High School.
       Jean A. M. Gordon..   "   "   "   "

MATHEMATICS.—Algebra.

XI.   John Roy..........New Glasgow High School.
       Donald Fraser. ....   "   "   "   "
X.   Hattie Roy........   "   "   "   "
IX.   Lillie Wilson ......   "   "   "   "

ARITHMETIC.

IX.   Lillie Wilson ......New Glasgow High School.
X.   Hattie Roy........   "   "   "   "
       Mabel Grenough ...   "   "   "   "
XI.   Donald Fraser ......   "   "   "   "
       John Roy ....   "   "   "   "

TRIGONOMETRY.

XI.   Donald Fraser......New Glasgow High School.
       John Roy..........   "   "   "   "

NATURAL SCIENCE.—MINERALOGY.

X.   Annie Keay ....New Glasgow High School.
       Mabel Grenough ...   "   "   "   "
       Specimens of Mica and Gypsum described.

CHEMISTRY.

IX.   Mary Murray ......New Glasgow High School.
X.   Hattie Roy ....   "   "   "   "

PHYSICS.

XI.   John Roy ....New Glasgow High School.

FOREIGN LANGUAGES.

XI.   *Greek*, Stanley McDonald, New Glasgow High Sch.
       Latin, John Roy ...   "   "   "   "
       French, Mary McLeod,   "   "   "   "

COMMON SCHOOL WORK.

WRITING.

VII.   Laura M. Wile . . . . . Old Barns, Colchester Co.
       Hattie D. McCurdy . "   "   "   "
III.   Blanche Bonnell . . . . South Branch, "   "
IV.   Maggie Dickie . . . . .   "   "   "   "
VIII. Lottie Burton . . . . . . Pine Tree School, Pictou Co.
       Annie B. Mitchell . . . "   "   "   "   "

MAPS.

VII.   Georgie Olding . . . . . Pine Tree School, Pictou Co.
VIII. Cassie Ray . . . . "   "   "   "   "
       Lottie Burton . . . . . . "   "   "   "   "
VII.   Georgie Burton . . . . . "   "   "   "   "
       Louisa J. Burgess . . Old Barns School, Col. Co.
VIII. Bessie Archibald . . . "   "   "   "   "
       Mabel Chisholm . . . . "   "   "   "   "
2 Copies " High School Monthly," New Glasgow High School.

DISTRICT NO. 2.

LUNENBURG AND QUEENS.

H. H. MacKintosh, Esq., *Inspector.*

COMMON SCHOOL WORK.

1. Copy Books, various grades.
2. Drawing, 12 pencil sketches.
3. Maps, Mar. Prov.; N. America; Queens Co.; Africa.
4. Accounts, 3 specimen accounts.
5. Arithmetic, grades II. to VIII.
6. Grammar, tabulated analysis.
7. Composition.

HIGH SCHOOL WORK.

1. Book-keeping, 2 sets, grades, IX. & X.
2. Composition.
5. Mathematics, various grades.
7. Foreign Languages, Latin Translations.
10. 2 Specimens Wood Work.
    Photographs of School Building.

DISTRICT NO. 6.

ANTIGONISH AND GUYSBORO'.

WM. McISAAC, B. A., ESQ., *Inspector.*

GRADE IX.

Grammar.—Examination Paper.

Composition.—Examination Paper and criticism on Reading Lesson Illustrated.

GRADES IX & X.

Drawing.—Freehand Drawing Books, Nos. 5, 6, 7, 8.

GRADES IX., X., XI., XII.

Languages.—Latin, Greek and French model exercises in answer to set questions.

Mathematics.—Trigonometry, Geometry, Algebra, Arithmetic, Exam. Papers.

GRADE IX.

Lessons on Nature.—Birds, one paper illustrated.

GRADE IX. & X.

History.—Answers to set questions.

GRADE XI.

History and Geography.—The Oriental Monarchies, illustrated by Maps.

GRADES X. & XI.

Chemistry.—Examination Papers.

Physics.—Examination papers.

GRADES X. & XI.

English,—Criticism and Essays.

Psychology.—Essay on Scope and Method of Psychology.

HALIFAX CITY.

MORRIS STREET SCHOOL.

Map of Europe (framed) .... Leo Michaels.
     "   Nova Scotia   "   .... S. Carman.
          Africa   "   .... S. Carman.
     "   England   "   .... Rea Dodge.
          Africa   "   .... Rea Dodge.
     "   N. America   "   .... Alex. Hobrecker.
          Asia   "   .... Alex. Hobrecker.
     "   S. America   "   .... Leo. Michaels.

Collection of Nova Scotia Plants, 67 different species from Grade VII.

Sewing.—Grace O'Connor, Percy Reynolds, Sadie Archard, Minnie Barnstead.

Relief Maps of North America, Nova Scotia and Halifax Co., by Willie Woodbury, Lancelot Purcell, Currie Michaels, Ethel Gardiner, Grace O'Connor, Annie Burgess, Emily Read, Lulie Blois, Helen Hermes.

Drawing Cards, full set.

Tonic Sol Fa, by Edgar Mason, Dan Horne, Helen Burton, Mamie Purcell, Ettie Bowser, James Elliott, Herbert Maynes, Gladys Wood, Robt. Burgess, Nellie Guild, Mabel Goudge, Geo. Ross, Geo. Hill, Geo. Woodman, Phoebe Hubley, Sam Brown, Susie Cornelius, Herbert Brown, Percy Dimock, Gertrude Bowser, Berbie Hopgood, John Gibb, Alice Wright, Harry Hilton, Percy Reynolds, Ethel Grant, Robert Hutchins.

Model Letters, by Nettie Dennis, Louise Read, Edith Archibald, Lon O'Donnell, Edith Read, Geraldine Murphy, Emily Angrove, Mabel Creighton, Clara Wier, Lena Pickering, Nita Caldwell, Jean Robinson, Hannah Hilton, Jessie Watt, Nellie Bowes, Bessie Cline, Etta Cornelius, Maude Anderson, Sadie Taylor, Ella Shields, Minnie Gammon, Eva Holloway, Mary Fraser, Emily Hilton, Bella Little, Kate Belcher, May Chambers, Clara Walters, Fannie Bliss, Elsie Vosnach, Maude Mosher, Josie Chamberlain, May Carman.

Arithmetic, by Louis Read, Nettie Bowes, Edith Archibald, May Fraser, Fanny Covey, Mabel Creighton, Edith Read, Minnie Gammon, Fanny Bliss, Etta Cornelius, Clara Wier, Lilian Reynolds, May Carman, Lousia O'Donnell, May Chambers,

Jean Robinson. Janie Share, Sadie Taylor, Lena Pickering, Josie Chamberlain, Maude Anderson, Katie Muirhead, Bessie Olive, Edith Brown, Ella Shields, Emily Coyle, Elsie Vosnach, Emily Hilton, Geraldine Murphy, Maude Simson, Eva Holloway, Clara Walter.

Analysis of Complex Sentences, Edith Read, Edith Archibald, Maude Anderson, Louise Read. Bessie Olive, Mary Carman, Nettie Bowes, Mabel Creighton, Fanny Bliss, Gertrude Currie, Etta Cornelius, Elsie Vossnack, Louise O'Donnell, Minnie Gammon.

Arithmetic, by Maude Simpson, Josie Chamberlain, Lena Pickering, May F. Chambers, Clara Walters, Emily C. Angrove, Katie Muirhead, Geraldine Murphy, J. Robinson, Etta Shields, Bella Little, Clara Wier.

CompTON AVENUE SCHOOL.

Map-sewing on Cloth.—Isabela Smith.
Map of N. S., Miriam Morash.
Map of North Am., Georgie Messervey.

Sewing.—Lottie Hart, Grace Hurshman, May Hurshman, Florence Cross.

Drawing Books.—Florence Mosher, Ethel Wollard, Emma Balcom.

Model Letter.—Eva Covey, Maude Nickerson, Clara Cunew.

Specimens of Writing.—Annie Forbes, Eva Covey, Maude Nickerson.

Arithmetic.—Minnie Maxwell, Maggie Kennedy, Ethel Brown, Florence Ireland, Gertrude Blakeney, Lillian Beattie, Bertram Goddard, Jessie Garrison, James Myers, Florence Ireland, Gertrude Blakeney, Lillian Beattie, Edna Boutilier, Gertrude Curren, Carrie Dauphinee, Jennie Taylor, Electa Dowden, Blanche Scriven, Grace Hurshman, Willie Hurshman, Charles Brinkman, Bessie Horne, Alfred Cross, George Mumford.

Square Decimeter.—Marion Dalton, Annie O,Donnell, Ethel Goudge.

Map of South America.—Annie Garrison.

Map of Australia.—May Ormeston.

Map of North America.—Clara Curren.

Map of Nova Scotia.—Carrie Dauphiney, Gertrude Curren, Edna Boutilier, Electa Dowden, Fred Edmunds, Ethel Beattie.

Original Design.—Ethel Brown, Pauline Parker, May Ormeston.

Drawing.—Charles Brinkman, Reginald Curren, Ethel Dauphiney, Nellie Grant, Alfred Cross, J. Tough.

RUSSELL STREET SCHOOL.

Drawing.—Rich. Westhaver, Albert Read, Jas. West, Francis Payne, John Guess, Edward Hinch, Geo. Wormell, Randall McGillvray, John McArran, Thos. Gorman, Chas. Hartlen, Sears Keating, Peter McGill, Chas. Keating, Chas. Pitman, Jos. White, Thos. McCarron, Geo. McSweeney, Chas. Purdy, Allan Hurley, Norman Oakes, Daniel Coleman, Jeremiah Mooney, Jas. Service, Wm. Morrow, Chas. Vincent, Hugh McDonald, Fred Griswold, Joseph Balfe, Chas. Purdy.

Writing.—Chas. Hartlen, John Cameron, Randall McGillvray, Rich. Westhaver, Peter McGill, Thos. Williamson, Thos. McCannon, Herbert Morrow, Thos. Haye, Fredk. Bowler, Jas. Hillman, Chas. Pitman, Geo. Evans, Jas. White, Geo. McSweeny, Chas. Keating, Allan Hurley, Norman Oakes, Daniel Coleman, Jeremiah Mooney, Thos. Malloy, John Walsh, Edward Weaver, Wm. Lovett, Fred. Griswold, Chas. Vincent, Hugh McDonald, Alex. Hector.

Arithmetic.—Albert Reed, Francis Payne, Randall McGillvray, Edward Hinch, Sears Keating, Robert Morrow, Jas. West, Chas. Hartlen, John Guess, Peter McGill, Geo. McSweeney, William Evans, James White, Francis McGillvray, Hubert Morrow, James Hillman, John Feely, Thomas Williamson, Edward Hartlen, Allan Hurley, John Jordan, Jas. Shea, Edward West, John Ahern, Norman Oakes, Daniel Coleman, Jeremiah Mooney, Thos. Malloy, John Walsh, Jas. Keating, Edward Weaver, Samuel Goodwin, Collingwood Clarke, Joseph Meehan, Henry W. Appleton, W. Lovett, Alex. Hector, Wm. Morrow.

Maps.—Allen Hurley, Jas. White, Norman Oakes, Daniel Coleman, Jeremiah Mooney, John Walsh, Geo. Reid, Allan Hurley, D. Coleman, Jas. Service, Louis Kaye, George Bede.

Tonic Sol Fa.—.Peter Mitchell.

Analysis and Parsing.—Allan Hurley, Norman Oakes, Jeremiah Mooney.

ST. MARY'S GIRLS' SCHOOL.

Original Design.—A. McEachren, M. Gorman, I. Thomas, M. Butler, M. Murphy, N. Sheehan, E. Mihan, A. Johnson, K. Lynch, B. Cannan, M. Dickson, M. E. White, M. Mills, M. Bennett, M. Murphy, M. Smith, I. Edwards, H. Larkin, A. Byers, G. Pickles, H. McNeil, L. Walker, F. Leddy.

Booklets of Mottoes, Original Designs,

Object Drawing.—J. McMannus, J. O'Brien.

26 maps by Jennie O'Brien and others.

Booklets of penmanship, paper cutting designs, maps, arithmetic, composition, commercial forms, etc., from whole classes in all grades.

ST. PATRICK'S BOYS' SCHOOL.

BOOK KEEPING.

IX.—John Fitzpatrick, Geo. B. Fitzpatrick.

ACCOUNTS.

IX.—Geo. J. Lynch, John F. Fitzpatrick, Thos. W. Lynch, Herbert Regan, Thos. W. Lynch,

GEOMETRY.

IX.—Thomas W. Lynch, J. W. Vales, Herbert J. Ryan, W. H. Campbell.

PHYSICS.

IX.   Thos. W. Lynch, V. J. Clancy.

ARITHMETIC.

IX.   J. J. Clancy.

Penmanship.—John Murphy, L. J. Quain, James Perrin.

Composition.—Lawrence McQuain, P. Mulchey, F. Walsh.

Arithmetic.—Ed. DeVanney, L. McLain, F. Kelly,

Commercial Forms.—L. McLain, F. Kelly, J. Murphy.

Original Designs.—John Murphy, L. McLain, E. Devanney.

Outline Maps.—L. McLain, J. Murphy, R. Shaw.

RICHMOND SCHOOL.

Oil Painting.—John Pickering,

Wall Maps.—Jas. Brodie, Fred Kelly, Harold Rogers.

ARITHMETIC—Grade V.

Isabella Smith, Mary Hartlen, Bessie Williams, Ada Jackson,

Composition.—Lena Smith, Anna McKenzie.

Designing.—Jas. Brodie, Jane Burgess, Willie Williams.

ARITHMETIC.—Grade V.

Nettie Blois.

Analysis.—Jeannie McKenzie, Ina Clarke.

DECIMETERS.—Grade VII.

Willie McLaughlin, Jos. Morley.

COMPOSITION.—Grade VII.

Irene Williams, Eva Green, Ina Clark, F. E. Stockall, Maude Hillis.

Forms of Account.—Jos. Morley, Ina Clarke, Maggie D. McLaughlin.

DECIMETERS.—Grade VI.

D. R. Turnbull.

ORIGINAL DESIGN.—Grade II.

Geo. Ryan, Cecil Blois, C. Hefler.

COMPOSITION.—Grade II.

Carvin Kelly, Ethel Norris, Edith Hartlen.

ARITHMETIC.—Grade IV.

Alice Morley, Beatrice Hartlen.

COMPOSITION.—Grade IV.

B. Hartlen, B. McLauchlin, Albert Clark, H. Hefler, D. Drysdale, Hilton Hann.

ARITHMETIC.—Grade IV.

Jenette Auld.

ORIGINAL DESIGN.—Grade III.

J. J. Abraham, Jas. A. Mowatt, J. Pickering, Percy Blois, Jas. Blackie.
Several sets of Copy Books.

ALEXANDRA SCHOOL.

ORIGINAL DESIGN.—Grade VIII.

Edith Harnel, L. Jost.

FREEHAND DRAWING.

L. Jost, Clara Boehner.

PENMANSHIP.—Grade III.

Daisy West, Mary Smith.

SEWING.—Grade VIII.

H. Dumaresq, J. Wilson, Georgie Moody.

MAPS.

B. B. Connor, Olive Smith, Edna Berringer, N. DeWolf, M. Lessel, M. Spencer, A. Sutherland, E. Taylor, G. Moody, E. Metzler, C. Boehner, J. Cives, L. E. Smith.

LE MARCHANT ST. SCHOOL.

WRITING.

Grade I.—E. Gebb, H. Grant, A. Veith; Grade II.—T. Hore, F. Sullivan, A. Rosengreen; Grade III.—B. Fry, M. Robinson, W. Irons; Grade IV.—A. Gibb, M. Laidlaw, A. Horn; Grade V.—M. Sullivan, J. Dunlap; Grade VI.—E. Rosengreen, J. Mellish, A. Yeaden, M. Carman.

Maps.—M. Morrison, E. Rosengreen.

Original Design.—N. Rosengreen, E. Parker, M. Morrison, R. MacKintosh.

HALIFAX ACADEMY.

Physiological Chart, by Grace Hart.

Plan of Academy Building, by Chas. Johnson.

School Song { Words by Gladys Fairbanks. { Music by Agnes Crawford.

School Song { Words by Jennie Morton.
{ Music by Wm. Chamberlain.

Mineral Map N. S., by Gordon Ferris.

General specimens of Latin, Greek, French, German, English Composition and Mathematical Exercises.

Several Original Designs and Freehand Drawings.

A box of Minerals.

One case of Manual Training Work and Drawings.

TRURO ACADEMY.

Drawing.—Leslie Smith.

Plan.—Jack Bentley.

Drawing. (Eye.) Grace Ross.

Original Design.—Blanch Smith, John Glassy.

Object Drawing.—Clara Linton, Louis Bradshaw.

Maps.—Blanche McKenzie.

     " *Canadian Railways.*—Delina Chisholm, Blanche Lee, Bessie McMullen.

Drawings. (Pencil.)—Gertie Christie, Mary Gillis, Raymond Cutten, Truman Bland, Alice McCallum, Fred Tupper.

LUNENBURG ACADEMY.

BOOK-KEEPING.

IX. Jennet Anderson, Marion C. McConnell.
X. Harry M. Hewitt.

BUSINESS LETTERS.

IX. Bernard C. Anderson, Sydney Morash, Jeannette Anderson,

GEOMETRY.

Marion C. McConnell, Jeannette Anderson.

ALGEBRA.

IX.   Marion C. McConnell, Jeannette Anderson, Violet M.
      Schwartz.
X.   F. E. Young, Ethel A. Scott.

ARITHMETIC.

X.   Frances E. Young.
IX.   Jennette Anderson, Lilla E. McLaughlin, Marion C
      McConnell.

MAPS.

IX.   Bernard C. Anderson.

LIVERPOOL ACADEMY.

ALGEBRA.

X.   Josie Henderson.
XI.   Josie Dauphiney, Mabel Thomas.

PRACTICAL MATHEMATICS.

XI.   Josie Dauphiney, George Harrington, Mabel Thomas.

ANALYSIS.

X.   Annie McLearn.
      Josie Henderson.
      Ethel Dauphiney.

LATIN.

XI.   Josie Dauphiney.
      J. Roland Morton.
      Georgie Harrington.

GEOMETRY

X.   Sadie Dexter, Josie Henderson, Lizzie Hemeon, Mabel
      Thomas.
XI.   Josie Dauphiney.

TRIGONOMETRY.

XI.   Mabel Thomas, Georgie Harrington, Josie Dauphiney.

ARITHMETIC.

X. Josie Henderson, Josie Leslie.
XI. Mabel Thomas.

MAPS.

IX. Arthur Drew.

DARTMOUTH HIGH SCHOOL.

SET OF BOOK KEEPING.—GRADE IX.

Annie Baker, Josie O'Toole.

PHYSICS.

Clara Miller, Josie O'Toole, Fred Gates, Grace Kingston, Maude Chisholm, Annie Baker, Gertie Gates.

ARITHMETIC.

Gertie Gates, Josie O'Toole, Annie Baker, Maude Chisholm, Laura Elliot, Ella Beck, Fred Gates, Della Phener.

Algebra.—Gertie Gates, Clara Miller, Ella Beck, Josie O'Toole, Fred Gates, Grace Kingston, Annie Baker.

Geometry.—Clara Miller, Josie O'Toole, Gertie Gates, Grace Kingston, Annie Baker, Fred Gates, Ella Beck, John Oland.

Drawing from the Flat.—Maude Chisholm, Gertie Gates, Ella Beck, Annie Baker, Ralph Elliot, Clara Miller, Allan Cunningham,

Drawing from the Object.—Clara Miller, Maude Chisholm, Annie Baker.

DARTMOUTH COMMON SCHOOLS.

WRITINGS.—Grade VIII.

Cassie Thomas, Bessie Harrison, Mary Bell, Lily Edgecombe.

COMPOSITION.

Lottie O'Toole, Arthur Winfield, Osmund Regan.

MERCANTILE FORMS.

Bertha Morrison.

MAPS.

Winfred A. Winfield, Leopold Graham.

ARITHMETIC.

Harry Murphy, Ethel Edgecombe, Rita Elliot.

MAPS.—Grade VII.

John Graham, Ed. Whebby, Hattie Webber, Frank Grant, Emma Burchell, George Wilson, Harry Black, Kate Dunbrack.

Designs.—James O'Toole, Hattie Webber, Harry Black, Emma Burchell.

Writing.—Hattie Webber, Emma Burchell, Katie Day, Idalia Innes, Laura Frazee.

Arithmetic.—Harry Hall, Hattie Webber, Harry Black, Florence McInnes, Florence Miller.

WRITING.—Grade VI.

Harry Storey, Ida Harlowe, Vincent Grant, Sadie Wisdom, Ida Glendenning, Etta Weston, Lizzie Lewis, Arthur Brown.

Composition.—Ida Harlowe, Alfred Davis, Beatrice Angwin, Ida Glendenning.

Arithmetic.—Martin Eager, Sadie Wisdom, Arthur Publicover.

Maps.—Harry Story, Blanche Eaton. Kenneth Forbes, Arthur Creighton.

Designs.—Bessie Collins, Stewart Wisdom, Stather Brown, Arthur Publicover, Eager Levy, Willie Bishop.

Maps.—Ida Harlowe, Mervin Hilton, Vincent Grant, Stather Brown, Arthur Publicover, George Whelpley, Chas. Allen.

WRITING.—Grade V.

Frank Lovett, Maurice Webber, George Short, Daisy Smith, Ethel Gates, James Stevens, Helen McLeod.

Arithmetic.—Laura Crimp, Minnie Marks, Jemima Myrer, Eva Sircom, Daisy Smith, Helen McLeod, Lulu Austen, Edith Ferguson, George Short, Florence Millard.

Maps.—Helen McLeod, Angus Hilton, Maurice Webber, Harry Richie.

Designs.—Frank Woodbury, James Stevens, Angus Hilton, Ernest Shrum, Laura Crimp, George Short, Lulu Austen.

WRITING.—Grade IV.

Frank O'Hanley, Murray Merson, Peter McInnes, Gertie Colbert, Percy Gammon, Nellie Bell, Eliza Devan, Eliza Graham, Alice Prescott, Mary Buchanan, Annie Power, Roy Forbes, Amy Gillis.

Arithmetic.—Jas. Colter, Elizabeth Courtney, Maude Griswold, Eliza Wilson, Mary Chapman, Percy Gammon, Florence Hunstone.

Penmanship.—Helen Vickery.

Arithmetic.—Nellie Bell, Annie O'Toole, Katie Miller, Frank O'Hanley, Wilfred Hilchey, Robert Strachan, Roy Forbes, Nellie Harlowe.

Maps.—Nellie Harlowe, Nellie Bell, Hugh O'Toole, Archie Zwicker.

Designs.—Warren Jenkins, Rita Loomer, Norman Merson, Laura Nauss, Wm. Martin, William Beehan, John Walker, Flory James, Brenton Eaton, Laura Monroe, Nellie Crocker, Frank O'Hanley, Murray Merson.

GRADE III.

Writing.—Janie McKay, Pearl Kenty, Ethel Hutchins, A. Graham, Archie Zwicker.

COLORED SCHOOL.

Composition.—Sarah Boulo, Fred Borden.

Designs.—Florencé Tynes, Clara Lee, Maggie Green.

Map.—Sarah Boulo.

BRIDGEWATER HIGH SCHOOL.

Bracket.—Fred. Beardsley.

Writing Desk.—Eddie Hoyt.

Drawing, Grade X.—Maud Hebb.

Business Letter, Grade X.—John Simonson.

Essay on Bridgewater, Grade X.—Bertha Simonson.

Geometry, Grade IX.—Grace Wagner.

Book-keeping, Grade X.—J. S. Simonson.

LUNENBURG SCHOOL.

COPY BOOKS.

Grade II. —Lillian Naas.
    IV. —Ada C. Stevenman, Eva B. Back.
    V. —Loretta Borgill.
    VI. —Mary Wilson.
    VII. —Kate Ross.

ESSAY ON "NATURE."

Grade VII. —Kate Ross.

BOOK-KEEPING.

Grade VIII.—Ella Smith.

BUSINESS ACCOUNTS.

Grade VIII.—Leone Mason, Jessie Smith, Maggie Silver.

ANALYSIS.

Grade VI. —Helen Wolfe, Flora Drew, Bessie Mullins.

    VIII.—Ellie M. Kempton.

ARITHMETIC.

Grade VI. —Helen Wolfe, Lillie Johnson, Flora Drew.

    VIII.—Ellie Kempton, Rose Ford, Everett N.
           Dominie, Chas. McL. Kempton, Jennie
           Smith.
    VII. —Kate Ross, Bertha Schnare, Maggie Silver.
    II. —Ralph Selig, Laura Smith.
    III. —Eva B. Beck, Hattie L. Young.
    IV. —Ina B. Prince.
    V.   —Evelina Eisenhauer.

ANALYSIS.

Grade VII. —Kate Ross.

MAPS.

Grade VIII.—Fred. Hewitt, Roslyn Haugle, Maggie Sil-
          ver, Leone Mason, Ellen Maxner.

HALIFAX LADIES' COLLEGE.

PHOTOGRAPHS.

1. Exterior of Buildings.
2. Entrance Hall.
3. Dining Hall.
4. Assembly Room.
5. English Class Room.
6. Studio.
7. Laboratory.
8. Calisthenics Class in Convocation Hall.

MICROSCOPIC SLIDES AND SALTS PREPARED BY THE STUDENTS IN THE LABORATORY.

Slides.

1- 8.—Sections of Kidney of Rabbit.
9-12.—   "   Tongue   "
13-16.—   "   Liver   "
17-19.—   "   Wall of Intestine of Rabbit.
20-21.—Muscle Fibres of Leg of Rabbit.
22-23.—   "   "   Heart   "
24.—   "   "   Œsophagus of Rabbit.
25-28.—Human Hair.
29.—Scales of Epithelium.
30-32.—Cross Section of Pine Stem.
33.—Longitudinal Section of Pine Stem.
34-35.—Epidermis of Pine Needle.
36.—Cross Section of Pine Needle.
37.—Epidermis of Fern.

Salts.

38.—Zinc Sulphate.	43.—Ammonium Sulphate.
39.—Lead Nitrate.	44.—Potassium Nitrate.
40.—Cupric Sulphate.	45.—Sodium Nitrate.
41.—Ferrous Sulphate.	46.—Sodium Sulphate.
42.—Ammonium Chloride.	47.—Potassium Chloride.

Art.

48.—Study in Charcoal from Cast. (Venus of Milo.)
49.—Still Life Study in Water color. (Oranges.)
50.—Still Life Study in Oils. (Vase of Crysanthemums.)

CHURCH SCHOOL FOR GIRLS.

WINDSOR, N. S.

PAINTINGS.

1. *Pansies.*—Sadie Forster.
2. *Two of the Fencing Class.*—Anna Sterns.
3. *Dog.*—Anna Sterns.
4. *Peaches.*—Ethel Davies.
5. *On Ferry Hill.*—Margaret Leckie.
6. *Stairway and Corridor.*—Edyth White.
7. *Study in Shading.*—Ethel Davies.
8. *Copy.*—Margaret Leckie.
9. *The Ferry Bridge.*—Louie Jack.

PHOTOGRAPHS.

1. Old and New Building.
2. New Building.
3. Entrance Hall, New Building.
4. Reception Room.
5. Corridor.
6. Class Room, No. 3.
7. Class Room, No. 4.
8. School Room.
9. Library.
10. Dining Room.
11. Corridor.
12. Lady Principal's Room.
13. Interior of Dormitory.
14. Bedroom.
15.   "
16.   "

ACADIA SEMINARY.

WOLFVILLE, N. S.

DRAWINGS AND PAINTINGS.

1. Ornament.—M. J. Eaton.
2. Ears and Eye.—J. Brison.
3. Models.—E. Shand.
4. Steps and Cube.—J. Brison.
5. Nose and Hand.—J. Brison and M. McKean.
6. Lily.—Edna Wyman.
7. Apples.—M. J. Eaton.
8. Monk.—G. Cunningham.

9. Model.—J. Brison.
10. Skeleton Cube.—J. Brison.
11. Apples.—Alice Bishop.
12. Banana and Lemon.—G. Cunningham and A. Bishop.
13. Apples.—Edna Wyman.
14. Acanthus Scroll.—G. Cunningham.

OILS.

1. Blue Heron.—Minnie Chipman.
2. Pansie and Mayflower.—Minnie Chipman.
3. Still Life.—Carrie Chute.
4. Apples, Still Life.—M. McKeen.
5. Still Life.—Bessie Hatfield.
6. Apples.—Jessie Burton.

VICTORIA SCHOOL OF ART AND DESIGN.

Frame Nos. 1, 2 & 3.—Six Diagrams each.
   "   " 4.—Power's Nut-lock (patent applied for).
   "   " 5.—Six Blue Prints, Tracings and Drawings.
   By J. Dustan, Senior Mechanical Class.

Frame Nos. 6 & 7.—Drawing of Spike and McLeod's Compound Fire
      Alarm Box.
   "   " 8 & 9.—Twelve Diagrams.
   By R. J. Wilson, Jr., Senior Mechanical Class.

Frame No. 10.—Pillow Block, etc.
   By F. M. Burton, Senior Mechanical Class.

Frame No. 11.—Plan and Section of Vertical Boiler.
   "   " 12.—Original Design High Pressure Engine.
   By B. A. Romans, Senior Mechanical Class.

Frame No. 13.—Throttle Valve.
   By T. W. Fulton, Senior Mech. Class.

ARCHITECTURAL CLASS.

Frame No. 14.—Permanent Fortification.
   By W. M. Doull.

Frame No. 15.—Permanent Fortification.
   By Percy Lea.

Frame Nos. 16 & 17.—Geometrical Drawings.
   By R. T. Gough.

Frame No. 18.—Original Design for an Artizan's Dwelling House, also
 " " 19.—Section and Framing plans.
  By L. G. Archbald.

FINE ART DIVISION.

Frame No. 21.—Original Study, View from Halifax County Academy,
  By Miss M. Graham.

Frame Nos. 21 & 22.—Original Studies, Flowers, Oak Leaves.
  By Miss A. Vondy.

Frame No. 23.—Original Studies.
  By Lewis E. Smith.

Frames Nos. 24 & 25.—Original Studies, Flowers from Nature.
  By Miss E. A. Smith.

PHOTOGRAPHS.

A.—PICTOU ACADEMY.

1. Pictou Town and Academy.
2. (Ink Drawing.) Pictou Academy.
3 & 4. Group of Mammalia. Pictou Academy Museum.
5. " Hawks, etc., " " "
6. " Eagles, "
7. " Fish Hawks, etc., "
8. " Pelican, etc.,
9. " Herons, etc.,
10. " Song Birds, "
11. " Nine cases of Insects, "

B.—KING'S COLLEGE.

1. King's College Buildings.
2. King's College.
3. Memorial Chapel, King's College.
4. " " (interior) King's College.
5. Convocation Hall, " "
6. " " (interior) " "
7. Library and Museum,
8. Students Reading Room, "
9. " Sitting "
10. " Dining "
11. Entrance Hall "
12 & 13. King George's Charter, "

C.—Church School for Girls, Windsor.

1, View of Old and New Buildings.
2.   "   New Building.
3.   "   Entrance Hall.
4.   "   Principal's Reception Room.
5.   "   Corridor.
6.   "   Class Room, No. 3.
7·   "   "   "   " 4.
8.   "   School Room.
9.   "   Library.
10.   "   Dining Room.
11.   "   Corridor.
12.   "   Principal's Room.
13.   "   Interior of Dormitory.
14.   "   Room with three Beds.
15, 16. "   Rooms with two Beds.
17.   "   Fencing Class.

D.—Acadia Ladies' Seminary, Wolfville.

1. Acadia Seminary Building.
2. Principal's Room.
3. Reception   "
4. Studio.
5. Alumnæ Hall.
6. Gymnasium.
7. Dining Hall.
8. Science Room.
9. Lower Corridor.
10, 11. Teachers' Rooms.
12. Class Room.
13. Student's Room.

E.—Acadia College, Wolfville.

1. Acadia College.
2. Convocation Hall.
3. Dining Room.
4. Library.
5. Ball Ground.

PUBLIC SCHOOLS.

1. Collingwood, Cum. Co. 2. Middleton, Anna. Co., (two depts). 3. Gowrie Mines, C. B, (four depts). 4. Bridgeport, C. B., (four depts.) 5. Berwick, Kings Co. 6. Bridgewate , Lun. Co. 7. Bridgetown, Anna. Co. 8. North Sydney, C. B., (sisters). 9. North Sydney, C. B. 10. Lunenburg. 11-16. Sydney, C. B. 12. Dartmonth

(Central Greenvale, North Park).   17. Barrington Passage, Shel. Co.
18. Lockeport, Shel. Co.   19 & 20. Springhill, Cum. Co., (H. Road,
Central).   21. Liverpool.   22. Yarmouth.   23. Lunenburg Academy.
24. Sydney Acad.   25. Digby Acad.   25. Amherst Acad.   26. Normal School.   27. Convent School, Sydney.   28. Convent School,
North Sydney.   29. Morris Street School, Halifax.   30 St. Mary's
Boys, Halifax.   31. St. Mary's Girls, Halifax.   32. Alexandra, Halifax.   33. Halifax County Academy.   34. Halifax Academy Cadets
and Armory.   35.   St. Ninian's Street School.

DEAF AND DUMB INSTITUTION.

36. Institution for the Deaf and Dumb, Halifax.   37. Teachers
and Pupils of the Institution for the Deaf and Dumb.   38. Deaf
and Dumb Spelling "Halifax."   39. Teaching "c" to Deaf and Dumb.
40. Teaching "o" to Deaf and Dumb.

HALIFAX LADIES' COLLEGE.

41.   Halifax Ladies' College Exterior.
42.   "   "   "   Entrance Hall.
43.   "   "   "   Dining Hall.
44·   "   "   "   Assembly Room.
45.   "   "   "   English Class Room.
46.   "   "   "   Studio.
47.   "   "   "   Laboratory.
48.   "   "   "   Calisthenics.

DALHOUSIE COLLEGE.

49.   Arts Library.   50.   Law Library.

---

51.   St. Francis Xavier's College.
52.   St. Bernard's Convent.
53.   Presbyterian College, Pine Hill, Halifax.

SCHOOL FOR THE BLIND, HALIFAX.

A fine assortment of special books and apparatus used in the
instruction of the blind, with specimens of pupils' work and photographs of buildings, rooms, etc.

DALHOUSIE COLLEGE.

Enlarged mounted photograph of building.

KING'S COLLEGE.

Engineering Department.—Large Mechanical Drawings, Design
for a Bridge.

OTHER EXHIBITS.

Large Map of Nova Scotia showing every School house, Academy, College, and University in the Province.

A collection of Photographs illustrating the scenery of the Province.
A collection of Enlarged and Mounted Photographs illustrating the Scenery of the Province.

●

BOUND VOLUMES.

1. University King's College Cal. 1890–3.
2.　　　"　　Acadia　　"　　"　1888–93.
3.　　 ·　"　　Presbyterian　　"　1889–93.
4.　　　"　　Dalhousie　　"　1878–93.
5. Courses of study, Acad., etc., '93·
6. University Periodicals, Dalhousie Gazette, Vols. XXIV.–XXV.
7. College Periodicals.
8. High School Periodicals.　(Pictou, Sydney, New Glasgow.)
9. Educational Reports (1878-1885).
10.　　　"　　　"　　(1885-1892).
11. Education Journal (1885-1892).
12. Copy Books.
13.　 "　　　"
14, 15, 16.　Exercises County Academies (Halifax, Antigonish).
17. Blank Forms Educational Department.
18. A case of the Books prescribed for the Public Schools of Nova Scotia.

NOTE.—It is unfortunate that a detailed list of the Normal School Exhibit cannot be given. No lists were supplied to me with the articles. The work, however, as already stated was particularly good. Deserving of special mention were the illustrated Nature Lessons, the clay modellings from the pupils of Miss O. Smith's Studio, a mineral map of Nova Scotia, and several freehand drawings and original designs in tinted papers.

Official information has not yet been received of the opinion of the judges, but by a private letter from the Superintendent of the Canadian Section of the Educational Department, Mr. Wm. Morton, I learn that we have won seven awards out of the ten classes into which the exhibit was divided. If this proves to be correct it will be most gratifying to you after your untiring efforts to have Nova Scotia well represented in the work of your department.

A. McK.

.HALIFAX, November, 1893.　　　　　　　*Adv. Com. for N. S.*

APPENDIX F.

SUMMER SCHOOL OF SCIENCE

FOR THE

ATLANTIC PROVINCES OF CANADA.

To A. H. MacKay, LL. D.,
          Superintendent of Education.

Sir,—

In the absence of the Secretary of the Summer School of Science, it is desirable that I should present a short report of the work of its last session.

An excellent calendar of twenty-four pages was published several months in advance. It gave a good outline of the various subjects to be studied and many interesting facts regarding the methods, of study, &c.

This enabled the students to read up in advance on the particular topics selected.

The School was opened in the Convocation Hall of Mount Allison University, Sackville, on Wednesday, the 5th of July and remained in session until the 21st.

There were 105 ladies and gentlemen enrolled as students, nearly all of them being teachers—49 from Nova Scotia, 52 from New Brunswick, 2 from Prince Edward Island, 1 from Newfoundland and 1 from the United States.

Several hours each day were devoted to class-room work—mostly laboratory work, conducted by some of the ablest Principals and Professors of the Maritime Provinces.

Excursions were made to various places of scientific or historical interest in the neighborhood of Sackville.

The students heard lectures from various distinguished speakers— among others, Attorney General Longley, on "Patriotism in the Public Schools."

They also enjoyed the hospitality of the citizens of Amherst, Sackville and other places, which vied with each other in showing them every attention. Foremost among those who thus honored them were President Allison and Dr. Borden of Mt. Allison.

An "Educational Symposium" and "Round Table Talk"—novel and most successful features of this season, were introduced by the president, Dr. Hall.

Most interesting and profitable discussion arose out of the reading of the following papers :

"University Extension," by Prof. Andrews, Mount Allison.
"Manual Training," by W. T. Kennedy, Halifax Academy.
"Comenius," by Principal Brown, Bridgetown.
"Herbart," by Miss Mosely, Morris Street School, Halifax.
"Pestalozzi," by B. F. Porter, Truro.

At the close of the school, certificates were awarded to those who passed their examinations as follows :—

Physics :—

W. E. Outhit, Halifax.
W. A. Warren, Sackville.

Physiology :—

Clara M. Archibald, Amherst.
Anna Creelman, Stewiacke.
Emma J. Bacon, Digby.
Sara J. Patterson, Linden, Cumberland Co.
Ethel Thompson, Sackville.

Zoology :—

K. A. McKenzie, North Sydney.
Edith A. Annis, Liverpool.
Sadie Hall, Port Hilford.
Victoria I. Ernst, Liverpool.
P. F. Martin, Harbor Grace, Newfoundland.

Mineralogy :—

Victoria I. Ernst, Liverpool.
Annie Creelman, Stewiacke.

The summer school is doing much to improve the teachers who attend it, and through them to raise the standard of science teaching among teachers generally throughout the Maritime Provinces.

Not being in possession of the Secretary's books, I am unable to present as full a report as I consider desirable.

The next session of the school will be held in Charlottetown, from the 4th to the 19th of July, 1894.

I append a list of officers and instructors to show that an institution under such management must be in the highest degree worthy of the confidence of the teachers' profession and of the educational authorities.

I have the honor to be

Your obedient servant,

A. McKAY,
Supervisor of Schools.

HALIFAX, N. S., November, 1893.

SUMMER SCHOOL OF SCIENCE, 1894.

The opening meeting of the Session will be held in the Philharmonic Hall, Charlottetown, P. E. I., on Wednesday, July 4th, at 8 p.m. D. J. McLeod, Esq., Chief Superintendent of Education, will preside. Dr. Anderson, President of Prince of Wales College, will welcome the School on behalf of the educationists of the Province, and Hon. L. H. Davies, M. P., on behalf of the citizens of Charlottetown. Replies will be given by members of the Faculty. Rev. W. W. Andrews, M. A., President of the School of Science, will deliver the opening address to the School.

Addresses will also be given by prominent gentlemen of the Maritime Provinces. Good music will be provided.

After the meeting, to permit the members of the School to become acquainted with each other and with the citizens, a reception will be held by the President of the School.

OFFICERS.—1894.

PRESIDENT.

Rev. W. W. Andrews, M. A., *Mt. Allison University.*

VICE-PRESIDENTS.

Prof. Brittain, *Provincial Normal School, Fredericton.*
Principal Lay, *Amherst Academy.*
F. Bain, Esq., *North River, Queens Co., P. E. I.*

SECRETARY-TREASURER.

J. D. Seaman, Esq., *Prince Street School, Charlottetown.*

EXECUTIVE COMMITTEE.

W. T. Kennedy, Esq.,   Principal Oulton,
Prof. Coldwell,   Miss L. J. Landers.
The President and Secretary-Treasurer.

· FACULTY.

ASTRONOMY.
PRINCIPAL A. CAMERON ....*County Academy, Yarmouth*

BOTANY.
G. U. HAY, PH. B.........................*High School. St. John*
NETTIE FORBES, B. A................*County Academy, Yarmouth*

CHEMISTRY.
PROF. BRITTAIN.....................*Normal School, Fredericton*

CIVICS.
W. T. KENNEDY, ESQ.................*County Academy, Halifax*

ELOCUTION.
MISS L. J. LANDERS ....*Mount Allison University, Sackville*

ENGLISH LITERATURE.
PRINCIPAL A. CAMERON.............*County Academy, Yarmouth*

GEOLOGY AND MINERALOGY.
PROF. A. E. COLDWELL................*Acadia College, Wolfville*

KINDERGARTEN.
Mrs. S. B. PATTERSON ....*Truro*

MUSIC (Tonic Sol-Fa.)
REV. JAS. ANDERSON, M. A........................ ....*Toronto*

PEDAGOGICS.
PROF. FRANK EATON...............................*Kentville*

PHYSICS.
REV. W. W. ANDREWS, M. A. ......*Mt.University Allison, Sackville*

PHYSIOLOGY.
JAS. DORSEY, M. D....... ....*Charlottetown*

PSYCHOLOGY.
J. B. HALL, PH. D. ....*Normal School, Truro*

ZOOLOGY.
PRINCIPAL G. J. OULTON ....*Dorchester*

PICTOU COUNTY ACADEMY, 1880.

ANNUAL REPORT

OF THE

SUPERINTENDENT OF EDUCATION

ON THE

PUBLIC SCHOOLS OF NOVA SCOTIA,

FOR THE YEAR ENDED 31st JULY,

1894.

HALIFAX, N. S.:
COMMISSIONER OF PUBLIC WORKS AND MINES, QUEEN'S PRINTER.
1895.

EDUCATION OFFICE.

HALIFAX, *January, 1895.*

SIR :—

I have the honor to transmit herewith, to be laid before His Honor the Lieutenant-Governor, my report on the Public Schools of Nova Scotia, for the School year ended July 31, 1894.

I am, with respect,

Your obedient servant,

A. H. MACKAY,
Superintendent of Education.

To the HON W. S. FIELDING, M.P.P.,
Provincial Secretary.

GENERAL CONTENTS.

PART I.—GENERAL REPORT.

PART II.—STATISTICAL TABLES.

PART III.—APPENDICES.

APPENDIX A.

APPENDIX B.

APPENDIX C.

APPENDIX D.

APPENDIX E.

GENERAL REPORT, 1894.

ANNUAL REPORT

ON THE

PUBLIC SCHOOLS OF NOVA SCOTIA,

1893-94.

To His Honor MALACHY BOWES DALY,
Lieutenant-Governor of Nova Scotia :

MAY IT PLEASE YOUR HONOR,—

I beg in accordance with the law, to submit my annual report on the Public Schools of the Province, for the School Year ended 31st July, 1894.

For much detail that might otherwise appear in this Annual Report, I refer you to the two numbers of the *Journal of Education,* issued according to law in April and October respectively, which contain, among other items, a list of teachers, with the amount of the Provincial Grant paid each, and of the school sections, with the amount of County Fund distributed to each.

As the previous school year was only three-fourths of a calendar year, on account of its being a transition term between the old and the new school year, there is the same inconvenience in the comparison of some of the statistics tabulated as was referred to in my last report. As will be seen from the reports of more than one of the Inspectors in Appendix B, the statistics taken this year from the Registers are not only more full but also more accurate than ever before. Special care is now taken to have as many items as possible compiled when there is leisure, and to have them in the Registers open to the inspection of all school visitors during the term.

The school year has been one of remarkable activity in every department of educational work.

Notwithstanding the possibiiity that the late changes in the law might produce a stringency beyond that estimated in the supply of teachers, before the country could adapt itself to the new conditions, the number of sections without school was 60 less than the previous term. The number of teachers also increased, the increase being mainly in teachers of experience, and those with Normal School training, the increase in the latter being 91 over the 408 of the previous term.

It is also satisfactory to note that the average salaries of the higher classes of teachers continue to rise, thus demonstrating a growing appreciation of their services on the part of the people, and holding out the hope that the profession of teaching may continue to attract into its ranks more and more of the men and women of culture, tact, and force.

As compared with the last *full* school year, the salaries of male teachers of the classes A & B advanced $32.06; of female B teachers, $23.45; of male teachers of class C, $20.31; of female teachers of class C, $3.69; of male teachers of class D, $0.65. But we must stop, for the average salary of class D female teachers, with their own consent, as well as with their trustees' estimate, decreased $1.93. It is gratifying to observe that this general advance had been going on before the increased provincial grant voted at the last session of the legislature began to affect salaries.

During the past two years I called attention to the remarkable interest shown in the improvement of school buildings. This interest, instead of abating, is still increasing, and at so remarkable a rate that I venture no further comment beyond the figures for the past four years.

Year.	Sections' Total vote Ann. Meeting.	Sections' vote for Buildings and Repairs.
1891	$341,655	$ 51,421
1892	313,229	96,788
1893 (¾ year)	413,448	95,6-7
1894	454,200	134,710

The estimated value of the literary and scientific equipments of the schools has also increased during the year from $28,728.36 to $33,589.58.

The common school course of study, outlining what experience in our best schools for a number of years suggested as the best co-ordination of school work from year to year for the first eight years of school life, so as to give, in the hands of a competent teacher, about enough work for the pupil of average ability without interfering with the proper amount of home recreations and moderate extra home studies, has been revised since its publication in the Education Report of 1885, ten years ago, principally with the object of reducing the memory work. This course was the outcome of a series of Provincial Educational Associations, in which committees representing all the leading schools in the province, and drawing on the experience of other countries, discussed and modified from year to year the original draft under the criticism of the teachers of the province in convention assembled. The lack of judgment on the part of untrained teachers, whom we must still accept in most of our schools, was since shown in the too great stress laid on the memorization of text books. The object of the revision was the lessening of such work, as is indicated by the omission altogether from the common school course of the "Advanced" Geography Text Book, the large British History, the Latin, (optional), &c. The only addition to the course has been the books made imperative by the Act of the Legislature of 1892. The council was fortunate in being able to comply with the law by prescribing two books acknowledged to be superior to those had in view by the promoters of the Act, and at nearly half the anticipated cost. These were introduced during this year, and it is found that they take the place of the former indefinite oral lessons prescribed on temperance and hygiene, and really add nothing to the difficulty of the course. By reference to the Inspectors' reports in Appendix B, it will be seen that they are well received as a rule in the schools.

In addition contracted courses of study, suggesting still further simplifications for common schools having less than eight grades, have been published in the *Journal of Education*, for the purpose of helping inexperienced or untrained teachers,—namely, one for a common school with four teachers, one for three teachers, one for two teachers, and one for the ordinary rural school with one teacher.

Although the common school course now does not appear so advanced on paper as those of some other countries or provinces, it is hoped that the increasing thoroughness of the work done under its general direction may prove it ultimately quite as serviceable.

Elsewhere in this report it will be found that for this school year the average proportion of time given in the school rooms of the province to the various subjects of the common schools, was as follows :—

1. English..........................42.7 per cent.
2. Mathematics (Arithmetic).........21.4 "
3. Geography and History...........14.4 "
4. Writing, Drawing, and Book-keeping.12.6 "
5. Observation Teaching and General
   Improvement Exercises, (Calisthenics, Music, Hygiene, Morals
   and Nature)................... 8.9 "

100.0 per cent.

A revision has also been made of the High School Course of Study, which lessens the range of studies on the part of a student in order to attain the highest certificate corresponding to the old grade A ; and although in some sections the local authorities, school commissioners or trustees, in the exercise of their powers, which are not narrowly limited by the general law, add more to the minimum course, yet in other sections it is possible for the teacher, through lack of judgment, to make even the minimum oppressive to the average pupil. There will, of course, be always some pupils for whom the average work will be too difficult, and both teachers and trustees should recognize that there is no provincial law countenancing pressure on those who from health, mental capacity, irregularities, or previous defective training are unable to keep up with any particular class. Nor, on the other hand, can we expect any sensible person to propose that the regular work for the whole school should be cut down to the fraction suiting only the invalid, or that the fractional work of the invalid should be considered the equivalent of the full work of the robust, when it is not and never can be. The intelligent and faithful teacher should carefully endeavor to discover those who are not able to do the average work without too much effort, and to give counsel to the parent if the parent should be so indifferent as to neglect consultation with the teacher.

No general regulation can supply the local administration of a school with a code of action for the innumerable anomalies which are likely to arise in various schools. They require the presence of an educationist with ready tact and sound judgment. And the number . of such teachers is, without doubt, steadily increasing in the more favored sections of the country.

A voluntary examination of the high school students is held at the close of the term, as an examination of that kind is necessary under any circumstances for testing the scholarship of those who are to become teachers. As may be pointed out more fully in the remarks on the statistics of this examination, the present form of the High School Course of Study is a very considerable simplification of the previous conditions; and the examination, which is granted without any cost to the candidate, has already lessened the necessity for the old time multiplicity of examinations in connection with the entrance of students into the universities and other institutions requiring a · recognized test of scholarship. The popularity of the privilege offered is shown by the large increase in the number of candidates who presented themselves this year, there being an advance of 416 over the 1,506 of the previous year. And as compared with the old teachers' examinations, we find that the proportion of male students coming up to the examination is very greatly increased, the increase noted above being, for example, male candidates, 202; female, 214.

The exhibit made by this Province at the Chicago Exposition was not at all arranged for the purpose of winning prizes in the various classes according to the catalogue divisions of the World's Fair. It was simply a single exhibit of educational work, representing as fairly as could be what was being done from the most elementary grades to the highest, as a duty Nova Scotia owed to the other countries of the world making an exhibit of their work for the general benefit. It is therefore specially gratifying to find that so large a number of awards has been given it. The seven awards cover the work of (1) the Kindergartens; (2) the Elementary rural schools; (3) the County Academies and High Schools; (4) the Normal School; (5) the Institution for the Deaf and Dumb; (6) the School for the Blind; and (7) the laws, school books, &c., of the province.

In the Blue Book "Report of the Executive Commissioner for Canada to the World's Columbian Exposition, Chicago, 1893," the

Superintendent of the Liberal Arts Department in his report has the following reference to the Nova Scotian Educational Exhibit :

" Nova Scotia had 352 exhibits, representing her schools, academies, and colleges. This exhibit was installed by Mr. A. McKay, Supervisor of Public Schools for Halifax, and he made a very neat and attractive court. While it was not so extensive as some other exhibits, yet for showing the thoroughness of Nova Scotia's school methods, the varied character of her educational institutions, and the wide diffusion of knowledge amongst her people, it answered the purpose most admirably, the kindergarten work especially of pupils five and six years' old being equal to that of pupils of seven and eight of the United States. It was the subject of much praise by visiting educationalists. Seven awards were given, and the diplomas testify in their wording to the correct method and the general excellence of Nova Scotia's school system."

STATISTICAL ABSTRACT.

For a general view of the more important details of the state and progress of education during the year, the following abstract of the statistical tables is presented here :

	1893.	1894.
1.—SECTIONS.		
School Sections in Province	1904	1891
Sections without school	196	136
2.—SCHOOLS.		
Schools in operation	2252	2292
" session 50 days or under. ...	37	16
" " 50 to 100 days	67	83
" " 100 to 150 "	219	139
" " 150 to 200 "	1929	280
" " 200 to 216 "		1157
" " full term 217 days		617
Average days in session	152.7	199.2
3.—TEACHERS.		
Number of Teachers	2319	2351
" " Normal trained	408	499
Class A, Male	45	46
" " Female	3	4
" B, Male	169	149
" " Female	169	162
" C, Male	216	199
" " Female	898	888
" D, Male	152	149
" " Female	667	756
New Teachers	288	255
Teachers, Service 1 year or under	325	297
" " 1 to 2 years	312	327
" " 2 to 3 "	304	309
" " 3 to 4 "	276	263
" " 4 to 5 "	211	205
" " 5 to 7 "	295	270

	1893.	1894.
Teachers, Service 7 to 10 years...... .	220	248
" " 10 to 15 "	199	186
" " 15 to 20 "	85	121
" " 20 or over...........	95	125

4.—ATTENDANCE.

	1893.	1894.
Pupils on Register, First Quarter......	......	75.821
" " Second "	78,121	86,700
" " Third "	84,238	89,939
" " Fourth "	93,248	97,920
Average Daily Attendance, First Quarter.	......	51,622
" " " Second "	49,887	47,183
" " " Third "	49,292	48,937
" " " Fourth "	48,991	51,492
Total Days' Attendance for year........	7,824,166	10,471,764

5.—CLASSIFICATION OF PUPILS.

	1893.	1894.
Grade I (and Kindergarten)............	18,020	18,908
" II............................	12,515	13,498
" III	11,653	12,184
IV............................	12,283	12,672
V	10,566	11,158
VI	9,296	9,202
VII...........................	9,831	9,409
VIII..........................	6,361	6,489
Total in Common Schools........	90,525	93,520
IX	2,506	2,922
X	1,206	1,186
XI	497	460
XII	37	82
Total in High Schools...........	4,246	4,650
" Public "	94,771	98,170
Full Academic High School Students....	1,351	1,371
" Non-Academic " "	1,250	1,860
Partial " "	1,645	1,419

6.—SECTION STATISTICS.

	1893.	1894.
Value of Property in Section...........$73,848,513	$73,848,513	$80,096,411
" School Property in Section.. ...	1,032,890	1,360,784
Total Vote at Annual Meeting..........	413,448	454,200
Voted for Buildings and Repairs........	95,687	134,710
Paid for Teachers' Salaries..............	279,355	339,848
Volumes in Library of School...........	4,183	6,537
No. of Maps, Charts, Globes, &c.........	7,108	7,161
Value of Scientific App. and Coll.........	6,577	8,277
Value of Total Literary and Scientific....	28,728	33,589

7.—TOTAL EXPENDITURE.

	1803	1894.
Total Provincial Grants	$ 166,040	$ 220,436
" County Funds	89,623	120,507
" Section Assessment	413,448	454,200
Total Expenditure, Public Education	$669,112	$795,144

PART II. of this Report commences with the Statistical Tables. These always form the most valuable part of every report, as they indicate quantitatively not only the absolute magnitude of each element tabulated, but also the direction and rate of change in each. They enable us to measure the tendencies exhibiting themselves in the system. From the same cause as last year, they will not so readily show the rate of change in every item, as the full school year of 1894 is compared with the short (transition) year of 1893. With the great majority of items this will make but little difference. In the other cases comparisons may be made with the statistics of the full year ended 1892, so far as they are given. With the present year this difficulty will disappear. I make a few notes on these tables in regular order. A close examination will reveal some discrepancies in minor points, such as were noticed last year, and are not yet entirely eliminated. The most of the Inspectors have been able to compile statistics from the returns sent in, which seem to show that all their teachers have not fully interpreted the meaning of these forms, or seen the importance of minute accuracy. One inaccurate return, if it cannot be corrected by the Inspector, will cause the sum for the county to fail in the test; and also, the sum for the Province. There are several columns which serve for the important purp s of checking the general accuracy of the statistics. One for instance, is the " Total on Register at end of Fourth Quarter" in Table IV., and total "Annual Enrolment" in Table V. The different totals in a few of the counties show that some teachers did not carefully follow the instructions given in the Register in the cases of pupils transferred from one room to another during the year. The error is not one affecting the accuracy of the figures on which public moneys are paid. And it would be wrong to manipulate the figures when editing to make them agree. The discrepancies themselves are most important statistics, because they point out weaknesses which would never be discovered in a simpler system of tables. As these discrepancies are very few comparatively speaking this year, it is hoped they may disappear altogether by next year. That in no country in the world is there a greater effort made to have minutely accurate statistics, is demonstrated by the statistical page in the Register of each school, a portion of which must be filled in, not hurriedly at the close of the school, when the teacher may be leaving the section for ever, but leisurely at the opening of the school, after which they stand open for inspection to every visitor and school officer during the year. There is, therefore, no temptation to fill in such statistics in the

" return " by a hurried estimate, when all that has to be done is to make an exact copy of the Register.

SECTIONS AND SCHOOLS.—I.

The decrease in the number of school sections from 1904 to 1891, would be a very promising feature were it due to the consolidation of weak sections into stronger ones. From special inquiry, however, I find it to be chiefly due to the rectification of the old number of sections in the County of Victoria.

The number of schools in session during the year was 40 greater than that of the previous year; and the number of schools in session for the shorter periods were generally less. The 1016 schools in session at the foot of the eighth column was the number of schools in session for the full term of 166 days in 1893, and they should more properly be added in with the seventh column, making 1929 schools between 150 and 200 days. Only 617 schools completed the full year to the 217th day it appears. By some means the figures 617, it will be noticed, have slipped down into the column noting " decrease." The increase of 32 in the number of teachers might be naturally expected from the greater length of the term.

NORMAL TRAINED TEACHERS.

There has been an increase of 91 in this class of teachers, and a diminution of 59 in the teachers without Normal school training. This shows a remarkable development of sentiment in favor of trained teachers. The number engaged in each county during the last two years is given below:—

COUNTIES.	1893.	1894.
Annapolis	25	25
Antigonish	2	7
Cape Breton	17	22
Colchester	63	67
Cumberland	75	83
Digby	17	14
Guysboro	2	13
Halifax Co	23	40
Halifax City	31	35
Hants	45	38
Inverness	7	7
Kings	23	35
Lunenburg	23	34
Pictou	20	33
Queens	5	7
Richmond	5	9
Shelburne	3	4
Victoria	4	4
Yarmouth	18	22
Totals	408	499

This showing is very satisfactory when we consider that there is no premium on Normal School training as against High School learning. The general principle of advance of class of license is as follows : A term at the Normal School may qualify for an advance of class ; or a term at the High School or County Academy with the M. P. Q. exam., by raising the general scholarship one grade. With those who do not intend to make teaching a profession, the latter course is at a premium, as it not only brings an advance of license, but also a year's advance towards their real profession. The term spent at the Normal School prepares specially but for one profession, that of teaching. I know of no model country where the profession of teaching is not only left open to those who have never taken a course of training, but where for those who wish to enter the profession but as a stepping stone, there is a premium on taking the non-professional course. The rule now everywhere is a professional course of training for a term of from one to three years. Until we can afford to do a little more in this direction in Nova Scotia, we cannot expect that the most perfect course of study in the world will produce good schools in every school section. The school can never be like anything else than the teacher. A reference is made in the report of the Supervisor of the Halifax schools to the high success attending the work of teachers who never passed through a Normal School. These facts specially emphasize the great value of selection when it can be applied. Halifax City, in virtue of a far-sighted policy, has been selecting a few of the teachers born with a special genius and developed by experience in various parts of the Province for its schools. But this selection from abroad cannot be imitated by every section. In the first place, few could afford to try it to any extensive extent. In the second place, should a movement to carry it out on any extensive scale be made, the supply would be exhausted right at the start. The stage immediately in advance of us is a supply of *trained* teachers. The next, more remote, but deserving of our most earnest efforts, is a supply of *selected* trained teachers. Before this stage arrives, salaries of teachers will rise, small sections must be consolidated or enlarged, and weak sections strengthened.

LIBRARIES AND COLLECTIONS.

The number of school libraries and scientific collections in the schools would appear to have decreased ; but this is more probably due to the growing feeling that a very small collection of books should not be called a school library, for from table VII. it can be learned that there was an increase of 2354 volumes in the libraries, that the scientific collections increased by the value of $1699, and the total literary and scientific equipment by $4861.

TEACHERS CLASSIFIED.—II. AND III.

We see from this table that female teachers are greatly in excess of male teachers, and still the disparity is increasing. The numbers in each class are shown in the following columns :—

Class A	44* Males.		4 Females.	
" B	149	"	162	"
" C	199	"	888	"
D	131	"	658	"
" D (Prov.)	18		98	
Totals	541	"	1810	"

The new teachers employed were 255, which is 33 less than last year: while the net number of experienced teachers increased by 65, the increase of those of over 15 years of experience being 66.

If we divide the teachers of the Province into two divisions, comparing the number with an experience of five years and under with the older teachers, we get the following proportions:—

	5 Years and Under. Male.	Female.	Over 5 Years. Male.	Female.
Classes A and B	66	71	127	95
Class C	102	478	97	410
Totals A, B and C	168	549	224	505
Totals of above	717		729	
Classes D	684		221	
Totals (all teachers)	1401		950	

That is, the majority of teachers of the three higher classes, A, B, and C, have been in the profession for over five years, by 729 to 717. Of the 905 of Class D, as we should expect, only 221 have been in the profession over 5 years.

GENERAL ATTENDANCE.—IV.

From this Table we find that the attendance was most irregular during the second quarter—November, December, and January—only 59.1 per cent. of those attending some time during the quarter being daily present, against 68 per cent. in the first quarter, and 64.2 in the third and fourth quarters. The largest attendance was in the fourth quarter, April, May, and June. Then come the second, third, and first quarters in order.

10,879 new pupils entered the schools during the second quarter, while 6,901 attending during the first quarter ceased to attend before the second quarter. 3,239 new pupils entered school during the third quarter; while 6,917 ceased attending school for the year; 7,981 new pupils entered during the fourth quarter; while 8,281 who attended the third quarter did not attend the fourth quarter.

In round numbers, the pupils enrolled during the year in all the public schools was nearly 100,000 (exactly 2,080 less than 100,000.)

* Should probably be 46, as two Class A teachers may have been counted as Class B teachers (having drawn only B grants) in a return, or in the Inspector's Abstract for Antigonish, which should therefore be credited with 5 instead of 3 A teachers in the Table.

The number who may be said to be in more or less regular attendance (average of those attending during the quarter) is about 80,000. The number actually present each day on an average is about 50,000.

Reducing the preceding figures to the simplest form, we find about 44 pupils enrolled during the year in the average Nova Scotian school; 35 were in more or less regular attendance; and 22 were present each day on an average. 5 pupils entered during the winter quarter who did not attend during the autumn quarter; while 3 who attended during the autumn quarter did not attend during the winter quarter. 1 or 2 new pupils entered during the spring quarter; while 3 left school before the spring quarter ended. 3 or 4 new pupils entered during the summer quarter; while nearly 4 ceased attendance before the commencement of the quarter.

CHANGES OF PUPILS BY HALF-YEARS.

During the last half of the year 11,220 new pupils entered the schools, while 15,198 who attended the first half year did not attend the second half year. Comparing this year with the last full year, under the old division of the school year, we find that while the withdrawals are practically the same, there is a difference of over 8000 in the new pupils. In 1892, the number of new pupils entering school during the second half of the year was 19,621, while the number of those who ceased attending before the end of the first half of the year was 15,397. It can be inferred from this that the time of the division of the school year formerly tended to inflate "the number of different pupils registered during the year;" and in the case of the years compared, to a considerable extent. Were the school year so divided that the number entering and leaving each half would be approximately equal, this inflation would be a minimum. Under our present system the total enrolment for 1894, which was 97.920, is practically the equivalent of the 102,586 of 1892. A test of the truth of this inference is found in the fact that the Grand Total Days' Attendance of 1892 was only 10,735,077; while that of 1894, with a nominal annual enrolment, 4000 less, and with an average of one week more of vacation, was 10,471,764.

SEMI-ANNUAL AND ANNUAL ATTENDANCE.—V.

The increase in attendance during the second half of the two last years—the only halves which can be compared—is a very decided one, 334,771 days. The 1631 pupils in the column "under 5 years of age," did not necessarily attend school while under 5 years. They were children who did not become 5 years of age until after the 1st day of August, and who entered school presumably on becoming 5 years old.

The total annual enrolment is given in this table as 98,710 against 97,920 in the previous table. This indicates an error in a few of the county tabulations of 790. Last year the corresponding error was 1651. The cause of this discrepancy has already been referred to.

ATTENDANCE OF PUPILS.—VI.

The first column of this table shows that during the year there were 9,625 pupils who attended school for only 20 days or less. It is an improvement on the previous year, however, when this class numbered 10,531.

It appears that 4,599 pupils attended school who did not belong to the section. The majority of these were probably attending County Academies or High Schools, when the section could not afford appropriate instruction for them at home.

The number of children between 5 and 15 years of age in all the sections is given as 93,938; while in Table V. we find the number enrolled between these ages to be 89,719. This would indicate at least 4,219 who did not attend school at all. As the 89,719 probably included a large number of the 4.599 attending from other sections, the figures 7,485 given as those between 5 and 15 years who did not attend school at all, are probably very nearly exact.

FINANCIAL STATISTICS OF SECTIONS.—VII.

All school property is found here to be valued at over $1,360,000. The valuation of school section property is about $80,000,000. The total amount voted at annual meetings for all school purposes nearly half a million dollars, $454,500 more exactly, a great increase over previous years, as is also the vote for buildings and repairs. Reference has already been made to this fact and to the increase in the literary and scientific equipment of the schools.

HOW THE TEACHER'S TIME IS SPENT IN THE SCHOOL ROOM.—VIII. and IX.

Table VIII. refers to the Common School subjects; but it also includes the time devoted to these subjects in the High Schools as well as the Common Schools. It includes every school room in the province in its sweep; while Table IX. refers only to the given number of schools in which the High School subjects are taught. We have here the average number of minutes of the teacher's time absorbed each week in giving instruction in each subject. Dividing these averages by 5, the number of teaching days in the week, we get the average number of minutes spent on each subject. It must be remembered that the subjects named in this table are not at all assumed to be co-ordinate in value; nor in the popular sense is each a separate subject. While English, Arithmetic, Geography, History and Writing are the main subjects which take up the time of both teacher and pupils, it is felt that monotonous drill on these alone would make the school work less interesting, and success in these fundamental subjects themselves less assured, than when attention is also paid to the all round development of the pupil, so as to prepare him for a healthy, moral, observing, and intelligent life.

CALISTHENICS.

Why should not the pupils in every school be trained to bear themselves in good form, to give the proper play to nature in developing a strong constitution which is so valuable in the fight for life, and in developing a graceful bearing which is so often a passport to the first stage of success? Why should not clownish habits when standing, slovenly habits in walking, injurious positions when sitting, be systematically watched for and corrected? Such is the mission of *Calisthenics*, (see General Directions Course of Study, No. 65.) When the pupil is wearied from the memorizing of his spellings or the solutions of his arithmetical problems, attention to this side of his training for a few moments adds nothing to his nervous exhaustion, or his load of books, or his home studies. On the other hand it is a nerve restorer, a glint of light in the darkness, an hour of life won from the dead. The time taken in the average school of the province for this work is less than *three* minutes during the whole long school day.

VOCAL MUSIC.

With respect to this subject it will suffice to quote the teaching of the late Dr. Forrester, one of the chief founders of our school system. It is now about thirty years since he set down in his Text Book for Teachers the following words when commencing the discussion of a proper course of study:

" Let us now briefly advert to each of these branches as enumerated, and this, as stated, entirely for the purpose of indicating their nature and utility in a complete and liberal course of education. I. Music. We have given music the precedence of all the others, not because it is here to be systematically taught, but because, *even when practically employed, it forms such a powerful auxiliary in the acquisition of all other branches—such a valuable* handmaiden in the ordering and regulating of the whole scholastic establishment. It has been said, that to attempt to conduct an infant or primary school without music is as impossible as to govern a nation without laws. This is strong language, but it is not, in our opinion, one whit overstated or exaggerated."

A generation has nearly passed away since these words were first impressed with earnest eloquence on the minds of Normal School teachers. Yet up to the present day hundreds of our schools remained songless, and thousands of parents and tens of thousands of pupils have suffered, and are suffering directly as well as indirectly from this great defect. The staff notation of music proved too cumbrous for successful application under our conditions. It is no wonder, then, that the tonic sol-fa notation, which has made possible so tremendous a revolution in school music in Great Britain, and even in Ontario, should be enthusiastically received here. It enables us to save very much time and effort, and accomplish results in the majority of schools impossible under the old conditions. And what is the time absorbed in the long school day of the average school in this health-giving, voice and ear training, and "nerve" restoring exercise? A very little more than *four* minutes.

HYGIENE AND TEMPERANCE.

The introduction of this subject as a distinct one, to be studied from text-books, with which the pupils must be provided, should be credited to the representatives of the people acting in the Provincial Legislature. We quote the Act, so that its full scope may be studied from the letter:

AN ACT TO PROVIDE FOR THE "MORE THOROUGH STUDY IN THE PUBLIC SCHOOLS OF THE EFFECTS OF ALCOHOLIC DRINKS ON THE HUMAN SYSTEM."

(Passed the 30th day of April, 1892.)

Be it enacted by the Governor, Council, and Assembly, as follows:

1. Appropriate instruction shall be given regularly in the public schools as to the nature of alcoholic drinks and narcotics, including tobacco, and special instruction as to their effect upon the human system in connection with the several divisions of the subjects of relative physiology and hygiene. Such instructions regarding physiological and hygienic laws and the effects of alcoholic drinks and narcotics, shall be given orally from a suitable text book in the hands of the teacher to pupils unable to read, and such instruction shall be given to all others with text-books in the hands of the pupils, and from text-books as well graded to the capacities of the pupils as other text-books are, and such instruction shall be given as aforesaid to the pupils in all public schools in the Province.

2. The text-books to be used for instruction required to be given by the preceding section of this Act shall be prescibed by the Council of Public Instruction, who shall notify the secretaries of the respective Boards of Trustees, and of the School Boards of the several incorporated towns and cities within the Province, of the choice of the text-books so selected by them as aforesaid, and said text-books used in the primary or intermediate grades shall give at least one-fourth of their space to the consideration of the nature and effects of alcoholic drinks and narcotics ; and the text-books used in the higher grades shall contain at least twenty pages of matter relating to this subject.

3. It shall be the duty of school officers and school inspectors to report to the Council of Public Instruction any failure on the part of the trustees or the teachers of the section under their control to carry out the provisions of this Act. Upon its being shown to the Council of Public Instruction, either by such school inspectors or school officers, or any ratepayer, that any teachers or trustees have failed to carry out the provisions of this Act, any such failure shall be deemed sufficient cause for withholding wholly or in part from any such teacher or trustees, provincial or county grants.

The Council of Public Instruction had then no alternative. Books must be prescribed, no matter how undesirable it might appear to any who might not understand the benefit of their use. After careful consideration and effort, Health Readers Nos. 1 and 2 were brought out on the lines of the most approved books on the subject, and at about one-half the price. They are with the pupils the best liked books on the prescribed list. They are attractive as readers, interesting as sources of information on common things, and beneficial in their influence. While some people may very naturally have been indulging in general protests against the addition of new subjects to the course, and the increase of the number of books required, none of them to my knowledge have been so *incautious* as to name these books, which have been the only additions made in late years to the common school course of study. I have in an editorial comment in the October *Journal of Education*, plainly pointed out to teachers and other school officers that the Education Office could not shield parties ignoring the obligations imposed upon them by the statute above quoted.

As these Health Readers also serve as reading books, the time absorbed in their study might to a great extent be counted as spent in the study of English. But the exercise is not, even under the most adverse circumstances, so exhausting as the regular reading book lessons, with their spellings and definitions. In the most of cases it will be found to be a pleasant and recreative oral or object lesson, and the average time per day given to this subject is hardly *six and one half* minutes.

MORAL AND PATRIOTIC DUTIES.

This is another heading which, under a possible perspective may be misunderstood by those who do not know what it is. There is no text-book. There is no lesson to be memorized at home. There may be no regular time each week for it on the school time table. Then it may be asked, why have it itemized in the Register, Returns and the Inspector's note book ? Just because it is an important element in school life which should never be lost sight of. And without having it itemized it would under many circumstances be omitted. If the young citizen is to be developed with a true patriotic spirit, he should naturally begin to show it in a disposition to sacrifice some of his time, his convenience, or his efforts, for that part of his country with which he comes first into contact. His first countrymen are his fellow-scholars; his first land the public school or play-grounds. If he can be inspired with the desire to make an effort to improve or beautify these surroundings for the common pleasure and pride of the school, he can do it for his town, his province, or the empire. This is next step to the recognition of the universal brotherhood of man, one at least of the fundamental elements of a good morality of which the teacher has already been certified to be a good example before being licensed. When a public holiday comes, here is a standing suggestion that its meaning should be impressed on the young pupils. When an incident in the history lesson offers to illustrate the duty of the citizen for the common weal, the occasion is taken. When geography points out our great resources, the opportunity occurs again. When an occasion requiring discipline arises, there is yet another chance to point an effective lesson on the principles of morality and public duty. The teacher's having to estimate the time on an average absorbed in such work, and to record the estimate on the Register, is the surest way we know of keeping the importance of such training always before them when an occasion arises to make such a lesson effective. What is education worth if the true spirit of a moral and patriotic citizen is not also simultaneously stimulated and developed ? Who is not in favor of the utilizing of every possible incident to develop such a spirit; more especially when it is not associated with the idea of being a task which must be gone through with at a certain minute, when there are no circumstances present to make the lesson of dramatic interest. This, too, is the commencement of the study of civics which is now receiving so much attention in other countries. The average time per day given to such work is hardly *five* minutes.

OBJECT LESSONS ON NATURE.

This is a subject introduced for the double purpose (1) of breaking the strain of exhaustive mental work in school by a light recreative exercise, and (2) of developing accurate observing power in the pupil, which book, and purely mental work alone, do not tend to stimulate. When Archbishop Walsh spoke in Dublin on the 25th of November last, and said, as reported, that he thought the whole system of primary education in Ireland to be little better than a gigantic mistake, he came down to particulars, stating that, in his opinion, primary education should not consist merely of teaching information which was to be found in books. " Children ought to be taught how to use their hands and to be accurate observers." This kind of training is becoming much more essential for success in the world now than it was formerly. While useful to all, it is especially important to the farming and horticultural industries. Why should not pupils travelling back and forward morning and afternoon from the schools in country sections be amusing and instructing themselves in noticing the wealth of beauty and natural law in the earth, rock, water, vegetation, air, and sky, around them? A few daily hints from a competent teacher would enable them to make their daily tramp to school more pleasant, and therefore their school more delightful. It would also open their eyes to the natural beauties of their own homestead, and to the laws which underlie the successful pursuit of those industries which are of primary importance in supplying mankind with the means of physical life, and in laying the foundation of a prosperous and happy country. To the lack of effective instruction of this kind in our primary schools we must attribute the tendency in the old solitary book drill, of making too many of the young pupils think more of city, foreign or professional life than of the possibilities of the intelligent development of farm life. And so of other industrial occupations. By developing this side of the school life, the tendency will be to increase the number of intelligent young men who will devote themselves to the producing industries. And at the same time, the standard difficult subjects of the school will also be more successfully mastered by the pupil, for the object lesson on nature is play or recreation, which will enable him to return to the severer work with renewed freshness. It is a play, but it is a useful play.

In order that even untrained teachers should not misapprehend the nature of this work, the amplified course of study printed in every Register indicates the trend of these lessons towards " Agriculture, Horticulture, or any local industry," under these general directions:—
. " 69. *Lessons on Nature.*—The noting, examination and study of the common and more important natural objects and laws of nature as they are exemplified *within the range of the school section* or of the pupils' observations. Under this head pupils should not be required

to memorize notes or facts which they have not at least to some extent actually observed or verified for themselves." And in the *Journal of Education*, in the contracted course suggested for country schools, directions are given, concluding with the following words :—

" It must be remembered that the memorizing of notes or facts merely stated to pupils is strictly forbidden under this head. Such memorizing is pure cram, injurious instead of being useful. These lessons are intended to show pupils how they may find out the facts and laws of the world for themselves. The lessons must be direct from nature itself, but under the guidance of the teacher who can save time in bringing the pupils to the point desired from his own more mature experience. They are intended to train the observing and inductive faculties, to show the true way of discovering something of the nature of the world which immediately surrounds us, and which is and will continue to be reacting upon us in one manner or another. This knowledge is so much power over nature from which we have to win our material existence."

The average time absorbed in this work daily is less than *six and one half* minutes.

A word may be here said on this *six and a half* minutes recreation, with respect to some of its peculiarities. A definite list of objects for each grade would be altogether out of place in a general provincial course of study, because the lessons must be taught from the object as in nature, and the natural environments of pupils in different sections of the country are different. The teacher, therefore, should select the objects from the most convenient and interesting within the pupil's scope of observation.

But the general course prescribed advises the teacher not to confine his attention to *one* division of nature alone, as if there were nothing of interest or value to be learned from any other division. Such specialization may be necessary at a later date in the university, or in preparation for the special occupation of life, or in amateur research work. In school life, the most salient features of nature on every side touching human interests, should, as far as there is time for it, be objectively and co-ordinately studied. A person who has not thought over the matter with some experience to guide him, might say now, " Is it not a 'smattering' of all the sciences you are attempting to give ? Would it not be better to be intensive and confined to one narrow line ?" Most certainly not, in the common school. Elementary comprehensive study is as genuine as intensive university work, if truly objective. In fact the narrow and intensive study at this stage would be (1) unscientific, and (2) the creator of a false general conception of nature. It is philosophically unscientific because it assumes that nature should be studied only in a narrow tunnel reaching down into the depths of the earth, far from the plane in which is the abode of human interest which the tunnel only intersects. Philosophically considered, it is just as sound to study the superficial plane which is the locus of our life, where we come into contact with the common mineral, plant, and animal ; mountain, wood, and

b

water ; sunshine, air, and cloud. Practically considered, it is very much more profitable. It also tends to give a truer conception of the laws of nature. The pupil is not so likely to think merely as a mineralogist who imagines the law of the universe to be that of crystalization, or a biologist who sees nothing in it but cell division, or the physicist who sees nothing in it but the effects of molecular motions, or a mythologist who sees nothing but the pranks of very human or bestial deities in it. Such teaching cannot be done by the purely professional minerologist, or geologist, or botanist, or zoologist, or chemist, or physicist. It can be done only by him who has an intelligent appreciation of the coördination of the common things around us, and who has the tact to open the eyes of his pupils to the nature of their surroundings. Nature is one. The artificial division of it is merely for the specialization of labor for its more complete exploration. But although children should follow the exploring method, they should not be confined to the simple tunnel of the laborer. That, with its one-sided wear, will come soon enough.

SPELLING (ORAL AND WRITTEN).

Although appearing here as a separate subject, Spelling for the most part is taken up with the Reading lesson. When the teacher's estimate is properly made it should include the average time he spends on spelling in connection with these lessons. The work of the spelling class is simply an examination on a definite spelling lesson, which is most commonly a home lesson, and in the lower grades one of the chief home lessons. Were English spelled phonetically, it would save two full years of school room and home time of study out of the first ten years of school life. To that extent every pupil having to learn English, as it is written, is handicapped as compared with pupils in Germany, Spain, and other countries where the written language is phonetically spelled, or nearly so. In 1880 the German orthography was simplified by decree of the Prussian Government after some four years study of the problem by conference and otherwise, under the direction of the Minister of Education. While the general principle laid down reads " express every sound you hear in correct and distinct pronounciation, by its proper sign " ; particular directions were given for the simplifications of certain classes of irregularities. The spelling is now very nearly phonetic, French spelling. which is nearly as irregular as English, has for some time been under the consideration of the reformer. Only two years ago the committee of the French Academy, on the revision of its great dictionary of the language for the new (eighth) edition, presented a report recommending important simplifications of French spelling. The object of the changes was stated to be " to make the task of learning the language more easy by making its orthography more logical, and thereby to facilitate its use by foreigners." The changes affect over one thousand common words, and are to go into use at once. The English language does not yet acknowledge an authority which can impress its views on all sections of the English world. Although an authority greater than ever represented in any English dictionary hitherto, is beginning to arise in the Philological Societies of England and America, the influence of which is apparent in the new *Standard Dictionary*; still there is no central, all compelling authority, to regulate extensive changes of orthography in the direction of simplification. To preserve the uniformity, if not the unity of the written language, it is our duty, therefore, to enforce attention to accurate spelling according to the best common usage, no matter what it costs. This is, therefore, the general direction given to teachers for Spelling and Dictation : —

" It should be strictly insisted upon that, from the very commencement in the first grade, the pupil should spell every word read in lessons, and common words of similar difficulty used in his conversation Writing words in the lower grades. Transcription and dictation in the higher grades should be utilized more and more as facility in writing increases."

The time devoted to the subject on an average in every school room in the Province, is a little over *thirty-one* minutes each day. As in the higher grades but little time is taken in the formal examination of spelling, the lower grades must take a correspondingly greater time than this average.

READING AND ELOCUTION.

Elocution is the name the subject takes in the higher grades of the High Schools. Were the language spelled phonetically, mechanical reading could be learned in a few weeks. Teachers could then have the time thus saved, as also that saved by the simple spelling, spent in studying the thought in the language, and its best expression. But mechanical reading must first be mastered, and then the spelling. Hence the class and the teacher are often so wearied by these necessary preliminaries, that the chief end of the lesson is too often reached under a state of exhaustion which robs the work of its freshness and interest. These are causes which undoubtedly tend to defeat the great effort made to secure excellence in this department in many schools. A proof that the effort is being made is given in the fact that about *sixty-one* minutes daily are absorbed in the schools in reading exercises alone, under the following general directions :—

" 1. Pupils must be enabled to clearly understand the portion to be read, then to read it with proper expression. 2. Faults of enunciation, pronunciation, etc., of tone, of posture and manner, etc., must be carefully noted and corrected. 3. Choice passages should be memorized occasionally for recitation with the proper expression."

ENGLISH COMPOSITION AND GRAMMAR.

" In all grades practice should constantly be given in expressing the substance of stories, lessons, or observations, orally in correct language, and in the higher grades in writing also. Discussion of subject matter of lesson. Attention to the use of capitals, punctuation marks, paragraphing, etc., should be introduced gradually and regularly, so that at the end of the common school course language in correct form can be fluently used in description or business letters, orally and in writing. The practical rather than the theoretical knowledge of English is what is specially required in the common school, and a large portion of the school time should be given to it. Pupils should be continually exercised in finding synonyms or substituting 'their own meanings' for difficult words in their reading lessons, instead of merely memorizing definitions often given at head of lesson."

Under these general directions over *twenty-two* minutes daily on an average are devoted to English language.

We thus see that more than 118 minutes per day on the average have been spent on these three divisions of English, which really form one subject,—*English Language.* That is about *two* hours a day. And in addition to this, these very same subjects require more effort from the pupils than any other as home work.

WRITING AND BOOK-KEEPING.

Paradoxical though it may appear, it is a fact that in many schools the legibility and beauty of writing are injured by the excess of writing. The devotion to written exercises for the purposeof developing accuracy of expression and rapidity of writing, always, when the teacher is not careful, ruins the hand-writing. Witness the cacography of the majority of our professional men. Like them the school boy is anxious to save time ; and therefore hurries through his written exercises, gaining rapidity at the expense of legibility. Hence the origin of the general directions :—

"Styles most easy to read should be cultivated. Simple vertical writing is generally preferable to the sloping styles. No exercise in writing should be accepted by the teacher from the pupil unless its form shows evidence of care. Should begin in the first grade with letters formed from the simple elements properly classified, and should be taught in the order of difficulty."

The average daily time taken by these two subjects in our schools is *twenty-six* minutes.

GEOGRAPHY AND HISTORY.

On account of the tendency to unnecessary memory work in these subjects with young children, the amount recommended in the course of study has been gradually reduced as compared with former years. In too many schools the pupils had, under fear of the task-master, to memorize great quantities of matter at home, in order to recite or be examined mechanically in class. The following general direction was therefore placed before the eyes of every teacher :—

"75 and 76. *Geography and History.*—The verbal memorizing of these lessons at home by the pupil is for the most part injurious to the character of the memory and useless as practical knowledge. For in spite of all cautions and instructions to the contrary, most pupils when left to themselves mentally associate the facts memorized with the wording, the paragraph and the page of a book, instead of with the proper locus in the map, or with the proper system of related facts. These lessons should therefore be prepared under the careful and philosophic direction of the teacher in the school room, at least until the pupils are trained how to study aright. The home work would then be only the review and perfecting of the lessons by the pupils in the proper manner by reference to the several items in the text. Local or current events, historical, economic or scientific, should be skillfully used to interpret the remote in time and place."

These two subjects during the school year have absorbed daily on the average about *forty* minutes.

DRAWING.

A very good series of Drawing Books has been prescribed; but on account of its price its use is not compulsory in the school room. We are awaiting an equally good, but cheaper series. The course of study prescribes not the Drawing Books; but Drawing *as in* the prescribed books. In many schools the drawing book, therefore, is home-made, at the cost of two or three cents. Some kinds of wrapping paper which take the pencil well, make very serviceable books. The teacher gives the drawing exercises on the black-board from her copy of the prescribed book. In the higher grades of the Common School the pupil is led up to understand the construction of plans according to scale, so as to enable him to solve readily by drawing, any easy work in land surveying, house building, maps, and the like. Drawing is also used in connection with object lessons, so as to train the eye in the habit of accurate seeing, as well as the muscles of the hand to the accurate execution of the idea. This work is light and recreative, more useful than writing in training the hand, and has taken up no more time on the average than *eight and a half* minutes a day.

ARITHMETIC.

This includes the all-important *mental* arithmetic as well as slate arithmetic. As, in all but the most elementary stages, the fundamental operations in Arithmetic must be so instantaneous as to depend for their accuracy altogether on an acquired mental habit which may make or mar forever the arithmetical success of the pupil, the following general direction is put before every teacher's eye :—

"78. *Arithmetic.*—It is of the highest importance to secure the habit of obtaining accurate answers at the *first* attempt. Every slip in mental or written arithmetical work is not only unnecessary, but is a positive education in a habit which will tend to render useless the most strenuous efforts afterwards to become accurate or even to make satisfactory progress in mathematics. Accuracy is of supreme importance from the first. Rapidity may then be neglected to look after itself. In the first four grades the teacher will have to prepare a great number of exercises of a nature not specially arranged for in the present prescribed text-book, so that the pupils may be accurate and rapid in their operations."

[Since the close of the school year on which I am reporting, the Council of Public Instruction has prescribed concurrently with the old text-book now for many years on the Common School Course, and having yet two years to run, a Common School Arithmetic which remedies the defect alluded to in the above direction. Not only is its price cheaper page for page than the old, the exercises more numerous, appropriate, and better graded, the paper and print superior, and the general treatment (barring minor defects which will be removed in the succeeding editions) equal to the best modern Common School Arithmetic in the English language; but it has another valuable feature new to us. It is published in three parts, each containing about two year's work. This feature, it is hoped, will be appreciated by those who have to buy the books. Instead of purchasing arithmetical text enough for six or seven years to be carried about until it is worn out or lost before the last of it is utilized, each part can be had fresh and new as it is required. It may also be mentioned here, that there are several books upon the prescribed list whose removal I shall recommend so soon as we can get the proper books to take their place. But as the annoyance caused by the change of a text-book is likey under any circumstances to be more or less felt, it is not desirable to make a change until something is found which is a very clear improvement, and is not likely to need revision for a long time.]

The time absorbed in teaching Arithmetic daily, on an average, was *fifty-nine* minutes—about an hour   This does not include " seat " study, which necessarily in rural schools takes up very much more of the time of the pupil than it does of the teacher—as it also does in most of the graded schools.

PERCENTAGE OF TIME TO EACH SUBJECT.

Trom this table we can calculate the number of minutes given to each subject of the so-called Common School subjects by the teacher out of every hundred minutes.   Here is the result :—

NAME OF SUBJECT.	Average percentage of school time taken by Teacher for each subject.
Calisthenics	1.
Vocal Music.	1.6
Hygiene and Temperance	2.3
Moral and Patriotic Duties	1.7
Object Lessons on Nature	2.3
Spelling	11.3
Reading, etc.	23.4
Composition and Grammar	8.0
Writing	7.2
Book-keeping	2.3
Geography	8.1
History	6.3
Drawing	3.1
Arithmetic	21.4
	100.0

The subjects which may be called the "nerve-exhausting ones" are given in italics. They also include those requiring "home lessons." The others are the "recreative" subjects. But, as explained before, each different heading is given here for the purpose of always keeping before the teacher every necessary side of his work. Some require the great bulk of the time, others require little time; but that little is very important for the attractiveness and usefulness of the school. To group them into subjects in the popular sense, we might do as follows :—

SUBJECTS OF COMMON SCHOOL COURSE OF STUDY AND PERCENTAGE OF TIME GIVEN TO THEM IN SCHOOL.

Percentage of Time.

1. English { Spelling...... 11.3 / Reading..... 23.4 / Composition .. 8.0 } 42.7
2. Arithmetic 21.4
3. Geography (8.1) and History (6.3).................... 14.4
4. Writing (7.2), Drawing (3.1), and Book-keeping (2.3)...... 12.6
5. General intelligence lessons and improvement exercises (Cal., Music, Hygiene, Morals, and Nature)........ 8.9

—
100.0

It must be remembered that this table was the average time given in the school rooms of the Province for the year ended July, 1894, every component item being to-day recorded in the school registers in every section in the Province, and sworn to as the most correct estimate the teacher could make in the returns transmitted to the Education Office. As in the olden time, English, Arithmetic, and Writing are the staple subjects of the schools. There is yet, perhaps, too much time spent in memorizing subject No. 3, Geography and History, at home. There is yet, also, a great lack of skill on the part of most teachers to utilize the recreative subjects (No. 5), so as to break the monotony and weariness of the school, to correct bad habits of body, and form good ones, and even to practise the expression of thought in good English in the most interesting and rational way possible—the description and explanation of what pupils see and understand in their surroundings. In the Common Schools, the best English will be found, as a general rule, where the best object and oral lessons are given. Language can be correctly learned only as it is used for the expression of ideas which are distinctly comprehended. In this and other ways, the *eight* or *nine* per cent. of recreative exercises indicated above, besides relieving the pressure, interesting the intelligence, and promoting health of body and mind, will enable the pupils to do better work in the old and staple subjects than was ever generally possible without them.

TIME IN DOING HIGH SCHOOL WORK.—VIII.

This table is interesting, perhaps not so much from the information it gives of the average amount of time absorbed in the teaching of each subject, as the information it gives as to the number of schools attempting to do more or less high school work.   There is a number of well known high schools besides the County Academies.   But such institutions are to be found only in the denser centres of population. But from this table it appears that there are 778 schools in which Algebra is taught.   This may include of course some of the elementary work in Grade VIII.   500 in which Geometry is taught.   This may include the practical Geometry of Grade VIII.   289 in which Physics is taught..   194 in which Physiology is taught.   169 in which Chemistry is taught.   119 in which Practical Mathematics is taught.   80 in which French is taught.   69 in which Latin is taught.   And 16 in which Greek is taught.

Teachers, as a general rule, like to encourage their pupils to advance as far as possible.   In country schools it is therefore not uncommonly found that there may be one or two pupils doing some high school work.   In a case of this kind any teacher of judgment will give but very little of the school time to the advanced pupil, who as a general rule, is an interested student, and can make progress by occasional momentary hints from the teacher.   In making an average, say of the 119 schools in which Practical Mathematics is taught, we get 16 minutes per day.   But as in mixed common and high schools the time given must be very short, the longer time given to the subject in the pure high schools is strongly masked in the " average " by the greater number of the partial high schools.   But still there is value in these statistics apart from the idea that it is useful to have the facts recorded in the Register as the history of the work of the school.   The product of the " average " by the number of the schools referred to, is an accurate quantitative statement of the time spent in the schools of the province in each of these subjects.   Owing to defective statistics in some teachers' returns from the Counties of Inverness and Victoria, their averages are omitted from this table, so as not to affect the provincial average.

It should not be surprising if the tendency of the teacher to encourage pupils to continue at school after finishing the work of the common schools in rural sections, should, under certain circumstances, give rise to complaints from certain parties that the common school work is neglected to too great an extent for the few doing advanced work.   Teachers should be careful not to give any just occasion for the neglect of the general school for any special section of it.

But just here comes up the question, should the teacher be prepared to distribute his attention evenly upon the pupils of a rural school containing all Grades from I to X or XI. ?   Yes, evenly upon the pupils, (not upon the subjects), if such has been the agreement with the trustees.   On the other hand, have the trustees the right to say to the teacher, you shall teach no higher subjects in this school than those of Grade VIII. ?   There are circumstances in which such a right might be sustained.   The Statutes and the Regulations of the Council of Public Instruction give very material aid to High Schools, County Academies in particular, to make provision for effective high school teaching, in order to obviate to some extent, the necessity of making a very poor provision for such instruction in every section. But so long as teachers are tactful and trustees judicious, there will be no demand for the Council of Public Instruction or a Statute to take away from sections the power of allowing more or less high school work to be done in rural (ungraded) schools.

CLASSIFICATION OF PUPILS.—IX.

605 are returned as Kindergarten pupils. From personal knowledge or reports made to me, I cannot say that all these are being trained in fully equipped Kindergartens. Cape Breton reports 60 in the Kindergarten, while Colchester, with its notable Truro Kindergarten, reports none, as the institution is not a public school. Halifax and Dartmouth are making very creditable provisions for free Kindergarten education. Adding in the number of pupils reported as belonging to public Kindergartens with those of Grade I, we have the following classification of the pupils of the public schools:—

```
Grade I.................................18,908
  "   II................................13,489
  "   III...............................12,184
  "   IV.................................12,672
  "   V..................................11,158
  "   VI.................................. 9,202
  "   VII................................. 9,409
  "   VIII................................ 6,489
        Total Common School Pupils...... ——  93,511
Grade IX................................2,922
  "   X..................................1,186
  "   XI................................. 460
  "   XII................................ 82
        Total High School Pupils........ ——  †4,650

        Total Public School Pupils............*98,161
```

These 4,650 high school pupils include 1,095 who are taking only a partial high school course.

Deducting from the general returns of pupils of high school grade, those returned as belonging to the County Academies, we find the number returned by teachers as of high school grade who are in attendance at the non-academic high schools and partial high schools. We must take this enumeration with some reserve, as the classification is based not upon the examination of a central board of examiners, but simply on the estimate of the teachers themselves throughout the country.

---

* The attention of Inspectors and Teachers is called to the discrepancy between the 98,161 of this table, the 93,710 of table V, and the 97,920 of table IV.

† Compare with sum of 15th column of table IX.

	General Returns, High School Students.	County Academic.	Non-Academic.
Grade IX	2,922	593	2,329
" X	1,186	423	763
" XI	460	303	157
" XII	82	52	30
Totals	4,650	1,371	3,279

All we can say for certain of these 3,279 non-academic high school pupils is, that they are all studying some high school subjects. From one column of this table we learn the additional fact, that of these 3,279 non-academic students 1,095 take only a partial course, which would leave the number outside of the County Academies taking full high school work at 2,184. Making due allowance for the discrepancies which we have noted, we are correct in sub-dividing into round numbers the pupils of the public schools as follows:—

```
Common Schools......... ........................93,500
Partial High School.... .... ..................... 1,100
Full High School......... ......... ............ 3,400
                Total ........................98,000
```

Analysis of High School Studies.—X to XIII.

Grade IX.

Here we find a general increase of between four and five hundred over last year.

Grade X.

Here there is a general decrease of between twenty and thirty, as compared with last year. But there is a decided increase in Latin.

Grade XI.

Here also there is a general decrease of between twenty and thirty, but as in the previous grade there is an increase in Latin.

Grade XII.

In this Grade there is a general increase of from twenty to thirty, while Latin, an optional, makes nearly the maximum increase.

Under this head I may mention, that the School Commissioners of Halifax, after a short and remarkably successful experience with this Grade, have nevertheless, after the present year, limited the high school work at the end of Grade XI. As the University of Dalhousie in its more elementary courses will cover the ground of Grade XII, the action of the Commissioners may be justifiable on economic grounds.

The number of high school students appears to have very largely increased on the whole as compared with former years, and even last year. This is no doubt due at least partly to the simplification of the High School Course of Study, and to the opportunity it gives students to prepare for the various colleges and other institutions in the same schools without following different courses of study as formerly, and to enter these institutions without undergoing special examinations. Further allusion to the High School Course of Study may be made when referring to the results of the Provincial Examination in table XXI.

AVERAGE SALARIES.—XIV AND XV.

To avoid the possibility of error on account of the fractional character of last year, it will be safer to draw comparisons with the figures of the last previous complete year which ended 31st October, 1892. As in the old tables classes A and B are taken together we must combine them in our present report for purposes of comparison.

Average annual salary, male " A " and " B " teachers 1892 . . . . $488 95
    "   "   "   "   "   1894 . . . . 521 01

                 Average increase . . . .$ 32 06

Average annual salary, female " A " teachers, 1892 . . . .$— — —
    "   "   "   "   1894 . . . . 652 00

Average annual salary, female " B " teachers, 1892 . . . .$295 77
    "   "   "   "   1894 . . . . 319 22

                 Average increase . . . .$ 23 45

Average annual salary, male " C " teachers, 1892 . . . .$255 45
    "   "   "   "   1894 . . . . 275 76

                 Average increase . . . .$ 20 31

Average annual salary, female " C " teachers, 1892 . . . .$224 24
    "   "   "   "   1894 . . . . 227 93

                 Average increase . . . .$ 3 69

Average annual salary, male " D " teachers, 1892 . . . .$180 05
    "   "   "   "   1894 . . . . 180 70

                 Average increase . . . .$ 0 65

Average annual salary, female " D " teachers, 1892 . . . .$158 43
    "   "   "   "   1894 . . . . 156 50

                 Average decrease . . . .$ 1 93

This comparison shows a decided and universal tendency to rise in the salaries of the better class of teachers. And it is a hopeful sign ; for otherwise we could not expect rapid improvement in the profession, as is pointed out in the report of Inspector MacIsaac. It is only in the very lowest class of teachers we find the tendency to accept lower salaries than formerly. Such teachers, while probably receiving as much as they are worth, by appealing to altogether false ideas of economy on the part of ignorant or unfaithful trustees, may have helped to throw out of the profession a teacher whom everyone would feel to be worth double the salary to the section had he been engaged.

AID TO POOR SECTIONS.—XVII. AND XVIII.

It will be seen from these tables that there is some diversity in the extra grants payable under the law to the different Counties. So far as the extra County Grant is concerned, the number of sections put on the "Poor List" is a matter for local municipal consideration alone. But when we come to the Provincial Grant, the putting of an extra section on the "Poor List" by a Board of School Commissioners is a tax put on the Provincial Grant of every teacher throughout the Province. This tax amounted to $3,647.31 last year. Boards of School Commissioners should therefore be careful that no section is put on this list unless there is a physical impossibility to have the section strengthened by union with another section, or by the consolidation of several sections into a fewer number by the revision of old boundaries. If this principle is not observed in any case, then a District Board of Commissioners is taxing, as the law now stands, every teacher in the Province on account of the selfish and unfair whim persisted in by a group of people entitled to no greater privileges than the rest of their countrymen.

COUNTY ACADEMIES —XIX.

During the year I have been able to visit all the County Academies, some of them more than once, with the single exception of Guysboro. This table gives so many details, covering so many points, that it is unnecessary, under the pressure of other departments of this report, to consider its suggestive points. These will be in order on a future occasion when the drift of some of the changes indicated may be more marked. High schools receiving no large grants such as are shown in a column on page 33 in this table, are now arising, some of them more fully equipped than many of the County Academies. This will eventually lead to a change in the mode of distributing the Academic grant, if not to its cessation altogether ; or else to an improvement in the poorer County Academies compatible with the provincial grant received. This grant is not merely a bonus given to the fortunate shire town section of a County for the purpose of reducing its local taxation for educational purposes. It must represent so much clear expenditure over and above the average expenditure of "non-academic" towns for education, in order to justify the system to the province at large. I am glad to say that in the majority of cases the "academic" towns do all that is here suggested and more. They are spontaneous leaders in the educational advance. Amherst Academy, elsewhere alluded to, was opened during the year with a luxurious accommodation compared with the best institutions a few years ago. Lunenburg has already commenced to lay the foundations of a building for its Academy and Common schools which will be an ornament to the town and a credit to the Province. Guysboro is also building anew, and Kentville is making an extensive addition to the Academy and Common school building in accordance with more modern ideas.

PROVINCIAL HIGH SCHOOL EXAMINATION.—XXI.

The Provincial High School Examination is another name for the old "Teacher's Examination." But with the same machinery it does more. It simplified the course of study by the assimilation of the old High School Course which had to be followed by the Academies on the pain of the loss of the Academic grant, with the syllabus of examination for teachers which had to be followed by the Academies on the pain of losing candidates for the teaching profession. It enables pupils in the same school to prepare for the different universities or other institutions requiring tests of scholarship, without adding a different course, or even an additional text-book to the course. A Provincial Examination was a necessity for the purpose of testing the scholarship of teachers. It is now opened for the admission of voluntary candidates from any school, or from private study, who would like to have a Provincial Certificate which can be used at home and abroad with a prestige which exempts the holder from examinations otherwise necessary. The system, therefore, has tended not only to the simplification of courses of study in the High schools, but to the reduction of the number of different examinations.

With respect to the value of the form of the certificate for the admission of students to colleges or universities of various standards of entrance, it may be explained, to clear away any misapprehensions, that the value of each of the candidates' examination papers is given on the document. A university may require a "pass" of 50 per cent., or 60 per cent., or 70 per cent., say, on the Latin of the course, or on any other subject. A candidate may fail in taking a "High School" Certificate at all; but yet his marks on the certificate "of his examination" may show sufficiently high marks on the *required* subjects to admit the candidate to college without any further examination. Each college may have a different standard of entrance, but the single Provincial Examination Certificate will do equally for each institution, as it will show whether the candidate has attained the proficiency required by its particular standard, as can be ascertained from the marks on the certificate and the examination papers which are always published.

That the institution in its present form is very popular, appears from the large increase in the number of candidates at the last examination. From the 1,506 of 1893 the number went up to 1922 in 1894, being an increase of 416, over 27 per cent.

Although, as Inspector Maclellan has pointed out in his report, the course of study evolved by the leading teachers of experience in the province, and subjected year after year to criticism, committees, and modifications at the Provincial Educational Conventions, can easily be carried out by the pupil of average ability under a teacher who understands his vocation, it should be expected that under certain conditions some pupils must have a painful experience. This thought leads to a consideration of the difficulties incident to all courses of study and the examinations upon them, which are a species of commentory upon the curricula as well as a test of proficiency in the candidates.

EXAMINATIONS IN GENERAL.

1. As testing the proficiency of a candidate. The *oral* examination is defective, because no single man or body of men can ask the same questions of each candidate coming up at any examination, without consciously or unconsciously changing the standard of value in a few hours. If the examiner becomes conscious of his drift he cannot review the earlier examinations to compare them with the later ones. It is defective on account of the time taken up. It is defective, because if the standard of one examiner is liable to vary, the standard and questions of the other independent oral examiners would have equally unmeasurable rates of variation. It is defective, as a great portion of the business of the world is done in written language, and many who would be at home in writing would be nervous and less collected in the hurry and "immediate presence" of an oral examination. The *written* examination is defective because the questions asked may be just those the candidate can or cannot answer. Another set of questions might result in a higher or lower mark. Of course these objections lie with still greater force against *oral* examinations, where the questions are likely to be given with even less careful consideration.

The estimate of a teacher who does not examine his students, would be a mass of prepossessions and prejudices, even were he (1) honest, and (2) possessed of the appropriate idea of proficiency.

The estimate of a teacher who is always examining his students while teaching them, and is constantly, as it were, posting up to date their several abilities in his mind, is the *best* estimate of all, providing (1) the number of his students is small so that he is always in touch with the mental development of each, (2) that he is honest and not subject to the tempting influence of the gain or loss of a grant of money, or of the applause or criticism of the world, and (3) that he has the proper conception of the standard required.

But even could we obtain an abundance of such teachers, the process of examination would be a long and expensive one. What then are we to do in the meantime? Simply what is practicable. The impossible must in the meantime be left in the region of speculation for the possible.

The written examination is therefore, in the High School grades, the fairest to all and the least open to criticism under present conditions. Even were an infallible divining process discovered which would instantaneously estimate every element of virtue in a candidate's personality and express the result in a percentage, those just below the line would be as discontented as ever, and in addition to their present advantage in tormenting the compiling authorities, they could cry out "produce my work in detail with the value for each item, to prove there has been no error not mine, no point overlooked, and I shall submit." But no record can be produced, and therefore no silence can be expected, even by the infallible process.

Now, the candidate knows that there is a concession made to one-sided humanity. His minor subject at 25 per cent. will not "pluck" him if his major stands at 75. If he falls a fraction of a point below the minimum, he feels he cannot ask for another examination, for by the same argument, were he a fraction above, he should be re-examined to see if he should not have really fallen below. He knows that there must be a line—a mathematical one—drawn some where for the purpose of decision ; that there is a wide range above this limiting line for properly qualified candidates, and that when anyone approaches the limit he has only technical rights, to be decided by the technical line. The examination test is not a long continued, expensive, closely testing one ; but it is sufficient as a useful estimate. which is all there is any real necessity for.

2. Examinations are useful as commentaries on a syllabus or course of study. If examination questions are carefully drawn up with such a view, its directive influence as an interpretation of the object and more important features of a syllabus is enormous. So much is this so, that there is a danger of the examination papers becoming the real syllabus. This danger is not so serious if the examination questions are so prepared that they do not always fall in the same narrow locus which might be termed the "question curve of the examiner." As soon as this " question curve " of an examiner is discovered, then the crammers can offer promotions at comparatively cheap rates.

COMMON SCHOOL COURSE.

This course has been already referred to with its *five* general subjects, namely. 1. English. 2. Arithmetic. 3. Geography and History. 4. Writing, Drawing (and in the highest grades Book-keeping). 5. Observation lessons, and health-preserving exercises. The examinations for the promotion of pupils from one grade to another is not controlled by provincial regulations at all. All this it is deemed can be safely left to the local authorities, the board of trustees and the Principal of the schools and his staff. The special duty of the Principal under the authority of the Board, is the grading of the various schools so as to have the work equally divided among his staff The Provincial Course of Study printed in the Register, fixes only one element, the coördination of studies. That program of eight annual divisions may have to be cut into seven, six, five, four, or less divisions, according to the number of pupils and the consequent number of teachers employed in the section. The pupil in the rural common school with one teacher, in the village school with two, three, or four teachers, or in the town with five, six, seven, or eight teachers, has the same general work to do, and may take eight, nine, or ten years—more or less—to accomplish it. The rural teacher has a class of 40, and has it for eight years. The city teacher has a different class of 40 each one of the eight years. The rural teacher's class consists of pupils from Grade I to VIII. The town teacher has but one or two grades of pupils. The main difference is that the town teacher can give from four to eight times the personal attention to a given lesson that the rural teacher can. The town teacher can force the attention of every pupil to his work whether he is interested or not. The rural teacher can do little more than endeavor to inspire every pupil with the spirit of his work, but if the inspiration does not take place he can not get the time for prolonged attention to the delinquent. Of the two teachers, the rural teacher requires both more force and tact. Between these extremes we find every possible gradation in different sections. The essential point is that whatever teachers do, they should not go ahead say with the English and leave Mathematics behind in one section, and do the reverse in another section. Such used to be the state of affairs in the olden days, and in many private schools at the present day. And the effect of it is always to cause the loss of a term when the pupil goes to another school, to an academy or to a college. He is more advanced than necessary in one subject, and not sufficiently advanced in another to enter a certain class. An ideal school would be a teacher with only from *five to ten* pupils. But the expense rules this ideal to be an impracticability. We cannot afford to give to one teacher much less than 40 pupils, who must in some manner or other be taught together. The necessity for the class produces these two general evils of all modern schools. The genius must mark time with the average boy. The dunce and the invalid are likely to be spurred up sometimes rudely to keep step with the class. The genius is thus often retarded to become a careless, lazy, ordinary man. The invalid, on the other hand, may have his health still further injured. What then must be done? The only general rule that suggests itself, is " the best possible." If the teacher, who is in a position to understand the peculiarities of each such case, cannot apply the general rule, then the rule is likely to be left unapplied, or a teacher with sound judgment or good common sense must be secured.

PROMOTIONS IN THE COMMON SCHOOLS.

In the ungraded school promotions are made by the teacher, and are generally made without a special examination, as the teacher is always examining while teaching the pupils.

In graded schools various methods are being tested in different towns. The following different general methods have come to my knowledge :—1. The teacher recommends to the principal at the end of the term a certain number of pupils as having completed satisfactorily the work assigned to the department. 2. The teacher makes monthly estimates of the work of the pupils, and at the end of the term gives to the principal a list of the pupils in the order of merit based on the monthly estimates. The principal then grades up as many as will approximately balance the attendance in the various rooms, beginning at the head of list and going down in order. 3. The teacher in the department the candidates expect to enter, examines the pupils and reports to the principal 4. The principal with a staff of examiners (teachers) examines the pupils in the lower grades orally, in the higher partly orally and partly in writing. 5. The same, only the general average of the principal's examination is combined with the teacher's estimate. In some towns an average of 60 or 65 per cent. used to be required for a pass. In others, 65 per cent. for the lower grades; 60, 55, and 50 for the higher grades, where the course is more extensive. In some cases only very rough estimates are made instead. It sometimes appears to be useful to change methods for the simple benefit of the alterative effect.

THE HIGH SCHOOL COURSE OF STUDY.

The High School Course in its first three years contains the following subjects, to which the values set after them are assigned in the Provincial Examinations :—

Imperative for High School Certificate.
1. English .... 200 each year.
2. Mathematics 300   "
3. Science and Drawing................ 200   "
4. Geography and History............. 100

Optional. 5.

GRADES.	IX.	X.	XI.
Latin.	100	100	200
Greek.......................	....	100	200
French	100	100	100
German..............	....	100	100

The four groups in the imperative portion are assumed to be a valuable, if not necessary, equipment for all passing through the High schools, and besides form a minimum which those who cannot do more may be able to master. It is found, as a general rule, that all the abler students take one or more of the foreign languages, which are optional Latin very properly leads, and during this year advanced from 1468 students to 1538. French comes next, and also advanced from 763 to 819. Greek comes third, and advanced from 158 to 169. German comes last, and advanced from 51 to 55.

With respect to the pronunciation of Latin and Greek, I am able to say that the question appears to be definitely settled for us. If there is to be any compromise between the five leading modern pronunciations, it can only be on the so-called ancient Roman or phonetic method. Our classical honor-men going to Harvard or Johns Hopkins, for instance, acquire the phonetic pronunciation of Latin, and read Greek according to the accent. At the Dominion Educational Convention three years ago, at Montreal, after a discussion opened by a classical professor of McGill, a resolution was carried *nem. con.* in favour of this usage of the leading universities. The leading High Schools in Ontario and Nova Scotia were then, or have since fallen into line, as have also the leading universities of this Province. The matter is a small one ; but a remark in one of the Inspector's reports suggested the comment at this point.

Some of our able classical scholars would prefer to have classics substituted for one of the imperative subjects, so as to be able to do more classics from the start. But in some of the smaller High Schools

c

an advance of the classical work would discourage many from taking the classics, when the whole work has to be done by one or two teachers at the most. While a minimum "core" of subjects, with options as we now have it, is very convenient for the certification of teachers who must be acquainted with all the imperative subjects, a course with substitutions would also have its good points. Such questions will be some of the problems to be considered by committees of the Provincial Educational Association, which I trust may be revived within the next year.

In Grade XII., popularly better known as the fourth year of the High School Course, there is a bifurcation into a classical and scientific side, which, while narrowing the range of the old Grade A, may eventually lead to greater thoroughness in each. This course, while optional on the part of the Academies, really belongs to the first year of our Colleges, which in their lower classes do the work of High Schools elsewhere. The bifurcation of our course begins, then, at the door of our university. Specialists often express themselves in favor of earlier bifurcation ; but general educationists appear to be ready to postpone the time of specialization as long as possible.

PROMOTIONS IN THE HIGH SCHOOLS.

High School work is often undertaken by a teacher who has all the work of the Common school grades in addition. In pure High Schools all the work is done either by one teacher, or by two, or three, or four, or even more. Halifax County Academy, for example, has a staff of eight or nine teachers, and their work is confined to Grades IX., X., and XI., omitting Grade XII. work, which is now relegated to the University. But in some of the Academies an attempt is made to do the work of Grades IX., X., XI., and XII., when there are no more than two teachers, and in at least one case aid was given students up to Grade XII. with only one teacher. It is only fair to the trustees of these sections to say that they did not ask the teacher to do so much work, even although he was able to aid the few advanced students who were in earnest by very brief hints from time to time, or by work after hours. Such work is voluntarily undertaken by the teacher to oblige students who cannot afford to go from home to a larger institution. The spirit of such teachers is most noble and self-sacrificing. But it is just possible that there may be in some cases too much sacrifice —of both the teacher and the majority of the school. But if the local authorities are content, it would ill become the Provincial authorities to interfere. And if the local authorities are not content, it is unnecessary for the Provincial authorities to interfere, for such matters are under the control of the local board of trustees or school commissioners. Now the numerous varieties of High Schools lying between the extremes alluded to, show at a glance that no general grading by Provincial examinations alone can be elastic enough to enable each institution to do its best.

Therefore promotions from one class to another in our Academies and High Schools must continue to be done by the Principal and his staff, utilizing, whenever it may be a means of saving labor, the results of the Provincial examinations. In some schools the Provincial examinations may just suit and do suit for grading purposes, the aggregate of 400 being adopted as the pass. In other schools 375 may give the distribution of pupils required for each room. In some others a different figure. The qualifications of those who hold no certificate of examination will of course have to be estimated by the Principal and his staff under the arrangement made between the Principal and the trustees. The main function of the Provincial Course of Study is merely the co-ordination of the various subjects of study.

The large increase in the number of candidates coming up to the Provincial examinations is not due to any pressure put upon High Schools, not even on County Academies, in the way of winning money grants. The largest grant given to a County Academy can be drawn under the law without a single student in its Grades XII, XI, or X. But notwithstanding this absolute freedom from central pressure to do advanced work in the High Schools, (which is deemed desirable, if not necessary, in some countries boasting of the best system of education in the world), the spirit of both teachers and students has so far shown that no such stimulus is yet called for here. It is to be expected that many people will endeavor to utilize the advantages offered by the High Schools in their vicinity who were not born for such a sphere, as will be proven by the impossibility of their attaining even the average proficiency after the most agonizing efforts. One such person in an average class of fifty can most feelingly complain of over pressure. But what would be thought of a management which would cut down for this one the average course of the forty and nine, one half of whom had reason to complain that the work of the class was already too slow, and thus add a year or years of worse than lost time to those who are capable of doing the whole work rapidly? Indeed, if we should depart from the course adapted to the average, it would be better to have a course suited to the requirements of those rather more clever than the average. For otherwise the clever students will be retarded, and run nearly an inevitable risk of acquiring idle habits, which is one of the greatest dangers in our public school system where pupils are restrained by the necessity of forming classes. The demoralization of our men of genius is the worst fate that can befal our country. Once our brightest students fall into the habit of passing time away their promise of useful power disappears, and rarely can the evil done be undone. The other difficulty, that of having the course of study of a school rather too heavy for a minority, which minority will include, (1) those of dull intellects, (2) those of bright intellect, but with a defective elementary education, sometimes due to premature promotion, (3) those morally wayward, and (4) those of good intellect and morals but of delicate physical health,—this difficulty can often with tact be tided over without making a separate class, by the teacher's exempting them from the severer work of certain subjects during the first course, leaving the full exactions for a second. What these young students omit during a first course, must be completed in a second over the same ground. It is as impossible, of course, to create something out of nothing, as to make a dullard or an invalid, or a pupil prematurely promoted or too young, who can only do half work, rank at the end of the year as if he did all the work. Tact on the part of a wise and sympathetic teacher can help many to bear this kind of failure not only submissively but with benefit to themselves. Often the most useful people fail in some tests. In fact there was never a genius in the history of man who would not fail in some test which could be passed by others.

One word more. Students may be found who may over exert themselves in order to win distinction. Teachers may be tempted to unduly press students in order to win renown for the school at the Provincial tournament. Just what people do in the pursuit of wealth, position and glory in other departments. As has already been pointed out, the principle of payment of Government Grants according to the results of this examination is not in existence here. In this respect our system, unlike that elsewhere prevalent, puts no premium on such pressure. I have a suspicion though, that there are some places where it would be desirable that a little more pressure should be put on. Now, it is possible that instead of laying the blame of the extremely few cases of over exertion from the causes above stated on the ambitious instinct which has not been subjected to due and discreet control, some person may think only of the system which furnishes the opportunity to these trespassers, and thoughtlessly blurt out an ejaculatory condemnation of an institution which is most useful for many, and absolutely necessary for some purposes. Shall we follow the principle of annihilating every good thing which may possibly tempt some to excess, or shall we endeavor to train erratic instincts and thus allow virtue still to exist?

At present the results of examination are duly published in the *Journal of Education*, a separate and independent list for each station. The institutions preparing candidates for examination are thus masked in these lists, for it is well known that in many of our larger institutions students leave for their own homes at the close of classes and attend an examination station, sometimes at the opposite end of the Province from the institution in which they studied. There are some people who would like to see each school obtain credit for the successful candidates in these lists. This would make the lists very bulky ; and worse than that, it would intensify that rivalry which tends to unjustifiable pressure. Others might say, " Do not publish the results of these examinations at all." That would appear on the other hand to be an extreme measure, and rather humiliating if it is thought to be necessary in order to curb the selfish instinct producing over-pressure in sporadic cases only ; for such an evil can not be very extensive in this country under such a system as ours. In schools making the very highest records at the Provincial examinations very few complain of over-pressure ; and those who do are usually not of normal character and health, or are taking optional subjects in addition to the imperative ones for a certificate. But it is the pained member we are most conscious of ; and we should never rest contented while there is pain we can relieve.

But is it necessary to abolish the publication of results of examination for this purpose? There are some who would like it, but they are too sensitive to express the wish. Inspectors and trustees want to know the facts. Teachers and candidates want to have an idea of the general results as well as of their own figures. The plan we have hitherto followed takes a middle course. It does not advertise the schools directly; although each school can collect its own statistics and publish them if it chooses. But it serves as a very convenient and authentic public record for all such as may have occasion for its use.

The following is a summary of the leading figures of the table :—

	1893.	1894.
No. of Candidates	1,506	1,922
No. received Grade applied for	598	760
" lower Grade than applied for	317	342
" Grade A	10	30
" " B	157	182
" " C	289	337
" " D	459	543
Total High School Certificates won	915	1,092

HISTORY OF OUR PUBLIC SCHOOL COURSE OF STUDY.

The first draft was presented at the request of Dr. Allison, then Superintendent of Education, and discussed at the Provincial Educational Association held in Truro on the 14th and 15th of July, 1880 (see Ed. Rep., 1880, XIII.—XV.). It was then referred to a committee for further consideration in order to be presented at the Provincial Association of 1881. The Common School Course after it left this Association, was presented by the Superintendent of Education to the Council of Public Instruction, which body referred it for special consideration to a committee of the Council and the Superintendent, the chairman of which was the late Right Honorable Sir John S D. Thompson.

The Course as it left this committee and the Council was published with comments in the Educational Report of 1881, pages XIII. to XXI. At the Provincial Educational Association of 1882 the committee on the Course of Study presented a detailed draft for the High Schools, which after discussion was remitted for further consideration of details to a new committee to report next year (see Ed. Rep., 1882, XXXV.).

At the Association of 1883 (See Ed. Rep., 1883, XVII.—XX.), after further discussion and modification, the Course was prepared for submission to the Council. In the Education Report of 1884, page XXVI., the Superintendent of Education discusses the Course of Study of 1881 in connection with the syllabus of examination of teachers and the text-books prescribed. In the Report of 1885, previously mentioned, pages XIV. to XXIX. are taken up with the presentation of the complete Common School and High School Courses in the general form in which they exist to-day.

In succeeding years such modifications as further experience suggested were made, and finally the assimilation of the teachers' scholarship examination and the High School Course was outlined in connection with other simplifications in 1892, (see Ed. Rep., 1892, pages XVII. to XX.). The minor adjustments made since that date have all been in the direction of lessening the tendency to unnecessary memory work as elsewhere specified.

MINIMUM PROFESSIONAL QUALIFICATION EXAMINATION OF TEACHERS.

Candidates for the teaching profession who do not elect to attend the Normal School, present themselves for examination on Teaching, School Law and Management, and Hygiene and Temperance. Those making as high as $33\frac{1}{3}$ per cent. but lower than 50 per cent. on each, receive certificates of the *third* rank. Those making from 50 to $66\frac{2}{3}$ per cent., receive a certificate of the *second* rank. Those making $66\frac{2}{3}$ per cent. or over, receive a *first* rank. These certificates rank one degree lower than the Provincial Normal School certificates in qualifying for a license. In many High Schools and Academies, lectures are given on the subjects required for this examination. To this extent many institutions play the role of a Normal School one degree lower than the Provincial institution.

Could a form of examination be discovered which would conveniently and with sufficient accuracy measure the subtle qualities which determine the value of a teacher, this examination might sometime evolve into the test of a system of elementary local training schools. If this could be done—if "a uniform government examination can test" the qualifications of a teacher, then we might easily solve the problem formulated in the report of the Supervisor of the Halifax Schools (Appendix, page 120). A government examination can approximately test the scholarship and educational theories of a teacher; but the difficulty comes in when the practical value of the teacher is to be tested. The only way the government attempts to do this now is by the establishment of a Provincial Normal School, with a staff of experts whose duty it is not only to train but to examine continuously and certificate in the theory and practice of education candidates for the teaching profession. Here is a government examining board already. This board now accepts, without question or examination, the advanced scholarship and mental maturity which graduation from our Provincial Universities implies, as equivalent to the greater part of the most advanced Normal School course. Examination as well as training has always been a function of this institution. It is true that the exclusion of the Normal School students from practice in the public school of Truro, may tend to reduce the Truro institution ultimately to the position of only a branch of the future provincial system, yet before making any change, we should have, at least, a substantial guarantee that some other headquarters would permanently continue to offer better facilities. There is no doubt that the great question in every educational system is the teacher. Normal School training of the proper kind will do one side of the work. But we must also have, as already intimated, strong school sections to justify the entrance of teachers of ability into the profession in the rural districts.

SUMMARY OF M. P. Q. EXAMINATIONS, 1894.

STATION.	Total.	RANK OF CANDIDATES.			
		First.	Second.	Third.	Failed.
Amherst	5	2	2	1	0
Annapolis	11	0	5	4	2
Antigonish	15	0	6	8	1
Arichat	7	0	2	3	2
Baddeck	12	0	4	8	0
Barrington	6	0	4	2	0
Bridgetown	23	0	17	5	1
Cheticamp	2	0	0	1	1
Clare	13	0	1	8	4
Digby	10	1	7	2	0
Guysboro	6	1	3	2	0
Halifax	26	7	18	1	0
Kentville	7	3	2	2	0
Liverpool	12	1	6	5	0
Lockeport	2	0	2	0	0
Lunenburg	23	0	11	12	0
Margaree Forks	3	0	0	0	3
New Glasgow	17	3	7	6	1
Parrsboro	8	0	7	1	0
Pictou	22	3	12	6	1
Port Hawkesbury	2	0	0	2	0
Port Hood	11	1	4	6	0
Shelburne	2	1	1	0	0
Sherbrooke	4	0	4	0	0
Springhill	4	0	2	2	0
Sydney	25	2	4	15	4
Tatamagouche	18	3	7	8	0
Truro	21	2	13	6	0
Windsor	11	4	4	3	0
Yarmouth	6	0	3	3	0
	334	34	158	122	20

That is, from the whole Province, out of 334 Candidates,

34 took *First* rank,
158 "   *Second* "
122 "   *Third* "

and only 20 failed altogether.

Teachers' Licenses Granted.

School Year, 1893-4.

	Males.	Females.	Totals.
Class A (Classical.	6	2	8
" A (Scientific)	2	0	2
" B.	10	27	37
' C.	18	54	72
' D.	16	67	83
" D (Provisional)	10	38	48 ·
Totals	62	188	250

Compared with the Previous Year.

	1892-3.	1893-4.
Class A (Classical).	7	8
" A (Scientific)	2	2
" B.	28	37
' C.	44	72
' D	48	83
" D (Provisional)	89	48
	218	250

In order to obtain a License for teaching the candidate must present, (1) the evidence of scholarship prescribed ; (2) the evidence of professional qualification prescribed ; and (3) the age and character prescribed. The form of the latter certificate is as follows :—

I, The undersigned, after due inquiry and a sufficient knowledge of the Character of the above named Candidate for a Teacher's License, do hereby certify.

1. That I believe the said Candidate........................ (name in full) is at date..........189....of the full age of........ (to be written out) years.

2. That I believe the moral character of the said Candidate is good, and such as to justify the Council of Public Instruction in assuming that the said Candidate will be disposed as a Teacher " to inculcate by precept and example a respect for religion and the principles of Christian morality, and the highest regard to truth, justice, love of country, loyalty, humanity, benevolence, sobriety, industry, frugality, chastity, temperance, and all other virtues.

.....................(Name and Title.)
.....................(Church or Parish.)
.....................(P. O. Address.)

(When this Certificate is signed by "two Justices of the Peace" instead of "a Minister of Religion" the word "I" should be changed by the pen into "we," and after the signature on the second line the words "Church or Parish" may be cancelled by a stroke of the pen.)

Cumberland County Academy and Public Schools of Amherst, 1893.

If our Clergy and Justices of the Peace do their duty well in this respect, the teaching profession will be composed of men and women who, even if they are not required to teach religion formally, will be themselves object lessons of due religious reverence and moral worth. And after all it is only the object lesson which the child can fully understand. He reads it without feeling it to be a lesson. It is assimilated into the texture of his life without the unpleasant flavor too often associated with a "task." The philosophy, the science, or the dogmatic principles of religion, pupils can in most cases more satisfactorily obtain from those specially qualified for that work.

SCHOOL BUILDINGS.

Following the chronological order of our most striking modern Public School buildings, the Pictou Academy, whose corner stone was laid on the 24th of May, 1880, appears this year as our frontispiece. The building is of brick trimmed with grey freestone, and is surrounded by ample grounds. It was designed for and is wholly devoted to academic work, the ordinary class-rooms being supplemented by laboratories, museum with collections of no inconsiderable completeness, magnitude and variety, library, special class-rooms and convocation hall. It is in many respects the best equipped building for academic work in the Province.

On another page is represented a building of another type. The Amherst Academy and Common School building is a grand structure of brick trimmed with brown freestone, designed to accommodate all the Public schools of Amherst. This it does in the most satisfactory manner, excelling in some respects all previous buildings, especially in the system of heating and ventilation, and the arrangements for the accommodation of pupils in the halls and cloak rooms. The Academic department is supplemented by laboratory, library, the commencement of a museum, and a convocation hall, all in keeping with the well finished character of the building. I had the pleasure of being present at the formal opening of this fine institution on the 4th of October 1893. Late in December following, I was present at the opening of the Wolfville public school, which although of wood, and not so large as that of Amherst, has an equally satisfactory system of thorough ventilation and heating. The superior High School building of New Glasgow, and the fine public school building of Parrsboro, and their inauguration, belong to the present year, and therefore must be referred to in my next report. The Lunenburg public school building is in the near future. Canso has also signalized its educational spirit by one of the best public school buildings in the eastern part of the Province.

RURAL SCHOOL BUILDINGS.

It is very desirable to assist trustees in building new school houses, by directing their attention to good plans. The greatest general defect is in the method of warming and ventilating the room in cold weather. It is possible that we may find at a cheap price a form of jacketed stove, drawing a supply of pure air from outside to be warmed

d

PART II.

STATISTICAL TABLES.

PUBLIC SCHOOLS, COUNTY ACADEMIES, ETC.

PART II.

STATISTICAL TABLES.

PUBLIC SCHOOLS, COUNTY ACADEMIES, ETC.

TABLE I.—SCHOOL SECTIONS, &c., (GENERAL).

Nova Scotia, Year ended July, 1894.

COUNTIES.	Total No. of School Sections.	No. of Sections without School any part of the year.	Total No. of Schools in Session during any part of year.	No. of Schools in Session 50 days or under.	Over 50 and up to 100 days.	Over 100 and up to 150 days.	Over 150 and up to 200 days.	Over 200 and under full year.	Full year of 217 days.	Average No. of days all schools were in session.	No. of Teachers.	No. of Licensed Assistants.	No. of Teachers holding Normal School Diploma.	No. of Pupils registered at School during year.	Proportion of Population (census of 1891) at School during year.	No. of School Libraries.	No. of School Scientific Collections.
Annapolis	107	7	119		3	5	10	56	45	205.6	122		25	4671	1 in 4.4	3	3
Antigonish	81	2	94	1	4	2	13	38	36	199.	97	2	7	3534	1 " 4.6	1	1
Cape Breton	132	23	157		6	1	20	56	56	198.5	157		22	6887	1 " 4.9	8	7
Colchester	122	6	143		3	10	18	93	19	194.2	147	1	67	6037	1 " 4.5	2	4
Cumberland	156	17	182		4	12	18	87	61	201.1	185	2	83	8624	1 " 4.3	3	7
Digby	80	4	100		2	6	8	52	31	203.3	103		14	4685	1 " 4.6	1	4
Guysboro	89	12	91		6	9	9	37	23	190.	94		13	3686	1 " 4.9	1	1
Halifax Cnty	131	19	145		7	15	15	57	42	205.	151		40	6600	1 " 5.		
Halifax City	1		129	1	1		18	115		200.	130	5	35	7412	1 " 4.3	2	40
Hants	99	7	122	3	4	5	8	69	34	202.5	126	1	38	5087	1 " 4.2	15	8
Inverness	176	1	170	5	16	14	38	42	58	173.	169		7	6095	1 " 4.3	9	
Kings	104	4	119	1	4	7	20	66	22	196.9	130		35	5235	1 " 4.7		2
Lunenburg	146	3	171	2	14	16	17	81	42	202.	180	2	34	7552	1 " 5.2		
Pictou	130	5	176		2	7	14	112	41	204.4	183		33	7283	1 " 4.9	2	2
Queens	47	10	56	1	1	1	3	39	12	208.	58		7	2023	1 " 4.3		2
Richmond	70	7	70		3	1	18	22	26	199.1	70		9	2928	1 " 6.5		
Shelburne	67		77		1	1	7	51	17	206.	77		4	3425	1 " 4.7		
Victoria	80		65			8	11	27	18	196.	66		4	2223	1 "		
Yarmouth	73	6	106	1	2	6	14	56	27	201.	106	1	22	4723	1 " 4.7	5	7
Total 1894	1891	136	2292	16	83	139	280	1157	617	199.2	2351	18	499	98710	1 in 4.5	55	91
" 1893	1904	196	2252	37	67	219	913	1016		152.7	2319	24	408	94899	1 " 4.7	89	96
Increase	13		40		16			141	617	46.5	32		91	3811	1 in 127		
Decrease		60		21		80	633					6				34	5

TABLE II.—TEACHERS EMPLOYED (CLASSIFICATION AND ANALYSIS).

Nova Scotia, Year ended July, 1894.

COUNTIES.	MALE.							FEMALE.							TOTAL.		
	Academic. A (cl. & sc.)	Academic. A (cl.)	Academic. A (sc.)	First-Class. B.	Second-Class. C.	Third Class. D.	Third (Prov.) D.	Academic. A (cl. & sc.)	Academic. A (cl.)	Academic. A (sc.)	First-Class. B.	Second-Class. C.	Third-Class. D.	Third (Prov.) D.	Males.	Females.	Total.
Annapolis		2		10	15	2	4				9	46	37	1	29	93	122
Antigonish		3		7	15	7	3				2	23	25	11	36	61	97
Cape Breton		3		21	23	16					6	42	40	3	66	91	157
Colchester		2		6	4	1	2				16	69	43	6	13	134	147
Cumberland		3		5	10	2	4				8	88	58	9	22	163	185
Digby		1		9	5	4	3				4	25	34	17	23	80	103
Guysboro		1		5	5	2					6	30	36	6	16	78	94
Halifax County		1			9	3			1		9	74	43	9	13	138	151
Halifax City		6		9	1						35	56	4	3	16	114	130
Hants		1		7	9	1					12	22	37		18	108	126
Inverness		2		16	33	49	1				11	55	47	2	100	69	169
Kings		2		14	12	3			1		8	64	31	14	31	99	130
Lunenburg		7		6	6	3					15	83	76		18	162	180
Picton		1		10	14	4					4	32	49	5	35	148	183
Queens		1		1	2	1						15	12	6	5	53	68
Richmond		2		9	11	13			1		5	38	15	1	34	36	70
Shelburne				2	7	2					1	10	20		13	64	77
Victoria		1		1	4	14							25		30	36	66
Yarmouth		3		11	4	4	1				11	40	28	5	23	83	106
Total 1894		44		149	199	131	18		4		162	888	658	98	541	1810	2351
" 1863		45		169	216	152	18		3		169	898	667		582	1737	2319
Increase		1							1				9	98	41	73	32
Decrease				20	17	21					7	10					

TABLE II.—TEACHERS EMPLOYED (CLASSIFICATION AND ANALYSIS.)—Continued.

Nova Scotia, Year ended July, 1894.

COUNTIES.	Licensed Assistants — Males.	Licensed Assistants — Females.	New Teachers.	Old Teachers, but new to Section.	Teachers continued in the same section as previous year.	No. whose total service as teacher was one year or under.	Over one and up to two years.	Over two and up to three years.	Over three and up to four years.	Over four and up to five years.	Over five and up to seven years.	Over seven and up to ten years.	Over ten and up to fifteen years.	Over fifteen and up to twenty years.	Over twenty years.
Annapolis			17	65	40	17	19	12	13	12	14	12	6	8	9
Antigonish	2		15	48	34	15	12	16	17	5	10	5	7	2	8
Cape Breton			11	65	81	11	18	16	24	12	17	13	20	14	12
Colchester			28	79	40	28	32	19	13	18	14	11	8	1	3
Cumberland		1	26	109	50	28	30	37	21	14	24	16	8	6	3
Digby		2	15	48	40	15	12	15	6	9	10	9	13	9	5
Guysboro			15	52	27	16	17	11	9	9	14	8	4	3	5
Halifax County			12	80	59	14	18	19	19	14	18	18	19	6	3
Halifax City		2	6		124	6	2	7	9	6	20	19	21	18	7
Hants		3	23	64	39	20	17	17	8	6	22	17	5	5	22
Inverness		1	16	109	44	18	18	25	19	18	12	20	20	16	2
Kings	2	1	5	89	36	12	19	21	22	12	13	15	5	5	14
Lunenburg			17	74	89	21	35	25	26	21	20	20	8	3	9
Pictou			2	102	79	23	35	29	12	14	16	17	9	8	5
Queens			9	17	32	9	6	8	9	7	3	8	3	2	6
Richmond		2	9	37	24	9	10	10	13	5	9	8	4	1	
Shelburne			10	40	27	9	15	7	12	6	12	4	2	5	5
Victoria			8	30	28	4	2	14	3	7	9	13	7	5	4
Yarmouth		1	11	33	62	24	10	12	3	10	6	15	17	4	3
Total 1894	4	14	255	1141	955	297	327	309	263	205	270	248	186	121	125
" 1893	6	18	288	910	1121	325	312	301	276	211	295	220	199	85	95
Increase				231			15	8				28		36	30
Decrease	2	4	33		166	28			13	6	25		13		

TABLE III.—TEACHERS EMPLOYED (ANALYSIS OF FIRST AND SECOND CLASSES).

Nova Scotia, Year ended July, 1894.

COUNTIES.	CLASSES A & B.—MALES.								CLASSES A & B.—FEMALES.							
	Service one year or under.	Over one and up to three years.	Over three and up to five years.	Over five and up to seven years.	Over seven and up to ten years.	Over ten and up to fifteen years.	Over fifteen and up to twenty years.	Over twenty years.	Service one year or under.	Over one and up to three years.	Over three and up to five years.	Over five and up to seven years.	Over seven and up to ten years.	Over ten and up to fifteen years.	Over fifteen and up to twenty years.	Over twenty years.
Annapolis		1	2	1				3		1		3	2	1		2
Antigonish			3	1				2			2		1			1
Cape Breton	1	2	4	1				5		1	3	3		3	1	
Colchester		2	2	1	1	2	2	1		6	2	2	3	3		
Cumberland	1			3	1		2	1	1				1	1		
Digby						2			1		3			9		
Guysboro					3					3	4	1	8		4	5
Halifax County			3		3					1	3	2			1	
Halifax City					2	1	3	5	2	2		5				
Hants			1	2		1		4					4	1	4	
Inverness	1	2	3	4		1	1	4		1	5	3	2	3	1	
Kings						1	3	3		5		3	1			
Lunenburg		1	3	2		1	1	3		3	3	2		1		
Pictou	2	3	5				2							3		
Queens												4			1	
Richmond	1			1	1	1	1						2		1	
Shelburne									2	3				2		
Victoria																
Yarmouth		3	3	1	1	3	1	2	2	3	4	2	2	2	1	
Total 1894	7	29	30	21	16	26	26	38	9	31	31	26	28	25	8	8
" 1893	10	33	36	24	16	35	26	34	11	35	44	23	24	24	4	7
Increase								4				3	4	1	4	1
Decrease	3	4	6	3		9			2	4	13					

TABLE III.—TEACHERS EMPLOYED, (ANALYSIS OF FIRST AND SECOND CLASSES.)—Continued.

Nova Scotia, Year ended July, 1894.

COUNTIES.	CLASS C.—MALES.								CLASS C.—FEMALES.							
	Service one year or under.	Over one and up to three years.	Over three and up to five y'rs.	Over five and up to seven years.	Over seven and up to ten y'rs.	Over ten and up to fifteen years.	Over fifteen and up to twenty years.	Over twenty years.	Service one year or under.	Over one and up to three years.	Over three and up to five y'rs.	Over five and up to seven years.	Over seven and up to ten y'rs.	Over ten and up to fifteen years.	Over fifteen and up to twenty years.	Over twenty years.
Annapolis	2	7		1	2	1		3	3	9	14	6	8	3	2	1
Antigonish	1	2	3	2	2		2	3	2	8	6	5	1	1	2	1
Cape Breton		2	8	1		4	5	2		10	8	6	7	7		2
Colchester	1	1		1	2	1			10	14	23	9	5	5	4	1
Cumberland		3	3	1		1			5	30	15	20	9	4	3	2
Digby		1			2	1			2	6	5	4	2	1	1	1
Guysboro		2							4	7	7	6	3			2
Halifax County	1	8	4	4	8	3	5	5	3	13	15	10	10	13	5	7
Halifax City	1	3	4	1	1	3	5	2	6	5	10	12	8	10	1	1
Hants	2	3		4					1	11	4	20	5	7	5	1
Inverness	1	3	4	1				5	4	2	15	4	7	3	2	
Kings	1	3	4		8		5	2	6	14	20	5	8	4		2
Lunenburg	2	3	1	3	1	3			4	16	17	12	14	1		2
Pictou	1	6	6	2				1	6	30	10	7	2	4		1
Queens									1	14	3	1	1	2		
Richmond		2	2			1			1	6	12	1	2	1		
Sel the	2	2	2	3	3			2	2	10	2	1	1	1	2	2
Victoria	1	1	3	2	1	2		3	3	2	3	1	1	1		1
Yarmouth	1	1	1		1	2	1		8	7	5	1	10		1	2
Total 1894	13	47	42	18	24	14	18	23	68	214	196	139	110	78	43	40
" 1893	25	63	39	20	17	20	16	16	99	222	176	147	100	83	38	33
Increase			3		7		2	7			20		10		5	7
Decrease	12	16		2		6			31	8		8		5		

TABLE IV.—ATTENDANCE, (QUARTERS).

Nova Scotia, Year ended July, 1894.

Counties	First Quarter — Total on register at end of quarter	First Quarter — Average daily attendance	First Quarter — Per cent. of pupils enrolled daily present on an average.	Second Quarter — Total on register at end of quarter	Second Quarter — No. attended during quarter	Second Quarter — Average daily attendance	Second Quarter — Per cent. attended daily present on an average.	Third Quarter — Total on register at end of quarter	Third Quarter — No. attended during quarter	Third Quarter — Average daily attendance	Third Quarter — Per cent. attended daily present on an average.	Fourth Quarter — Total on register at end of quarter	Fourth Quarter — No. attended during quarter	Fourth Quarter — Average daily attendance	Fourth Quarter — Per cent. attended daily present on an average.
Annapolis	3735	2538.6	70.7	4133	3819	2324.7	60.9	4272	3559	2308.1	64.9	4671	3763	2428.5	64.
Antigonish	2594	1530.8	53.2	3029	2774	1806.2	45.3	3236	2961	1602.5	54.3	3534	2896	1677	52.2
Cape Breton	5297	3368.3	63.6	6009	5541	3086.6	52.8	6273	5003	3150.6	62.9	6587	5686	3355.4	58.9
Colchester	4779	3346.6	70.	5321	4592	2885.3	57.9	5526	4458	2864.4	64.2	6037	4922	3294.7	66.9
Cumberland	6341	4277.	66.4	7355	6517	3736.	56.8	7495	6240	3901.2	62.	8308	6757	4265.	62.5
Digby	3339	2451.9	60.2	4010	3630	2094.1	57.5	4338	3655	2275.5	62.3	4485	3814	2467.4	64.7
Guysboro	2513	1596.5	64.5	3068	2871	1637.	55.6	3311	2867	1788.9	58.9	3886	3030	1810.5	58.7
Halifax County	5250	3760.	71.	5742	5267	3414.	64.	5942	5153	3553.	69.	6690	5559	3890.	70.
Halifax City	6371	4966.2	78.	7120	6370	4357.2	68.4	6725	6276	4746.6	76.5	7412	6737	5059.8	75.
Hants	4003	2796.8	69.8	4469	4078	2400.4	58.8	4619	3691	2375.6	64.4	5002	4195	2705.9	65.
Inverness	4028	2245.	55.7	4803	4392	2289.	52.3	5400	4627	2591.	56.	6085	4819	2534.	52.6
Kings	3681	2476.8	67.3	4640	4235	2517.7	59.4	4771	3894	2454.2	63.	5235	3768	3508.8	66.6
Lunenburg	5729	3880.8	67.7	6778	6240	3760.8	60.1	7062	6067	3833.4	63.2	7150	5781	3635.1	63.8
Pictou	5950	4202.6	69.4	6589	6173	3649.4	58.8	6789	5724	3716.4	64.6	7283	6162	4079.3	65.6
Queens	1001	1080.8	67.4	1811	1669	1046.4	63.9	1881	1740	1092.1	62.5	2013	1576	1076.3	68.3
Richmond	2187	1432.6	65.5	2466	2259	1256.4	55.6	2610	2171	1346.4	62.	2928	2495	1338.7	53.2
Shelburne	2746	1897.	69.	3138	2948	1837.	61.	3221	2765	1766.	63.	3407	2676	1826.	67.
Victoria	1526	898.	58.8	1899	1727	923.	53.4	1990	1655	974.	58.8	2223	1815	990.	54.5
Yarmouth	3841	2776.	71.	4320	4077	2602.	63.	4446	3915	2593.	63.	4534	3637	2460.	66.
Total 1894	75821	51622.3	68.	86700	79799	47183.2	59.1	89939	76121	48937.3	64.2	97920	80123	51492.4	64.2
" 1893				78121	78121	40987.2	63.8	84238	76928	49292.9	64.	93248	77773	48991.4	62.9
Increase				8579	1678			5701			.2	4672	2355	2501	1.3
Decrease						2704.	4.7		807	355.6					

TIME TABLE.—ATTENDANCE, (SEMI-ANNUAL AND ANNUAL).

Nova Scotia, Year ended July, 1894.

Counties	Days taught first half year	Days taught second half year	Total days' attendance first half year	Total days' attendance second half year	Under 5 years of age	Between 5 and 15 years	Over 15 years	Total annual enrolment	Boys	Girls	Total days' attendance for year	Days taught during year	Days present on an average during year	Average of quarterly percentage of attendance
Annapolis	12142.5	12326.	261284.	251570.	89	4129	453	4671	2417	2254	512834.	24468.5	2456.9	62.8
Antigonish	9143.	9520.	152729.5	174331.5	41	3294	199	3534	1961	1573	327061.	18963.	1560.5	51.2
Cape Breton	13163.	16014.5	342264.	345437.	87	6386	414	6887	3687	3200	687701.	31177.	3438.1	59.5
Colchester	13673.	14081.5	318063.	316111.	81	5425	531	6037	3121	2916	634174.	27754.5	3226.3	64.6
Cumberland	17934.5	18677.	425527.	429455.	107	7951	566	8624	4476	4148	854982.	36611.5	4132.	61.8
Digby	9879.	10455.	240397.	250178.	96	4187	402	4685	2406	2279	490575.	20334.	2409.9	62.3
Guysboro	9051.5	9074.	159986.	193722.	44	3373	269	3686	1977	1709	349708.	17125.5	1785.	57.1
Halifax County	13596.	14612.	390945.	418131.	151	6192	257	6600	3370	3221	808676.	28208.	3774.	68.
Halifax City	12560.	13292.	478155.	510420.	116	6905	391	7412	3726	3686	988575.5	25852.	4942.	75.
Hants	12264.5	12438.	274621.5	266057.5	109	4551	427	5087	2620	2467	540679.	24702.5	2609.8	64.5
Inverness	15339.	15994.	237566.	284332.	80	5426	589	6095	3592	2803	521598.	31333.	2505.	54.1
Kings	11603.	11827.	253107.5	251787.5	69	1490	676	5235	2742	2493	594895.	23430.	2530.7	54.1
Lunenburg	16872.5	17441.5	388765.	400865.	223	6873	456	7552	3915	3637	789630.	34314.	3890.	61.7
Pictou	17800.	18068.	409824.	412079.	53	639	591	7283	3842	3441	821903.	35868.	3960.5	64.6
Queens	5736.5	5907.5	115072.	115102.	16	1849	158	2023	1032	991	230174.	11644.	1033.1	63.6
Richmond	6599.	7343.	136352.	146240.	73	2683	172	2928	1595	1333	282592.	13942.	1368.	59.1
Shelburne	7995.	7964.	195108.	190916.	78	3099	248	3425	1816	1609	386024.	15963.	1827.	65.
Victoria	6171	6648.	94482.	105869.	34	2000	189	2223	1171	1052	200351.	12819.	983.	56.4
Yarmouth	10699.	10595.	276247.	262745.	84	4267	372	4723	2409	2314	538952.	21294.	2651.	65.
Total 1894	223922.	232281.5	5146416.	5325348.5	1631	89719	7360	98710	51584	47126	10471764.5	454503.5	51152.8	62.1
" 1893	119124.5	229051.5	2800799.5	4990577.5	1221	85990	7688	94899	49775	45124	7824166.	349020.5	50103.5	63.5
Increase	104097.5	4230.	2335616.5	334771.	410	3729		3811	1809	2002	2647508.5	106483.	1049.3	
Decrease							328							1.4

TABLE VI.—STATISTICS, (VARIOUS).

Nova Scotia, Year ended July, 1894.

COUNTIES.	20 days or less.	Over 20 and up to 50 days.	Over 50 and up to 100 days.	Over 100 and up to 150 days.	Over 150 and up to 200 days.	Over 200 days.	Belonging to this School Section.	From beyond limits of Section.	No. of children in the Section from 5 to 15 years of age.	No. of those who did not attend school at all during the year.	Deaf.	Blind.	No. of visits by Trustees and Secretary.	No. of visits by Inspector and school officials.	No. of visits by other visitors.	No. of Parents and visitors at Public Examination.	No. of prizes awarded.	Value of prizes awarded.
Annis	401	741	997	1089	1268	225	1469	202	4362	246	4	1	392	143	1926	736	71	$35 60
Antigonish	446	753	825	776	571	163	3197	337	2900	210	1		480	127	1292	323	35	17 05
Cape Breton	840	1193	1522	1524	151	257	6501	386	5367	606	7	2	997	256	1961	2237	120	166 25
Colchester	515	1001	1338	1382	1577	224	5715	322	5895	416	4		406	90	1831	891	184	71 15
land	964	1530	1807	1956	2039	328	8205	419	8546	595	6	2	560	291	2873	1725	77	42 15
Digby	446	723	1140	1098	1076	202	4578	107	4574	383	4	1	312	145	1576	538	149	34 00
(Guyaboro)	446	722	896	834	703	75	3510	176	3615	294			357	113	1754	598	54	22 25
Halifax County	485	1003	1225	1444	2105	338	6464	135	6644	567	4		472	313	2421	2161	267	122 90
Halifax City	315	676	830	1610	3532	399	7266	146	7505	146			277	574	84	1078	68	73 45
Ants	484	845	1117	1213	1336	207	1880	207	4798	369	2	2	409	261	2013	1218	143	45 80
Iness	995	1319	1491	1098	933	144	5501	84	5237	543			899	88	2865			
Kings	560	985	1335	1147	1120	88	1885	350	4663	374	2		470	218	1695	1424	65	32 08
Lunenburg	730	1276	1578	1696	1973	299	7380	172	7580	677	8		617	218	2907	2242	233	72 35
Pictou	567	1069	1650	1670	923	304	891	392	7116	466	1		675	268	3324	2170	238	210 25
Queens	144	325	377	439	532	156	1934	69	904	216	1		175	68	888	615	23	15 60
Richmond	378	656	449	569	632	144	2780	148	3048	411	5	1	535	133	1263	218	92	17 50
Shelburne	286	507	656	761	966	249	360	65	3344	234	4		304	100	1136	872	96	36 15
Ofia	304	486	604	468	317	44	1953	268	2041	183			380		660			
with	319	710	950	1103	1395	246	4620	103	4699	549	2		235	176	1880	1714	114	58 25
Total 1894	9625	16420	21027	21847	25699	4092	94111	4599	93938	7485	55	9	8952	3676	35479	20750	2029	$1072 78
" 1893	10531	19665	26553	30494	7656		90959	3940	84978	8166	70	10	8011	2865	26963	17312	1760	791 53
Increase					18043	4092	3152	659	8960				941	811	8516	3438	269	$281 25
Decrease	906	3245	5526	8647						681	15	1						

TABLE VII.—SECTION STATISTICS, (FINANCIAL).

Nova Scotia, Year ended July, 1894.

SECTION STATISTICS.

Counties.	Value of all School property, (ground, buildings, fixtures, &c.,) belonging to the Section.	Valuation of property in Section according to last Assessment Roll.	Total amount voted at last annual meeting for all School purposes.	Portion voted for building and repairs.	Total amount of Teachers' salaries paid during the year by Section, not including the Provincial Grant to Teachers.	No. of Volumes in Library (if any), belonging to School.	No. of Wall Maps, Globes and Charts.	Estimated value of all Scientific Apparatus and Collections.	Estimated value of total Literary and Scientific School Equipment.
Annapolis	$65,813 00	$4,486,763 00	$18,991 00	$4,159 00	$17,343 91	120	354	$297 50	$1265 70
Antigonish	24,723 00	1,643,892 00	9,284 00	1,411 00	8,522 82	2030	236	709 00	4276 75
Cape Breton	61,433 00	2,907,971 00	25,005 00	2,228 00	24,124 00	308	310	375 00	1511 60
Colchester	79,554 00	4,192,184 00	34,743 00	2,830 00	20,508 00	242	670	1271 00	2837 00
Cumberland	127,241 00	6,593,715 00	41,291 00	15,109 00	26,630 00	166	674	764 00	2483 00
Digby	43,049 00	2,109,288 00	13,839 00	4,247 00	14,556 00	66	249	210 00	881 25
Guysboro	38,770 00	1,253,761 50	12,811 00	683 00	10,062 00	170	214	91 00	414 85
Halifax County	94,776 00	3,659,534 00	32,009 50	9,517 90	20,876 78	57	511	220 50	1463 48
Halifax City	244,000 00	22,952,237 00	88,663 63	22,000 00	47,089 21	1548	410	1162 00	3094 00
Hants	68,735 00	4,556,330 00	20,105 00	3,863 00	18,802 00	52	455	146 00	1392 00
Inverness	31,060 00	1,246,892 00	13,644 00	2,295 00	17,146 00	......	261	25 00	818 00
Kings	74,497 00	5,139,621 00	18,983 00	5,300 00	17,915 00	108	463	251 00	1707 00
Lunenburg	63,412 00	4,289,870 00	15,292 00	26,392 00	15,690 00	7	457	92 50	1460 00
Pictou	135,342 00	4,682,622 00	52,740 00	26,401 00	26,198 00	1265	611	1760 00	5043 00
Queens	24,695 00	1,018,715 00	6,186 00	303 00	6,744 00	3	178	233 00	779 30
Richmond	12,588 00	741,582 00	6,507 00	990 00	7,000 50	102	170	60 00	551 50
Shelburne	46,021 00	1,442,299 00	11,071 00	1,582 00	10,696 00	49	365	100 00	1130 60
Victoria	17,005 00	520,169 00	7,033 00	1,427 00	7,915 00	......	101	57 09	291 00
Yarmouth	108,140 00	6,659,366 00	25,912 00	3,973 00	22,029 00	244	472	453 00	2149 65
Total 1894	$1,360,784 00	$80,096,411 50	$454,200 13	$134,710 90	$339,848 22	6537	7161	$8,277 50	$33,589 58
" 1893	1,032,890 42	73,848,513 00	413,448 85	95,687 09	279,355 00	4183	7108	6,577 65	28,728 36
Increase	$327,893 58	$6,247,898 50	$40,751 28	$39,023 81	$60,493 22	2354	53	$1,699 85	$4,861 22
Decrease									

TABLE VIII.—TIME TABLE.

Nova Scotia, Year ended July, 1894.

Average No. of Minutes per Week taken by Teacher during the Year in giving Instruction in the various Groups of Subjects specified below. (*For all Schools in each County.*)

Counties.	Calisthenics and Military Drill.	Vocal Music.	Hygiene and Temperance.	Moral and Patriotic Duties.	Object Lessons on Nature.	Spelling and Dictation.	Reading and Elocution.	English Composition, Gram., Lit.	Writing.	Book-keeping.	Geography.	History.	Drawing.	Arithmetic.
Annapolis	9.3	17.	37.	25.	30.5	150.	295.	118.	85.	30.	135.	106.	49.	291.
Antigonish	9.3	8.4	20.4	23.1	28.5	121.3	369.1	137.2	93.	31.9	96.7	73.3	22.3	344.3
Cape Breton	33.8	38.2	32.8	33.7	47.6	156.8	343.6	124.5	105.2	51.3	100.	89.3	62.	318.4
Colchester	16.9	34.8	36.8	27.6	32.1	174.7	329.6	112.3	75.9	32.1	112.	82.5	51.2	279.1
Cumberland	21.	32.	43.	26.	34.	163.	370.	116.	103.	52.	123.	92.	43.	316.
Digby	8.	17.	35.	29.	39.	166.	394.	93.	104.	14.	104.	72.	46.	315.
Guysboro	6.9	13.5	25.9	22.8	28.1	160.4	360.8	109.2	104.8	21.4	115.8	88.5	29.9	304.4
Halifax County	13.	20.	23.	21.	26.	165.	296.	115.	120.	14.	110.	110.	29.	318.
Halifax City	42.	48.	30.	31.	52.	116.	260.	105.	141.	41.	78.	82.	70.	305.
Hants	13.6	29.8	45.1	25.7	30.6	166.7	334.3	120.5	90.1	27.2	206.3	93.9	50.8	289.1
Inverness	11.	14.	24.	25.	18.	116.	223.	92.	95.	19.	82.	73.	18.	239.
Kings	7.2	17.2	44.3	20.3	30.7	166.5	351.8	119.4	34.3	82.9	139.4	97.1	48.1	262.
Lunenburg	8.2	26.1	30.	18.	29.3	212.9	399.2	92.	102.4	26.1	119.5	76.2	52.	312.
Pictou	8.1	15.6	25.8	20.7	25.5	176.1	333.2	113.9	103.	28.9	107.3	79.5	34.1	294.2
Queens	7.7	9.4	29.6	15.	49.3	141.	244.	89.5	99.6	30.	101.5	82.	37.4	230.
Richmond	29.2	37.6	38.2	33.1	45.9	125.5	296.	112.4	106.3	44.3	84.2	84.3	38.6	382.7
Shelburne	4.	13.	33.	22.	31.	182.	337.	112.	95.	16.	131.	101.	59.	306.
Victoria	12.	15.	26.	25.	31.	138.	236.	128.	105.	21.	95.	78.	31.	231.
Yarmouth	10.	19.	36.	21.	35.	173.	290.	106.	106.	21.	106.	78.	53.	309.
Total 1894	14.2	21.9	32.4	24.5	32.3	156.3	323.5	111.3	98.3	31.8	112.9	86.2	43.4	295.
" 1893	9.3	15.2	22.8	21.8	32.5	151.	311.9	108.1	100.3	30.	106.9	82.6	36.9	264.4
Increase	4.9	6.7	9.6	2.7		5.3	11.6	3.2		1.8	6.	3.6	6.5	30.6
Decrease					.2				2					

TABLE VIII.—TIME TABLE.—*Continued.*

Nova Scotia, Year ended July, 1894.

AVERAGE NO. OF MINUTES PER WEEK TAKEN BY TEACHER DURING THE YEAR IN GIVING INSTRUCTION IN THE VARIOUS GROUPS OF SUBJECTS SPECIFIED BELOW.

COUNTIES.	Practical Mathematics.	No. of Schools.	Algebra.	No. of Schools.	Geometry.	No. of Schools.	Botany, Zoology, Geology, etc.	No. of Schools.	Physiology.	No. of Schools.	Physics.	No. of Schools.	Chemistry.	No. of Schools.	Latin.	No. of Schools.	Greek.	No. of Schools.	French.	No. of Schools.	German.	No. of Schools.	Manual Training.	No. of Schools.
Annapolis	71.	15	104.	77	74.	6	38.	60	31.	23	43.	38	65.	30	90.	7	83.	3	68.	2			15.	1
Antigonish	266.7	3	166.5	4	81.1	38	47.6	21	60.5	9	62.2	13	161.7	3	972.5	2	570.	1	338.3	3			90.	2
Cape Breton	69.2	14	109.9	109	72.	65	29.	70	46.	32	57.	26	59.4	12	135.	5	77.5	1	100.	2	25.	2		
Colchester	39.	4	65.	82	56.5	66	32.6	89	31.	37	36.9	28	50.	13	91.5	5	430.	1	117.5	37				
Cumberland	86.	4	65.	37	48.	29	28.	27	18.	7	25.	20	39.	11	116.	3			243.	1				
Digby	63.	3	70.	16	64.	51	37.	13	41.	1	37.	4	37.	4	95.	1				6		37		
Guysboro	115.	1	223.5	1	133.6	1	54.9	1	88.5	10	61.3	11	129.	9	225.	1	176.	1	24.	2				
Halifax County	18.	2	46.	19	38.	10	12.	29	18.	21	24.	30	24.	23	24.	9	60.	8	155.		160.	3	73.	30
Halifax City	142.	17	70.	67	113.	63	34.	64	33.		82.		26.		190.				92.5		90.	1		
Hants	85.		80.5		68.8		35.5		27.9		31.4		51.7		77.5									
Inverness	61.6	10	88.9	70	79.	70	40.	62	79.	13	47.	34	69.8	16	96.7	6		2	36.5	2		2	30.	1
Kings	54.	17	92.2	62	66.2	35	53.5	29	40.	6	35.6	18	51.3	4	60.	1	70.	1		1				
Lunenburg	69.9	12	109.	102	74.	89	32.	67	40.	18	40.	24	77.	14	159.	8	33.	2	218.	2				
Pictou	54.	5	89.6	25	69.5	20	43.	17	30.	4	53.5	10	34.	7	60.	2	162.		120.					
Queens	40.		140.3	47	72.5	36	33.5	28	10.		35.2		60.		43.3				181.6					
Richmond	61.	4	88.		66.		25.		27.	8	29.	16	48.	10	79.	5	62.		62.	3				
Shelburne																								
Victoria																						2	30.	2
Yarmouth	66.	8	77.	60	63.	39	45.	30	27.	10	40.	16	40.	12	115.	4			273.	18	12.3		90.	1
Total 1894	80.	119	99.1	778	72.9	580	36.6	607	34.1	194	43.5	289	59.5	169	154.6	69	171.5	16	144.9	80	99.5	6	59.6	34
" 1893	72.1	112	85.3	678	70.8	634	39.1	524	37.7	228	42.7	173	62.4	129	143.6	75	142.	22	138.8	61	69.6	8	57.5	57
Increase	7.9	7	3.8	100	2.1			83			.8	116		40	11.		29.5		6.1	19	20.9		2.1	
Decrease						54	2.5		3.6	34			2.9			6		6				2		23

TABLE IX.—CLASSIFICATION OF PUPILS.

Nova Scotia, Year ended July, 1894.

No. of Pupils in each Grade according to Provincial Course of Study. — Grades IX to XII. — Transfers.

Counties	Kindergarten	Grade I	Grade II	Grade III	Grade IV	Grade V	Grade VI	Grade VII	Grade VIII	Grade IX	Grade X	Grade XI	Grade XII	No. holding Provincial Certificates	Total No. High School Pupils	No. High School Pupils taking full course	No. High School Pupils taking partial course	No. of Pupils transferred out of school	No. of Pupils transferred into school
Annapolis		679	534	445	512	556	438	526	485	314	131	49	1	29	495	330	165	5	12
Antigonish	60	598	699	381	516	382	363	359	231	155	36	45	25	30	143	140	3	20	20
Cape Breton		1538	980	826	807	665	695	642	385	223	86	16			325	235	90		
Colchester		824	702	688	779	721	573	814	554	210	92	52	3	70	321	287	34	12	26
Cumberland	10	1766	1309	1193	1078	1028	778	852	390	132	64	24		30	220	198	22		
Digby		943	684	580	665	544	470	384	275	105	39	14		3	158	97	61	78	83
Guysboro	19	655	544	518	436	495	356	376	170	71	43	3		30	101	86	15		
Halifax County	112	1270	830	860	989	869	679	610	252	94	35				129	129			
Halifax City	256	1787	977	891	970	654	643	500	364	176	99	71	24	16	370	311	59	793	746
Hants	13	774	583	598	615	571	462	669	462	244	76	18	3		341	226	115	5	14
Inverness		1375	924	799	815	726	461	442	276	139	27	9	1	10	37	37			
Kings	5	633	532	527	580	600	540	650	660	376	103	39		17	518	261	257	27	46
Lunenburg	26	1263	1029	1035	1065	984	778	990	368	136	42	15	15	96	161	118	43	84	84
Pictou		1031	988	798	859	736	728	276	665	215	174	57		15	461	387	74	96	96
Queens	18	330	276	249	253	175	192	244	121	74	13	20			94	62	32	3	3
Richmond		836	443	467	382	271	181	200	99	44	5			5	49	27	22		
Shelburne	2	532	468	488	441	433	288	353	277	124	32	10	8		160	121	39	3	3
Victoria		436	308	280	317	268	227	183	118	66	28	1	1	8	36	28	8		
Yarmouth	85	1033	699	561	593	480	386	339	387	134	61	17	6		207	151	56	101	98
Total 1894	605	18303	13489	12184	12672	11158	9202	9409	6489	2922	1186	460	82	349	4396	3231	1095	1227	1231
" 1893	898	17122	12515	11653	12283	10566	9296	9831	6361	2506	1206	497	37		3549	2601	921	1023	926
Increase		1181	974	531	389	592			128	416			45	349	777	630	174	204	305
Decrease	293						94	422			20	37							

TABLE X.—ANALYSIS OF HIGH SCHOOL STUDIES, (GRADE IX. OR D).

Nova Scotia, Year Ended July, 1894.

COUNTIES.	English.	Latin.	French.	History.	Geography.	Botany.	Physics.	Drawing.	Book-keeping.	Arithmetic.	Algebra.	Geometry.	Manual Training.	Total No. High School Pupils.	No. Pupils taking full regular course	No. taking partial or special course.
Annapolis	309	47	9	307	310	218	202	261	265	307	282	270	12	314	188	126
Antigonish	43	31	23	43	43	43	43	43	43	43	43	43		43	43	
Cape Breton	220	13	12	217	217	170	151	118	195	222	218	200		223	158	65
Colchester	171	101	76	172	172	156	127	156	170	173	172	166		193	146	47
Cumberland	122	53		122	122	122	122	122	119	124	125	125		130	122	8
Digby	104	6	7	100	104	79	83	92	93	105	92	87		105	54	51
Guysboro	62	10		56	56	51	55	19	37	59	55	56		71	59	12
Halifax Co.	86	44	50	84	84	48	51	77	77	86	84	84		94	74	20
Halifax City	169	165	3	167	167	170	165	170	169	170	170	170	9	170	163	7
Hants	208	26	19	224	234	151	142	188	205	242	209	199	7	247	122	125
Inverness	129	40	4	23		135	140	75	95	59	88	96		62		
Kings	368	38	12	356	363	271	208	252	340	372	305	218		372	189	183
Lunenburg	103	14		103	104	80	76	58	106	108	101	92		100	58	42
Pictou	212	72	76	186	199	179	161	188	194	200	195	209		218	174	44
Queens	45	8	10	48	52	33	29	38	51	53	43	41		54	31	23
Richmond	44	6	5	44	44	33	34	30	36	44	44	32		44	22	22
Shelburne	104	39	26	112	113	98	91	100	109	114	110	109		114	79	35
Victoria	22	12	4		22	22		20	22	22	22	21		20		
Yarmouth	129	17	33	127	129	100	101	120	125	129	126	124		129	90	39
Total, 1894	2650	742	373	2491	2535	2162	1991	2147	2451	2632	2484	2342	27	2703	1772	849
" 1893	2233	722	246	2123	2140	1757	1482	1682	2110	2219	2113	1956	49	2217	1519	698
Increase	417	20	127	368	395	405	499	465	341	413	371	386		486	253	151
Decrease													22			

TABLE XI.—ANALYSIS OF HIGH SCHOOL STUDIES, (GRADE X OR C).

Nova Scotia, Year Ended July, 1894.

Counties	English	Latin	Greek	French	German	History	Geography	Chemistry	Drawing	Book-keeping	Arithmetic	Algebra	Geometry	Manual Training	No. holding Prov. High School Certificates	Total No. High School Pupils	No. Pupils taking full regular course	No. taking partial or special course
Annapolis	130	29		3		120	120	105	115	125	130	130	127		3	131	95	36
Antigonish	41	31	7	57		41	41	41	41	41	41	41	41		19	41	40	1
Cape Breton	85	12	2	18		83	82	65	58	90	85	82	79			86	72	14
Col ... land	79	61	13	22		79	79	80	79	79	79	79	79		41	88	79	9
Digby	62	36				62	62	58	57	59	62	62	61		10	62	46	16
Guysboro	39	11		2		38	39	32	30	36	39	37	37		1	39	29	10
Halifax Co.	35	14				39	39	36	30	39	39	39	39		6	27	24	3
Halifax City	35	35		35	24	35	35	35	35	35	35	35	35	15		35	85	
Hants	90	55	18	67		90	90	85	90	82	90	90	90			90	68	5
Inverness	75	31	4	14		80	77	75	76	79	80	80	80			80		12
Kings	99	22			8	98	98	80	87	86	102	92	96	9	126	102	58	44
Lunenburg	41	13		7		41	41	35	41	41	41	41	41		9	45	44	1
Pictou	170	84	5	42		168	169	163	161	169	174	173	169		4	174	149	25
Queens	20	1				20	20	14	14	12	19	17	20		23	20	11	9
Richmond	5			5		5	5	5	5	5	5	5	5		15	5	5	
Shelburne	30	11	3			30	30	24	20	32	33	30	32			33	25	8
Victoria															2			
Yarmouth	55	15		19		54	54	40	45	49	52	53	49		2	55	38	17
Total, 1894	1055	461	52	261	32	1093	1091	973	982	1049	1106	1086	1080	24	261	1113	903	210
" 1893	1140	444	52	307	21	1139	1142	984	1008	1120	1160	1078	996	14		1142	926	216
Increase		17			11							8	84		261			
Decrease	45			46		46	51	11	26	71	54			10		29	23	6

TABLE XII.—ANALYSIS OF HIGH SCHOOL STUDIES (GRADE XI OR B).

Nova Scotia, Year ended July, 1894.

Counties	English	Latin	Greek	French	German	History	Physics	Algebra	Geometry	Prac. Mathematics	Physiology	Manual Training	No. holding Prov. High School Certificates	Total No. High School Pupils	No. Pupils taking full regular course	No. taking partial or special course
Annapolis	49	24	13	5		49	48	49	49	47	46		25	49	46	3
Antigonish	47	43		43		18	46	38	38	46			11	47	46	1
Cape Breton	16	7	4	1		16	6	15	15	10	10			16	5	11
Colchester	52	43	9	8		52	51	52	52	52	51		27	52	50	2
Cumberland	18	19				24	24	24	24	28	24		10	24	24	
Digby	14	5	2		1	14	14	14	14	14	14			14	14	
Guysboro	3					9	3	3	3	3	3		2	3	3	3
Halifax City	62	46	28	26	9	62	59	59	59	59	59			62	59	13
Halifax Co	14	6	3	2	1	14	12	14	14	14	11		7	14	14	2
Hants																
Inverness	36	23				35	37	36	36	35	33		6	38	25	
Kings	16	9	9	10		16	16	16	16	16	16	20	11	16	16	
Lunenburg	56	35	12	2		53	56	56	56	56	31		13	57	55	
Pictou	20	8		29		20	20	20	20	20	20		15	20	20	
Queens				13												
Richmond													2			
Shelburne	8	2				10	10	10	10	10	4	13		10	8	2
Victoria													3			
Yarmouth	16	8		10	6	16	17	17	17	16	1			17	16	1
Total, 1894	427	278	80	151	17	408	419	423	423	424	323	33	122	439	401	38
" 1893	468	272	88	194	27	454	442	435	437	413	219	6		469	407	62
Increase		6								11	104	27	122			
Decrease	41		8	43	10	46	23	12	14					30	6	24

2

TABLE XIII.—ANALYSIS OF HIGH SCHOOL STUDIES (GRADE XII OR A).

Nova Scotia, Year ended July, 1894.

Counties	English	Latin	Greek	French	German	History	Botany	Physics	Chemistry	Algebra	Geometry	Psychology	Sanitary Science	Zoology	Geology	Astronomy	Navigation	Trigonometry	Manual Training	No. holding Prov. High School Certificates	Total No. High School Pupils	No. of Pupils taking full regular course	No. taking partial or special course
Annapolis	1	1				1	1	1	1	1	1	1	1	1	1	1	1	1		1	1	1	1
Antigonish	12	12	4	10		4		8	10	2	3	12	8					5			12	11	
Cape Breton	3	3	3			3		3		3	3							3		3	3	3	
Colchester																							
Cumberland																							
Digby																							
Guysboro																							
Halifax County																							
Halifax City	22	21	18	4	2	22	4	16	14	15	21	22	22	4	2	6	4	16			24	22	2
Hants		3		3		3		3		3	3										3		3
Inverness																							
Kings																							
Lunenburg																							
Pictou	14	12	9	9		14	1	9	5	11	10	12	11			3		6		9	15	10	5
Queens																							
Richmond																							
Shelburne	3	3	3			3				3	3		3								3	3	
Victoria																							
Yarmouth	6	2		5	4	5	5		1	6	1	5		5		5		5		1	6	5	1
Total, 1894	61	57	37	31	6	55	11	41	31	44	45	54	45	10	4	16	5	36		14	67	55	12
" 1893	40	30	18	16	3	15	6	12	13	29	33	27	16	6	6	6	9	24			37	27	10
Increase	21	27	19	15	3	40	5	29	18	15	12	27	29	4		10		12		14	30	28	2
Decrease															2		4						

TABLE XIV.—AVERAGE SALARY OF MALE TEACHERS.

Nova Scotia, School Year ended July, 1894.

Counties.	Class A—(Male).			Class B—(Male).			Class C—(Male).			Class D—(Male).		
	Prov. Grant.	From Section.	Total.	Prov. Grant.	From Section.	Total.	Prov. Grant.	From Section.	Total.	Prov. Grant.	From Section.	Total.
Annapolis			$855 12	$111 88	$338 50	$450 38	$83 90	$208 06	$291 96	$55 94	$149 00	$204 94
Antigonish			750 00	111 88	229 29	341 17	83 90	138 00	221 90	55 94	112 40	168 34
Cape Breton			865 60	111 85	265 62	377 50	83 90	128 91	212 81	55 94	98 42	154 36
Colchester			900 00	111 88	493 33	605 21	83 90	126 65	210 55	55 94	120 00	175 94
Cumberland			836 78	111 88	394 00	505 88	83 90	170 80	254 70	55 94	196 25	252 19
Digby			750 00	111 88	334 44	446 32	83 90	193 24	277 14	55 94	183 75	239 69
Guysboro			750 00	111 88	337 00	448 88	83 91	151 80	235 70	55 94	81 40	137 34
Halifax County			1085 12	111 88	661 00	772 88	83 90	200 50	284 40	55 94	140 00	195 94
Halifax City			1081 00	111 88	338 57	450 45	83 90	410 00	493 90	55 94	115 00	170 94
Hants			1000 00	111 88	300 00	411 88	83 90	237 22	321 12	55 94	90 00	145 94
Inverness			750 00	111 88	261 90	373 78	83 90	200 00	283 90	55 94	128 33	184 27
Kings			850 00	111 88	250 83	362 71	83 90	185 33	269 23	55 94	113 75	169 69
Lunenburg			852 26	111 88	314 00	425 88	83 90	148 00	231 90	55 94	126 00	181 94
Pictou			788 37				83 90	184 75	268 65	55 94	130 00	185 94
Queens			750 00	111 88	250 00	361 88	83 90	175 00	258 90	55 94	105 69	161 63
Richmond			231 88	111 88	196 11	307 99	83 90	136 54	220 44	55 94	122 50	178 44
Shelburne			611 85	111 88	232 50	344 38	83 90	213 00	296 90	55 94	90 00	145 94
Victoria			750 00	111 88	290 00	401 88	83 90	160 00	243 90	55 94	143 20	199 14
Yarmouth			776 88	111 88	384 36	496 24	83 90	277 50	361 40			
Total, 1894			$801 89	$111 88	$326 19	$438 07	$83 90	$191 86	$275 76	$55 94	$124 76	$180 70
" 1893			675 85	83 19	264 86	348 05	62 39	142 88	205 27	41 59	110 58	152 17
Increase			$126 04	$28 69	$61 33	$90 02	$21 51	$48 98	$70 49	$14 35	$14 18	$28 53
Decrease												

XV.—AVERAGE SALARY OF FEMALE TEACHERS.

Nova Scotia, School Year ended July, 1894.

COUNTIES.	CLASS A—(FEMALE).			CLASS B—(FEMALE).			CLASS C—(FEMALE).			CLASS D—(FEMALE).		
	Prov. Grant.	From Section.	Total.	Prov. Grant.	From Section.	Total.	Prov. Grant.	From Section.	Total.	Prov. Grant.	From Section.	Total.
Annapolis				$111 88	$178 33	$290 21	$83 90	$126 79	$210 69	$55 94	$85 85	$144 79
Antigonish				111 88	135 00	246 88	83 90	116 55	200 45	55 94	90 73	146 67
Cape Breton				111 88	211 67	323 55	83 90	158 26	242 16	55 94	92 70	148 64
Colchester				111 88	228 57	340 45	83 90	149 87	233 77	55 94	91 16	147 10
Cumberland				111 88	183 77	295 65	83 90	145 21	229 11	55 94	103 02	158 96
Digby				111 88	138 75	250 63	83 90	121 76	205 66	55 94	109 05	164 99
Guysboro				111 88	215 83	327 71	83 90	140 40	224 30	55 94	97 28	153 22
Halifax County				111 88	174 50	296 38	83 90	154 50	238 40	55 94	94 00	149 94
Halifax City			$800 00	111 88	369 12	481 00	83 90	231 10	315 00	55 94	201 06	257 00
Hants				111 88	193 75	305 63	83 90	180 32	284 22	55 94	105 38	161 32
Inverness				111 88	280 00	391 88	83 90	150 00	233 90	55 94	80 00	135 94
Kings				111 88	223 00	334 88	83 90	131 24	215 14	55 94	95 64	151 58
Lunenburg				111 88	162 14	273 94	83 90	129 47	213 37	55 94	100 34	156 28
Pictou			505 00	111 88	181 25	293 13	83 90	125 50	209 40	55 94	94 50	150 44
Queens				111 88	185 00	296 80	83 90	84 20	168 10	55 94	87 44	143 38
Richmond							83 90	125 25	209 15	55 94	86 14	142 08
Shelburne				111 88	172 00	243 88	83 90	135 00	218 90	55 94	87 38	143 32
Victoria				111 88	290 00	401 88	83 90	161 00	244 90	55 94	90 00	145 94
Yarmouth				111 88	209 54	321 42	83 90	170 25	254 15	55 94	116 00	171 94
Total, 1894			$652 50	$111 88	$207 34	$319 22	$83 90	$144 03	$227 93	$55 94	$100 56	$156 50
" 1893			564 49	83 19	156 45	239 64	62 39	116 58	178 07	41 59	80 29	121 88
Increase			$87 01	$28 69	$50 89	$70 58	$21 51	$27 45	$48 98	$14 35	$20 27	$34 62
Decrease												

TABLE XVI.

APPORTIONMENT OF COUNTY FUND TO TRUSTEES FOR YEAR ENDED JULY, 1894.

MUNICI-PALITIES.	Grand total days' attendance made by all the pupils.	On account of Teachers employed.	On account of average attendance of Pupils.	On account of Pupils attending Halifax School for Blind.	On account of Pupils attending Deaf and Dumb Institution, Halifax.	Total amount appropriated.	Amount per Pupil in attendance the Full Term.
Annapolis ..	512,854	$ 2,849 49	$2,833 55	....	$120 00	$ 5,806 04	$1 26
Antigonish..	327,061	2,249 49	2,486 61	$ 37 50	60 00	4,833 60	1 61
Cape Breton.	687,701	3,679 00	6,378 77	....	240 00	10,297 77	1 96
Colchester ..	634,174	2,972 06	2,925 46	300 00	420 00	6,617 52	1 22
Cumberland.	854,982	4,543 57	5,635 06	....	180 00	10,358 63	1 20
Digby	295,818	1,574 06	1,806 94	44 37	106 50	3,531 87	1 32
Clare	194,757	976 91	1,356 06	30 63	73 50	2,437 10	1 53
Guysboro ...	261,298	1,508 98	2,202 89	112 52	45 01	3,869 40	1 80
St. Mary's ..	88,410	521 47	715 16	37 48	14 09	1,289 10	1 75
Halifax Co..	808,676	2,912 21	5,077 79	....	300 00	8,290 00	1 86
Hants, East.	235,752	1,406 57	1,638 41	....	59 02	3,104 00	1 48
" West	304,927	1,289 22	1,888 80	....	60 98	3,239 00	1 74
Inverness. ..	521,898	3,700 27	3,759 53	75 00	180 00	7,714 80	1 59
Kings	504,895	2,881 39	3,590 61	225 00	60 00	6,757 00	1 48
Lunenburg.	655,687	3,375 65	4,050 19	123 92	148 71	7,698 47	1 30
Chester.....	134,263	763 40	800 46	26 08	31 29	1,621 23	1 19
Pictou	821,903	4,257 73	5,675 27	375 00	60 00	10,368 00	1 48
Queens	230,174	1,475 10	1,707 36	....	....	3,182 46	1 49
Richmond ..	282,592	1,678 77	2,788 00	....	60 00	4,526 77	2 08
Shelburne .	201,095	1,020 53	1,150 47	....	155 50	2,326 50	1 24
Barrington..	184,929	854 40	1,232 50	....	144 50	2,231 40	1 56
Victoria	200,351	1,504 52	2,236 48	....	....	3,741 00	2 38
Yarmouth .	311,764	1,496 51	2,257 06	43 51	69 62	3,866 70	1 54
Argyle	227,228	1,038 11	1,679 02	31 49	50 38	2,799 00	1 57
Total, 1894..	9,473,189	$50,529 41	$65,875 45	$1,462 50	$2,640 00	$120,507 36	$1 57
" 1893..	7,085,436	38,126 23	48,200 88	956 25	2,340 00	89,623 36	1 16
Increase	2,387,753	$12,403 18	$17,674 57	$506 25	$300 00	$30,884 00	$0 41
Decrease....	....	....	....				....

TABLE XVII.

Special Government Aid to Poor Sections.

COUNTIES.	Paid by Government over and above the ordinary Grants, towards Salaries of Teachers employed in Poor Sections.		TOTAL.
	First Half Year.	Second Half Year.	
Annapolis	$134 92	$ 133 53	$268 45
Antigonish.............	118 01	119 04	237 05
Cape Breton	77 08	79 31	156 39
Colchester	140 81	132 28	273 09
Cumberland............	117 98	117 02	235 00
Digby	114 74	137 35	252 09
Guysboro	51 57	75 42	126 99
Halifax	99 96	121 65	221 61
Hants................	76 64	80 57	157 21
Inverness.............	107 47	128 94	236 41
Kings	132 41	140 83	273 24
Lunenburg	154 41	145 59	300 00
Pictou	97 86	103 59	201 45
Queens...............	102 63	109 93	212 56
Richmond	73 91	94 22	168 13
Shelburne.............	26 57	19 03	45 60
Victoria..............	75 24	67 84	143 08
Yarmouth	72 08	66 88	138 96
Total 1894........	$1774 29	$1873 02	$3647 31
" 1893........	892 10	1789 49	2681 59
Increase	$882 19	$83 53	$965 72
Decrease........			

TABLE XVIII.

POOR SECTIONS—SPECIAL COUNTY AID.

MUNICIPALITIES.	Number of these Sections having Schools.	Amount of County Assessment paid to these Schools over and above ordinary allowance.
Annapolis, County of..........	21	$219 82
Antigonish, "	16	173 33
Cape Breton, "	18	203 18
Colchester, "	22	239 95
Cumberland, "	17	190 67
Digby, District of	15	183 84
Clare, "	5	82 02
Guysboro, "	8	88 86
St. Mary's, "	2	30 34
Halifax, County of..........	17	201 20
Hants, District of, East......	11	107 86
" " West.....	8	126 59
Inverness, County of.......	19	215 76
Kings, "	24	290 17
Lunenburg and West Dublin, District of...............	18	195 45
Chester, District of..........	8	88 73
Pictou, County of	19	198 43
Queens, "	16	195 72
Richmond, "	14	180 56
Shelburne, District of	2	17 33
Barrington, "	3	41 55
Victoria, County of	9	140 33
Yarmouth, District of	8	72 24
Argyle, "	4	41 60
Total 1894............	304	$3525 63
" 1893............	290	2573 15
Increase	14	$952 48
Decrease...........	....	....

TABLE XIX.—COUNTY ACADEMIES.

Academy.	Instructors.	Class of License.	Annual Salary.	Department, or subjects taught, (subjects may be given briefly by Nos. 65 to 90, as in following table.)	Hours per day.
Annapolis	W. M. McVicar, A. M	A. cl.	$ 900 00	All subjects	5¼
Antigonish	Rev. Daniel A. Chisholm, D. D	B.	500 00	Nos. 87, 88	1
	Rev. Alex. Chisholm, D. D.	A. cl.	750 00	No. 86	4
	Rev. Alex. Thompson, D. D	A. cl.	750 00	Science and Higher Mathematics	4
	Hugh McPherson, B. A	A. cl.	750 00	English and Junior Mathematics	4
	Daniel MacNeil, B.A.	B.	300 00	Nos 74, 77, 82, 84, d.	4
	Sr. St. Margaret	B.	160 00	Junior English and Mathematics	4
Cape Breton	E. T. MacKeen	At cl.	950 00	Nos. 67, 68, 70, 71, 72, 75, 76, 83, 86, 90	5
	Frank J. Stewart, A. B	A. cl.	750 00	69, 74, 77, 78, 79, 80, 81, 82, 84, 85, 87, 88, 89.	5
Colchester	W. R. Campbell, B. A	A. cl.	1050 00	82, 85, 86, 87	4¾
	James Little	B.	975 00	78, 80, 81, 84	4½
	M. D. Henninson, A. B	A. cl.	750 00	72, 75, 76, 79	4½
	Josephine Upham	B.	500 00	65, 67, 71, 74, 77, 78	4¾
Cumberland	E. J. Lay	A. cl.	1290 00	71, 72, 76, 78, 79, 80, 81, 82, 83, 86	5
	A. S. Ford	B.	720 00	72, 74, 75, 77, 78, 80, 81, 84, 85	5
Digby	J. M. Longley, B. A	A. cl.	750 00	All subjects	4¾
Guysboro	Edmund B. Smith, B. A	A. cl.	750 00	Nos. 66 to 85	5

County	Teacher	Grade	Salary	Nos.	
Halifax	Howard Murray, B. A.	A. cl.	1800 00	Nos. 86, 87	4
	Kate Mackintosh, ...n, M. A.	A. cl.	800 00	67, 70, 71, 72, 73, 75, 76, 83	4
	Silvanus A.	A. cl.	1200 00	74, 77, 78, 79, 80, 81, 82, 84	4
	William T. Kennedy,	A. cl.	1250 00	71, 75, 76, 81, 85, 86	4
	Florence A.	B.	700 00	72, 74, 78, 80, 82, 84	4
	...her Von et Groeben		300 00	No. 89	4
	Kate F. Hill		250 00	77	2
	Jean V. ...on		400 00	88	4
	Nelson H. Gardner		500 00	90	4
Hants	John A. Smith, B. A.	A. cl.	1000 00	Nos. 65 to 90	4½
Inverness	D. S. ... Mosh, B.A.	A. cl.	750 00	" 67 to 88	5
Kings	Angus ... D...l	A. cl.	1000 00	" 74, 76, 78, 79, 80, 81, 83, 86, 88	4½
	E. Hart ...	A. cl.	700 00	" 71, 74, 75, 77, 82, 84, 85, 86, 87	4½
Lunenburg	B. McKittrick, B. A.	A. cl.	1000 00	All subjects	5
Pictou	Robt. McLellan	A. cl.	1200 00	Nos. 105, 106, 107	4
	Charles B. Rubinson, B.A	A. cl.	700 00	" 114, 115, 116, 117, 120, 124	4
	A. C. L. Oliver, B.A.	A. cl.	850 00	" 104, 109, 110	4
	Clarence L. Moore, B.A.	A. cl.	800 00	" 111, 112, 113, 118, 119, 121, 126	4
Queens	J. D. Sprague	A. cl.	750 00	" 67 to 88	5½
Shelburne	C. ...t ...ey Bruce	A. cl.	750 00	All subjects	5
Victoria	Thos. C. ...ly, B.A.	A. cl.	750 00	Nos. 65 to 88	4⅜
Yarmouth	A. ...n	A. cl.	1200 00	" 72, 75, 76, 79, 80, 81, 83, 84, 85, 89	5
	Antoinette Forbes, B.A.	A. cl.	900 00.	" 72, 74, 76, 77, 78, 82, 83, 84, 86	5
	Paul J. B. Kurtzer, B.A., B.Sc.		600 00	No. 88	1½
	Beatrice Tooker	B.	60 00	Nos. 72, 75, 76	1/16

TABLE XIX.—COUNTY ACADEMIES.—(Continued).

ACADEMY.	First Quarter 16 Total pupils on Reg. at end of quarter.	17 Average daily attendance.	18 Per cent. of pupils enrolled daily present on aver. age.	Second Quarter 19 Total pupils on Reg. at end of quarter.	20 No. attended during quarter.	21 Average daily attendance.	22 Per cent of those attended during quarter daily present on aver. age.	Third Quarter 23 Total pupils on Reg. at end of quarter.	24 No. attended during quarter.	25 Average daily attendance.	26 Per cent. attended during quarter daily present on an average.	Fourth Quarter 27 Total pupils on Reg. at end of quarter.	28 No. attended during quarter.	29 Average daily attendance.	30 Per cent. attended during quarter daily present on an average.	Half Year 31 Days open first half year.	32 Days open second half year.	33 Total days' attendance first half year.	34 Total days' attendance second half year.
Annapolis	37	31.5	85.2	39	38	24.6	64.7	39	32	23.9	74.7	39	29	21.5	74.1	102	103	2939	2340.5
Antigonish	116	90.2	77.7	136	133	110.7	83.2	139	131	110.6	84.6	141	110	95.9	87.1	104	108	9911	9961.5
Cape Breton	30	24.5	81.8	38	35	27.8	77.3	50	46	41.6	83.4	51	44	31.	70.5	99	103	2542	3772.
Colchester	178	140.2	81.7	195	188	133.8	69.8	202	185	149.1	80.6	206	180	137.	77.2	100	102	13874	14020.
Cumberland	66	54.5	82.2	74	72	50.4	70.	74	67	51.9	77.5	74	58	48.6	93.7	102	101	5352	5085.
Digby	22	14.2	64.5	24	21	15.9	75.7	25	20	15.4	78.	25	17	15.2	90.	107	101	1609.5	1683.5
Guysboro	36	26.1	72.5	36	35	23.7	67.7	38	36	28.5	78.9	40	38	27.	72.1	103	103	2560.5	2882.5
Halifax	271	242	89.3	276	267	219.8	82.3	280	240	205.8	85.7	280	230	194.8	84.7	97	101	22291	20263.
Hants	36	27.2	75.5	42	41	28.6	70.	42	33	27.	81.8	42	30	23.1	77.	101	108	2820.5	2741.
Inverness	29	17.8	61.4	35	34	23.4	68.8	35	32	25.6	80.1	37	32	26.7	83.4	104	103	2155	2589.5
Kings	65	62.5	80.7	72	67	49.4	73.7	72	62	49.3	79.5	75	35	38.5	69.8	101	102	5144.8	4492.5
Lunenburg	38	32.	84.3	42	36	31.1	86.4	48	40	34.2	85.5	49	38	33.2	87.4	98	103	3090	3475.
Pictou	165	129.9	78.4	189	179	126.4	69.	195	167	124.4	74.4	197	133	100.1	73.7	103	97	13180	11018.
Queens	32	29.1	90.9	32	31	25.9	83.5	32	27	22.3	82.6	32	36	21.5	97.7	104	108	2851.5	2365.
Shelburne	39	29.6	75.9	42	42	26.8	63.8	44	42	29.	69.	44	30	25.5	70.8	103	102.5	2914	2802.
Victoria	28	15.7	56.	36	35	22.2	63.4	38	36	26.7	74.2	38	35	19.	63.4	103	108	1984.5	2373.5
Yarmouth	48	41.6	86.7	48	47	36.5	77.6	49	41	31.5	76.3	49	35	29.7	81.9	87.5	101.5	3252	3004.
Total, 1894	1236	908.6	80.8	1356	1301	977.	75.	1402	1237	997.1	80.6	1419	1117	887.3	79.4	101.1	103.	98363	95428.5
" 1893	1236	908.6	80.8	1324	1324	1039.3	78.4	1365	1256	989.	78.8	1395	1091	839.9	77.	56.6	102.7	96741	93829.
Increase				32				37		8.1	1.8	24	26	47.4	2.4			99692	1599.5
Decrease					23	62.3	3.4		19							44.5			

TABLE XIX.—COUNTY ACADEMIES.—(Continued).

ACADEMY.	WHOLE YEAR.									No. on Register whose Attendance During the Year was						No. of Pupils on Register.		
	Between 5 and 15 years.	Over 15 years.	Total annual enrolment.	Boys.	Girls.	Total days' attendance for year.	Days taught during year.	Daily present on an average during year.	Average of quarterly percentages of attendance.	20 days or less.	Over 20 and up to 50 days.	Over 50 and up to 100 days.	Over 100 and up 150 days.	Over 150 and up to 200 days.	Over 200 days.	Belonging to this School Section.	From beyond limits of Section, but within County.	From beyond limits of the County.
	36	37	38	39	40	41	42	43	44	45	46	47	48	49	50	51	52	53
Annapolis	15	24	30	16	25	5179.5	205.	25.3	74.7	3	3	9	9	16	2	29	9	1
Antigonish	33	108	141	103	38	19772.5	212.	102.5	83.2	1	8	18	29	77	6	43	35	63
Cape Breton	13	38	51	37	14	6314.	202.	31.	78.	5	4	14	11	19	2	32	13	6
Colchester	75	131	206	83	123	28494.5	202.	141.1	77.3	1	12	27	47	113	2	125	66	15
Cumberland	38	36	74	26	48	10437.5	210.	51.4	78.3	3	5	12	14	40		50	24	
Digby	4	21	25	16	9	3193.	208.	15.2	77.	2	3	3	4	12		20	5	
Guysboro'	15	25	40	17	23	5443.	206.	26.4	72.8	6	2	3	13	20		35	3	2
Halifax	100	180	280	132	148	42554.	198.	214.9	85.5	1	8	31	49	186		211	47	22
Hants	15	27	42	18	24	5410.	204.	26.5	76.1	1	5	9	7	20		33	8	1
Inv'ss	14	23	37	18	19	4896.	207.	23.6	73.4		5	6	6	19	1	56	13	1
Kings	27	46	75	36	39	9637.	203.	47.4	75.9	4	10	12	21	31	1	56	18	1
Lunenburg	17	32	49	15	34	6565.	201.	32.7	85.9	15	4	6	6	26	3	36	12	25
Pictou	69	128	197	113	84	24206.5	200.	121.1	73.4	1	18	32	44	88	13	102	70	
Queens	5	27	32	7	25	5216.5	212.	24.6	88.6			8	3	9		20	11	
Sh'lb'ne	24	20	44	18	26	5716.	205½	27.8	69.9	2		8	13	20	1	39	4	3
Victoria	12	28	38	25	13	4342.	206.	21.1	20.9	1	4	9	12	10		27	8	
Yarmouth	17	32	49	16	33	6316.	189.	33.4	80.8		5	10	5	28	1	45	4	
Total, 1894	493	926	1419	696	723	193,692.5	204.	966.	78.9	46	99	215	293	734	32	926	350	143
" 1893	518	879	1397	682	715	152,561.	159.4	960.8	78.	47	153	284	669	244		930	342	125
Increase		47	22	14	8	41,131.5	44.6	5.2	.9					490	32		8	18
Decrease	25									1	54	69	376			4		

TABLE XIX.—COUNTY ACADEMIES.—(Continued).

AVERAGE No. OF MINUTES PER WEEK TAKEN BY TEACHER DURING THE YEAR IN GIVING INSTRUCTION IN THE VARIOUS GROUPS OF SUBJECTS SPECIFIED BELOW.

ACADEMY.	65 Calisthenics and Military Drill	66 Vocal Music	67 Hygiene and Temperance	68 Moral and Patriotic Duties	69 Object Lessons on Nature	70 Spelling and Dictation	71 Reading and Elocution	72 Eng. Composition, Gram., Lit., &c.	73 Writing	74 Book-keeping	75 Geography	76 History	77 Drawing	78 Arithmetic	79 Practical Mathematics	80 Algebra	81 Geometry	82 Botany, Zoology, Geology, &c.	83 Physiology, Psychology	84 Physics	85 Chemistry	86 Latin	87 Greek	88 French	89 German	90 Manual Training
Annapolis	15		40				40	150		60	80	80	80	80	50	150	150	30	30	40	80	200	100	120		
Antigonish		120	70	65		15	40	1200		103	140	230	170	360	360	540	600	55	258	360	360	1800	570	480		
Cape Breton	10		25	15	15	30	50	180		50	70	140	40	480	90	180	180	40		90	40	450	150	100	25	
Colchester	30		20	15	10	45	100	650		55	525	405	205	450	135	450	415	30	90	255	165	750	300	495		
Cumberland								400		120	120	200	120	300	90	200	280		90	90	120	270				
Digby		15	20	15		15		160		60	60	90	30	120	60	120	180	40	40	70	60	225		480	480	
Guysboro		25	95	15			20	200		40	150	150	60	100	100	100	150	50	25	70	75			25	90	
Halifax						10	80	865		210	210	430	255	470	85	455	595	188	110	120	102	970	530			1200
Hants		4	20	10		45	80	120		15	60	120	21	135	90	60	120	18	90	60	85	150	60			
Inverness			3	2			20	200		60	60	240	30	60	20	40	240	30	40	60	40	225	85	100		
Kings			15	5		10	135	560		25	120	135	120	180	100	180	180	83	135	141	81	60	80	375		
Lunenburg							60	240		40	130	450	90	180	120	160	250	50	25	35	75	630	195	120		
Pictou			15	15				690		95	50	90	40	275	50	650	625	25	135	178	210					
Queens			10			10	40	160		50	80	90	30	70		100	180	90	90	30	60	140		5		
Shelburne			21	25		4	25	160		30	90	58	89	138		88	240	50	30	33	103	60	45	360	120	70
Victoria	12					10		337		32							162	32				56				70
Yarmouth							43	425		150	135	175	150	215	240	185	310	250	85	110	60	270				
Total, 1894	4	10	21	11	1	11	45	394	20	70	129	188	92	209	108	218	285	68	77	115	101	378	124	160	42	70
" 1893	6	11	26	14	6	39	93	315		89	135	199	93	217	113	230	274	98	98	131	115	257	155	128	29	70
Increase								79	20								11					21		32	13	
Decrease	2	1	5	3	5	28	48			19	6	11	1	8	5	12		30	21	16	14		31			

TABLE XIX.—COUNTY ACADEMIES.—(Continued).

ANALYSIS OF HIGH SCHOOL STUDIES.

ACADEMY.	English IX	English X	English XI	English XII	English Total	Latin IX	Latin X	Latin XI	Latin XII	Latin Total	Greek IX	Greek XI	Greek XII	Greek Total	French IX	French X	French XI	French XII	French Total	German IX	German XI	German XII	German Total	History IX	History X	History XI	History XII	History Total
Annapolis	25	6	8		39	20	5	8		33			6	6	9	3	5		17					25	6	8		39
Antigonish	43	39	47	12	141	31	31	43	12	117	7		4	11	23	39	45		107			2	2	43	39	18	4	104
Cape Breton	31	16	4		51	9	5	4		18	1	3		4	11	8	1		20	1	1		2	31	16	4		51
Colchester	90	61	51	3	205	96	49	43		181	13	9	3	25	75	21	8		104		51		51	90	61	51	3	205
Cumberland	40	18	16		74	23	7	13		43														40	18	16		74
Digby	5	13	7		25	2	10	5		17		2		2		2			2					5	13	7		25
Guysboro	14	23	3		40																			14	23	3		40
Halifax	118	75	62	22	277	117	51	46	21	235	18	28	18	64		54	26	4	84	17	9	2	28	116	75	62	22	275
Hants	24	8	10		42	13	8	4		25		3		3	8	2			10				1	24	8	10		42
Inverness	18	14	4	1	37					5		3	1	4										17	14	4	1	36
Kings	29	22	21		72	21		19		39		7		7	15				20					29	22	21		72
Lunenburg	27	14	8		49	8	4	2		14					10				10					24	14	8		46
Pictou	60	84	35	14	193	48	28	28	8	109	1	8	9	17	15	24	15	9	63					60	82	32	14	188
Queens	12		20		32	8		8		16														12		29		32
Shelburne	27	10	4		41	15	2			17			1	1				5	4					27	10	6		43
Victoria	22	15			37	12	8	1		21					4				4					22	14			37
Yarmouth	23	13	8	5	49	14	4	6	1	25					21	10	6	5	42	5			7	23	13	8	5	49
Total, 1894	608	431	308	57	1404	383	248	233	51	915	40	63	41	144	182	161	135	28	508	18	65	6	89	602	428	278	50	1358
" 1893	581	463	309	34	1387	377	261	205	28	871	28	72	18	118	177	218	134	15	544	13	23	3	39	581	462	303	15	1361
Increase	27			23	17	6		28	23	44	12		23	26	5		1	13		5	42	3	50	21			35	
Decrease		32	1				13					9				57			36						34	25		3

TABLE XIX.—COUNTY ACADEMIES.—(Continued).

ANALYSIS OF HIGH SCHOOL STUDIES.

Academy.	Geography Grade IX.	Geography Grade X.	Geography Grade XI.	Geography Total.	Botany Grade IX.	Botany Grade XII.	Botany Total.	Physics Grade IX.	Physics Grade XI.	Physics Grade XII.	Physics Total.	Chemistry Grade X.	Chemistry Grade XII.	Chemistry Total.	Drawing Grade IX.	Drawing Grade X.	Drawing Grade XI.	Drawing Total.	Book-keeping Grade IX.	Book-keeping Grade X.	Book-keeping Total.
Annapolis	25	6	8	39	25		25	25		8	33	6		6	25	6		31	25	6	31
Antigonish	43	39	12	94	43		43	43	46	8	97	44	10	54	43	39		82	43	39	82
Cape Breton	31	16		47	31	16	47	31			31	16	1	17	31	16		47	31	20	51
Colchester	90	61	3	154	90	51	141	90	6	3	99	62		62	90	61		151	90	61	151
Cumberland	40	18		58	40		40	40	16		56	18		18	40	18		58	40	18	58
Digby	5	13	7	25	4		4	5	7		12	13		13	5	13		18	5	13	18
Guysboro	14	23	3	40	14		14	14	3		17	22		22	14	22		36	14	23	37
Halifax	116	75	62	253	119	4	123	117	59	16	192	70	14	84	119	75	17	211	118	67	185
Hants	24	8	10	42	24		24	24	10		34	8		8	24	8		32	24	8	32
Inverness	18	14	5	37	17	1	18	17	4	1	22	15		15	18	14		32	18	14	32
Kings	29	22	21	72	29		29	29	21		50	22		22	25	22		47	25	18	43
Lunenburg	24	14	8	46	24		24	24	8		32	14		14	27	14		41	27	14	41
Bu.	60	81	32	173	59	1	60	60	35	9	104	81	7	88	61	80		141	61	84	145
Queens	12		20	32	12		12	12	20		32	10		10	12			12	12		12
Shelburne	27	10	6	43	27		27	27	6		33	20		20	27	10		37	27	10	37
Victoria	22	14	1	37	17		17	22	1		23	13		13	20	13		33	22	15	37
Yarmouth	23	13	8	44	23	5	28	23	8		31	13		13	23	13		36	23	13	36
Total, 1894	603	427	206	1236	598	78	676	603	250	45	898	434	32	466	604	424	17	1045	605	423	1028
" 1893	581	462	231	1274	643	6	649	581	303	23	907	450	12	462	581	444	50	1075	581	465	1046
Increase	22					72	27	22		22			20	4	23				24		
Decrease		35	25	38	45				53		9	16				20	33	30		42	18

TABLE XIX.—COUNTY ACADEMIES.—(Continued).

ANALYSIS OF HIGH SCHOOL STUDIES.

ACADEMY.	ARITHMETIC.				ALGEBRA.					GEOMETRY.					Prac. Mathematics.	Physiology.	Psychology.	Sanitary Science.	Zoology.	Geology.	Astronomy.	Navigation.	Trigonometry.	Manual Training.
	Grade IX	Grade X	Grade XI	Total	Grade IX	Grade X	Grade XI	Grade XII	Total	Grade IX	Grade X	Grade XI	Grade XII	Total	Grade XI	Grade XI	Grade XII	Grade XII	Grade XII	Grade XII	Grade XII	Grade XII	Grade XII	Grade X
Annapolis	25	6	8	39	25	6	8		39	25	6	8		39	6	8						12	17	
Antigonish	43	39		82	43	39	38	2	122	43	39	41	3	126	46	20	12	8				4	5	
Cape Breton	31	16	4	51	31	16	4	3	51	31	16	4		51	4	4	2	12		2			3	
Colchester	90	61	54	205	90	61	51		205	90	61	51		205	50	51								
Cumberland	40	18	16	74	40	18	16		74	40	18	16		74	6	16						4	16	19
Digby	5	13	7	25	5	13			25		13	7		25	7	5						4	5	
Guysboro	14	23	3	40	14	23	3		40	14	22			40	8	3								
Halifax	119	75	59	253	119	75	59	15	268	119	75	59	21	274	59	62	22	22	4	2	6	4	16	
Hants	24	8	10	42	24	8	10		42	17	14	10	1	42	10	10	1							
Inverness	18	14		32	18	14	4		36	29	14	4		36	5	4								
Kings	29	22	21	72	29	22	21		72	27	22	21	1	72	21	21							6	
Lunenburg	27	14		49	27	14	8		48	61	14	8		49	8	8	12		5					
Pictou	61	85	34	180	61	85	35	11	192	61	83	35	10	189	35	31		11		1	3		6	
Queens	12		20	32	12		20		32	12		20		32	20	20	12							
She...	27	11	6	44	27	11	6		44	11	6		44		1	6	5		5			5	5	
Vic...	22	14	1	37	22	14	8	5	37	21	14	8		36	8	8								
Yarmouth	23	13	8	44	23	13	8		49	23	13	8		44	1									
Total, 1894	610	432	259	1301	606	432	299	37	1374	608	429	302	38	1377	305	277	54	53	9	3	14	24	57	19
" 1893	581	464	299	1344	581	461	309	27	1378	581	461	308	31	1381	309	302	26	15	6	33	6	31	45	39
Increase	29				25			10		27			7				28	38	3		8		12	
Decrease		32	40	43		29	10		4		32	6		4	4	25				30		7		20

TABLE XIX.—COUNTY ACADEMIES.—(Continued).

ACADEMY.	No. in each Grade Admitted by Provincial Certificate.					Total No. High School Pupils.					No. High School Pupils taking full regular course.					No. taking partial or special course.				
	Grade IX.	Grade X.	Grade XI.	Grade XII.	Total.	Grade IX.	Grade X.	Grade XI.	Grade XII.	Total.	Grade IX.	Grade X.	Grade XI.	Grade XII.	Total.	Grade IX.	Grade X.	Grade XI.	Grade XII.	Total.
Annapolis		1	4		5	25	6	8		39	25	6	8		39					
Antigonish		13	19	11	43	43	39	47	12	141	43	38	46	11	138		1	1	1	3
Cape Breton		1	4		5	31	16	4		51	31	16	4		51					
Colchester		38	27	3	68	90	62	51	3	206	90	61	50	3	204		1	1		2
Cumberland		17	16		33	40	18	16		74	39	17	16		72	1	1			2
Digby		4	2		6	5	13	7		25	5	13	7		25					
Guysboro		6	2		8	14	23	3		40	14	22	3		39		1			1
Halifax	1	65	37	23	126	119	75	62	24	280	115	75	59	22	271	4		3	2	9
Hants		3	7		10	24	8	10		42	24	8	10		42					
Inverness		3	3	1	7	18	14	4	1	37	18	14	4	1	37					
Kings		3	17		20	29	22	24		75	29	22	21		72			3		3
Lunenburg		8	8	9	17	27	14	8		49	24	14	8		46	3				3
Pictou		14	12		35	61	85	36	15	197	59	82	34	10	185	2	3	2	5	12
Queens			15		15	12	11			32	12	10			32					
Shelburne		1			5	20	14	1		44	27	12	4		41				1	3
Victoria		5	4	1		23	13	8	5	36	15	13			28			5		8
Yarmouth		7	7	5	19	23	13	8	5	49	23		8	5	49					
Total, 1894	2	189	184	53	428	608	433	315	61	1417	503	423	303	52	1371	15	10	12	9	46
" 1893	1	32	89	12	134	580	466	313	35	1394	573	451	303	28	1355	7	15	10	7	39
Increase	1	157	95	41	294	28		2	26	23	20			24	16	8		2	2	7
Decrease							33					28					5			

TABLE XIX.—COUNTY ACADEMIES.—(Continued).

ACADEMY.	AVERAGE AGE OF TOTAL PUPILS IN EACH GRADE. (On first day of School Year.)				REVENUE.					EXPENDITURE.					
	Grade IX.	Grade X.	Grade XI.	Grade XII.	Provincial Grant.	School Section Fund.	Fees.	Other Sources.	Total.	Salaries.	Apparatus.	Building and Repairs.	Fuel and Attendance.	Miscellaneous.	Total.
	Yrs.	Yrs.	Yrs.	Yrs.											
Annapolis	14.87	15.62	16.72		$500 00	$400 00		$75 00	$975 00	$900 00	$75 00	$200 00	$100 00	$20 00	$975 00
Antigonish	17.08	17.7	18.77		1500 00	700 00	$20 00	1260 00	3480 00	3110 00	50 00	150 00	160 00	1525 00	3480 00
Cape Breton	16.45	17.83	17.36	18.8	500 00	3000 00			3500 00	1650 00	15 00	200 00	400 00	200 00	3500 00
Colchester	15.25	17.94	16.8	18.8	1500 00	2725 00			4225 00	3275 00	150 00		100 00		4225 00
Cumberland	14.64	15.59	16.22		*500 00	1440 00			1940 00	1800 00	40 00		40 00		1940 00
Digby	15.83	17.4	19.79		500 00	295 00			795 00	750 00	15 00	25 00	30 00	13 74	795 00
Guysboro	13.71	15.9	16.8		500 00	388 74			888 74	750 00	50 00		50 00		888 74
Halifax	14.7	15.51	17.6	18.03	1720 00	6814 00	300 00	1076 00	9910 00	7124 00			487 00	2299 00	9910 00
Hants	15.45	15.68	15.75		500 00	520 00			1020 00	1000 00	10 00	250 00	85 00	10 00	1020 00
Inverness	14.41	16.18	15.74	16.84	500 00	590 00			1090 00	750 00	5 00		100 00		1090 00
Kings	14.9	15.54	17.32		1000 00	805 00			1805 00	1700 00	5 00		100 00	50 C0	1805 00
Lunenburg	15.01	15.9	16.08	20.55	500 00	650 00			1150 00	1000 00			285 00	65 00	1150 00
Pictou	15.17	16.6	18.96		1720 00	3028 00	252 00		5000 00	3550 00	50 00	1050 00	30 00		5000 00
Queens	16.18		16.7		500 00	355 00			855 00	750 00	75 00		120 00	180 00	855 00
Shelburne	14.94	17.42	17.67		500 00	800 00			1300 00	750 00	10 00	240 00	30 00	6 00	1300 00
Victoria	15.06	18.2	17.25	16.93	500 00	388 00			888 00	750 00	4 00	90 00	38 00		888 00
Yarmouth	15.46	15.79	15.87	18.2	500 00	2260 00			2760 00	2760 00					2760 00
Total 1894	15.24	16.55	17.14	18.22	$13440 00	$25158 74	$572 00	$2411 00	$41581 74	$32369 00	$554 00	$2205 00	$2085 00	$4368 74	$41581 74
" 1893	14.88	16.17	17.46	19.51	10830 00	16571 79	475 16	9250 43	37127 38	24422 50	412 51	9044 02	2628 54	619 81	37127 38
Increase	.36	.38			$2610 00	$8586 95	$96 84		$4454 36	$7946 50	$141 49			$3748 93	$4454 36
Decrease			.32	1.29				$6839 43				$6839 02	$543 54		

* $250 of this amount was paid after the close of the fiscal year, September 30th.

TABLE XIX.—COUNTY ACADEMIES.—(Continued).

ACADEMY.	GROUND. Dimensions of (grounds on which building is situated). Decimetres.	REGULAR TEACHING ROOMS. Number of.	REGULAR TEACHING ROOMS. Average dimensions of. Decimetres.	ASSEMBLY ROOM. Dimensions of (if there is a special room). Decimetres.	LIBRARY. Dimensions of room (if there is a spec'l one), or of cabinet, cases or shelving (if no special room). Decimetres.	LIBRARY. No. of Volumes.	LIBRARY. Estimated Value of the Books.	MUSEUM OF NATURAL HISTORY, PHYSIOLOGY, &c. Dimensions of room (if there is a spec'l one), or of cabinet, cases or shelving (if no special room). Decimetres.	MUSEUM. Estimated Value of Collections, Models, &c.	LABORATORY. (Chemical.) Dimensions of room (if there is a spec'l one), or of cabinet, cases or shelving (if no special room). Decimetres.	LABORATORY. Estimated Value of Apparatus, &c., kept here.
Annapolis	980 x 125	1	31 x 54 x 110	37 x 109 x 178	33 x 52 x 78	2030	$3000 00	33 x 52 x 78	$100 00	33 x 78 x 104	$ 30 00
Antig nish	100 x 160	6	33 x 64 x 96		42 x 40 x 40	280	355 00			42 x 40 x 30	550 00
Cape Breton	900 x 400	3	42 x 90 x 90		42 x 45 x 45	180	250 00		50 00	42 x 45 x 45	155 00
Colchester	682 x 1364	4	42 x 83 x 92	40 x 92 x 218	39 x 51 x 85	70	80 00	50 x 80 x 121		39 x 61 x 107	200 00
Cumberland	909 x 1818	2	39 x 90 x 111	50 x 137 x 196						20 x 10 x 25	480 00
gly	331 x 455	1	38 x 90 x 90	36 x 74 x 198	24 x 30 x 30	170	50 00			24 x 3 x 15	10 00
Guysboro	403 x 694	1	45 x 82 x 97		42 x 40 x 55	800	900 00	9 x 7 x 94	200 00	42 x 40 x 60	20 00
it	157 x 140	6	42 x 83 x 97	52 x 196 x 160						40 x 41 x 46	200 00
Hants	850 x 590	1	40 x 79 x 99								50 00
Inverness	166 x 178	1	40 x 74 x 89								25 00
Kings	364 x 667	2	40 x 78 x 87					42 x 55 x 72	1200 00	45 x 52 x 50	20 00
Lunenburg*											
Pictou	650 x 1150	4	45 x 85 x 97	42 x 95 x 213	42 x 55 x 73	1175	1000 00			28 x 19 x 5	200 00
Queens	96 x 314	1	42 x 86 x 110					14 x 10 x 3	20 00	20 x 6 x 38	
Shelburne	732 x 732	1	46 x 110 x 120			4	20 00	9 x 8 x 37	30 00	21 x 4 x 22	30 00
V ton in	603 x 1426	1	34 x 74 x 82	44 x 89 x 183	14 x 3 x 15	70	60 00	21 x 4 x 22	50 00		22 00
Yarmouth	640 x 1460	2	44 x 83 x 91								250 00
t 1894		36				4779	$5715 00		$1650 00		$2242 00
" 1893		37				4610	5425 00		1615 00		2155 00
Increase						169	$290 00		$35 00		$87 00
Decrease		1									

* House destoyed by fire September 28th, 1893.

TABLE XIX.—COUNTY ACADEMIES.—(Continued).

ACADEMY.	LABORATORY. (Physical.) Dimensions of room (if any) or of cabinet, cases or shelving (if no special room). Decimetres.	Estimated Value of Apparatus kept here.	GYMNASIUM OR PLAY-ROOM. Dimensions of room (if any). Decimetres.	Estimated Value of Apparatus.	GENERAL. No. of Wall Maps, Charts and Globes.	No of reference books, &c, for teachers' desks.	Estimated Value of the same.	TOTAL VALUE. Estimated Value of all collections, apparatus, &c., (not including furniture, &c., seats, desks, &c.,) used for teaching purposes.
Annapolis		$120 00			19	5	$ 50 00	$ 200 00
Antigonish			44 x 90 x 166	$60 00	30	30	90 00	3900 00
Cape Breton	42 x 45 x 45	155 00			40	10	40 00	800 00
Colchester		200 00			20	12	20 00	1070 00
Cumberland	36 x 20 x 20	480 00	30 x 80 x 100		10	15	50 00	600 00
Digby		10 00			12	1	60 00	170 00
Guysboro	29 x 7 x 24	27 00			15	2	38 00	155 00
Halifax		150 00	32 x 83 x 95		33	8	120 00	1750 00
Hants		25 00			12	3	25 00	100 00
Inverness					4	1	20 00	45 00
Kings		70 00			22	6	103 00	187 00
Lunenburg					10	15	75 00	75 00
Picton	42 x 52 x 52	500 00			56	4	100 00	300 00
Queens	42 x 40 x 40	100 00			4	2	40 00	140 00
Shelburne					26	4	120 00	180 00
Victoria					18	12	40 00	107 00
Yarmouth					30	10	100 00	460 00
Total, 1894		$1837 00		$ 60 00	366	140	$1091 00	$12849 00
" 1893		1060 00		100 00	372	164	1037 00	12203 00
Increase		$777 00					$54 00	$646 00
Decrease				$40 00	6	24		

TABLE XX.—GOVERNMENT NIGHT SCHOOLS.

County	Section	Teacher	Assistant	Pupils Enrolled.	Average Attendance.	No. of Sessions.
Cape Breton	Gowrie	J. J. Macaskill		40	23	24
"	Big Lorraine	diry D. Scott		40	18	12
"	Low Point	Murdoch		70	23	53
"	Sydney Mines	Wm. Haggarty	James Conners			27
"	"		Charles A. Burchell	48	26	51
"	Bridgeport	Wm. Young		43	21	45
"	West Louisburg	Lawrence D. Bates		35	25	48
"	Barachois	?ex. J. ?ld		30	23	39
"	"	Duncan Matheson		25	10	48
Inverness	North Sydney	John D. McNeil		30	21	9
"	Red Banks	John A. ?nald		41	24	48
"	Millan	?thel C. McDonald		58	28	27
Victoria	S. W. Bridge	P. A. Murphy		45	26	52
"	?e Intervale	Alex. D. McDonald		74	43	33
"	Nw ?n	John M. ?e		38	22	33
"	French River	?n. J. ?son		37	18	43
Pictou	Englishtown	?lin C. ?n		26	18	30
"	Westville	A. ?. Ml ?ie		56	29	36
"	Albion Mes	J. W. Henderson		41	28	51
Lunenburg	Thorburn	Bruce ?d		63	25	38
"	Tancook	Diadem Bell		25	19	50
Digby	Westport	Go. M. Huggins		34	26	25
Cumberland	Springhill	W. W. ?ey		78	25	46
"	"		Lou. Ella Logan			40
						37

TABLE XXI.—PROVINCIAL HIGH SCHOOL EXAMINATION, JULY, 1894.

Station.	Male Candidates.	Female Candidates.	Total Candidates.
Amherst	20	44	64
Annapolis	14	24	38
Antigonish	28	36	64
Arichat	9	11	20
Baddeck	21	21	42
Barrington	5	5	8
Bridgetown	38	63	101
Cheticamp	5		
Clare	4	17	21
Digby	27	38	65
Guysboro	16	24	40
Halifax	116	172	288
Kentville	51	70	121
Liverpool	6	37	43
Lockeport	12	14	26
Lunenburg	26	66	92
Margaree Forks	4	11	15
New Glasgow	37	73	110
Parrsboro	2	94	96
Pictou	47	49	96
Port Hawkesbury	6	17	33
Port Hood	19	23	43
Shelburne	13	32	35
Sherbrooke	7	8	9
Spring Hill	18	18	35
Sydney	40	52	92
Tatamagouche	7	30	37
Truro	77	147	224
Windsor	20	43	63
Yarmouth	31	56	87
Total, 1894	707	1215	1922
" 1893	506	1001	1506
Increase	202	214	416

TABLE XXI.—PROVINCIAL HIGH SCHOOL EXAMINATIONS, JULY, 1894.—(Continued).

STATIONS.	MALE C. Candidates for Grade C.	MALE C. Received Grade C.	MALE C. Received Grade D.	MALE C. Failed.	FEMALE C. Candidates for Grade C.	FEMALE C. Received Grade C.	FEMALE C. Received Grade D.	FEMALE C. Failed.	MALE D. Candidates for Grade D	MALE D. Received Grade D.	MALE D. Failed.	FEMALE D. Candidates for Grade D.	FEMALE D. Received Grade D.	FEMALE D. Failed.	Total received Grade A.	Total received Grade B.	Total received Grade C.	Total received Grade D.	Total received Certificates.	No. received Grade applied for.	No. received lower Grade than applied for.	No. failed.
Amherst	4	3		1	14	8	8	4	11	5	6	25	11	14		6	14	19	39	33	6	25
Annapolis	3	1	6	2	5	1	1	3	4	1	3	11	3	8		7	5	7	19	13	11	19
Antigonish	13	4	2	3	13	2	2	4	10	1	8	17	7	10	4	4	8	18	34	23	4	30
Arichat	4	1	3	1	7		1	5	4	1	3	8	1	7	1	2	2	9	7	12	5	13
Baddeck	9	1	3		9		2	5	9	2	7	14	2	12				9	17	12	1	25
Barrington	2				7	1	1		1	1		3	1	3			2	1	3	2		6
Bridgetown	8	3		1	2		1		8		8	24		18				2	1		1	36
Cheticamp	3	1	8	2	34	15	7	6	18	9					1	9	26	30	66	41	24	72
Clare									2			15		13				1	1			4
Digby					18	7	2	9	2	1		16	2	11	1	12	12	6	31	35	6	18
Guysboro	9	4	4	5	14	5	4	8	3	3		13	1	11	1	8	8	10	19	19	10	34
Halifax	35	21	9	18	62	25	19	18	46	33	13	74	40	34	11	38	56	109	212	166	50	21
Kentville	20	7	8	4	21	10	6	4	20	5	15	34	7	27	1	18	21	31	65	42	24	65
Liverpool	1	1	1	5	10	4	2	6	5	1		15	10	5	1	3	7	14	30	21	7	12
Lockeport	8	1	1	1	3	2	1		3	3		10		8			5	6	14	12	1	12
Lunenburg	4	1		1	19	6	7	6	13	1	11	36	13	27		9	14	25	46	32	14	46
Margaree Forks	16	8	1						5		2	10		9		3	3	1				14
New Glasgow					23	8	11	6	13	6	8	29	6	23	1		20	27	61	39	23	18
Parrsboro	20	11	1	4	7	9	12	9	19	2	12	14	3	14		4	4	7	18	11	24	38
Pictou	1	1	5	2	26	1	1	5	6	1	13	9	4	9			25	24	58	34	7	33
Port Hawkesbury	8	1	1	1	9	3	1	4	1	1	4	11	1	11		2	5	5	11	11	1	21
Port Hood	2	2	1	1	9	1	2	1	9	2	10	16		16		4	12	10	18	10	8	24
Shelburne	1	1	5	1	3	3	2	2	5	1	3	2		2		2	6	16	22	17	5	13
Sherbrooke	14	3	2	1	10	5	12	4	11		17	11		11			7	6	12	8	3	4
Springhill	4		1	7	64	21	12	20	8	2	16	30	3	19	2	3	12	24	34	8	4	13
Sydney					10	10	12	9	3		9	19	1	15		8	11	8	34	13	13	58
Tatamagouche	23	14	1	1	90	64	22	20	30	14	2	58	25	33	2	35	42	69	147	106	43	90
Truro	14	6	5	7	9	4	8	2	20	4	16	16	3	13		5	9	17	31	17	14	75
Windsor	6	5	2		16	11	3	2	13	4	7	27	14	13	1	5	20	30	56	40	18	29
Yarmouth																						
Total, 1894	**237**	**107**	**72**	**58**	**443**	**164**	**141**	**188**	**298**	**110**	**188**	**574**	**183**	**391**	**30**	**182**	**337**	**543**	**1092**	**760**	**342**	**830**
" 1893	**174**	**62**	**63**	**49**	**422**	**142**	**138**	**142**	**197**	**88**	**109**	**403**	**147**	**261**	**10**	**157**	**289**	**469**	**915**	**698**	**317**	**601**
Increase	**63**	**45**	**9**	**9**	**21**	**22**	**3**		**101**	**22**	**79**	**166**	**36**	**130**	**20**	**25**	**48**	**84**	**177**	**162**	**25**	**229**
Decrease								**4**														

TABLE XXII.—Expenditure of Government Funds for Public Schools, County Academies, &c.

School Year ended July, 1894.

County.	Population.	No. of Schools in session.	No. of Pupils registered.	Sum of Government Grants.	Cost to Government per pupil.	County Academies.	Total assignable to Counties.
Annapolis	19,350	119	4671	$9,340 48	$1 99	$500 00	$9,840 48
Antigonish	16,144	94	3534	6,490 67	1 83	1,500 00	7,990 67
Cape Breton	34,244	157	6887	11,656 90	1 69	500 00	12,156 90
Colchester	27,160	143	6037	10,294 64	1 70	1,500 00	11,794 64
Cumberland	34,529	182	8624	13,139 68	1 52	250 00	13,389 68
Digby	19,897	100	4685	6,968 54	1 49	500 00	7,468 54
Guysboro	17,195	91	3686	5,901 74	1 60	50C 00	6,401 74
Halifax County	32,863	145	6600	10,570 56	1 60		10,570 56
Halifax City	38,495	129	7412	11,320 49	1 53	1,720 00	13,040 49
Hants	22,052	192	5087	9,112 46	1 79	500 00	9,612 46
Inverness	25,779	170	6095	10,607 13	1 73	500 00	11,107 13
Kings	22,489	119	5235	9,069 67	1 73	1,000 00	10,069 67
Lunenburg	31,075	171	7552	11,888 86	1 57	500 00	12,388 86
Pictou	34,541	176	7283	13,645 22	1 87	1,720 00	15,365 22
Queens	10,610	56	2923	4,306 74	2 12	500 00	4,806 74
Richmond	14,399	70	2928	5,000 90	1 71		5,000 90
Shelburne	14,956	77	3425	5,871 22	1 71	500 00	6,371 22
Victoria	12,432	65	2223	4,176 62	1 88	500 00	4,676 62
Yarmouth	22,216	106	4723	8,092 33	1 71	500 00	8,592 33
Total, 1894	450,396	2292	98710	$167,452 85	$1 69	$13,190 00	$180,642 85
" 1893	450,396	2252	94899	125,632 20	1 32	11,807 15	137,429 35
Increase		40	3811	$41,830 65	$0 37	$1,382 85	$43,213 50
Decrease							

Other Services and Total Expenditure for Education.

Inspectors' Salaries	$12,300 00
" Stationery, Postage, &c.	500 00
Examination	2,235 37
Travelling Expenses—Normal School Pupils	1,510 05
Salaries	3,400 00
Travelling Expenses—Superintendent	400 00
Office Expenses, (Registers, Register Covers, Postage, Expressage, Telegrams, Stationery, &c)	1,735 19
Total	$22,080 61
Last column	180,642 85
Total for Public Schools, 1894	$202,723 46
Institution for the Deaf and Dumb	4,125 00
Halifax School for the Blind	1,725 00
Normal and Model Schools	8,900 00
School of Agriculture	1,500 00
Government Night Schools	1,463 44
Total Government Expenditure, 1894	$220,436 90
" " 1893	166,040 49
Increase	$54,396 41

TABLE XXIII.

SUMMARY OF GOVERNMENT GRANTS FOR EDUCATION,
YEAR ENDED, JULY 1894.

Common Schools	$167,452 85
Normal School	8,900 00
Institution for Deaf and Dumb	4,125 00
Halifax School for the Blind	1,725 00
County Academies	13,190 00
Inspection.	12,800 00
Expenses (offices)	1,735 19
Salaries	3,800 00
Examination	2,235 37
School of Agriculture	1,500 00
Travelling Expenses, Normal School Pupils	1,510 05
Government Night Schools	1,463 44
	$220,436 90

PART I.II.

APPENDICES.

APPENDIX A.

REPORT OF NORMAL SCHOOL.

SESSION OF 1893-94.

To A. H. MacKay, Ll.D.,

Superintendent of Education, Halifax, N. S.

Dear Sir,—I have the honor to submit my report of the Provincial Normal School for the Session ended June 28th, 1894.

The total number of students enrolled was one hundred and thirty. Of these eight were graduates ot colleges,—three from Acadia, two from St. Francis Xavier, and three from Mt. Allison.

One hundred and twenty-three diplomas were awarded, of which fifty-three were of First Rank, fifty-six of Second Rank, and fourteen of Third Rank.

The work of the year was, on the whole, highly satisfactory. Indeed, estimated on the basis of effectiveness, I believe it was the most successful in the history of the Institution. As compared with any former year, in my opinion the students gained a more complete and thorough grasp of the principles underlying good teaching, and attained to higher skill in the application of those principles to practical work in the presentation of knowledge, and in class management.

In making this statement I speak of the School as a whole, in regard to its general average, rather than of the special and exceptional excellence of individuals.

It is not difficult to account for this advance. In fact, it was what was to be expected from the changed conditions under which we have been working. The new arrangement of requiring the scholarship qualifications for license of those admitted to the various classes, while it secured enlarged mental power and equipment on the part of the students under training, at the same time allowed more freedom for attention to that professional training which constitutes the special function of the Institution.

It must not be supposed, however, that advancement in scholarship formed no considerable element in our work. With the view of introducing the new system with the least possible friction, and of avoiding those disturbances which are likely to arise out of abrupt transitions, the standard of admission to the various classes was somewhat relaxed, by which applicants were received whose qualifications were not quite up to the requirements of the syllabus. This, of course, implied the consequent obligation of doing some Academic work to prepare such students for the High School examination. This modification of the terms of admission must, however, be held under restriction as a mere temporary expedient to meet present conditions.

There is also another, and as I regard it, a permanent obligation to extend the scholarship of our students. If the professional treatment of the various subjects of the School curricula is rightly conducted, there must be more or less review of facts and principles belonging to those subjects, as well as a certain amount of new ground covered through the discussion of related knowledge. The subjects which more especially received attention were English (including Grammar, Composition, and Literature), Physics, Chemistry, Botany, and the use of the microscope.

In the subjects of Vocal Music, according to the Tonic Sol-fa System, and Drawing, the students generally have little practical knowledge or skill, so that the work done is almost entirely from rudimentary stages. I may note here, however, that the progress in these departments last year was especially gratifying.

The Manual Training Department, which was added to the Institution last year, was very successfully conducted by Mr. Lee Russell, in addition to the Practical Chemistry conducted in the Chemical Laboratory. The time of our students is so fully occupied that only two hours in each week could be found available for this work. The Department was very popular, and excellent work was done. I may say, however, that considering all the varied studies and exercises required in the Normal School for the proper equipment of our students for their future calling, and taking into account the short time at our disposal to secure this equipment, it is open to reasonable question whether we can, in the near future, devote any more attention to this work than we are now giving.

The changes made in the building, by which we had four additional class rooms, were found very serviceable in enabling us to carry on our work with much more comfort and effectiveness.

A course of lectures on educational and literary topics delivered by various gentlemen, formed an interesting feature of the session. Ths gentlemen who favored us in this way, were His Lordship Bishop Courtney, President Sawyer of Acadia, President Allison of Mt. Allison, Dr. MacKay, Superintendent of Education, and Hon. Attorney-General Longley.

The closing exercises of the Session, held on the morning of June 28th, were exceedingly interesting, and were witnessed by a large number of visitors. The first hour was spent in specimen teaching by students selected from the various classes. The exercises were carried on simultaneously in ten or twelve different rooms, and comprised lessons in Geography, History, Literature, Natural Science, Music, Drawing, Microscopy, Laboratory work, and Manual Training. At the close of these exercises the Rev. President Forrest of Dalhousie University, delivered before the assembled faculty, students, and visitors a very able address. Among the visitors present were Hon. Provincial Secretary Fielding, Hon. Attorney-General Longley, His Lordship Bishop Courtney, Dr. A. H. MacKay, Superintendent of Education, and A. McN. Patterson, Principal of Acacia Villa Seminary.

I am, yours respectfully,

JOHN B. CALKIN,

NORMAL SCHOOL, Truro, N. S.   *Principal.*

STUDENTS OF SESSION 1893-'94.

AWARDED FIRST RANK DIPLOMAS.

(The figures show the number of the Diploma.)

Armstrong, Tremain E.... 30.... Kingston Station.... Kings.
Begg, Ellen C .... 9.... Kentville .... "
Bell, Mary F............ 21.... Dartmouth .... Halifax.
Best, Lillian G.......... 24.... Grafton............ Kings.
Boehner, Reginald S..... 39.... Paradise .... Annapolis.
Blackadar, Ross.......... 41.... Hebron .... Yarmouth.
Callaghan, Minnie........ 11.... Pleasant Hills...... Colchester.
Congdon, Hattie......... 12.... Port Williams ..... Kings.
Chamberlain, Lois D ..... 27.... Halifax .... Halifax.
Crowe, Henry S .... 35.... Central Onslow. .... Colchester.
Cameron, Edward H..... 37.... Yarmouth......... Yarmouth.
Crosby, Frank R .... 40.... Hebron .... Yarmouth.
Creed, John N........... 42.... Canso. .... Guysboro'.
Crandall, Ella D......... 43.... Wolfville .... Kings.
Dauphinee, A Josephine.. 2.... Liverpool .... Queen's.
Doherty, D. Philip ...... 28.... Halifax .... Halifax.
Dunlop, Allen E .... 48.... Shelburne......... Shelburne.
Foote, Cora A .... 17.... Grafton........... Kings.
Gillis, Ewen.... .... 31.... Baddeck Forks..... Victoria.
Harrington, Georgie M.... 3 ... Liverpool .... Queens.
Hart, Grace M.......... 8.... Halifax .... Halifax.
Harlow, Leslie E .... 32.... Lockeport......... Shelburne.
Kinley, Thos. J......... 34.... Paradise .... Annapolis.
Kinney Julia........... 44.... Weymouth .... Digby.
Lewis, Kate A......... 20.... Centreville .... Lunenburg.
Longley, Robert S.. .... 38.... Paradise .... Annapolis.
McCallum, Myrtle D..... 1.... Truro .... Colchester.
McIsaac, Mary.......... 4.... Caledonia Mills..... Antigonish.
McVicar, Maggie M...... 5.... Annapolis .... Annapolis.
MacKay, Jessie G........ 7.... Shubenacadie...... Colchester.
Macleod, Mary E ...... 15.... New Glasgow ..... Pictou.
McIntosh, Beachell...... 18.... Halifax .... Halifax.
McColough, Agnes M..... 19.... Halifax .... Halifax.
Miller, Bessie........... 22.... Miller's Creek ..... Hants.
McNealy, Clara A........ 23.... Summerville....... Hants.
Moody, Ida G........... 26.... Halifax .... Halifax.
McLeod, Albert C....... 29.... Brookfield .... Queens.
Matheson, Alfred L ..... 45.... Barrington .... Shelburne.
Moore, Warren I. .... 46.... Wolfville .... Kings.
Murray, Archibald ..... 47.... Yarmouth......... Yarmouth.
McNealy, Murray....... 49.... Summerville....... Hants.
McNeil, Daniel .... 51.... Bridgeport .... Cape Breton.
McTavish, Neill D ...... 53.... Carriboo.......... Pictou.
Osborne, Norman A..... 33.... Waterville .... Kings.

Patterson, Samson A. .....50.... Aylesford .... Kings.
Phalen, Thomas M........52.... Little Bras d'Or. ....Cape Breton.
Redding, M. Bell ....10.... Kentville .... Kings.
Ross, Christina M........14.... New Glasgow. ..... Pictou.
Robbins, Welton H.......36.... Rossway .... Digby.
Starratt, Helen M........16.... Paradise .... Annapolis.
Trefry, Amy G .... 6.... Milton .... Yarmouth.
Troop Wilhelmina.......13.... Granville Centre.... Annapolis.
Webster, Winnifred M....25.... Brooklyn St........ Kings.

AWARDED SECOND RANK DIPLOMAS.

Angus, Julia ....13.... Shinimicas .... Cumberland.
Allan, Libbie............36.... Dartmouth .... Halifax.
Black, Jessie F ....27.... Glendyer.......... Inverness.
Barclay, Della...........32.... Eureka............ Pictou.
Benjamin, Lena.. ....50.... Gaspereau .... Kings.
Chisholm, E. Maud. ......28.... Great Village ...... Colchester.
Douglas, Christie B...... 8.... River John .... Pictou.
DeLong, Maud E. ....16.... New Germany ..... Lunenburg.
Doucet, Emily. ....18.... Tusket. .... Yarmouth.
Daniels, Edith D. ....29.... W. Paradise .... Annapolis.
Eaton, Grace I........... 5.... Truro .... Colchester.
Fulton, Mary............21.... Newton Mills ...... Colchester.
Ford, Carrie M..........31.... Milton .... Queens.
Goudey, Alice A. .... 1.... Port Maitland ..... Yarmouth.
Hall, Bertie M. ....14.... Kingston.......... Kings.
Healy, Katie E...........34.... Halifax .... Halifax.
Hartigan, Mary E........51.... North Sydney ...... Cape Breton.
Ibbitson, Celia A........53.... Springhill Mines ....Cumberland.
Jacques, Frank B.......42.... Auburn .... Kings.
Johnson, Minnie G. ......12.... Lower Canard ..... Kings.
King, Ida M ....33.... New Glasgow ...... Pictou.
Lewis, Anna .... 6.... Cow Bay .... Cape Breton.
McLauchlin, Zilla........ 2.... Great Village....... Colchester.
Maclean, Mary L .... 4.... Meadowville........ Pictou.
MacVicar, Margaret A.... 7.... Cow Bay .... Cape Breton.
McDonald, Wilhelmina.... 9.... Lockeport.......... Shelburne.
Marchant, Laura L. ......10.... Brooklyn St........ Kings.
Marchant, Ethylberta L ..11.... Brooklyn St........ Kings.
McBride, Hattie L. ......45.... Harborville .... Kings.
McAlpine, Emma ....15.... Shelburne.......... Shelburne.
Meek, Geddie............40.... Brooklyn .... Hants.
Morash, Jessie H. ....47.... Lunenburg......... Lunenburg.
Morash, Clara M. ....19.... Great Village....... Colchester.
Minard, Clara V. ....54.... South Brookfield....Queens.
Mason, Ernest S. ....37.... Springfield .... Annapolis.
McLeod, Daniel F........38.... Union Centre. ...... Pictou.
Morse, Egbert P.........43.... Paradise .... Annapolis.
Munro, John A..........55.... Pugwash .... Cumberland.
Nichols, Clarence ....39.... Aylesford .... Kings.

Oulton, Lissie R........23....Springhill.........Cumberland.
Parker, Adelia M ....22....Granville Ferry.....Annapolis.
Roy, Alice G............20....Maitland ....Hants.
Roy, Sarah D............24....Merigomish ....Pictou.
Robb, Sarah ....25....Oxford ....Cumberland.
Rines, Leonard D........44....Maitland. ....Hants.
Sibley, Lulu ....52....Wittenburg ....Colchester.
Stuart, Mary E.........35....Truro ....Colchester.
Smith, M. Myrer ....48....Lunenburg........Lunenburg.
Swim, Lina ....26....Swansburg........Shelburne.
Scott, Hannah P.........30....Kelley's Cove......Yarmouth
Skinner, Henrietta ......41....Port Hastings .....Inverness.
Sutherland, Marian ...... 3....Earltown ....Colchester.
Thomas, Bessie ....56....Dartmouth. ....Halifax.
Tompkins, Rebecca ......17....E. Margaree........Inverness.
Tobin, Gertrude.........49....Town Plot.........King's.
Young, Frances E........46....Lunenburg.........Lunenburg.

AWARDED THIRD RANK DIPLOMAS.

Bruce, Christy ....Moose Riv. G. Mines..Halifax.
Drinnan, Isabelle ....Upper Nine Mile Riv.Hants.
Hamilton, Alma L........ 7....Truro . ...Colchester.
Morse, Chas. D .... 1....Sandy Cove ....Digby.
Martell, Eliza ....Arichat ....Richmond.
Murray, Sadie ....West Merigomish....Pictou.
McIntosh, Euphemia...... 3....Pleasant Bay ......Inverness.
McDonald, Sadie .... 5....Shubenacadie ......Colchester.
Rutherford, Ada M. ....Middle Stewiacke ...Colchester.
Shipley, Lillie M......... ....Nappan Station. ....Cumberland.
Shipley, Laura A .... 4....Nappan Station. ....Cumberland.
Thompson, Minnie ...... 6....Nine Mile River ....Hants.
Totten, Annie ....East Folly Mountain. Colchester.
Webber, Hattie.......... 2....Chester ....Lunenburg.

COURSE UNCOMPLETED.

Cooke, Alex. D ....Halifax...........Halifax.
Coates, Clara May........ ....Amherst..........Cumberland.
Gardner, Harold W ....Antigonish........Antigonish.
Mosher, Frederic T. ....Windsor..........Hants.
McLeod, Susan A........ ....Wittenberg........Colchester.
Taylor, Annie M. ....Earltown ....Colchester.
Thomas, Ella M.......... ....Truro ....Colchester.

STUDENTS IN KINDERGARTEN AWARDED DIPLOMAS.

Gertrude Cunningham.... ....Guysboro'.........Guysboro'.
Lena L. Woodill ....Halifax...........Halifax.
Edith S. Stewart......... ....St. John..........N. B.

NORMAL SCHOOL.

YEAR.	PUPILS.			EXPENDITURE.				
	No. of Teachers.	Total number enrolled.	Received Diploma.	Salaries of Teachers.	Salary of Janitor.	Cost of Fuel.	Contingencies,—Stationery, etc.	TOTAL.
1893	6	163	154	$5400	$400	$219 47	$382 82	$6402 29
1894	7	130	123	6600	400	284 75	616 10	7900 85

MODEL SCHOOL.

YEAR.	PUPILS.			EXPENDITURE.			
	No. of Teachers.	Average daily attendance.	Total number different Pupils registered.	Salaries of Teachers.	Amount received from Province.	Amount received from Truro.	TOTAL.
1893	2	87	119	$1100	$600	$500	$1100
1894	2	79	109	1100	600	500	1100

SCHOOL OF AGRICULTURE,

A. H. MACKAY, LL.D.,
       Superintendent of Education.

DEAR SIR :—I have the honor to submit the following report upon my work in connection with the Provincial Normal School and the Local Agricultural Schools.

     I am, Sir,

         Your obedient servant,

            H. W. SMITH, *Principal.*

PROVINCIAL SCHOOL OF AGRICULTURE, Truro, N. S.

PART 1.

THE NORMAL SCHOOL STUDENTS AT THE SCHOOL OF AGRICULTURE.

Most of the students attending the Normal School during the past year received some scientific instruction in the Provincial School of Agriculture. .With few exceptions, every week day afternoon was given to these 'students. They received instruction in Microscopy, Structural Botany, Vegetable Anatomy and Physiology, Systematic Botany, and General Chemistry. It was necessary to divide the first and second classes into sections in order to provide them with sufficient room, apparatus and instruction. As a result, three classes attended once a week. The " A " class and the first division of the the third class twice a week, and the second division of the third class once a week. Fifteen Normal students registered for special work in the School of Agriculture. Of these, twelve took Chemistry, and three Botanical work. Of those taking Chemistry, one studied Quantitative Analysis, three Advanced General Chemistry, and the others Introductory Chemistry.

The following shows the regular Normal classes which attended, the number of students in them, and the number of times they attended :

" A " Class.............10 students attended 24 times.
1st   " 46   "   "   30   "
2nd   " 55   "   "   19   "
3rd   "   (1st Div.)......10   "   "   10   "
3rd   "   (2nd Div.)..... 6   ··   "   8   "

4

TABLE SHOWING THE ATTENDANCE IN THE CLASSES IN AGRICULTURE IN THE LOCAL AGRICULTURAL SCHOOLS.

		TOTAL ATTENDANCE.	CLASS IN			
			BOTANY.	CHEMISTRY.	PHYSIOLOGY.	AGRICULTURE.
Middleton	1st Term	36	.....	9	2	10
	2nd "	53	13	13	3	12
*Richmond	1st Term	46	35	40	40	40
	2nd "	45	37	.....	37	47
*Roger's Hill	1st Term	40	40	40	40	40
	2nd "	65	65	60	60	60
Antigonish	1st Term	50	22	20	10	20
	2nd "	42	.....	20	12	20
Beaver's Cove	1st Term	50	9	9	9	26
	2nd "	.....	17·	17	.....	17
Little Glace Bay	1st Term	30	26	20	8	26
	2nd "	36	30	20	8	30

*Nearly all the Pupils in the School took part in these studies.

APPENDIX B.

REPORTS OF INSPECTORS OF SCHOOLS.

DISTRICT No. 1.—CITY AND COUNTY OF HALIFAX.

HINKLE CONDON, *Inspector.*

SIR :—

I have the honour of presenting my Annual Report on the condition of the Public Schools of Halifax, District No. 1, for the year ended July, 1894.

NEW HOUSES.

We have much reason for satisfaction in the improved character of the School Buildings, especially in the case of those erected within the last few years. Nine new houses have been built during the last school year.

WESTERN DISTRICT.

Sections:—St. James, at the Head of St. Margaret's Bay, with two departments, is delightfully situated on a healthy spot which commands a fine view of the Bay. These rooms are fitted with modern desks.

West Dover, after wasting the school life of a generation of *children*, has, at last, a good substantial house, and arrangements have been made to open a school in August, 1894.

Spryfield, within five miles of Halifax City, has nearly finished what will be a commodious house, well furnished with the most approved desks. A school has been in session for three months of the year. This is the first public school for the section, and represents no small amount of laborious perseverance on the part of those who have, for years, been trying to secure the benefits of our school system. The annual meeting is reported to have been a stormy one, almost ending in an old fashioned row, but, as the result proved, the party of progress won.

DARTMOUTH.

Dartmouth has added six (6) new rooms, well-arranged in regard to light and ventilation. Two of these are at Woodside, in a neat house, where a miscellaneous school is taught in the first six grades, after which the scholars are promoted to the other regularly graded schools. Greenvale has had four (4) rooms added to its accommoda-

tion by raising the roof.   Principal Miller and Miss Findlay each
have rooms in this building, in addition to the Principal's office.   The
office has communication by telephone with all·the schools in the
town.   The expenses of this great improvement, which will add
much to the Principal's efficiency, were met by the proceeds of a
lecture delivered by Principal Miller, and a concert given by the
teachers, which netted a considerable sum.   The Free Kindergarten,
under Miss Hamilton's able directorship, is also in this building.

East Chezzetcook (Hope Ridge) has added a separate class-
room.

South East Passage, Cow Bay, and Hope Ridge have improved by
putting in the patent desks.

Arrangements have been made at Foot Porter's Lake, Head
Chezzetcook, and Eastern Passage to erect houses suitable to the
requirements of the law.   The two latter sections will also each provide a class-room for an assistant.

Ketch Harbor, Portuguese Cove, and Herring Cove have pledged
themselves to put in suitable furniture.

The notice given in the *Journal of Education* for 1893, that the
County Grant will be withheld if school buildings are in an insani-
tary condition, the Inspector being the judge, has already begun to
work well, and, in District No. 1, the penalty, if deserved, will be
enforced.

EASTERN DISTRICT.

Tangier has completed a good house, but, unfortunately, the
desks (home-made) are a wretched failure.

Musquodoboit Harbour and Pope's Harbour are now well
furnished.

RURAL DISTRICT.

There is only one section to report as having made any material
improvement, either in the houses or furniture, and that is "Dutch
Settlement," No. 1, where the house has been ceiled and new desks
put in which, although not of the most approved pattern, are superior
to the old ones.

SECTIONS.

Sections may be classed as follows:

First, those in which trustees and ratepayers take a pride in their
schools, and need no importunate urging to comply with the requirements of the law.   Some very poor sections, to their honour be it
spoken, come under this class.

A second variety, with constant official suggestion and urging,
will be induced to make suitable educational arrangements.

But a third class, even after their school house has been condemned, are perfectly indifferent, and will take two or three, and, in
more cases than one, even five years, before they take steps to

provide the needed school accommodation. It does not need argument to show the cruel and irreparable wrong done the children, but it will need some planning to circumvent this selfish folly.

We cannot, perhaps, have compulsory attendance outside of the City and Dartmouth, but, certainly, we can have the law made so plain and unmistakable on the point that it shall not be in the power of an ignorant and selfish majority to prevent the keeping of a school during, at least, some portion of the year, where there are parents who are anxious to educate their children.

Study the following cases :—

1. A section with upwards of 50 children of school going age, with virtually no school for five years.

2. Another, with 70 or more children, with the school closed for three-fourths of the time for the last fifteen years.

3. Still another section, within ten miles of Halifax, closing their school from year to year because they were asked by the Commissioners to substitute for their miserable, clumsy desks some well proportioned ones, no matter how plain. In my next report, I propose to give the names of these and any other sections guilty of such dereliction of duty. May I suggest that our Legislators, at the coming session, remedy this and other deficiencies in our school law ?

SCHOOLS IN OPERATION.

We have had 145 schools, with 6600 children in attendance during some portion of the year. These 145 schools have been taught by 151 teachers. Thus it will be seen that six teachers failed to fulfil their agreement. In one case the teacher left at the Christmas vacation, and substituted another teacher of a lower grade and inferior qualifications. Another, at the end of the quarter, having married, resigned. Out of the six cases, not one, according to my judgment, had a valid reason for breach of agreement. Certainly the law should annex some penalty for these breaches of contract, for they affect our schools injuriously.

Another point of uncertainty in the school law which needs clearing up, is the ground on which trustees may dismiss a teacher. The law says: " For gross neglect of duty or immorality." But this is too vague, as one of the sections of this County knows to its cost.

The GRADES of the teachers are as follows :—

    Grade A............................. 2
       "   B............................. 9
       "   C............................. 85
          D............................. 55

CLASSIFICATION.

This is steadily improving, and specially marked in the case of the teachers trained in the Normal School, and also those who have passed through the city schools.

SCHOOL WORK.

As regards vocal music, while very few of our schools fail to have more or less singing, which is recognized as an aid to discipline, the scientific teaching is largely dependent upon the teacher. If he or she has been at the Normal School, or has had the advantage of being educated in the schools of Dartmouth or Halifax, you will probably find a good deal of enthusiasm thrown into the teaching of vocal music.

HYGIENE AND TEMPERANCE.

The prescribed text books are now in all the schools, with less than half a dozen exceptions, and will undoubtedly have a profound moral effect.

MORAL AND PATRIOTIC DUTIES.

Good faithful teachers have always endeavoured to inculcate correct notions and practice upon these points.

READING, WRITING, AND ARITHMETIC.

So far as my experience goes, if Nos. 71, 72, 73, and 78 of the *Course of Study* are faithfully attended to, so solid a foundation is laid that the scholar who has profited by such instruction has the power to strike out for himself new paths of discovery, but nothing can compensate for a slip-shod treatment of these fundamental subjects of instruction. It is, therefore, a pleasure to see the increasing skill and care exercised in the teaching of these subjects.

PRIMARY WORK.

After a long experience of teaching and inspection, if I were asked for the greatest improvement which has been made in our school system, I should unhesitatingly place it in the Primary work, which is wonderfully good in some of our schools, and greatly improved in all. *Scientific Pedagogy* has displaced the unnatural methods of our young days, and there is no pleasanter duty than the inspection of many of our Primary Departments.

THE COLORED SCHOOLS.

Out of the eight sections in this County only one had school during the year. The African section above Hammond's Plains, with a school population of upwards of 50, has been without a school for the last five years. After much laudable effort they have succeeded in providing suitable accommodation, and will commence a school in August, 1894. The Lucas Settlement has a comfortable house and kept a school for the year.

Maroon Hill, with a poor school house, kept a school open for only one term in the last seven years.

Cobequid Road with a fair house, has been closed for the year.

Beech Hill, with some aid from the Commissioners, has put up a small house, and will shortly open a school.

Lake Loon, with a pretty good house, has been closed.

Preston, with children enough for a large school, has no school house, and has had no school open for the last fifteen years. I have repeatedly visited this section, and done my best to create an interest, but have hitherto utterly failed.

Partridge River (Preston), with upwards of 60 children, had their house destroyed by fire in 1892, but at the last annual meeting they voted money to erect a new one.

But suppose we had in each one of these sections a well equipped school house, the question arises, how are we to get good teachers, such as these poor people require ; for unless such special aid is given as will induce competent teachers to take charge, the colored people, of whom there are upwards of 300, will be left to struggle on in their ignorance.

INDIAN SCHOOL.

This school is doing very well under the care of the teacher, who is eminently adapted to the work. They have just received valuable gifts of books, kindergarten material, and a fine collection of wall pictures from George Philip & Son, of 32 Fleet St., London, to whom our sincere thanks are tendered for their generous gifts.

Mr. Barnes, of the *Presbyterian Witness*, has also sent them colored papers for decoration, etc., and has presented the teacher with a copy of Dr. Rand's " Mic-Mac Dictionary."

CITY SCHOOLS.

I spent March, April, and part of May in the city schools, and note here with pleasure their steady progress. While the teaching of some branches, reading and arithmetic, for example, quite hold their own in many of our county schools, in calisthenics, music, and drawing the city schools are far ahead, for the advantages are very great and are made much of. The vertical style of writing is proving a success, as was to be expected, from its superiority in legibility, dispatch and simplicity. At the risk of repeating myself, I may say that my inspection of the Primary Departments has been both pleasant and profitable, as I often obtain hints and suggestions that enable me the better to advise the teachers in our country schools.

Respectfully submitted,

H. CONDON.

To A. H. MacKay, Esq., Ll. D.,
        Supt. of Education.

DISTRICT No. 2.—LUNENBURG AND QUEENS.

H. H. MacIntosh, *Inspector.*

SIR :—

I beg to submit the following report on the Public Schools of Inspectoral District No. 2, for the year ended July 31st, 1894.

Two new sections were organized during the year, Upper Woodstock in Lunenburg, and Bang's Falls in Queens, the number of sections in the district now standing at 193, as follows :

Lunenburg and New Dublin............ 117 sections.
Chester.............................. 29 "
South Queens .... 26 "
North Queens 21

The following sections were without school during the year: Lower Northfield and North-West Cove, in Lunenburg Co., and Western Head, Riverdale, Denmark, Fifteen Mile, and Albany New, in Queens. Two of these were unable to secure suitable teachers, while the others were closed chiefly on account of the very small number of pupils in the sections.

The number of schools in operation, number of pupils registered, and attendance are shown in the following table :—

LUNENBURG COUNTY.

DISTRICT.	No. of Schools.	Pupils Reg stered.	Attendance.
Lunenburg & New Dublin	141	6175	654,778
Chester	30	1377	135,172
Total	171	7552	789,950

QUEENS COUNTY.

South Queens..........	37	1476	177,833
North "	19	547	52,332
Total	56	2023	230,165

The various graded schools throughout the district comprise 58 of the 227 reported in the above table, or 25 per cent. of all the schools. Lunenburg Academy has 12 departments; Liverpool Academy 8; Bridgewater 7; Mahone Bay 5; Milton, Mill Village, Port Medway, and Chester, 3 each; Brooklyn, Petite Riviere, West Dublin, Conquerall Bank, Summerside, Ritcey's Cove, and Tancook, 2 each. These schools enrol 3067 pupils, over 32 per cent. of the total number registered, and make over 41 per cent. of the total attendance.

The proportion of the population attending school was 1 in 4.1 in Lunenburg County, and 1 in 5.2 in Queens County. In Lunenburg County the average quarterly per centage of attendance was 61.7, and in Queens 63.6.

The number of children between 5 and 15 years of age not attending school at all, is given as 677 in Lunenburg County, and 216 in Queens. Out of the full term, 217 days, the schools in the district of Chester were open on an average 213.5 days; in South Queens, 211.5; in North Queens, 201.5; and in Lunenburg and New Dublin, 200 days.

During the past year, 239 teachers were employed, 181 in Lunenburg County, and 58 in Queens—only 23 of these being males. Comparing the number of teachers employed with the number of schools open shows a change of teacher in 12 sections during the year.

The various grades were represented as follows :—

	A	B	C	D
Lunenburg County....	2	14	72	. 93
Queens County.......	1	5	34	18

Compared with 1893, the year just closed shows an *increase* of *2 sections, 2 schools, 266 pupils, and more than a corresponding increase in attendance.*

Every settlement in Lunenburg County has now its public school, and every one of the 146 sections is organized and active. Upper Woodstock, the last to provide school privileges for the rising generation, has at length succeeded in building a very neat and substantial school house, and, next term, school will be opened for the first time in this section.

In Queens County, also, schools are within easy reach of every inhabitant, and every section is organized. Denmark and Riverdale, in South Queens, and Fifteen Mile and Albany New, in North Queens, have not had school in regular operation for the last two years, chiefly on account of the small number of children in each section. Two of these, however, Denmark and Albany New, will have school next term.

Besides the new school house in Upper Woodstock, already referred to, Mader's Cove has just completed a fine new building adapted for two departments when necessary, and furnished it with modern seats and desks. The ratepayers of this section did not wait, as is usually the case, for the old school house to be condemned. They saw that a new one was needed and built it.

School was opened last April in the new school house at Bang's Falls, the section lately organized in North Queens. A school was much needed in this settlement, and both parents and pupils seem greatly interested in its success.

The Lunenburg Academy, after an existence of nearly thirty years, was destroyed by fire on the 28th of last September, and the sum of $25,000 has been voted for a new building, which is now in course of construction. This promises to be a modern building in every respect, and will be one of the largest public school buildings in the province.

Considerable has been done the past year in the way of repairs to buildings and improvement of grounds, $1695 having been spent for this purpose. The following may be noted here :—

Chester.—Partial repairs to interior of rooms, to be completed duing the winter months.

Clearland.—Building raised, new foundation, grounds levelled and fenced, making a very creditable appearance.

Lower LaHave.—Building put in thorough repair.

Liverpool.—General repairs to Academy, amounting to about $400.

Milton.—$145 spent in improving grounds and out-buildings.

Port Medway.—Very necessary repairs to building.

Mill Village.—General repairs to buildings and premises.

Greenfield.—Over $70 spent in general repairs.

Bridgewater.—Grounds improved, and $100 voted for seating High School.

Park's Creek, Penny's, Knock's, and a number of other sections have made less extensive repairs, while the minutes of the last annual meetings show that Conquerall Mills, Petite Riviere, and several others have made provision for improvements during the next school year.

Nearly all the graded schools are fairly well supplied with apparatus. Liverpool Academy has received an outfit of scientific apparatus costing about $150. Many of the larger miscellaneous schools have a good outfit of maps, but the smaller schools of the poorer sections are still scantily supplied. More attention is being paid to providing materials and helps for use in the lower grades.

I can report a generally satisfactory year's work in the schools. The good teachers have done good work—always do. They *know how* to teach, are successful under any circumstances, and their work always tells. Other teachers are just as faithful and work just as hard, but *not knowing how*, their energy is mis-applied, and the results are unsatisfactory and discouraging. Without a practical training, the teacher is heavily handicapped. Many of this class, after years of experience, make excellent teachers, but what about the pupils' loss of time and teacher's loss of effort in the meantime ? The poor teacher is still with us, careless, without any ambition, full of excuses, placing the blame everywhere but in the right place. It is encouraging, however, to find that every year we have more good teachers and fewer poor ones. In this respect the premium on attendance at the Normal School has, even already, done this district good service. In 1890, only three students from Lunenburg and Queens are reported attending the Normal School; in 1893 there were 17, and this year, I think, even a greater number. Previous to 1893 the number of Normal School teachers employed in both counties ranged from 20 to 25; this year there were 41.

I have given much time and attention to the teaching of reading, writing, and arithmetic in the schools, and am pleased to be able to report improvement in these branches. Language and geography are also better taught than formerly. In many schools much good has been done by means of language lessons, composition, letter-writing, etc. In regard to geography, more attention is being given to our own country, its resources, industries, etc.,—in many cases history is taught in connection with geography, and with good results. Certainly, more oral work is being done every year, but the progress in this respect still seems too slow. The hints and directions on the teaching of the different subjects, given in the school register, have been of great assistance to many of our teachers, and if this idea were carried out more fully in manual form, as suggested by an Inspector in last year's report, I am confident it would do an immense amount of good to the teaching profession throughout the province. Something like this, to show the untrained and inexperienced teacher what intelligent teaching really is, would, in my opinion, have a widespread and beneficial effect.

In the past, the supply of teachers in this district was always largely in excess of the demand, but this year a sufficient number of teachers could not be got to fill the schools, particularly those opening after the beginning of the term. On this account a number of permissive licenses had to be issued, and judging from the continued scarcity, the same thing will have to be done next year. This scarcity of teachers is easily accounted for. The number of schools is increasing, more teachers from the district are attending the Normal School, and there are fewer candidates for license.

As you have personally inspected the County Academies in this district during the year, there is no necessity of any remark from me.

At the Provincial Examination, there were 92 candidates at Lunenburg station and 43 at Liverpool, 50 per cent. of the former and 72 per cent. of the latter being successful in obtaining some grade.

With a single exception, the returns of the past year were received within the specified time and, compared with those of last year, were superior in point of completeness, correctness, and neatness. Strange to say, the most of the incorrect and untidy returns came, year after year, from the same teachers — so much so, indeed, that I could make a pretty accurate list of " Unsatisfactory Returns " before examining them. In a number of the shore sections all the trustees, or a majority of them, were away at the close of the school year, and no arrangement had been made for the signing of returns. In such cases we had to be content with the certificate of the remaining trustee or secretary.

At date of writing, a copy of the minutes of the annual meeting from every section in the district is on file. No certificate for the payment of County Fund is issued to any section failing to comply with the law in this respect. This insures the filing of the minutes at least by the time of the division of the County Fund. The form for minutes of annual meeting in the April *Journal of Education* has been extensively followed, and no doubt the note at the bottom, " Copy of this to be sent Inspector within one week," had a good effect.

The regulation allowing sections so desiring to hold the annual meeting in March instead of June, was a great convenience and gave much satisfaction throughout the district. Thirty-six of the shore sections took advantage of the privilege, and in nearly every instance the meeting could not have been held in June on account of the ratepayers being away on the fishing grounds at that time. Already, applications are in from a number of sections asking the same permission next year.

At the meeting of the Commissioners for the District of Lunenburg and New Dublin, a petition was received asking for the formation of a new section to the north of Stanbourne Section, No. 38, to include a number of the ratepayers of Stanbourne Section and several families not in any section. The prayer of the petition was granted on condition that the bounds of the proposed section should be so amended at the next meeting of the board as to include several other families in that neighbourhood.

At the same meeting, the school house in Falkland Section, No. 35, was condemned.

The Chester Commissioners also condemned the school house in Back of Lake Section, No. 13.

New buildings will likely be completed in both these sections before August, 1895.

The change from semi-annual to annual terms has not, to my knowledge, called forth a single complaint in this district, and after two years' trial its many advantages are evident. It may have disadvantages, but they have failed to materialize with us.

Details affecting the different sections will be found in the statistical tables and notes of inspection already in your hands.

Your obedient servant,

H. H. MacINTOSH.

To A. H. MacKay, Esq., Ll. D.,
Superintendent of Education.

DISTRICT No. 3.—YARMOUTH AND SHELBURNE.

JAMES H. MUNRO, *Inspector.*

SIR :—

I intend this to be a brief report. The main features of the school year were so much like those of the preceding year, that to comment on them would be merely a repetition of what was previously said. The most noticeable difference was a scarcity of teachers, on account of which several boards of trustees were hard pressed to provide schools. Argyle Sound, Maple Grove, Gavelton, and North Kempt were all vacant, though repeated efforts were made to procure teachers. Indeed, other schools would have been vacant had not trustees succeeded in attracting teachers from other counties.

This deficiency in the supply contrasts oddly with the abundance of former years, and is accounted for, in part at least, by the large number of female teachers who have lately exchanged the school room for the domestic sphere, and by deaths.

Miss Philomena Babin, an excellent French teacher, died after a few weeks' sickness. Miss Georgina Trask and Miss Jessie MacCallum, young and promising teachers, became the victims of typhoid fever early in the year. Miss Ethel MacAlpine died a few months ago. She was esteemed for her faithful services.

It should be added that since the recent changes few candidates have come forward to qualify for licenses. At the last examination there were only sixteen in the whole district.

In one instance only have the boundary lines of sections been seriously changed. For several years I kept urging the ratepayers of Power's Brook and Enslow's Point to amalgamate their sections, since their united length was barely three miles, and the valuation of their properties about five thousand dollars. In both sections the school houses were very poor buildings, and while Power's Brook managed to have a school pretty regularly, Enslow's Point rarely had a school. After several disappointments, petitions in favour of union, signed by a majority of the ratepayers, were at the last annual meeting laid before the school commissioners, who readily acceded to the request of the petitioners. Power's Brook and Enslow's Point have now given place to " Upper West Jordan," No. 14½.

In a former report I referred to Belleville as coming under the review of the Argyle school commissioners. The present accommo- dation is insufficient, and three parties in the section have each a proposal. One would make three sections out of the present one ; another would make two, and the third would organize a graded school of two departments. The final deliverance of the board was to the effect " That unless the ratepayers organize a graded school, the commissioners at their next meeting will divide Belleville into two new sections." At the same meeting the following resolution was unanimously adopted : " That the time to expect gratuitous services is past, and that the Government should indemnify the school commissioners for the time spent, and expenses incurred in connection with meetings of the board."

All the boards in the district discussed the condition of the school buildings, and condemned the worst. It is up-hill work to persuade trustees and ratepayers that school houses and their surroundings should be neat and attractive. While other public buildings receive a lavish application of paint, school houses stand as monuments of solitary neglect. Still, as if to encourage the hope of improvement, a section here and there shows a consciousness that something better is needed. At Charlesville and Upper and Lower Wood's Harbour, I saw men to work levelling and smoothing the school grounds. In the town of Shelburne the trustees applied during the year two hundred dollars in this way, and intend to expend more money. Yarmouth town school houses are always well up to the standard. They are now as handsome as the hands of carpenters and painters can make them. Their fine grounds and trim hedges attract the attention of many tourists.

It is a perplexing question what to recommend where school houses are too good to be condemned, and yet too small for the needs of the section. Were there a stringent law compelling attendance, new buildings would have to be erected at once, and in other cases new apartments as attachments to the old buildings. But where the intelligent foresight of a generation that is passing away provided ample space in the building for the accommodation of another department, no tolerance should be given to that penuriousness which would crowd eighty or ninety children into a room which can hold comfortably only half that number. This is just what is being done in a section in this district. For the present the County Fund is withheld from the trustees.

I hope to see an amendment to the law whereby an annual meeting will be prevented from reducing unnecessarily the number of departments in the school. I have known a good graded school, at the freak of a few ratepayers, changed in a night to a miscellaneous school.

For simplicity, clearness, and completeness, so far as they go, as well as for their excellent print, the new Health Readers deserve commendation. They have been pretty generally introduced into the schools of this district, and were it not for a hitch in the supply, the cause of which I cannot explain, very few schools would be without them. I am pleased to notice that teachers and pupils study them carefully, and that the lessons are given with the feeling that there is a moral obligation to impress the facts on the minds of their pupils. I must confess my partiality to No. 1. Seven or eight years ago I recommended to teachers what was substantially the same book, and I have the gratification of seeing it on a good many school desks.

As regards the general work of teachers, there need be no hesitation in saying there is obvious improvement. The following points are quite discernible: More readiness in adopting practical suggestions, discarding books while teaching classes, completing to a figure the registers, making out correct returns, better oversight of school houses, apparatus, and out-buildings, a more accurate knowledge of the course of study, and an intelligent endeavor to carry out its requirements. I wish I could add regular habits of reading and study. Of course there is a minority to whom these remarks do not apply. Their registers are blotted, and though sworn to, are scribbled over, indicating a mental feebleness characteristic of little children, and their returns have mistakes which proclaim the domination of careless habits. The essential subjects are much better taught. One no longer sees classes huddled round the teacher's desk. Instead, they take their position in a remote part of the room, hold their books at an even height, and put force into their voices so as to be heard distinctly. Arithmetic, too, is receiving the time and attention it requires. In my opinion the teaching of arithmetic is the grand test of a teacher's ability and success. Show me a school where this branch is efficiently taught, and I shall draw the inference that the teacher is methodical in her work, clear in explanation, apt to illustrate, and she is not soon weary of repetition. No subject will be slighted, for her energy will quicken every class.

I have reviewed carefully the table showing how teachers apportion their time in their school rooms. Owing to the diversity of pupils, attainments, and other differences, a uniform allowance in all the schools for the same subjects cannot be expected. Nevertheless, the time in different schools often varies too largely. The differences, indeed, would suggest that there is a misunderstanding in some minds as to what is really wanted. For instance, a late graduate of the Normal School has entered 30 minutes as the allotment *per week* to writing, while another teacher would have to encroach on a second week for the sum of the minutes devoted to the subjects she taught. After all, the time apportioned among the different subjects in the average school makes a reasonable showing, and though it is not the same in both Counties, there is in some things an approximation.

This table shows the average number of minutes per week teachers have given to the subjects I have selected :—

	Nature Lessons.	Dictation.	Reading.	Grammar, etc.	Writing.	Geography.	History.	Drawing.	Arithmetic.
Yarmouth County....	35	173	290	106	106	106	78	53	309
Shelburne County....	31	182	337	112	112	131	101	59	306

Though music is receiving more attention, there are two many schools in which it is neglected. In Shelburne Municipality there are 23 schools which have no singing; in Barrington 10 ; in Argyle 7 ; and in Yarmouth 18. Thirty per cent. of all the schools make no pretence

5

to cultivate music. In Milton and Central schools, teachers give a training in the theory of music, and the singing is very fine. Miss L. Ada Goudey, Lower Town school, is an enthusiastic teacher, and her pupils share her enthusiasm. The melody and harmony of their singing it is delightful to listen to.

The number of candidates for the Provincial Examination was nearly equal to that of last year. As I believe their names were forwarded in good faith, and that the absences were due to sickness or other unavoidable causes, I submit the sections to which they belonged, and the grades of certificates applied for:

YARMOUTH STATION.

	A	B	C	D	TOTAL.
Academy	6	7	7	16	36
Milton..............................	....	4	8	6	18
Hebron.............................	1	2	4	9	16
Maitland............................	....	....	1	6	7
Tusket.............................	....	1	....	5	6
Ohio...............................	....	....	2	....	2
Wellington..........................	....	....	1	1	2
East Glenwood	....	....	....	2	2
Upper Eel Brook.....................	....	....	....	2	2
Plymouth...........................	....	....	....	1	1
Rockville...........................	....	....	....	1	1
Carleton............................	....	....	1	....	1
Private students	1	....	2	....	3
Total......................	8	14	26	49	97

SHELBURNE STATION.

	A	B	C	D	TOTAL.
Academy............................	....	4	7	23	34
Jordan Falls........................	....	....	....	2	2
Clyde River.........................	....	....	....	2	2
Private Students	....	1	....	1	2
Total.......................	....	5	7	28	40

LOCKEPORT STATION.

	A	B	C	D	TOTAL.
Lockeport	....	3	6	13	22
Osborne	....	....	2	3	5
Middle Sable	....	....	....	1	1
Total......................	....	3	8	17	28

BARRINGTON STATION.

	A	B	C	D	TOTAL.
Lower Wood's Harbor			2		2
West Pubnico			2		2
Passage			1		1
Head			1		1
Cape Negro				3	3
Clark's Harbor				1	1
Stony Island				1	1
Baccaro				1	1
Port La Tour				2	2
Pubnico Head				2	2
Total			6	10	16

It will be noted that in Yarmouth County there is only one examination station, and that in Shelburne there are three. Aggregating all the candidates belonging to the latter County for whom applications had been made, they will stand thus: for B 8, for C 19, for D 53 ; in all eighty.

It is hardly necessary to make special reference to the County Academies. The tables I have given indicate in a general way the attendance and degrees of proficiency. Besides, at your recent visits you had the opportunity of inspecting the equipment, and of becoming acquainted with the management of these institutions. As you are aware, the average attendance at the Yarmouth Academy fell short of the legal number, resulting in the loss to the town of one-half the former Provincial allowance.

I am in a position to state that in the preparatory departments of both the Academies and High Schools in the district excellent work is being done. The teachers are intelligent and energetic, and modern in their methods. The examination of the preparatory taught by Miss Emily R. Lyle is always gratifying, the pupils doing the given exercises with an accuracy and dispatch which leave the impression of a reserve of mental power and knowledge.

In Shelburne County there are a few miscellaneous schools which deserve notice. These are Black Point, taught by Miss Augustus Hogg ; Jordan Falls, of which Mrs. L. F. Holden is the teacher ; Cape Negro, taught by Miss Ella Sutherland ; and Middle Sable, taught by Miss Linda Best. Baccaro people made a grave mistake. They erected a building for one school, whereas two departments are needed for the comfortable accommodation of all the children in the section. Considering the attendance, the teacher— Miss Annie Bingay—makes a good show of work.

In Yarmouth District, Messrs. N. Hilton, C, E. Brown, J. W. Moody, and R. B. Brown have been for years the only active school commissioners. At the last meeting, Mr. J. W. Moody was absent, and a few days later his death was announced. Mr. Moody was for nearly thirty years a member of the board, and, as the records show, a regular and useful member. Though the powers of the board are being gradually eliminated, he knew that what remained had to be exercised, and his attendance was prompted by a sense of duty There is now a bare quorum. The recent appointments do not value the honour; at any rate they have never attended a meeting.

With assurances of much esteem,

I have the honor to remain,

Your obedient servant,

JAMES H. MUNRO.

To A. H. MacKay, Esq., Ll. D.,
Superintendent of Education.

P. S.—The statement in my last year's report that there were three hundred children in the town of Yarmouth, between the ages of five and fifteen years, who did not attend school at all, received some attention. As I dealt with figures officially supplied, though I believed them to be approximately correct, I did not consider myself responsible for them. The town commissioners having appointed responsible men to take a census of the children between the age limits, from five to fifteen years, the number was found to be more than a hundred less than that previously estimated. Notwithstanding this, and the fact that the attendance for the last year was a little better, any persons philanthropically inclined can find an ample field in the town for the exercise of their activities. Every observing ratepayer knows that there is a very large number of children that do not pass the threshold of a school room.

J. H. M.

DISTRICT No. 4.—DIGBY AND ANNAPOLIS.

L S. Morse, A. M., *Inspector.*

Sir :—

The following report on the state of the public schools in Inspectoral District No. 4, is hereby submitted. My monthly reports are already in your hands, and my notes of inspection, and the tables of statistics are forwarded herewith.

Reference was made in my report for last year to Annapolis Section No. 19, A. W. That portion of said original Section No. 19, lying south and west of the Allen River, and excluded from the section by the incorporation of the town of Annapolis, was at the time of writing that report without an organized existence as a school section, or a part thereof. The ratepayers, deeming such a condition prejudicial to their best interests, succeeded in having a special meeting of the board of school commissioners convened on the 11th day of September last. At this meeting petitions were presented by some of the ratepayers asking for the formation of a new section, and by other ratepayers praying the board to recommend union with the town of Annapolis for school purposes. A large part of this day was spent by the board in hearing the arguments of the petitioners and of the representatives of the town, and in considering the proper course to be pursued in the matter. As it was not certain whether a majority of the ratepayers favoured union with the town for school purposes or not, in consequence of some ratepayers having signed both petitions, the board deemed it advisable to adjourn until the 25th of the same month, in order that new petitions might be prepared, and the true sentiment of the district affected might be ascertained. At the adjourned meeting the matter again came before the board by petition and was again discussed, and the will of the board was finally expressed by the passage of a resolution recommending the securing of legislation to readmit the severed portion of the original section to the town of Annapolis for school purposes. In pursuance of the recommendation of the board as then expressed, a bill for effecting the union aforesaid was submitted to the Legislature at its last meeting, and was unanimously passed in the Lower House, but was defeated in the Legislative Council, in consequence of the opposition of the councillors residing in the County of Annapolis. The recommendation of the board of commissioners was therefore rejected, and matters remained in *statu quo* until the annual meeting of the board in May last. At this meeting the matter again came before the board by petition, and largely through the earnest advocacy of two commissioners appointed since the date of the special meetings in September, the board by a vote of *five* to *three*, formed a new section to be known as Allen River Section, No. 48. This action of the board was submitted to the Council of Public Instruction, as required by law, and received the approval of that body. The first annual meeting under the law was regularly called, at which trustees were appointed, and money voted for a school house and for general school purposes. The ratepayers who opposed the formation of the new section did not attend this meeting. The trustees at once selected a site for school house and grounds which was approved of by me. As the owner of part of said site refused to sell the same, it was expropriated under sub-section 4 of section 27 of the school law, as amended by the Acts of 1889 and 1890. An action of trespass is the result, and further proceedings are delayed awaiting a final decision of this suit by the Supreme Court.

The new school house in Bear River section, referred to in my last report, is not yet completed. This building is adapted for a school of eight departments, and is the best planned school building in this Inspectoral District. In addition to the eight school rooms, there is a large room in the third story suitable for any purpose for which a public hall may be required. The school rooms are detached from each other by halls—the side halls being intended for cloak rooms. The building will be warmed by furnaces in the basement. At the annual meeting in June, 1893, the sum of $5000.00 was voted for the school site and building, but the sum was found to be insufficient. Some difficulty was experienced in getting a supplementary appropriation from the section, owing to fact that the trustees had expended money in completing the hall in the third story, which many of the ratepayers considered to be unnecessary at the present time. The difficulty was finally arranged at the last annual meeting, at which $1800.00 was voted to finish and furnish the building. The work of completion is now being pushed forward as rapidly as possible, and for a few weeks longer, until that is accomplished, the schools will occupy the old school houses as usual.

There are now *one hundred and eighty-seven* school sections in this Inspectoral District, *six* of which are not organized and do not maintain schools. Several other sections are thinly settled, and are not able to sustain schools continuously. During the year *fifty-one* sections were entitled to receive aid as "poor sections," of which *nine* only were without schools during the whole year. Some others were able to maintain schools for a part only of the year, and were granted permission accordingly. In a few cases teachers were not available at the beginning of the year, and sections were therefore obliged to have school for a shorter period than was originally intended.

No new school houses have been erected during the year, with the exception of that at Bear River and one at Phinney's Cove. A new building has been commenced in Forest Glen Section No. 34. in the District of Clare, and it is hoped that it will be ready for occupation at some time during the ensuing year. This is the last section created in that district, and it is situated on the Tusket river between lake Wentworth and the Yarmouth County line. It is now erecting its first school house. Preparations are being made for building new houses in Torbrook West, Tiddville, Freeport, and Meteghan sections. In the last named section an agitation for the division of the section has arisen, which will doubtless be settled by the board of commissioners and the Council of Public Instruction before another year passes. If the section remain as at present, a new school house for four departments must 'be provided. If a division be made, two new school houses will be required. At Weymouth Bridge, a prosperous and wealthy community, new school grounds and buildings are much needed and must soon be provided. The present school house and its environments are by no means creditable to the section.

In many schools the supply of apparatus should be largely increased in order that the teachers may be in a position to perform more effective work. Trustees and ratepayers are in many cases unwilling to vote an adequate appropriation for this purpose. The recommendations of the Council of Public Instruction on this subject are good, but there appears to be no definite machinery provided for enforcing them. Some enactment or additional regulation on the subject is needed.

The condition of the schools, so far as the work of teachers and pupils are concerned, may be more definitely ascertained by consulting my notes of inspection for the year. Generally speaking, a few may be classed as superior, some good, some fair, and a few very poor. Due allowance being made for local conditions, it may safely be said that the teacher makes the school. Where energy and enthusiasm are exercised on her part good results may be expected. The lack of these essential qualities causes failure.

Two hundred and seventy candidates applied for scholarship certificates at the four stations in this district, of whom *fifty-nine* only took the *minimum professional qualification* examination. A considerable number of these latter may be expected to fail, and unless the attendance at the Normal School be increased a scarcity of licensed teachers may soon occur.

In the municipality of Clare about thirty schools require French speaking teachers. Licensed teachers cannot be found for all of these schools, in consequence of which " permissive licenses " are a necessity. Fifteen of these " permissive licenses " were issued during the year in order that the French schools might be supplied with teachers. Difficulty is undoubtedly experienced by French candidates in passing the Provincial Examination ; but when it is seen that the same candidates come up for examination year after year, and show but little or no improvement in their work, there is great reason to suspect that no proper effort is being made to qualify themselves for examination. It is evident that some of these candidates make but little effort to obtain a regular license, relying upon the issue of " permissive licenses," which place them upon an equal footing financially . with a majority of the teachers of that district. It is to be hoped that the County Academy, about being established in Clare, will provide a remedy for this necessary evil. It is also very desirable that the French schools become more efficient and do more advanced work than that which has been done in a majority of these schools in the past, in order that they may act as feeders for this academy. Under present regulations this academy must soon cease to exist, unless a large proportion of 'its pupils are drawn from sources other than French common schools of Clare.

The registered attendance at the schools was fairly satisfactory. In this Inspectoral District the number of children between five and fifteen years of age reported in sections having schools, was 8936, of which number 8316 attended school during some portion of the year. The total annual enrolment was 9356, being 553 more than the annual enrolment of the previous year. The per centage of enrolled. pupils daily present at school, however, was 62.6 only, showing an irregularity in attendance far too great. There is yet much room for improvement in this regard.

The course of study is producing beneficial results. A uniformity of work now prevails which was unattainable under the old system. Occasionally, however, a teacher is found who fails to comprehend the design of the course of study, and causes such disarrangement and disorder as will give her successor much trouble to eradicate. The text-book studies are receiving due attention. In some cases the prescribed oral lessons are being taught very successfully, but in many schools the work in this line is crude and unsatisfactory. This is no doubt the result of inexperience and lack of training. A normal training is certainly most desirable, but greater ambition and determination to succeed in the line of oral instruction would soon cause many of the teachers to do far better work than they have hitherto accomplished.

With one or two exceptions the annual returns came to hand promptly. Most of these were carefully prepared and correct. A few required revision, and were promptly sent back for that purpose, with instructions to correct the registers also. When visiting the schools special pains was taken to explain the registers and to prevent, as far as possible, the possibility of mistakes. The sequel has proved the wisdom of this course.

The County Academy at Annapolis was taught by Principal McVicar. The attendance was large, and the work done was, as usual, highly efficient and satisfactory. About one-half of the candidates who applied for examination at Annapolis station in July, were students of the Academy.

At Digby, the County Academy was taught by Principal Longley, an experienced and successful teacher. The attendance was small, owing to circumstances over which the Principal had no control. At the entrance examination at the close of the preceding year, three pupils only passed into the Academy— a number insufficient to keep the attendance at its normal standing. Mr. Longley discharged his duties efficiently and satisfactorily. Fourteen of his pupils applied for examination in July, some of whom made a creditable record. A lack of ambition on the part of some of the young people of this town militates against the success of this Academy.

All schools were inspected once during the year, and some visited a second time. More would have been accomplished if a bad cold had not made it expedient for me to remain at home for about two weeks during the winter. Correspondence and other clerical work has claimed very much time and attention.

Very few complaints have reached me regarding the one term system. Some of the "poor sections" prefer the old system, and also some teachers who wish to engage schools during the summer only. Other sections and teachers, so far as I have ascertained, are satisfied. The Superintendent and Inspectors have more reason to complain, owing to the fact that they are necessarily kept so busily engaged during the greater part of the summer vacation.

In conclusion, permit me to recommend that a revision of the school law and regulations be undertaken as soon as leisure can be found for that purpose. The confusion now resulting from the many amendments made since the revision causes serious difficulty to all having occasion to consult the law and regulations in the form in which they now exist. Feeling confident that this recommendation will commend itself to your judgment,

I have the honour to be, Sir,

Your obedient servant,

L. S. MORSE.

A. H. MacKay, Esq., Ll. D.,
   Superintendent of Education.

DISTRICT No. 5.—HANTS AND KINGS.

COLIN W. ROSCOE, A. M., *Inspector.*

SIR :—

I respectfully submit the following report of the schools in Inspectoral District No. 5, for the year ended July 31st, 1894 :

This district includes three School Commissioners' Districts, viz. : Kings, West Hants, and East Hants. There were in operation for the whole. or some part of the past year, 241 schools. In these schools 256 teachers were employed, 10,322 pupils attended, making an attendance of 1,045,574 days. That 56 of these schools were in operation the full term of 217 days ; 135 for over 200 days, but less than the full term ; 29 for 150 to 200 days ; 12 for 100 to 150 days, and 1 under 50 days, shows their regularity, and to some extent the working of the one term system. A large percentage of the schools employed their teachers for the full term. Some could not secure teachers at the outset, and thus were compelled to have schools for a shorter period than was desirable. A few had my consent for a period shorter than a year. These cases have already been reported to you. Failures in health, or in the ability to conduct the schools undertaken, made it necessary to have a change of teachers in a few instances. Of the 43 " poor sections " in this district having schools, 28 engaged their teachers for the full year, and 4 more for over half the year, thus leaving but 11 which adopted the minimum length of term allowed. I regard the foregoing as evidence that the change in the length of term is meeting with a good degree of approbation on the part of trustees and people. A few complain that the term does not suit ; but in most of these cases the Inspector can consent to a period that will meet the wants of those concerned. The objections, so far, are only imaginary.

Black Rock Mt., Australia, E. Pereaux Mt , and Kellyville Sections in Kings County, and Mt. Summerville, Lakelands, Dawson Road, Upper Nine Mile River, Renfrew, Milford, and Rawdon Gold Mines, in Hants, had no schools for the past year. All of these, except one, are " poor sections," and most of them have a very small number of children, and are weak financially for such sections, which may be assigned as the causes of their failure to have schools. Upper Nine Mile River was building a school house, and thought best to drop their school for the time. Milford was required by the board of commissioners to put their house on a site sanctioned in a regular way, and because they did not do so the school was not started. Rawdon Gold Mines and Renfrew closed down their schools when the mines were closed down. Almost every one of these will re-open their school next term.

The schools in the three commissioners' districts may be reported as follows :—

	No. Schools.	No. Teachers.	No. Pupils.	Attendance.
Kings......	119	130	5235	504,895 days.
West Hants..	62	65	2391	242,809 "
East Hants ..	60	61	2696	297,870 "
Total....	241	256	10322	1,045,574 days.

TEACHERS.

	A.	B.	C.	D.	Male.	Female.	Total.
Kings	2	25	67	36	31	99	130
West Hants	1	13	36	11	10	51	61
East Hants.....	0	6	29	30	8	57	65
Total	3	44	132	77	49	207	256

Seventy-three of the teachers employed hold Normal School Diplomas. These are only 26 per cent. of the whole—a much smaller number than should be found in the schools at this date.

Of the schools as a whole I am pleased to report progress. There is a disposition on the part of most of the *teachers* to advance as the way is opened to them. The *trustees* and too many of the *parents* question the utility of some of the new subjects and changes being introduced. This opens the way for teachers to exercise their influence in creating a healthful educational sentiment in the section, and making the work of the schools understood and appreciated. In so so far as the teacher rises to the importance and true dignity of his office, he leads his pupils and the section too, to estimate at their right value the subjects he is required by the C. P. I. to teach. It is a pleasure to be able to report that the teachers in this district who expect to meet difficulties, and are prepared to combat them wisely and overcome them, are in the majority. Of the work of these in the school room and in the section, I have words of commendation only. They are popular educators, and the people among whom they labor are not likely soon to forget their efforts for the well-being of their constituents. The few pessimistic teachers who are not in touch with the onward march of the schools, who see no need of change from the old ways and methods of days long past, and who will not be at the pains to learn what is required of them, are fast going to the rear. They do not realize it, but 'Ichabod" is written on their work, and none too soon ; for the good of the schools, they must seek employment congenial to their tastes.

The shire towns of Windsor and Kentville, in which are situated the County Academies, are to be commended for the intelligent view they take of the importance of maintaining the best kinds of schools in their midst. In both these towns much caution is observed in selecting teachers who will bring to their work ability, experience, and the tact so essential to success in school teaching.

I shall only be stating what you already know by personal examination of the work of these Academies, when I say that the high standing won by them heretofore has been fully sustained during the year just closed. With the academies there may be grouped the schools of Hantsport, Berwick, Maitland, Wolfville, and Canning, the efficiency and management of which differ very slightly from the academies. The difference is seen principally in the number of pupils in attendance and in the number of teachers employed. The character of the work done and the interest manifested by the town commissioners and trustees, in most of these, compare favorably with the academies.

Other schools, graded and miscellaneous, have succeeded during the year in maintaining efficiency and advancing upon their previous record. Space would fail to speak of each of them separately, and it may suffice to say that most of them have made progress proportionate to the money expended in their behalf. The lack of equipment retards progress more than any other hindrance I have to report. It would pay to invest 50% more capital in all our schools.

BUILDINGS.

New school houses have been erected in W. Black Rock, St. Mary's, and Upper Nine Mile River during the year, and, in accordance with the vote of the school commissioners, Kingsport has added a new room to its house; Three Mile Plain has built a new house and graded its school; St. Croix divided its house into two rooms, added entrance halls, &c., and graded the school, and Cheverie has enlarged the room for the advanced department and added new entrance ways. Hantsport has joined their two two school houses together, re-arranged the rooms and halls, and thoroughly repaired so as to accommodate all their schools—five in number—under the same roof. They also put in a hot air furnace. By these improvements the expense of heating is much lessened and the management of the school facilitated. The houses of Weston, Brooklyn (A), and Brooklyn (C), Sheffields Mills, Upper Gaspereaux, Tremont, Lakeville, New Minas, and Dempsey Corner, in Kings, and Wentworth and Urbania in Hants County, have undergone considerable repairs, and been furnished with new furniture of an improved style. Lower Canard, Falmouth Village, Coldbrook, Martock, Poplar Grove, and Mt. Pleasant have repaired to some extent. The improvements thus made are of a durable character. The rooms have been ceiled or sheathed with matched wood, and the furniture is of a make and pattern to last and give comfort in its use.

WOLFVILLE SCHOOL BUILDING.

The formal opening of the new school house in the town of Wolfville took place in College Hall on the evening of December 21st, 1893. The Superintendent of Education; Mr. E. W. Sawyers, chairman of the town commissioners; Dr. J. B. Hall; Dr. A. W. Sawyer, President of Acadia University; Prof. F. H. Eaton, Prof. Faville, and Prof. E. M. Keirstead, addressed the meeting. The history of the school house, its cost, ventilation, school grounds, civics, &c., &c., were discussed briefly. All united in congratulating the town on the advance step made in the matter of improved school accommodation. The system of heating and ventilation was particularly referred to. After one year's trial the house, in all its equipments, is pronounced entirely satisfactory. It is one of the few houses in the Province ventilated to secure the health and comfort of the pupils attending according to the most improved method. The system is recommended to other sections building new school houses.

Kentville is now erecting an addition to the academy building that will contain four rooms.

HEALTH READERS.

At my first visit to the schools for the year, I called special attention to a law recently passed, requiring instruction to be given in all the schools upon Health and Temperance. At my second visit I found the prescribed Health Readers in general use. They were used as readers, and then the pupils questioned upon lessons read. A good elementary knowledge of the structure of the human body, and its principal organs and their functions, has thus been given. The chapters on foods, alcohol, tobacco, and other narcotics, have been dwelt upon. I believe an impression is being made in regard to the injurious effects of narcotics more lasting than that made by the lectures upon these subjects to adults, because given at an age when impressions are easily made. The aim is to *prevent*, not to *cure*. I believe success will result.

SCHOOL VISITATION, ETC.

I made 460 visits for the purpose of inspection, and several others in *re* matters pertaining to schools which seemed to need my attention at the time. My first visit to the schools was announced by a post card to the teacher containing the following :—

" I intend to visit your school on the .... day of ...., 1894, at .. o'clock, .. M., and wish you to have present for inspection the register for past term, your license, agreement, and the books of the secretary of trustees. Please notify the trustees of my visit and intention to make a thorough examination of the school buildings, and premises, in order to report upon their condition.

Yours very truly,
COLIN W. ROSCOE,
Inspector of Schools."

Wolfville............1894.

The inspection of the registers for the year ended July, 1893, discovered a large number not complete and not at all creditable to the teachers, who had charge of the schools, and who had in their returns sworn that the prescribed register had been faithfully and correctly kept by them. These were sent to the teachers who had begun them to be completed, and they were warned of the result of having the register in such a condition. For the past year it was the exception not to find the register completed to the date of my visit. These will be called up on my first visit next year, and all delinquents reported to you.

I find the inspection of the licenses occasionally a necessity. It is seldom when the license is thus called for that any one attempts to impose upon me in regard to the class held. Written agreements have become the rule since teachers understand they are expected to produce them for inspection, and this notice gives them time to attend to that duty if they have not had them written and signed before.

The system of book-keeping by the secretaries of trustees is almost as varied as the number of secretaries. Your form for keeping the section's accounts, in the last *Journal*, will be suggestive, and very helpful to many.

The notice concerning school buildings and premises had the effect of calling the attention of trustees to their condition, and having them put in order, often, previous to my visit. When more was needed than could be done at so short a notice, I told the trustees what was needed and required, and in most cases I am able to report that it has been done or arranged for.

SCHOOL RETURNS.

I had intended to report all cases of incomplete or incorrect school returns at this time, but there are too many of them to report here. From 241 schools, 87 returns needed corrections or additions. The teachers or trustees had to be written to, and often the sheet sent back before they could be passed. Perhaps in half of these cases the defects were either omissions of some small item that seemed of no value to the teacher, but which made no small amount of labor for me to secure the information needed for reports being prepared for the Education Office ; or the neglect to give " Totals of every column which can be added." It seems to me the instruction is too plain to need a word of comment, and yet it is not attended to. Instead of reporting individual cases this time, I will use my best efforts, for another year, to make teachers understand their duty in this regard. One encouraging feature, however, is that, bad as the returns were, they were much better than last year. And 154 returns were models of neatness and correctness— a testimonial of no little value of how these teachers will do all their work. All teachers who have not been notified by me of defects in their returns may regard themselves as belonging to the 154 mentioned above.

TEACHERS' ASSOCIATION.

The teachers of Hants and Kings Counties held a very successful Association in Wolfville, just before the closing of the schools for the Christmas vacation.

Programme.

"The School Master and His Work" .... JOHN N. STURK.
"Scientific Temperance" .... MISS L. A. SCOTT.
"The Prescribed Speller" .... I. CROMBIE.
"Relation of Parents to the School" .... STEPHEN H. ROGERS.
"Mathematical Problems" .... ANGUS McLEOD.
"Address on Science" .... DR. A. H. MACKAY.
"Tonic Sol Fa Notation" .... MISS N. A. BURGOYNE.
"Chemical Apparatus" .... PROF. A. E. COLDWELL.
"Lesson in English" .... DR. J. B. HALL.
"Dr. Arnold as a Teacher" .... JOHN F. GODFREY.
"Normal School" .... E. H. NICHOLS.
"Metric System" .... J. A. SMITH.

All the work of the Association was interesting and profitable to the teachers. The Superintendent of Education put himself in touch with the teachers and their work, and won golden opinions from all. His willingness to answer questions, and his brief addresses on the subjects discussed, were of value to the Association. Miss Burgoyne presented the history, merits, and popularity of the Tonic Sol-Fa notation in so clear and convincing a manner that, by the unanimous vote of the Association, she was pursuaded to publish her paper.

This extract is taken from a Halifax paper :— "Dr. J. B. Hall then gave a lesson in English to a class of Grade 9 pupils. The lesson combined reading, literature, and analysis, and was taught in the doctor's usual happy style. He has the faculty of being pleasant himself and of making others feel pleasant— two strong points in good teaching. The doctor is always welcome at teachers meetings." Space forbids to speak of the merits of all the papers. The teachers of the district did their part nobly and well as usual.

For detailed information regarding the time spent in giving instruction in the various school studies, the number of pupils engaged in them, the expenditure for the schools for all purposes, etc., etc., etc., I refer you to the tables of statistics sent herewith. I have exerted myself to present in these all the reliable information possible.

In conclusion, I wish to refer to the attention all my communications to you have received, and to say in that regard my work has been made most pleasant and agreeable.

I have the honor to be, Sir,

Your obedient servant,

COLIN W. ROSCOE.

To A. H. MACKAY, ESQ., LL. D.,
Superintendent of Education.

DISTRICT No. 6.—ANTIGONISH AND GUYSBORO.

W. MacIsaac, B. A., *Inspector.*

Sir:—

Following is my report on the schools of Inspectoral District No. 6, for the year ended July, 1894.

The total number of schools in operation in Antigonish was 94, and in Guysboro 91. The number of teachers employed in Antigonish was 97, in Guysboro 94. There were three sections without school in Antigonish during some portion of the year, and twelve in Guysboro.

The total annual enrolment in Antigonish was 3236; in Guysboro 3341. Grand total of attendance : Antigonish, 327,469 ; Guysboro, 345,995.

Average annual salaries paid to the teachers, including government grants :—

	MALES.			FEMALES.		
	B	C	D	B	C	D
Antigonish..	$341 17	$221 90	$168 33	$246 88	$200 45	$146 67
Guysboro...	$448 88	$234 70	$137 34	$327 71	$224 30	$153 22

Number of teachers employed of different grades and sexes :—

ANTIGONISH COUNTY.

	A	B	C	D
Male	3	7	15	11
Female	..	2	23	36
Totals	A 3	B 9	C 38	D 47

GUYSBORO COUNTY.

	A	B	C	D
Male	1	5	5	5
Female	..	6	30	42
Totals	A 1	B 11	C 35	D 47

A new school section was established at Indian River at the last meeting of the school board in Sherbrooke. There are but a few ratepayers in the section so created ; but as they are all beyond three miles from the nearest school, the commissioners deemed it nothing but justice to give them a school of their own.

A new school house has lately been built at Greenfield in the same municipality. The unsuitable character of the one replaced, coupled with local difficulties, retarded the progress of education in the section for a considerable time. These difficultes having now happily disappeared, it is to be hoped that the section will endeavor to make up, as far as possible, for lost opportunities by employing only the best available teachers.

I am happy to report that the inhabitants of Dover, in the Municipality of Guysboro, replaced the school house which was burnt last year by a large and handsome building worthy of its predecessor.

Repairs and improvements, more or less extensive, were made during the year to several school buildings in the two counties, but, it is needless to say, that much remains yet to be done.

A few weak and straggling sections have unfortunately been practically closed in this inspectorate for a few years past, and external efforts made to revive them are met with the old-time argument that the pupils are few and that the parents cannot afford to pay a teacher. It is unpleasant to refer to such a state of things; but it is only too true that people are to be found here and there who though thoeretically in favor of a school, prefer to see it closed to making even a small pecuniary sacrifice to keep it open. Nor does it unfrequently happen that the public spirit of a few ratepayers in some sections, supported by the provisions of the school law, which contemplates that every child in the county shall receive, at least, an elementary education, is brought actively into play to prevent the closing of schools in sections which cannot by any means plead real poverty or fewness of pupils.

With regard to the general character of the work of our schools, I think I can fairly say that it is improving from year to year. Many of our teachers, however, do not fully apprehend the true place or function of the text-book, or of oral instruction in the school room. They seem to fear that if they devote a half hour now and then to a talk on a suitable topic with a view to arouse a thoughtful or questioning mental attitude on the part of the pupil, they will be considered by both the pupils and parents as wasting time because not occupied in the beaten track of the text-book. Instead of following the text in teaching a lesson on Manitoba, for example, the pupils would be benefitted very much more by approaching the special lesson for the day by a talk on flour—why so cheap as compared to its price in years gone by, what makes an article cheap, why it is more abundant and less expensively carried now than in past years, advantages of improved implements of agriculture, the wonderful part steam power plays in our social economy, new wheat regions put under cultivation, location and extent of Manitoba as shewn on maps, rail and water routes by which flour is carried thence to Nova Scotia, giving names and distances of the principal railways and rivers. A map could be drawn on blackboard showing position of railroads, rivers, and coast waters. Important points in history and commerce could be easily inwoven in a lesson conducted on this or similar plan, and the interest of the pupils could be strongly enlisted because the lesson would place them in a certain and definite relation with the province whose geography they are studying. It is needless to say that classes taught in a conversational way like this become more intelligent, fonder of school and reading, an object that should be always kept'in view in school work.

The opinion is quite prevalent that rural sections do not need as good teachers as the town schools. Nothing could be more erroneous. In the towns, schools are more carefully graded ; and usually only a few grades are assigned to a teacher. In the ordinary miscellaneous school in the country, the teacher has often all the grades of the common school course, and not unfrequently a few high school pupils. The town teacher has, besides, better appliances and facilities for work ; and if he do well, his labors receive more commendation, if ill, more discriminative censure.

On this matter I cannot do better than quote from the report of James F. Crooker, Superintendent of Schools for the State of New York, for the school year ended July, 1893 :—

"It is in the country district where the mental and physical " strength of the teacher is heavily taxed and strained to secure good " results, and where the most meagre, and, in many cases, shamefully " paltry wages are paid for his services. The deplorable practice of " parsimony in teachers' wages on the part of trustees is the chief " reason for the lack of interest in education, and the cause of failure " to have good, profitable schools in many country districts. The " character of the school depends on the efficiency of the teacher, and " the quality of the teacher employed generally corresponds to the " amount of salary offered for services. Through the employment of " incompetent teachers a great wrong is done not only to the children, " but to the public generally. There is not only waste of public " funds, but a sacrifice of valuable time which properly belongs to the " youth of our land in which to be prepared and trained to become " intelligent and useful citizens. The period for this purpose is " necessarily limited, and none of it should be wasted. It should be " remembered that parsimony in furnishing the youth of our land " with educational facilities is dangerous, and that stint in teachers' " wages is foolish frugality."

All of which is respectfully submitted.

I have the honor to be, Sir,

Your obedient servant,

W. MacISAAC.

A. H. MacKay, Esq., Ll. D.,
     Superintendent of Education.

DISTRICT No. 7.—CAPE BRETON AND RICHMOND.

M. J. T. MACNEIL, B. A.. *Inspector.*

SIR :—

I beg to submit the following report on the schools and educational affairs of District No. 7 for the year ended July last.

In the County of Cape Breton there was school in 109 sections out of the 132, leaving 23 sections without any school any part of the year. In these 109 sections there were 157 schools or departments, as compared with 161 the year previous, and 6887 pupils enrolled (as against 6848 in 1893) or 1 in 4.94 of the population.

In Richmond County there were 70 schools in operation in 60 of the 70 sections, ten consequently having remained vacant, while the previous year there were 70 schools in 61 sections : one of the closed departments of the Arichat schools was re-opened at the beginning of the year.

Twenty-three sections vacant in one county and ten in the other. There must be some good reason for so many schools being closed. Let us see. Barachois No. 5, Macadam's Lake No. 97½, Ben Eoin No. 87, Rear Eskasoni No. 110, and Juniper Mount. No. 127, have not had school for years—have, in fact, practically fallen into desuetude. Four of them have no school buildings and are not likely to have any for some time to come. One of the above named, Rear of Eskasoni, is agitating for a union with the neighboring section of Rear of Beaver's Cove. Ben Eoin has been making spasmodic efforts to build a school house for the last ten years, but that desirable object seems to-day as difficult of accomplishment as ever. No. 76½, Gabarus Bay, is a new section whose school house has only recently been erected, and will come in for inspection the current year and notice in next report. No. 73, Trout Brook ; 84, Grand Mira North ; 91, Huntington's Mountain ; 122, Little Pond ; and 129, Brickyard, have all lost their school houses through forest fires within the last four or five years. They are none of them overburdened with wealth, and have been unable to rebuild in a hurry, but three or four, if not the whole five, will most probably have new school houses and have schools in operation in the course of the current year. Thus are eleven out of the twenty-three accounted for ; for the remaining twelve, which are for the most part isolated sections, no better excuse could be offered than the difficulty of securing teachers—with one exception, however, Catalone No. 59, whose trustees have assumed a grave responsibility in closing the doors of the school in a section having 61 pupils enrolled the last term it was in operation, and an assessment roll of from $9,000 to $10,000 wherewith to support it.

Of the ten vacancies in Richmond County, No. 52½, Caledonia, and 60, Macnab, might as well be dropped off the list for some time to come, if not for good, being too weak to support a school. No. 12, Richmond Mines, and 68, Hureauville, had their school houses condemned at the meeting of the board in 1893. No. 36, Loch Lomond North, occupies a site that was never officially approved, and though a suitable one was selected and duly expropriated according to law about two years ago, the trustees have so far failed to proceed further. No. 21, Cape George, has a new school house in course of construction, the old one having served its time and been torn down. No. 65, Port Richmond, had its school house burnt in a forest fire some five years ago, since which time it has only had school two terms (half-years) in temporary quarters, and only during the year just closed have the people, urged on by one or two of the more public-spirited ratepayers, made up their minds to build, and I hope to find a good modern school building occupied in the course of this year. No. 35, Loch Lomond —here the school house was destroyed by fire (let us hope accidentally) in the autumn of 1892, and this thriving settlement, with a good record for its enlightened interest in education in the past, has been ever since, and is till now, without a school on account of a disagreement about a site arising from disputed boundaries. The matter has been before the board of commissioners at each annual session for several years past, and finally at a special meeting recently held for the purpose, when it was, presumably, definitely settled, and in all probability a site will shortly be chosen and building operations commenced. No. 37, Red Islands—here also school matters have been in a very unsatisfactory condition for several years owing to the alleged inconvenient location of the school house. A proposed readjustment of boundary lines with neighboring sections has been occupying the attention of the commissioners for some time, which it is claimed would enable the placing of school houses in the different sections in question more in accordance with present requirements. The inconvenient location of a school house may not be a sufficient cause to justify trustees in keeping its doors closed, but in this case a change or reconstruction of boundaries would mean the building of several new school houses, the necessity for which in any case is recognized by all, and it is urged that in view of such a contingency the repairing of a building, now unfit for occupation, would be but a useless waste. There remains to be accounted for No. 29, Point Micheau, and I know of no more valid reason why the school remained vacant than that the trustees made no special efforts to secure a teacher when none came to offer his services. In the above enumeration, I have not included section No. 16½, Macpherson, which never organized after having secured its autonomy some five years ago. The majority of the people seem to have secured the object aimed at, viz., immunity from taxation for schools and school purposes, and to be content to allow their children to grow up without education, save the little smattering they can pick up by occasional visits to the school of a neighbouring section. Several efforts have been made to restore the original order of things, but so far the majority refuse to sign the petition necessary, according to law, to accomplish that object; and those ratepayers who were really anxious to have a school to which to send their children, have been compelled to apply individually to be restored to their former sections. Promoters of such divisions occasionally succeed in convincing a board of commissioners that they are imbued with the liveliest interest in education, and that the scheme they are promoting is absolutely necessary to secure educational privileges for a few unfortunately or inconveniently situated children, and that, finally, they and their supporters are prepared to make extraordinary sacrifices for the attainment of so worthy an object. The board, even against its better judgment, yields the point; pressure is brought to bear on the Council of Public Instruction, a new section is established, and— there's an end of it. When the mistake is discovered, the only remedy is to apply to the board by petition of a majority of the ratepayers of the sections concerned for re-union, which virtually means that there is no remedy, because the necessary signatures cannot be obtained. Surely then some remedy should be devised whereby such a blunder, committed in good faith and with the best intentions, could be rectified. I cannot see any harm likely to arise from an amendment of the law such as I have already suggested, that, namely, a new section failing to organize and to establish a school within a reasonable specified time, should revert to its original status.

The following table will show the number, class, and sex of the teachers employed, and the attendance at school of the pupils as compared with the previous year:

CAPE BRETON COUNTY.

	MALE.				FEMALE.				TOTAL.		
	A	B	C	D	A	B	C	D	M	F	TOTAL.
1894....	3	21	23	19	....	6	42	43	66	91	157
1893....	4	20	26	23	....	7	42	39	73	88	161

RICHMOND COUNTY.

	A	B	C	D	A	B	C	D	M	F	TOTAL.
1894....	....	9	22	12	....	....	12	15	43	27	70
1893....	1	9	11	13	....	....	15	21	34	36	70

CAPE BRETON COUNTY.

	No. of Boys.	No. of Girls.	Total.	Grand total days' attendance.	No. children in section, 5 to 15 years of age.	No. of those who did not attend school during year.
1894	3687	3200	6887	687,701	7078	646
1893	3685	3163	6848	533,886	6754	672
Increase ..	2	37	39	153,815	324	....
Decrease..	......	....	....	....	....	26

RICHMOND COUNTY.

1894	1595	1333	2928	282,592	3048	411
1893	1504	1226	2730	200,462	2918	402
Increase ..	91	107	198	82,130	130	9

The number of students returned as pursuing the High School Course in any of the schools, including several miscellaneous rural schools, was, in Cape Breton County 325, 235 of whom were following the full prescribed, while the remaining 90 were taking only a partial course. This shows a falling off of 31 from the figures of last year, which I doubt not may be partly accounted for by omissions in the returns of some of the miscellaneous schools. Last year the number of High School pupils returned for all the schools of Richmond County was only 12, due largely to omissions which were noticed too late to have them supplied; for this year the number given is 49, 27 of whom were taking the full course, and 22 only a partial one.

I think that, in the main, much greater accuracy has been secured in the returns of the past year than, probably, ever before. This object has not, however, been attained without a great expenditure of time and labor. If one could expect the improvement to be permanent, one's time and labor so expended would not be begrudged, but with a continual change of teachers, trustees, and secretaries it can scarcely be counted upon. This conviction leads me to wish for some medium of intercommunication between trustees and teachers on the one hand, and inspectors on the other. During his visits to the schools an inspector is so pressed for time in which to do the ordinary work of inspection and examination that often many points which he intended bringing to the notice of the teacher or of the trustees in connection with the carrying out of the school law or regulations are forgotten, and the only recourse then left him is to write, perhaps, a long letter, which, in many instances, may remain a long time unwritten. The *Journal of Education* cannot fill the requirement owing to its infrequent issue. No one newspaper of the provincial or local press reaches very many of the teachers or other school officials, and as a matter of fact, very many teachers do not take any periodical, alleging that they cannot afford the expense. Could the trustees be induced or compelled (if necessary) to subscribe for one good educational journal—the *Educational Review* for instance—for the use of the school and the teacher, at the expense of the section, payable out of the county fund or otherwise, the desired medium would be established, besides securing to the teacher and the school valuable and profitable articles and exercises without any appreciable burden to anybody. Many official notices and editorial notes appearing in the *Journal of Education*, the official organ of the Council of Public Instruction, are glimpsed over by the secretary of trustees, and in many cases soon forgotten; the paper is passed over to the teacher who, in his turn, gives it a hasty perusal, and forgets or neglects to familiarize himself with its contents when more at leisure. I am led to this conclusion by the very many letters of inquiry from time to time received, which a careful perusal of the *Journal* would have rendered unnecessary — letters which often can be answered by a single reference to regulation so and so, or to page so and so of the *Journal.* An opportunity of impressing such messages at shorter intervals as occasion might require would be a vast benefit and convenience to inspectors.

I am frequently asked what subjects of the common school course teachers, especially young and inexperienced teachers, display the least aptitude for teaching, and the greatest lack of improvement in their methods as they acquire experience generally, and I have come to the conclusion that those subjects are *History* and *Geography.* Except in comparatively rare cases, the lessons on these subjects consist simply in recitations memorized from the text, without note or ·comment on the part of the teacher ; and while the map is sometimes called into requisition in the teaching of the latter, for the former it is very seldom, if ever used to connect the event with the place. An occasional interruption of the parrot-like answer by a question of the kind indicated too often reveals the fact that both subjects are being very imperfectly taught. *Composition*, perhaps, comes next, receiving altogether too little attention in connection with the language lessons ; and coming into the course as a separately specified subject so late as the seventh grade, it would often be willingly relegated to the High school. The teaching of *Arithmetic* is often done without sufficient system—not enough of class work and thorough grounding in first principles—but generally speaking, more time is devoted to it than, perhaps, to any other single subject, and it gets drummed in after a while, even if more or less mechanically. At any rate, it seems to me that arithmetic is the average country boy's strong point. *Grammar* and *Analysis* are receiving more and more intelligent treatment, and are in the majority of cases found nearly, if not quite. up to the requirements of the grade. *Reading* gets its full share of time, and perhaps more. That the results are proportionately good I hesitate to say, for in the great essential—expression—far too many teachers fail. While satisfactory progress can be noticed from one visit to another in distinctness of articulation, correct accent and pronunciation, too often the admission has to be made : " I have failed to break them of that monotone." And I am forced to confess that I, too, have found it a difficult matter where the habit is once acquired, and I find that the best remedy is to guard against its introduction by insisting on requiring correct expression the moment classes pass from the disjointed phrases and sentences of the primers to the connected stories and selections of the first reader. *Spelling*—as I take it last, it may be inferred that I find it the best taught subject. I fear we have too many poor spellers in the country to warrant that conclusion, but spelling must be admitted to be the most *easily taught* of all subjects though not necessarily the most easily learned. Nothing but incessant practice, both oral and written, makes a good speller, and in proportion to the amount of exercise given, in spelling and dictation, to the ear and the eye, will be the measure of success in this subject so indispensable to a finished education— if there can be such a thing.

During the year I attended public meetings as follows :—On August 2nd, a meeting of ratepayers of section No. 9, Little Ance, County of Richmond, called for the purpose of discussing a proposed division of the section and other sectional disputes. On Aug. 7th, a meeting of ratepayers of Point Michaud, section No. 29, for the purpose of settling disputed accounts, and deciding as to the legality of the last previous annual meeting, and the consequent legality of the board of trustees. On November 4th, a meeting of ratepayers of St. Peter's, section No. 44, to settle a dispute in the order of succession of trustees arising from the filling of " occasional vacancies " caused by death and removal from the section. Many other meetings of a less public character with trustees and secretaries, selecting or examining sites, discussing old and new school houses, plans, &c., and settling difficulties of different kinds, were held from time to time, of which no record can be made in the monthly reports. I am pleased to say that generally these meetings have been productive of the desired results.

In connection with the election or appointment (by commissioners) of trustees, a legal question has arisen which, in my opinion, calls for an authoritative decision, or possibly an amendment of the law to meet the case. Sec. 20 of the School Act enacts that " One trustee may be chosen from the poll-tax payers authorized as hereinafter provided, to vote in the election of trustees." Sec. 46 defines what shall qualify such poll-tax payer to vote in such election and thereby make him eligible as a trustee, viz. : " depositing with the secretary of trustees previous to or at any annual school meeting, the sum of one dollar," and " having paid all poll-taxes previously imposed, including that of the year just closing. . . ." Now, at an annual meeting, a poll-tax payer who was not qualified as above, not only not having deposited his dollar, but being actually in arrears for "poll-taxes previously imposed," was proposed for trustee and, receiving a majority of votes, was declared elected. On being appealed to and furnished with sufficient proofs of the facts as above stated, I decided that the election was null and void, and put the machinery of the law in motion to have the vacancy filled under sections 16 and 12. The nature of the vacancy, and the alleged election by the ratepayers were set forth in the requisition and in my accompanying certificate, so that the committee of the board acted with the facts of the case before them, and appointed as trustee the nominee of the requisition,— a person other than the choice of the annual meeting. It is now contended by persons whose opinions are entitled to respect, that the election by the ratepayers was an election *de facto* which remains in force till voided by some competent tribunal, and that there are now really *four* trustees in the section. If legal authority sustain this view, the law as it stands makes it possible for serious complications to arise from such cases as the above.

Five new school houses have been erected and occupied in the county of Richmond during the year, one being at West L'Ardoise, section No. 67, a neat building, well finished exteriorly, but very inadequate, both as to plan and size, to the requirements of so large a section ; and what is even worse, built on a site altogether in contravention of the regulations of the Council of Public Instruction on the subject—on the very verge of the public highway. Though not approved, its use is being allowed temporarily under promise of removal at a convenient season. Brae, section No. 49, entered a new school house on the first of November, erected on the site of the one burnt in 1893. This also is a good building, but poorly planned. On Nov. 6th, the pupils of Black River, section No. 25, occupied, for the first time, their new though rather diminutive quarters. There being, however, only fourteen of them of school going age in the section, they will likely have room enough for some time to come. Petit-de-Grat, section No. 9, enjoys the distinction of having erected the first school house in the district according to one of the official plans of the Province of New Brunswick, suggested some time ago for use in this Province, pending the preparation and adoption of plans of our own. It is a neat and convenient building, light and airy, well finished outside and inside, and reflects much credit on the thriving settlement it adorns. Much praise is due especially to the tact and enterprise of Councillor Thomson, the energetic secretary of trustees, for the carrying out of the plans to so successful an issue. Nothing is wanting now but a set of patent desks to make it one of the most comfortable and commodious school building of its size in the district. In the latter part of November, a good substantial new building was occupied at Grand River, section No. 30, supplying a long felt want. At the time of my visit, Feb. 2nd, it was ceiled overhead and the walls up to the window-sills, with a fairly good ante-room partitioned off. It is of a suitable size, and when completely finished and furnished, as I expect to see it at no distant day, it will meet the educational requirements of this picturesque section for a good many years. No new buildings were occupied during the year in the County of Cape Breton, but I expect to find several in the course of my next year's visitation. With the exception, then, of minor repairs here and there, with an occasional new set of desks and the erection of several much needed outhouses, the above are all the improvements I have to report in school buildings. In the matter of out-buildings, trustees are being awakened to the necessity of stricter compliance with their duties, and with the requirements of the law. In the matter of improved furniture, maps, and other school apparatus and appliances, there is still a great deal to be done, but having regard to the circumstances of the country generally, I think we are moving along, on the whole, about as well as can be expected.

I have the honor to be, Sir,

Your obedient servant,

M. J. T. MACNEIL.

A. H. MACKAY, ESQ., LL. D., &C.,

Superintendent of Education.

DISTRICT No. 8.—INVERNESS AND VICTORIA.

JOHN Y. GUNN, *Inspector.*

SIR :—

As required by law, I beg respectfully to submit the following condensed annual report, showing the present general condition of education within the Counties of Inverness and Victoria—together with a synopsis of progress made during the school year ended in July, 1894.

This district embraces a larger extent of territory than any other field of inspection in the Province. It includes a slice of Richmond, North Inverness, South Inverness, and the whole of Victoria.

School sections have been established in every settlement, and even to the adjacent islands the privilege of autonomy has been extended. Port Hood Island within the present century was connected with the mainland, making the harbor *Chestico* one of the most capacious in the Province. A gale, however, of unprecedented severity swept away the isthmus, and what was at one time a safe refuge from the tempest is now, in the words of the poet, a mere "*sinus et mala fida carinis.*" Further north are Seal Island and Cheticamp Island. A number of years ago the superintendent of the light house at Seal Island applied to the board of school commissioners for leave to have a school established principally for the training of his own family. This was granted for one term only, but he was informed that a school could be opened at any time on the island, with the understanding that it would be considered as a department of the mainland school at Broad Cove Marsh. Under similar circumstances a school was in operation for a term or two at Bird Islands, in the County of Victoria, being temporarily considered a department of Cape Dauphin School Section, No. 40.

At the regular semi-annual and annual meetings of the school boards the following sections were established :—

In South Inverness.. Port Hood Island, No. 63, in 1865.
" Victoria.........St. Paul's Island, " 87, " 1883.
" North Inverness.. Cheticamp Island, " 47, " 1884.
" South Inverness .. Smith Islands, " 89, " 1884.

To these I should perhaps add the island of Boularderie, named in honour of the Marquis de la Boularderie, and one of the most beautiful spots the eye of man ever rested upon. This island is partly within the limits of the adjoining county of Cape Breton—the Victoria portion consisting of *nine* distinct school sections.

Schools have also been established on the mountains in each of the sub-districts :

SOUTH INVERNESS.

Campbell's Mountain....	No. 33½	Skye Mountain	No. 65
Mount. Young..........	" 28	Scotch Hill	" 64
River Dennis Mount....	" 66	Mount Noah	" 69
South Highlands	" 61	McIntosh Mount	" 95
North Highlands	" 62		

NORTH INVERNESS.

Pembroke	No. 5½	S. W. Egypt	No. 40
Lewis Mount	" 27	Piper's Glen	" 48
Campbelltown	" 38	McLellan's Mount	" 49
Whycocomagh Mount	" 39		

VICTORIA.

Crowdis Mount,   Gairloch Mount,
Big Bras d'Or Mount,   Cain's Mountain,
Hunter's Mount,   Smith's Mountain.
Gillander's Mount,

These elevations, although dignified with the names of mountains, would be called mere hills in southern Europe or central Asia—none of them having a greater altitude than 1200 feet, but all have the distinction of being nearer the sun than any other region in the Province. The tops are invariably flat and the surface corrugated, indicating glacial action in the earlier periods of the country's history. In all the more elevated portions of the district the rock is either precambrian or metamorphic, with an occasional outcropping of *trap* and *dolerite*. Along by the seashore, and also by the margins of lakes and rivers, the formation is generally lower carboniferous.

Ethnologically, the great majority of the people of both counties are the descendants of the 'original settlers who emigrated to this country from the highlands and islands of Scotland more than half a century ago. There are also important settlements at Port Hood, Hillsboro, and North-East Margaree of Loyalist extraction. At Big Brook, in North Inverness, and at Lake O'Law, so famed for its beautiful chain of lakes, the people are natives of the Emerald Isle. At Margaree and Cheticamp the people are generally French—descendants of the Acadians who were expelled from Grand Pre in 1755. The island of St. Johns being then a demesne of the French crown, the exiles took refuge among their countrymen. But in 1758 another change occurred, and, like the Trojans of ancient story, they transferred their *lares et penates* to the adjacent island of Cape Breton. They landed at Cheticamp, which they so named on account of its being at that time such a-miserable place, although now one of the finest country districts in the Province. Soon afterwards some of the party landed at Margaree, which was named on account of the fertility of the soil—Mon-gre.

The original settlers had been generally crofters and fishermen in their native land, and knew absolutely nothing about the cultivation of the soil. Every tree seemed to be in the way, and they did not at all regret to see forest fires destroy not only the forests themselves, but also the mould and moss and decayed vegetation which the Giver of all Good had been accumulating for beneficent purposes through ages of ages. Verily "if ignorance is bliss," it compels its votaries to offer many a sacrifice to an avenging *Nemesis*.

The lists of the "poor sections" in both counties were revised by the school boards of each sub-district in May, and a copy sent to the

Education Office for the purpose of testing the accuracy of entries in the semi-annual and annual distribution sheets.

In this district there are now 257 distinct school sections, one of the number having been created during the past summer in the sub-district of South Inverness, under the name and number of Rodena, No. 76.

During the past year there were 239 schools in session within the district—174 in Inverness, and 65 in Victoria. In Inverness there were :—

Teachers, Grade A............................. 2
" " B............................. 16
" " C............................. 56
D............................100

In Victoria there were :—

Teachers, Grade A............................. 1
" " B............................. 2
" " C............................. 24
D............................. 38

Salaries paid to teachers in the district amounted to $25,061— $17,146 in Inverness, and $7,915 for Victoria, making an average salary of $105 to each teacher irrespective of grade held. To the above may be added the Provincial Grant at the rate of $110 for Grade B; $90 for Grade C, and $58 for D.

The funds in the hands of the trustees of the district amounted to $11,455.80—the amount to the credit of the municipality of Inverness being $7,114.80, and for Victoria, $3,741.

In Inverness the distribution was effected in accordance with the following scale :—

1000 days.................................$7 40
100 " 74

And in Victoria the following scale was employed :—

1000 days $11 02
100 " 1 10

The three sections in Inverness drawing the highest appropriation for full term were :—

Port Hawkesbury $266 80
Port Hood 232 20
Mabou 171 51

The three lowest :—

Big Brooklyn, North Inverness.............. $30 36
Cody Settlement 31 84
McLellan's Mount 41 08

In Victoria the highest were :—

Baddeck $363 68
New Haven............................. 110 36
Englishtown 92 55

The three lowest :—

Gillis Point $39 98
McKenzie................................. 40 25
Big Baddeck 47 60

Only *two* sections took advantage of the proviso authorizing the annual meeting to be held in March—one in Inverness, the other in Victoria. The meeting in Inverness was held at N. W. Arm, No. 57, S. Inverness, that in Victoria was held at New Haven, No. 73. The regular annual meeting in June was held in nearly all the sections on the day by law appointed. Of course there were a few laggards as usual. But they were afterwards put in line with the rest.

The County Academies at Port Hood and Baddeck continue to flourish. Both institutions unquestionably exercise a potent influence in enhancing the cause of education in the respective counties of the district. This is evinced by the unprecedentedly large number of candidates from the county capitals who presented themselves for examination in July last. The results will appear later on. Mr. McIntosh has been re-engaged at Port Hood, and Mr. Robert S. Campbell at Baddeck.

The Indian schools in both counties are in charge of teachers of the second class. Wagamatcook was officially visited in June, and Micmac in October.

Early in April, Victor Christmas, the only Indian teacher, I believe, in the Province, died. He was succeeded by Mr. P. A. Murphy, a highly successful teacher, who has the enviable distinction of being, perhaps, the best English reader in the county.

The Indian is constitutionally lazy and listless—and when the poor children are taught in a language essentially foreign to them, it is not surprising that indications of progress should not be more manifest. The philanthropy of the Dominion Government, in furnishing their dusky wards with school buildings, which serve also for church purposes on Sundays, is worthy of unstinted praise.

By present appearances it is not at all probable that poor Lo will continue long to be a source of anxiety. On the occasion of my recent official visit to Wagamatcook I obtained the following statistics :—

Total number of families..................... 17
      "   "   children 68
                                                        ——
                Total population 85

There were 13 deaths on the reservation during the year ended 30th April last. Now a family of *four* is usually considered small—but when the fact is added that nearly all the deaths resulted from *phthisis*, it appears to me that it will not take " many more moons and many more winters " for them all, Hiawatha like, to "vanish in the glory of the sunset, in the purple mists of evening."

The High School examination was largely attended, and exhibited the following results :—

The first place on the roll of honour is assigned to J. M. McRitchie, examined at Baddeck for Grade A, making a total aggregate of 1238.

The three candidates making the highest average at Port Hood were :—

A. Beatrice McDonnell .... 579 B.
John Angus McDougall.................... 509 C.
Mary A. McLellan........................ 492 D.

At Baddeck the three highest were :—

John McRitchie .... 1238 A.
Arthur Douglas Blanchard................. 654 B.
Charles Jacob Crowdis .... 600 C.

At Port Hawkesbury the three highest were :—

Ora P. Lamey .... 577 B.
Annie L. Mack .... 537 B.
Bessie Lamey .... 475 C.

Margaree Forks.—At this station there were 15 candidates of whom 14 failed—there being only one successful :—

Michael Coady........................... 473 D.

Cheticamp.—At this station also the shewing was poor—5 candidates—only one successful :—

John P. LeBlanc......................... 514 C.

It is, however, to be remembered that High School examination results are by no means sufficient criteria to judge of educational success. Take for example North Inverness, a sub-district famed for the general success of its schools. Here there are *two* examination stations which have been notoriously unsuccessful at the July examination.

Margaree Forks, B. C. Marsh, N. E. Margaree, and Cheticamp have magnificent school-buildings, good teachers of a superior order, and general equipment first class in every respect, and yet the public examination showed up very unfavourably. The object of the school law is to banish illiteracy out of the land, and its mission is especially to relieve the educational exigencies of the poor. Years before the school law became a legislative enactment those in independent circumstances were in a position to give a fair education to their families, but since the inception of existing school act, high and low, rich and poor are placed on the same level, so that now the aphorism, "there is no royal road to learning," is more literally true than it was when first uttered two thousand years ago.

If a teacher wishes his classes to succeed at the public examination, he must accord their legitimate place to dictation and general preparation on the lines of the prescribed syllabus of examination ; he must insist on thorough accuracy and neatness in every exercise, and he must confine the work of his instruction to four days in the week, the fifth to be devoted exclusively to reviewing.

The Roman pronunciation of Latin has been attempted in a a number of our advanced schools. I need hardly say that the effort has been a signal failure. The system is supposed to be based upon the Italian, which language I have had an opportunity of studying with a native of Tuscany some years ago, and I can certify that the late fad is not Latin, neither is it English, nor yet Italian. To have the question definitely settled would it not be wise to call a convention of experts with a view to have the matter thoroughly ventilated.

When I attended college the classical professor got a native Greek who called to see him to read for the benefit of the Greek class, and it is perhaps unnecessary to say that his style was very different from what the students were accustomed to. I may also say that I have had the distinguished honour of corresponding with Professor Blackie upon his favourite study. His reply was nearly as undecipherable as Horace Greely's. But I made out that in his opinion a better knowledge of Greek could be obtained by mingling with the *suns cu ottes* of Athens for six months than could be derived from taking the full curriculum in any Scotch or English University.

Education may be regarded as being moral, physical, and intellectual. The Greeks and Romans showed the present and the past of all ages that their heads were level when they combined both the moral and physical elements in the education of their youth. Indeed the Olymphic and Nemean games were largely of a religious character. To this fact we owe the imperishable story of the Horatii and Curatii together with the magnificent tragedies depicted so gracefully in the pages of Aeschylus, Sophocles, and Euripides.

But to the masses education means "a preparation for life," and anything which does not conduce to that end is regarded with more or less contempt. The most rudimentary knowledge that a boy gets in school enables him to read advertisements, written directions, and orders, &c. ; to write letters, and to keep track of his earnings and expenses. Physiology is accorded its appropriate place in the curriculum of studies, but I regret to say it is not invested with one half the importance it merits. Hygiene, if the entries in the school returns are to be credited, is taught in a large number of schools. What is especially needed is that the pupils should be habituated to right conduct in every act of their school life. They should be taught to prefer right to wrong through the exercise of their reasoning faculties, rather than be put under the restraint of a set of autocratic commands.

The school returns you will find, on examination, to be much improved, both in accuracy and general neatness. When errors occur they are traceable to the fact that some teachers do not keep accurate *time tables,* and do not seem to realize that school returns should always be a mere transcript of the School Register.

I regret very much that the exigencies of the service compelled me to apply for a larger number of permissive licenses than on former years. I think the privilege should not be accorded any longer.

In the October number of the *Journal of Education* the suggestion is made that the duties of the school boards might be delegated to the municipal councils. I need not say that such a departure from established usage would be most unwise. The school commissioners are generally clergymen, members of the legal and medical professions, together with the foremost representatives of the mercantile and agricultural industries. These gentlemen have as much respect for their decisions as Judges of the Supreme or County Courts have for theirs. The municipal councils are, on the other hand, so saturated with political rancour that party interests are considered to be paramount to every other consideration. During my official supervision of the public schools hundreds of clergymen, lawyers, doctors, and graduates in arts have been teachers in the public schools of the district, and some of the number have been conspicuously fortunate in attaining to high positions not only within the Dominion, but also in the neighbouring Republic. At this moment one is a Judge of the Supreme Court in a Western State; another is Chief Commissioner of Crown Lands in British Columbia; two are College Professors; two are Senators of the Dominion, and two are members of the Federal Parliament; four are members of the Local Parliament, three government and one opposition.

I do not mean to say that I have been a *Maecenas* to them all. But I do say that whenever I discovered a glimmering ray of talent imbued with energy and application, I did everything in my power to promote its development.

One of the greatest leaders of men who ever lived required of all candidates for his profession to answer the following questions in the affirmative: Is the applicant physically and mentally sound? Has he parts? If either of these queries were answered in the negative, the candidate was summarily dismissed. This serves to show the overwhelming importance attached by one of the greatest of men to physical and mental stamina.

I am gratified to learn of British success anywhere. I am proud when I see a Nova Scotian succeed, and my blood fairly thrills with pleasure when a Cape Bretonian is crowned with laurels either in college halls or in the gladiatorial arena.

Here, I may be allowed to make a personal reference. My first license was of the second class, passing fourth on the published list. I afterwards passed for Grade B being the second on the list. After attending college for a couple of terms, I went up for Grade A, passing at the head of the list for the whole Province, a distinction rarely attained to by any person now in the educational field.

I have been over a quarter of a century in harness. My first appointment was received from the Vail Government, and after the lapse of a decade or so the County of Victoria was added, both constituting Inspectoral District No. 8. A new appointment was of course necessary. On this occasion my commission was issued by the Holmes-Thompson Government. I have found the position both irksome and laborious. Suavity and firmness are absolutely necessary. Time and again have I had to sail between *Scylla* and *Charybdis*, but never have I met with a single serious collision. The school commissioners were always my warmest friends, and in the discharge of professional duty I was allowed untrammelled action in dealing with any infringement of the law. Personally I have many friends in every locality in the district, but professionally my motto has always been '*Tros Tyriusve mihi nullo discrimine agetur.*"

To school commissioners, clergymen, and other friends who have invariably treated me with much kindness both personal and professional, I am under lasting obligations. I owe a deep debt of gratitude, especially to my friends in Victoria. My Inverness friends I may hope to meet again, and pay them back in their own coin, but those in Victoria to whom I am under the greatest obligations, I never expect to meet again.

I have served under four superintendents—Dr. Rand, firm and unflinching in his adhesion to the requirements of the school act ; Rev. Mr. Hunt, a gentleman in every sense of the word ; Dr. Allison, a man who combined suavity of manner with rare executive ability ; and the present incumbent, whom I have always found inflexible but just. May his firm hand long continue at the educational helm in the schools of his native province.

Respectfully submitted,

JOHN Y. GUNN.

To A. H. MacKay, Esq., LL. D.,
    Superintendent of Education.

DISTRICT No. 9.—PICTOU AND SOUTH COLCHESTER.

W. E. MacLellan, LL. B., *Inspector.*

Sir :—

I have the honor, in accordance with law, to submit the following report of my inspectorate for the school year ended July 31st, 1894.

In several respects the year has been one of considerable activity and progress.

The new section established at Eureka and Ferrona, in the County of Pictou, towards the close of the preceding school year, promptly completed its organization and erected a suitable building, which has been well furnished and equipped. It contains rooms for two departments, which have been in successful operation since early in the year. The formation of this section has, however, apparently demoralized Riverton section, which formerly included Eureka. The latter section has had no school during any portion of the year. But possibly this is not much to be regretted, since most of the children in said section are within reach of the schools of Stellarton, or Eureka and Ferrona.

The Bridgeville school house has been removed to a new and much better site ; it has been thoroughly repaired and a new wing added, giving ample accommodation for the two departments into which the school has been graded.

New Glasgow has put up and almost completed a new high-school building, which, when ready for occupation, as it will be shortly after the commencement of the new school year, will have cost the town some twenty-five thousand dollars. No effort is being spared to make it a model of its kind and a credit to eastern Nova Scotia.

Westville has added a comfortable two-roomed building to its school equipment, and another teacher to its staff, which now numbers ten.

Ste llarton is talking of building, and will no doubt soon follow the lea d of its sister towns in the direction of improvement.

Pictou has repaired its western building besides purchasing, grading, and enclosing suitable grounds about it.

In the rural districts of Pictou County no new buildings have been erected, with the exception of a temporary one at East French River, to replace the one destroyed by fire; but there has been unusual activity in repairing and re-furnishing existing buildings, a number of which have been made quite presentable without, and thoroughly comfortable within.

In the district of South Colchester, Riverside section is building, and Shubenacadie has voted money for that purpose. Camden has created a creditable new house. Crowe's Mills and North River have thoroughly repaired and re-furnished. Liberal amounts have been voted for repairs by a number of sections.

I am glad to be able to report the growth, throughout my district, of interest in school grounds and surroundings. Trees are being planted in increasing numbers. Unsightly fences are giving place to less objectionable ones. Several sections have been at considerable pains and expense during the past year in grading and improving their grounds. These are encouraging signs, and point, I trust, to a not distant day when the school house will at least cease to be the most unattractive in the section.

Trustees are also showing more liberality in supplying necessary apparatus. In most cases my suggestions concerning such matters have been promptly attended to.

In the County of Pictou, every organized section has had school during some portion of the year, with the single exception of Riverton, already referred to. The disorganized sections are Fraser's Mountain, which has not had school for many years, and probably will not have

7

again, as its needs are supplied by New Glasgow, and Carriboo Island, closed for several years on account of non-attendance of pupils, but likely to re-open next year.

In the district of South Colchester, all organized sections have had school with the exception of South Vale and Riverside. South Vale lost its school house by fire some two years ago and has not yet re-built, owing to disputes in the section. I understand that arrangements are now being completed and that school will re-open next year. Riverside's old building has been torn down to give place to the new, and the section allowed the year to go by without school.

The sections of Kemptown and Springmount, disorganized long before I became inspector of the district, and without school ever since, have been got into working order again, and will both open their schools next year, when I hope to have every school in my district in operation.

In school-room work there is observable, if slow, progress. Too close adherence to text-books, and failure on the part of teachers to appreciate the relative importance of the various subjects of the prescribed course of study, continue to be the chief obstacles to more rapid advancement. The work marked out for common schools is by no means too difficult, and could easily be accomplished by pupils of average ability. In fact it is so accomplished in well-taught schools. But it is far otherwise where teachers regard themselves as mere hearers of tasks, as they persist in doing in many cases. I think I may safely assert that a considerable majority of teachers do not consider educating or even instructing as among their functions. They believe their whole duty discharged in requiring the child to learn set lessons—chiefly at home. When insisting on compliance with the requirements of the law concerning the giving of " lessons on nature," I am frequently asked for a text-book on the subject. If such a book were available it would be directly placed in the hands of pupils with a demand that they should memorize its contents. It is so at least with the examples of oral lessons on language, given in in the prescribed text-book in grammar.

I am strongly of the opinion that it would be better to prohibit the use by common-school pupils of all text-books, except such as are necessary in connection with the teaching of reading, writing and arithmetic. History as it is taught, or, rather, as it is learned from the text-books, is one of the heaviest and most time-consuming burdens which common-school children have to bear. Is the information, if any, gained and retained worth what it costs in time, labor, and lasting dislike of the subject? Geography ranks second as a consumer of time and labour. The children, in spite of all that can be said, being required to commit to memory the mere names of places and the words of the text. Could not these two subjects be better taught together—geography from the surrounding country from globes and maps, and history in connection with it, or in connection with civics ? A good text-book in civics, *for the use of teachers*, is, by the way, urgently needed.

The use of the prescribed text-book in grammar, so far as I can judge, seems to operate as an almost complete bar to the acquisition of any practical knowledge concerning the ordinary use of language. I am also of the opinion that it must have so operated for a good many years past, judging from the " dialect " in which teachers not infrequently conduct so-called lessons in grammar. I find pupils memorizing definitions which they do not in the least understand, and rules which they cannot comprehend, and in so doing satisfying themselves, their parents, and their teachers that they are " learning grammar." In very few schools do I hear even an attempt to correct or improve the language of pupils. I have to ask you, then, if common-school pupils should be allowed to waste their time in generally misdirected and futile attempts to pry into the scientific structure of their mother tongue before they have acquired more than a mere rudimentary idea of its correct and effective everyday use ? In other words, should not the grammatical text-book be banished from our common schools ?

My excuse for setting forth the foregoing opinions is the fact that they have been forced upon me by observation and experience in the schools. It seems to me that reform, or some vigorous attempt at reform in the direction I have indicated, is urgently demanded. Reading, writing, arithmetic, and language are being neglected or " scamped " that a mere exhibition of learning in geography, history, and grammar may be made.

Temperance as required by law is, I believe, being faithfully taught in the schools of my district. Most teachers appear to be more earnest in the discharge of this than of almost any other of their duties.

Some progress is being made in the teaching of music, but it is not great, owing to lack of knowledge or capacity, or both on the part of teachers. In drawing there is more headway. In both subjects it will probably be rather slow and up-hill work for some time.

It is unnecessary for me to report specially on the work done by the academies and high-schools of my district. They all came out most creditably from the searching test of the provincial examination, the results of which you know.

Few questions of importance were discussed at the annual meetings of the various boards of school commissioners of my district. In South Colchester it was even more difficult than usual to secure a quorum for the transaction of business. The last two or three annual meetings which that board has held have been largely due to the untiring energy and earnestness of its chairman, R. Craig, Esq., of Truro.

With reference to my work of visitation, I have to report that I went over my whole district once, and a large portion of it twice, visiting all the schools in session. I was greatly hindered by the unusual severity of last winter. Repeated snow storms made the roads in many places impassable during the months of February, March, and April.

The statistical tables sent you herewith, furnish detailed information concerning the schools under my charge.

. I have the honour to be,

You obedient servant,

W. E. MACLELLAN.

To A. H. MacKay, Esq., Ll. D.,

Superintendent of Education.

DISTRICT No. 10.—CUMBERLAND AND N. COLCHESTER.

Inglis C. Craig, *Inspector.*

Sir :—

In conformity to the requirements of the Department of Public Instruction, I have the honor to transmit information touching the operations of the public schools in the County of Cumberland and that part of Colchester embraced in the Districts of Stirling and West Colchester, for the school year commencing August 1st, 1893, and ending July 31st, 1894, together with the statistical abstracts and notes of inspection :—

There are 156 sections in Cumberland and 61 in the Districts of Stirling and West Colchester. Twenty of these have had no school during the year. In the case of five, new school-rooms were being built, which precluded a school, either through the builders operations or the extraordinary demand upon the finances of the section for their erection.

Lower Southampton 65, and Black River 115, in Cumberland District ; Two Islands 54, and North Port Greville 26, in Parrsboro District, have had no school for several years. Indeed, the last two named may be scored from the lists ; in the one case the population has left the section, and in the other no school room was ever built.

Greenville Cross Roads 100; South Branch Shinemacas 103; Rushtons 110 ; Salt Springs 116, and Athol Mills 1, in the District of Cumberland ; Sugar Hill 20 ; Eatonville 22 ; Allen Hill 24 ; Moose River 25, in Parrsboro ; Folly Lake 23 ; New Britain 28, and Beaver Meadow 27, have schools intermittently.

These sections, with many others in this inspectorate, suffer through the operations of the Act which requires a freeholder to pay school taxes in the section in which he is domiciled, whether the property be within or without the section in which he resides. Intentionally made in the interests of these rural sections at first, it, in the majority of cases, operates against them now, so that every year special legislation is asked to free sections from the operation of the Act, and make them a unit in the possession of property within the bounds of the section. The tendency of the present Act is to build up the wealthy section at the expense of the poor; this is especially true of lumbering and suburban districts. If the sparsely settled districts were made financially stronger by giving them the benefits of all the public school funds to which they are rightfully entitled, many would not give up their country homes and move to centres of population where continued free school privileges may be enjoyed.

I am aware of the confusion any change in the assessment law would make, especially in marsh districts, where proprietorship is represented in contiguous sections ; but as these are so few compared with those crippled by the present law, that it seems only apparent justice to have the present enactment the exception and sectional unity the rule.

Another cause of financial weakness is the sub-division of sections. There is not the same disposition to put up with the privations and hardships of even three decades ago.

These demands upon commissioners for local accommodations in large sections can be met only by giving relief in some way by reduced taxation to those beyond reasonable walking limits. It is to the advantage of children to go a little farther to a good school than to spend their time in small schools where young and inexperienced teachers are employed, and where too often unprofitable results are the issue.

One new section, known as Wentworth Lake Road, was formed at the last meeting of the Cumberland board of commissioners.

SCHOOL BUILDINGS.

Improvements in school buildings is keeping pace with other advanced steps towards a more perfect system. Twenty-five new school rooms in one year is a tribute to the intelligence and educational progress of this district.

Sections erecting or have completed school rooms in the course of the year are :—

Cumberland District.—Wallace Bay 10 ; Middleboro 43 ; Nappan 44, two departments ; Joggins 5, four departments ; Mapleton 63 ; South Brook 112.

Parrsboro District.— Parrsboro Town (1) high school of eight departments ; Diligent River 7 ; Salem 16 ; Wharton 23.

Stirling District.—Tatamagouche (1) two departments ; Henderson 16 ; The Falls 23.

The building at Tatamagouche is not exactly new, but has been completely reconstructed at an expense of $1000.

All the graded schools are heated by furnaces.

Reconstructed or Improved. — Malagash 1, renovated and refurnished. Southampton 60, refurnished and renewed. Fenwick 71, and Oxford 79, are much improved. Millvale (room) in Stirling, and Lower Five Islands in West Colchester, have been remodeled, and the former refurnished.

Much attention has been given to provide comfort and convenience, and in some instances it has been done at a moderate cost. In the majority of cases trustees have applied to me for help in plans. I have given all the advice and assistance my experience enabled me to do ; yet this is not practical, and in some instances not plain to those not apace with modern school architecture.

I think it would be provincial economy for the department to provide plans and specifications for four or five types of buildings suitable for miscellaneous schools and graded systems up to five departments. These plans should be modern, and well adapted for good light and ventilation, with perfect heating systems, while convenience and architecture need not be sacrificed to either. Good school rooms do not make good schools, but the physical environment of teachers and pupils have a potent influence in the right direction.

The towns of Parrsboro and Joggin Mines have done especially well during the past year. The former has erected a new High School at a cost of about $10,000, including cost of site ; the latter $4,000. Both buildings have commanding positions, and are conspicuous on account of their sites and as the best buildings in either town. The one overlooks Minas Basin, the other Chignecto Bay. Both buildings are modern in their design and equipment, and bear striking contrast to those occupied in past years. It is a goodly sight in these mixed communities to witness the unity which all creeds and classes display about the common point, the comfort and educational advancement of their children.

The total amount voted in Cumberland alone for buildings and repairs was $15,109, and in West Colchester and Stirling, $2,470.

TEACHERS.

There were 251 teachers employed in the district during the year, and five substitutes. This is one regular teacher less than last year. In West Colchester fewer schools have been in operation than in past years. Five Islands and Folly Village, formerly two department buildings, are now miscellaneous schools. Great Village and Central Economy, three department systems, have cast off a room each. Depletion in the attendance is the cause assigned by the different boards of trustees. In two instances the economy practiced was questionable.

Divided according to the sexes, there were 26 males and 225 females. The male teachers are slowly and surely being supplanted by their sisters. I am not prepared to say that the educational status of the district is falling thereby ; rather there are many proofs that it is rising. The day for physical force in the management of the school room has passed away, the schools having by their own reflex influence brought about a sentiment for order and obedience.

Little change has been made in the classes of teachers employed. The returns show an increase in those having a Normal School rank. This is a gratifying feature, inasmuch as these teachers adapt themselves more easily to the requirements of the Course of Study, and moveover, have a more intelligent grasp of its recent requirements.

SALARIES.

No marked difference is shown in the amount given teachers. If there is any change it is against them, presuming this department of the returns of 1893 to be correct. The yearly engagement would seem to be financially in the interests of the section. When the semi-annual salary of the past is doubled it becomes unduly out of proportion in the opinion of the parsimonious school board. Sectional pay to teachers for the past year was $34,410. Government aid $18,287.37, or $52,697.37, amount of full salaries.

The following table gives the salaries per day for both years :—

CUMBERLAND.

GRADE.	SEX.	PER DAY, 1893.	PER DAY, 1894.
A	Male......	$4 00	$3 85
B		2 54	2 33
C		1 02	1 17
D		1 32	1 16
B	Female. ...	1 50	1 36
C		1 07	1 06
D		74	73

STIRLING AND COLCHESTER WEST.

GRADE.	SEX.	PER DAY, 1893.	PER DAY, 1894.
B	Male......	$2 37	$2 30
C		1 37	....
B	Female. ...	1 30	1 24
C		1 00	99
D		65	66

SCHOOL POPULATION.

The whole number of persons reported as attending school during the year in this district was 11,409, giving an increase in Cumberland of 493, and a decrease in North and West Colchester of 35. Just 25 per cent. of the population of Cumberland attended school during the year. This is a high percentage, and is an indication of the growing interests in schools in this part of the province.

TEACHERS' ASSOCIATION.

The District Association met in Spring Hill on December 8th and 9th in annual session.   From the many favorable opinions that have reached me from teachers and others in attendance, I am freely convinced that the association is of inestimable value to the district's educational interests. It gave the teachers under my supervision the first opportunity to meet you in your official capacity. It is not flattery, sir, to say that the part you bore while in attendance gave those present assurance of your sympathy and confidence in your superintendentship.   The association's thanks must here be recorded to Prof. Lee Russel for the interest he contributed to the various meetings by his addresses on manual training.

Programme.

An Address of Welcome ....PRESIDENT.
The Teaching Profession......................W. M. FERGUSON.
The Effect of Alcohol on the Tissues...........W. R. SLADE.
Lessons illustrative of the Tonic sol-fa System....A. S. FORD.
The Educational Exhibit at the World's Fair....M. SCANLAN.
Short Cuts in Arithmetic ....W. W. TOREY.
The School Section as an Educator............R. S. CAMPBELL.
The Teaching of Mathematics ....A. W. HEALY.
Illustrative Lesson on Writing ....L. RUGGLES.

HIGH SCHOOLS.

By reference to the accompanying tables it will be noted that only 2.7 per cent. of the pupils registered are doing high school work, and that a little more than 5 per cent. are in the last grade of the common school course   The attendance is well maintained until this grade is reached, when the break from school is very abrupt.   These facts should disabuse the extremist's mind that it is possible for the high school work to monopolize the time of the common course.   Deduct the attendance of high school pupils from a few centres of population as Amherst, Parrsboro, Acadia Mines, and Oxford, and the high school attendance is practically nothing.   Of the 2.7 per cent. of high school pupils not more than 1 per cent. took the government examination.

The results, as far as could be learned from the leading schools, are as follows :—

GRADES OBTAINED.

HIGH SCHOOL.	B.	C.	D.
Amherst	6	12	17
Parrsboro....................	2	4	4
Springhill	....	4	4
Oxford.......................	....	3	3
Acadia Mines	....	1	3
Pugwash	....	2	1
Tatamagouche	....	1	1
Great Village	....	3	1

This does not include a number from the common schools, nor those attending institutions beyond the district.

COURSE OF STUDY.

By observation, and the statistics at my command, I find little tendency for the ornamental (?) branches to yield to those considered by many only essential. Arithmetic and reading alone consume two-fifths of the school week. The methods generally employed in teaching reading are open to criticism, and is the greatest disturbing element in the proper gradation of the miscellaneous school. Without any other ability save that of an imperfect pronunciation, pupils are hurried from reader to reader without reference to the composition or meaning of the subject, or the hearing of collateral subjects. The fault is mainly attributable to teachers themselves, who, to gain a short-lived notoriety, advise the use of readers unfit for the child's attainments. I believe it is the gravest fault in this district's schools. It creates an aversion for school life, especially in the sixth and seventh grades where the studies are multiplied, and, as a result, the course of study gets out of balance.

The subject of temperance at one bound has leaped into the foreground, and has laid claim to its full share of time. From personal knowledge I believe the most sanguine and enthusiastic temperance advocates could not have expected more.

The same cannot be said of music and calisthenics. While the former subject in many schools is intelligently taught, and with beneficial results, the majority of teachers seek immunity from the demands of the course of study in ignorance or physical disabilities.

Drawing has not netted the results that it should for the time that it has been on the course of study. Teachers meet with much opposition in introducing the subject into schools. Its utility is not known.

The leading subjects of the course, such as arithmetic, writing, geography, history, language, are more intelligently presented. This is especially true of language and composition. Teachers are discovering the fact that as in the mechanical arts we learn by doing, so skill and accuracy in the use of English is only acquired by constant practice in expression.

Amherst Academy is steadily growing in public favor, and is beginning to attract pupils from all parts of the county. The county has implicit confidence in Mr. Lay's principalship. The academy is qualifying for the support of two academic grades. N. D. Mactavish, A (Sc.), the efficient principal of Springhill for two years, has been taken upon the competent staff of the academy.

Parrsboro High School is a strong rival to the academy. Now with increased facilities for better work, and under the enthusiastic principalship of T. C. McKay, B. A., A (Cl.), may be expected to be favorably reported another year.

Oxford and Pugwash High Schools, under the management of Messrs. Slade and Healy, passed 90 per cent. of candidates presented for examination this summer. Indeed, there are only words of commendation for all of the schools given in the tables. Their teachers are generally experienced and select.

This is no reflection upon the scores of efficient miscellaneous schools throughout the district. The town systems have no more devoted servants than the majority of rural sections. I would that they were as well equipped, for it is from the country come the distinguished men and women who, in the majority of instances, fill the roll of honor, and give to their country the most valuable element of citizenship.

Yours very respectfully,

INGLIS C. CRAIG

To A. H. MacKay, Esq., Ll. D.,
Superintendent of Education.

APPENDIX C.

REPORT OF THE BOARD OF SCHOOL COMMISSIONERS

OF THE

CITY OF HALIFAX,

(YEAR ENDED JULY 31st, 1894.)

(I.)

CHAIRMAN'S REPORT.

OFFICE OF SCHOOL COMMISSIONERS,
Halifax, November, 1894.

A. H. MacKay, Ll. D.,
    Superintendent of Education.

Sir :—

I have the honor to submit herewith the statistical and financial returns relating to the public schools of the city. The statistical tables are for the school year ended July 31, and the financial returns are for the official year ended Oct. 31, 1894.

The appropriations are made for the civic year, which commences on the first day of May and extends to the thirtieth day of April in the following year.

The estimated amount required for maintenance for the year ended April 30th, 1894, was $101,500 ; and for the year ending April 30th, 1895, $98,200. I give the estimated expenditure for the two years, for the reason that the official year comprises the last half of the civic year 1893-94, and the first half of the civic year 1894-95.

Of the $98,200 estimated as being required for the current civic year, $85,600 was assessed on the city.

The balance due the board from the city assessment, as per ledger Oct. 31, 1894, was $84,750.41, made up as follows :—

Due for the year 1892-93................$ 5,575 75
    do.   1893-94................ 14,934 31
    do.   1894-95................ 64,240 35

$84,750 41

As a result of this indebtedness, and having no other available source of revenue, the board, in order to meet its obligations for the first six monhts of the currént civic year, was compelled to overdraw its account at the Union Bank to the extent of $37,101. The interest on overdrafts for the twelve months ended July 31, 1894, amounted to $1681.59. If the whole sum assessed and collected for school purposes was paid over to the school board, it would materially decrease the cost of our schools.

The following table, covering a period of ten years, discloses (1) the amount asked for and paid to the school board, (2) the amount added by the city council for short collection, and (3) the total assessment for school purposes for the period named :—

YEAR.	Amount asked for and paid to the Board.	Added for short collection.	Total assessment.
1884-85	$ 66,820 00	$ 3341 00	$ 70,161 00
1885-86	67,700 00	3385 00	71,085 00
1886-87	68,600 00	3430 00	72,030 00
1887-88	70,600 00	3530 00	74,130 00
1888-89	72,000 00	3600 00	75,600 00
1889-90	74,000 00	3700 00	77,700 00
1890-91	78,900 00	3945 00	82,845 00
1891-92	84,000 00	2100 00	86,100 00
1892-93	85,000 00	2125 00	87,125 00
1893-94	88,500 00	2212 00	90,712 00
	$756,120 00	$31,368 00	$787,488 00

The first column shows the actual cost to the city of the schools for the ten years.

On referring to the annual reports of the city government we find that the actual loss from short collection was in the vicinity of one per cent. on the total assessment, so that in the ten years the schools contributed between $20,000 and $25,000 to the city council's unexpended balance fund, and which was used by the council to reduce its own rate of taxation.

The valuation for assessment purposes for the civic year ending April 30, 1895, are as follows :

Real Estate...$15,795,810
Personal Property............................ 5,003,650

Total Real and Personal...........................$20,799,460
Banks and Companies exclusive of Real Estate 2,152,777

$22,952,237

The school rate for the current civic year ending April 30, 1895, is 43 cents on the one hundred dollars, and was levied on the above valuation of real and personal property.

The amount expended for maintenance during the official year just ended was $101,488.16, appropriated as follows:

To Common Schools....................$ 91,204 21
County Academy..................... 9,677 43
Manual Training Department 606 52

$101,488 16

The income for the same period was $98,061.84, derived as follows:

From City Assessment $83,984 09
" Government Grant to Common Schools .. 11,320 49
" " " Academy 1,720 00
" Fees, etc., Academy.................... 552 05
" " Common Schools 485 21

$98,061 84

Deducting its income from the expenditure, we find that the County Academy proper cost the citizens of Halifax for the year just closed, $7,405.38.

The opponents of free higher education object to this expenditure on the ground of its being burdensome to the poorer class of the tax payers. A glance at the following table, which includes at least three-fourths of the tax payers—both direct and indirect—will show the fallacy of this contention. Basing the rate per centum on the valuation of the city for the current year ($20,799,460) we find that the individual tax payer who owned or occupied property valued at

$1000, contributed $0.36 towards its maintenance.
2000, " 0.72 " "
3000, " 1.08 " "
4000, " 1.44
5000, " 1.80
6000, " 2.16

The total funded debt due for schools on the 31st October was $254,600, the yearly interest on which amounts to $11,797. A sinking fund should be provided for the extinguishing of at least one-half of this debt.

The city of Halifax is, I believe, the only school section in the province excepted from the operation of the clause in the Education Act which provides that, " All moneys borrowed for the purchase or improvement of grounds for school purposes, or for the purchase or building of school houses, should be paid by equal yearly instalments not exceeding twelve, to be assessed upon the section."

When trustees are allowed to create a permanent debt for school purposes, the amount borrowed should be limited to the market value of the real estate owned by the section, otherwise the burden of paying the principal—as we are to-day, the interest —will fall upon

those receiving little or no benefit from a large portion of the
expenditure. To justify this conclusion I give below a summary of
the debenture debt to October 31, 1874, from which it will be seen
(1) that $12,259 was disbursed for repairs to school houses, more than
one-half of which amount was laid out on buildings, which in consideration of the expenditure were leased to the board either free
or at a reduced rental ; (2) that $14.898 was paid for furniture, nearly
all of which has long since been replaced with new ; and (3) that at
least $13,000 of the original cost of the Brunswick street school
disappeared with the building when it was pulled down to give
place to the Alexandra school.

The Richmond school was completed and occupied in the year
1868, the Morris street school in 1869, and the Albro street school in
1870. In estimating their value, an allowance should be made for
depreciation brought about by the wear and tear of twenty-five
years use. In recent years all expenditure for repairs and for furniture have been charged to maintenance account.

Expenditure on Debentures Account to October, 1874.

School.	Land.	Construction.	Repairs.	Furniture.	Total.
Acadian.................	....	....	$ 2,497 38	$ 415 52	$ 2,912 90
Albro Street...........	$ 3,617 00	$ 21,233 83	208 52	1,920 33	26,979 68
Brunswick Street........	*11,600 00	4,048 90	1,594 61	1,989 07	19,232 58
Campbell Road..........	....	....	12 33	13 37	25 70
Colonial Market.........	....	....	83 48	60 97	144 45
Convent.................	....	....	8 88	300 52	309 40
City Street..............	....	....	69 14	264 02	333 16
Inglis	....	....	71 38	67 51	138 89
Mason Hall............	....	....	29 08	409 62	438 70
Morris Street	8,830 70	30,738 73	537 52	3,012 30	43,119 25
National	....	....	3,031 84	711 00	3,742 84
Richmond, Old	....	....	81 23	6 00	87 23
Richmond, New	....	15,637 93	631 27	809 05	17,078 25
St. John's	....	....	219 76	531 23	750 99
St. Luke's	....	....	408 99	366 60	775 59
St. Mary's	....	....	911 32	937 42	1,848 74
St. Patrick's............	....	....	1,549 17	2,524 36	4,073 53
Three Mile	....	....	7 40	10 70	18 10
Lot on Common	806 00	....	....	....	....
Bloomfield..	1,900 00	....	....	....	....
Vinecove Hall	....	....	1 00	....	1 00
Zion	....	....	46 03	12 20	58 23
Russell Street...........	....	....	259 12	536 86	795 98
Tower Road	1,200 00	....	....	....	1,200 00
D. Sterling, architect....	....	613 00	....	....	613 00
C. Dart, clerk	....	453 50	....	....	453 50
	$27,953 70	$72 725 89	$12,259 45	$14,898 65	$127,837 69

* Building included.

The nine department building to replace the Russell St. school and
rooms, reported last year as being in the course of construction, was
completed and occupied in March last. The building, out-buildings,

grounds, and fences cost $15,028, for which sum debentures at $4\frac{1}{2}$ per cent. interest per annum were issued. A further sum of about $300 was charged to maintenance, and expended for plank walks and grading. The rent paid for the buildings which constituted the Russell St. school, so-called, was $705 per annum; the interest on cost of new building will amount to $676 per annum.

On the completion of the three room addition to Compton Avenue school, the class-rooms in the Victoria and Curren halls were closed, and the teachers and children transferred some to Compton Avenue, and some to Bloomfield schools. The addition cost $4196, the interest on which, at $4\frac{1}{2}$ per cent. per annum, amounts to $188.82. The rent paid for the two rooms vacated was $240 per annum, and included heating in one and attendance in both. The Compton Avenue school is now an eight department building.

The total enrollment for the year was 7,412, with an average daily attendance of 5,001, or 67 per cent. of the whole number on the registers. The table also show that 1,803 pupils attended less than 100 days out of a possible 208 days.

Apathy and indifference on the part of parents, truancy especially among the boys, and perhaps in some cases carelessness on the part of teachers, are chiefly responsible for this want of regularity in the attendance. It is unnecessary for me to here point out the evil effects arising therefrom, they have been freely commented upon in nearly every annual report since the introduction of our free school system.

We have now a remedy in the Compulsory Attendance Act, which came into full operation in August last. A vigorous and systematic enforcement of the clauses of the Act which make the parent or guardian responsible for the irregular or non-attendance of children under their care or control, will soon bring about this much needed reform.

A "Home," having for its object the care, management, and education of habitual truants, is an urgent necessity if the truancy clauses of the Act are to be rigorously enforced. The only institutions at present available for the reception of truants are the reformatories for boy criminals, and even, if they were in other respects suitable, the propriety of compelling those who are not criminals to associate with those who are, is to say the least questionable.

In his report to the Board for the year 1890-91, Supervisor McKay called attention to this difficulty, and as his remarks are so appropriate and to the point, I cannot refrain from again bringing them to your notice. He said : "Very properly the commissioners hesitate in many "cases to press our law because * * * a serious objection arises, "when to convict means that the boy whose only offence is truancy is "made to associate with criminals. Besides the stigma that attaches to "such association there is a very great danger of moral contamination. "It is a principle of reformatory institutions that success means the "classification of criminals. How important then, that boys who are "not criminals should not be so classed—that those who are only wild

"and wayward should not almost certainly be hastened on a downward
"career. Let them be saved to society and their parents."

He then goes on to suggest that "A parental home should be
"established for truants and incorrigible boys. Parents, whose boys
"are there, should be compelled to contribute to their maintenance,
"according to their means, the rest of the cost would have to be borne
"by the city. The institution should be in charge of a superior
"teacher, and under the management of the school board. In such a
"school the boy would be restrained, protected, taught self-control,
"habituated to obedience, instructed in industrial work as well as in
"books, and above all, by being guarded from all imputation of
"criminality while in school, dismissed therefrom with more than an
"even chance of doing well in after life."

A "Home," such as outlined in the foregoing extract, provincial in
its character and under the management of the Council of Public
Instruction, would not only be more likely to secure the confidence of
the public than if a private undertaking, but would at the same time
place at the disposal of every school section in the province an
institution having for its sole object the moral, mental, and manual
training of truant and incorrigible boys committed to its care.

St. Mary's boys school-house has been leased by the board for a
further period of ten years, at a rental of $1,025 per annum. The
building is to be kept in repair by the owner, who is also to keep it
insured.

A new arrangement has also been effected with the owners of the
Dutch Village school-house by which the board will in future pay a
rental of $110 per annum for the building, and collect the regular
tuition fee from children attending the school whose parents or
guardians reside outside the city limits. Previous to this arrangement the board occupied the building free of rent, and children of
non-resident parents attending the school enjoyed equal school privileges with those of citizens.

For all further information respecting the condition of our city
schools, I would respectfully refer you to the exhaustive report of the
Supervisor, which, with the detailed financial statements prepared by
the Secretary, will in the course of a few weeks be published in the
Commissioners' Annual Report.

In conclusion, it affords me pleasure to testify to the zealous
and energetic manner in which the Supervisor, Mr. A. McKay, continues to discharge the important duties pertaining to his office.
I am also pleased to be able to report that the board have in their
Secretary, Mr. R. J. Wilson, a painstaking and careful executive officer,
and one who may always be relied upon to combine economy with
efficiency in all matters of expenditure committed to his management.

I have the honor to be, Sir,
Your obedient servant,
JNO. P. LONGARD,
Chairman.

(II.)

SUPERVISOR'S REPORT.

To the Chairman and Members of the Board of School Commissioners for the City of Halifax:

GENTLEMEN :—

Herewith I submit for your information statistical tables relating to the attendance and studies of the pupils of the Halifax public schools for the year ended July 31st, 1894.

There were throughout the year 123 regular departments, and one department at the Industrial school. There were, besides, for about one-fourth of the year, supplementary departments in Albro street, Alexandra, Compton avenue, Morris street, Richmond, and Young street schools. Besides the teachers required for these departments, there were three teachers of special subjects, who were employed on certain days of the week.

There were employed in all, 132 teachers, of whom one acted in a dual capacity. Of these, 17 were males and 115 females. Of the males, 4 held grade "A"; 10 grade "B"; 1 grade "C"; and 2 no license valid in this province. Of the females, 1 held grade "A"; 35 grade "B"; 74 grade "C"; 4 grade "D"; and one no license.

Of the teachers now on the staff, about one-half have been employed in our schools over ten years, and 22 over twenty years. 35 have diplomas from the Normal school at Truro. 28 received their professional training at Mount St. Vincent. 68 have had no professional training at a Normal school. Of those holding Normal school diplomas from Truro, 2 are principals of schools. Of those having no Normal school diplomas, 11 are principals. The self-taught teachers, whose preparation for their work consists of scholarship and experience, have taken somewhat higher rank than those trained theoretically at the Normal school. The teachers from Mount St. Vincent, carefully selected as to their natural aptitudes, and practically trained, have for several years been ranked higher, on an average, than any other class of our teachers. 22 teachers are marked superior; 34 very good ; 48 good ; and the rest below the average.

The total number of pupils registered was 7,412, or 279 more than during the preceding partial year. Of these, only 391 were over fifteen years of age. The average daily attendance was 4,942 : the average of quarterly percentages being 75,— a considerable improvement on that of last year. The sexes were very nearly equally divided in respect of numbers, there being 11 more boys than girls. But not so in scholarship. In the 8th grade there were twice as many girls as boys, and in the academic grades 86 more girls than boys. Boys not preparing for college leave school at an earlier age than girls.

8

VISITS.

Not many of the teachers are careful to enter the names of visitors. According to their reports, however, there were 574 inspectoral visits; 272 commissioners' visits; and less than 2,000 by all other visitors.

APPORTIONMENT OF TIME.

If we are to judge of the relative values of school studies by the amount of time devoted to them, the three R's are still looked upon as fundamental. During the past year 20 minutes per week more than formerly were devoted to copy-book writing. In the attention given to other subjects, there seems to have been very little change, except that chemistry, Latin, and Greek apparently take much less time than before.

On an average, 30 minutes per week are devoted to health, includ-temperance, in nearly every department. This is ample time in which to do the subject full justice, seeing that the pupils have Health Readers for home study.

An hour each week has been devoted to drawing lessons. In a few departments only have the results been quite satisfactory. The same might be said of the object lessons given. In penmanship there has been a marked improvement. So far as I know no other schools in the province can show so large a proportion of neat, well-written copy-books.

There has been a decline in pure kindergarten work. It has been found very difficult to keep it up in connection with first grade reading and arithmetic; yet it has had a marked influence in improving primary work.

In the higher grades there was no special change, except that Grade XII. had more than twice as many pupils as before,—many of whom, however, took only a partial course. This grade, which is collegiate rather than academic, has been discontinued.

TEACHERS' SALARIES.

Grade B male teachers average $769 per year.
    " B female   "   " $481   "
    " C "   "   " $315   "

The other grades are exceptional. There has been no increase in the average of teachers' salaries for several years.

ACADEMIC EDUCATION.

For the July provincial examination of 1893, I reported that of the Academy pupils 159 had passed in the various grades. In the July examination of this year 139 have succeeded,— 7 A's; 29 B's; 40 C's, and 63 D's.

The system of government examinations enables us to judge of the state of education in the various educational centres. In the province there are 30 stations at which candidates are examined. The majority of them are usually from the academy or high school at the station. I will limit my estimates to a few of the larger centres of population that show the best percentages.

STATION.	No. of Candidates.	Per cent receiving the grade applied for.	One grade below.	Unsuccessful in the grade applied for.
Halifax	288	57 %	15 %	43 %
Amherst	61	51 "	7 "	49 "
Truro	224	47 "	16 "	53 "
Yarmouth	87	45 "	1 "	55 "
New Glasgow......	110	35 "	17 "	65 "
Pictou	96	35 "	35 "	65 "
Lunenburg........	92	35 "	13 "	65 "
Antigonish........	64	35 "	15 "	65 "
Kentville	122	34 "	14 "	66 "

From this table it appears that Halifax leads the province in academic education. It is but fair to say that if the comparison had been confined to grades B and C Truro Academy would have surpassed all its competitors. Antigonish sent up 4 A's,—all successful; Pictou, 4 A's,—all successful; and New Glasgow, 5 A's,—4 successful. But Halifax sent up 16 A's, of whom 11 were successful, besides 8 candidates for a partial A course, of whom 2 succeeded.

Your action a year ago in discontinuing the grade A work of the academy has, I believe, met with the approval of the great majority of those interested. Yet there are many who look upon it as a retrograde movement. It is therefore desirable to state the reasons which led to the discontinuance of one of the most prosperous classes of the academy.

1. As already stated, the work of this class was collegiate rather than academic. In Classics, Mathematics, and English it included the first year's work of our provincial colleges, and in Science and some other subjects much more. It seemed a waste of energy to make provision in our academies for work which was done much more thoroughly in our colleges. The only advantage that appeared was that no fees were required of the pupils. But the great majority of our people believe that the state has done enough for higher education when it has made it free to the gates of the universities. The disadvantage of the old plan was the lack of thoroughness, and consequently of genuine culture.

2. It seemed to be a great injustice to the other grades of the school numbering 94% of the attendance, that nearly one-third of the teachers' energies should be devoted to 6% of the class. There are academies in the province dissipating their energies on a few grade A pupils, doing them as well as the rest of their pupils a great wrong. In Halifax Academy the case was not quite so bad, for the class

numbered 11 and subsequently 22, and the teaching staff was such as to admit of division of labor to a greater extent. Still it was not considered right to devote as much time to one class of 22 as to another of 72.

3. The course for grade A includes more than can be fairly accomplished by the average pupil in the fourth and fifth years of high school study,—more than can be fairly comprehended by pupils of the average age of from 16 to 18. It was thought that it would be to the advantage of higher education if candidates for grade A were required to take a college course in connection with, or previous to, their grade A studies. That would imply sufficient maturity and culture in those who are to occupy the highest positions in our public schools.

4. It is true that by closing grade A work, grade B loses the stimulating effect of having a higher class to strive for, and the academy loses many of its country students whose industrious habits, scholarship, and example were most beneficial to our city pupils. But if the extra time to be hereafter devoted to the other grades is judiciously used it should more than compensate for this loss.

The public school system is greatly simplified by the withdrawal from it of all the formidable subjects required in grade A. In grade B there are but seven compulsory subjects,—English, History, Physics, Physiology, Practical Mathematics, Algebra, and Geometry, with some review of Geography and Arithmetic. The ancient and modern languages are optional. Many look upon the study of the classics as practically useless for the great majority of our pupils, if not for all,— not only useless but a positive loss. Those who come so easily to that conclusion should remember that the determining of the best course of study to develop the child is the most difficult and profound of all problems. It requires the highest qualifications,—a thorough knowledge of human nature in all its complexity, and a comprehensive acquaintance with the educational experience of past ages.

The members of the Government, as possessing more than the average intelligence of those whom they represent, might be deemed qualified to draw up a course of study suited to the average needs of our citizens. But they have never ventured to do so. This task they very wisely leave to experts, and we are required, in the meantime, to accept their conclusions.

I have always been, as many of you are, one of those whose sympathies were drawn to the so-called practical and scientific studies. But I must admit that it is much more difficult and unusual to get as good results from them as from the classical studies. That I may be able to give a satisfactory reason for this does not change the fact.

When you go into a school and find that, as a class, the boys who devote themselves exclusively to your practical studies do not make nearly as good progress mentally or physically as those who study Latin and Greek, you stop to think, and you hesitate to recommend *changes* of which you do not know the effect.

It is a surprising fact that out of 370 academic pupils from the most intelligent homes in the city, 287 deliberately choose Latin, although it is one of their most difficult studies. They give as a reason that the study of Latin " does them more good," by which they mean that it gives them better habits of study, and strengthens their intellects more than the substitutes that are offered for it.

It is true, as some one says, that " if we are seeking for an ideal curriculum we shall fail, as the wisest men in all ages have failed. A healthy discontent with our present circumstances is wise, but it is also wise not to be too discontented. No practical system of education produces ideal results, and it is very easy to criticise present work from an ideal standpoint. The reformer in education has always the advantage. The actual results produced by present arrangements are not as good as they might be; and as the subjects proposed have not been subjected to the crucial test of actual experience, it is easy to predict that under the new system there will be no friction, and that the calculated results are sure to be obtained. This is a time of progress and great pedagogical activity ; but we must not after all expect too much of it."

COMMON SCHOOL STUDIES.

The common school course of study is also charged with being overloaded with subjects of which many are said to be useless. Let us inquire into the facts. The 25 teaching hours of the week are thus divided : about 8 hours are devoted to reading, spelling, and the meanings of words ; 7 hours to arithmetic ; 2 hours to copy-book writing ; 1 hour to information on general things—useful knowledge ; 1 hour to drawing ; 2 hours to lessons on moral and patriotic duties, and restful movements ; 3 hours to geography and history ; and 1 hour to singing.

Suppose we dropped any one of these subjects, what is the other subject to which the time could be devoted without wearying the pupil ? And which of these subjects could be dropped without a serious loss in the all-round development specially required by the child who leaves at the end of the common school ? Which subject could be omitted without a protest long and loud from a majority of the parents ? And they would be right. There are not too many subjects, nor do any of them receive too much attention or time. When the importance of incidental teaching—the concentration of studies—comes to be properly understood and practised by teachers, our common school curriculum will be found to be scientifically grounded on the soundest educational principles. It will then be found possible to master all the subjects which it now includes, and also to give much more attention to English and the study of things instead of vocables, making and doing rather than memorizing.

THE TEACHER.

In a system of education it is desirable to have good school houses. They should be in healthful localities, should be well ventilated, warm, and properly lighted. If they can be made to minister to the pupil's aesthetic culture so much the better but we must not forget that nearly all our greatest scholars and best men were educated in very plain buildings, with poor furnishings, and possessing but few comforts. It is therefore plain that elegant buildings and costly furniture are not essential to the training necessary to produce great men and women.

A good course of study and good text-books are very desirable. Much time, no doubt, has been wasted on the study of subjects not suited to the child's mental development, and by the use of uncouth text-books, which fail to present even good subjects so that they can be appropriated. But there is so little yet understood of the disciplinary value of any subject of study, and so little known of child-nature, that even the best curriculum cannot differ so very much from the poorest. At all events we find that, of our great men, some are trained by one system, and some by another, and some without the help of any system. It is evident then that the curriculom is not, any more than the school house, the important thing in education. But if there is any one thing in education that is transcendentally more important than another, it is the teacher. From log school houses, with a poor course of study and a dearth of text-books, there came forth the greatest, best, and even the most refined men of the last generation in Canada and the United States.

The disadvantages of which we sometimes complain so much, sink into insignificance in the presence of the strong personality of a great teacher. Let us then look to our teachers as the vital part of our educational system. Let them be "apt to teach," of strong character, and well-trained, and we need not fear for our schools.

This brings me to an important subject, at which I have occasionally hinted in my former reports,—

THE TRAINING OF CITY TEACHERS.

Naturally before taking action on such an important matter, we should avail ourselves of the experience and wisdom of other countries. In Prussia, candidates for the teaching profession are required to have a good elementary education before their professional training begins. The professional course of study is for three years. Throughout the last year the student must practise teaching for not less than six hours per week. The Normal schools are small, and there are many of them. Evidently there is no desire manifested to build up one great central institution with a maximum of theory and a minimum of practice. At the age of twenty, and after three years special study, the student passes his first examination, which tests not only his theoretical knowledge, but also his skill in teaching. The second examination must take place after two years' teaching, and not more than five years after the first.

In England, teachers in order to obtain certificates must be at least twenty years of age, must pass two examinations at an interval of one year or more, and must have given satisfactory proofs of their professional ability in actual service for two years, as provisionally certificated, or for one year as assistants, before they can be admitted to the first examination. Many of the Normal schools are attached to some university, and the students may be certificated chiefly on the results of the university examinations. This is regarded as an important advantage, opening before the student a wider range of knowledge, and promising the stimulus of broader and freer views on those subjects. There are on an average eighty pupils in each training school.

The United States are dotted over with Normal schools. There are State Normal schools— sometimes several in one State. There are City Normal schools in nearly every large town. Of these Dr. Harris, the United States Commissioner of Education, says: " If any schools for the training of teachers in this country ought to deserve the name of professional, it is the class known as City Normal schools. A system of city schools is an educational unit. It is natural that the upper class of the High school should be looked to for the material of which to make teachers, and that finally a Normal school should be the result of the attempt to train High school pupils for teaching." It is urged that the State Normal schools are inadequate to supply the city's wants, or to supply the kind of training specially needed in the city. Although in the United States the professional training of teachers does not receive one tithe of the attention which it should, yet there are 130 Normal schools, which in 1891 sent out five thousand graduates, or an average of less than 40 from each school. In cities of the size of Halifax the training schools will average about 10 graduates each. They have, therefore, abundant opportunities for practice under skilled supervision before they receive their appointments.

On this point Dr. Larkin Dunton says : " A practice school is to a Normal school what a hospital is to a medical school. It is a place for verifying and illustrating principles. It is an opportunity to reduce theory to practice. The theoretical side of education is never fully understood till it is supplemented by the practical side. Beginners in education, like beginners in everything else, need to see the truth at first in the concrete. A principle of teaching or of discipline has a new meaning when seen in its application. Then, too, the novice never knows what children really are till he sees live children in action. The sympathy of numbers, the contagion of intellectual activity, the power of example, the force of public opinion, these and similar factors in a working school, must be learned in the school itself. Power and skill in teaching and governing are developed by teaching and governing. The development of skill is more rapid if practice is done under the direction of experts. The acquisition of skill is less expensive to the children if skill is gained in the practice school. Practice work by the Normal pupils should be so arranged that only one Normal student will be in a room at a time, and she should remain for several successive weeks. Thus no more Normal pupils can be trained in the practice school at the same time than there are classes in the practice school. The practice school should be supplemented by teachers in various parts of the city selected for their theoretical knowledge of education, and practical skill in teaching and governing. The classes under the charge of these teachers should be used for purposes of practice, the same as the classes in the practice school itself. By this means the poor work of novices will not fall heavily upon the pupils in the regular classes in the practice school."

In Ontario there are 50 training schools, with an average attendance of 25 students each. Over three months' attendance is compulsory before beginning to teach. But in Toronto and Hamilton the time is extended to one year. In Hamilton the pupil teachers are required during the last half year to spend one-half of every day in actual teaching. Inspector Ballard says :—" The power to handle a class or a school cannot be learned theoretically. There is no royal road to it, only by experience extending over some definite considerable time. Nor can it properly be allowed that a class should be sacrificed in order that a teacher may obtain this experience. A city system of education may very properly embrace within its autonomy all the machinery necessary for the adequate training of its own teachers."

From all that I have said it is evident that for the proper professional training of teachers there is needed ample opportunity for extended practice in normal conditions.

There is a Normal school at Truro. It is an excellent institution, well equipped, and with a staff of earnest, able, and enthusiastic professors. But it lacks the essential element,—an opportunity to give to its students adequate practice of the educational theories which it propounds,—a defect which it can never overcome. Shut out from the public schools of Truro, for some years now, its 140 students have scarcely one pupil apiece on an average on which to practice, and the larger it becomes·the worse its plight in this respect.

The Truro school board, influenced by its past experience, would scarcely feel justified in again opening its schools as a practice-ground to more than about 15 pupil teachers. That number might have a stimulating effect on the schools and be themselves greatly benefited. An overwhelmingly greater number they might fail to assimilate, as was the case before in these schools.

Concentration may sometimes become a great evil. Normal school training, to become effective, must become decentralized. Every considerable community with scholastic advantages must become a practice field for would-be teachers. If there must be a weakness in the teacher's training let it, by all means, be in the theory rather than in the practice. But there need be no great weakness in either,—for a uniform government examination can test both, no difference from what source they come.

Halifax, as the capital of the province, has exceptional opportunities for the training of its teachers :—

1. *Manual Training* is given by Mr. Nelson Gardner, class A. To the skill of a practical workman he has added a theoretical study of a modified Sloyd, and has had one year's successful practice in teaching it.

2. *Music.*—Miss Ryan, one of our teachers, is an excellent musician. After an extensive study of the staff notation, and of instrumental music, she devoted much attention to tonic sol-fa, and passed several grades of examinations from the Tonic Sol-fa College, London, England. She has had great experience as a choir trainer and a teacher of teachers.

3. *Drawing.*—The Victoria School of Art and Design is able to meet any demands made upon it by teachers for painting, drawing, or modelling. Besides, our teachers are now enjoying an admirable course of lessons taught by Sister Colomba of Mount St. Vincent Academy, and founded on the system of drawing used in the Chicago schools. Other institutions in the city could also furnish excellent courses in drawing.

4. *Calisthenics.*—Miss Holmstrom, a thoroughly qualified graduate of Baron Nils Posse's Gymnasium, Boston, teaches the Swedish system of calisthenics to several classes in Halifax. There are likewise other teachers of this subject here.

5. Well-equipped laboratories and the most skillful teachers supply Practical Chemistry and Practical Physics in Dalhousie College.

6. There are also courses of lectures on Psychology, Pedagogics, and the History of Education. Professor Murray, who lectures on Psychology and the Theory of Education, has no superior in his own subjects in this country.

7. Courses of lectures are to be given by such eminent educationists as Professors Macdonald, H. Murray, MacGregor, MacMechan, Lawson, President Forrest, and Principals Kennedy and O'Hearn.

8. There would be ample opportunity for practice under the supervision of skilled teachers. The 129 departments of our city schools would be able to assimilate the new material required,—say a class of 10 or 15 student-teachers. The renewed and increased attention given to method would greatly stimulate the regular as well as the prospective teacher.

I have now shown that, judging by our city schools, a Normal school training devoid of practice is of little benefit to our city-trained girls; that careful selection and much practice are the common-sense elements in securing the best teachers; that across the Atlantic the Normal schools are small, with a two or three years' course, and extended normal practice in normal conditions; that in America the tendency is towards city Normal schools, and the associating of theory with an apprenticeship at teaching; that in our city there exists the greatest facilities for the complete professional training of our Academic and High school graduates—facilities which are never likely to become less.

When a vacancy occurs in any of our schools it is but natural, right, and economical of time and energy that it should be filled by one trained in our own graded schools, and familiar with our system and environments. Those likely to make the best teachers cannot always afford to go to Truro Normal school, where the opportunities do not exist for an ideal professional training; nor should they be compelled to go contrary to the general tendencies shown to result from experience elsewhere. That we will appoint them to our schools is certain. Then we should also train them under certain government restrictions; and our training should be recognized as sufficient for our purposes. It would greatly benefit the general education of the province if work of this kind, wherever done, were tested, and when efficient, recognized. Difficulties in the way ;—well it seems that they can be overcome elsewhere.

Apart from this local practical work, the Truro Normal school will always have its own special field,—the province in general. There it has all it can accomplish and, no doubt, it will always do its work well. It should lead in securing this reform which covers work that it cannot itself accomplish. It would then retain its hold on professional training, and be the heart of the system for the province; influencing and largely determining the direction of advanced educational thought.

COMPULSORY ATTENDANCE.

In last year's report I spoke of our compulsory attendance law as being the best that I had seen. With no material change it was adopted by the town of Dartmouth, where it has been vigorously enforced with the best possible results, proving its efficiency when properly administered. We should have this wholesome Act enforced, in a humane and considerate manner it is true, but enforced. We should not make

> "A scarecrow of the law,
> Setting it up to fear the birds of prey,
> —till custom make it,
> Their perch and not their terror."

It should be incumbent on every parent to shew that his children are receiving at least the minimum education required by this board. Every child has a right to an education that will help to make it self-supporting and a useful citizen. Riches are not a substitute for education, although education is a good substitute for riches. Riches may fail and leave the possessor dependent on charity, as is often the case. Poverty should not be a bar to education. Public or private charity should step in at a time when prevention is tenfold better than cure.

An English member of parliament, who made a study of the German schools, says that in Germany there is no such thing as an uneducated class, and no uncared-for children. He believes that it is owing to the system of thorough education that Germany has almost extinguished the pauper and semi-pauper class, which is the bane and disgrace of England. An education of the proper kind, given to every child, would create such habits of industry, mental application, and self-control as would place every one above want, and make our city prosperous.

In the administration of this law there should be no delays. It loses all its point and efficacy when the punishments for gross carelessness are either uncertain or long deferred.

There is one amendment most urgently needed. When badly disposed children approach the age of fourteen their conduct in school frequently becomes almost intolerable. They become indifferent because they feel that they are soon to be free, or if they are fourteen that they can leave at any time. Many of them have attended so badly through their school career that they can scarcely read; yet they leave, and spend two or three years in idleness and vice, in training for Rockhead.

The same evil has been experienced elsewhere, and has been largely prevented by requiring the attendance at school from the ages of fourteen to sixteen of all who are not up to a certain standard of education, unless they are actually engaged at work. I would strongly recommend this amendment, as being justified by experience and common sense. In the upper departments of our schools there are ample accommodations, and every other required facility, provided and paid for by the board, and they should be utilized to the fullest extent.

THE SCHOOL SAVINGS' BANK.

The benefit arising to pupils and parents from a well-conducted school savings bank are so great that I think it my duty again to call your attention to this subject by repeating what I said in 1892.

In Europe the school savings bank is a fully recognized educational and economic institution. To manage it takes but fifteen minutes a week, and no time is better spent. It is an incentive to industry and study. This teaching of thrift is usually introduced through the practical interest of school directors or bankers, who are quick to see the benefit it necessarily brings a community. Frequently, mostly in fact, the savings bank to have the school deposit in trust takes the expense of furnishing the teacher's roll-books, blanks, cards, envelopes, and slips as adapted to the system. When a child's savings reach one dollar he is given a separate bank book by the bank, and stands in the light of an adult depositor acting through the school facilities. When he has three dollars he is allowed an interest of three per cent. on his deposit. The boys and girls are thus taught how money grows with care. They are told from time to time the advantage of industry, thrift, and business knowledge. By the interest thus aroused parents, who never had a dollar ahead, have started savings' banks accounts for themselves. "The school savings' bank is a relief measure for pauperism, a preventive of crime, a developing force of honesty, sobriety, and peace."

THE SCHOOL LIBRARY.

In our public schools there are several small libraries aggregating 1600 volumes. Of these the academy owns 800 valuable, carefully selected books. They have been of the greatest benefit to the pupils, as they are extensively read and used in connection with their school work.   The libraries at St. Mary's, Summer street, St. Patrick's, and Le Marchant street schools are doing good work.   The pupils, teachers, and parents should be encouraged to add to existing libraries and to form others where none now exist.

Unfortunately, bad books are cheaper and more accessible than good ones.   The teacher has scarcely a more sacred or more important duty than to protect his pupils from the seductive, soul-destroying literature that abounds on every side.   He should pre-occupy the child's mind,—creating and fostering a desire for good reading.   He should help to cultivate a taste that will aid the pupil in his studies while at school, and protect him after he leaves school.   Happily there never was a time when it was so easy to procure classical master-pieces suited to children of every grade and disposition.

In some schools we find mottoes on the blackboards, pictures on the walls, plants in the windows,—all tending to moral culture and proving the deep interest of the teacher in something higher than the mere routine of lessons.   We praise all this, but much more let us encourage the teacher whose interest in her pupils leads her to have them supplied with pure literature,—a good, less showy, but deeper and more permanent in its effects.

EXHIBITS.

You will be pleased to hear that some of our school exhibits at the World's Fair were considered worthy of the award of a diploma. Also that our schools were successful in taking the greater part of the medals offered at the late Provincial Exhibition for school work.   Of course there was not much competition, but some of the work in writing, sewing, drawing, and mapping, was most creditable.

All of which is most respectfully submitted.

ALEXANDER McKAY,

Supervisor.

HALIFAX, *November, 1894.*

APPENDIX D.

SPECIAL PROVINCIAL INSTITUTIONS.

(I.)

HALIFAX INSTITUTION FOR THE DEAF AND DUMB, 1894.

The total attendance for the year has been seventy-seven, viz.: forty-five boys and thirty-two girls, of whom sixty-five belong to Nova Scotia, nine to Newfoundland, two to New Brunswick, and one to Prince Edward Island. The following table gives in detail the whole attendance :—

	Boys.	Girls.	Total.
Pupils of previous years still in attendance..	30	25	55
Additions during the year................	8	4	12
Absentees expected to return	1	2	3
Left school during the year	6	1	7
	45	32	77

The Institution is called the " Institution for the Deaf and Dumb at Halifax, N. S." The name of the Principal is James Fearon. The names of the teachers are : Miss J. Bateman, Mr. Lawrence, Miss M. Mosher, Miss L. Mahony, and Mr. A. G. Forbes. As regards subjects— arithmetic, geography, and history are taught, but every subject is made subservient to the teaching of language. The following table refers to the ages of the pupils and the time under instruction :—

Number of pupils under fifteen years old...................	44
" " over " " "	33
Average age of pupils	13
Number of pupils less than one year at school...............	12
" " one year and less than two years at school....	9
" " two years and less than three years at school	10
" three years and less than four years at school	8

HEALTH.

It is gratifying to be able to report that though a considerable amount of sickness of an infectious nature was present in the city throughout the year, the health of the pupils in the institution has been remarkably good. Only one case of serious illness appeared during the year. In the early part of the present session one pupil contracted pneumonia, but he is now quite recovered, and is back in the school-room.

THE SCHOOL-ROOM.

The work of the school-room has been going on satisfactorily. The teachers, one and all, have been faithful and energetic in the discharge of their duties, and good progress is being made in the several classes. Thirty-one pupils are receiving instruction in articulation and speech-reading, and the remainder are being taught under the manual system.

NEW BUILDING.

A new building is in contemplation, and it is expected that operations will begin early in the spring.

(II.)

HALIFAX SCHOOL FOR THE BLIND, 1894.

ATTENDANCE.

The table of attendance shows that 59 blind persons have been under instruction during the past year, 43 of whom were males and 16 females. Seven of these have since graduated or left the school, making the total number in attendance on December 1st, 1894, 52 ; of whom 37 are males and 15 females. Of these, 28 are from the province of Nova Scotia, 12 from New Brunswick, 4 from Prince Edward Island, and 8 from Newfoundland.

The table of attendance is as follows :

	Boys.	Girls.	Adults.	Total
Registered Dec. 1, 1893	32	13	2	47
Entered during the year	9	3	0	12
Graduated or remained home	5	1	1	7
Registered December 1, 1894......	36	15	1	52

It is gratifying to report that the past school year has been one of steady and satisfactory effort upon the part of both teachers and pupils. The teachers have brought to their work added experience, zeal for the progress of their pupils, and ambition to have the school retain its good name and reputation. Imbued with the spirit of the new education, they have faithfully striven to discharge their responsible duties, so as to secure the best results, and I am satisfied that the respect and esteem in which they are held by the pupils is well deserved.

MODERN LANGUAGES.

Recognizing the desirability of opening up to our graduates special literary callings, and availing ourselves of the experience of similar institutions abroad, a regular course in modern languages has been adopted, and instruction has been given to four of the older pupils with a view to their becoming teachers of French and German.

Prof. Lanos has undertaken the instruction in French, and Fraulein Œllars in German. In this new department one practical end is kept steadily in view, namely, preparing our pupils to earn their own livlihood. If the experiment proves as great a success as we anticipate, a new and wide field of usefulness will be opened to the blind.

TECHNICAL DEPARTMENT.

Work in the electrical department has passed beyond the experimental stage. S. J. Harivel, the enthusiastic instructor, has himself exploited this new field of occupation for the blind, and inspired by his success and enthusiasm, the pupils of his class are ambitious to prove that they, too, can become experts in special electrical work. In our workshop several young men are being trained as willow basket makers ; while others are being taught the re-seating of canebottom chairs.

ENLARGED BUILDING, ETC.

One of the difficulties with which we have to contend in educating the blind arises from the fact that many of the best years for educational work are lost. Our pupils enter the school at ten years of age. Prior to that time they have received no training whatever, and many of them are the victims of indulgence, ignorance, or neglect. No argument is necessary to prove that these little blind children suffer physically, mentally, and morally during these years of inactivity. If this be true, and it surely is, it would not be asking too much of the governments and legislatures of the Maritime Provinces and Newfoundland to allow us to take the children at six instead of ten years of age.

In our present school buildings, the maximum number of pupils that can be accommodated is sixty, and having due regard for the health and comfort of all within the establishment, the number of resident pupils should not exceed fifty-six. Of the fifty-two pupils now on the register, fifty-one are resident in the school, and already we have found it necessary to turn our trunk room into a dormitory for the domestics.

Judging from the number of names of probable pupils now on the books, I feel satisfied that the school will continue to increase in numbers for several years to come. This being the case, it is evident that some measure should soon be taken to provide increased accommodation. In the meantime the friends of the blind should unite in subscribing towards a building fund, in order that the board of managers may see their way clear to meet the emergency at the threshold.

(III.)

VICTORIA SCHOOL OF ART AND DESIGN.

To A. H. MacKay, Ll. D.,

Superintendent of Education.

Sir:—I beg to submit for the information of the Council of Public Instruction the report of the Treasurer of the Victoria School of Art and Design, for the year ended June, 1893-94.

The attendance of students in the regular classes was as good as usual. There was besides a special class of 50 teachers, who took a course in Object Drawing. This class was of great benefit to the public schools. It enabled many teachers to teach drawing from the object instead of from the flat—thus making this subject of much greater educational value. There was also the usual class from the Institution of the Deaf and Dumb. The mechanical class numbers about 60, nearly all of whom are apprentices, and therefore receive their tuition free. There were in all about 200 students. At the Provincial Exhibition several of them were awarded medals. The work of the school as a whole was also creditable, and was awarded a diploma.

TheArt School is gradually, though slowly, growing in favor with mechanics. The want of proper accommodation is a serious loss, and greatly hinders more rapid development.

Respectfully submitted,

A. McKAY,

Secretary.

Halifax, *January, 1895.*

VICTORIA SCHOOL OF ART AND DESIGN, HALIFAX.

(Incorporated 1888.)

DIRECTORS, 1893-94.

Ex-Officio . { THE SUPERINTENDENT OF EDUCATION,
{ THE MAYOR OF HALIFAX.

MRS. LEONOWENS,	MR. J. M. SMITH,
MRS. H. H. FULLER,	MR. J. C. MACKINTOSH,
MRS. J. F. KENNY,	MR. E. P. ARCHBOLD,
MISS E. RITCHIE,	MR. GEO. HARVEY,
MISS H. ALLISON,	MR. D. KEITH,
MR. J. DEMPSTER,	HON. SENATOR POWER,
DR. J. G. MACGREGOR,	MR. M. DWYER.
MR. A. MCKAY.	

Auditors.

MR. THOMAS BROWN,
MR. R. J. WILSON.

President . . . . MAYOR KEEFE.
Vice-President . . . . DR. MACKAY.
Treasurer . . . . MR. J. M. SMITH.
Secretary . . . . MR. A. MCKAY.

TEACHING STAFF.

Head Master.

MR. OZIAS DODGE, (Yale Un.)

Assistant Teachers.

Mechanical Drawing . . . . J. T. LARKIN, *Engineer,*
Architectural Drawing . . . .

Saturday Class.

MISS M. GRAHAM.

9

TREASURER'S REPORT.

THE TREASURER IN ACCOUNT WITH THE VICTORIA SCHOOL OF ART
AND DESIGN.

Endowment Fund :—
    Amount from 1893............................$ 7,702 40
Building Fund :—
    Amount from 1893............................ 8,000 00
Current Account-Receipts :—
    School Fees, etc...................... $221 50
    Government Grant 600 00
    City Grant 500 00
    Membership Fees...................... 15 00
    Interest 551 55
                                             1,888 05

                                              $17,590 45

Disbursements :—
    Salaries............................ $1575 00
    Rent............................... 200 00
    Fuel and Light..................... 79 28
    School Supplies 40 80
    Janitress 114 08
    Sundries 5 60

                               $2014 76
    Balance, September, 1893 .... 3228 80

                               $5243 56

Town of Kentville Bonds $5100 00
City of Halifax Consols............ 4950 00
Deposit Receipts Bank N. S........ 2200 00
Open account ...., 96 89
                                  12,346 89
                                         $17,590 45

JOHN M. SMITH,
Treasurer.

HALIFAX, N. S., *29th Sept., 1894.*

APPENDIX E.

EDUCATIONAL INSTITUTES.

(I.)

SUMMER SCHOOL OF SCIENCE FOR THE ATLANTIC PROVINCES.

To A. H. MacKay, Esq., Ll. D.,
Superintendent of Education.

SIR:—I beg leave to submit the following report of the Eighth Annual Session of the Summer School of Science for the Atlantic Provinces of Canada, held at Charlottetown, P. E. I., July 4th—19th, 1894.

The usual Calendar was issued in October, 1893, giving an outline of the subjects to be studied, and other matters of interest to those preparing to attend the school. Students were thus enabled to read in advance the subjects to be studied at the school. The school was opened by a public meeting in the Opera House, Charlottetown, on Wednesday, the 4th of July, and closed on the 19th. Classes were conducted in the Prince Street school. There were 93 students enrolled, the greater number of whom were teachers—49 from Prince Edward Island, 25 from New Brunswick, 18 from Nova Scotia, and 1 from the United States. Eight hours each day were devoted to lectures and laboratory work, conducted by specialists in the subjects undertaken by them, and the acknowledged leading educationists of the Maritime Provinces in their several departments.

Opportunities for excursions to places of scientific interest are fewer in P. E. Island than in the neighbouring provinces ; the excursions undertaken by the school were consequently not so successful as in former years.

Arrangements had been made with Rev. Dr. McIntyre, of Denver, Col., for a series of lectures on " The Creative Week." Shortly before the meeting of the school circumstances arose which prevented Dr. McIntyre's coming. It was then too late to arrange for any lecture.

Among the prominent citizens showing attention to the school were Lieut.-Governor Howlan, Ex-Governor S. Heath Haviland, Hon. D. Laird, Wm. Heard, Esq., and others.

The " Round Table Talks," begun last year, were continued. Most interesting and profitable discussion was had on the following subjects :—

"Music as an Educational Factor ".......Introduced by REV. JAS. ANDERSON, M.A.
" Humanitarian Influence of Science Teaching"   "   PROF. J. BRITTAIN.
" The Kindergarten ".....................Papers by MRS. S. B. PATTERSON, and
                                                        MISS MACKENZIE.

At the close of the school, certificates were awarded to those who passed examinations on the courses followed.

The Summer School of Science is now an established educational agency, and is yearly increasing in usefulness. . The management is gradually enlarging the scope of the work undertaken, and modifying it to suit the changing educational conditions of the time.

Patrons of the school were elected this year for the first time as follows :—

For Nova Scotia . . . . . GENERAL MONTGOMERY MOORE, Commander-
                    in-Chief of the Forces, British North America.

For New Brunswick . . SIR S. L. TILLEY.

For P. E. Island . . . . . . HON. T. HEATH HAVILAND.

The next session of the school will be held in Amherst, N. S. from the 3rd to the 18th of July, 1895.

The following is a list of officers and instructors for 1895 : —

OFFICERS:

President.

REV. W. W. ANDREWS, M. A. . . . . Mt. Allison University, Sackville.

Vice-Presidents.

PRINCIPAL A. CAMERON . . . . County Academy, Yarmouth. •
PROF. J. BRITTAIN . . . . Normal School, Fredericton.
E. STEWART, ESQ. . . . . Supervisor Schools, Charlottetown.

Secretary-Treasurer.

PRINCIPAL J. D. SEAMAN . . . . Prince St. School, Charlottetown.

Executive Committee.

J. K. DORSEY, M. D.,   MRS. S. B. PATTERSON,
REV. G. J. OULTON, B. A.,   INSPECTOR CRAIG,
        THE PRESIDENT, AND SECRETARY-TREASURER.

FACULTY:

Astronomy.

PRINCIPAL A. CAMERON ....County Academy, Yarmouth.

Botany.

ANTOINETTE FORBES, B. A.......County Academy, Yarmouth.
N. D. MACTAVISH.............   "   Amherst.

Chemistry.

PROF. BRITTAIN ....Normal School, Fredericton.

Civics.

PRINCIPAL W. T. KENNEDY......County Academy, Halifax.

Elocution.

MRS. L. J. LANDERS'...........Mt. Allison University, Sackville.

English Literature.

PRINCIPAL A. CAMERON ....County Academy, Yarmouth.

Geology and Mineralogy.

PROF. A. E. COLDWELL.........Acadia College, Wolfville.

Kindergarten.

MRS. S. B. PATTERSON..........Normal School, Truro.

Music (Tonic Sol-Fa).

REV. JAMES ANDERSON, M. A....Toronto.

Pedagogics and Psychology.

J. B. HALL, PH. D............:Normal School, Truro.

Physics.

PROF. W. W. ANDREWS, M. A....Mt. Allison University, Sackville.

Physiology and Hygiene.

PRINCIPAL E. J. LAY..........County Academy, Amherst.

Zoology and Entomology.

PRINCIPAL G. J. OULTON, B. A. ..County Academy, Dorchester.

I have the honor to be,

Your obedient servant,

J. D. SEAMAN,

CHARLOTTETOWN, P. E. I., *Dec., 1894.*   *Secretary.*

(II.)

TEACHERS' ASSOCIATIONS.

CUMBERLAND COUNTY AND WEST COLCHESTER.

The Teacher's Association for district No. 10 met in annual session at Springhill on Thursday and Friday, December 8th and 9th, about one hundred and ten teachers being present. Besides the teachers, Superintendent of Education (Dr. MacKay), Prof. Lee Russell of the Provincial Normal School, Truro, and Inspector Craig were present. The session was one of the most profitable and interesting yet held.

On Wednesday evening a reception was tendered the visitors by the Springhill teachers. A good programme was furnished by the orchestra, assisted by the leading musical talent of the town.

Inspector Craig, president of the accociation, opened the first session on Thursday morning with a short address of welcome, after which the programme of the session was taken up, the first being a paper on "The Teaching Profession," by Mr. W. M. Ferguson of Tatamagouche. W. R. Slade of Oxford, read an excellent paper on "The Effect of Alcohol in the Tissues." These papers elicited more or less discussion. Mr. A. S. Ford gave a lesson illustrative of the tonic sol-fa system.

At the afternoon session Prof. Lee Russell gave a splendid paper on "Manual Training." Miss Peppard of Onslow, read a very interesting paper. In the evening a rousing educational mass meeting was held in Fraser's Hall, town clerk McLeod presiding. Addresses were given by the chairman, Dr. MacKay, Prof. Lee Russell, and Inspector Craig and Rev. Mr. Wright. Splendid music was furnished by the Springhill orchestra.

The first matter of business taken up the next morning was the election of the following officers:

      President..........................MR. CRAIG.
      Vice-President.....................A. S. FORD.
      Sec.-Treasurer ....A. D. ROSS.

The *Executive* consist of the above officers, and MESSRS. FERGUSON (Tatamagouche), CAMPBELL (Parrsboro), SLADE (Oxford), and MISSES WEST (Amherst), GRANT (Springhill), CAMERON (Parrsboro), and CRANDALL, (Oxford).

After the election Mr. A. S. Ford gave another lesson in the tonic sol-fa system. Mr. Scanlan of Nappan, who spent a large portion of his vacation at the World's Fair, three days of which were spent in the educational department, read a very interesting and instructive paper on "The Educational Exhibit at the World's Fair." Principal Ruggles of Acadia Mines, with a class tron the Springhill academy, gave a lesson illustrative of his method of teaching writing. Principal Torey of Springhill, read a paper, "Short Cuts in Arithmetic." The discussion of these papers occupied considerable time and were very interesting. Inspector Craig gave a valuable talk on "School Returns."

At the afternoon session Principal Campbell, Parrsboro, read a paper on "The School Section as an Educator." This paper called forth much praise, and by request of the convention will be published in the EDUCATIONAL REVIEW. A paper on "The Teaching of Mathematics" was read by Principal Healy, Pugwash. After the discussion of these papers and on the suggestion of Dr. MacKay, "The Course of Study" was thrown open for discussion, and all seeming difficulties, as presented by the different teachers present, were explained away by the Superintendent, Dr. MacKay, to the entire satisfaction of the convention.

The usual votes of thanks to Dr. MacKay and Principal Russel for their valuable assistance, the railways for reducing fares, the teachers and town council for their reception, etc., were passed. Much regret was expressed that Mr. E. J. Lay, principal of the Amherst academy, was prevented from being present by the serious illness of Mrs. Lay

In the absence of Mr. Lay, Mr. A. S. Ford, on behalf of the Amherst teachers, extended a hearty invitation to the convention to meet at Amherst at their next session, and by a unanimous vote of the convention the invitation was accepted—*Halifax Herald.*

HANTS AND KINGS COUNTIES.

The teachers of Inspectoral District No. 5 concluded a very successful Association on December 22nd, 1893. The meetings were held, principally, in the new Wolfville school. About one hundred teachers were in attendance. After the enrolment of members Inspector Roscoe, in a few well chosen words, welcomed the Association to the university town of Wolfville, and hoped the surroundings might be congenial to all. He welcomed their teachers to their homes, and to the meetings of this educational gathering, and felt assured from the deep interest each had in the work to be done, no one would leave a word unsaid that may bring help to a fellow-teacher.

Mr. Stephen Rogers of Habitant, read the first paper on "The Relation of Parents to the School." In early times the education of the child was entirely in the hands of the parents. Even now, when teachers are specially trained to teach, young parents often persist in interfering with the teacher in his duties. He maintained that parents had no right to interfere with the teacher in the selection of studies and text-books, so long as he follows the course of study as a guide. The studies of the course—imperative and optional—were wisely selected and adapted to the needs of the pupils of *public schools.*

Miss Lily A. Scott of Wolfville, gave a very interesting lesson on "Scientific Temperance" to a class of Grade IV pupils. She illustrated by the use of a microscope how alcohol is made, explained its poisonous effects upon muscle, brain, etc. She declared it a thief, and proved the truth of Shakspeare's lines: "Men put an emeny in their mouth to steal away their brains." She showed the necessity of protection against this thief. The door must be locked. The key was the temperance pledge.

Mr. Isaac Crombie, B. A., of Hantsport, gave a paper on "Spelling." In a concise and practical manner he described his experience in teaching this difficult subject to Grades IX and X. He said that having learned that memorizing long lists of words—minus sense and context—was a failure, he adopted the dictation method. This was best performed by assigning a number of words which the pupils were to use in sentences that would clearly illustrate their meaning. As a means of arriving at the meaning of the words he required his pupils to learn the *roots, prefixes,* and *suffixes,* and derive their meaning from the original language. This plan worked well with him. Mr. C. urged the importance of the use of the Superseded Speller in our Schools.

On Wednesday evening the teachers were entertained by Inspector Roscoe, where they met Dr. A. H. MacKay, Superintendent of Education; Professor Tufts and Coldwell of Acadia College; Prof. Oakes of Horton Academy; Prof. Faville of the Horticultural School, and Dr. Hall of the Normal School. Music, games and the discussion of educational topics were heartily engaged in; and all seemed to extract pleasure from the occasion.

Thursday, a. m., Mr. J. M. Sturk read a paper on "The School Master and his Work." He showed the important mission of the teacher, how he moulded the youthful mind when it is "wax to receive, but marble to retain." This paper was well received from a teacher so young as the writer.

The Association then repaired to Prof. Coldwell's laboratory in the college, and were entertained and instructed in the Professor's happy method of presenting a subject. He exhibited a cheap set of apparatus and illustrated its use by various experiments. By having the apparatus in readiness, with the aid of some of the teachers, the experiments followed in quick succession, and much was accomplished in the hour. The Professor showed how to construct such apparatus as an ordinary school needs. The lesson was suggestive and will be very valuable to all who are trying to do work of this kind. The Association evinced their interest by the closest attention.

The Museum, library, seminary, and manual training schools were visited by the teachers through the courtesy of Dr. Sawyer, Miss Graves, and Prof. Oakes.

Thursday, p. m., Mr. J. F. Godfrey read an excellent paper on "Dr. Arnold as a Teacher." Education has ever been the most difficult field in which to display originality, because in this field there was the greatest temptation to conservatism ; and innovation meets the strongest opposition among educationists themselves. Among those teachers who have triumphed over ignorance and prejudice, the foremost stands Dr. Arnold of Rugby. This great man had as his motto—good order, willing obedience, active work. His success depended not on tact, but solely upon industry and attention. Unflagging industry must succeed. Study the minds of and seek to understand the children and their wants ; expect from boys the work of boys only, not men. Ever seek to improve ; be not satisfied with what has been done.

Dr. J. B. Hall of the Normal School, then gave a " Lesson in English " to a class of grade IX. pupils. Howe's poem, "My Country's Streams," formed the basis of the lesson. The exercise combined reading, literature, analysis, and parsing, and was taught in the Dr.'s happy style. He has the faculty of being pleasant himself, and of making his pupils feel pleasant—two strong points in good teaching. The audience enjoyed the lesson very much. Dr. Hall is always welcome at teachers' meetings.

Miss N. A. Burgoyne, at this stage, read a paper and taught a lesson on the " Tonic Sol-Fa Notation." The history, the popularity, and the merits of this notation were clearly presented in a carefully prepared paper. She quoted many distinguished musicians as authority for the statements made. At the suggestion of Dr. MacKay, the Association by vote, requested Miss Burgoyne to consent to the publication of this valuable paper. The lesson took the Association through some of the elementary stages of the notation in Miss Burgoyne's clear and concise method of presenting a subject, and was a delight to all who had the pleasure of hearing it.

On Thursday evening a public educational meeting was held in College Hall in connection with the formal opening of the new schoolhouse In the absence of Mayor Bowles, Inspector Roscoe presided. Mr. E. W. Sawyer, of the school board, was called upon and spoke of the great improvement made in educational facilities in connection with public school instruction in the last decade. He referred to the history, etc., of the new house, and said the people had unanimously voted money for its erection, and for heating and ventilating it in the most approved way, as soon as the need of such a building was intelligently placed before them. Dr. A. H. MacKay, Superintendent of Education, congratulated the school board and town upon having erected a building so well adapted for school purposes. He attributed the sentiment of such preparation for the public schools to the presence of such magnificent buildings as the one in which we were assembled, and the adjoining institutions. He dwelt upon the method of heating and ventilating by the improved system. Amherst, Yarmouth, and Wolfville had introduced this system, and were setting examples worthy of imitation by other towns and sections. He compared the educational advantages of the present with those of the past, and showed the superiority of the former.

Dr. Hall described his visits to the schools of the various European countries as well as those of Canada and the United States, and noted the points of contrast.   While in many respects our schools are superior to those of Germany, we can with profit imitate the Germans in physical training, school etiquette and the study of horticulture.

Dr. A. W. Sawyer, while engaged in university education, sympathized with his fellow-teachers in all their endeavors to advance the interests of the public schools.   He congratulated the school board upon the fine house just completed, and expressed a hope that they might set an example to the governors of the college in the matter of beautifying and improving the grounds.

Prof. Oakes spoke at some length on the importance of Civics as a subject of study in the schools.   He thought that every school boy should be taught his duty and responsibility as a citizen.

Prof. F. H. Eaton urged the importance of optional studies in the public schools.

Prof. Faville, who is to have charge of the Horticultural school to be opened in Wolfville in January, was introduced and spoke for a short time in regard to the work he came to do.

Prof. E. M. Keirstead was the last speaker.   He emphasized the importance of good ventilation in school buildings, and referred to the paper and lesson of Miss Burgoyne in very complimentary terms. Excellent vocal and instrumental music was furnished by Mrs. Witter, Mrs. Crandall, and Miss Fitch.

Friday, a. m.   The session began by voting that the next meeting of the Association be held in Windsor.

The following are the officers :—

> *President*.................... INSPECTOR ROSCOE.
> *Vice-President*................. J. A. SMITH, B. A.
> *Sec.-Treasurer*................ C. E. SEAMAN, B. A.

Executive Committee.—PRINCIPAL CROMBIE; PRINCIPAL ROBINSON ; MISS BURGOYNE ; MISS MCINTOSH.

Mr. E. H. Nichols, B. A., of Kentville, read a paper on " Normal Schools."   He advocated the necessity of teachers having professional training to place them on an equality with the other professions.   Mr. J. A. Smith, B. A., of Windsor, introduced the " Metric System " by a short paper, in which he gave its history and claims upon us ; and taught an excellent lesson illustrating the system.   He thinks it must soon come into general use.   The Superintendent of Education followed, showing the necessity of maintaining this simple system, and thanking Mr. Smith for presenting it so clearly.   The discussion of the various subjects was an interesting feature of the Association.   Messrs. McLeod, Smith, Robinson, Lee, Sturk, Dr. Hall, Prof. Coldwell, Prof. Oakes, Dr. MacKay and others participated in it.

The Superintendent of Education preferred to come in incidentally to answer questions, instead of giving a formal address or paper on " Science."   A number of such questions came up during the meeting, which were readily and very satisfactorily answered by Dr. MacKay. He is certainly at home, with chalk in hand, before the blackboard, elucidating some perplexing point of science. At all these meetings Dr. MacKay put himself in touch with the teachers and their work, and seemed to delight to answer questions put to him. The teachers of this District hold the Superintendent in high esteem. To quote from two of their reports: (1) To the Hants *Journal*, " It is needless to say that Superintendent MacKay has won the respect and esteem of all." (2) To Halifax *Herald*, " It was an inspiration to the teachers to come in contact with him who is now the head of our public school system. Dr. MacKay will always be welcome among us."

A vote of thanks to the people of Wolfville for free entertainment, and short addresses by Dr. MacKay and Inspector Roscoe, brought the Association to a close.—*Educational Review.*

ANNAPOLIS AND DIGBY COUNTIES.

The fifteenth annual meeting of the Teachers' Association for District No. 4, was held at Weymouth on May 24th and 25th. The first session was called to order at 9.30 A. M. by L. S. Morse, Esq., inspector for the district. The following officers were appointed :—

Vice-President ....I. M. LONGLEY.
Secretary-Treasurer ....J. H. CROWE.

Executive Committee.—B. S. BANKS, NELSON CHURCHILL, MRS. BENSON, MISS MABEL FASH, and W. M. McVICAR.

The Executive Committee thought it advisable this year to change the order of work, and instead of papers and discussions thereon, to introduce Science Teaching. The first lesson taught was one in Physiology, by O. P. Goucher, Principal of the Lawrencetown school. Subject : " The Anatomy of the Human Skeleton," and " The Heart." Mr. Goucher presented the subject in an interesting and practical manner, illustrating his lesson with parts of a skeleton, a dissected bullock's heart, and drawings. The subject was discussed by Principals Banks, Longley, Prof. Smith of Truro, and others.

The Association cordially welcomed Prof. Smith for the first time to its gathering. The Professor gave evidence by his manner of entering into the discussion that he came to help, and many valuable hints were given by him.

Principal McGill of Middleton, was to present the subject of " Chemistry," but was unable to attend ; and Professor Smith kindly filled in the gap with a talk on " The Sciences," discussing the difficulties, and best methods of teaching them. He emphasized the fact, that art must precede science, but eventually they would go hand in hand. He claimed that drawing must play an important part in teaching the sciences.

At the afternoon session, Miss Addie Parker gave a lesson on the " Tonic Sol-Fa." She first gave a short historical sketch of the origin and growth of the system, and then proceeded to teach a lesson to the Association as a class. Miss Parker was fully acquainted with her subject, and presented the same in a very pleasing and plain manner to her appreciative class.

It being impossible to obtain a suitable building for the usual public educational meeting on Thursday evening, an informal meeting of teachers was held in Weymouth Bridge school room, when questions of a miscellaneous nature were presented and discussed.

At Friday morning's session, Principal Cameron of Yarmouth, who was present as a substitute for Principal McVicar of Annapolis, gave an interesting and useful lesson on " Physical Geography." Mr. Cameron presented his subject in his own unique and characteristic manner. Papers were then read by Principal Woodman of Weymouth, and Mr. Hogg of Digby. Mr. Woodman discussed the subject of " Attention " in a practical and helpful manner. Mr. Hogg gave a sketch of the life of Pestalozzi, and an outline of his work as an educator.

The remainder of the session was occupied by Principal Cameron on " Literature," subject, " Gray's Elegy," which he presented in his usual interesting and instructive manner, showing that he was master of his subject.

After the customary votes of thanks, the Association adjourned to meet in Bridgetown, in May, 1895.

The work this year was prepared for the purpose of aiding and stimulating teachers in scientific work. Owing to lack of time, a number of subjects could not be taken up.

The teachers separated to return to their respective schools feeling strengthened and inspirited for the work of the coming year.— *Educational Review.*

- - - - -

(III.)

TONIC SOL-FA NOTATION.

By Miss Burgoyne, before the Teachers' Association at Wolfville.

- - - - -

When asked to bring before this Association the claims of the Tonic sol-fa Notation of Singing, it was with much hesitation that I consented to do so. The principal reason for my reluctance was the fact that so many teachers know much more about it than I do. I feel sure that some present here to-day need no help on this subject, but for the sake of your sisters and brothers who want a little assistance and encouragement in starting to teach music, will you bear for a short time with the tedium of a few remarks from me. It was supposed that I should give a lesson, and so I will if you will constitute yourselves my class. We shall in this way save much time. I thought it would be more helpful to those who need help to give a few thoughts on this beautiful subject first.

I shall not attempt to soar to any great heights or to descend to the depths, for 1 am only a beginner myself ; and I shall speak only of things which I know by experience to be practicable. So I begin by putting in a plea for the tonic sol-fa notation, so simple yet so grand, and growing in importance as the years go by.

Some will say we need not waste time in advocating this system, because the fiat has gone forth that it must be taught in our public schools. It is now a part of our school course, and it is not for us to decide whether we will or will not teach it. Neither can we choose between this and the staff notation. But as we do not wish to be like dumb, driven cattle, and as we do like to enter cheerfully into our work, let us set aside all prejudice, and let us look a little at this system in its true light.

" To know it is to love it."

Some teachers unhesitatingly say they do not like it, and on enquiry we find that they have not taken the trouble to look into its merits. Long ago doubts were entertained by a part of the musical profession as to the soundness of the system ; but a great change of opinion in its favor has set in. The musical scientists are all on its side, and some of the stiffest staff notationists loud in its praise. These were the last to give way, because they felt that tonic sol-fa was intended to supersede the common notation. But not so ; it should be regarded as a stepping stone to the staff notation. Hear what some celebrated musicians, whose eyes have been opened, say concerning it :—

Sir John Stainer, doctor of music in England, says : "The ordinary notation will be infinitely better understood and mastered by those who have passed into through the gates of the tonic sol-fa, and it is important to note that all that is learned by the tonic sol-faist is of value when studying the staff; nothing has to be unlearned."

Dr. Stannard, professor of music at Cambridge University, says : "For school purposes and for vocal music always it is simply invaluable."

Henry Leslie, conductor of one of the largest choirs in the old country, says : "The cause of musical education is very dear to me. I have been watching the working of the two systems, and I must say that tonic sol-fa has carried the day entirely."

A. J. Ellis, F. R. S., says : "The tonic sol-fa is the best and happiest guide to the old notation."

Orton Bradley, M. A., director of music at the People's Palace, London, says : "Tonic sol-fa is a most magnificent introduction and a most unfailing one to the staff notation."

Mr. Sedley Taylor, in his work on "Sound and Music," says : "I have watched carefully both the old and the new notations and assert, without the slightest hesitation, that as an instrument of vocal training the new system is enormously, overwhelmingly superior to the old."

Mrs. Curwen says that she strongly advises a year of tonic sol-fa training, as preparatory to piano lessons. "Here eye and ear are trained while the child is using the simplest and most beautiful of all instruments, his own little voice-box. The tiny tonic sol-faist starts with a stock-in-trade of real musical knowledge, which he quickly learns to apply to his new study. He knows what pulse, accent, and measure mean ; his time names fit the crochets and quavers as well as the letter notation, and he has only to learn some new signs which represent facts that he already knows. To those who affect to despise tonic sol-fa," says the same lady, ' I will quote the words of St. Augustine : ' A golden key which does not fit the lock is useless ; a wooden key which does is everything.' To which the celebrated Thring adds : ' Despise not the wooden key because it is wooden.' To which I add again. Apply the tonic sol-fa notation to the highest problems of harmony and you will call it the golden key unlocking all its difficulties."

Dr. Wm. Mason, an eminent American musician, was at first unfavorable to it ; but now speaks in the highest terms of it. He says it carries out the Pestalozzian principle consistently and educationally, and thus affords a most thorough and valuable preparation for the study of the staff.

Mr. E. J. McGolrick, for several years organist and director of music in a Boston church, writes : " I regard the tonic sol-fa system as the singer's best friend."

Mr. William T. Meek of the celebrated Ruggles street church male quartette, says : " I have always found the tonic sol-fa system to be of the greatest service to me in reading music."

We could multiply these testimonies many many times, but have given sufficient to show what is the opinion of those who occupy a high place in the musical world. Now, do you wonder that the C. P. I. chose this notation for us instead of the other ?

Sometimes the inspector visits a school and sees staff music beautifully written on the board. He asks : " Why do you not teach the prescribed ?" The answer sometimes is : " I do not know the other." It would be a matter of no time for that teacher to gain a knowledge of it if he so desired. Another says : " I do not like the tonic sol-fa." Have you made its acquaintance ? I am sure you have not or you will be filled with admiration of it.

But what makes this such a desirable system ?

First. Its simplicity. It is adapted to all from the infant to the adult. I have heard pupils of our own primary grade in Windsor sing sweetly and correctly by note, and I know no prettier sight than that of an infant school beating time with their little index fingers and singing a tune printed on the blackboard. There is much diversity of opinion about beating time. My experience has been that as soon as the pupils know how, let them beat. It makes them independent. If they want to learn a piece, and have been taught correctly how to beat the time, they can do so without the teacher's aid. But do not permit any slovenly beating.

Secondly. This is a time-saving system. Music has been on our school course for years, but a very small percentage of our children have been taught to sing. Why? Because the staff-notation required so much time to master it. No striking results would be noticeable after several years of school life; but by the tonic sol-fa delightful music may be produced in a year with only the ordinary amount of time.

Thirdly. Another point in its favor is the enjoyment it gives the children. As there is no drudgery connected with it, the children hail their singing hour with delight; even the boys do not hang back, but feel it to be a punishment should they be deprived of their singing lesson.

Fourthly. It gives the children a power of expression and purity of tone as nothing else does. This, at least, has been my experience. Rote-singing is much better than none, but it has a tendency to coarsen the voice. The tonic sol-fa singing makes a specialty of sweetness of execution.

Fifthly. It oils the machinery of school life and acts as an incentive to good work. "We have no time for singing in our school" should never be uttered. It is a mistake. Make time for it, and other studies will not suffer in consequence. I have been told by the inspector that schools which he found doing good work in music were invariably well up in their other studies.

Sixthly. It strengthens the pupils in habits of attention and concentration. The hand-signs are valuable mostly on this account, because the pupil must keep his attention on the teacher, or the result will be disastrous, and in these fly-away times the habit of fixedness is a good one.

Seventhly. The music which we are teaching the little ones is carried into the homes, and it will be, and has been, in many cases that have come under my own notice, taken up by the parents, and have become students *en famille,* and in those families a concert is possible and practicable whenever they so desire.

Eighthly. There is so much tonic sol-fa literature obtainable at a very low cost, and pupils who sing from their little books seem to value them very highly. I could give many more reasons, but these are sufficient to justify the place which this system occupies in our school course. Our aim is not to make great musicians or musical composers, but to educate the masses in the line of music.

We do not expect to make singers like Patti and Sims Reeves, any more than we aim at making great artists, when we teach our children to draw; yet there is always a chance of discovering a talent which is worthy of cultivation, and it is good to know that our notation will not block the way of one possessed of this talent, but on the contrary will help him towards his goal.

This notation is an infant in our country. In the United States it is a strong and vigorous youth. In the old countries it is more advanced in life, but increasing in vigor and popularity all the time.

In England, at the present time, over two million school children are being taught to read music at sight by this system. Six millions, including adults, sing by it in the old home country. The last blue book states that where one sings by the staff seven use the new notation. Before I left home, seventeen years ago, nearly all the church choirs sang by it, and yearly concerts were given in the Crystal Palace by over 4,000 children, all singing by the tonic sol-fa. This was at first merely tentative. The Handel orchestra was standing empty, and the question was asked: " Why not fill it with children?" In about a month appeared the announcement that a tonic sol-fa concert would be given by 3,000 children. The result was an overwhelming success, and the annual concert is one of the events to which Londoners, as well as their country cousins, look forward with intense interest.

The month of March, 1861, was a memorable one for tonic solfaism. The officials of the Paris International Exhibition sent a letter to Sir Sterndale Bennett, principal of the Royal Academy of Music, stating that a musical competition would take place, and that they would be pleased if any English society would compete. A prize of $1,000 and a gold wreath were to be won. The Tonic sol-fa Association sent a mixed choir of 70. There had never been a case of an English choir leaving home before to compete for musical honors. On Saturday, July 6th, the English choir arrived in Paris, and surprised the French very much by declining to take part in a musical competition on the Sabbath day. Next day came the trial, the turn of the English came last, and the first burst of song from them brought the audience to their feet. The first verse brought down thunders of applause, and ⋅ the end of the piece convinced the French that the English can sing. The audience jumped in their seats, waved their hats, and insisted on more. The choir and its conductor, Mr. Proudman, were again and again re-called. The next day they were presented to the Emperor in the presence of 20,000 people, and came away laden with prizes and gifts. For weeks the Parisians talked of that English choir. Yet this is the notation that some people despise. Simply because they know not what they say.

This system is wonderfully adapted to church music. The church of Scotland uses ten sol-fa copies of the hymn book to one of the staff notation. This system has found its way into nearly every part of the world. Australia, Madagascar, Hong-Kong, Palestine, Fiji, Kaffraria, Burmah, Chili, and Zululand. It is taught in the New England Conservatory of Music, and in the Michigan University, and now we are going to teach it in our schools of Nova Scotia.

It might be interesting just here to mention that Miss Glover, an English lady, was really the originator of this system. John Curwen is generally spoken of as its founder, but he was not. He developed the system, and gave Miss Glover a great deal of happiness in doing so. She was the daughter of a clergyman and full of philanthropic works. In trying to teach some Sunday school children to sing, it occurred to her to place some letters on the keys of the piano and slide them up and down for the different keys.

From this simple beginning the world-renowned letter-notation has envolved, and all its improvements are due to Mr. Curwen, of whom Miss Glover was never jealous, but on the contrary, grateful. She died at the age of 82, having worked at her beloved music to the last without any pecuniary remuneration. Her plan, as is also Mr. Curwen's and ours, was to teach that simple and beautiful thing, music, and postpone the old form of writing it until the pupil has mastered the thing itself. Just before her death she said to Mr. Curwen, " Let the question be, not who was the first to invent the Tonic sol-fa, but is the thing itself good, and true and useful to the world ?"

Now having considered the merits of this new notation, shall we not take up the work with more courage, and cheerfulness, and dismiss the . coldness and lack of interest of the past, feeling that it is one of the oases in the desert of our school life. But how shall we begin ? Do you remember one of Jacotot's principles ? Learn one thing well, and learn everything else by the help of that. This will apply to more. Learn a little well, teach it well, and keep somewhat in advance of your pupils, and you will be suprised at the result. You will find the aid you need in the " Teacher's Companion," and the Standard course.

But commence : hang up a modulator and begin, for the approach to a subject is half the battle. Having begun you and your pupils will have a desire to go on. Then as soon as you can begin to prepare for certificates, even if you do not expect an examiner to come your way. They are everything to aim for, and you know what an incentive that is to young people.

The qualifying for certificates supplies the teacher also with a plan of work, and gives him the satisfaction of knowing that his teaching is not mere desultory work, but that his pupils are acquiring real practical knowledge. But what about the teachers who cannot sing ? I hardly know what to say. A great many think they cannot sing when they can. Some have a musical ear, and that is a precious gift, but they cannot rely on their voice. Well, put yourselves in a true light before your class, and they will be willing and anxious to give you voice. There are always some who can sing up and down the natural scale ; make a combination of your ear and their voice, and you will accomplish great results. (If none can sing, obtain a dulcimer and strike the notes from it writing the names on the board.) One of the most successful Tonic sol-fa teachers I ever knew had an exquisite ear but no voice.

If there are teachers with neither ear nor voice I have never met them. I believe that nearly every one who can be taught to speak can be taught to sing. The same voice-box produces both speech and singing ; but the training must commence early. Just think what a grand influence for good music is, how it softens and humanizes the world, and God speaks to mankind through music. Let us try to do our little share in making the world better, and leading it upward through the channels of music to God.

PUBLIC HIGH SCHOOL, NEW GLASGOW, NOVA SCOTIA, 1894.

ANNUAL REPORT

OF THE

SUPERINTENDENT OF EDUCATION

ON THE

PUBLIC SCHOOLS OF NOVA SCOTIA,

FOR THE YEAR ENDED 31st JULY,

1895.

HALIFAX, N. S.:
COMMISSIONER OF PUBLIC WORKS AND MINES, QUEEN'S PRINTER.
1896.

EDUCATION OFFICE.

HALIFAX, *January, 1896.*

SIR :—

I have the honor to transmit herewith, to be laid before His Honor the Lieutenant-Governor, my report on the Public Schools of Nova Scotia, for the School year ended July 31, 1895.

I am, with respect,

Your obedient servant,

A. H. MacKAY,

Superintendent of Education.

To the HON W. S. FIELDING, M. P. P.,
    Provincial Secretary.

GENERAL CONTENTS.

PART III.—APPENDICES.

APPENDIX A.

APPENDIX B.

APPENDIX C.

APPENDIX D.

APPENDIX E.

APPENDIX F.

APPENDIX G.

GENERAL REPORT, 1895.

ANNUAL REPORT

ON THE

PUBLIC SCHOOLS OF NOVA SCOTIA.

1894-95.

To His Honor Malachy Bowes Daly,
Lieutenant-Governor of Nova Scotia:

May it Please Your Honor,—

I beg in accordance with the law, to submit my annual report on the Public Schools of the Province, for the School Year ended 31st July, 1895.

For much detail that might otherwise appear in this Annual Report, I refer you to the two numbers of the *Journal of Education,* issued according to law in April and October respectively, which contain, among other items, a list of teachers, with the amount of the Provincial Grant paid each, and of the school sections, with the amount of County Fund distributed to each.

GENERAL SUMMARY.

During the year very substantial progress has been made in nearly every department. The number of schools increased from 2292 to 2305; the pupils enrolled from 98,710 to 100,555; the number of teachers from 2351 to 2399; the number of Normal School trained teachers from 499 to 616; and the total days' attendance of pupils from 5,325,348 to 5,342,309.

The amount of $77,838 voted by the school sections for building and repairs, while not so large as the abnormal amounts of the previous two years, is nevertheless much greater than the old normal of $51,000 of each of the first two years of this quinquennial period.

The amount voted by the school sections for teachers' salaries is reported to have increased more than $35,000 over the $339,848 of last year. The Provincial Grant to teachers was also increased to the extent of $14,970 over the $167,452 of the same year, giving the teachers the largest Provincial Grant yet paid them, by a small amount—38 cents to class D, 57 cents to class C, and 77 cents to class B, over the original maximum. Thus, while the average salaries of teachers in various counties, or of some classes in the whole Province, have not advanced, there has been an advance in the sum total. This is a very encouraging feature, for without better salaries we cannot expect an improved class of teachers to continue in the profession. From the Inspectors' reports it will be seen that the reason why there are yet sections with no school is not the scarcity of teachers, but the weakness or smallness of many sections. This is often due to the reprehensible selfishness of parties wishing to have the schools near their own doors, and to the altogether inadequate salaries offered. It is also gratifying to notice that the tendency of the late changes has been to diminish the previously decreasing number of male teachers. For the present year the diminution in the number of male teachers has been only *one* as against 41 the previous year. The impression prevalent at first in some quarters, that the new order is not so favorable to male as to female teachers, is being modified; and there are indications that during the next year the number of male teachers will increase, instead of following the general law of diminution prevalent everywhere during the past quarter of a century or more.

The reports of the several Inspectors on the Common Schools indicate improvement in teaching methods and general equipment. In the High Schools there was never so much effort displayed on the whole, either by the trustees or teachers. The superior buildings going up in every quarter of the Province attest to the one, while the ever-increasing number of candidates at the Provincial Examinations, and the sensitiveness of teachers with respect to the character and results of examination, prove the other. There can be no better evidence of the existence of the conditions most compatible with high and rapid progress than the live and universal interest in what should be taught in the schools, and how the teaching should be done. The large attendance at the several Teachers' Institutes in most of our progressive inspectorates, and at the Provincial Educational Association, as well as the desultory discussions in the public press, all show that the present is not a time of stagnation, but of rapid development.

The consolidation of the Education Acts, and of the Regulations of the Council of Public Instruction, and their issuance in the new Manual of the School Law, during the course of the year, has already shown good results in diminishing the correspondence with Inspectors and the Education Office; and it is hoped that during the incoming year it will very much smooth the difficulties inseparable from the conditions necessarily prevailing before.

STATISTICAL ABSTRACT.

For a general view of the more important details of the state and progress of education during the year, the following abstract of the statistical tables is presented here:

1.—SECTIONS.

	1894.	1895.
School Sections in Province............	1891	1894
Sections without school	136	161

2.—SCHOOLS.

	1894.	1895.
Schools in operation..................	2292	2305
" session 50 days or under	16	16
" " 50 to 100 days	83	55
" 100 to 150 "	139	127
" 150 to 200 "	280	294
" 200 but under full term.	1157	955
" " full term 216 days	617	858
Average days in session	199.2	198.7

3.—TEACHERS.

	1894.	1895.
Number of Teachers...................	2351	2399
" " Normal trained.....	499	616
Class A, Male	44	49
" A, Female	4	6
" B, Male	149	142
" B, Female	162	183
" C, Male	199	178
" C, Female	888	900
" D, Male	149	171
" D, Female	756	770
Total Male Teachers..................	541	540
" Female Teachers...............	1810	1859
New Teachers	255	345
Teachers, Service 1 year or under......	297	389
" " 1 to 2 years........	327	239
" " 2 to 3 "	309	276
" " 3 to 4 "	263	281
" " 4 to 5 "	205	224
" " 5 to 7 "	270	310
" " 7 to 10 "	248	255
" " 10 to 15 "	186	202
" " 15 to 20 "	121	113
" " 20 or over...........	125	110

4.—ATTENDANCE.

	1894.	1895.
Pupils on Register, First Quarter	75,821	77,566
" " Second "	86,700	88,177
" " Third "	89,939	91,136
" " Fourth "	97,920	99,625

	1894.	1895.
Average Daily Attendance, First Quarter.	51,622	53,673
" " " Second "	47,183	51,748
" " " Third "	48,937	48,344
" " " Fourth "	51,492	52,349
Total Days' Attendance for year........	10,471,764	10,773,255

5.—CLASSIFICATION OF PUPILS.

	1894.	1895.
Grade I (and Kindergarten)............	18,908	19,470
" II...........................	13,498	13,042
" III	12,184	12,361
" IV........	12,672	13,011
" V	11,158	10,833
" VI............................	9,202	9,711
" VII.........	9,409	9,854
" VIII.......................	6,489	6,745
Total in Common Schools........	93,520	95,027
" IX............................	2,922	3,553
" X.......	1,186	1,331
" XI......	460	576
" XII....	82	68
Total in High Schools	4,650	5,528
Total in Public Schools.........	98,170	100,555
Full Academic High School Students....	1,371	1,492
" Non-Academic " "	1,860	2,593
Partial " "	1,419	1,443

6.—SECTION STATISTICS.

	1894.	1895.
Value of Property in Section.........	$80,096,411	$78,702,374
" School Property in Section....	1,360,784	1,401,155
Total Vote at Annual Meeting.........	454.200	453,144
Voted for Buildings and Repairs........	134.710	77,838
Paid for Teachers' Salaries	339,848	375,725
Volumes in Library of School	6,537	8,274
No. of Maps, Charts, Globes, &c........	7,161	7,138
Value of Scientific App. and Coll........	$ 8,277	$ 7,106
Value of Total Literary and Scientific ..	33,589	33,703

7.—TOTAL EXPENDITURE.

	1894.	1895.
Total Provincial Grants	$ 220,436	$ 238,760
" County Funds	120,507	119,900
" Section Assessment	454,200	453,144
Total Expenditure, Public Education....	$795,144	$811,804

THE STATISTICAL TABLES.

To be of any value these tables must be based on accurate individual returns. No amount of care on the part of the great majority, and on the part of the various compilers, can eliminate the taint of error originating in the lack of thought or care of a single blundering teacher, or the criminal laziness of the person who inserts an inaccurate or merely approximate estimate, when the exact figures to the degree of accuracy prescribed could be had by some effort. To take away any necessity of undue hurry in the collecting and accurate recording of section and school statistics, they are required to be entered in the register—as many as possible at the opening of the school—so that they can be examined by the authorities and school visitors. And the Return must be a copy of the Register. There have been cases of teachers in some inspectorates who evidently thought at first that some of the directions for accuracy to the *day* or the *decimal* were unnecessarily precise. When such a speculative notion reveals itself in the character of a Register or Return, the Inspector is responsible if such teacher continues longer in the profession. Cases of misunderstanding for carelessness were not uncommon in some inspectorates two years ago. Now, all the Inspectors report that the inaccurate teacher is disappearing, and that never before were the statistics more universally accurate. Were this not the case, much of the time and effort of accurate compilation would be useless, and the statistics, instead of indicating the true direction and rate of development, might be misleading. We require statistics not only for the purpose of showing the number of days a teacher taught and the attendance of pupils in order to determine the gross though very material question of how much money is to be paid ; but for the more subtle purpose of knowing as many as possible of the numerous changes going on, some of them so slow that it may require the accumulation of years of precise statistics to demonstrate their existence.

SECTIONS AND SCHOOLS.—I.

A discrepancy suggests itself in a column of this table when we find that although the number of schools increased 13, that the number of sections without school increased also, and to the extent of 25. It might be explained by supposing that while there was an increase of 25 in the sections without school, additional departments to the number of 38 were opened in sections having graded schools. But the true explanation is not so simple. There may have been an increase in the number of new departments opened in graded school sections, but not to the extent of 38, I would think. On comparison of this column with the corresponding one of 1894, in the said year there was only 1 section without school in Inverness, and 0 without school in Victoria, while in 1895 there were 12 in the former county and 21 in the latter, thus showing only *one* section in the two counties to have been without school in the former year, while there were *thirty-three* without school in the latter. In the rest of the Province there was a decrease of the number of sections without school to the extent of 7, which shows progress in the right direction. But if the

EDUCATION—SUPERINTENDENT'S REPORT.

statistics of Inverness and Victoria for the previous year were correct, they were in this respect the most favored counties in the Province, having only *one* section without school, while the rest of the Province had *one hundred and ninety-five* without school. This suggests a slip in the summation of the figures for these counties in 1894. To compare the figures of 1893 with those of 1895, there is a decrease of 35 sections without schools in the two years.

The number of departments in which school was kept for the complete school year of 216 days rose from 617 to 858; and the number of schools in session under 200 days diminished by 26. The total number of teachers increased by 48. In all these cases the changes are in the right direction.

NORMAL TRAINED TEACHERS.

There has been an increase of 117 in this class of teachers, and a diminution of 69 in the teachers without Normal school training. This shows a remarkable development of sentiment in favor of trained teachers. The number engaged in each county during the last three years is given below :—

COUNTIES.	1893.	1894.	1895.
Annapolis	25	25	33
Antigonish	2	7	6
Cape Breton	17	22	29
Colchester	63	67	85
Cumberland	75	83	95
Digby	17	14	14
Guysboro'	2	13	18
Halifax Co	23	40	57
Halifax City	31	35	34
Hants	45	38	48
Inverness	7	7	17
Kings	23	35	48
Lunenburg	23	34	38
Pictou	20	33	41
Queens	5	7	7
Richmond	5	9	6
Shelburne	3	4	5
Victoria	4	4	9
Yarmouth	18	22	26
Totals	408	499	616

This table shows that the character of the Normal School trained teachers is now rapidly improving, for they are being retained longer and in an increasing number in the service of trustees. Still nearly three-fourths of the teaching staff of the Province have received no special training for the profession. Among these there are, of course, many who have been trained in good schools, under good teachers, and some who have naturally the teacher's tact. But the educational interests of the Province are still suffering from the prevalence of the incompetent teacher. The improvement taking place is satisfactory at present, although we have not made professional training a necessary condition to the securing of a license, as is done in every other equally advanced country.

VOLUNTARY PROFESSIONAL TRAINING.

The efforts being made by the teachers throughout many districts to improve themselves at their own expense should not be passed without notice. There were the 128 teachers from Colchester and Cumberland who met at Amherst in November for Institute work ; those from Kings and Hants who met. in April at Windsor ; those from Annapolis and Digby who met in May at Bridgetown ; and the 250 from the Province generally, who with the 150 at the Normal School, made up the 400 at the Provincial Association in Truro last October. In addition, I find that in Halifax there is always at least two or three different classes of teachers engaged every year in studying practically such school subjects as Calisthenics, Drawing, Vocal Music, Elocution, Natural Science, etc. And the following quotations from Inspectors' reports show a similar activity in many other places :—

Inspector Munro says, page 63 :

" The unequivocal remarks in the October *Journal of Education* in regard to calisthenic and musical exercises have been fruitful of good results. Music, which was cultivated in comparatively few schools, and calisthenics, which was seldom practised, are now receiving a good measure of attention. Many teachers who used to prefer the excuse that they could not sing, found that by stirring up the gift that was in them they could sing, and also teach their pupils to sing. There were some who made use of all the helps within their reach, even going long distances to get instruction in the new notation. In Christmas week a number of rural teachers in Shelburne district formed a class and hired an instructor, and bore all the expenses incident to travelling to and residing in the shire town. The singing of the pupils proved how much they had benefited by the enterprise of their teachers. In Mr. John B. LeBlanc's department, Lower Wedge, I heard stirring music when the pupils sang with patriotic fervour " Our own Canadian Home," and the National Anthem. At Barrington Passage, where Mr. W. B. Parker is principal, the singing was first-class. Pupils took their parts, as tenor, alto, bass, and sang with fine effect.

" Teachers volunteered the acknowledgment that they could discern the good effect on their pupils of the calisthenic practice, in correcting a stooping tendency in the shoulders, ungainly attitudes, and a slouching gait in walking. To teachers generally praise is due, but if I had a prize to offer I would award it to Miss Amy Hilton's department, where the exercises, conducted to the music of a phono-harp, were marked with a precision and gracefulness of motion almost perfect."

Inspector Roscoe says, page 72 :

" I am able to report a more general conformity to the course of study than heretofore. Subjects that hitherto were regarded of less importance than many others, came in for a fair share of time and attention. Among these calisthenics, music, moral and patriotic duties, and lessons on nature, may be referred to. The excuse for not teaching these in the past was 'want of time.' When the *Journal of Education* for October, 1894, came to hand, all the teachers, with few exceptions, set about preparing to teach these subjects. Those who have been most careful to divide their time so as to give each subject a fair proportion, and who have endeavored to make the best use of the time assigned to the various subjects, report in substance as follows :—

" *Calisthenics* secures the strictest attention of all the pupils, exercises the muscles of all parts of the body, gives an agreeable relaxation from work, and so enlivens the pupils that they can do much more and much better work after engaging in this exercise than they otherwise could do. So far then as time is concerned this drill results in gain ; and so far as the habit of attention, correct form and position enter into this matter, great advantage is gained.

" *Music* is more enjoyed than any other exercise in the school. All *want* to sing and *do sing* when properly taught. The Tonic Sol-Fa notation is easily learned, and the pupils are so inspired while singing, and the exercise leaves them in such a happy state of mind, that other and harder work is easily performed. In this too there is a gain in all that pertains to the management of the school. Any time spent in singing is more than compensated for by the increased ability it gives to perform other duties. It is understood that but a short period is to be devoted each day to calisthenics and music, and this at a time when relaxation is most needed.

" *Moral and Patriotic Duties,* so far, is taught principally in connection with other lessons, and at times when some incident suggests a lesson. Occasionally a set lesson is given on such topics as 'Truth,' 'Honesty,' 'Industry,' 'Our Flag,' 'Our Great Men,' &c. There are plenty of topics, full of interest, affording as much real education as can be secured in any other way.

" *Nature Lessons,* when thoroughly and properly prepared, and adapted to the age of the pupils, produce most beneficial results in the mastery of other subjects, as well as in awakening and developing the power of the mind. All these subjects have proved failures in the hands of some teachers, because the main aim seemed to be to do enough to have something to report and thus have their schools accepted. It is questionable whether any one should receive license to teach when he has never demonstrated, by actual practice, that he *can* teach. And it seems to me that those who have defects which will prevent them from teaching a subject essential to the well-being of all schools, should not think of teaching as a profession.

" I am pleased to report that so large a number of teachers in this district have made a success of these so called new subjects. Many of them spent their Saturdays and holidays in going to places at some distance to be taught music, so that they could teach it in their own schools. In this way they have been benefited themselves by the new order of things, while they were preparing to teach others. It is not now an uncommon thing to have quite young pupils write from memory the music of some of the national songs, and sing them both by note and words. We have made commendable progress along these lines. I may add that the schools in which most has been done in the subjects referred to, have made the best progress in all the other required subjects."

School Libraries and Collections.

School libraries have increased from 55 to 90, and school scientific collections from 91 to 133. From Table VII. the volumes in the libraries have increased from 6537 to 8274—an increase of 1737 volumes. But on the other hand the estimated value of all scientific apparatus and collections has decreased from $8277 to $7106. The 42 new collections then have not equalled in value the depreciation in the old collections, if we assume the estimates to be made exactly on the same principles as last year.

Small School Sections.

In the Regulations of the Council of Public Instruction it is very clearly implied that four miles is not an excessive diameter for the school section, especially where the population is sparse. Now, while a distance of two miles from the school makes attendance, especially for young pupils, impossible in stormy weather and in certain seasons of the year, it has been found from experience that such a distance has some compensation as compared with the too often longed for position near the school house. An hour's walk to school in the morning, and another back again in the afternoon, give the very best opportunities for health and strength-developing exercise in the open air, give good chances for the practical study of nature along the road, and prepare the pupil for the enjoyment of physical rest and mental work in the school room, and also at home when such work is required. Still so many parents can only think of the discomfort of the distance in bad weather that they are ready to create a weak section, which can never be in a position to keep a good school regularly, for the sole purpose of saving a portion of the distance, as if the additional distance were of so much importance once the pupil is on the road.

It sometimes happens that an apparent mania takes possession of some people whose fathers and mothers were content for over a quarter of a century to attend school perhaps two miles distant, to have the school near them. Such people sometimes persist for years in agitating for the division of the section, or the changing of boundaries, and the consequent disarticulation of several neighboring sections. As a general rule, the various boards of District School Commissioners, assisted by the Inspectors, resist any extreme or unwise demands for such re-organizations of boundaries as will increase the number of sections. And it is most necessary. For while the law leaves it comparatively easy to divide a section, it is extremely difficult, if not practically impossible, to consolidate again. At some future time it may be the desire of the great majority of two sections to unite ; but a small minority, which may nearly always be had, can prevent it. In other cases three sections should be consolidated into two, or four into three. But such a move would require concerted and practically unanimous action on the part of each three or four sections, involving the change of their boundaries and of the school houses, each of which would affect several individuals unfavorably. When sections are subdivided, then, it should not be merely to suit the present generation. The interests of succeeding generations should be held in view as well as the present fugitive circumstances. But, unfortunately, in many parts of the country, and in some counties to a greater extent than others, the mischief has been done already. For example, Inverness, with its area of 1,270 square miles, has no less than 176 school sections, although a large part of the interior is unsettled. That would give about $7\frac{1}{2}$ square miles to each section, a diameter of only about $2\frac{3}{4}$ miles each. As a large part of the county has no school sections, it follows that the majority of school sections cannot be very much over 2 miles in diameter. Now there is no county in the Province in which the young children have greater intellectual ability. But let us study the result of this petty school section system.

In my general summary I have already called attention to it as the chief cause of the scarcity of suitable teachers. Inspector McKinnon, on page 80, says :

" A very considerable number of sections are too weak financially, and too small, to maintain an efficient school, hence in a great degree the large number of sections vacant during the year now expired.

" The smallness of so many sections is an evil for which some remedy should be provided, and as a step in that direction I think that discretionary power should be vested in the school commissioners to unite two weak sections when, in their opinion, the educational interests of the locality manifestly require it."

And on page 81 :—

" The extremely low salaries offered by many sections lead to a scarcity of teachers both in Inverness and Victoria, and no alternative presents itself except to leave the schools closed, or issue permits to a number of persons indifferently qualified for the teaching profession. No remedy for this state of affairs can be suggested until parents and trustees are willing to tax themselves a little heavier for the education of their children than they do at present, unless, indeed, the legislature step in and substantially increases the amount at present collected by the county authorities for educational purposes."

It may be said that the county is not yet so wealthy as some of the more western. Even if that be granted, it only goes to show that its school sections should be larger than the western ones instead of being smaller. In some places, where the pioneers are making new settlements, the conditions for having strong sections are impossible, as they are in every other county. And we must always be prepared to assist sections weak from their geographical and geological condi- tions. If the 176 school sections of Inverness could be amicably consolidated into 100 or less, the educational interests of the people would be greatly advanced. While Inverness appears to be the most generally affected by the system of small school sections, the evil exists to some extent perhaps in every county, and the argument is for the Province at large.

Some of the injurious effects can be seen in the following statistics. The average of salary from the section for a male " B " teacher in Halifax city is $661 ; in Colchester County, $560; in Yarmouth County, $409 ; in Cumberland, $345 ; in Lunenburg, $317 ; in Guysboro', $297 ; in Richmond, $207 ; in Inverness, $113. There can be no inducement for a clever young man to aspire to become a class " B " teacher in a county of small school sections. There is no fair general chance for the young people to become qualified to enter the County Academy, or stand well at the Provincial Examinations. Yet when students from this county have the opportunity they find their way into the very first rank.

From Tables XIV. and XV., pages 19 and 20, it can be seen that all the other classes of teachers fare in a similar manner. While the male class " C " teacher gets from the section in Halifax City $440, in Hants $271, in Shelburne $225, he gets in Inverness but $97. While the male class " D " gets $203 in Cumberland, he gets in Inverness but $64. But even in Cumberland, Inspector Craig says, see page 86 :

" There is a scarcity of teachers this year, especially in the third class. There are enough teachers resident in the two counties forming this district to fill all positions, but they will not engage for amounts insufficient for a living."

More than from any other remediable evil Inverness is suffering from its many school sections so snug and neat that very few pupils are two miles distant, or even over one and a half miles from the school. They have the school houses at their doors. They have that with all it is worth.

I trust that School Inspectors and District Commissioners may make a special study of this question with a view to remedy the evil wherever it exists. In many places we find efforts now being made to unite several school sections into a large union or district section under one board of trustees. This policy was advocated in this Province no later than last year in the Legislative Council. It has, no doubt, some points of advantage as compared with the normal or standard school section at present. But whether the advantages are great enough to press the consideration of such a policy now or not, there can be no doubt that every effort should be put forth immediately to enlarge and strengthen weak sections wherever they may be found. That involves the increase of territory within the school section, which in turn involves increasing the distance of some parties from the school. And this will always become, as a general rule, a source of contention and opposition to improvement. In order to offset to some extent the disadvantage of distance, the Act of 1895,

EDUCATION—SUPERINTENDENT'S REPORT.

sec. 14, allows Boards of District School Commissioners to exempt from sectional taxation in whole or in part, persons dwelling more than two and one quarter miles from the school house. Perhaps it might still further aid reform in this direction if the commissioners were allowed, in addition, to exempt those over *two* miles from the school, say, from one-half of the sectional taxation.

TABLE II.

The most important point in this table appears to be the fact that the male teachers employed have decreased by only *one* during the year. The decrease occurred in classes B and C, and were nearly balanced by the increase in the classes A and D. This suggests a turn in the tide ; and the fact that the increase in the D class male teachers is greater than that of the corresponding D class female teachers, who stand as 770 to 171 males, leads us to hope that the late modifications make the profession more attractive to the latter. The problem is one, of course, which time will solve for us. The variation of a single year may suggest a tendency, but does not prove it.

CHANGE OF TEACHERS.

Inspector MacIsaac says, page 77 :

" While it must be admitted that the change from the two-term year to the one-term has diminished the evil of frequent changes of teachers, I am convinced that our schools still suffer too much injury. A teacher has no sooner become acquainted with the powers, dispositions, habits, and attainments of his pupils than his term closes; and the trustees often, on the plea of saving money to the section, employ another who must gain the knowledge of the school which his predecessor acquired before he can effectually do his work."

Inspector McKinnon, page 80 :

" A serious drawback to the interests of schools in this district is the frequent change of teachers. From 60 to 70 per cent. change their situations every year. This unfortunate practice is not so much the fault of the teacher as that of the ratepayers and trustees. Given a comfortable school house and fair salary and there will be no difficulty in retaining the services of a good teacher for years."

Inspector Craig, page 86 :

" Twenty-five per cent. of the teachers of 1893-94 continued in the service of the same section in 1894-95. Changes take place most frequently among the poorer schools and often to their disadvantage. In the graded schools seventy-five per cent. re-engaged in the same sections."

The table shows us that, taking the Province as a whole, we have made an advance over last year in the right direction, and last year was the best in the history of the Province. The number of old teachers who have removed to new sections has diminished 83. And the number of teachers engaged in the same section as last year has increased 41.

TABLE III.

This table shows a decrease in the number of male and female teachers between the limits of one and three years' service. A series of years will be necessary to indicate the full significance of this fact. Does it mean that more teachers than usual have spent their first year in teaching and the next at the Normal School ? The provisional class D was formed for the purpose of allowing young teachers to earn money for a year in order to enable them to attend the Normal School during at least a portion of the second year.

During the year the number of teachers of 5 years' experience and under, increased from 1401 to 1409, an increase of 8 ; but teachers of over five years of experience, from 950 to 990, an increase of 40.

ATTENDANCE—TABLES IV., V. AND VI.

We find that the best attendance during the year was made in the first quarter, and the worst in the third quarter. The previous year the worst attendance was in the second quarter ; thus showing how the attendance is affected by the prevalence of stormy weather.

Inspector Maclellan says, page 82 :

"The attendance of pupils for the year has been satisfactory, although there was a falling off in the third quarter owing to storms and bad roads. The one-year term has undoubtedly improved the attendance. This fact is, I think, generally recognized. Nearly all seem satisfied with the change. I seldom hear complaints concerning it, except from the few teachers who have the boldness to confess that they would enjoy a change of location every six months, or from trustees who are unwilling to abide by the consequences of engaging, without enquiry, the cheapest and frequently the most incompetent available teacher."

The attendance during the year is probably the best in the history of the Province.

The enrolments for the half years are greater respectively than those of 1886, when the total enrolment for the year, calculated according to the approximate method then in use (see " Changes of Pupils by Half Years," page x., report of 1894) was 105,410, the greatest total on our records. Our grand total attendance of 10,667,657 days is nearly equal to that of 1886, although the number of school days in the year is now less. It would appear then that with a total enrolment of 100,555 this year, we are not only 1845 ahead of last year, but had a larger number present every day of the school year than in 1886.

The difference between the total enrolment, 100,555, and the total on register at the end of the fourth quarter, 99,625, represents the enrolments of sections having school during the first part of the year, but no school in the second half year, or during the last quarter. This difference is 930.

The number of children who attended school under 50 days during the year decreased 137 ; thus indicating more continuous attendance than during the previous year. The number of children belonging to the section increased by 1700 ; while those from beyond the section also increased to the extent of 145. The number of children between 5 and 15 who did not attend school is set down at 6835, as compared with 7485 last year. The visits of trustees and parents increased during the year, showing more local interest in the schools, which is also evidenced by the 400 additional prizes offered and their value increased by $196.

ATTENDANCE BY QUARTERS.

77,566 pupils attended during the first quarter. 10,611 new pupils came in during the second quarter, while 7,270 ceased attending. 2959 new pupils came in during the third quarter, while 7136 old pupils ceased attending. 8489 new pupils came in during the fourth quarter, while 4151 old pupils ceased to attend.

The counties having the largest number of pupils attending school from beyond the limits of the section, are Inverness with 575, and Pictou with 460. The large number attending the Pictou Academy, the New Glasgow High School, and other smaller good schools in the latter county, from beyond their respective sections, accounts for the larger part of the 460. A similar explanation will not do for every county. Where there are too many small sections children can conveniently attend school in the neighboring section, especially if their own section is too weak to support a school.

COMPULSORY ATTENDANCE.

Quite a large number of sections promptly adopted the new Compulsory Attendance sections of the Education Act of 1895. Inspectors will now be required to keep a careful record of each section adopting the law, for once adopted it is in force so long as the law remains. Each year all sections which have not adopted the law must re-vote on it at the annual meeting, or be held in default of observance of the law, and therefore not entitled to receive any public money. The law is also more stringent than the old one, requiring a minimum attendance of 120 days each year. The fines are to be added to and collected with the sectional rates of the following year. The law was not passed in time for action upon it during this year in certain "fishing" sections in which the Annual Meeting was authorized to be held on the last Monday of March. But the number of sections adopting the law so soon after its promulgation proves that it is considered to be more efficient than the old law which was adopted in very few, if any, sections during the last few years. The success of the law will altogether depend on the character of the administration of the trustees of the section, which it often requires as much genius to govern effectively as some sovereign state. As a general rule, the best sections within each inspectorate are among those which have already adopted the law, and many have voted funds to carry the law out. From the Annual Directory prepared by the Inspectors after the Annual Meetings of the sections, each county appears to have led off with the following numbers :—

Annapolis and Digby	89	Kings	53
Antigonish	1	Lunenburg	47
Cape Breton	47	Pictou	10
Colchester	16	Queens	18
Cumberland	47	Richmond	26
Guysboro'	?	Shelburne	3
Halifax Co	?	Victoria	?
Hants	44	Yarmouth	10
Inverness	?		

The Towns' Compulsory Attendance Act has been adopted in several towns, such as Halifax, Dartmouth and Amherst.

FINANCIAL STATISTICS OF SECTIONS.—VII.

It will be interesting to follow a series of this table for a few years. From the figures of this year it would appear that while school property rose over $40,000 in value, the assessable property fell over $1,390,000. The total assessment on the section is very nearly the same as last year, only $1000 less. This is an average of from forty to fifty cents less in each section. This diminution appears to have been due to the less need for repairs and buildings, and amounts to an average of $30 for each section. But on the other hand, the average section has increased its vote of money for the teacher's salary by over $19. It should be noted here, however, that although there has been retrenchment in building and repairs as compared with the previous year, which was 170 per cent. greater than the normal of the first two years of this five-year period, the sections are still expending 50 per cent. more than the normal in this work. The other points in this table have been already referred to in a former paragraph.

HOW THE TEACHER'S TIME IS SPENT IN THE SCHOOL.

Time Table.—VIII. AND IX.

So much space was given in my last report to the explanation of the object of estimating the amount of time spent in the school room in the various subdivisions of that comprehensive unity—an education,—and to the object of the specific subdivisions themselves, that it is not desirable to add anything so soon to what was then said; and more especially as the matter has been so much before educationists in the discussions on the Course of Study at the Provincial Association in Truro. I would refer those who read this with the desire for more detail, to my report of last year, beginning at page xxii.

PERCENTAGE OF TIME TO EACH SUBJECT.

This table shows the number of minutes given to each subject of the so-called Common School course by the teacher out of every hundred minutes. Here is the result compared with the previous year:—

NAME OF SUBJECT.	Average percentage of school time taken by Teacher for each subject.	
	1894.	1895.
Calisthenics	1.	1.5
Vocal Music	1.6	2.1
Hygiene and Temperance	2.3	3.1
Moral and Patriotic Duties	1.7	1.6
Object Lessons on Nature	2.3	2.3
Spelling	11.3	11.1
Reading, etc.	23.4	23.7
Composition and Grammar	8.0	8.1
Writing	7.2	6.8
Book-keeping	2.3	1.8
Geography	8.1	7.2
History	6.3	6.0
Drawing	3.1	3.5
Arithmetic	21.4	21.2
	100.0	100.0

The subjects which may be called the "nerve-exhausting ones," are given in italics. They also include those requiring "home lessons." The others are the "recreative" subjects. But, as explained before, each different heading is given here for the purpose of always keeping before the teacher each necessary side of his work. Some require the great bulk of the time, others require little time; but that little is very important for the attractiveness and usefulness of the school. To group them into subjects in a popular sense, as follows:

SUBJECTS OF COMMON SCHOOL COURSE OF STUDY AND PERCENTAGE OF TIME GIVEN TO THEM IN SCHOOL.

		Percentage of time.	
		1894.	1895.
1.	English { Spelling...... 11.3 Reading...... 23.4 Composition .. 8.0 }	42.7	42.9
2.	Arithmetic	21.4	21.2
3.	Geography (8.1) and History (6.3)	14.4	13.2
4.	Writing (7.2), Drawing (3.1), and Book-keeping (2.3)	12.6	12.1
5.	General intelligence lessons and improvement exercises (Cal., Music, Hygiene, Morals, & Nature).	8.9	10.6
		100.0	100.0

Comparing the average distribution of time during the past two years, it would appear that on the average, 2 minutes more in every

1000 minutes were given to English, and 2 minutes less in every 1000 to Arithmetic. Geography and History took up 12 less in every 1000; Writing, Drawing and Book-keeping, 5 less in the 1000; while the General Oral Lessons and Exercises took 17 minutes more in every 1000 minutes of school.

If we take a day's work to include 5 hours without intermission, that is 300 minutes, then during the past year the average time given to English each day increased a little over half a minute. Arithmetic lost the same time. Geography and History lost a little over three and a half minutes. Writing, Drawing, and Book-keeping all together, lost a minute and a half per day. While Calisthenics Music, Hygiene, and Temperance, etc., gained about 5 minutes a day

'DISTRIBUTION OF TIME IN HIGH SCHOOLS SUBJECTS.

This portion of the table is interesting because it gives us a glimpse into the number of partial High Schools, that is the number of schools doing some High School work in addition to the common school work; and because it shows us whether the schools in the various counties, as well as in the Province as a whole, are endeavoring to do more advanced work in obedience to popular demand, or are cutting down their curricula to that of the simple common school.

We see, for instance, that the average number of minutes given per week to Practical Mathematics, which is a grade xi. subject, has diminished from 80 minutes to 62. But, on the other hand, the number of schools teaching the subject has increased from 119 to 235. That is, the number of schools teaching this advanced subject has about doubled in the year; but it is evident that most of the additional schools have not been able to give more than an average of 40 minutes per week to the subject. The inference from this single column is that in 1894 one school in twenty was doing or attempting to do High School work of the "third year"; and that in 1895 one in ten were attempting to do the work. It is possible that some schools counted mathematical drawing under this head. Whether these conditions are the best for thorough High School work remains to be demonstrated. That they are good conditions for thorough common school work in many sections we do not know. But that there is a local demand for advanced work in many rural schools we know to be a fact. There is very full "home rule" in each school section, however; and in the meantime we may assume that trustees are working in accordance with the general desire of their several constituencies.

The next column shows a similar tendency. The number of schools in which Algebra is studied rose from 778 to 1124 during the year, and 82.7 minutes per week are devoted to it. The average time per day spent on common school work in all the schools of the Province is 295.6 minutes without intermission. That is about 4 or 5 minutes less than 5 hours a day. But in addition to this we must add the High School work done in many of these schools. In very nearly one-half of the schools of the Province, 82.7 minutes

b

per week, that is, 16.5 minutes per day is given to Algebra. And so with regard to each of the other subjects.

In Geometry, which is a pure High School subject, the number of schools introducing it went up from 580 to 875.

Natural Science, a subject involving a great deal of labor to teach, and one in which our teachers as a mass have had the poorest opportunities to attain excellence, has also been introduced to a greater extent, but much more moderately, the increase being only from 607 to 778.

Physiology went up from 194 to 214 schools. Physics, from 289 to 478. Chemistry, from 169 to 274. Latin, from 69 to 109. Greek, from 16 to 24. Modern Languages, no change practically.

The general conclusion is that from at least 100 to 200 common schools have during the year commenced to do High School work. Here it might be well to quote a sentence or two from my discussion of the subject last year, and a note from the report of Inspector MacIsaac, bearing on the same point, this year :

"Teachers, as a general rule, like to encourage their pupils to advance as far as possible. In country schools it is therefore not uncommonly found that there may be one or two pupils doing some high school work. In a case of this kind any teacher of judgment will give but very little of the school time to the advanced pupil, who as a general rule, is an interested student, and can make progress by occasional momentary hints from the teacher."

"The Statutes and the Regulations of the Council of Public Instruction provide for very material aid to High Schools. County Academies in particular, to make provision for effective High School teaching, in order to obviate to some extent, the necessity of making a very poor provision for such instruction in every section. But so long as teachers are tactful and trustees judicious, there will be no demand for the Council of Public Instruction or a Statute to take away from sections the power of allowing more or less High School work to be done in rural (ungraded) schools." — *Report, 1894, page xxiv.*

And from the Inspector's Report, page 78 :

" In a few schools I have found too much time given to one or two, or three of the more advanced pupils who were preparing for the teachers' examination. Individual teaching is very good in its place, but it should not be done at the expense of a large majority of the pupils. Teachers who undertake to make their mark by successfully preparing pupils for these examinations, should endeavor to understand the art of profitably employing and interesting the primary grades in the school while they are engaged in High School work."

CLASSIFICATION OF PUPILS.—IX.

Adding in the number of pupils reported as belonging to public Kindergartens with those of Grade I, we have the following classification of the pupils of the public schools :—

	1894.		1895.	
Grade I	18,908		19,470	
" II	13,489		13,042	
" III	12,184		12,361	
" IV	12,672		13 011	
" V	11,158		10,833	
" VI	9,202		9,711	
" VII	9,409		9,854	
" VIII	6,489		6,745	
Total Common School Pupils.		93,511		95,027
Grade IX	2,922		3,553	
" X	1,186		1,331	
" XI	460		576	
" XII	82		68	
Total High School Pupils....		4,650		5,528
Total Public School Pupils		98,161		100,555

These 4,650 and 5,528 High School Pupils include 1,095 and 1,174 respectively, who are taking only a partial High School course.

Deducting from the general returns of pupils of High School grade, those returned as belonging to the County Academies, we find the number returned by teachers as of High School grade who are in attendance at the non-academic High Schools and partial High Schools. We must take this enumeration with some reserve, as the classification is based not upon the examination of a central board of examiners, but simply on the estimate of the teachers themselves throughout the country.

GENERAL CLASSIFICATION OF HIGH SCHOOL STUDENTS.

	1894.		1895.
Full Course Academic Grade IX...	593	633	
" " ' " X...	423	453	
" XI...	303	357	
" XII...	52	49	
" Total	1371	Total..	1492
" Non-Academic, Total	1860	"	2593
Partial Course, Acad. and Non-Acad. ..	1095	"	1174
Errors in Classification	324	"	269
Totals	4650	.	5528

From this it appears that there were, according to the estimates of the teachers themselves, 2593 "full course" High School students studying outside the County Academies which have altogether but 1492. The 324 and 269 are the sums of the students enrolled each year in columns 10 to 13 of the table, which have not been counted in column 15. The discrepancy is less this year than last year, and probably indicates " partial course " students.

GRNERAL CLASSIFICATION OF ALL PUPILS.

	1894.	1895.
Common Schools and Kindergartens	93,511	95,027
Partial High School Pupils	1,419	1,443
Non-Academic High School Pupils	1,860	2,593
Academic High School Pupils	1,371	1,492
Totals	98,161	100,555
Candidates at Prov. Examination	1,922	2,399

ANALYSIS OF HIGH SCHOOL STUDIES.

Tables x. to xii.

The authorities governing the Halifax County Academy which last year furnished the largest quota to the highest grade, decided to take advantage of the optional character of the said grade xii., and have confined the attention of its large staff of instruction to the grades ix., x., and xi., during the present year. This is responsible for the decrease in the number of students in this grade. In the opinion of some it is desirable. These hold that the subjects of grade xii. are likely to be studied to greater advantage in the universities, and that the extensive range of subjects in the said grade took too large a portion of the time of the teaching staff for a disproportionately small number of students.

The number taking optional subjects did not increase so fast as those taking the imperative. In some cases they have actually diminished. This may be caused to some extent by the fact that at the Provincial Examination no credit is given for any marks in optional subjects which fall below 25.

SALARIES OF TEACHERS.—XIV. AND XV.

The average salaries of male teachers of classes A, C and D, have substantially increased. The average of class B has decreased principally owing to the heavy fall in a few counties. In a majority of the counties there was an increase. But the fall in Antigonish from $341 17 to $293.77, in Inverness from $411.88 to $233.77, and in Victoria fiom $401.88 to $267.77, neutialized large increases in other counties in this class.

The average salary of female class A has diminished on account of the increase of the number of the teachers, the new teachers engaging at a lower salary than the old teachers whose salaries have not declined. There has been a decrease in the average salaries of classes B and C; but the average salary of class D has increased.

On the whole, there has been a general rise in the rate of salaries, which corresponds with the increase in the amount voted by the sections for salaries—$35,876.80, and the increase in the Provincial Grant—$14,970.91; which indicates a total increase of $50,847.71.

County Academies.—XIX.

A valuable feature in this table not found in the general tables, is the average age of each grade on the first day of the school year. These figures are correct to two decimal places; and as they are the calculations of the leaders of the teaching profession in our Province, their absolute accuracy can be relied upon. From this it appears that the average of the average age of grade ix. in each Academy of the Province, is about 15 years and 5 months at the opening of the school year; grade x., about 16 years and 9 months; grade xi., about 17 years and 10 months; and grade xii. about 19 years. Candidates have gone up to the last Provincial Examination at 12 years of age, and some candidates between 12 and 13 were successful in obtaining grade D; but three years ago males were not allowed to present themselves at the Provincial (then Teachers') Examination until they were 17 years of age, and females 16 years. The sound judgment of the Academy headmasters, I trust, is not in favor of this attempt at rapid advancement characteristic of many schools doing High School work during the last year. In fact, in the Academies, the average age of grade ix. has advanced 47 days as compared with the previous year; grade x., 57 days; grade xi., 230 days; and grade xii., 277 days.

The difference between the average ages of each grade in the different Academies will depend somewhat on the source of supply of the students. If they all come from the graded schools of the town the average age is likely to be low. If many come from beyond the section the average age will be greater as a rule. Then again, the degree of severity with which the examiners mark the County Academy Entrance Examination papers at the different institutions, tends to affect the average age of those admitted.

The Provincial Grants to the Academies are greater this year by $2,610.

I was not able to visit all of the County Academies during the year. But I am able to report that the Provincial Examinations are supplementing the inspection method to such an extent that the work done by each can be more accurately estimated than ever before. In some cases the buildings and equipment are not up to the standard, while the teacher is doing all that is possible under the circumstances. The authorities have been notified of these defects, and reasonable time will be given in accordance with the law to have them removed. When buildings of good architectural appearance, with superior heating and ventilating arrangements, and other modern conveniences, are being erected where no Academic Grant is given, the County Academies must speedily come up to the same standard or excel it, otherwise the continuance of the grant cannot be justified.

The Academy at Sydney has been extensively renovated and improved during the year. The Academy at Antigonish, St. Francis Xavier's College, is superior in every respect; and the common school buildings, it is hoped, may some day do credit to the town. Guysboro has erected a well warmed, ventilated, and modern building of fine appearance, on one of the most beautiful sites. Lunenburg has done the same on a larger scale ; and while the structure is one of our best examples of the new school, its site and proportions add conspicuously to the beauty of one of our most picturesque towns. The opening of this Academy, after the close of the school year, will bring a reference to it into my next report.

Digby has only lately erected its pretty brick public school, which contains the County Academy as a department. Kings County Academy at Kentville has nearly doubled the size of the original building during the year, and it is fitted up with a hot air and ventilating system, and a chemical laboratory. Beautiful grounds have also been purchased around its interesting site. The Amherst Academy has also only lately been completed as the best finished and equipped public school in the Province at the date of its completion. The Colchester Academy at Truro, too, has only lately arisen as a separate building from those of the common schools, and has taken its rank among the largest of our Academies.

The Pictou Academy which, when built fifteen ago, was the best of its kind, had been undergoing during the year still further enlargement, more especially for laboratory extension. A stroke of lightning early in the morning of the 26th of October, set the building on fire and reduced it to ruins. In my next report I hope to be able to say that the restored building will be the best of its kind in the Province. This I infer from the manner in which its restoration and enlargement have been commenced.

PROVINCIAL HIGH SCHOOL EXAMINATION.—XXI.

In my last report so large a space (pages xxix. to xxxix.) was devoted to a discussion of the principles involved in examinations, promotions, and the course of study, that it is sufficient now to call attention to but a few points. The course of study is now undergoing the usual annual revision, to embody the results of our latest experience as indicated in conference and otherwise.

The following is a summary of the leading figures of the table compared with the previous years :

	1892.	1893.	1894.	1895.
No. of Candidates	1,431	1,506	1,922	2,399
No. received Grade applied for	175	598	760	684
" lower Grade than applied for.	209	317	342	325
" Grade A	5	10	30	15
" " B	66	157	182	189
" " C	330	289	337	277
" " D	430	459	543	854
Total High School Certificates won	831	915	1,092	1,070

In 1892 the certificates were Licenses, and male candidates were required to attain the age of 17, and female candidates the age of 16 years, before being admitted to the examination. Now there is no limitation of age for examination or certificates of scholarship. The age limit is required only for the issuance of Licenses for teaching.

This year candidates went up to examination as young as the age of 12 years; and a aggregate of over 1000 was successfully made on A (classical) by a candidate of 16 years and 4 months. It should be expected that the proportion of successful candidates admitted only after the mature age of 16 and 17 years should be very much greater than when there is no such limitation. There are, however, many advantages in favor of the general usefulness of our present system. The increasing number coming up each year proves its popularity. The only danger is, that teachers may in some cases advance pupils too rapidly. But with experienced teachers of good judgment there will be no ill-advised attempts at promotion. The following remarks of Inspectors may be quoted on this point.

Inspector Craig, page 90, says:

" While no official information touching the results of the exami‑nation has been received, I have been able to learn that, generally, they were disappointing. This I anticipated in my last report when alluding to indifferent promotions on the course of study.

" Children get the impression that they are going to be advanced after spending a year in a certain grade, and, whether meriting or not, they are hurried on to the high school course at such a pace that they are to be found there at the tender age of twelve and thirteen years, trying to do the work which requires maturer minds to grasp. A boy of average ability, with special training, may pass the 9th grade, but the step is a long one for the same pupil to the 10th in another year. I do not argue that the standard is too high, but I require more thorough work in the common school grades and more discrimination among teachers in making promotions."

Inspector Morse, page 67 and 68, says:

" *Three hundred and ten* candidates applied for examination for scholarship certificates at the four stations in this Inspectoral District, of whom *fifty-nine* took the *minimum professional examination* in addition. The number applying for Grade A, was 13; for Grade B, 58; for Grade C, 84; and for Grade D, 155. It is to be expected that a considerable proportion of these candidates will fail in securing certificates, for the reason that many of them are quite young and have not had sufficient mental development to enable them to deal with original questions in a logical manner. This must be expected so long as candidates come from miscellaneous as well as graded schools, and are certified by inexperienced as well as experienced teachers. Further, all teachers are not equally judicious in certifying to the fitness of applicants for examination."

" The prescribed Course of Study is being fairly well followed. In many of the schools the work of the course is being more or less thoroughly and systematically done. Some inexperienced or untrained teachers are to be found, however, who partially neglect the oral work, and who promote their pupils far more rapidly than their attainments warrant. To this fact may be attributed a large proportion of the failures to pass the Provincial Examination. As the number of Normal trained teachers is gradually increasing, it is fair to expect more thorough work in the common school department of the Course of Study, and consequently fewer failures to obtain scholarship certificates."

Another point has also to be taken into consideration. This is the first year that no relaxation had to be made by the Council of Public Instruction with respect to candidates falling below the minimum of 25, (for which regulations see October *Journal of Education* for 1893 and 1894). We have this year outgrown the necessity of any further allowance on account of the transition from the old to the new system. The fact that the results of the examination are in some respects even superior to those of the previous years, although the conditions in some respects were more severe, is a very creditable testimony to the progressive spirit of the body of our teachers.

Inexperienced teachers who are preparing candidates, have to be reminded of the fact that in testing their own candidates as to their fitness for the Provincial Examinations, they should remember that they are not likely to put questions on points which escaped their own attention when teaching. Furthermore, that they will be prone to put questions to their own candidates on points on which while teaching they laid special stress. Candidates are therefore likely to have their records at the school examinations under perhaps the great majority of teachers, all of whom are both capable and honest, reduced at the Provincial Examinations from 10 to 40 per cent., according to the care of the teacher in guarding against the tendency referred to. As soon as this principle is more fully apprehended by teachers as a whole, the results of the Provincial Examinations will not so often be disappointing to them.

Written examinations cannot test every qualification of a scholar equally well. It is, however, our most convenient approximative test of scholarship. It is more particularly defective in testing practical scientific ability, and accomplishments of voice and manner. Such subjects are therefore in the more especial domain of the official inspections and public examinations in each school.

In Appendix G. is given a table showing the average mark of candidates on each subject at each station ; and also as a measure of the approximate easy or difficult character of each examination paper, the highest mark on each made by a candidate. Where schools have been under the charge of experienced and effective teachers whose pupils had had a thorough grounding in all the common school subjects, the candidates were as generally successful as could be desired. Such schools are found in various counties of the Province, and are indisputable evidence of the fact that neither the Course of Study nor the standard of the examiners, as a general rule, is too advanced for our present conditions.

The following table of the average of Station Averages (Provincial Average) made on each subject of the B, C, and D grades, may be interesting for the purpose of the comparison of "marks" made by candidates. It will show whether any particular "mark" is above or below the Provincial average on the subject. An improvement on these averages is reasonably expected in 1896. The highest "mark" made on each subject is given in the lines below :

Average Provincial value of each subject in Grade B, C, and D, 1895. Also highest "mark" made by any Candidate.

Average of Station Averages.	Eng. Language.	Eng. Grammar.	Hist. and Geography.	Science.	Physiology.	Draw. & Book-keeping.	Arithmetic and P. M.	Algebra.	Geometry.	Latin (c.)	Latin (au.)	Greek (c.)	Greek (au.)	French.	German.	Aggregate.
Grade B......	55.3	52.7	51	39.5	34	....	37.8	43.5	47.5	27	35.7	28.7	51.6	38.9	42.7	390.8
" C....	36.5	48.8	48.1	30.2	...	26.9	42.4	37.4	40	24	....	32.8	...	35.5	34 3	319.9
" D.....	40.7	49.2	38.5	33.6	...	25.2	39	40.7	43.9	23.5	....	....	....	33.8	....	319.3

HIGHEST "MARK."

Average of Station Averages.	Eng. Language.	Eng. Grammar.	Hist. and Geography.	Science.	Physiology.	Draw. & Book-keeping.	Arithmetic and P. M.	Algebra.	Geometry.	Latin (c.)	Latin (au.)	Greek (c.)	Greek (au.)	French.	German.	Aggregate.
Grade B.....	88	98	90	89	79	....	92	100	98	76	82	75	84	91	97	858
" C......	81	99	95	82	..	81	100	100	100	91	..	84	..	93	84	770
" D.....	86	92	95	79	..	86	97	100	100	88	..	..	..	96	..	730

MINIMUM PROFESSIONAL QUALIFICATION EXAMINATION.

The number of candidates who went up to this examination shows an increase of 65 on the previous year. 354 were successful in taking some rank as compared with 314 last year. A summary of the examination compared with that of 1894 is here given :

	1894.	1865.
Candidates obtaining First Rank..........	34	10
" " Second Rank........	158	152
" " Third Rank	122	192
" failed	20	45
Total candidates........	334	399

These certificates, with the appropriate High School certificates, are conditions necessary for securing a teacher's License ; but they rank one degree lower than the corresponding diplomas from the Normal School.

CONSPECTUS OF M. P. Q. EXAMINATION RESULTS BY STATIONS.

STATION.	1894.					1895.				
	Total.	Rank of Candidates.			Failed.	Total.	Rank of Candidates.			Failed.
		First.	Second.	Third.			First.	Second.	Third.	
Amherst	5	2	2	1	....	7	....	2	5	....
Annapolis	11		5	4	2	12	1	..	9	2
Antigonish	15		6	8	1	27		6	15	6
Arichat	7		2	3	2	7	....	1	5	1
Baddeck	12		4	8	....	20	....	6	12	2
Barrington	6		4	2	....	12	....	1	10	1
Bridgetown	23		7	5	1	31	1	18	12	....
Canso	..			....	....	6		6	..	..
Cheticamp	2	....	...	1	1	4		1	3	....
Clare	13	....	1	8	4	11	....	2	4	5
Digby	10	1	7	2	....	7	...	3	4	....
Guysboro	6	1	3	2	....	7	..	2	5	....
Halifax	26	7	18	1	....	21	1	8	12	....
Kentville	7	3	2	2	....	30	4	18	8	....
Liverpool	12	1	6	5	....	9	1	3	5	....
Lockeport	2	....	2	..		2	....	2		.....
Lunenburg	23	....	11	12	....	18	....	6	9	3
Maitland	..		...	....		1	....	.	1	....
Margaree Forks	3	....	...	...	3	3	....	.	1	3
New Glasgow	7	3	7	6	1	20	....	7	12	1
Parrsboro	8	....	7	1	....	5	...	3	...	2
Pictou	22	3	12	6	1	29	1	15	12	1
Port Hawkesbury	2	....	...	2	....	9	....		4	5
Port Hood	....	1	4	6		9	....	4	5	....
Shelburne	2	1	1	....		..				
Sherbrooke	4	....	4	....		6	....	2	3	1
Springhill	4	....	2	2	....	2	....	2	...	....
Sydney	25	2	4	15	4	32	....	9	18	5
Tatamagouche	18	3	7	8	....	15	....	4	7	4
Truro	21	2	13	6	....	23	1	15	6	1
Windsor	11	4	4	3	....	10	....	8	2	....
Yarmouth	6		3	3	....	10	....	4	3	3
	334	34	158	122	20	399	10	152	192	45

TEACHERS' LICENSES GRANTED.

In order to obtain a License for teaching the candidate must present, (1) the evidence of scholarship prescribed; (2) the evidence of professional qualification prescribed; and (3) the certificate of age and character prescribed.

Three hundred and sixty-five licenses were granted during the year as compared with 250 the previous year. These figures indicate that the province is recovering from the threatened stringency in the supply of teachers due to the shock of change. As no more licenses should be granted than is sufficient to supply the schools of the province, whenever there appears to be over-production, all the change required to check it will be to require teachers to make an aggregate of at least 450 or 500, as circumstances may require, instead of the 400 necessary for the High School pass certificate in each grade. Regulations 7, 8, 9, and 10, page xxix, School Law Manual of 1895, have been drawn up with a special view to their easy amendment by simply changing the figures, and thus raising the scholarship standard of the profession without raising the standard of the "pass" in the High Schools, which may remain at the original 400, the equivalent of 50 per cent of the possible "marks" on the imperative subjects of the course of study.

LICENSES GRANTED IN 1894 AND 1895 COMPARED, SHOWING THE PROPORTION OF SEXES.

	1894.			1895.		
	M.	F.	Totals.	M.	F.	Totals.
Class A (Classical)	6	2	8	6	2	8
" A (Scientific)	2	0	2	3	0	3
" B	10	27	37	21	31	52
" C	18	54	72	38	68	106
" D	16	67	83	23	75	98
" D (Provisional)	10	38	48	29	69	98
Totals	62	188	250	120	245	365

	M.	F.	Total.
Increase in 1895	58	57	115

We discover from this table that during the year there was actually a greater increase of male than of female teachers. The difference is only one in favor of the male; but that there is a difference in his favor is the remarkable point.

COMPARED WITH THE TWO PREVIOUS YEARS.

	1893.	1894.	1895.
Class A (Classical)	7	8	8
" A (Scientific)	2	2	3
" B	28	37	52
" C	44	72	106
" D	48	83	98
" D (Provisional)	89	48	98
	218	250	365

OPENING OF NEW SCHOOL BUILDINGS.

On the first of November, 1894, I had the pleasure of being present at the formal opening of the New Glasgow High School. The occasion was one of wide-spread interest, as was manifested by the notable array of the public men of the province present. A view of the building is given in the frontispiece. It is designed for High School work alone, and is furnished with a very complete suite of rooms, laboratories, class-rooms, &c., such as are necessary for convenient and thorough work to day. The building is of brick, trimmed with brown stone, on a fine site, well finished in hardwood within, halls so arranged as to separate the sexes until the class-room is entered, heating and ventilation on the most approved system and ample. It is at present the best modelled High School building in the province.

On the 11th of January, 1895, I was present at the opening of the public school building of Parrsboro. It contains departments for all the schools, including the High School department. The building is of wood, but it is well furnished within, and is warmed and ventilated by a very effective system of hot air from furnaces in the basement. Good grounds have also been secured, but they have only just been set out with trees. The lithograph opposite gives a good idea of the size and appearance of the building which is a credit to the educational sentiment of the community, and an important addition to the public school architecture of the province.

APPENDICES.

It remains for me to make some allusions to the subject matter of the various appendices, to which I must refer you for details. First in order come the reports, pages 43 to 55, of the Principals of the

PROVINCIAL NORMAL SCHOOL AND OF THE SCHOOL OF AGRICULTURE,

institutions which henceforward are to be more intimately associated together than in the past. The attendance of pupils at the former increased from 130 of the previous year to 177 of this year. The good spirit of the students towards the institution was appropriately demonstrated by the presentation of statuary for its adornment. Following this the government procured the first supply of plaster casts for the Art Department. The spirit of the instructors is admirable ; for several of them have come forward to study practically with their classes departments of Natural Science which the smallness of the staff in the School of Agriculture made it impossible otherwise to overtake. It would be very desirable to have all the available space in the hallways and other suitable places, appropriately adorned with as complete a collection as possible of the various natural productions of the province scientifically named and classified, for the purpose of aiding in the effective study of all our natural resources.

The report of the Principal of the School of Agriculture, which is affiliated with the Normal School, gives an idea of the character of the students' work in this department. In his suggestions he complains with justice of the " tendency to be superficial in our education, and particularly," he says, " is this true of the present studies of botany and physiology." But there is even more truth in the paradox that there is not superficiality enough after all in the study of these same subjects. When practical knowledge lies so deep that it can never be utilized in the constant contact with our environment on the superficial plane of human daily use and labor, it may be said to be buried, so far from superficial is it. With intensive work on a few types there must be combined the comprehensive co-ordination of observations on all the natural elements lying openly at the base of industrial and social life. The teacher, as a botanist, should not only know

PUBLIC SCHOOL, PARRSBORO, NOVA SCOTIA, 1894.

some methods of investigating the hidden structure and marvellous genesis of typical forms of vegetable life, but should also have an outline knowledge of the classification, functions, and industrial uses of the flora indigenous to the rural school section. Although the equipment of the School of Agriculture is the best in our province for such work, the time which the student can spend in it is comparatively very short. But the most is being made of that short time.

With advancing salaries for 'our teachers we may soon, perhaps, be able to insist on a more extended course in which the prospective teacher may acquire a fuller and more practical training for the development of such classes of citizens as the country stands in need of. Such a teacher can conduct his lessons on nature in the rural school so as to lay the scientific foundation of domestic economy, of agriculture, of horticulture, of mining, of fishing, of mechanics and the like. The farmers are calling for a text book in agriculture, as if that would be likely to make the boys love the farm. The housewives want a text book to exploit the elements of the household chemistry, physics and biology, and so on. But when every class in the country has its industrial text book in school, the work will become too mnemonical and divided, and the instruction will tend to cause every living soul to forswear the cause of its infantile torture for ever after.

There is but one book of nature; and for man and maid, farmer and fisher, miner and mechanic, its alphabet is the same. Its 'a, b, abs," are the same. If the farmer lad goes to any agricultural college, he must commence by studying the ground, the stones, the hills, the swamps, the blades of grass and corn, and the beasts of a thousand hills which feed thereon. Why should he not do this elementary work in school? And so with each of the other classes. The elements of all industrial science are the same. It is but the accurate observation of the manner in which the forces of nature work, and the classification of the principles observed so that the individual can easily remember and apply the knowledge gained. The teacher may change his nature lessons into any or every local industry in which his pupils can be made to take an interest.

Inspector Craig, in his report, has well taken the point for the farmer, see page 89, as follows:

"There is but one subject in the course of study which I wish to refer to briefly, that is agriculture, which is first mentioned in the 8th grade. I beg leave to suggest its place in all the grades. The nature work may be so adapted that its trend may be in this direction. Let the lessons in botany, ornithology, entomology, chemistry, have a bearing on the agricultural life of the section. There is no factor so potent to popularize that calling, from which we have been drifting away so long, as the profession of teaching.

The very nature of an inspector's duties gives him the best opportunity to know the conditions and requirements of rural life. Associated a greater portion of the year with the farming class, he hears their grievances and discovers their wants. It is strikingly noticeable the improvidence displayed in the homes and upon the farms of 50 per cent. of the people. This arises mainly from an ignorance of the first principles taught in the elementary sciences.

Ninety per cent. of the farmers do not now enjoy the luxuries which Providence has placed within reach of their hands were they taught how to extend them. The delicacies of a good garden are almost unknown. The continual and injudicious cropping of farms in the first settled portions of the county, have forced hundreds to leave them for the precarious living of city. or town. But our teachers need first to be taught. Few, though coming from country homes, have a practical, much less a theoretical knowledge of farming The excellent institution at Truro affiliated with the Normal School, has been munificently equipped for an agricultural education, and the fullest advantage should be taken of it. No teacher should leave the training school until he or she has completed a course in some branch of agriculture.

The action of a number of teachers in voluntarily taking a course during the summer holidays, suggests an extension of the Normal School term in this department through the months of July and August, when there is much to be seen and learned."

When education is becoming universal, as it is with us, we must cease to develop it solely on the good old road leading directly to the comparatively few old-time learned professions, or else we will inevitably injure our country. In addition to the old road we must have those radiating to the wide fields of all possible industries which skirt the horizon. To captain intelligent labor is as noble as to lead a band of patriots. To develop property is as noble as to be able to write instruments to convey it. To study the very works of the Creator of all things in the search for truth is as noble as studying the conceptions of seers who dreamed instead of observing.

SCHOOL OF HORTICULTURE.

Under section 4 (8) of the Education Act of 1895, I am required "to collect as far as possible the statistics of all educational institutions in the province."

As the report of Professor E. E Faville, of the Nova Scotia School of Horticulture, is published by the department of Agriculture, it is not appended hereto. The school was established at Wolfville by the Fruit Growers' Association, and was opened in January, 1894. It receives a grant from the provincial treasury in proportion to the number of persons taking the course of instruction—$50 for each full course student up to the maximum of $2000. The attendance each year has been as follows :

	Students.
1894	33
1895	43
1896	49 (at opening).

A four month's winter course opens in January of each year. The full course of study is two years, with a diploma at completion. The work comprises a practical study of horticulture and its kindred branches, including small fruit, as well as large. The school has accessory aid for practical work, such as a library, laboratory, greenhouse, orchard, nursery, garden, &c. Professor Faville also delivered from two to three lectures in each county in the province during the past year as a part of his regular work. Were it possible to have the schools of Agriculure and Horticulture consolidated, there would be much advantage in dealing with the elements of science common to them both, and more time set free for the treatment of special subjects. And when the common school pupils receive generally the proper kind of object lessons from teachers who know how to investigate their surroundings, these schools can commence their work at a more advanced stage.

INSPECTION.

Appendix B, commencing at page 56, contains the reports of Inspectors. It must not be thought that these documents are the sum total of their communications with the department. Every month detailed reports of the conditions of the schools inspected by them are transmitted. All the returns from teachers within their inspectorates are examined by them, verified, and finally summed up in appropriate form for the central office. At the beginning of the school year they are acquainted with the action of the annual meetings in all the school sections under their charge, and are notified promptly when each school is opened. They have thus a directory of the condition of the schools within their district kept always posted up to date, and transmit a copy of the same, with monthly corrections, to the Education Office. Then there are the numerous incidental problems which come up with infinite variations from time to time from different sections of the province. For the proper growth and development of the schools, the inspector and his influence is the greatest controling power. The reports will disclose to some extent the character of the interest taken in the schools by each. It will be readily seen that the most fluent writer may not always be the most interested educationist, or the most useful inspector. One excels in one department, and another in a different but equally valuable direction. From year to year it will also be noticed that different phases of educational work may be engaging their chief attention. This is not only natural, but sometimes for effective work, necessary. The real gauge of the success of the inspector is the character he is developing in the educational work within his inspectorate. But even by this criterion it is hard to judge of the magnitude of his labor. For the fundamental educational conditions of each inspectorate are neither equal nor similar to start with. When we estimate the amount of work done, we must not only consider where it ended, but where it began.

Owing to the death of Hinkle Condon, Esq., Inspector of schools for Halifax city and county, on the 26th of July, just before the end of the school year, there is no report from his inspectorate. His successor, Graham Creighton, Esq., was not able to commence inspection until November. Mr. Condon continued, although in his sixty-ninth year, in the most active discharge of his duties until a few months before his death. His last work in the field was the inspection of the schools in the rural districts of the county, during the early winter, where some of the sections in his extensive inspectorate were very difficult of access. But he performed his duties with the same enthusiasm, sound judgment, and happy manner which characterized all his work from his appointment. The results of his service fully justified the action of the Council of Public Instruction over twenty-three years ago, when they refused to restrict their choice to the limits of the county, but took the best man the province could afford from the High School of Yarmouth. In educational council he was equally valuable, for with extensive information and a sympathetic nature, he combined rare diplomatic tact. His presence will be greatly missed not only by trustees, teachers and the other educational officials, but by the public at large throughout the inspectorate.

The report of the inspector for the counties of Richmond and Cape Breton, having been unavoidably delayed by unusual circumstances, was not received in time to be published in its proper place. It will be found at the end of the appendices, beginning at page 144.

No report is of more value than that of the Supervisor of the Halifax schools. The Board of Commissioners and its officers show an activity unexcelled in any other part of the province in studying the latest educational developments, and in testing many of them in actual application. The present report has the average quota of suggestive ideas for the consideration of the practical educationist of the province.

Institutions with Provincial Affiliations.

These affiliations consist in some form of recognition or degree of aid. Reference has already been made to the School of Horticulture, following the reference to the School of Agriculture.

At page 110 is a short report of the work of the *Halifax Institution for the Deaf and Dumb*. The event of the year is the new building, which will be shortly opened.

At page 111 a fuller report of the *Halifax School for the Blind* commences. These two institutions are subsidized by grants from the provincial treasury, and from public school county funds from the several counties from which their pupils come. This is virtually an extension of the free school system to the blind, and deaf and dumb of the province. Hence the statistical item required in each public school return with reference to these classes of pupils in each section.

At page 119 there appears a report on the *Victoria School of Art and Design*, which is subsidized to a small extent by both the province and the city.

The *Halifax Medical College* has a brief summary of its statistics on page 122.

The *Summer School of Science for the Atlantic Provinces of Canada*, which is really a voluntary Normal School, supported at the expense of those attending it, has its report for the year at page 123.

Commencing at page 126 are reports of the different *Teachers' Institutes* and *Associations* which are virtually teachers' training schools supported at the expense of those attending. Two days' attendance at the Institute, or three at a Provincial Association, or five at the Summer School of Science are allowed to count as so many teaching days, provided there be no more than five in any one year. This is the chief extent of recognition accorded these institutions.

The *Dominion Educational Association,* which was organized under the presidency of the Hon. D. Ross, Minister of Education for Ontario, held its first triennial session in Montreal, from the 5th to the 8th of July, 1892. The second session was held in Toronto from the 16th to the 18th April, 1895, in conjunction with the Ontario Educational Association. The third session will be held at Halifax, Nova Scotia, early in August, 1898. The attractive character of the Atlantic seaboard at that season of the year will help to draw a large number of the leading educationists of the west to this Canadian convention. It is expected that arrangements will be made, especially in the Atlantic provinces, to have this Dominion Association take the place and enjoy the privileges of the several Provincial Associations for 1898.

On page 26, Table xx gives the statistics of the 26 *Government Night Schools* established during the year in localities where there were large numbers of adult laborers who had no opportunity previously to acquire an elementary education.

In addition to such schools, there are established in the vicinity of the collieries *Mining Schools,* under the charge of competent instructors and boards of examiners who grant certificates. The following lists give an idea of the number and distribution of these institutions:

1895.

Instructors of Candidates for Certificates as Underground Managers and Overmen.

Jno. Johnson	Westville.
J. W. Sutherland	Thorburn.
Angus McKay	Stellarton.
A. D. Ferguson	Springhill.
T. Blackwood	Joggins.
Jno. Caddegan	Bridgeport.
G. W. Greenwell	Reserve.
Jno. Carey	Sydney Mines.
M. Morrison	Cow Bay.
Peter Currie	Victoria.
Isaac Greenwell	Caledonia.
W. S. Wilson	Glace Bay.

1895.

Board of Examiners for Colliery Officials

W. B. Wilson	Springhill.
James Baird	Maccan.
R. O'Rourke	Springhill.
R. McKenzie	Westville.
A. B. McGillivray	Glace Bay.
Henry Mitchell	Old Bridgeport.
I. Rutherford	Stellarton, *(Chairman.)*
H. S. Poole	Stellarton.
E. Gilpin, Jr	Halifax, *(Secretary.)*

1895.

Board of Examiners for Granting Certificates to Engineers.

DAN. MURRAY.................Springhill.
I. G. BARRINGTON ....North Sydney.
JAS. FLOYD ....Westville.

INSTITUTIONS NOT CONNECTED WITH THE PUBLIC SYSTEM OF EDUCATION.

These institutions all coöperate harmoniously with those under public control ; and it is in the interests of all public systems to carefully study such institutions. In their freedom from central control they may be able to adapt themselves more readily to peculiar circumstances and new conditions. Their very existence demonstrates the demand for them. In order to show the extent of this demand it has been deemed advisable to have their statistics presented as fully as possible with those of the public educational system. I addressed a "circular" request to the principals of all the institutions known to myself, the inspectors and others from whom information could be obtained. The circular sent to the institutions within the province having the power of conferring degrees—the universities, six in number—was accompanied with the tabular form shown in Appendix F, (I,) page 137. The tabular form sent with the circular to all the other institutions—the private schools, seminaries and colleges without degree conferring powers—was that shown in Appendix F,(II,) page 138. The terms of the "circular" request were as follows :

"Under the Amended and Consolidated Act of 1895, relating to Public Instruction, the Superintendent of Education is required ' to collect as far as possible the statistics of all educational institutions in the province.'

"I have therefore the honor of asking you to favor me with such statistics of your institution as may enter into the following tabular form, to be published in my report ; and I hope your kindness may prove useful to your institution by keeping its existence and work before the public at home and abroad, as it will also be an important contribution to the educational statistics of the province.

"These statistics are entirely supplementary to those of the public schools, and therefore should include only those who have *not* been registered and returned as belonging to any public school while in attendance at your institution."

PRIVATE SCHOOLS, SEMINARIES, &C.—APP. F. (II).

It would appear from this table that there were 1612 pupils for some portion of the year studying in institutions having no connection with the public school system. By examination of the figures it will be seen that the work of many of these institutions is not at all parallel to that of the public schools. But it is desirable that the general standing of the pupils should be approximately known. An effort has been made by nearly all to indicate this standing. It must not be assumed that this classification is anything more than approximate. Some classified according to the pupils' work in English; some according to the mathematics, chiefly; some according to the classics; some according to a general balancing of subjects; some according to the maturity or age of the pupils (having reference to the fact that the average of grade XII in our academies is about 19 years; grade XI, 18 years; grade X, 17 years, and grade IX, 16 years). But there were some cases, more especially the commercial and business colleges, where no attempt at the classification could well be made unless it were purely on the age principle. The average daily attendance at all these institutions is 1156. Approximately, it may be said that for every 1000 attending the public schools there are 16 attending private schools, seminaries, and special collegiate institutions. The females are in excess, being 857, as against 755 males. Of these 1259 are estimated to be mainly doing work of common school grades, 372 work of high school grades, while the remaining 353 are engaged in studying some special subjects.

University Colleges.—App. F. (I).

We have six colleges with university powers of conferring degrees. St. Anne's College, at Church Point, Digby County, was established quite lately, and with a very commendable caution has not yet commenced to confer degrees. The institution has been affiliated according to law with the Clare County Academy, which has already commenced to do good work for French students, some of whom are preparing to become teachers in the public schools. As the advanced students have been returned as in attendance at the county academy (for which see county academy tables, page 24 to 33), they cannot be entered into this table for summation.

St. Francis Xavier's College is affiliated with the Antigonish County Academy, which is doing very valuable service in the eastern portion of the province, giving thorough scholarship to many of the teachers in our public schools. Although the advanced classes do university work in addition to the imperative academic work, the numbers of students are not entered into these columns for general summation, as in the case of St. Anne's College.

For the other institutions the table is self-explanatory. The totals returned as professors for the six colleges are 55, and as lecturers, 19. From an actual comparison of these institutions it may be found that the class of work done by the "professor" in one institution is quite different from that done by the "professor" in another. Also, the grade of work peculiar to each "year" may be different in the different institutions, as well as the character of scholarship necessary for graduation. Each institution has its own standard, so that the same nomenclature may not identically connote the same ideas or facts. With this explanation the table gives these statistics perhaps as accurately as they can be presented to the public. The students attending the colleges within the province may be classified thus, for the year ended summer of 1895:

Undergraduates in Arts.

```
1st  year ........................ 67
2nd   "   ........................ 72
3rd   ..   ....................... 58
4th   "   ........................ 58
Graduates........................ 11
         Total regular in Arts ..........  — 266
         Total general    "    .... .....     58
            Total in Arts ............    — 324
              "     Science ..........        36
              "     Medicine .........        45
              ..    Law .............        53
              "     Theology .........        60*
         Total (with duplicate registration)..  — 518
         Students registered in two faculties..   23
```

Total students in the *four* colleges.. 495

Total number of graduates from the colleges in Nova Scotia up to date, 1778.

Degrees conferred in 1895.

B. A., 60; B. L., 2; M. A., 23; B. Sc., 3; B. Eng., 1; M. Eng., 1; LL. B., 13; B. C. L., 5; D. C. L., 5; Ph. D., 1; M. D., C. M., 7; D. D., 4. Total, 125.

The Provincial High School Certificates which, from the method of examination and the wide publication of the syllabus and examination papers, have well known and definite values, are accepted in lieu of portions or all of many entrance examinations into the various colleges. This arrangement virtually affiliates every one of the foregoing institutions with the public school system so far as admission examinations are concerned, and obviates the difficulty formerly felt in the different standards required by each. These certificates contain the values of the examination work of each candidate on each subject; so that each institution can make its standard a mark of 40, or 50, or 60 per cent. or more on such subjects as it requires. There is, therefore, no further necessity for high school masters to have their pupils reading different authors, &c., according as some of them are preparing to enter one or another college. The prescribed high school course, which is more extensive than the requirements, perhaps, of any one institution, is accepted when the certificate granted by the Board of Provincial Examiners indicates a mark high enough for the standard set by each separate institution. The arrangement simplifies the work in many high schools, lessens the number of written examinations for both candidates and colleges, and gives the pupil the fairest possible chance, by allowing him the examination upon the full regular work of his school.

All of which is respectfully submitted.

I have the honor to be, your obedient servant,

A. H. MACKAY,

Superintendent of Education.

---

* 65, when including theological students in St. Anne's.

PART II.

STATISTICAL TABLES.

PUBLIC SCHOOLS, COUNTY ACADEMIES, ETC.

TABLE I.--SCHOOL SECTIONS, &c., (GENERAL).

Nova Scotia, Year ended July, 1895.

Counties	Total No. of School Sections	No. of Sections with School any part of the year	Total No. of Schools in Session during any part of year	No. of Schools in Session 30 days or under	Over 50 and up to 100 days	Over 100 and up to 150 days	Over 150 and up to 200 days	Over 200 and under full year	Full year of 217 days	Average No. of days all schools were in session	No. of Teachers	No. of Licensed Assistants	No. of Teachers holding Normal School Diploma	No. of Pupils registered at School during year	Proportion of Population (census of 1891) at School during year	No. School Libraries	No. of School Scientific Collections
Annapolis	107	9	117		4	4	15	61	33	199.8	118		33	4741	1 in 4.1	2	3
Antigonish	81	5	93			3	14	33	42	157.	97		6	3551	1 " 4.5	1	1
Cape 1 Bon	132	25	158	2	5	6	20	47	78	199.9	158	1	29	7391	1 " 4.6	8	7
Colchester	122	7	145	1	6	12	42	63	23	194.4	161	1	85	6123	1 " 4.4	3	3
Cumberland	158	15	191	2	4	14	17	114	38	196.1	207		95	8772	1 " 3.9	5	7
Digby	80	4	102		6	13	6	44	39	200.7	104	3	14	4717	1 " 4.2	1	4
Guysboro	90	10	92	2		4	20	30	32	190.5	98		18	3871	1 " 4.8		
Halifax County	131	11	149		4	7	23	61	67	200.4	153	1	57	6876	1 " 4.8	7	5
Halifax City	1		134	4			10		119	201.	134		34	7524	1 " 5.	17	68
Hants	99	3	125		9	7	8	63	38	194.5	133	4	48	5092	1 " 4.3	25	14
Inverness	176	12	164			18	33	52	61	197.	167		17	6086	1 " 4.2	1	
Kings	104	5	122	1	5	6	9	61	40	190.6	131		48	5294	1 " 4.2	10	8
Lunenburg	146	8	167		4	16	12	60	75	198.	174		38	7434	1 " 4.8	2	2
Pan	131	3	173		7	9	13	82	62	203.2	184		41	7285	1 " 5.	2	2
Queens	47	2	59			2	4	31	22	206.5	62	1	7	2128	1 " 4.7		
Richmond	70	11	70	1	1	2	8	23	35	202.2	70		6	3034	1 " 4.3	2	2
Sel rbe	66	5	78		1		4	46	27	209.8	78		5	3509	1 " 5.6		2
Victoria	80	21	59	3		2	23	12	18	193.	63	1	9	2199	1 " 4.5		
Yarmouth	73	5	107		2	2	13	71	19	207.	107	3	26	4928	1 "	2	4
Total 1895	1894	161	2305	16	55	127	294	955	858	198.7	2399	15	616	100555	1 " 4.4	90	133
** " 1894**	1891	136	2292	16	83	139	280	1157	617	199.2	2351	13	499	98710	1 " 4.5	55	91
Increase	3	25	13				14		241		48	3	117	1845	1 " 243	35	42
Decrease					28	12		202		5							

TABLE II.—TEACHERS EMPLOYED (CLASSIFICATION AND ANALYSIS).

Nova Scotia, Year ended July, 1895.

COUNTIES	MALE							FEMALE							TOTAL		
	Academic A (cl. & sc.)	Academic A (sc.)	Academic A (cl.)	First-Class B.	Second-Class C.	Third-Class D.	Third (Prov.) D.	Academic A (cl. & sc.)	Academic A (cl.)	Academic A (sc.)	First-Class B.	Second-Class C.	Third-Class D.	Third (Prov.) D.	Male.	Females.	Total.
Annapolis		1	2	14	14	2	1				14	38	30	2	34	84	118
Antigonish			4	5	16	10	3				2	21	27	9	38	59	97
Cape Breton			4	18	18	17	4				8	45	36	8	61	97	158
Colchester			2	5	5	2			1		16	70	57	3	14	147	161
Cumberland		1	3	4	10	3	1				15	98	62	9	22	185	207
Digby		1	2	10	5	5	5		1		4	21	38	14	27	77	104
Guysboro			1	2	6	3	1				6	30	36	12	14	84	98
Halifax County			1	3	1	3	2		1		13	70	50	6	14	139	153
Hfx City			5	9	6						37	74	4	1	17	117	134
Hants			2	6	8	4					12	57	37	6	20	113	133
Inverness			2	15	30	41	9				1	21	43	5	97	70	167
Kings			3	11	9	2	1		1		13	63	28	1	26	105	131
Lunenburg			2	4	7	3					9	70	66	13	16	158	174
Pictou			7	10	13	7			1		14	74	53		37	147	184
Queens			1	2	2		1				3	33	14	6	6	56	62
Richmond				1	13	13	7					12	15	3	40	30	70
Shelburne			2	5	2	3			1		3	47	15	1	12	66	78
Victoria			1	2	10	9	1				2	11	27		23	40	63
Yarmouth			2	10	3	6	1		1		11	45	26	2	22	85	107
Total 1895		3	46	142	178	133	38		6		183	900	669	101	540	1859	2399
" 1894			44	149	199	131	18		4		162	888	658	98	541	1810	2351
Increase		3	2			2	20		2		21	12	11	3		49	48
Decrease				7	21										1		

TABLE II.—TEACHERS EMPLOYED (Classification and Analysis)—Continued.

Nova Scotia, Year ended July, 1895.

COUNTIES.	Licensed Assistants Males	Females	New Teachers	Old Teachers, but new to Section	Teachers continued in the same section as previous year	No. whose total service as teacher was one year or under	Total Period of Service Over one and up to two years	Over two and up to three years	Over three and up to four years	Over four and up to five years	Over five and up to seven years	Over seven and up to ten years	Over ten and up to fifteen years	Over fifteen and up to twenty years	Over twenty years
Annapolis			23	46	49	23	5	24	10	8	12	13	5	5	13
Antigonish			13	49	35	13	16	7	16	10	10	6	9	2	8
Cape Breton		1	19	49	90	22	15	8	14	17	16	15	22	21	8
Colchester		1	19	87	55	31	16	20	14	16	22	25	12	2	3
Cumberland			36	121	50	36	27	26	29	23	34	15	8	5	4
Digby		2	16	43	45	16	7	13	14	7	8	13	13	8	5
Guysboro			15	58	25	15	11	13	12	10	15	16	2	3	1
Halifax County	2	1	30	77	46	30	26	15	20	9	22	11	11	5	4
Halifax City			6	2	126	7	3	7	10	7	16	22	24	18	20
Hants			22	73	38	22	16	13	25	9	19	11	14	3	1
Inverness		2	29	79	59	29	17	18	15	19	20	18	14	9	8
Kings			18	68	45	20	10	18	15	8	25	12	13	2	8
Lunenburg			17	76	81	23	20	23	18	25	25	21	9	7	3
Pictou			23	72	89	35	17	25	25	23	17	17	10	8	7
Queens			8	24	30	16	4	8	11	9	4	3	6		1
Richmond		1	16	23	31	16	5	7	7	6	9	9	5	2	4
Shelburne			9	39	30	9	6	6	8	8	20	13	2	3	3
Victoria			14	33	16	14	4	9	13	4	6	6	4	1	2
Yarmouth		3	12	39	56	12	14	16	5	6	10	9	19	9	7
Total 1895	2	12	345	1058	996	389	239	276	281	224	310	255	202	113	110
" 1894	4	14	255	1141	955	297	327	309	263	205	270	248	186	121	125
Increase			90		41	92			18	19	40	7	16		
Decrease	2	2		83			88	33						8	15

TABLE III.—TEACHERS EMPLOYED (ANALYSIS OF FIRST AND SECOND CLASSES).

Nova Scotia, Year ended July, 1895.

COUNTIES.	Service one year or under.	Over one and up to three years.	Over three and up to five years.	Over five and up to seven years.	Over seven and up to ten years.	Over ten and up to fifteen years.	Over fifteen and up to twenty years.	Over twenty years.	Service one year or under.	Over one and up to three years.	Over three and up to five years.	Over five and up to seven years.	Over seven and up to ten years.	Over ten and up to fifteen years.	Over fifteen and up to twenty years.	Over twenty years.
	CLASSES A. & B.—MALES.								CLASSES A. & B.—FEMALES.							
Annapolis	2	1	1	3	2	1	2	5	4	2	1	2	1	2		2
Antigonish		1	1	1	1	4		1						1		1
Cape Breton		1	4	2		4	7	4	1	2	1	1		3		
Colchester		1	2			3		1	1	4	4	3	4		.1	
Cumberland	1	2		2			1	2	3	2	3	3	3	2		
Digby	1	2	3	1		3	2					2		2		
Guysboro			1		3					1	2	1	1	1		
Halifax County		2						1	3	1	3	3	2	1		
Halifax City		1	1	3	2	2	2	3	2	2	3	5	7	11	3	5
Hants		1	2		1	3		3	1	2	6	2		2		
Inverness	2			1	3	6	2	3			1					
Kings			3	3		3	1	4	3	1	2	4		3		
Lunenburg			1	1	1	2		1		1	4	2		2		
Pictou		2	6	1	1		2	5	4	1	3	1	4			
Queens	1					1		1	2		1					
Richmond		1	2			1	1	2					1	2		
Shelburne	1	1	2		2			1					1	2		
Victoria		2	1						1					1		
Yarmouth	1	2	2	1		3	1	2	1	2	2	1	2	2	2	
Total 1895	9	20	32	19	16	36	24	35	26	21	37	32	24	35	6	8
" 1894	7	29	30	21	16	26	26	38	9	31	31	26	28	25	8	8
Increase	2		2			10			17		6	6		10		
Decrease		9		2			2	3		10			4		2	

TABLE III.—TEACHERS EMPLOYED (ANALYSIS OF FIRST AND SECOND CLASSES).—*Continued.*

Nova Scotia, Year ended July, 1895.

COUNTIES.	CLASS C.—MALES.								CLASS C.—FEMALES.							
	Service one year or under.	Over one and up to three years.	Over three and up to five years.	Over five and up to seven years.	Over seven and up to ten years.	Over ten and up to fifteen years.	Over fifteen and up to twenty years.	Over twenty years.	Service one year or under.	Over one and up to three years.	Over three and up to five years.	Over five and up to seven years.	Over seven and up to ten years.	Over ten and up to fifteen years.	Over fifteen and up to twenty years.	Over twenty years.
Annapolis	5	3	1	.	2	.	.	3	2	11	8	6	3	2	2	2
Antigonish	.	2	4	2	2	3	2	3	1	6	8	3	1	1	.	1
Cape Breton	.	1	5	1	.	1	5	1	2	5	10	7	8	9	3	1
Colchester	2	2	2	.	2	.	.	.	9	12	10	17	12	7	2	2
Digby	1	.	1	.	.	.	.	.	7	29	28	18	8	5	2	.
Guysboro	1	.	.	2	.	.	2	.	1	2	4	3	5	2	4	.
Halifax County	4	2	3	2	.	3	5	.	3	18	8	6	7	.	12	.
Halifax City	3	2	4	.	.	.	.	3	.	5	12	10	7	1	2	.
Hants	1	3	3	5	1	.	.	.	10	10	13	8	13	7	1	.
Inverness	2	2	4	2	5	.	.	.	5	4	4	6	3	1	.	.
Kings	.	3	3	.	1	2	5	.	3	16	12	9	9	6	1	3
Lunenburg	.	.	5	.	.	.	.	.	9	22	15	14	3	1	.	1
Pictou	1	.	1	.	.	1	1	3	5	19	18	10	6	6	8	1
Queens	2	.	3	2	3	.	.	1	1	9	12	8	1	4	.	.
Richmond	.	.	.	.	.	.	.	.	2	9	2	4	2	1	2	.
Shelburne	.	2	3	2	3	2	.	.	1	8	9	14	8	2	.	2
Victoria	.	.	.	.	.	.	.	2	2	6	3	2	8	2	.	2
Yarmouth	1	.	3	.	1	.	.	.	.	9	8	5	4	4	5	.
Total 1895	22	28	39	17	23	15	16	18	76	191	194	155	119	82	47	36
" 1894	18	47	42	18	24	14	18	23	68	214	196	139	110	78	43	40
Increase	9		8			1			8			16	9	4	4	
Decrease		19		1	1		2	5		23	2					4

TABLE IV.—ATTENDANCE (QUARTERS).

Nova Scotia, Year ended July, 1895.

COUNTIES.	First Quarter			Second Quarter				Third Quarter				Fourth Quarter			
	Total on register at end of quarter.	Average daily attendance.	Per cent. of pupils enrolled daily present on an average.	Total on register at end of quarter.	No. attended during quarter.	Average daily attendance.	Per cent. attended during quarter daily present on an average.	Total on register at end of quarter.	No. attended during quarter.	Average daily attendance.	Per cent. attended during quarter daily present on an average.	Total on register at end of quarter.	No. attended during quarter.	Average daily attendance.	Per cent. attended during quarter daily present on an average.
Annapolis	3752	2620.3	69.8	4310	3846	2470.3	64.3	4345	3569	2237.7	62.7	4746	3701	2376.1	64.2
Antigonish	2785	1757.4	63.1	3111	2797	1629.2	58.2	3254	2620	1475.	56.3	3551	2960	1612.3	56.3
Cape Breton	5673	3775.1	66.5	6352	5743	3614.	62.7	6431	5354	3426.7	64.	7391	6058	3748.2	61.8
Colchester	4743	3414.6	71.9	5372	4843	3383.9	68.	5509	4503	2910.8	64.4	6093	5063	3336.3	65.8
Cumberland	6785	4614.	68.	7536	6747	4128.1	61.1	7705	6319	3931.	62.2	8772	6877	4594.1	63.8
Digby	3575	2385.2	66.7	4158	3787	2396.5	63.3	4341	5686	2280.3	61.9	4712	3784	2383.3	62.9
Guysboro	2513	1647.3	65.5	3257	2984	1851.9	62.	3530	2984	1779.3	59.6	3871	3231	1859.7	57.5
Halifax County	5586	3967.7	71.3	6142	5700	3764.4	66.	6368	5384	3444.3	63.9	6864	5716	3856.7	67.4
Halifax City	6543	5153.5	78.	6703	6469	4702.4	72.	6744	6272	4594.8	73.	7255	6663	4983.8	74.
Hants	3915	2724.4	69.6	4351	3952	2473.7	62.6	4649	3960	2402.	62.2	5037	4144	2690.8	64.7
Inverness	4145	2527.3	60.9	4997	4516	2739.9	60.9	5432	4581	2763.4	60.3	6030	4965	2939.1	59.2
Kings	3760	2477.4	63.9	4638	4204	2504.9	59.6	4746	3814	2246.3	61.5	5245	3786	2319.8	61.2
Lunenburg	5534	3772.2	68.2	6574	6243	3679.9	62.2	6636	5607	3658.6	62.	7109	5475	3457.2	63.1
Pictou	6113	4381.2	71.5	6581	6061	4007.1	66.1	6721	5605	3673.6	63.6	7199	6098	4079.2	66.2
Queens	1720	1220.	71.	1902	1781	1177.5	61.	1978	1709	1110.8	65.	2128	1692	1168.4	69.
Richmond	2289	1533.8	67.	2652	2443	1457.6	61.5	2748	2296	1338.8	59.	3034	2534	1524.3	60.1
Shelburne	2852	1983.2	69.5	3212	2910	1792.	60.7	3294	2705	1636.7	59.4	3509	2731	1823.7	66.7
Victoria	1477	1953.8	64.6	1669	1706	1037.		1957	1596	991.6	62.1	2199	1733	1000.5	57.7
Yarmouth	3906	2745.	72.1	4460	4174	2797.9	67.	4548	3946	2443.2	61.9	4880	3937	2906.7	71.2
Total 1895	77566	53673.4	69.2	88177	80007	51748.2	63.9	91136	76730	48344.9	63.	99625	81068	52349.2	64.5
" 1894	75821	51622.3	68.	86700	79799	47183.2	59.1	89939	76121	48837.3	64.2	97920	80128	51492.4	64.2
Increase	1745	2051.1	1.2	1477	1108	4565.	4.8	1197	609		1.2	1705	940	856.8	.3
Decrease										592.4					

TABLE V.—ATTENDANCE (SEMI-ANNUAL AND ANNUAL).

Nova Scotia, Year ended July, 1895.

COUNTIES.	HALF YEAR				ANNUAL ATTENDANCE OF PUPILS.									
	Days taught first half year.	Days taught second half year.	Total days' attendance first half year.	Total days' attendance second half year.	Under 5 years of age.	Between 5 and 15 years.	Over 15 years.	Total annual enrolment.	Boys.	Girls.	Total days' attendance for year.	Days taught during year.	Daily present on an average during year.	Average of quarterly percentage of attendance.
Annapolis	11,708.	11,782.	264,245.	224,882.	104	4149	488	4741	2314	2427	509,129.	23,490.	2472.	65.2
Antigonish	8.803.	9,322.	177,192.	161,425.	43	3044	464	3551	1838	1713	338,617.	18,125.	1635.3	58.5
Cape Breton	15,235.	16,345.	384,434.	384,467.	117	6708	476	7391	3873	3518	768,901.	31,580.	3766.1	63.8
Colchester	13,659.5	14,479.	347,545.	321,171.	89	5448	586	6123	3169	2954	668,716.	28,138.5	3353.1	67.5
Cumberland	18,785.5	18,692.5	450,142.	439,395.	150	7898	724	8772	4496	4276	889,537.	37,478.	4352.9	63.8
Digby	10,061.	10,401.5	248,210.	246,887.	78	4222	417	4717	2398	2319	495,097.	20,462.5	2462.2	63.7
Guysboro	8,194.	9,340.5	172,975.	196,206.	55	3513	303	3871	2068	1803	369,181.	17,534.5	1910.2	61.1
Halifax County	14,506.5	15,252.	392,417.	386,107.	132	6473	271	6876	3495	3381	778,524.	29,858.5	3804.4	67.1
Halifax City	12,888.	13,655.	489,321.	504,470.	107	7022	395	7524	3636	3888	993,791.	26,543.	4863.9	73.
Hants	11.881.	12,427.	270,940.	267,769.	79	4576	437	5092	2565	2527	538,709.	24,308.	2679.4	64.8
Inverness	13,936.	15,586.	267,212.	301,131.	109	5852	625	6086	3285	2801	568,343.	29,522.	2836.	58.5
Kings	12,165.	12,094.	258,615.	247,213.	73	4478	743	5294	2800	2494	505,828.	24,259.	2529.5	62.1
Lunenburg	16,521.	16,454.	296,562.	384,437.	198	6751	485	7434	3842	3592	780,999.	32,975.	4325.8	63.9
Pictou	17,716.5	17,447.5	443,740.	408,141.	43	6471	771	7285	3879	3406	851,881.	35,164.	4073.6	66.8
Queens	6,007.	6,168.5	126,378.	121,495.	32	1908	188	2128	1079	1049	247,873.	12,175.5	1106.5	67.8
Richmond	6,780.	7,375.	157,283.	151,925.	61	2776	197	3034	1662	1372	309,208.	14,155.	1732.8	61.8
Shelburne	8,089.5	8,278.5	196,801.	185,503.	99	3115	295	3509	1810	1699	385,304.	16,368.	1827.1	64.2
Victoria	5,164.	5,831.	99,885.	102,943.	49	1961	189	2199	1165	1034	202,828.	10,995.	1039.	59.1
Yarmouth	40.912.	11,234.	287,049.	283,742.	123	4416	389	4928	2511	2417	570,791.	22,146.	2738.	68.
Total 1895.	223,112.5	232,165.	5,430,946.	5,342,309.	1741	90371	8443	100555	51885	49670	10,773,255.	455,277.5	54006.8	65.1
" 1894.	223,222.	232,281.5	5,146,416.	5,325,348.5	1631	89719	7360	98710	51584	47126	10,471,764.5	455,503.5	51152.8	62.1
Increase			284,530.	16,960.5	110	652	1083	1845	301	1544	301,490.5		2854.	3.
Decrease	109.5	116.5										226.		

TABLE VI—STATISTICS, (VARIOUS).

Nova Scotia, Year ended July, 1895.

COUNTIES.	20 days or less	Over 20 and up to 50 days	Over 50 and up to 100 days	Over 100 and up to 150 days	Over 150 and up to 200 days	Over 200 days	Belonging to this School Section	From beyond limits of Section	No. of children in the Section from 5 to 15 years of age	No. of those who did not attend school at all during	Deaf	Blind	No. of visits by Secretary, Trustees and	No. of visits by Inspector and school officials	No. of visits by other visitors	No. of Parents and visitors at Public Examination	No. of Prizes awarded	Value of Prizes awarded
Annapolis	430	779	1047	1030	1244	211	4508	233	4281	239	1		379	126	1947	744	111	93 22
Antigonish	425	628	849	829	716	104	3219	332	3214	246			457	102	1278	769	88	78 15
Cape Breton	834	1141	1547	1612	2023	234	6932	459	7164	662	2	1	971	212	1907	2169	149	168 70
Colchester	488	957	1380	1407	1661	230	5763	360	5607	211	1		397	181	1919	879	130	52 40
Cumberland	1005	1570	1943	1843	2161	250	8391	381	8461	563	6		631	273	2691	1699	94	44 47
Digby	385	798	1120	1023	1120	271	4616	101	4600	342		4	358	130	1561	483	107	37 95
Guysboro	404	774	966	797	815	115	3706	165	3799	331	3		411	112	2042	842	44	22 65
Halifax County	492	1123	1356	1629	1965	311	6706	170	6754	456	3	1	476	166	1784	1633	315	115 13
Halifax City	325	699	891	1135	3503	370	7429	93	7522	200			349	536	1100	987	77	34 90
Hants	542	851	1629	1207	1381	154	4896	196	4785	343			379	228	1997	1704	97	30 67
Inverness	857	1155	1394	1109	1184	289	5321	565	5437	421	1	1	1353	165	2541	2028	36	88 80
Kings	577	1014	1365	1500	1141	88	4923	371	4622	328	7	1	966	225	1695	1615	111	31 60
Lunenburg	777	1579	1479	1689	1899	410	7239	175	7485	636	5	4	554	229	2628	2196	163	65 00
Pictou	514	978	1526		2234	344	6325	460	6681	490	6		605	256	2899	2219	384	259 40
Queens	159	305	406	430	662	148	2065	73	2051	171			169	72	1066	726	48	25 00
Richmond	373	501	670	601	979	227	2851	183	2756	320	3	1	546	108	1232	286	84	24 65
Shelburne	293	550	751	739	662	197	3430	79	3417	323	3		252	116	1379	983	123	88 96
Victoria	278	478	494	496	372	81	1942	287	1980	163			390	47	882	274	17	18 00
Yarmouth	345	725	978	1066	1613	201	4830	89	4756	370	4	2	347	161	2032	1766	229	69 72
Total, 1895.	9503	16405	21190	21878	27343	4235	95811	4744	94422	6835	43	15	9460	3425	34390	24344	2437	1269 37
" 1894.	9625	16420	21027	21847	25699	4092	94111	4599	93888	7485	55	9	8932	3676	35479	20750	2029	1072 78
Increase.			164	31	1644	143	1700	145	484			6	508			3794	408	196 59
Decrease.	122	15								650	12			251	1089			

TABLE VII.—SECTION STATISTICS, (FINANCIAL.)

Nova Scotia, Year ended July, 1895.

SECTION STATISTICS.

COUNTIES.	Value of all School property (ground, buildings, fixtures, &c.,) belonging to the Section.	Valuation of property in Section according to last Assessment Roll.	Total amount voted at last annual meeting for all school purposes.	Portion voted for building and repairs.	Total amount of Teachers' salaries paid during the Section, including the Provincial Grant.	No. of Volumes in Library (if any), belonging to School.	No. of Wall Maps Globes and Charts.	Estimated Value of all Scientific Apparatus and Collections.	Estimated value of total Literary and Scientific School Equipment.
Annapolis	$70,674 00	$4,356,910 00	$18,771 00	$3,390 50	$17,978 75	124	398	$310 60	$1,438 00
Antigonish	23,644 00	2,569,803 00	8,491 00	637 50	27,828 75	3032	219	793 50	4,820 00
Cape Breton	60,933 00	3,032,452 00	25,545 00	3,341 00	22,248 00	307	299	430 00	1,973 00
Colchester	81,519 00	4,584,276 00	27,654 00	3,624 00	20,172 00	275	595	559 00	2,453 25
Cumberland	136,653 00	6,635,128 00	29,835 00	4,745 00	27,597 00	301	681	715 00	2,151 00
Digby	43,994 00	2,074,262 00	15,458 39	4,935 00	15,162 69	135	275	165 50	1 047 00
Guysboro	41,263 00	962,054 00	17,987 00	5,152 40	11,511 00	192	228	167 50	609 00
Halifax County	49,356 00	3,523,666 00	25,862 75	1,932 50	22,270 68	95	475	99 50	1,659 85
Halifax City	250,000 00	21,143,500 00	98,200 00	4,000 00	60,462 50	1710	411	438 00	1,673 00
Hants	71,345 00	4,448,461 00	19,596 00	2,196 00	18,526 00	68	396	407 00	1,513 00
Inverness	35,190 00	1,163,571 00	13,729 00	2,277 00	10,452 50	22	283	35 00	1,352 50
Kings	68,717 00	4,881,748 00	20,060 00	2,545 00	18,302 00	143	476	398 00	1,926 00
Lunenburg	67,566 00	4,135,082 00	44,392 00	26,742 00	12,375 00	7	452	250 00	1 361 75
Pictou	169,325 00	4,656,503 00	31,065 00	4,526 00	28,178 00	1343	609	1110 00	4,598 00
Queens	25,850 00	1 104,515 00	6,391 00	116 00	7,588 50	5	168	185 00	781 00
Richmond	15,231 00	820,248 00	7,530 70	1,975 00	6,743 65	204	188	319 00	752 50
Shelburne	47,290 00	1,424,481 00	11,502 00	1,608 00	10,993 50	53	393	120 00	1,175 00
Victoria	15,831 00	453,112 00	5,111 00	906 00	5,962 00		112	50 00	284 25
Yarmouth	126,654 00	6 720,602 00	25,961 00	3,190 00	22,306 00	258	480	534 00	2,135 00
Total 1885	$1,401,155 00	$78 702,374 00	$453,144 84	$ 77,838 00	$375,725 02	8274	7138	$7106 60	$33,708 10
" 1894	1,360,784 00	80,096,411 50	454,200 13	134,710 90	339,848 22	6537	7161	8277 50	33,589 58
Increase	$40,371 00		$1,055 29		$35,876 80	1737		$1170 90	$113 52
Decrease		$1,394,037 50		$56,872 90			23		

TABLE VIII. — TIME TABLE.

Nova Scotia, Year ended July, 1895.

AVERAGE NO. OF MINUTES PER WEEK TAKEN BY TEACHERS DURING THE YEAR IN GIVING INSTRUCTION IN THE VARIOUS GROUPS OF SUBJECTS SPECIFIED BELOW. *(For all Schools in each County.)*

COUNTIES.	Arithmetic.	Drawing.	History.	Geography.	Book-keeping.	Writing.	English Composition, Gram., Lit.	Reading and Elocution.	Spelling and Dictation.	Object Lessons on Nature.	Moral and Patriotic Duties.	Hygiene and Temperance.	Vocal Music.	Calisthenics and Military Drill.
Annapolis	288.	51.	102.	125.	25.	83.	119.	300.	147.	32.	25.	44.	25.	19.
Antigonish	293.	34.	66.	78.	25.	97.	136.	356.	117.	33.	29.	32.	16.	13.
Cape Breton	320.3	32.	66.	91.6	13.3	103.5	113.6	365.4	140.	27.	29.2	38.	25.	10.
Colchester	288.5	55.5	99.	115.	31.	91.5	127.	323.5	167.	34.5	22.	110.	43.	22.
Cumberland	314.	54.	89.	115.	38.	98.	125.	360.	185.	37.	18.	40.	38.	23.
Digby	309.	66.	75.	106.	38.	94.	99.	356.	168.	41.	29.	39.	30.	12.
Guysboro	334.	42.	103.	64.	18.	63.	130.	424.	217.	39.	19.	42.	22.	12.
Halifax County	294.	56.	77.	93.	30.	104.	94.	348.	159.	31.	28.	44.	33.	22.
Halifax City	368.	64.	84.	80.	34.6	143.	100.	254.	124.	52.	25.4	29.	54.	45.
Hants	353.5	76.4	122.7	153.4	19.	116.1	146.9	361.1	204.5	43.6	25.	63.5	53.	35.6
Inverness	291.	32.	79.	85.	44.5	97.	117.	402.	126.	31.	30.6	32.	16.	10.
Kings	317.4	68.1	127.5	175.8	21.	101.8	147.1	406.9	174.4	41.6	17.6	57.2	39.4	30.6
Lunenburg	352.	59.	87.	131.	32.	123.	111.	385.	236.	36.	19.7	60.2	37.	19.3
Pictou	279.	41.	81.	101.	17.	100.	111.	328.	173.	30.	15.7	35.	28.	19.7
Queens	330.	65.	94.	122.	17.3	99.	112.	319.	197.	30.4	16.	38.7	30.	15.8
Richmond	319.	34.7	47.9	58.3	22.	81.5	136.5	383.7	119.2	24.	16.	43.4	19.3	20.4
Shelburne	278.	71.	103.	125.	24.	96.	116.	314.	187.	34.	20.	45.	31.	30.
Victoria	301.	85.	93.	101.	24.	100.	130.	347.	124.	31.	20.	26.	18.	10.
Yarmouth	331.	62.	92.	116.	29.	100.	115.	312.	170.	36.	24.	39.	30.	25.
Total 1895	313.7	52.	88.8	107.2	26.1	99.8	120.3	349.7	164.4	35.	23.	45.6	30.9	22.
" 1894	295.	43.4	86.2	112.9	31.8	98.3	111.3	323.5	156.3	32.3	24.5	32.4	21.9	14.2
Increase	18.7	8.6	2.6				9.	26.2	8.1	2.7		13.2	9.	7.8
Decrease				5.7	5.7	1.5					1.5			

TABLE VIII.—TIME TABLE.—Continued.

Nova Scotia, Year ended July, 1895.

AVERAGE No. OF MINUTES PER WEEK TAKEN BY TEACHER DURING THE YEAR IN GIVING INSTRUCTION IN THE VARIOUS GROUPS OF SUBJECTS SPECIFIED BELOW.

Counties	Practical Mathematics	No. of Schools	Algebra	No. of Schools	Geometry	No. of Schools	Botany, Zoology, Geology, etc.	No. of Schools	Physiology	No. of Schools	Physics	No. of Schools	Chemistry	No. of Schools	Latin	No. of Schools	Greek	No. of Schools	French	No. of Schools	German	No. of Schools	Manual Training	No. of Schools
Annapolis	64.	18	8.	81	75.	68	41.		43.	58	28.	21	48.	49	63.	33	63.	12	100.	3			15.	8
Antigonish	145.	3	38.	43	84.	31	54.		65.	18	68.	5	18.	12	665.	4	640.	3	292.	1				4
Cape Breton	51.2	12	115.7	72	75.3	48	33.5		36.	90	50.	8	51.7	22	125.	17	10.	5	63.5				27.5	3
Colchester	103.	6	66.	90	59.	73	29.		25.	77	27.	25	52.8	39	21.2	19	27.	8	255.	2			46.	2
Cumberland	52.	4	58.	78	54.	63	40.		28.	89	37.	36	38.	36	107.	16			22.	1			40.	1
Digby	21.	4	70.	38	68.	27	61.		34.	23	31.	3	58.	20	106.	7		4	266.	2			58.	1
Guysboro	45.	35	92.	45	75.	32	29.		21.	20	33.	8	34.	13	83.	7	10.	4	136.5		110.	2	10.	4
Halifax County	42.	19	61.	64	55.	40	35.		33.	46	38.	8	38.	18	57.	7	40.	4	111.	1	60.	1	587.	23
Halifax City	3.	3		19	105.	10			32.	3		2		3	135.	3		3	60.				56.	2
Hants	70.8	24	78.2	70	62.7	67	28.		31.1	64	33.8	19	46.	38	3.	20	110.	9	17.	1			150.	7
Inverness	6.	14	52.	81	28.	61	40.6		2.	30	8.	7	4.	26	86.2	11	10.	10	82.5	1			2.	
Kings	54.1	13	84.4	74	79.2	73	8.		41.4	66	39.4	15	40.	51	100.	41	3.	9	75.	4			15.	2
Lunenburg	104.	32	88.	69	60.	47	34.		28.	46	43.	10	49.	23	81.	12	4.	2	147.					
Pictou	51.6	17	96.3	106	73.	93	40.		9.	74	33.	17	44.	42	115.	29	120.	15	70.	3	30.	1	60.	1
Queens	18.	4	111.	21	84.	18	37.		30.	19	46.	6	6.	10	50.	8		2	196.					
Richmond	50.	9	100.6	34	53.2	26	31.7		2.	13	31.5	4	31.6	13	91.	14	18.	4	30.	1			7.	2
Shelburne	30.	4	67.	47	65.	36	22.		28.	40	25.	9	2.5	23	3.	3	132.	2	20.	2				
Victoria	4.	8	70.	38	24.	20	10.		3.	18	9.	6	2.	12	18.	18	2.5	4	113.	1			10.	1
Yarmouth	52.	6	57.	54	63.	39	33.		29.	44	34.	7	41.	25	96.			6			51.	2	120.	
Total 1895	62.6	235	82.7	1124	65.4	885	33.8	778	30.3	778	35.8	216	46.1	475	116.6	274	130.	109	108.	24	62.5	6	80.2	63
" 1894	80.	119	99.1	778	72.9	580	36.6	607	34.1	607	43.5	194	59.5	289	154.6	169	171.5	69	144.9	16	99.5	6	59.6	34
Inc. / Dec.	17.4	116	16.4	346	7.5	95	2.8	95	3.8	171	7.7	22	13.4	186	38.	105	41.5	40	36.9	8	37.		20.6	29

TABLE IX.—CLASSIFICATION OF PUPILS.

Nova Scotia, Year ended July, 1895.

Counties	Kindergarten	No. of Pupils in each Grade according to Provincial Course of Study												Grades IX to XII				Transfers	
		Grade I	Grade II	Grade III	Grade IV	Grade V	Grade VI	Grade VII	Grade VIII	Grade IX	Grade X	Grade XI	Grade XII	No. holding Provincial certificate	Total No. High School Pupils	No. High School Pupils taking full course	No. High School pupils taking partial course	No. of Pupils transferred out of school	No. of Pupils transferred into school
Annapolis		749	509	456	473	515	508	482	479	358	149	60	3	72	570	413	157	13	13
Antigonish		585	446	438	507	380	393	341	249	99	54	46	13	51	212	163	49	178	178
Cape Breton	60	1830	958	1028	872	678	534	653	451	204	91	22	10		319	284	35	43	23
Colchester		922	703	713	744	690	681	730	509	290	71	57	13	12	431	332	99	156	159
Cumberland		1902	1189	1142	1175	967	763	879	448	198	82	27		52	307	233	74	81	81
Digby	54	914	669	638	615	512	470	423	289	139	35	13		7	187	111	76	5	4
Guysboro	111	748	550	469	507	396	412	352	240	91	32	20		7	143	120	23	30	17
Halifax County	407	1259	954	908	1033	895	681	638	247	127	23			6	127	98	29		
Halifax City		1620	1028	872	1022	713	609	527	342	193	112	79		149	384	372	12	666	735
Hants		740	610	583	644	617	481	563	498	305	77	36		33	418	285	133	10	9
Inverness		1336	876	853	771	592	583	530	389	94	25	12		15	65	49	16	10	10
Kings		645	432	440	609	961	673	631	548	506	162	56		50	724	518	206	57	57
Lunenburg	30	1270	964	942	1064		784	812	370	150	73	14	18	36	236	174	62	14	14
Pictou		907	899	899	888	761	638	984	709	313	193	76		229	520	464	56	55	55
Queens	2	325	319	248	279	186	252	234	154	94	25	10		20	125	76	49	3	3
Richmond		926	431	464	387	289	226	162	90	49	7	3			51	44	7		
Shelburne		654	459	410	522	399	343	348	282	126	49	14	3	21	188	154	34	57	57
Victoria		422	292	280	274	245	226	197	158	69	25	11			31	18	13	12	12
Yarmouth		1152	754	578	625	482	454	368	293	148	46	20	8	26	221	177	44	104	111
Total 1895	664	18806	13042	12361	13011	10533	9711	9854	6745	3553	1331	576	68	786	5259	4085	1174	1494	1538
" 1894	605	18303	13489	12184	12672	11158	9202	9409	6489	2922	1186	460	82	349	4326	3231	1095	1227	1231
Increase	59	503		177	339		509	445	256	631	145	116		437	933	854	79	267	307
Decrease			447			625							14						

TABLE X.—ANALYSIS OF HIGH SCHOOL STUDIES (GRADE IX OR D).

Nova Scotia, Year ended July, 1895.

COUNTIES	English	Latin	French	History	Geography	Botany	Physics	Drawing	Book-keeping	Arithmetic	Algebra	Geometry	Manual Training	Total No. High School Pupils	No. Pupils taking full regular course	No. taking partial or special course
Annapolis	356	29		349	354	264	275	315	324	357	315	290	12	358	247	111
Antigonish	54	30	16	56	56	42	38	42	45	59	54	45		59	39	
Cape Breton	210	19	27	210	210	204	204	195	184	202	206	292		210	180	30
Colchester	289	130	73	280	290	225	200	274	278	286	285	270	1	290	207	83
Cumberland	180	47	9	191	193	147	146	171	186	198	178	162	32	198	136	62
Digby	140	20	4	124	140	89	102	122	135	140	114	111		140	75	65
Guysboro	73	8		70	67	43	54	60	73	73	67	59		73	70	3
Halifax County	98	20	42	109	112	101	94	111	111	112	112	109		112	84	28
Halifax City	193	158	69	193	193	193	193	193	193	193	193	193	18	193	193	
Hants	277	27	4	281	292	201	203	237	287	299	268	243		300	172	128
Inverness	73	17	40	73	63	61	61	61	63	63	63	61		65	49	16
Kings	494	63	23	479	497	353	313	384	432	498	439	310	61	505	291	214
Lunenburg	130	7	5	146	146	89	74	96	140	147	133	133	13	150	90	60
Pictou	291	83	66	283	285	245	238	260	284	296	278	268		305	234	71
Queens	75	6	3	77	81	64	49	63	79	84	61	56		90	38	41
Richmond	41	2	7	41	41	40	40	40	39	41	41	40		41	38	3
Shelburne	122	27	3	122	122	109	99	114	120	122	113	111		122	94	28
Victoria	18			18	18	18	18	18	18	18	18	18		18	10	8
Yarmouth	140	9	37	142	146	106	117	133	138	147	146	144		147	108	39
Total 1895	3264	702	428	3257	3906	2594	2518	2889	3099	3335	3088	2834	137	3376	2386	990
" 1894	2650	742	373	2491	2535	2162	1981	2147	2451	2632	2484	2342	27	2703	1772	849
Increase	614		55	766	771	432	537	742	648	703	604	492	110	673	614	141
Decrease		40														

TABLE XI.—ANALYSIS OF HIGH SCHOOL STUDIES. (GRADE X OR C.)

Nova Scotia, Year ended July, 1895.

Counties	English	Latin	Greek	French	German	History	Geography	Chemistry	Drawing	Book-keeping	Arithmetic	Algebra	Geometry	Manual Training	No. holding Prov. High School Certificates	Total No. High School Pupils	No. pupils taking full regular course	No. taking partial or special course
Annapolis	147	41	1	4		148	148	133	132	135	149	146	143	15	33	149	122	27
Antigonish	48	52	8	24		46	46	44	42	45	48	48	45		15	52	52	
Cape Breton	87	16	1	24		87	87	85	82	82	87	87	87			87	82	5
Colchester	71	46		28		71	71	71	70	71	71	71	71		8	71	70	1
Cumberland	81	35	12	22		79	78	78	80	80	81	81	78		32	82	74	8
Digby	35	12		7		35	35	31	33	35	35	34	34		3	35	31	4
Guysboro	31	12				28	28	29	21	28	30	31	30		5	31	31	
Halifax County	20	1	6	7	2	19	20	20	19	19	21	21	19		6	21	18	3
Halifax City	112	82	16	51	16	110	110	111	112	110	112	111	109	6	81	112	105	7
Hants	73	9	1	11	3	72	73	63	72	71	73	72	67		2	73	60	13
Inverness	24	15	1	11		30	30	19	21	21	24	24	22			24	16	8
Kings	148	42	6	4		148	148	120	126	146	148	139	141		11	149	127	22
Lunenburg	72	14		55		73	73	72	72	71	70	72	72		26	73	71	2
Pictou	186	79	27	1	7	181	189	146	178	193	190	189	181		87	201	176	25
Queens	25	3				23	25	21	22	25	25	23	23		13	25	18	7
Richmond	7	3	3	4		7	7	6	7	6	7	7	7			7	6	
Shelburne	49	7				49	49	42	47	49	49	49	49		9	49	46	1
Victoria	9	8				9	9	9	9	9	9	9	9					
Yarmouth	46	6		16		46	44	45	43	43	46	46	45		16	46	42	3
Total, 1895	1271	483	82	268	28	1261	1270	1145	1188	1299	1275	1260	1232	21	347	1287	1147	140
" 1894	1095	461	52	261	32	1093	1091	973	982	1049	1106	1086	1080	24	261	1113	903	210
Increase	176	22	30	7		168	179	172	206	190	169	174	152		86	174	244	
Decrease					4									3				70

TABLE XII.—ANALYSIS OF HIGH SCHOOL STUDIES (GRADE XI OR B.).

Nova Scotia, Year ended July, 1895.

COUNTIES.	English	Latin	Greek	French	German	History	Physics	Algebra	Geometry	Prac. Mathematics	Physiology	Manual Training	No. holding Prev. High School Certificates	Total No. High School Pupils	No. Pupils taking full regular course	No. taking partial or special course
Annapolis	60	16	2	3		59	58	60	60	59	55	7	36	60	54	6
Antigonish	43	20	2	21		18	40	37	37	35	35		25	46	45	1
Cape Breton	22	6	3	3		22	22	22	22	22	22			22	22	
Col᷏der ᷏land	57	44	13	16	1	57	57	57	57	57	57		4	57	57	4
Digby	27	16		7		28	27	28	25	28	14		20	27	23	4
Guysboro	13	7				13	13	13	13	13	9		7	13	9	
Halifax County	20	10		8	20	19	20	20	20	19	12	6		17	17	5
Halifax City	79	49	15	31	4	76	77	77	78	77	71		68	79	74	2
Hants	34	5	1			29	34	35	35	34	27		21	35	33	
Inverness	13	7	3	7		13	13	13	13	13	3	3	3	13	13	7
Kings	54	25	7			55	50	64	53	49	42	8	33	56	49	4
Lunenburg	14	8	22	26	6	14	14	14	14	14	14		14	14	14	1
I᷏tou	75	49	2			69	20	73	74	71	70	1	56	78	72	3
Queens	10	2	2			10	9	10	10	9	8		8	10	9	3
R᷏nd	3	5			2	3	3	3	3	3				3		
᷏le	12	4				11	11	12	12	13	2			14	11	1
V᷏ ta	4	2		12		4	4	4	4							
Yarmouth	20					15	20	20	20	19	10	8	10	20	19	
Total 1895	560	275	72	134	33	513	492	550	550	533	453	95	313	562	521	41
Total 1894	427	278	80	151	17	408	419	423	423	424	323	33	122	439	401	38
Increase	133				16	105	73	127	127	109	130	8	91	123	120	3
Decrease		3	8	17												

2

TABLE XIII.—ANALYSIS OF HIGH SCHOOL STUDIES (Grade XII or A).

Nova Scotia, Year ended July, 1895.

Counties.	English	Latin	Greek	French	German	History	Botany	Physics	Chemistry	Algebra	Geometry	Psychology	Sanitary Science	Zoology	Geology	Astronomy	Navigation	Trigonometry	Manual Training	No. holding Prov. High School Certificates	Total No. High School Pupils	No. of pupils taking full regular course	No. taking partial or special course
Annapolis	3	3	3	3		3			3	1	3	3	3				3	5		3	3	1	2
Antigonish	15	13	5	10		5		12	2	5	5	12	5				1	5		11	13	13	
Cape Breton	7	18	10			9		9		10	10	5									13		13
Colchester																							
Cumberland																							
Digby																							
Guysboro																							
Halifax County																							
Halifax City																							
Hants																							
Inverness																							
Kings																							
Lunenburg																							
Pictou	15	14	6	8	2	15	11	9	12	13	13	14	14	7	10	11	8	10		18	18	17	1
Queens																							
Richmond																							
Shelburne	3	3	3			9				3	3							3		3	3	3	
Victoria																							
Yarmouth	8				6		8	8	9	8	8	8	8	8	8	8	8	8			8	8	
Total 1895	51	46	27	21	8	30	19	38	35	40	42	42	30	15	18	19	20	31		35	58	42	16
" 1894	61	57	37	31	6	55	11	41	31	44	45	54	45	10	4	16	5	36		14	67	55	12
Increase	10	11	10	10	2		8		4					5	14	3	15			21			4
Decrease						16		3		4	3	12	15					5			9	13	

TABLE XIV.—AVERAGE SALARY OF MALE TEACHERS.

Nova Scotia, School Year ended July, 1895.

Counties.	Class A—(Male) Prov. Grant	From Section	Total	Class B—(Male) Prov. Grant	From Section	Total	Class C—(Male) Prov. Grant	From Section	Total	Class D—(Male) Prov. Grant	From Section	Total
Annapolis			$854 72	$120 77	$266 29	$387 06	$90 57	$195 71	$286 28	$60 38	$140 00	$200 38
Antigonish			687 30	120 77	173 00	293 77	90 57	138 94	229 51	60 38	116 16	176 54
Cape Breton			850 00	120 77	274 05	384 82	90 57	145 27	235 84	60 38	101 20	161 58
Cumberland			1000 00	120 77	550 44	671 21	90 57	197 50	288 07	60 38	140 00	200 38
Digby			865 20	120 77	345 00	465 77	90 57	173 30	263 87	60 38	203 75	264 13
Guysboro			750 00	120 77	333 00	453 77	90 57	161 00	251 57	60 38	168 30	228 68
Halifax County			620 40	120 77	297 50	418 27	90 57	168 83	259 40	60 38	76 75	137 13
Halifax City			980 00	120 77	206 33	327 10	90 57	199 16	289 73	60 38	158 75	219 13
Hants			1218 00	120 77	661 00	781 77	90 57	440 00	530 57	60 38	119 75	180 13
Inverness			675 00	120 77	329 67	450 44	90 57	271 25	361 82	60 38	64 00	124 38
Kings			750 00	120 77	113 00	233 77	90 57	97 00	187 57	60 38	116 67	177 05
Lunenburg			823 00	120 77	246 55	367 32	90 57	190 22	280 79	60 38	83 33	153 71
Pictou			910 00	120 77	317 50	438 27	90 57	123 00	213 57	60 38	142 91	203 29
Queens			914 74	120 77	312 80	433 57	90 57	194 30	284 87	60 38	115 00	175 38
Richmond			750 00	120 77	207 50	328 27	90 57	262 50	353 07	60 38	102 75	163 13
Shelburne			585 00	120 77	263 60	384 37	90 57	140 40	230 97	60 38	111 33	171 71
Victoria			750 00	120 77	147 00	267 77	90 57	225 00	315 57	60 38	94 00	154 38
Yarmouth			1100 77	120 77	409 50	530 27	90 57	278 33	368 90	60 38	130 00	190 38
Total 1895			$837 99	$120 77	$298 50	$419 27	$90 57	$197 14	$287 71	$60 38	$121 92	$182 30
" 1896			801 89	111 88	326 19	438 07	83 90	191 86	275 76	55 94	124 76	180 70
Increase			$36 10		$27 69	$18 80		85 28			$2 84	
Decrease				8 89			$6 67		$11 95	$4 44		$1 60

TABLE XV.—AVERAGE SALARY OF FEMALE TEACHERS.

Nova Scotia, School Year ended July, 1895.

COUNTIES.	CLASS A—(FEMALE).			CLASS B—(FEMALE).			CLASS C—(FEMALE).			CLASS D—(FEMALE).		
	Prov. Grant.	From Section.	Total.	Prov. Grant.	From Section.	Total.	Prov. Grant.	From Section.	Total.	Prov. Grant.	From Section.	Total.
Annapolis				120 77	157 32	278 09	90 57	125 13	215 70	60 38	88 10	$148 48
Antigonish				120 77	155 00	275 77	90 57	124 33	214 90	60 38	93 09	153 47
Cape Breton				120 77	206 87	327 64	90 57	160 06	250 63	60 38	93 13	153 51
Colchester			$525 00	120 77	181 38	302 15	90 57	144 78	235 35	60 38	93 88	154 26
Cumberland			310 77	120 77	179 66	300 43	90 57	141 31	231 88	60 38	107 32	167 70
Digby				120 77	101 25	222 02	90 57	133 00	223 57	60 38	109 42	169 80
Guysboro				120 77	187 50	308 27	90 57	152 43	243 00	60 38	98 83	159 21
Halifax County			800 00	120 77	207 30	328 07	90 57	180 98	271 55	60 38	128 47	188 85
Halifax City			551 39	120 77	356 00	476 77	90 57	267 00	357 57	60 88	194 00	254 38
Hants				120 77	189 16	309 93	90 57	168 00	258 57	60 38	105 02	165 40
Inverness				120 77	100 00	220 77	90 57	85 00	175 57	60 38	56 00	116 38
Kings				120 77	186 10	306 87	90 57	130 43	221 00	60 38	98 76	159 14
Lunenburg				120 77	167 23	288 00	90 57	123 50	214 07	60 38	97 55	157 93
Pictou			481 15	120 77	174 39	295 16	90 57	131 50	222 07	60 38	93 45	153 83
Queens				120 77	211 67	332 44	90 57	128 00	216 57	60 38	92 65	153 03
Richmond							90 57	76 66	167 23	60 38	91 90	152 28
Shelburne				122 77	188 33	309 10	90 57	131 50	222 07	60 38	106 63	167 01
Victoria				120 77	237 00	357 77	90 57	120 00	210 57	60 38	77 00	137 38
Yarmouth				120 77	218 18	338 95	90 57	169 66	260 23	60 38	123 50	183 88
Total 1895			$543 66	$120 77	$189 13	$309 90	$90 57	$141 64	$232 21	$60 38	$102 56	$162 94
" 1894			652 05	111 88	207 34	319 22	83 90	144 03	227 93	55 94	100 56	156 50
Increase				8 89			6 67		4 28	4 44	2 00	$0 44
Decrease			$118 84		18 21	9 32		2 39				

TABLE XVI.

APPORTIONMENT OF COUNTY FUND TO TRUSTEES FOR YEAR ENDED JULY, 1895.

MUNICI-PALITIES.	Grand total days' attendance made by all the pupils.	On account of Teachers employed.	On account of average attendance of Pupils.	On account of Pupils attending Halifax School for Blind.	On account of Pupils attending Deaf and Dumb Institution, Halifax.	Total amount appropriated.	Amount per Pupil in attendance the Full Term.
Annapolis...	509,127	$ 2,749 37	$ 2,755 90	....	$ 300 00	$ 5,805 27	$ 1 20
Antigonish..	338.617	2,233 51	2,405 09	$ 75 00	120 00	4,833 60	1 44
Cape Breton	768,901	3,789 71	6,185 29	....	300 00	10,275 00	1 70
Colchester	668,716	2,981 13	2,916 02	300 00	420 00	6,617 15	1 41
Cumberland.	889.537	4,465 02	5,593 75	....	300 00	10,358 77	1 31
Digby	297,479	1,554 90	1,861 31	44 37	71 00	3,531 58	1 19
Clare......	197,618	1,024 38	1,333 36	30 63	49 00	2,437 37	1 29
Guysboro...	278,766	1,523 51	2,143 35	112 52	90 02	3,869 40	1 61
St. Mary's..	90,415	602 29	619 35	37 48	29 98	1,289 10	1 44
Halifax Co..	778,524	3,094 95	4 695 05	....	360 00	8,150 00	1 59
Hants, East.	239,264	1,416 80	1,285 65	....	147 55	2,850 00	1 13
" West	299,445	1,246 93	1,839 62	....	152 45	3,239 00	1 73
Inverness ..	568,343	3,862 04	3,676 65	75 00	120 00	7,733 69	1 29
Kings	505,828	2,987 31	3,544 69	225 00	....	6,757 00	1 46
Lunenburg..	647,548	3,287 44	4,092 47	123 92	198 28	7,702 11	1 34
Chester.....	133,451	661 00	892 21	26 08	41 72	1,621 01	1 41
Pictou.....	851,881	4,159 18	5,773 82	375 00	60 00	10,368 00	1 43
Queens......	247 873	1,529 49	1,577 71	75 00	....	3,182 20	1 32
Richmond..	309,208	1,753 20	2,319 09	75 00	180 00	4 327 29	1 48
Shelburne...	202,486	1,062 98	1,139 12	....	124 40	2,326 50	1. 21
Barrington..	182,818	891 66	1,224 14	....	115 60	2,231 40	1 53
Victoria	202,828	1,377 23	2,352 31	....	....	3,729 54	2 36
Yarmouth	327,760	1,547 57	2,118 98	130 53	69 62	3,866 70	1 14
Argyle.....	243,031	1,074 50	1,579 65	94 47	50 38	2,799 00	1 39
Total, 1895..	9,779,464	$50,876 10	$63,924 58	$1,800 00	$3,300 00	$119,900 68	$ 1 43
" 1894	9,473,189	50,520 41	65,875 45	1,462 50	2,640 00	120,507 36	
Increase	306,275	$ 346 69	....	$ 337 50	$ 660 00	....	
ecrease..	....	....	$ 1,950 87	....	....	$ 606 68	

TABLE XVII.

SPECIAL GOVERNMENT AID TO POOR SECTIONS.

COUNTIES.	Paid by Government over and above the ordinary Grants, towards Salaries of Teachers employed in Poor Sections.		TOTAL.
	First Half Year.	Second Half Year.	
Annapolis................	$ 95 45	$ 97 77	$193 22
Antigonish	135 70	143 87	279 57
Cape Breton...........	103 88	134 93	238 81
Colchester.............	123 39	166 77	290 16
Cumberland., ...	139 59	112 26	251 85
Digby.................	140 00	144 87	284 87
Guysboro	57 29	84 93	142 22
Halifax	103 60	130 79	234 39
Hants.................	119 98	147 72	267 70
Inverness..	134 19	159 21	293 40
Kings.................	118 74	120 64	239 38
Lunenburg	148 30	130 61	278 91
Pictou	102 34	122 73	225 07
Queens................	117 38	124 75	242 13
Richmond	88 63	103 05	191 68
Shelburne.............	39 76	45 38	85 14
Victoria..............	61 01	63 39	124 40
Yarmouth.............	59 52	71 25	130 77
Total, 1895	$1888 75	$2104 92	$3993 67
" 1894	1774 29	1873 02	3647 31
Increase	$ 114 46	$ 231 90	$ 346 36
Decrease			

TABLE XVIII.

POOR SECTIONS--SPECIAL COUNTY AID.

MUNICIPALITIES.	Number of these Sections having Schools.	Amount of County Assessment paid to these Schools over and above ordinary allowance.
Annapolis, County of	19	$ 185 10
Antigonish, "	18	201 88
Cape Breton, "	19	242 26
Colchester, "	24	219 78
Cumberland "	22	203 72
Digby, District of	15	185 13
Clare, "	6	84 13
Guysboro, "	8	110 34
St Mary's, "	4	40 91
Halifax, County of..........	18	233 60
Hants, District of, East	13	110 21
" " West.	8	106 47
Inverness, County of	21	252 53
Kings, "	26	291 18
Lunenburg and New Dublin, District of	15	148 34
Chester, District of..........	5	47 93
Pictou, County of	19	183 15
Queens, "	16	174 34
Richmond, "	13	162 85
Shelburne, District of........	3	43 07
Barrington, "	4	45 79
Victoria, County of..........	8	114 65
Yarmouth, District of.... ...	7	82 86
Argyle, "	5	54 39
Total, 1895	316	$3524 61
" 1894	304	3525 63
Increase............	12	....
Decrease............	.. ..	$ 1 02

TABLE XIX.—COUNTY ACADEMIES.

Academy.	Instructors.	Class of License.	Annual Salary.	Department, or subjects taught, (subjects may be given briefly by Nos 65 to 90, as in following table).	Hours per Day.
Annapolis	W. M. McVicar, A. M.	A. cl.	$ 900 00	All subjects	5¼
Antigonish	Rev. Daniel A. Chisholm, D. D	B.	500 00	3rd and 4th year Greek	2
	Rev. Alex. Chisholm, D D	A. cl.	750 00	Latin	4
	Rev. Alex. Thompson, D. D.	A. cl.	760 00	Physics, Higher Mathematics and English	4
	Edward Wm. Connolly. B. A.	A. cl	750 00	Junior English and Mathematics	4
	Sr. St. Margaret	B.	200 00	Mathematics, History and Geography	6
Cape Breton	E. T. MacKeen	A. cl.	900 00	Nos. 67, 68, 70, 71, 72, 75, 78, 83, 86	5
	F. I. Stewart, B. A (London)	A. cl.	750 00	" 69, 74, 77, 78, 79, 90, 81, 82, 84, 85, 87, 88.	5
Clare	T. M. Phalen	A. cl.	750 00	" 70, 71. 72, 74, 77, 81, 8? 84, 85, 67, 68.	3½
	J. C. McKinnon			" 75, 76, 78, 80.	3
Colchester	W. R. Campbell, M. A	A. cl.	1200 00	" 81, 82, 86, 87, 88	4¾
	Jas. Little	B.	1050 00	" 78, 80, 81, 83, 84	4¾
	M. D. Hemmeon, B. A.	A. cl.	800 00	" 72, 75, 76, 79, 83, 91	4¾
	Ellen M. Mackenzie M. A	A. cl.	525 00	" 71, 72, 78, 82, 86, 87, 89	4¾
	Ella Rettie	B.	350 00	" 71, 72, 74, 75, 76, 77	4¾
Cumberland	E. J. Lay	A. cl.	1200 00	" 71, 72, 76, 78, 79 80, 81, 82, 83, 86	6
	N. D. MacTavish	A. sc.	700 00	" 72, 74, 75, 77, 78, 80, 81, 84, 85	5
Digby	J. M. Longley, B. A.	A. cl.	750 00	All subjects	4¾
Guysboro	Edmund B. Smith, B. A., (Harvard)	A. cl.	750 00	All subjects	5

County	Name	Class	Salary	Subjects	No.
Halifax	Wm. T. Kennedy*	A. cl.	1600 00	Nos. 71, 75, 76, 81, 70, 68, 65, 81, 82	4
	Silvanus A. Morton, M. A	A. cl.	1250 00	" 74, 78, 79, 80, 84, 85	4
	Kate Mackintosh	A. cl.	840 00	" 66, 67, 63, 70, 71, 72, 75, 76, 83.	4
	Florence A. Peters	B. cl.	700 00	" 72, 74, 78, 90, 82, 84	4
	Jotham W. Logan, B. A.	A. cl.	1100 00	" 86, 87	4
	Kate F. Hill		250 00	" 77	2
	Jean V. Plotton		400 00	" 88	4
	Gunther Von der Groeben		300 00	" 89	4
	Nelson H. Gardner	A. cl.	540 00	" 90	4
Hants	John A. Smith, B. A.	A. cl.	1000 00	All subjects	4?
Inverness	D. S. McIntosh, B. A.	A. cl.	750 00	All subjects	5
Kings	Angus McI	A. cl.	1000 00	Nos. 66, 67, 68, 72, 74, 76, 78, 79, 80, 81, 83, 86.	5
	E. Hart Nichols	A. cl.	750 00	" 71, 72, 75, 76, 77, 82, 84. 85, 86, 87.	5
Lunenburg	Burgess McKittrick, B. A.	A. cl.	1000 00	All subjects	5
Pictou	Geo. B. Robinson, B. A.	A. cl.	750 00	Nos. 74, 77, 78, 80, 83	4
	Clarence L. Moore, B. A.	A. cl.	850 00	" 75, 79, 81, 82, 84, 85	4
	A. C. L. Oliver, B. A.	A. cl.	850 00	" 72, 76	4
	Robt. McLellan	A. cl.	1200 00	" 86, 87, 88, 89	4
Queens	J. D. Sprague	A. cl.	750 00	All subjects	5
Shelburne	C. Stanley Bruce	A. cl.	750 00	All subjects	5
Victoria	Robert S Campbell	A. cl.	750 00	All subjects	6
Yarmouth	A. Cameron	A. cl.	1200 00	Nos. 72, 75, 76, 79, 80, 81, 83, 84, 88, 89	5
	Anto cate Forbes, B. A.	A. cl.	900 00	" 67, 74, 76, 77, 78, 80, 82, 83, 84, 85, 86	5
	Beatrice Tooker		125 00	" 72, 80, 82, 85, 88	2

TABLE XIX.—COUNTY ACADEMIES.—(Continued).

ACADEMY.	16	17	18	19	20	21	22	23	24	25	26	27	28	29	30	31	32	33	34
Ann apolis	30	23.1	77.	34	32	24.4	76.3	35	29	20.9	72.1	36	26	22.4	86.2	103	102	2449.5	2204.5
Antigonish	135	114.6	82.5	152	149	124.3	83.6	100	145	115.2	86.5	164	133	114.7	85.8	103	108	11730	1486.5
Cape Breton	46	38.8	84.	60	60	49.8	83.	63	55	49.	89.	63	50	40.	80.	99	103	4440.	1720.
Clare	17	15.4	90.6	18	18	17.4	96.6	18	17	15.7	92.2	15	15	14.8	98.7	97	101	1605.	1539.
Colchester	203	164.4	80.2	212	204	158.9	73.9	218	195	145.6	74.	172	144	144.7	78.3	100	102	16009.	14808.
Cumberland	72	56.	83.3	79	73	36.4	77.1	83	71	56.5	70.5	67	67	54.	80.6	103	98	5818.5	6418.5
Digby	26	19.5	75.	27	25	20.1	80.	28	31	19.7	73.	25	25	18.9	76	103	101	2044.	1936.5
Guysboro	44	30.8	70.	46	43	32.2	74.9	46	42	30.5	72.6	39	39	30.9	79.2	103	99	3247.5	3038
Halifax	265	239.8	90.5	272	270	239.4	88.1	275	261	224.2	84.6	283	241	217.6	83.1	98	101	23492	22387.
Hants	34	25.7	84.4	50	33	39.	76.9	41	39	29.6	76.	41	33	27.2	82.4	99	101	2907.	2486.5
Inverness	18	12.5	63.4	20	20	16.6	2.8	23	22	17.3	78.7	23	19	15.5	81.6	103	103	1507.	1694.
Kings	83	61.2	76.5	92	80	44	76.8	99	84	67.2	80.	103	81	69.2	85.4	103	103	6299.5	903.
Lunenburg	42	33.7	80.3	42	35	28.5	80.2	44	57	31.	84.	47	40	31	77.6	104	108	3225	3200.
Pictou	188	157.	83.5	230	214	162.5	75.8	236	234	154.6	84.	229	165	119.4	71.8	108	108	17197	15202.
Queens	27	25.1	93.	27	27	23.6	87.4	27	26	22.3	85.8	27	24	22.	91.5	103	108	2904.5	2393.6
Shelburne	32	24.4	76.3	36	36	22.9	63.6	30	34	26.3	77.4	36	31	23.1	74.5	102	98	409.	2527.
Victoria	27	15.3	56.7	30	30	21.2	70.7	30	28	22.1	78.9	31	26	20.1	77.3	103	108	1828	2186.
Yarmouth	40	35.5	88.8	43	41	34.1	83.1	46	37	28.1	73.9	46	33	30.4	92.2	98	101	3341	2945.
Total, 1895,	1326	1099.8	82.9	1440	1396	1123.6	80.5	1498	1354	1078.8	79.6	1526	1220	1016.	83.2	101.5	102.5	112061.5	107478.
" 1894.	1236	993.6	80.8	1356	1301	977.	75.	1402	1237	937.1	80.6	1449	1117	887.3	79.4	101	103.	983363	96428.5
Increase	90	101.2	2.1	93	95	146.	5.5	96	117	81.7		107	103	128.7	3.8	.4	.5	13699.5	12049.5
Decrease											1.								

TABLE XIX.—COUNTY ACADEMIES.—(Continued.)

ACADEMY.	Between 5 and 15 years. [36]	Over 15 years. [37]	Total annual enrolment. [38]	Boys. [39]	Girls. [40]	Total days' attendance for year. [41]	Days taught during year. [42]	Daily present on an average during year. [43]	Av. of quarterly percentages of attendance. [44]	20 days or less. [45]	Over 20 and up to 50 days. [46]	Over 50 and up to 100 days. [47]	Over 100 and up to 150 days. [48]	Over 50 and up to 200 days. [49]	Over 200 days. [50]	Belonging to this School Section. [51]	From bey'nd lim-its of S. Sec., but within County. [52]	From beyond lim-its of Coun'y. [53]
Annapolis	7	29	36	13	23	4,654.	205	22.7	77.9	1	6	3	10	16	11	22	10	4
Antigonish	11	153	164	106	58	23,216.5	211	118.6	84.6	2	14	18	40	79	3	41	50	73
Cape Breton	12	51	63	40	23	9,160.	202	45.3	84.	2	2	8	16	32		42	13	8
	3	15	18	18		3,744.5	98	15.9	94.5			2	1	15	3		10	8
Colchester	84	137	221	87	134	30,817.	201	153.3	78.1	6	12	31	48	121		135	69	17
Cumberland	35	48	83	27	56	11,237.	193	56.7	80.1	2	6	14	17	44		60	23	
Digby	9	20	29	16	13	4,020.5	204	19.7	76.		3	4	7	15		23	5	1
Guysboro	24	22	46	23	23	6,285.5	202	31.1	74.2	3	5	5	13	22		37	8	
Halifax	106	177	283	127	156	45,879.	199	230.5	79.9	1	13	16	30	221	2	216	52	15
Hants	10	31	41	12	29	5,803.5	200	29.	79.0			7	8	24	1	33	8	
Inverness	7	16	23	16	7	3,201.	206	15.5	78.1	1	4	1	3	12	5	16	7	
Kings	42	61	103	51	52	13,204.5	204	64.7	79.7	7	11	13	20	51		62	37	4
Lunenburg	12	35	47	16	31	6,425.	207	31.	81.	3	7		6	25	8	34	13	
Pictou	48	181	229	125	104	32,399.	216	150.	76.4	11	18	30	57	113		102	83	44
Queens	6	21	27	6	21	4,894.	211	23.2	89.5			1	2	16		15	12	
Shelburne	10	26	36	16	20	4,936.	200	24.7	72.9	4	2	6	10	18		31	5	
Victoria	10	21	31	16	15	4,042.5	211	19.	71.2		1	7	9	13		20	11	
Yarmouth	18	28	46	21	25	6,286.	199	31.6	85.		2	8	2	30		39	7	
Total 1895	454	1072	1526	736	790	220,179.5	204	082.5	80.5	45	107	175	299	867	33	928	423	175
" 1894	493	926	1419	696	723	193,692.5	204	966.	78.9	46	99	215	293	734	32	926	350	143
Increase		146	107	40	67	26,487.		116.5	1.6		8		6	133	1	2	73	32
Decrease	39									1		40						

TABLE XIX.—COUNTY ACADEMIES.—(Continued).

AVERAGE NO. OF MINUTES PER WEEK TAKEN BY TEACHER DURING THE YEAR IN GIVING INSTRUCTION IN THE VARIOUS GROUPS OF SUBJECTS SPECIFIED BELOW.

ACADEMY.	65 Calisthenics and Military Drill.	66 Vocal Music.	67 Hygiene and Temperance.	68 Moral and Patriotic Duties.	69 Object Lessons on Nature.	70 Spelling and Dictation.	71 Reading and Elocution.	72 Eng. Gram., Lit., &c. Composition.	73 Writing.	74 Book-keeping.	75 Geography.	76 History.	77 Drawing.	78 Arithmetic.	79 Practical Mathematics.	80 Algebra.	81 Geometry.	82 Zoology, Botany, Geology, &c.	83 Physiology, Psychology.	84 Physics.	85 Chemistry.	86 Latin.	87 Greek.	88 French.	89 German.	90 Manual Training.
Annapolis	20	140	40	60			40	150		60	80	270	120	80	40	150	150	50	50	80	100	200	100	150		
Antigonish		60	150	15	80	30	60	1140		120	330	330	120	360	270	600	660	105	200	400	320	1800	640	420		
Cape ...ton		60	25	20	15	30	50	180		50	70	140	120	290	90	180	180	40	40	40	40	150	150	100		
Clare			10	10		60	90	210		60	60	60	60	135	180	90	120	120	145	60	90	170	170	170	30	
Colchester	30		15		30	45	300	832		290	240	745	350	385		615	600	150		240	130	1065	435	285		600
...Island				50			20	330		100	120	200	130	310	80	200	280	90	40	90	120	200		40		
Digby		10	10	10		10	20	160		60	60	90	40	120	100	120	180	90	40	70	80	180		40		
Guysboro		50	50	50	30	10	30	200		50	160	150	315	160	90	90	180	50	30	70	70					
Halifax	50		10			85	265	570		210	315	315	55	750	100	570	660	125	350	80	625	715	600	600	600	
Hants			50	5		10	20	100		30	50	100	60	150	100	100	150	34	60	80	100	60	80	45	60	
Inverness			12	4			135	220		90	90	100		60	30	70	180	13	3	60	30	225	40	150		
Kings		3	20	5		15	50	615		90	120	270	120	130	130	180	130	90	40	130	80	180	50			
...nenburg			15				60	230		30	80	120	70	240	90	100	160	54	40	40	80	60				
...bou						10	60	600		90	30	540	30	270	60	365	550	277	120	173	210	630	260	310		
Queens			10				30	200		10	100	290	64	270	108	220	200	75	5	5	100	200		70		
Shelburne			10			10	20	165		35	150	100	75	45	45	40	300	33	30	60	90	40	80	43		
Victoria		5						400		15	50	100	20	300	75	200	180	10	15	115	100	20	40			
Yarmouth			20			10		500		150	60	130	70	150	90	415	270	220	90	170	200	325	50	415	20	
Average, 1895	6	18	22	10	7	17	73	382		80	121	220	93	226	120	250	295	91	82	132	143	362	141	155	39	33
" 1894	4	10	21	11	1	11	45	394		70	129	188	92	209	108	218	285	68	77	115	101	378	124	180	42	70
Increase	2	6	1		6	6	28	12		10		32	3	17	12	32	10	23	5	17	42	16	17	5	3	37
Decrease				1							8															

TABLE XIX.—COUNTY ACADEMIES.—(Continued.)

ANALYSIS OF HIGH SCHOOL STUDIES.

ACADEMY.	ENGLISH Grade IX.	Grade X.	Grade XI.	Grade XII.	Total.	LATIN Grade IX.	Grade X.	Grade XI.	Grade XII.	Total.	GREEK Grade X.	Grade XI.	Grade XII.	Total.	FRENCH Grade IX.	Grade X.	Grade XI.	Grade XII.	Total.	GERMAN Grade X.	Grade XI.	Grade XII.	Total.	HISTORY Grade IX.	Grade X.	Grade XI.	Grade XII.	Total.
Annapolis	16	11	9		36		3	4		12		2		2	12	4	1		17					16	11	9		36
Antigonish	54	48	43	15	160	30	52	20	13	5	5	9		15	16	24	21	10	71					51	46	18	5	120
Cape Breton	31	21	11	7	63	12	7	5		24	5	3		8	10	7	2		19					31	21	11		63
Clare	12	6			18	4	6			10				10	12	5			17					12	6			18
Colchester	110	46	52		215	110	37	41	13	201	12	12	10	34	78	23	16		112			20		110	46	52	8	216
Cumberland	38	33	14		83	23	17	10		50						22	7		29	4	4			36	33	14		83
Digby	12	8	9		29	7	6	7		20						2			6	3				12	8	9		29
Guysboro	28	9	9		46																			28	9	9		46
Halifax	125	84	74		283	107	64	47		218	16	15		31	8	36	26	8	70	28		2	28	125	82	71		278
Hants	18	9	14		41	14	1	5		20		1	1	2	1				1	7		7		18	4	14		41
Inverness	10	4	9		23	3	4	7		14		3		4		4	7		11					10	4	9		23
Kings	40	30	33		103	25	23	22		70		6		6										40	30	33		103
Lunenburg	16	23	23		47	4	8	8		14														16	23	8		47
Pictou	70	83	55	15	223	19	43	42		118	18	20		31	21	31	16	8	76	2	10	2		67	79	50	15	21
Queens	10	9	8		27	6	3	1		10					3	1	2		6					10	9	8		27
Shelburne	16	14	6		36	5		4		6		1		1										16	14	5		35
Victoria	18	9	4		31		8	4		12						10	6							18	9	4		31
Yarmouth	18	12	8	8	46	9	9	3	14	22	18				14				38	18	63	6	8	18	12	8	8	46
Total 1895	640	459	366	45	1510	383	291	221	41	936	58	63	21	144	174	169	114	26	473	7	10	28	45	634	451	332	36	1453
" 1894	608	431	308	57	1404	383	248	233	51	915	40	63	41	144	182	161	135	28	506	18	63	6	89	602	428	278	50	1358
Increase	32	28	58		106		43			21	18					8						22		32	23	54		95
Decrease				12				12	10				20		8		21	2	33	11	55		44				14	

TABLE XIX.—COUNTY ACADEMIES.—(Continued).

ANALYSIS OF HIGH SCHOOL STUDIES.

ACADEMY.	Geography Grade IX.	Geography Grade X.	Geography Grade XI.	Geography Total.	Botany Grade IX.	Botany Grade XII.	Botany Total.	Physics Grade IX.	Physics Grade XI.	Physics Grade XII.	Physics Total.	Chemistry Grade X.	Chemistry Grade XII.	Chemistry Total.	Drawing Grade IX.	Drawing Grade X.	Drawing Grade XI.	Drawing Total.	Book-keeping Grade XI.	Book-keeping Grade X.	Book-keeping Total.
Annapolis	16		9	38	16		16	16	9		25	11		11	16	11		27	16	11	27
Antigonish	51	46	18	115	37		37	33	40	12	85	44	12	56	37	42		79	40	45	85
Cape Breton	30	21		51	31		31	31	11		42	24		24	31	21		55	31	21	52
Clare	12	6		18	18		18	12			12	6		6	12	6		18	12	6	18
Col bester	110	46		156	110	1	111	110	32		171	46		46	110	46		156	110	46	156
Cu rberland	36	33		69	36		36	36	14		50	33		33	38	33		69	38	33	69
Digby	12	8	9	29	12		12	12	9		21			9	12	8		20	12	8	20
Guysboro	28	9	9	46	28		28	28	9		37	9		9	28	9		37	28	9	37
ax	125	82	71	278	125		125	125	72		197	84		84	125	84		209	125	82	207
Hants	18	9	14	41	18		18	18	14		32	9		9	18	9		27	18	9	27
Inverness	10	4	9	23	8		8	8	9		17	4		4	8	4		12	10	4	14
Kings	40	30		70	40		40	40	33		73	30		30	35	30		65	40	30	70
Lunenburg	16	23		39	16		16	16	8		24	23		23	16	23		39	16	23	39
Pictou	65	81		146	118	11	129	66		9	75	79	12	91	67	81		148	68	82	150
ns	10	9	8	27	10		10	10	8		18	9		9	10	10		19	10	9	19
Shelburne	16	14	5	35	16		16	16	5		21	14		14	16	14		30	16	14	30
Victoria	18	9		27	18		18	18			18	9		9	18	9		27	18	9	27
Yarmouth	16	12	16	46	18	8	26	18	8	8	34	12	8	20	18	2	16	46	18	12	30
Total 1895	631	453	168	1252	675	20	695	613	301	38	952	454	32	486	613	451	19	1083	624	453	1077
" 1894	603	427	206	1236	598	78	676	603	250	45	898	434	32	460	604	424	17	1045	605	423	1028
Increase	28	26		16	77		19	10	51		54	20		20	9	27	2	38	19	30	49
Decrease			38			58				7											

TABLE XIX.—COUNTY ACADEMIES.—(Continued.)

ANALYSIS OF HIGH SCHOOL STUDIES.

ACADEMY.	ARITHMETIC Grade IX	X	XI	Total	ALGEBRA Grade IX	X	XI	XII	Total	GEOMETRY Grade XI	X	IX	XI	Total	Prac Mathe matics Grade IX	Physiology Grade XI	Psychology Grade XI	Sanitary Science Grade XI	Zoology Grade XII	Geology Grade XII	Astronomy Grade XII	Navigation Grade XII	Trigonometry Grade XII	Manual Training Grade X
Annapolis	16	11	9	36	16	11	9		36	16	11	9		36	9	9						9	36	
Antigonish	54	48		102	49	48	37	5	139	40	45	37	5	127	36	25	12	5				34	35	
Cape Breton	31	21	11	63	31	21	11		63	31	21	11		63	11	11		11			1	11	11	
Clare	12	6		18	12	6			18	12	6			18										
Colchester	110	46		156	110	46	52	10	218	46	46	52	10	218	52	52	5	46				13	7 13	
Cumberland	36	33	14	83	36	33	14	5	83	36	33	13	13	82	82	13								52
Digby	12	8	9	29	12	8	9		29	12	8	9		29	9	9								
Guysboro	28	8		46	28	9	9		46	28	9	9		46	9	9						33	9	
Halifax	125	84		209	125	83	72		280	125	81	73		279	72	71			7	80		8	8	
Hants	18	9	14	41	18	9	14		41	18	9	14		41	14	14						8	6	
Inverness	10	4		14	21	4	9		21	8	4	9		21	9	9								
Kings	40	30	28	98	40	30	33		103	40	36	33		103	33	33	14						10	17
Lunenburg	16	23	8	47	16	23	8		47	16	23	8		47	8	5						8	8	
Pictou	70	82	54	206	68	81	53	13	215	67	81	54	13	215	51	51				10		8	10	
Queens	10	9	8	27	10	9	8		27	10	9	8		27	8	5			8		8	8	6	
Shelburne	16	14	6	36	16	14	6		36	16	14	4	8	36	6	6	14	14				5	6	
Victoria	9	9	4	31	16	9	4		31	10	18	4		31	4	4								
Yarmouth	18	12	8	38	18	12	8	8	46	18	12	8	8	46	4	8	8	8	8	20	8	8	8	39 19
Total 1895	640	658	182	1280	631	456	336	36	1479	621	451	357	36	1465	421	338	39	84	15	110	20	138	143	39
" 1894	610	432	259	1301	606	432	299	37	1374	608	429	302	38	1377	305	277	54	53	9	3	14	24	57	19
Increase	30	26			25	24	57		105	13	22	55	2	88	115	61		31	6	107	6	114	86	20
Decrease			77	21				1									15							

TABLE XIX.—COUNTY ACADEMIES.—(Continued).

ACADEMY	No. in each Grade admitted by Provincial Certificate.					Total No. High School Pupils.					No. High School Pupils taking full regular course.					No. taking partial or special course.				
	Grade IX.	Grade X.	Grade XI.	Grade XII.	Total.	Grade IX.	Grade X.	Grade XI.	Grade XII.	Total.	Grade IX.	Grade X.	Grade XI.	Grade XII.	Total.	Grade IX.	Grade X.	Grade XI.	IIX Grade.	Total.
Annapolis		5	7		12	16	11	9		36	16	11	8		35			1		1
Antigonish		15	25	11	51	54	51	46	13	164	54	51	45	13	163			1		1
Cape Breton		6	3	2	11	31	21	11		63	30	21	11		62	1				1
Clare						12	6			18	12	6			18					
Colchester		37	46	13	96	110	46	52	13	221	110	46	52	11	219				2	2
Cumberland		10	11	5	26	36	33	14		83	36	32	12		80		1	2		3
Digby		3	4		7	12	8	9		29	12	8	9		29					
Guysboro		2	9		11	28	9	9		46	28	9	9		46					
Halifax		81	68		149	125	84	74		283	125	78	70		273		6	4		10
Hants		1	12		13	18	9	14		41	18	9	14		41					
Inverness		1	7		8	10	4	9		23	8	4	9		21	2				2
Kings		3	22		25	40	30	33		103	40	30	33		103					
Lunenburg		13	8		21	16	23	8		47	16	23	8		47					
Pictou		84	56	18	158	71	84	56	18	229	66	81	52	17	216	5	3	4	1	13
Queens		7	4		11	10	9	8		27	10	9	8		27					
Shelburne		11	2		13	16	14	6		36	16	14	5		35			1		1
Victoria		7	3		10	18	9	4		31	18	9	4		31					
Yarmouth		5	7	7	19	18	12	8	8	46	18	12	8	8	46					
Total, 1895	2	291	294	56	641	641	463	370	52	1526	633	453	357	49	1492	8	10	13	3	34
" 1894		189	184	53	428	608	433	315	61	1417	593	423	303	52	1371	15	10	12	9	46
Increase	2	102	110	3	213	33	30	55		109	40	30	54		121			1		
Decrease									9					3		7			6	12

TABLE XIX.—COUNTY ACADEMIES.—(Continued).

Academy	IX Grade (Yrs.)	X Grade (Yrs.)	XI Grade (Yrs.)	XII Grade (Yrs.)	Provincial Grant	School Section Funds	Fees	Other Sources	Revenue Total	Salaries	Apparatus	Building and Repairs	Fuel and Attendance	Miscellaneous	Expenditure Total
Annapolis	14.92	16.84	17.77		$500 00	$750 00			$1250 00	$900 00		$150 00	$200 00		$1250 00
Antigonish	15.88	19.30	19.82	20.23	1500 00	500 00	$150 00	$1500 00	3650 00	3400 00	$100 00	40 00	100 00	$10 00	3650 00
Cape Breton	15.82	16.27	16.95		1000 00	1395 00			2395 00	1750 00	45 00	350 00	250 00		2395 00
Clare	17.15	19.9			500 00	250 00			750 00	750 00					750 00
Colchester	15.12	17.08	17.45	17.67	1720 00	2780 00			4500 00	3925 00	50 00	75 00	400 00	50 00	4500 00
Cumberland	14.91	15.72	16.8		1000 00	1000 00			2000 00	1900 00			100 00		2000 00
Digby	15.2	16.18	16.8		500 00	350 00			850 00	750 00			75 00	25 00	850 00
Guysboro	14.39	16.	16.62		500 00	250 00		4086 50	4836 50	750 00	44 00	4000 00	22 50	20 00	4836 50
Halifax	15.1	15.77	17.28		1720 00	7875 00	139 00	340 00	10074 00	6966 00		192 00	639 00	2277 00	10074 00
Hants	15.14	16.04	19.73		500 00	1397 00			1897 00	1000 00		179 00	600 00	118 00	1897 00
Inverness	16.84	15.81	17.39		500 00	286 00			786 00	750 00	5 00	6 00	25 00		786 00
Kings	14.06	15.79	17.65		1000 00	1000 00		2606 00	4606 00	1730 00	56 00	2000 00	100 00	700 00	4606 00
Lunenburg	15.38	16.32	16.54	19.89	500 00	625 00		20000 00	21125 00	1000 00		20000 00	100 00	25 00	21125 00
Pictou	15.28	17.12	18.27		1720 00	2855 00	388 00		4963 00	3650 00	25 00	466 00	822 00		4963 00
Queens	15.33	16.7	18.38		500 00	405 00			905 00	750 00		125 00	30 00		905 00
Shelburne	15.22	15.66	19.64		500 00	300 00			800 00	750 00	5 00	15 00	25 00	5 00	800 00
Victoria	15.64	17.67	16.7		500 00	622 00			1122 00	750 00	25 00	212 00	135 00		1122 00
Yarmouth	15.33	16.38	15.34	18.15	500 00	1875 00			2375 00	2225 00	100 00		50 00		2375 00
Total 1895	15.37	16.69	17.77	18.98	$15160 00	$24515 00	$677 00	$28532 50	$68884 50	$33716 00	$455 00	$27810 00	$3673 50	$3230 00	$68884 50
" 1894	15.24	16.55	17.14	18.22	13440 00	25158 74	572 00	2411 00	41581 74	32369 00	554 00	2205 00	2085 00	4368 74	41581 74
Increase	.13	.14	.63	.76	$1720 00		$105 00	$26121 50	$27302 76	$1347 00		$25605 00	$1588 50		$27302 76
Decrease						$643 74					$99 00			$1138 74	

8

TABLE XIX.—COUNTY ACADEMIES.—(Continued).

ACADEMY.	GROUND. Dimensions of Grounds on which building is situated. (Decimetres.)	REGULAR TEACHING ROOMS. Number of.	REGULAR TEACHING ROOMS. Average dimensions of. (Decimetres.)	ASSEMBLY ROOM. Dimensions of (if there is a special room). (Decimetres.)	LIBRARY. Dimensions of room (if there is a spec'l one), or of cabinet, or of shelving (if no special room). (Decimetres.)	LIBRARY. No. of Volumes.	LIBRARY. Estimated Value of the Books.	MUSEUM OF NATURAL HISTORY, PHYSIOLOGY, &c. Dimensions of room, etc. (Dms.)	MUSEUM. Estimated Value of Collections, Model, &c.	LABORATORY. (Chemical.) Dimensions of room, etc. (Decimetres.)	LABORATORY. Estimated Value of Apparatus, &c., kept here.
Annapolis	980 x 125	1	31 x 54 x 110	37 x 109 x 178	33 x 52 x 78	3052	$3500 00	33 x 52 x 78	$100 00	33 x 78 x 104	$ 30 00
Antigonish	1429 x 750	5	33 x 64 x 98			280	355 00				200 00
Cape Breton	900 x 400	2	42 x 90 x 90		42 x 45 x 45	100	54 00			42 x 45 x 45	155 00
Clare	920 x 920	2	40 x 72 x 80			220	350 00				500 00
Colchester	882 x 1364	5	42 x 83 x 92	40 x 92 x 218	38 x 51 x 85	70	90 00	39 x 80 x 121	50 00	39 x 61 x 107	490 00
Cumberland	900 x 1818	2	39 x 90 x 111	50 x 137 x 196							15 00
Digby	351 x 455	1	36 x 90 x 90	36 x 74 x 198		172	51 00			36 x 36 x 66	32 00
Guysboro	893 x 694	1	36 x 97 x 84	52 x 160 x 196	36 x 36 x 56	720	600 00	9 x 7 x 94	100 00	42 x 40 x 60	200 00
Halifax	157 x 140	6	42 x 83 x 97		42 x 40 x 55					40 x 41 x 46	50 00
Hants	590 x 850	1	40 x 79 x 99							17 x 5 x 12	35 00
Inverness	180 x 220	1	39 x 72 x 87							40 x 59 x 88	70 00
Kings	1097 x 1828	2	40 x 78 x 87								
Lunenburg											
Pictou	650 x 1150	4	45 x 85 x 97	42 x 95 x 213	42 x 55 x 73	1175	1000 00	45 x 55 x 72	1200 00	45 x 52 x 50	200 00
Queens	304 x 960	1	42 x 86 x 119					14 x 3 x 10	20 00	42 x 44 x 46	20 00
Shelburne	732 x 732	1	56 x 100 x 115					3 x 9 x 32		28 x 5 x 19	30 00
Victoria	615 x 923		31 x 62 x 108		14 x 3 x 15	100	125 00				
Yarmouth	640 x 1460	3	44 x 83 x 91	44 x 89 x 183				21 x 4 x 22	50 00	21 x 4 x 22	280 00
Total, 1895.		39				5889	$6115 00		$1520 00		$2297 00
" 1894.		36				4779	5715 00		1650 00		2242 00
Increase		3				1110	$400 00				$55 00
Decrease.									$130 00		

TABLE XIX.—COUNTY ACADEMIES.—(Continued).

COUNTIES.	LABORATORY, (Physical). Dimensions of room (if any) or of cabinet, cases or shelving (if no special room).	LABORATORY, (Physical). Estimated Value of Apparatus kept here.	GYMNASIUM OR PLAY-ROOM. Dimensions of room (if any).	GYMNASIUM OR PLAY-ROOM. Estimated Value of Apparatus.	GENERAL. No. of Wall Maps, Charts and Globes.	GENERAL. No. of reference books, &c., for teachers' desks.	GENERAL. Estimated Value of the same.	TOTAL VALUE. Estimated Value of all collections, apparatus, &c.	TOTAL VALUE. Total Value of furniture, &c., (not including seats, desks, &c.,) used for teaching purposes.
Annapolis	33 x 78 x 104	$120 00		$70 00	19	5	$50 00		$200 00
Antigonish		400 00	44 x 90 x 166		34	50	160 00		4400 00
Cape Breton					40	10	40 00		550 00
Clare		200 00			8	10	20 00		40 00
Colchester	36 x 20 x 20	25 00			20	12	20 00		1100 00
Cumberland		39 00			10	15	50 00		600 00
Digby	29 x 7 x 24	150 00			15	1	60 00		170 00
Guysboro		25 00	32 x 83 x 95		16	2	44 00		200 00
Halifax					30	5	80 00		1600 00
Hants					12	3	25 00		100 00
Inverness		70 00			4	1	20 00		55 00
Kings					22	6	103 00		243 00
Lunenburg	42 x 52 x 52				10	15	75 00		3100 00
Pictou		600 00		100 00	55	4	100 00		160 00
Queens					4	2	40 00		150 00
Shelburne				50 00	26	3	18 00		70 00
Victoria					10	1	20 00		550 00
Yarmouth					30	10	100 00		
Total 1895		$1629 00		$220 00	366	155	$1025 00		$13288 00
" 1894		1837 00		60 00	366	140	1091 00		12849 00
Increase				$160 00		15			$439 00
Decrease		$208 00					$66 00		

TABLE XX.—GOVERNMENT NIGHT SCHOOLS.

County	Section	Teacher	Assistant	Pupils Enrolled.	Average Attendance.	No. of Sessions.
Cape Breton	West Louisburg	Lawrence D. Bates		33	20	51
"	Barachois	A. J. McDonald		31	24	48
"	New Victoria Mines	Murdoch Matheson		69	20	51
"	Bateston	Michael Mullins	James Connors	31		31
"	Gowrie	J. J. Macaskill		19	15	25
"	Sydney Mines	Wm. Haggarty		40	14	5
Inverness	North Sydney	John D. McNeil	John A. Lamond	33	24	45
"	Red Banks	John A. McDonald		39	20	38
"	Julique Intervale	Alex. D. Macdonald		78	25	36
"	Millan	Andrew McLellan		44	46	48
"	Brook Village	Dan. C. McDonald		37	22	52
"	S. W. Margaree	A. S. Macdougall		29	19	52
"	S. W. Bridge	Raymond Murphy		37	20	50
"	Judique	Duncan Chisholm		43	27	30
Picton	Westville	Michael Muir		33	26	51
"	Lyons' Brook	A McArthur		26	23	33
"	Stellarton	Fred. W. Mitchell		70	10	40
"	New Glasgow	Wm H. Magee	Murr y Douglas	42	26	44
"	Thorburn	G. E. Forbes		51	16	36
Lunenburg	Ritcey's Cove	John M. Gow	Katie J. Carroll	33	24	24
"	East Chester	Diadem Bell		40	21	50
"	Chester	Eva A. Webber		23	32	42
Richmond	River Bourgeois	John W. McIsaac		35	13	32
"	Macdougall	Alex. D. McNeill		25	25	43
Digby	Westport	Geo. M. Huggins		31	12	45
"	Corberrie	Augustin F. Haché		28	18	51

TABLE XXI.—PROVINCIAL HIGH SCHOOL EXAMINATION, JULY, 1895.

STATION.	Male Candidates.	Female Candidates.	Total Candidates.
Amherst	18	47	65
Annapolis	34	36	69
Antigonish	43	45	85
Arichat	18	10	28
Baddeck	31	25	56
Barrington	9	25	34
Bridgetown	39	91	130
Canso	6	12	18
Cheticamp	8		8
Clare	15	12	12
Digby	22	30	57
Guysboro	15	18	32
Halifax	117	215	332
Kentville	74	99	173
Liverpool	15	46	61
Lockeport		31	31
Lunenburg	28	62	90
Maitland	8	6	47
Margaree Forks		6	11
New Glasgow	39	76	115
Parrsboro	7	23	30
Pictou	61	82	143
Port Hawkesbury	17	21	38
Port Hood	20	33	53
Shelburne	11	18	29
Sherbrooke		3	11
Spring Hill	9	25	34
Sydney	55	74	129
Tatamagouche	5	46	51
Truro	88	159	247
Windsor	22	51	72
Yarmouth	36	64	100
Total, 1895	883	1516	2399
" 1894	707	1215	1922
Increase	176	301	477
Decrease			

TABLE XXI.—PROVINCIAL HIGH SCHOOL EXAMINATION, JULY, 1895.—(Continued).

STATIONS.	Candidates for Grade C.	Received Grade C.	Received Grade D.	Failed.	Candidates for Grade D.	Received Grade D.	Failed.	Candidates for Grade D.	Received Grade D.	Failed.	Total received Grade A.	Total failed Grade A.	Total received Grade A "Partial."	Total failed Grade A "Partial."	Received Grade B on A examination.	Received Grade B on B examination.	Total received Grade B.	Total failed Grade B.	Received Grade C on A examination.	Received Grade C on B examination.	Received Grade C on C examination.	Total received Grade C.	Total failed Grade C.	Received Grade D on B examination.	Received Grade D on C examination.	Received Grade D on D examination.	Total received Grade D.	Total failed Grade D.	Total received certificates.	No. received Grade applied for.	No. received one Grade lower than applied for.	No. received second Grade lower than applied for.	Total No. failed.
Amherst	19	1	7	11	8	1	7	22	7	15						3	3	5		1	4	5	13	1	8	8	17	22	25	15	9	1	40
Annapolis	9		4	5	7	2	5	21	1	20	1		1	2	2	4	6	1		5	5	11	1	4	3	8	25	21	9	11	1	39
Antigonish	18	2	6	10	17	6	11	21	1	19	1		2		1	6	7	1	3	6	9	16		7	8	16	30	35	23	11	1	50
Arichat	2			2	11	1	10	8	1	7				1		4	4	1			3	3		4	17	6	3		3		22
Baddeck	10		1	9	14	2	12	17	8	9						4	4	1		5	5	12	2	1	10	13	21	22	14	6	2	34
Barrington	10	2	1	7	6		4	13	2	11								1	1	2	3	10		3	5	15	8	5	3		26
Bridgetown	29	2	5	22	15	2	13	43	5	38					13		13	4	2	8	13	26	5	11	7	23	51	49	25	19	5	81
Canso	6	1		5	3	1	2													3	5	5	3		1	3	3	6	1	2		12
Cheticamp	1		1		3	1	2													3	2	2			2	2	2	6	4	2		3
Clare	2	1		1	12	4	8	10	3	7										4	1	1		1	7	9	15	11	9	2		16
Digby	11		4	7	9	1	8	13	3	10	1			3	1	4	5	2	6	1	7	8	2	6	3	11	15	24	9	13	2	28
Guysboro	5		2	3	9	1	8	12	2	10						5	5				3	3		5	3	8	18	14	8	6		21
Halifax	64	21	21	22	57	37	20	108	44	64	1		3	4		36	36	3	14	43	57	26	8	29	81	118	84	215	164	43	8	117
Kentville	35	7	8	20	31	3	28	43	6	37	1				1	10	11	4	11	8	19	36	11	16	9	36	66	67	28	28	11	106
Liverpool	13	7	2	4	8		8	24	9	15			1	1		8	8	2	1	9	10	5		2	9	11	23	30	26	4		31
Lockeport	3	1		2	6		6	17	3	14								3		1	3	4		3	4	20	5	4		1	26
Lunenburg	30	6	12	12	11	5	6	25	5	20			1		1	5	6	2	4	7	11	20	1	14	10	25	26	42	22	19	1	48
Maitland	14	3	4	7	11	5	6	12	3	9						2	2			5	5	12	1	4	8	13	20	15	4	1		27
Margaree Forks	1			1	7		7	5		5						1	1				1	1			12	1		12	1	1		13
New Glasgow	22	1	5	16	20	4	16	43	5	38						1	1	6	3	2	5	28	1	8	9	21	54	27	12	11	4	88
Parrsboro	9	2	4	3	16	2	14	12	2	10						1	1		1	3	3	9		4	7	8	14	12	7	5		18
Pictou	30	7	8	24	18	4	14	32	4	28	2	2	1	2	1	16	17	2	6	10	16	35	3	13	8	24	42	60	37	20	3	83
Port Hawkesbury	7		3	4	10		10	12	1	11						1	1	2	1		5	5		3	5	8	21	10	2	6	2	28
Port Hood	11	1	6	4	11	1	10	17	5	12						2	2	4		1	3	9	2	6	5	15	22	18	7	8	3	35
Shelburne	10	4	1	5	5	2	3	8	6	3						2	2			3	5	6	3	7	10	6	17	17	14	3		12
Sherbrooke	2		1	1	1		1	7		7										1	1	1		1	1	8	1	6			10
Spring Hill	8	2	3	3	4	2	2	13	1	12						3	3		1	2	3	4	2	3	10	14	16	8	6	2	18
Sydney	28	9	4	15	20	5	15	40	1	39	1				1	5	6	3	6	14	20	25	4	10	6	20	54	47	26	17	4	82
Tatamagouche	13	3	3	7	4	2	2	33	10	23						4	4			3	12	15		4	7	15	19	16	3		32
Truro	54	16	14	24	43	30	13	72	30	42	5		1		4	30	34	6	2	7	27	36	29	21	60	81	55	157	123	32	2	90
Windsor	12	3	2	7	11	1	10	20	6	14	1					7	7	6		6	9	9		7	7	15	24	32	18	10	4	40
Yarmouth	19	4	6	9	16	6	10	34	11	23	1		1	3	5	4	9	3	4	7	11	14	1	7	17	25	33	47	30	16	1	53
Total, 1895	516	106	138	272	409	130	279	759	185	574	15	2	10	17	18	171	189	68	2	101	174	277	388	59	205	315	579	854	1070	684	325	61	1329
" 1894	443	164	141	138	298	110	188	574	183	391	30		10	12	18	165	182	31	2	63	271	337	196	37	213	293	543	579	1092	760	294	39	820
Increase	73			134	111	20	91	185	2	183		2		5		6	7	37		38			192	22		22	36	275			31	22	509
Decrease		58	3								15										97	60			8				22	76			

XXII.—Expenditure of Government Funds for Public Schools, County Academies, &c.

School Year ended July, 1895.

Counties	Population	Common Schools				County Academies.	Total assignable to Counties.
		No. of Schools in session.	No. of Pupils registered.	Sum of Government Grants.	Cost to Government per pupil.		
Annapolis	19,350	117	4,741	$10,033 17	$2 11	$ 500 00	$10,533 17
Antigonish	16,144	93	3,551	6,920 12	1 94	1,500 00	8,420 12
Cape Breton	34,244	158	7,391	12,747 21	1 72	1,000 00	13,747 21
Col tar	27,160	145	6,123	10,860 30	1 77	1,720 00	12,580 30
Cumberland	34,529	191	8,772	14,814 01	1 68	*1,250 00	16,064 01
Digby	19,897	102	4,717	7,421 22	1 57	1,000 00	8,421 22
Guy boro	17,195	92	3,871	6,472 08	1 67	500 09	6,972 08
Halifax County	32,863	149	6,876	11,867 40	1 72		11,867 40
Halifax City	38,495	134	7,526	12,466 30	1 65	1,720 00	14,186 30
Hants	22,052	125	5,092	9,844 34	1 93	500 00	10,344 34
Inverness	25,779	164	6,086	12,018 27	1 97	500 00	12,518 27
Kings	22,489	122	5,294	10,210 04	1 92	1,000 00	11,210 04
eburg	31,075	167	7,434	12,568 70	1 69	500 00	13,068 70
Pictou	34,541	173	7,285	14,248 80	1 95	1,720 00	16,968 80
Queens	10,610	59	2,128	4,821 68	2 26	500 00	5,321 68
Richmond	14,399	70	3,034	5,312 84	1 75		5,312 84
Shelburne	14,956	78	3,509	6,665 57	1 90	500 00	7,165 57
Vta	12,432	59	2,199	4,103 10	1 89	500 00	4,603 10
Yarmouth	22,216	107	4,928	9,028 61	1 83	500 00	9,528 61
Tal 1895	450,396	2303	100,555	$182,423 76	$1 81	$15,410 00	$197,833 76
" 1894	450,396	2292	98,710	167,452 85	1 69	13,190 00	180,642 85
Increase	......	13	1,845	$14,970 91	$0 12	$2,220 00	$17,190 91
Decrease							

Other Services and Total Expenditure for Education.

Inspectors' Salaries	$12,558 33
Stationery, Postage, &c...	500 00
Examination	2,704 87
Travelling Expenses—Normal School Pupils	2,089 00
Salaries	3,403 00
Travelling Expenses—Superintendent.	400 00
Office Expenses, (Registers, Register Covers, Postage, Expressage, Telegrams, Stationery, &c.	1,413 30
Total	$ 23,045 50
Last column	197,833 76
Total for Public Schools, 1895	$220,879 26
Institution for the Deaf and Dumb.	3,480 00
Halifax School for the Blind	2,025 00
Normal and Model Schools	9,178 81
School of Agriculture.	1,500 00
Government Night Schools	1,697 54
Total Government Expenditure, 1895	$238,760 61
" " " 1894	220,438 90
Increase	$18,324 71

* $250.00 of this amount was for the previous school year.

TABLE XXIII.

SUMMARY OF GOVERNMENT GRANTS FOR EDUCATION,
YEAR ENDED JULY, 1895.

Common Schools	$182,423 76
Normal and Model Schools	9,178 81
Institution for Deaf and Dumb	3,480 00
Halifax School for the Blind	2,025 00
County Academies	15,410 00
Inspection	13,058 33
Expenses (Office)	1,413 30
Salaries	3,800 00
Examination	2,704 87
School of Agriculture	1,500 00
Travelling Expenses, Normal School Pupils	2,069 00
Government Night Schools	1,697 54
	$238,760 61

PART III.

—————

APPENDICES.

APPENDIX A.

REPORT OF NORMAL SCHOOL.

To A. H. MacKay. Ll.D.,
   Superintendent of Education, Halifax, N. S.

SIR,—I have the honor to submit the following report of the session of the Normal School begun October 17th, 1894, and ended June 27th, 1895.

The total number of students enrolled was one hundred and seventy-seven. Of these eighteen were graduates of colleges—eight of Dalhousie, four of Acadia, three of St. Francis Xavier, two of Mount Allison, and one of Toronto University.

Five were admitted on a license of the first class, fifty-five on the high school certificate of grade B, and forty-one on either a license of the second class or a high school certificate of grade C, and twenty-seven on a high school certificate of grade D. The remaining thirty-one were admitted on examination. This is a smaller number than we have heretofore in any one year admitted in this way.

As the high school examination in July affords every reasonable facility for obtaining the required scholarship certificate, which entitles the holder to be admitted as a student at the Normal School without examination, it would seem that only exceptional circumstances could justify us in obstructing our work at the first of the session by entrance examinations.

College graduates have hitherto been admitted to the three months' course without the grade A certificate. Then, subsequently to the completion of the Normal School course, these students have been accustomed to go up for the high school examination. This has not proved at all satisfactory. The students have a divided interest, and a large portion of their time and energy is given to private study in preparation for the July examination. A period of three months when given wholly to professional training, is all too little for securing satisfactory results. Hence it seems advisable that this class, as the others, shall be required to present the scholarship certificate on entering the Normal School.

Out of our one hundred and seventy-seven students, one hundred and seventy-one received diplomas of the various ranks,—seventy-one of first rank, sixty of second rank, and forty of third rank. Of the remaining six some left the Institution without completing the term, and others failed to reach the required standing for diploma of any rank. Several of those who received diplomas did not secure the rank for which they were working. Thus, fifteen of those who competed for diploma of first rank were placed in second rank, and ten of those who competed for second rank 'were awarded third rank, while three failed to receive any diploma.

It should be observed further that of the fifteen referred to as having failed to take diplomas of the first rank, thirteen reached the required standing in the matter of theoretic qualification or knowledge of principles, their shortcomings being in practical skill. The Faculty could not take the responsibility of certifying them as teachers of the first class, and yet it seemed scarcely advisable to require them to return to the Normal School for a supplementary course. We have accordingly placed these students in the second rank, with the recommendation that after one year's successful practice in teaching, duly certified to by an inspector, they shall be granted diplomas of first rank. It may indeed be worth considering whether in all cases successful experience for a short period under a lower class of license ought not to be an essential condition for a higher class.

The successful competitors for the Governor General's medals were the following :—

> Miss Annie A. McNeill, of North Range, Digby County, (silver medal).
> Miss Anne Campbell, of Tatamagouche, Colchester County, (silver medal).
> Miss Agnes B. Scott, of Poplar Grove, Hants County, (bronze medal)

It is with much pleasure and appreciation that I here acknowledge the interest in the Normal School on the part of the students of the session under report, shown by their gift of casts of Shakespeare, Locke, and Scott. I trust that these busts may form the beginning of contributions which will at no distant day greatly adorn our halls and class rooms.

Having thus briefly described the leading features of the past session, I desire to say a few words bearing on the relation of the Institution to the public schools of the Province. My colleagues and myself have a deep interest in the way in which our graduates acquit themselves after they leave us, and we feel like following them to their various spheres of labor and taking careful note of what they are doing for the advancement of sound education. Favorable reports of their work give us gratification and encouragement, and their failures bring us sorrow and shame. Adverse criticism of their work has sometimes been made, it appears to me, without that fair discrimination which should characterize a well-balanced judgment.

The finished product of the Normal School, as of any other institution, largely depends on the material furnished for it to work on. Our students receive their academic education in the high schools of the Province, and they come to us with certificates of scholarship in the various subjects of the course of study provided for the public schools. Our business mainly is to give professional training. It is not an easy matter to develop the power of teaching any given subject in one who is greatly deficient in the knowledge of that subject. The knowledge of what to teach is a necessary preliminary in learning how to teach. Unfortunately many of those who enter the Normal School, duly certified as possessed of the required scholarship, are exceedingly weak in certain subjects. This deficiency is more marked in vocal music, drawing, physical geography, English grammar, composition, chemistry, and physics. The scientific knowledge of our students in most cases consists wholly of what has been gained from text-books, and shows entire lack of acquaintance with laboratory methods. These statements are made in no censorious spirit, or with desire to expose the weaknesses of the educational institutions of the Province. Taken all in all, our schools are perhaps doing their work as well as circumstances permit. I believe that they are making steady progress towards a higher plane.

In the meantime, however, the Normal School should not be held responsible for defects which lie outside its province, and are in a measure incident to the immature condition of our educational system. And yet the Normal School is doing very much in the way of strengthening what is weak and supplying what is wanting as regards the subject matter of what our students will be called on to teach when they go out to take charge of schools. While exercising our special function of training our students in professional skill, and striving to develop in them higher conceptions of the responsibilities of the teacher's office and work, we are seeking in many ways to broaden and enrich their scholarship. There is scarcely a subject in the course of study provided for the public schools which is not brought under review, some of them with great minuteness and care

In closing I shall venture to make two suggestions, the carrying out of which will, I believe, tend to advance the educational interests of the Province :—

1. I suggest that the standard of scholarship as regards the minimum pass marks be raised in certain important subjects in which, at least in the teacher, " *little* learning is a dangerous thing." Under present arrangements, a person having an aggregate of 400 in all subjects, and not falling below 25 in any subject, is entitled to the scholarship certificate demanded for a first class license. But a person whose knowledge of English Grammar, or indeed of almost any other subject in the syllabus, is adequately represented by such a mark, can scarcely be competent to take charge of a school.

2. I suggest that some of our high schools restrain their ambition in the matter of taking up the work of grade XII. In my opinion it would be vastly wiser to expend their surplus energy in the way of securing greater thoroughness in the work of the other three grades. Could they not, with much greater advantage to their students, do some laboratory work in botany, chemistry, and physics, and give more attention to physical geography, English subjects, drawing, and music ?

Respectfully submitted,

JOHN B. CALKIN,

Principal.

NORMAL SCHOOL, TRURO, N. S., Aug. 1, 1895.

STUDENTS OF SESSION 1894-'95.

AWARDED FIRST RANK DIPLOMAS.

(The figures show the number of the Diploma).

MacPherson Margaret C .. 1 .... New Glasgow ...... Pictou.
Hensley, Winifred M...... 2 .... Windsor .... Hants.
Lloyd, Katie A............ 3 .... Brooklyn Street .... Kings.
Harrington, Edna B....... 4 .... Liverpool .... Queens.
Crouse, Annie............ 5 .... Lapland .... Lunenburg.
Edwards, Elizabeth ...... 6 .... Truro .... Colchester.
Spurr, Margaret C........ 7 .... Melvern Square .... Annapolis.
Bishop, Annie M. .... 8 .... Somerset .... Kings.
Morse, Flora M.... ...... 9 .... Nictaux West...... Annapolis.
Banks, Aurelia B .... 10 .... Kingston .... Kings.
Bool, Evelyn J.... ...... 11 .... Truro .... Colchester.
Dempsey. Isabel .... 12 .... Halifax .... Halifax.
Phelan, Margaret .... 13 ....   "   ....   "
Anderson, Teresa .... 14 ....   "   ....   "
Mills, Hattie .... 15 .... Chester .... Lunenburg.
McLean, Cassie .... 16 .... Fraser's Mt .... Pictou.
Baxter, Agnes L.......... 17 .... Amherst .... Cumberland.
Johnson, Carrie .... 18 .... Sandy Cove........ Digby.
Vroom, Cassie............ 19 .... Deep Brook........ Annapolis.
Leslie, Josephine .... 20 .... Liverpool.......... Queens.
Chisholm, Emma .... 21 .... Salt Springs ...... Antigonish.
McLane, Harriet E. ...... 22 .... Stillwater .... Guysboro.
Cameron, Margaret ...... 23 .... Sherbrooke ....   "
Chute, Lalia M. .... 24 .... Bear River .... Digby.
Fash, Mabelle........... 25 .... Bridgetown .... Annapolis.
Wade, Louisa............ 26 .... Belle Isle..........   "
Angwin, Edith .... 27 .... Burlington .... Hants.
Mack, Annie .... 28 .... North River .... Colchester.
Campbell, Anne M........ 29 .... Tatamagouche......   "
MacKean, Mary H........ 30 .... West LaHave Ferry..Lunenburg.
Wakely, Agnes .... 31 .... Halifax .... Halifax.
Kelly, Jessie .... 32 ....   "   .... "
Bigney, Ella M. .... 33 .... Mount Denson...... Hants.
Wardrope, Annie H. ...... 34 .... Milford ....   "
Scott, Agnes B. .... 35 .... Poplar Grove ......   "
Morse, George........... 36 .... Melvern Square .... Annapolis.
Phinney, Willoughby .... 37 .... South Farmington ..   "
McKenzie, George P....... 38 .... North Shore ...... Cumberland.
Cunningham, George D .... 39 .... Tatamagouche Bay .. Colchester.
Beveridge, William R...... 40 .... Hebron........... Yarmouth.

Matheson, Donald F......41....St. Peter's.........Richmond.
Ruggles, Arthur G........42....Annapolis ....Annapolis.
Faulkner, Fred R.... ....43....Truro ....Colchester.
Fulton, Silas A...........44.... " .... "
Robinson, William C.....45....North Sydney.....Cape Breton.
Craig, Nelson R.......... 46....Lockeport ....Shelburne.
MacKean, James A........47....LaHave ....Lunenburg.
Allen, Shenton B..........48....Milton ....Yarmouth.
Sargent, Joseph H........49....Barrington ....Shelburne.
Crosby, Leander.........50....Hebron............Yarmouth.
Wickwire, Bessie H........51....Canning ....Kings.
Roop, Agnes H.......... 53....Clementsport ......Annapolis.
Ross, Jennie W ....54....Bedeque ....P. E. Island.
Jordan, Edward E........55....Bridgetown ....Annapolis.
Shankel, Bolton W. ......56....Hubbard's Cove ....Halifax.
Nickerson, Alex. W.. ....57....Ohio.............Yarmouth.
Webb, John W...........58....Halifax ....Halifax.
Connolly, James P.......59....Antigonish ....Antigonish.
Haycock, Ernst ....60....Westport ....Digby.
Trefry, James H.........61....Barrington ....Shelburne.
Benoit, Alphonse ....62....Arichat ....Richmond.
Chisholm, Roderick D.... .63....Glassburn ....Antigonish.
Tompkins, James J. ......64....Margaree Forks ....Inverness.
Putnam, James F.... ....65....Maitland ....Hants.
Haynes, Ralph E. ....66....Hill Grove ....Digby.
Harvey, Basil C. H......67....Watford ....Ontario.
Duchemin, Henry P......68....Charlottetown.....P. E. Island.
Horner, Albinus W.... ...52....Yarmouth ....Yarmouth.
Moses, Judson A..........70....Hebron .... "
Lockhart, Nathan J.. ....69....Aylesford.........Kings.
Layton, James S ....71....Halifax ....Halifax.

AWARDED SECOND RANK DIPLOMAS; BUT QUALIFIED FOR FIRST RANK AFTER ONE YEAR OF SUCCESSFUL TEACHING.

MacDonnell, Beatrice ...... 1....Port Hood ....Inverness.
Allen, Stella .... 2...Halifax ....Halifax.
Henderson, Annie I. ...... 3....Truro ....Colchester.
Crowe, Winnifred A...... 4.... " .... "
O'Brien, Katie E. .... 5...Noel.............Hants.
Donovan, Florence E...... 6....Truro ....Colchester.
Park, Florence M......... 7....Beaver Brook...... "
Black, Sadie E. .... 8...Amherst ....Cumberland.
Graham, Jessie E. .... 9...Bear River ....Digby.
Pippy, Fredk. G..........11...Springhill ....Cumberland.
MacArthur, Olive E......12...Pictou ....Pictou.
Morton, Rupert F.........48...Milton ....Queens.
Starratt, Harry J. ....49....Paradise ....Annapolis.

AWARDED SECOND RANK DIPLOMAS.

MacKenzie, Margaret......46....Dartmouth ....Halifax.
Bishop, Ida M............47....Truro ....Colchester.
Brown, Maud S...........1....Tusket............Yarmouth.
Bond, Anna B. ....2.... " .... "
Fraser, Lillian S..........44....River Philip ......Cumberland.
Creelman, Laura ....3....Portaupique ......Colchester.
Currie, Griselda B........4....Waugh's River .... "
Crosby, Emma ....5....Port Morien........Cape Breton.
Macaulay, Jean C.........6.... " .... "
Maxwell, Martha J........7....Mount Thom ......Pictou.
Cruikshank, Maggie ......8....Sunny Brae........ "
MacDonald, Mary A.......9....Antigonish ....Antigonish.
Grant, Christina..........10....Springville ....Pictou.
Shaffner, Thirza B........11....Granville Centre....Annapolis.
Parker, Van Esse ....12....Berwick ....Kings.
Hennigar, Effie S. ....13....Chester Basin......Lunenburg.
Ernst, Phebe ....14....Pleasantville ...... "
Jordan, Jennie E. ....15....Grafton ....Kings.
Gammell, Jeannette ......16....Newton Mills ......Colchester.
MacLellan, Winifred......17....Noel Shore ....Hants.
Freeman, Mary E.........18....Greenfield ....Queens.
Shaw, Nina V...........19....Avonport..........Kings.
Cox, Effie L. ....20.... " .... "
McGill, Winifred ....21....South Farmington..Annapolis.
Bond, Mary G............22....Tusket...........Yarmouth.
O'Neil, Annie H..........23....Westville..........Pictou.
Duff, Catharine I.........41.... " .... "
Ward, Corabel ....24....Advocate..........Cumberland.
Ward, Lillian J...........25.... " .... "
Martin, Maria I..........26....Shelburne ....Shelburne.
Smith, Ella A............27....Lunenburg ....Lunenburg.
Fisher, Laura F..........28....Sheet Harbor ......Hants.
Laws, Sophia S. ....29....Windsor .... "
Wallace, Effie B..........30....West Gore .... "
Borden, Minnie L.........31....Pugwash ....Cumberland.
MacKay, Christina........43...Earltown..........Colchester.
Fullmore, Della M........32....Five Islands........ "
McLeod, Katie J..........33....Port Morien........Cape Breton.
Peters, Annie M..........34.... " .... "
Dick, Jane D............35....Springhill ....Cumberland.
MacLean, Dan ....36....Fourchee ....Richmond.
Webb, Warren S..........37 ..Wallace Bay ......Cumberland.
Redmond, James A........38....Pugwash .... "
Gould, Susan J...........39....River John ....Pictou.
McNeill, Anna A. ....45....North Range ......Digby.
Grant, Stella J. ....40....Hardwood Land....Hants.
Cossaboom, Annie F......42...Tiverton ....Digby.

AWARDED THIRD RANK DIPLOMAS.

Ward, Lavinia O. ....36....Melvern Square ....Annapolis.
Faulkner, Beatrice.... ...37....Chelsea ....Lunenburg.
Maxwell, Ella............27....Westville..........Pictou.
MacPherson, Maggie ......28 ...   "   ....   "
Sutherland. Roberta ......29....   "   ....   "
MacDonald, Minnie ......30....Port Morien.... ...Cape Breton.
Huskins, Ansell G........31....Lockeport ....Shelburne.
Scott, George ....32...Selma ....Hants.
Munro, George L. ....33....Pugwash :........Cumberland.
Layton, Mary...........34...Elmsdale ....Hants.
Parker Alice ....35...Tenny Cape........   "
Brown, Maggie ....18....Dean Settlement....Halifax.
Ross, Annie J...........1....Hildon...........Colchester.
Miller, Bertha...........2...Noel Shore ....Hants.
Marshall, Caroline........3...Beaver Brook......Colchester.
MacKenzie, Sarah ....4....Princeport ....   "
MacVicar, Bessie A. ......5....Port Morien.......Cape Breton.
Jackson, Martha E........6...Dalhousie West ....Annapolis.
MacGibbon, Mary E......19...Cloverville ....Antigonish.
MacDonald, Anastasia ....20....West Lakeville ....   "
Hamm, Lilla E. ....7....Mahone Bay. ....Lunenburg.
O'Brien, Janie L. ....21....Moose Brook ... ..Hants.
Doyle, Sarah J. ....8....Margaree Forks ....Inverness.
Mallett, Hattie ....9....South Range ......Digby.
Weston, Mary L........10...Rockville..........Yarmouth.
MacKay, Maggie A........22....Earltown..........Colchester.
Lewis, Eliza . ...11....Point Edward.....Cape Breton.
Martell, Phœbe ....12....Port Morien........   "
McDonald, Lina J........23...Concord .. ..Pictou.
Cameron, Jennetta R. ....24....Cameron Settlement. Guysboro.
MacKay, Maria ....25...Tatamagouche.....Colchester.
Barnes, Nettie M. ....13....Nappan ....Cumberland.
Farrell, Annie...........14...Parrsboro' ....`.   "
McLeod, Johanna ....26....Westville..........Pictou.
MacDonald, Laura C..:....15....Truro ....Colchester.
Dennis, Jessie P..........16....Middle Stewiacke ..   "
MacCabe, Clara M........38....Advocate Harbor...Cumberland.
Petipas, Mary M..........39....East Tracadie......Antigonish.
Coady, Peter W ....17 ...S. W. Margaree ....Inverness.
Hennigar, Grace D........40....Chester Basin......Lunenburg.

COURSE UNCOMPLETED.

Crowe, Ella J............ ....Truro ....Colchester.
MacVicar, John E........ ....Annapolis ....Annapolis.
Mosher, Fredk. P. ....Windsor ....Hants.
Parker, Phebe S.......... ....Tenny Cape........   "
Rutherford, Blanche ....Truro ....Colchester.
Murphy, Bella P.......... ....Truro.... ....   "
4

NORMAL SCHOOL.

YEAR.	No. of Teachers.	PUPILS.		EXPENDITURE.				TOTAL.
		Total number enrolled.	Received Diploma.	Salaries of Teachers.	Salary of Janitor.	Cost of Fuel.	Contingencies,—Stationery, etc.	
1895	7	177	171	$6800	$400	$249 95	$477 41	$7927 36
1894	7	130	123	6600	400	284 75	616 10	7900 85

MODEL SCHOOL.

YEAR.	No. of Teachers.	PUPILS.		EXPENDITURE.			TOTAL.
		Average daily attendance.	Total number different Pupils registered.	Salaries of Teachers.	Amount received from Province.	Amount received from Truro.	
1895	2	87	108	$1100	$600	$500	$1100
1894	2	79	109	1100	600	500	1100

SCHOOL OF AGRICULTURE.

,DR. A. H. MacKay,
  Superintendent of Education.

SIR :—I have the honor to submit to you the following report upon the work of this School for the past year.

Part I relates to the Normal School work.
Part II. relates to the Local Agricultural Schools.
Part III. relates to the Provincial School of Agriculture.

I am, sir, your obedient servant,
  H. W. SMITH, *Principal.*

PART I.

The " A " class, first class and second class of the Normal School, received instruction in scientific subjects in this building. Of these three classes, one hundred and fifty-four pupils studied biology or chemistry, or both.

All three classes studied biology, but as they were here for different terms and seasons, the course had to be modified to meet their needs and conditions.

The " A " Class.—This class, entering as it did in April, had an excellent opportunity to do good work. But for three things that interfered they might have done so. These were : (1st), that they were admitted irregularly ; (2nd), they did not all have certificates, and of those who had, many were classical students and some scientific, and therefore not equally prepared for the work ; (3rd), many of those not having " A " certificates were more desirous of getting these than of obtaining knowledge of the sciences. The result was that while the work of some members of the class was excellent, many did very little beyond what was necessary to "get through." The work covered by a majority of the class was : A study of yeast, bacteria (briefly), liverworts, mosses, ferns, flowering plants, a study of protozoa, worms, fishes, and frogs. Each of these studies consisted of laboratory work and field work, collecting, dissecting, and to a very limited extent microscopic examination of the object. These studies were of course accompanied by lectures and recitations upon these and allied forms.

Besides the above the class received a course of lectures upon general physiography. Some of the students in this class did considerable special work besides the regular work of the class, a full account of which will be given under " special work " in this report. This class attended two afternoons a week for the months of April, May and June.

The First Class.—This class comprised nearly one-half of the Normal students who came here. They attended one afternoon per week for the entire Normal School year. They studied biology and chemistry.

In biology they took up a few lessons in Microscopy, then a thorough study of *Raphanus raphanistrum,* a comparative study of leaves, stems, roots, fruits, etc., etc., substances essential to plant life, the general principles involved in the growth and propagation of plants, comparison with animal life, study of ferns, liverworts, mosses, worms, spiders, insects, fishes, and frogs.

These studies consisted, as stated above, in collecting and noting the habits, situation, etc., of the specimen, then a thorough study of its anatomy and parts of its histology. This work was accompanied by lectures and recitations.

In chemistry they should have had a good general knowledge upon entering the school, but unfortunately only a few had ever performed any experiments, and these not many, while the larger portion of the class had never *seen* any number of experiments performed. I can scarcely withhold comment upon the worse than useless character of such methods of teaching chemistry, or any science for that matter, as it is actually an injury to the student. Such a student scarcely ever progresses as well or obtains as much benefit for the first few months of proper teaching of the subject as would have been obtained if he had never seen a text-book. With the class in such condition it was necessary to begin with the most elementary work. They studied by experimental methods the following substances and some of their more important compounds, hydrogen, oxygen, sodium, magnesium, calcium, carbon, nitrogen, sulphur, and chlorine.

The Second Class.—This class followed nearly the same course as the first class in biology, but leaving early in the spring they of course were not able to take up the flowering plants, except for a short time in the autumn. They attended from November to March, inclusive, one afternoon per week.

SPECIAL WORK.

Special facilities are offered to Normal students to do extra work or advanced work in the sciences at this school. Many students, so far as their time permitted, took advantage of this opportunity and did extra work, each student taking up some particular line of work independent of the regular class work or suggested by it. This work included among various subjects chosen—general chemistry as required for " A," qualitative and quantitative analysis, organic chemistry of drugs and medicine, their analysis and synthesis, analysis of minerals, etc. In Biology it included a detailed study of the gross and minute anatomy of typical plants of the various divisions of the vegetable kingdom, a study of the leguminous plants, the collection of insects and study of their habits, history, and characters.

SUGGESTIONS.

I would like to offer the following suggestions : That the first class receive a course of instruction in agriculture, horticulture, and dairying.   Without entering into the details of such a course, I might point out that it was the original intention in establishing this position and school to give such a course to these teachers.   I think it would be feasible and of great benefit to the students.   It should be made of such a character that it would interest and instruct them, and at the same time develop their mental powers by accurate observation and reasoning.

That this class be given more time to study chemistry.   The great need of this I need not emphasize, as I know that it is appreciated.

That instead of studying biology as in the past, the class should take up only a few of the most common plants and animals, and make a *thorough* study of these.   There is too great a tendency to be superficial in our education, and particularly is this true of the present studies of botany and physiology.   A thorough study as proposed would help to counteract that tendency.

The fourth suggestion I have to make is that a regular summer course for teachers be given at the School of Agriculture.   The course to afford teachers facilities to pursue any line of scientific work they may desire.   Our excellent equipments for chemistry, botany, and biology, would be of great value to our teachers if they would take advantage of it during their vacations.   This summer a number of students and teachers asked permission to work in the laboratories, and I granted it.   The result was an excellent summer's work.   I should propose that such a course should begin on the Tuesday follow ing the Provincial Examinations, and continue for a term of four weeks.

PART II.

LOCAL AGRICULTURAL SCHOOLS.

Three local schools were in session during the past year.   One at Richmond and two in Cape Breton.   I have little to add to the remarks concerning these schools made in my last report.   They have been successfully conducted, and are of great value to the communi-ties in which they are situated.   I frequently receive letters from sections asking for agricultural teachers to conduct their schools.   The three schools are taught by : G. R. Marshall, at Richmond, Halifax Co. ; J. D. McKinnon, at Beaver Cove, C. B ; J. W. Edwards, at Little Glace Bay, C. B.   I extract the following from Mr. Marshall's excellent report :

" The first two months of the term were devoted to the study of Zoology.   The parts dwelt upon particularly were the classes Aves and Hexapoda.   The pupils were required to notice as many facts as they could respecting the anatomy and habits of wild birds.   The interest they evinced in this subject was very gratifying to the teacher, for it proved to him that it had been presented to them in the natural way.

This place being so favorably situated for marketing poultry and eggs, a large amount of attention was given to the raising of domestic fowls. The exhibition in Halifax during the month of September facilitated the study of this subject very much.

A number of insects collected and mounted by the pupils received creditable mention at the last Provincial Exhibition.

The advancement made in the study of Chemistry was not so great as I could have wished, owing to our want of suitable apparatus. The work outlined in the first 150 pages of Johnson's "How Crops Grow," was used as a guide, though it was not thought wise to take it up in just the same order as it was in the book. This also is a subject pupils are very fond of if they are allowed to do practical work, and as an aid to intelligent farming it is second to none.

During March and April the work was on farm crops and how to raise them. As the farms here are small, most of the attention was given to the culture of small fruits and vegetables. There is quite a large amount of land within a few miles of the city of Halifax now lying idle that might be made to produce very profitable crops if the owners would attend to it. Fertilizing substances can easily be obtained, and with but a small effort lots now waste and unsightly might be made to become beautiful and productive.

The last two months of the term were devoted to the study of Botany. An effort has been made to get the children to see, handle, and know the truly beautiful wild flowers."

Mr. McKinnon had the following classes besides his regular school classes : In Agriculture, 14 ; Chemistry, 3 ; Botany, 10 ; Anatomy and Physiology, 3 ; Vet. Med., 2 ; Stock Feeding, 12. He advised and treated about twenty cases of sick stock, and thus saved hundreds of dollars to the district. He gave a number of public lectures in the evening to the farmers of the community. But, perhaps, best of all is the object lessons which his farm affords, and the experiments which he and the pupils of the school are conducting. They afford an object lesson in teaching and practice which it would be hard to excel.

One of the best schools in the eastern part of the Province is that conducted by Mr. J. W. Edwards. He has had from twenty-five to thirty pupils studying agriculture, agricultural chemistry, and allied sciences. That he is appreciated is evinced by the fact that although he has taught there continuously for a number of years, he has had his salary increased every year.

Ninety pupils in these schools received instruction in agriculture during the past year.

Eight hundred and twelve pupils have received the equivalent to one year's instruction in agriculture in the local schools since they were established, and about sixteen hundred and forty children have attended these schools and indirectly received benefit from them.

PART III.

THE PROVINCIAL SCHOOL OF AGRICULTURE

Began its annual session last November. Thus far forty pupils have been enrolled. The year has been quite successful, particularly in the high character of the work done by the pupils.

Two hundred and sixty students have attended this school, an average of twenty-six per year for the ten years of its existence, as follows :—

1885-86	7 pupils.
1886-87	8 "
1887-88	12 "
1888-89	18
1889-90	23
1890-91	25
1891-92	26
1892-93	59
1893-94	42
1894-95	40
Total	260

Adding to those studying Agriculture in the local schools we have :

Local schools	812
Provincial schools	260
Grand total of	1072

Or an average of over one hundred and seven per year who have received instruction in agriculture directly or indirectly from this institution since its establishment. This is in addition to all the Normal students, nearly two thousand, who have received more or less agricultural instruction here, which would make a total of about three thousand students who have received some instruction in these subjects. An average of about three hundred per year—a record of which I think we might be justly proud.

H. W. SMITH, B. S.,

Principal Prov. School of Agriculture.

APPENDIX B.

REPORTS OF INSPECTORS OF SCHOOLS.

DISTRICT No. 1.—CITY AND COUNTY OF HALIFAX.

(No Report).

DISTRICT No. 2.—LUNENBURG AND QUEENS.

H. H. MacIntosh, *Inspector.*

Sir :—

I respectfully submit the following report on the Public Schools of Inspectoral District No. 2, for the school year ended July 31st, 1895.

One new section was added during the year, known as Rosebud, No. 109, District of Lunenburg and New Dublin, making a total of 194 sections in the inspectoral district, as follows :—

Lunenburg and New Dublin............	118 sections.
Chester	29 "
South Queens......:...............	26 "
North Queens......................	21 ..

Eight sections were without school during the year, viz, Beech Hill, Sherwood, Lower Northfield, Cook's Branch, Lakeville, and Bush's Island in Lunenburg Co., and Riverdale and Fifteen Mile in Queens. Lower Northfield, Riverdale, and Fifteen Mile have had no school for several years, owing to scarcity of pupils, and may be considered dormant sections. In Beech Hill section the school house was burnt two years ago, and has not yet been replaced. I know of no good reasons why the other four sections should not have had school for at least a part of the year.

A number of sections had school for part of the year only. Three of such sections could not secure teachers for the full year. In some of our island sections there is sufficient attendance only in the winter months to warrant keeping school open. Others were financially unable to support a school for the full term.

In Lunenburg Co. there were 167 schools in operation, with 7434 pupils, and an attendance of 780,999 days. Compared with the preceding school year this shows a *decrease* of 4 schools, 118 pupils, and an attendance of 8,951 days.

In Queens Co. there were 59 schools in operation, with 2128 pupils, and an attendance of 247,871 days, showing when compared with the preceding year an *increase* of 3 schools, 105 pupils, and 17,706 days attendance.

From the above it will be seen that compared with 1894 the school year just closed shows for the *whole district* a *decrease* of 1 school and 13 pupils, and an *increase* of 8755 days' attendance.

The proportion of population attending school was 1 in 4.2 in Lunenburg Co. and 1 in 5 in Queens. The average quarterly percentage of attendance was 65.6 in Lunenburg Co., and 65.3 in Queens. The annual returns report 636 children in Lunenburg Co., and 171 in Queens, not attending school.

In Lunenburg Co. the schools were open on an average 198 days, and in Queens Co. 206.5 days, the full term being 216 days.

Of the 236 teachers employed in the district during the year, only 20 were males. The various grades were represented as follows :—

	A	B	C	D
Lunenburg Co.	2	13	77	82
Queens Co.	1	5	35	21

Forty-five of these were Normal School graduates.

The following are the average salaries for the year :—

LUNENBURG CO.

	A	B	C	D
Males	$910	$438 27	$213 59	$157 93
Females	——	288 00	214 07	153 91

QUEENS CO.

	A	B	C	D
Males	$750	$328 27	$353 07	$175 38
Females	——	332 44	216 57	153 03

Compared with 1894 there has been a noticeable *increase* in the average salary of A and B males and B females, a *decrease* in that of C and D males, and scarcely any change in the case of C and D females.

Every year shows advancement in the class of school buildings, grounds, and surroundings. New school houses are being built every year, old ones repaired and enlarged, school grounds graded and fenced, trees planted, etc. The general tendency is in the line of making the school room and its surroundings more comfortable, convenient and homelike. There are at present at least 10 school buildings altogether inadequate for the requirements of the sections to which they belong, and generally unfit for school purposes. The Boards of Commissioners have deferred condemning these, owing to the general complaint of hard times. A number of miscellaneous schools too large for one teacher have not been divided for the same reason. These matters, however, will be remedied in the near future. I am pleased to see that trustees show a disposition to provide a better class of outbuildings than formerly, and know of only two sections unprovided in this respect.

The new County Academy occupies the most commanding site in the town, and no finer view can be had in the Province than that afforded from the roof of this building. It is a large, handsome, and commodious structure, 125 ft. in length and 100 ft. in breadth. The basement contains the furnaces, latrines, etc. The Smead-Dowd system of heating and ventilating has been adopted. There are twelve large school rooms, each with separate cloak rooms for boys and girls, a well arranged laboratory, a library, and a large assembly hall capable of seating at least four hundred. The whole building is beautifully finished in hard wood. This, with the handsome wooden ceilings, renders each room most attractive. There are six entrances, affording a complete separation of boys from girls, except when under the teacher's eye. Four towers adorn the building, in one of which is placed a 650 lb. bell. It is the most conveniently arranged and best finished school building in the Province, and marks well the enterprise and progress of the town of Lunenburg. A complete outfit of scientific apparatus, costing $550, has just been received.

The school house in Back of Lake section, Chester District, has been enlarged and repaired, so as to give the section virtually a new building at a very moderate cost.

School was opened in the new school house at Upper Woodstock in November last.

Harmony Section, North Queens, boasts of a new school house. About $1800 was spent in repairs and improvements during the year. The following may be noted here :—

Chester—Completion of repairs to interior of building.

Conquerall Mills—Building repaired and patent seats and desks supplied.

Petite Riviere—New furniture for primary department.

Port Medway—Completion of repairs to building and improvement of grounds.

Blue Rocks, North River, Niniveh, Martin's Point, Leville, and several other sections, have made various repairs and added to the appearance of their school premises during the year.

The meetings of the several Boards of Commissioners were well attended, except in South Queens, where for some years past we have been indebted to a few interested commissioners for a quorum and the transaction of necessary business. In making future appointments, care should be taken that they be men interested in education, and who can attend the annual meeting without too great inconvenience.

At the Lunenburg and Chester meetings important business was transacted. Both these boards are composed of excellent business men, and all matters for consideration are handled expeditiously and with good judgment and tact.

The same may be said of the board for North Queens. I inspected all the schools in the district open at the time of my visit, and a number of them a second time. It sometimes happens that a school in session for part of the term is not open, or perhaps is closed at the time of my visit to the neighborhood. Some of these can be visited later, others cannot.

Owing to a scarcity of teachers, several permissive licenses had to be granted, chiefly in sections where school did not open at the beginning of the term.

The leading features of the past school year were so much like those of the preceding, that there is little new to report. Our schools have done at least a fair year's work. Glancing back over the past five years there is much to encourage. Every year has been marked with improvement, not only in buildings and other school equipments, but also in the character of the work done. Yet it must not be inferred that our schools are in every way satisfactory. I find from notes made on my rounds of inspection that for the year just closed 26 per cent. of the schools in the district are marked *good*, 23 per cent. *poor*, the remainder *fair*. This means, according to my rating, that of every four schools one is good, one is poor, two are fair. From the above I think it is very evident that while good buildings and proper apparatus are very desirable and important factors in successful work, what we need more than anything else is good teachers. We cannot have good schools without good teachers. If we could retain all our good teachers and increase their number every year by the addition of ten or fifteen good ones, we would soon have an ideal state of educational affairs.

The returns show that nearly one-fourth of the whole school time is spent on reading. I have marked reading *good* in about 30 per cent. of the schools. This looks small, but there has been marked improvement to reach even this point.

In teaching arithmetic there has been progress all along the line, and over one-third of our schools may be marked *good* in this subject. The fundamental rules are more thoroughly taught, more mental exercises are given, and the work is made more practical throughout.

Except in a limited number of the schools, writing is poorly taught, especially to beginners. More use should be made of the blackboard in explaining principles and teaching the formation of the letters, and the spacing and connecting of them. The penmanship of many high school pupils is poor, in some cases almost illegible, and no doubt assists in making failures at the Provincial Examination.

In the common schools English Grammar is largely taught orally, the text-book being seldom used below the 8th grade.

History and Geography are intelligently taught in many schools ; in others the time is largely wasted. In the latter case a lesson generally consists of repeating barren dates and unimportant details concerning foreign countries. I find that, as a general rule, the Normal trained teacher excels in teaching these subjects.

In Drawing and Music the past year's work was satisfactory, and these subjects may be considered pretty well established throughout the district.

For the length of time " Lessons on Nature " has been a subject of the Course of Study, there should be better results. Instead of the child being led to observe and investigate, the process too often consists of memorizing a mass of dry and uninteresting facts.

The number of candidates attending the Provincial Examination is increasing every year. In 1893 there were 55 applications at the Lunenburg station, this year there were 101. At the Liverpool station the number increased from 32 to 67 during the same time.

With one exception, the annual returns were received within the specified time. Nearly all were practically correct, but too many were carelessly made up. I trust you will find the abstracts of the same, already forwarded to the Education Office, more correct than in any former year.

One hundred and fifteen sections voted on the Compulsory Attendance Act, with the result that sixty-six adopted it. I have no doubt that next year the Act will be generally adopted throughout the district.

Every Board of Trustees was supplied with a copy of the Revised School Act during the year. The effect of this has been to considerably lessen my correspondence on questions of school law, and makes a reply to such questions much easier and more satisfactory.

For detailed information concerning individual sections, I will refer you to the Statistical Tables and Notes of Inspection already forwarded.

Your obedient servant,

H. H. MacINTOSH.

To A. H. MacKay, Esq., Ll.D.,
        Superintendent of Education.

DISTRICT No. 3.—YARMOUTH AND SHELBURNE.

JAMES H. MUNRO, *Inspector.*

SIR :—

Notwithstanding the fact that in many sections the past was a very unhealthy year, and January and February unusually stormy months, a comparison of the statistical tables will show that fair progress was made. In Yarmouth County 107 schools were open more or less of the year, and in Shelburne 78, giving an addition over the previous year of one school for each county. The best that could be attained in Yarmouth County is 112 schools, and in Shelburne 80 or 81. Then, why were Lake George, Forest Glen, Canaan, Greenville, and Morris Island sections in the former county, and Big Port L'Hebert, West Green Harbour, McNutt's Island, Ensor, and Granite Village sections in Shelburne County without schools? My intimate knowledge of these sections enables me to give a direct reply.

As a rebuke to the ratepayers of Lake George for the irregular attendance of their children, the commissioners withheld the special grants which the section was accustomed to receive. In a fit of sulky humour they refused to provide a school. As the commissioners have put the school on trial again, the usual allowances were voted at the annual meeting in June. For some years the people of Forest Glen have had no school house. Last year they reorganized and voted money, but owing to misunderstandings little work was done. In midsummer I attended a public meeting, and succeeded so well in harmonizing differences that work has been resumed with a will, which leaves no doubt that school will be kept some part of the year closing July, 1896. The trouble in Canaan was to agree upon the season of the year when school should be kept, for, being "a poor section," it could content itself with a six months' school. Alas! the seasons came and went, but no season saw Canaan's school in operation. Greenville is a school section of coloured people. Up to last year they had the use of a building owned by private parties, but being debarred from the further use of it, they resolutely set to work, with the result that the new building will be ready for occupation at the beginning of the year. I have more than once referred to Morris Island and its scattered roadless settlements. I have to repeat that it is still without a school house. The bridge, which was built a few years ago by the local government, connecting it and Suret's Island, has given a few families the privilege of access to the school of the latter place. So much for the sections in Yarmouth County without schools.

Big Port L'Hebert is a small place, and at best can support a school part of the year. Indeed, there is only one family of children in it, but that is a big one. Two years ago the father, acting on a whim, withdrew his children in the middle of the term, leaving the trustees to settle accounts with the teacher as best they could. Lately they offered to hire a teacher for six months, but the haughty sire rejecting the maxim that half a loaf is better than no bread, stoutly

insisted : a school for the year, or no school at all. A serious calamity
overtook West Green Harbour ; a new school house, which had been
occupied only nine months, was destroyed by fire. As a heavy debt
was still due on the building, the people were almost driven to despair.
What aggravated the loss was the morally certain fact that it was a
resident who applied the fire. There is no school accommodation yet
on McNutt's island. A few months ago I sounded a ratepayer who
I knew was anxious to get school privileges for his children. His
answer was not encouraging ; it was the old story, " Those who have
the most property have no direct need of a school." Ensor should no
longer be numbered among the sections, as family antagonisms will
ever prevent co-operation. The children near the post road attend
Clyde River school, and those near the lake a shore school. As
regards Granite Village, I have only to repeat what I stated in a previous report, that since the properties changed ownerships there seems
to be no material for a school.

I have dwelt at considerable length on sections without schools, in
order to draw attention to the fact that they are under watchful
supervision, and that there is a solicitude to assist and direct any
movement towards starting a school.

New school houses have been already referred to. The coloured
people of Greenville have erected a nice building on a site with
grounds which can be easily improved. These people illustrate the
power of union, for it is by acting together that they have succeeded.
The liabilities assumed by the trustees will be promptly met at the
proper time. At Forest Glen the site was well chosen, and I hope in
my next report to speak in satisfactory terms of the new school house.

The need of repairs and improved furniture was felt by a few
sections. Richmond, Riverdale, North Kempt, and Comeau's Hill
have provided modern seats and desks, and as the rooms were previously sheathed, they are very comfortable and present an attractive
appearance. Other sections made repairs more or less extensive, such
as Bloomfield, Osborne, Tusket, and some that I cannot just now
recall. The Tusket trustees made a good job of the room. At a
future day a new suit of furniture will be in order. Bell Neck, Birch-
town, and West Head have very poor structures, and if not improved
they must be condemned.

Ratepayers move slowly when they are urged to improve the
school grounds, and the exterior of the school house. Still, they are
moving, for one can see here and there a newly painted school house
and a neatly constructed fence. To save expense, and to enable ratepayers to dispense finally with the cost of keeping up fences, I have
made this recommendation : Provide suitable posts and sufficient
smooth wire to make a fence of four strands. In the fall or spring
plant small spruce trees about three feet apart inside the grounds and
close to the fence. Once a year at least clip the trees so that the
branches may grow thick, and interpenetrate each other. In a few
years a beautiful hedge will enclose the grounds, and its impenetrable

tangle will bar the encroachment of cattle. With good gates no better protection can be effected.

It seems to me no section should be without an outbuilding for fuel. Many a time a visitor's equanimity is disturbed on coming to a school to find the lobby dirty, the floor strewed with chips, wood piled up in the corner, and hacked doors and walls, due to the rough hand-ling of the wood. At a small cost the fuel could have its proper place, and if it were provided a year ahead the saving and convenience would more than pay for the outlay.

Two sections have provided for another department, namely, Jordan Falls and Clark's Harbour. For some years past Jordan Falls has shown a public spirit in the management of its school affairs. It has made extensive repairs, procured the best furniture to be had, engaged good teachers, and it is now preparing for a graded school. No section in Barrington has such educational possibilities as Clark's Harbour. With four departments it should be to the west what Lockeport has been to the east of the county. It has a large popula-tion, plenty of children, bright and intelligent, and citizens capable of making a first-class school if their minds were once set on it. In a few years it would attain a grade *A* standing, and become a centre to which would be drawn from other sections young men and women ambitious to qualify for responsible positions.

The unequivocal remarks in the October *Journal of Education* in regard to calisthenic and musical exercises have been fruitful of good results. Music, which was cultivated in comparatively few schools, and calisthenics, which was seldom practised, are now receiving a good measure of attention. Many teachers who used to prefer the excuse that they could not sing, found that by stirring up the gift that was in them they could sing, and also teach their pupils to sing. There were some who made use of all the helps within their reach, even going long distances to get instruction in the new notation. In Christmas week a number of rural teachers in Shelburne district formed a class and hired an instructor, and bore all the expense incident to travelling to and residing in the shire town. The singing of the pupils proved how much they had benefited by the enterprise of their teachers. In Mr. John B. LeBlanc's department, Lower Wedge, I heard stirring music when the pupils sang with patriotic fervour "Our own Canadian Home," and the National anthem. At Barrington Passage, where Mr. W. B. Parker is principal, the singing was first-class. Pupils took their parts, as tenor, alto, bass, and sang with fine effect.

Teachers volunteered the acknowledgment that they could discern the good effect on their pupils of the calisthenic practice, in correcting a stooping tendency in the shoulders, ungainly attitudes, and a slouching gait in walking. To teachers generally praise is due, but if I had a prize to offer I would award it to Miss Amy Hilton's depart-ment, where the exercises, conducted to the music of a phono-harp, where marked with a precision and gracefulness of motion almost perfect.

To all the other subjects of the course the usual time has been given. In the rounds of one year I may think the reading is improving, and that teachers are attending to those principles that underlie good reading. In the next, perhaps, I may have reason to change my estimate, and draw the inference that reading is receiving proper attention only by fits and starts, and that the supreme importance of boys and girls leaving their schools good readers is not adequately realized. If the simple fact were kept in view that reading ought to give pleasure to the listener, the standard would be much higher than it is, and teachers would have a ready test of its quality. I wonder in how many schools the pupils have been drilled to apply the rules for reading in the Fifth Royal Reader ? In most of the French schools the reading is better than an Englishman would expect to hear, considering that the children know little or no English when they first come to school. I have thought that in the primary rooms more might be done to cultivate English. This remark does not apply to Upper East and Middle West Pubnico, for the little folk are taught to read and speak English well.

The vertical style of writing is coming into use gradually. At first I was averse to a change, but the favourable account received from those who are using it, backed by specimens of writing and comparisons with the slanting hand, has modified my views. As it appears that it is going to supersede the other, I will make the suggestion that it should le imperative in the case of the first, second and third grades. When promoted, they would still cultivate that hand, and ere long it would be in universal use. In the case of senior pupils I observed that though they practised the vertical hand in their copy books, they reverted to the slanting when writing dictation, &c.

Drawing is no longer regarded as a new subject; the belief is that it has come to stay. Consequently it is a rare thing to find a school without books. Teachers, too, are becoming better acquainted with the subject, as one can see in the improved work of their pupils. In some schools the drawing may be characterized as beautiful. In view of artistically executed work of this kind, every reasonable person will concede that the school of to-day is conferring a special boon, and that to know how to draw will ere long be a valuable element in the average pupil's equipment.

The applications for the provincial examination in July were rather larger than usual. There were at—

Yarmouth Station, for A, 11, for B, 14, for C, 30, for D, 50. Total, 105.
Barrington   "   "   0,   " 1,   " 15,   " 18.   " 34.
Shelburne   "   "   0,   " 2,   " 14,   " 15.   " 31.
Lockeport   "   "   2,   " 4,   " 6,   " 25.   " 37.

Total for A, 13, for B, 21, for C, 65, for D, 108. Total, 207.

The majority of students came from the Yarmouth Academy and Milton High School, the other sources of supply being chiefly Hebron, Port Maitland, Ohio, and Tusket. From what I saw of the Shelburne

Academy I would expect to hear that a good percentage of the pupils had made " a pass."

In Yarmouth town schools we have some teachers that, in my opinion, are equal to any in the province. They have knowledge, experience, skill; they are faithful workers, judicious in discipline, and feel that the formation of character is a matter of the first importance. The work of their pupils is tested by competent principals, and it always gives satisfaction. A brief visit to these schools is profitable. What a great benefit then young people looking to teaching would receive, if, as a condition of getting a license, they had to pass two or three months in these schools, not as lookers on, but doing the work themselves under the direction of the teachers. With this training they would enter their own schools, grounded in the fact that to drill is the main business of the teacher—not merely to hear lessons. There are some departments in Shelburne town school to which these remarks also apply.

In most of the graded schools in the District good work is being done. Teachers of the higher departments often complain that advanced studies are out of the question, because the children leave school at such an early age. I am told that it is not an unusual thing in fishing settlements to withdraw boys eight or nine years old in order that they may engage in their parents' occupation. As the period is short between the closing season and the time to start anew, they are practically without educational advantages. The future of those children is not bright. At Lower Woods' Harbour there are excellent schools, taught by Mr. and Mrs. A. B. Huestis. The trustees have shown good judgment by retaining their services. At the south end of Yarmouth the commissioners have added the eighth department.

During the year I visited all the schools, with the exception of Hawthorn and Lower Wedge primary, which were not at work when I was in the vicinity, and 40 per cent. of the whole a second time.

In conclusion, I beg to refer you to the sheets and book of tables lately forwarded to the Education Office, for further confirmation of my initial statement that fair progress has been made.

I have the honor to remain,

Your obedient servant,

JAMES H. MUNRO.

To A. H. MacKay, Esq.. LL.D.
Superintendent of Education.

5

DISTRICT No. 4.—DIGBY AND ANNAPOLIS.

L. S. MORSE, A. M., *Inspector.*

SIR:—

In addition to my monthly reports, which you have already received, and my Notes of Inspection and Statistical Tables, which are forwarded herewith, the following general report for the year ended July 31st, A. D. 1895, is presented for your consideration.

Reference was made in my last report to the formation of Allen River 'section, No. 48, in the District of Annapolis West, and to the action of trespass which resulted in consequence of the expropriation of land for school purposes. Before coming to trial this action was settled, and all proceedings in the formation of said section and in obtaining a site for the school house and grounds, were subsequently ratified and confirmed by a special Act of the Legislature passed last winter. A new school house was promptly built, and school was kept during the greater part of the year. In Bear River section, to which reference was also made in my last report, all cause of friction has been removed, and the school buildings have been completed and occupied since November last. The school house is more convenient and better adapted for school purposes than any other school building in this Inspectoral District. The section has good reason to be proud of the fine accommodation provided, and of the efficient school of five departments now being maintained. The head department, taught by Principal Shields, has been doing High School work exclusively, and bids fair to become a successful rival of the County Academies.

Meteghan Section, also referred to in my last report, remains as it was. The action of the Board of Commissioners in dividing the section was not sanctioned by the Council of Public Instruction, as you are aware, for the reason that no valid ground for the division could be shown. At the annual meeting in June last money was voted for a new school house of four departments, and the work of construction is to begin shortly. A new site has been chosen by the trustees, and has received my approval.

New school houses have been erected during the year in Torbrook West, Salem, Victory, Tiddville, Freeport, and Forest Glen sections, suitable to the requirements of those sections. The house at Freeport is large and convenient, and is intended for four departments. The other houses referred to are creditable to the sections for which they are intended. At Weymouth Bridge the school accommodation has been poor for some years past, but at the last annual meeting the rate-payers voted *two thousand* dollars to provide new grounds and buildings. Before another year passes it is expected that a school house will be erected which will reflect credit upon that prosperous village. Some difficulty is being found, however, in getting a suitable site, as the title to the best available location is so entailed as to render it probable that recourse will be had to the Legislature for a special Act for expropriating the same. At Church Point also, in

Clare, a new school house is in course of erection, and will no doubt be ready for occupation before another year closes. The school houses in Salem and Albany North sections, were burned during the year. In the former case the fire, which is generally supposed to have been of incendiary origin, occurred in midwinter. In the latter case the loss was occasioned by a forest fire in the early part of summer. In both sections the ratepayers, with commendable promptitude, have provided suitable buildings, which will be ready for occupation at or shortly after the close of the summer vacation. Repairs more or less extensive have been made in various other sections. A very creditable degree of progress may, therefore, be reported in the matter of school buildings.

As regards apparatus and general school equipment other than buildings, no marked improvement can be reported. The attention of trustees has been called to this matter, but, except in a few cases, no heed has been paid to my suggestions. All schools have more or less necessary apparatus, but in most sections the quantity should be supplemented. This matter will continue to receive my attention, and, in cases where necessary articles are not supplied, it will become necessary to ask your permission to withhold payment of the County Grant.

There has been no increase in the number of sections during the year—the number remaining at 187 as last reported. *Six* sections are not at present organized and do not maintain schools. Several other sections are thinly settled, and are able to sustain school for a part of the year only. *Thirteen* sections were without schools any part of the year. *Fifty* sections were entitled to receive extra aid as "*poor*" sections, of which number twelve were without schools. In some cases teachers were not available at the beginning of the year, and some sections were, therefore, obliged to have schools for a shorter period than was intended. In a few cases, for valid reasons, sections were granted permission to maintain schools for part of the year only.

You are referred to my Notes of Inspection for the year for definite information regarding the condition of each school. Generally speaking, schools of all sorts are to be found. The condition of each school depends very largely upon the teacher in charge. A large proportion of the teachers are energetic and successful, both in imparting instruction and in governing their pupils. Their success in some cases is limited by want of sufficient apparatus and by other local conditions. As a class their educational qualifications are increasing year by year. Poor teachers are, also, to be found, but they are not so numerous as formerly. Higher scholastic attainments and better professional training of the present day are producing legitimate results. The number of Normal trained teachers is increasing, and the influence of their training is to be seen in the work of the young teachers who are entering the profession.

Three hundred and ten candidates applied for examination for scholarship certificates at the four stations in this Inspectoral District, of whom *fifty-nine* took the *minimum professional examination* in addition. The number applying for Grade A, was 13; for Grade B, 58; for Grade C, 84; and for Grade D, 155. It is to be expected that a considerable proportion of these candidates will fail in securing certificates, for the reason that many of them are quite young and have not had sufficient mental development to enable them to deal with original questions in a logical manner. This must be expected so long as candidates come from miscellaneous as well as graded schools, and are certified by inexperienced as well as experienced teachers. Further, all teachers are not equally judicious in certifying to the fitness of applicants for examination.

The registered attendance of pupils during the year was fairly good. The annual returns show that there were in this District at the beginning of the year 8,881 children between five and fifteen years of age in sections having schools. The total annual enrolment was 9,458, being 102 more than were registered last year. The average of quarterly percentage was 64.5, being *one and nine-tenth* per cent. higher than last year. It is satisfactory to report a gradual advance in this regard, but there is still room for improvement. A percentage of at least 75. should be attained in all schools. Some have already exceeded that standard.

The prescribed Course of Study is being fairly well followed. In many of the schools the work of the course is being more or less thoroughly and systematically done. Some inexperienced or untrained teachers are to be found, however, who partially neglect the oral work, and who promote their pupils far more rapidly than their attainments warrant. To this fact may be attributed a large proportion of the failures to pass the Provincial Examination. As the number of Normal trained teachers is gradually increasing, it is fair to expect more thorough work in the common school department of the Course of Study, and consequently fewer failures to obtain scholarship certificates.

There are about thirty schools in the District of Clare for which French-speaking teachers are required. To supply this demand there were but fifteen licensed French teachers available. It was necessary to engage others to supply the remainder of these schools, and to apply for " *permissive licenses* " for that purpose. Several of those who taught during the year under " permits " are experienced teachers who did creditable work, and in this regard compared favorably with those holding regular licenses. It is to be hoped, however, that the Academy opened this year at Church Point will, within a couple of years at most, enable French students to obtain regular licenses in sufficient numbers to supply all the French schools.

In my last report I inadvertently omitted any reference to the meetings of our Teachers' Association, held at Weymouth in the month of May. As a synopsis of the proceedings was published in the " Educational Review " and in the local papers, it will not be necessary at this late date to refer to them at any great length. It will be sufficient to say that the subject of Science Teaching and Tonic Sol-Fa occupied the attention of the Association, and proved exceedingly beneficial in aiding inexperienced teachers in introducing the oral lessons on Nature and Music into their schools. The Association was on this occasion particularly indebted to Principal Goucher of Lawrencetown, Prof. Smith of Truro, and Principal Cameron of Yarmouth, for their aid in the departments of Science and Literature, and to Miss Addie Parker for her admirable lessons on the Tonic Sol-Fa system of teaching music. Papers were also read by Principal Woodman of Weymouth Bridge, and Mr. Hogg of Digby.

The meetings of the Teachers' Association—to be known hereafter by virtue of recent regulations as the "Teachers' Institute"—were held this year at Bridgetown, on the 30th and 31st days of May. An interesting programme was presented, including the following papers and lessons, viz. :—

"Practical Teaching," by Mrs. Ida M. Benson.
An illustrative lesson in Botany on "The Lily of the Valley," by Miss Margaret B. Redding.
" Tonic Sol-Fa "—a paper—by Miss Jennie A. Hall.
An illustrative lesson in Botany on "The Apple," by Principal Dunlop.
Literature—"Goldsmith's Traveller," by Principal Brown.
"Tonic Sol-Fa "—a lesson—by Miss Hattie Congdon.
"Tardiness and Irregular Attendance," by Jos. Crowe.
"The causes of unequal length of Day and Night," by Principal McVicar.

"The "Metric System" was to have been présented by Principal Longley of Digby, but illness prevented.

About one hundred teachers were present at the various meetings, and much enthusiasm was manifested. The discussions which followed the presentation of the various papers were practical and instructive. The teachers present were much indebted to Dr. MacKay, the Superintendent of Education, and to Principal Patterson and Mr. McGill, of Acacia Villa Seminary, for their presence and assistance, which contributed largely to the success of the Institute. A public meeting was held in the Baptist Church on the evening of the 30th, which was attended by a large audience. The principal speakers were Dr. MacKay, the Supt. of Education, and Principal Patterson of Acacia Villa Seminary. Short addresses were also given by Principals McVicar, Longley, Shaffner, Dunlop, Mr. McGill, and Rev. Geo. E. Tufts of Belfast, Maine. Dr. MacKay spoke of the educational affairs of this Province as compared with those of Ontario, and while he believed the high school system of that Province to be superior to our own, yet he was certain that the common school system of this Province was superior to that of Ontario. He spoke at length of the old system of education and of the new, and emphasized the necessity of instilling into the minds of pupils the spirit of patriotism. Principal Patterson's address was enthusiastic and interesting, as his public addresses always are. Several pieces of music rendered in a superior manner by the church choir, contributed much to the interest of the occasion. The meetings of the Institute on this occasion may be considered among the best yet held, and will tend yet further to engender an *esprit de corps* among the teachers, and to furnish incentives to more energetic and successful work in their profession. The large attendance of teachers at these meetings entitled the Institute to send *four* delegates to the Provincial Association, and Principals Brown, McVicar, and Longley, and Mrs. Benson, were elected for that purpose.

Of late years the Optional Compulsory Attendance law has not engaged the serious attention of the rate-payers in this Inspectoral District, and few sections only have voted on the resolution as required by law. According to instructions received, all sections which had not voted on this question at the annual meetings in June were promptly notified to call a special meeting for that purpose. At this writing reports have been received from 172 sections, showing that compulsory attendance, as defined by the law, was adopted in 89 and rejected in 83 sections. It may be fair to assume that the remaining sections will be divided in about the same proportion. In very many sections the vote was unanimous, either for or against the Act.

With one or two exceptions the Annual Returns came to hand promptly. Most of these were carefully prepared and correct. Several required revision or completion, and were sent back for that purpose. A few teachers fail to comprehend that the returns, so far as the tables are concerned, is to be a copy of the register, although they have been instructed that such is the case.

The County Academies at Annapolis and Digby were taught by Principals McVicar and Longley respectively. Excellent work was done at both of these academies. The attendance was good considering the large amount of high school work being done in many of the common schools, particularly in the head departments of most of the graded schools.

The County Academy at Church Point, in connection with Ste. Anne's College, was taught by Principal Phalen. As this is the first year in the history of that Academy as much could not be expected as will be looked for later on. Those who succeeded in passing the entrance examination were the college students. No candidates from the common schools were successful. Mr. Phalen did as good work as could be expected. Quite a number of his pupils were not very familiar with the English language and this made his position more difficult to fill with satisfaction. As you have visited all three of these Academies, it will not be necessary to say more in this connection.

All schools were inspected during the year except that in Salem Section, in Annapolis East. The destruction of the school house by fire, and the closing of the school in consequence thereof, prevented an inspection of that school. Some were visited a second time, and more would have been accomplished if an accident in the early part of June, while in the discharge of my duty, had not compelled me to remain at home during the remainder of the school year.

The Health Readers are now being used in most schools of this district with very beneficial results. A large amount of useful knowledge is thus being imparted in a more systematic manner than was possible to be given by inexperienced teachers without the aid of such books. A very few schools have not introduced these readers, but these will probably do so before another year passes.

Reference has been made to the thirty purely French schools in this district. For these schools no French books have been prescribed, except the bilingual series of Royal Readers. As the series does not extend beyond the No. 3 Reader, the advanced classes in these schools have been using such books as the "Nouveau Traité," and "Telemaque." I have ordered the " Nouveau Traité " to be discontinued, as its use clearly contravenes the spirit and intention of the school law. In view of these facts an advanced French reader should be prescribed, in order that those classes which get beyond the third bilingual Readers may have some authorized reading book available for use. A French grammar should also be prescribed for use in these schools. Hoping that these recommendations may commend themselves to your judgment,

I have the honor to be, Sir,

Your obedient servant,

L. S. MORSE.

A. H. MacKay, Esq., Ll..D.,
Superintendent of Education.

DISTRICT No. 5.—HANTS AND KINGS.

Colin W. Roscoe, A. M., *Inspector.*

Sir :—

As required, I submit a report of the schools under my supervision in District No. 5, for the year ended July, 1895.

The information contained in the statistical tables, sent herewith, affords a detailed statement of all matters connected with the schools in the three school commissioners' districts included in my inspectorate. I need not therefore repeat much of this information. Those who desire to go somwhat into such details as are given in a school report, are invited to study what had been prepared for the counties of Hants and Kings.

For comparison with 1894 A. D., I report for the two counties as follows :—

Date.	No. Schools.	No. Teachers.	No. Pupils.	Attendance.
1895.............	247	264	10,394	1,044,537
1894.............	241	256	10,322	1,045,574
Increase......	6	8	72	....
Decrease				1,037

TEACHERS.

Date.	A.	B.	C.	D.	Male.	Female.	Total.
1895	6	42	137	79	46	218	264
1894	3	44	132	77	49	207	256
Increase ..	3	......	5	2	......	11	8
Decrease..	......	2	.....	.....	3	....	......

Eight sections—three in Hants and five in Kings—did not open schools during the year. These were Mt. Summerville, Lakelands, and Rawdon Gold Mines, in Hants, and Fair View, Black Rock Mt., Baxter's Harbor, Town Plot, and East Pereaux Mt., in Kings. There was a somewhat reasonable excuse given in each case for not having a school, and I am expecting schools in most of these sections next year. The schools in operation made a good record as a whole. Most of them fully sustained their previous good standing, and in some notable respects did work of a superior character. I am able to report a more general conformity to the course of study than heretofore. Subjects that hitherto were regarded of less importance than many others, came in for a fair share of time and attention. Among these calisthenics, music, moral and patriotic duties, and lessons on nature may be referred to. The excuse for not teaching these in the past was " want of time." When the *Journal of Education* for October, 1894, came to hand, all the teachers, with few exceptions, set about preparing to teach these subjects. Those who have been most careful to divide their time so as to give each subject a fair proportion, and who have endeavored to make the best use of the time assigned to the various subjects, report in substance as follows :—

Calisthenics secures the strictest attention of all the pupils, exercises the muscles of all parts of the body, gives an agreeable relaxation from work, and so enlivens the pupils that they can do much more and much better work after engaging in this exercise than they otherwise could do. So far then as time is concerned this drill results in gain ; and so far the habit of attention, correct form and position enter into this matter, great advantage is gained.

Music is more enjoyed than any other exercise in the school. All *want* to sing and *do sing* when properly taught. The Tonic Sol-fa notation is easily learned, and the pupils are so inspired while singing, and the exercise leaves them in such a happy state of mind that other and harder work is easily performed. In this too there is a gain in all that pertains to the management of the school. Any time spent in singing is more than compensated for by the increased ability it gives to perform other duties. It is understood that but a short period is to be devoted each day to calisthenics and music, and this at a time when relaxation is most needed.

Moral and Patriotic Duties, so far, is taught principally in connection with other lessons, and at times when some incident suggests a lesson. Occasionally a set lesson is given on such topics as "Truth," " Honesty, " Industry," " Our Flag," " Our Great Men," &c. There are plenty of topics, full of interest, affording as much real education as can be secured in any other way.

Nature Lessons, when thoroughly and properly prepared and adapted to the age of the pupils, produce most beneficial results in the mastery of other subjects, as well as in awakening and developing the power of the mind. All these subjects have proved failures in the hands of some teachers, because the main aim seemed to be to do enough to have something to report and thus have their schools accepted. It is questionable whether any one should receive license to teach when he has never demonstrated, by actual practice, that he *can* teach. And it seems to me that those who have defects which will prevent them from teaching a subject essential to the well-being of all schools, should not think of teaching as a profession.

I am pleased to report that so large a number of teachers in this district have made a success of these so called new subjects. Many of them spent their Saturdays and holidays in going to places at some distance to be taught music, so that they could teach it in their own schools. In this way they have been benefitted themselves by the new order of things, while they were preparing to teach others. It is not now an uncommon thing to have quite young pupils write from memory the music of some of the national songs, and sing them both by note and words. We have made commendable progress along these lines. I may add that the schools in which most has been done in the subjects referred to, have made the best progress in all the other required subjects.

Upper Canard and Lower Canard sections, after several years of miscellaneous school life, have graded their schools again. These sections are situated in the wealthiest part of Kings county ; and twenty years ago their schools were among the best graded schools in the county. For want of pupils the schools became miscellaneous, and for some years, until now, they enjoyed but one teacher each. They are now returning to their former good standing.

SCHOOL BUILDINGS.

The improvement in school buildings continues. During the past year several houses have been re-seated with an improved kind of seat and desk. To make the house compare with the furniture necessitated considerable repairs and painting. Piedmont, Waterville (Primary), Lakeville, Centreville, Lower Canard (Primary), and Upper Church Street may be mentioned as those that have done most in improvements of this kind.

Kentville has built a large addition to the school house, and thereby nearly doubled the school accommodation. In this a room has been fitted up as a laboratory, and another for the use of one of the large classes of the academic department. There remains two large unfinished rooms which will be finished as soon as needed. The accommodation is now ample for some years to come. The town has increased the school grounds by the purchase of a large lot of land. Now it consists of two acres or more.

One hundred and three were enrolled in the academic department during the past year, and the prospects are so good for an increase that a third grade A teacher has been engaged for the incoming year. In equipment, teachers, and otherwise, this school holds a first-class position.

A good school house was completed in Aylesford, the new section formed by the school commissioners in May, 1894, and occupied for a school at the beginning of 1895. This school raised funds, by an entertainment to purchase apparatus and chemicals for experiments in chemistry and physics. In this respect it is now the best equipped of any miscellaneous school in the district.

Lakeville, also, by means of a school entertainment, supplied maps and some much needed apparatus for the school. Occasionally this might be done to advantage in many sections.

The school house in West Branch, Falmouth, was burned near the end of the first half year of the past term, and the school conducted in a dwelling house for the remainder of the term. This is a small poor section. The school made an average of about 12 for the past year. Arrangements have been made for rebuilding. To do this the people contribute lumber, shingles, and such material as they have, and then do most of the work among themselves.

INDIAN RESERVE.

There is a settlement of Indians about five miles west from Shubenacadie, on a tract of reserved land in East Hants. The Dominion Government's agent built a school house and engaged to pay a teacher's salary, and the trustees of East Indian Road section, which includes this Indian Reserve, have recognized the school by signing the "Returns." The board of school commissioners decided that the grant from the County Fund on account of this school should be used for its equipment and benefit, and not for general school purposes in East Indian Road section. The school was in session for nine months of the past year. Thirty-eight pupils were enrolled. The attendance, as was expected, was somewhat irregular. Mr. Robert J. Logan was the teacher. He did good work, and the children seemed delighted to be taught. At the request of the agent I inspected the school. I think it will prove a great boon to these Indian people.

ARBOR DAY.

Some schools are in the habit of observing "Arbor Day" once a year. The day is spent in setting trees, preparing beds and sowing flower seeds, and in clearing up and improving the appearance of the school grounds. This is done by the sanction and help of the trustees and section. The day is either begun or concluded by addresses, recitations, songs, etc., and thus throughout is one of pleasure and profit. I am in favor of the day thus spent. In too many cases the teachers give the impression that a day is set apart as an arbor holiday. Without consultation with the trustees, teachers and what few pupils think it worth while to come, spend an hour or so in some little work about the grounds, go home and report that " Arbor Day " was observed. I cannot believe the day was intended to be used in this way, and will not encourage teachers to spend it thus. If for any one day more than another a surplus of work is provided, this day is " Arbor Day." The teacher should prepare for it before hand, and make his lessons on plants, etc., for this day, worth much to the pupils, and the work done on the grounds should be of such a kind as to prove a constant source of instruction.

TEACHERS' INSTITUTE.

A successful Teachers' Institute was held in Windsor on Thursday and Friday, April 26th and 27th, 1895. One hundred and ten enrolled as members, and many others were in attendance. The papers, lessons and addresses were of a highly instructive character. The presence and aid of Dr. A. H. MacKay, Superintendent of Education, Prof. Roberts of Kings College, Prof. Haley of Acadia College, Prof. Faville of the Horticultural School, and other eminent educationists, made the meetings of great value to the teachers. The evening of Thursday was devoted to a public meeting. A prominent feature of this meeting was the singing of one hundred of the pupils of the Windsor schools, directed by Miss N. A. Burgoyne. The singing was interspersed by speeches from Dr. MacKay, Professors Roberts, Haley and Faville, and Rev. Mr. Archibald. Mayor Wilson was requested by the president to preside, and he did so in a most satisfactory manner. The singing and addresses were listened to and much enjoyed by the largest audience that could be accommodated in the largest hall of the town, and some hundreds could not gain admittance.

The next meeting of the Institute will be held in Berwick.

For details I refer you to the Statistical Tables and Notes of Inspection in your hands.

Your obedient servant,

COLIN W. ROSCOE.

A. H. MacKay, Esq., LL.D.,
    Superintendent of Education.

DISTRICT No. 6.—ANTIGONISH AND GUYSBORO'.

W. MacIsaac, B. A., *Inspector.*

Sir:—

I beg leave, in compliance with the law, to submit my report on the schools of District No. 6 for the year ended July, 1895.

A new section was organized at North Branch, Ogden, at the last meeting of the school board at Guysboro. Steps have been already taken to build a school house, which will be finished at an early date.

There were 93 schools in operation in Antigonish, with a total enrolment of 3551, and a grand total attendance of 338,617.

The number of schools in session in Guysboro was 92; the total enrolment 3871; and the grand total of attendance, 369,181.

The proportion of population at school in Antigonish was 1 in 4.51, and in Guysboro 1 in 4.44.

In Antigonish the average of quarterly percentages was 54.4, and in Guysboro 60.2.

The number of children between 5 and 15 years of age not attending school at all in Antigonish was 246; in Guysboro, 331.

Number of teachers employed of different grades is as follows:—

ANTIGONISH.

A	B	C	D
4	7	37	49

GUYSBORO'.

A	B'	C	D
2	8	36	52

The number of schools in session for full year of 216 days in Antigonish, was 42; in Guysboro, 32.

Average number of days all the schools were in session in Antigonish was 187; in Guysboro, 190.5.

There are 81 sections in Antigonish, of which 76 had school; in Guysboro 90, of which 80 had school.

Average salary paid the teachers, including Government Grant:—

ANTIGONISH.

	B	C	D
Male......	$293 77	$229 51	$176 54
Female....	275 27	224 88	153 47

GUYSBORO.

	B	C	D
Male......	$418 77	$269 40	$137 13
Female....	308 27	243 00	159 21

In the matter of school buildings, and better equipment and accommodation, some improvement has been done during the year. It would be pleasant to record as evidence of increasing intelligence, humanity and liberality on the part of the people, that better efforts are being made in the construction, ventilation, heating, and furnishing of school houses on modern and approved plans. But this is generally difficult of accomplishment for financial reasons, except in the case of the principal towns.

The new Academy in Guysboro', which has been erected during the year, is an excellent specimen of the ideal school building. It commands a beautiful position near the site of the old academy, and has four large and commodious departments. It is an ornament to the town, and a lasting testimony of the public spirit and generosity of its citizens.

Although there are many schools furnished with the necessary aids and appliances such as books, maps, and other school apparatus, there are still a few in the rural districts presenting nothing more attractive than the bare walls and the old-fashioned black-board. This neglect is frequently brought to the attention of the trustees and teachers—the latter generally blaming the former, and the former justifying their apathy on the ground of lack of funds. It is gratifying to note, however, that it is only in a comparatively few schools that such an undesirable state of affairs exists.

One cannot help noticing how much the success of our common schools depends upon the excellence with which our academies and high schools, in which our teachers are usually prepared for their scholarship examination, do their work. Indeed the more the academic standard of work is raised, the more surely will our teachers in the lower schools and grades possess ability for their work. And this is true not merely in the matter of scholarships, but with regard to methods of teaching as well. The teacher very naturally endeavours to make his own the method pursued in the schools that enabled him to pass from the position of a pupil to that of a teacher. Of course, if all our teachers had the benefit of a Normal School training, this dependence of the common schools on the high schools in the matter of professional skill would in a large measure cease.

While it must be admitted that the change from the two-term year to the one term has diminished the evil of frequent changes of teachers, I am convinced that our schools still suffer too much injury. A teacher has no sooner become acquainted with the powers, dispositions, habits, and attainments of his pupils than his term closes ; and the trustees often, on the plea of saving money to the section, employ another who must gain the knowledge of the school which his predecessor acquired before he can effectually do his work. The time consumed in this continued routine of repetition, which should add vastly to the power and acquirements of the youth under instruction, is too precious to be passed without notice.

It too often happens that parents and trustees expect results of a striking character at the public examination of the school, and that the absence of such results is regarded by them as a proof of inefficiency on the part of the teacher, when conclusions quite different would be formed by people understanding correctly the true test of the teacher's work. They forget that true education only aids the healthy growth of the mind which is slow, and not of a nature to be exhibited in a startling fashion. The full value of the incorporation into the mind of principles, and the formation of tastes and habits, will only appear after the mature years shall have developed their tendencies. Indeed, the highest and best parts of education are incapable of exhibition. The show made in examination days, which often proves so interesting to the children and visitors, is frequently but the frost-work of education, which vanishes with the occasion. The inferences drawn by parents from these occasions encourage, or perhaps create a tendency on the part of many teachers, to give undue prominence and too much time to mere mechanical drill and memoriter work.

In a few schools I have found too much time given to one or two, or three of the more advanced pupils who were preparing for the teachers' examination. Individual teaching is very good in its place, but it should not be done at the expense of a large majority of the pupils. Teachers who undertake to make their mark by successfully preparing pupils for these examinations, should endeavor to understand the art of profitably employing and interesting the primary grades in the school while they are engaged in high school work.

I am glad to be able to say that arithmetic on the whole is well and practically taught; but in many schools the recitations in some of the other subjects of the course, particularly in language teaching, are poor. The text-book is still far too dominant; and teachers, in giving direct information, do not always confine themselves to the limits which should leave an inviting field for the pupil's own investigations, and secure his personal interest in pushing inquiry further.

On the whole, progress is being made in nearly all our schools. Our teachers in general are devoted to their calling, and our school system is producing a fair measure of success all along the line.

I have the honor to be, Sir,
*   Your obedient servant,

W. MacISAAC.

A. H. MacKay, Esq., Ll.D.,
      Superintendent of Education.

DISTRICT No. 7.—CAPE BRETON AND RICHMOND.

M. J. T. Macneil, B. A., *Inspector.*

(Report not received in time for publication.)

DISTRICT No. 8.—INVERNESS AND VICTORIA.

J. McKinnon, *Inspector*.

SIR :—

I beg to submit the following brief report on the state of the public schools in Inspectoral District No. 8, comprising the counties of Inverness and Victoria, for the school year ended July, 1895.

No new sections were created during the year. There are, therefore, as reported in 1894 by my respected predecessor, 257 sections— 177 in Inverness, and 80 in Victoria.

The total number of schools in operation in Inverness during the year, or any part of it, was 164, and in Victoria 59, leaving 13 vacant sections in the former and the large number of 21 in the latter county. A majority of these are weak and more or less disorganized, and unable or unwilling to hire teachers.

The date of my appointment (December 1st) did not permit me to visit all the schools in my district before the close of the school year, and it being my first year of inspectoral work, I am not in a position to report accurately as to the year's progress, or to make comparisons between the present condition of the schools and the past. I shall therefore confine myself to a few observations of a general character, founded upon what I have noticed during my school visits.

The County Academies at Port Hood and Baddeck, the High Schools at Port Hawkesbury and Mabou, each having four departments, are efficiently conducted, and are doing good and satisfactory work. The graded schools at Port Hastings, Whycocomah, Eastern Harbor, and Belle Côte with two departments each, are also doing well.

The condition of the miscellaneous schools varies very greatly. A considerable number, in spite of many drawbacks, are giving satisfactory results, the teachers being well trained and painstaking, but too many are in a very unsatisfactory condition. The fault is not always, not even generally with the teachers. The equipment of the great bulk of the smaller schools is very meagre, or is entirely wanting. The trustees in many cases grossly neglect their duties. Parents manifest no interest in the school, hence the children attend very irregularly, and entirely neglect home preparation of lessons. All this leads to the utter discouragement of the teacher, and disposes him, so soon as his engagement expires, to seek another school, leaving his successor to travel the same disheartening round again.

The teachers as a rule desire to do their duty and are anxious to succeed, but many lack experience and skill. The salaries to be obtained in the lower grades hardly compensate for the time occupied and the expenses incurred in taking a course at the Provincial Training Institution at Truro, and until trustees and ratepayers are willing to pay higher salaries for the education of their children than they do at present, they cannot expect efficient and well-trained teachers to offer their services.

At present too many teachers, in the lower grades especially, are mere hearers of lessons learned by rote from text books, and they quite misapprehend the proper function of the teacher. There are others, however, I am glad to say, who without any special aid or training, have developed into teachers of a high order, showing what original capacity developed by experience can attain to.

A very considerable number of sections are too weak financially, and too small, to maintain an efficient school, hence in a great degree the large number of sections vacant during the year now expired.

The smallness of so many sections is an evil for which some remedy should be provided, and as a step in that direction I think that discretionary power should be vested in the school commissioners to unite two weak sections when, in their opinion, the educational interests of the locality manifestly required it.

A serious drawback to the interests of schools in this district is the frequent change of teachers. From 60 to 70 per cent. change their situations every year. This unfortunate practice is not so much the fault of the teacher as that of the ratepayers and trustees. Given a comfortable school house and fair salary and there will be no difficulty in retaining the services of a good teacher for years.

The School Returns nearly all came to hand within the time allotted. A large number were correctly made up, but a considerable minority showed haste and culpable carelessness, being wanting in neatness and accuracy.

Owing to the large number of sections without schools the attendance for the past year shewed no appreciable increase. The following being the figures :—

	1895.		1894.	
	Boys.	Girls.	Boys.	Girls.
Inverness	3285	2801	3292	2803
Victoria.................	1165	1034	1171	1052

The compulsory clauses of the Education Act have been adopted in a considerable number of sections. I do not anticipate that the power thus acquired will be exercised to any material extent in the meantime. A more coercive enactment is needed to accomplish the desired reform.

The schools in the three commissioners' districts in this inspectorate may be reported as follows :

	No Schools.	No. Teachers.	No. Pupils.	Days' Attendance.
North Inverness....	65	71	2731	267,953
South Inverness....	85	96	3355	304,147
Victoria	59	63	2199	201,808

TEACHERS.

	A.	B.	C.	D.	Male.	Female.	Total.
Inverness	2	16	51	98	97	70	167
Victoria	1	4	21	37	23	40	63
Total......	3	20	72	135	120	110	230

The salaries, I regret to say, do not appear to be increasing in amount. According to the returns they average as follows, including government grants :

MALES.

	A.	B.	C.	D.
Inverness	$750 00	$233 77	$187 57	$124 38
Victoria	750 00	267 77	234 57	154 38

FEMALES.

	B.	C.	D.
Inverness	$220 77	$175 57	$116 38
Victoria	237 77	210 57	137 38

The extremely low salaries offered by many sections lead to a scarcity of teachers both in Inverness and Victoria, and no alternative presents itself except to leave the schools closed or issue permits to a number of persons indifferently qualified for the teaching profession. No remedy for this state of affairs can be suggested until parents and trustees are willing to tax themselves a little heavier for the education of their children than they do at present, unless, indeed, the legislature step in and substantially increases the amount at present collected by the county authorities for educational purposes.

The statistical tables, already forwarded to your office, will supply further details, and make it needless to extend this report to a greater length.

I have to thank you, Sir, for much valuable assistance and kindness during this my first year of office.

Your obedient servant,

J. McKINNON.

A. H. McKAY, ESQ., LL.D.,
Superintendent of Education.

6

DISTRICT No. 9.—PICTOU AND SOUTH COLCHESTER.

W. E. MACLELLAN, Lt.B., *Inspector.*

SIR :—

I have the honour to submit the following report of my Inspectoral District for the past school year.

The number of schools in operation has been unusually large—the largest, I believe, in the history of the district. In South Colchester, every school, with the exception of Green's Creek, was open during some portion of the year. The section named is a poor one, and was engaged in repairing its school house. In South Pictou, every organized section had school. The two disorganized sections in this district are Fraser's Mountain and Riverton. The former has been without school for years, its few pupils finding accommodation in the schools of neighbouring sections. The latter was so reduced in strength by the formation of Eureka section that it has not since opened its school. Its pupils, however, are within reach either of Stellarton or Eureka.

North Pictou had two sections without school—Central Carriboo, closed on account of repairs to school house, and College Grant, because its trustees were unwilling to pay the sum necessary to secure the services of a teacher. The last named is one of those sections which seem to consider themselves entitled to a school without cost to their ratepayers. It receives special aid from the county fund, and has usually managed, I am informed, to keep its expenditures within the limits of its puplic grants. Authorized by the board of school commissioners, I have notified the trustees that more energy and liberality will be required of them hereafter.

The attendance of pupils for the year has been satisfactory, although there was a falling off in the third quarter owing to storms and bad roads. The one-year term has undoubtedly improved the attendance. This fact is, I think, generally recognized. Nearly all seem satisfied with the change. I seldom hear complaints concerning it, except from the few teachers who have the boldness to confess that they would enjoy a change of location every six months, or from trustees who are unwilling to abide by the consequences of engaging, without enquiry, the cheapest and frequently the most incompetent available teacher.

I have to report continued and highly gratifying progress in the matter of improving school buildings and premises. Shubenacadie section, in the district of South Colchester, has completed a most creditable building—furnace-heated, well ventilated, handsomely furnished, altogether the best country school house in my district. Lower Stewiacke Village has enlarged its building and graded its school. Riverside has put up a new and comfortable school house. Green's Creek has renovated and refurnished its room. Nuttby has made substantial repairs. A number of sections have voted liberal sums for improvements during the coming year.

In the County of Pictou, Moose River section has completed a comfortable new building to replace the one destroyed by fire last winter. Rossfield has a new building ready for occupation. New Glasgow has occupied its new high school building. The following sections have thoroughly repaired and re-furnished their school houses, namely, River John, Lyon's Brook, Central Carriboo, Marshdale, and Roger's Hill. Less extensive but important repairs and improvements have been made by a number of other sections, and many have been aroused to the necessity of providing better out-house accommodation. The sums voted at the last annual meetings give promise of increased activity in school-house improvement for the coming year.

I am trying to interest pupils and teachers, as well as parents and trustees, in the good work of increasing the attractiveness of school-rooms and premises. In not a few instances I have met with gratifying success, and I am not without hope that a movement has begun which may soon become general.

In the matter of providing maps, globes, and other necessary apparatus, I have to report increasing willingness on the part of trustees to comply with the requirements of the law. A large number of schools have had their equipment materially improved during the year.

In the district of South Colchester, two sections—Kemptown and Springmount—which had long been disorganised, have again got into working order, and maintained school during part of the year. Carriboo Island, in the county of Pictou, is about to reorganize and will build a new school-house.

With four exceptions—Pictou Island, Merigomish Island, Kemptown and Brookland, I visited once all the schools in my district open at the time of my rounds; many of them I visited twice; some, three or four times. Pictou Island was omitted because of the difficulty of reaching it at times when 1 could leave my other work. My last visit to this section cost me a whole week. Merigomish Island was left at the time of my visit to Merigomish on account of bad weather. I intended to revisit Merigomish at a better season and to inspect the island school then, but was unable to do so. I missed Kemptown and Brookland schools by reason of an accident to my horse when on the way to them.

The supply of teachers in my district has been sufficient and on permissive licences have been granted, although a number of applications for them were made by trustees who were unwilling to take the trouble or reluctant to pay the salary necessary to secure regularly licensed teachers.

Of the work done in and by the schools I need say little. In its high-school departments it was tested by the Provincial examinations, the results of which you know. Change in the character of the common school work is so slight as to be scarcely perceptible from one year to another. I trust, however, that it is in the direction of

nation of learning among all classes makes an incompetent teacher no longer tolerable. About the only criticisms upon the system of yearly engagements come from those who are the victims of a bad bargain.

SERVICE.

Twenty-five per cent. of the teachers of 1893-94 continued in the service of the same section in 1894-95. Changes take place most frequently among the poorer schools and often to their disadvantage.

In the graded schools seventy-five per cent. re-engaged in the same sections.

Forty-three inexperienced teachers were engaged this year There are only twenty-four who have been in the service over ten years and but five veterans, namely, those who have taught more than twenty.

SALARIES.

	MALES.				FEMALES.			
GRADES	A.	B.	C.	D.	A.	B.	C.	D.
Cumberland........	$865 20	$465 77	$263 87	$264 13	$310 77	$300 43	$231 88	$167 70
Colchester.........	.....	512 43	320 57	200 38	......	280 77	224 72	150 98

But little change is noticeable in this direction. Whatever little advance there is it is chiefly due to the increase in the Government allowance, which was the largest amount ever given to individual teachers in the history of our free schools. This reversion to the former grant was a comely act on the part of the Government, and was much appreciated by the teachers.

It seems to me there should be a regulation governing in some way the amount each section having property to the value of $20,000 or more, should contribute to teachers' salaries. In sections able to pay liberal salaries, the lowest grades and the most incompetent teachers are frequently employed. The fallacious argument is sometimes used that the class of children attending school is young and does not need scholarship or skill.

There is a scarcity of teachers this year, especially in the third class. There are enough teachers resident in the two counties forming this district to fill all positions, but they will not engage for amounts insufficient for a living.

SCHOOL BUILDINGS.

There was not so much activity in building as last year.

Stake Road has erected a new house and equipped it with modern furniture.

Shinimicas has enlarged the school room and provided better entrances.

Wallace is maintaining rooms in a more efficient state, and has refurnished one department.

Lower Gulf Shore has refurnished school room and improved appearance of school grounds.

At Shinimicas Bridge, school room was enlarged to accommodate increased attendance.

Southampton section has completely remodelled and refurnished its house.

River Philip (82) having lost its house by fire, has built one of the best school rooms in the county and upon a better site.

Having liquidated the debt upon the new building at North Wallace Bay, the section has refurnished it.

Port Greville has a school of two departments. These have been so remodelled as to better accommodate the primary department.

Black Rock section, on West Bay, has built a neat house at a great sacrifice.

At Fox River a modern house of two departments has been built.

The school room in Halfway River had some repairs made upon it. This school is attended by a number of Indian children from the neighboring Reserve. They have made considerable progress in reading, writing, and numbers. The district commissioners, through the Indian agent at Parrsboro', have solicited the co-operation of the Indian Department in the maintenance of the house. The section is poor, and it is with great difficulty that a school can be supported the year round. There are 16 Indian children between the ages of 5 and 15 living in the section.

In Yarmouth section (30) the last log school house in the district has been displaced by a framed structure.

Lower Economy has opened a branch school in Gerrish Valley. The people in this remote part of the section have not been able to enjoy school privileges until their children were past the school-going age. With laudable generosity the ratepayers have accorded this part of the section a school part of the year.

Under the efficient management of Principal Harlow, Great Village school presents a new appearance. The high school department has been equipped with considerable apparatus. This is also one of the few schools in the district which had any marked success at the recent examinations.

The school room at Eastville has been completely repaired and very comfortably furnished.

In Mill Brook section the school house has undergone substantial repairs, and has been refurnished.

At Oliver's Bridge repairs were made upon the school buildings, but not of so thorough a nature as in the last named.

The long standing feud which deprived Truro Road section of a school for two years, and led to the burning of the school house, has been settled. A new house here is in course of construction, and will be occupied in the latter part of the year.

BUILDINGS CONDEMNED.

At the last annual meeting of the commissioners, the school houses in Upper Linden (32), and Minudie (50), in the district of Cumberland, and Point Brule, in the district of Stirling, were condemned.

On January 10th, the new high school in Parrsboro' was dedicated by interesting and appropriate exercises. Some of those who took part were Dr. MacKay, the Superintendent of Education, Chairman Nicholls of the Board of School Commissioners, Principal Mackay, and the local clergy. This beautiful building is now without a superior among the high schools of the province in furnishings and suitable surroundings.

Westchester Station and DeBert River's large miscellaneous schools should be graded. In the former there were 65 pupils registered with a grand total of 7313 days' attendance, and in the latter 81 with 11,100 days. In neither section have the ratepayers made any provision for another department, although it has been pressed upon their attention by the commissioners. Both schools have ten grades. Westchester sent five " C " high school pupils for examination, and passed four for the grade applied for, and one for " D." Yet after this excellent record the ratepayers choose rather to reduce the efficiency of their school than make the suggested changes.

REGISTRATION.

There were 11,530 pupils registered during the year—5926 boys and 5604 girls; cost to the province per pupil is $1.72; to the sections, $3.39: Total attendance for the year is 1,179,775 days, and 49,279 more than last year.

In Cumberland County 12.6 per cent. of the population was in school the entire year, and 25.4 per cent. some time during the year.

TIME TABLE.

In the school week of 27½ hours, the greater part of the time is spent as follows:

Reading, etc.	6 hours.
Arithmetic	5 "
Spelling, etc.	3 "
English Language, etc.	2 "
Geography	2 "
Writing	1¾ "
History	1½ "
Drawing	1 "
Temperance, etc.	¾ "
Music	¾ "
Calisthenics	½ "
Book-keeping.	½ "
Moral and Patriotic Duties	⅓ "

The average amount of time spent upon these subjects varies but little in the two counties of this district; the uniformity is even remarkable.

Returns show much more care in their compilation. A few exaggerations appear in them. Occasionally some young grade D teacher endeavours to make me believe that she has taught all the sciences and classics in the course of study. Happily these instances are rare. There is but one subject in the course of study which I wish to refer to briefly, that is Agriculture, which is first mentioned in the 8th grade. I beg leave to suggest its place in all the grades. The Nature work may be so adapted that its trend may be in this direction. Let the lessons in botany, ornithology, entomology, chemistry, have a bearing on the agricultural life of the section. There is no factor so potent to popularize that calling, from which we have been drifting away so long, as the profession of teaching.

The very nature of an inspector's duties gives him the best opportunity to know the conditions and requirements of rural life. Associated a greater portion of the year with the farming class, he hears their grievances and discovers their wants. It is strikingly noticeable the improvidence displayed in the homes and upon the farms of 50 per cent. of the people. This arises mainly from an ignorance of the first principles taught in the elementary sciences.

Ninety per cent. of the farmers do not now enjoy the luxuries which Providence has placed within reach of their hands were they taught how to extend them. The delicacies of a good garden are almost unknown. The continual and injudicious cropping of farms in the first settled portions of the county, have forced hundreds to leave them for the precarious living of city or town. But our teachers need first to be taught. Few, though coming from country homes, have a practical, much less a theoretical knowledge of farming. The excellent institution at Truro affiliated with the Normal School, has been munificently equipped for an agricultural education, and the fullest advantage should be taken of it. No teacher should leave the training school until he or she has completed a course in some branch of agriculture.

The action of a number of teachers in voluntarily taking a course during the summer holidays, suggests an extension of the Normal School term in this department through the months of July and August, when there is much to be seen and learned.

HIGH SCHOOLS.

There were 429 pupils in this district doing high school work. 20 pupils, residents of the district, were either in Pictou or Truro Academies; 126 were taking a partial course, and 64 held provincial certificates.

Applicants for high school examination were distributed as follows:—Amherst Station, 81; Tatamagouche, 58; Parrsboro, 37; Springhill, 36; and Truro, 31. A few of these failed to present themselves.

While no official information touching the results of the examination has been received, I have been able to learn that, generally, they were disappointing. This I anticipated in my last report when alluding to indifferent promotions on the course of study.

Children get the impression that they are going to be advanced after spending a year in a certain grade, and, whether meriting or not, they are hurried on to the high school course at such a pace that they are to be found there at the tender age of twelve and thirteen years trying to do the work which requires maturer minds to grasp. A boy of average ability, with special training, may pass the 9th grade, but the step is a long one for the same pupil to the 10th in another year. I do not argue that the standard is too high, but I require more thorough work in the common school grades and more discrimination among teachers in making promotions.

DISTRICT INSTITUTE.

On November 7th, 8th, and 9th, the Teachers' Institute met in the commodious rooms of the Amherst Academy. Notwithstanding the season on which it fell being one of the most unpleasant of the year, 128 teachers registered. The meeting was highly successful and fraught with many good influences to those in attendance. I regret that there are few teachers in this district who are willing to teach year after year and not avail themselves of this privilege of association. At the risk of being too freely spoken, I may say that the great majority of failures are among those who stay at home. After attending these institute meetings even the most successful teachers sometimes admit their deficiencies, a confession which implies that their professional horizon has been enlarged.

" If teachers would grow they must use the means of growth. They must associate with their fellow teachers and discuss with them the principles which underlie all true teaching and all true discipline. They must make themselves familiar with that marvel of marvels, the human mind, and with the laws which govern its growth."

" They must make a constant study of the methods by which instruction may be most effectively given to a child."

PROGRAMME.

November 7th. For the observation of methods employed by the Amherst staff, the Academy was opened from 2.20 to 4 p. m. to visiting teachers.

On Wednesday evening, prior to the formal opening of the Institute, a reception was given to the teachers by the residents of Amherst· Mayor Curry presided.

November 8th—Morning Session. Enrolment of Teachers ; Inspector Craig's address ; Patriotism, Miss Augusta Pipes ; Relation of Education to Agriculture, Col. W. M Blair ; The best way to Maintain Discipline, Miss Lucretia Dawson.

Afternoon Session. The importance of Civics in Common Schools, Miss Margaret Graham; Research Work, Prof. Andrews, Mt. Allison; Advantages of Written Spelling, Miss Cassie McKenzie.

November 9th—Morning Session. Natural Phenomena, Principal MacKay; Lesson in English, Miss Julia Dickson; Primary Arithmetic—a talk, Prof. A. G. Macdonald; Teacher's Influence, Miss Bessie Douglass.

Afternoon Session. Drawing, A. Murray, B. A.; Business of Association.

The Educational meeting, presided over by Wm. Read, Esq., chairman of the local school board, was one of the largest ever held in the town. Speakers of the evening were Dr. MacKay, Prof. Macdonald, Hon. A. Dickey, Minister of Militia, T. R. Black, M. P. P., and Hon. H. Black.

The Summer School of Science, which met in Amherst this year, was quite liberally patronized by the teachers of Cumberland and Colchester. Over half the attendance was from these two counties.

The permanent location of the school in Parrsboro' I believe to be in its interests. Geographically it is in the centre of its constituency, and can be reached by rail and boat daily from almost any point of the Atlantic Provinces. The surrounding country affords the very best opportunities for study either in geology, mineralogy, or botany. To these must be added the attractions of a clean seaport town, charming scenery unsurpassed by any other parts of the provinces, scenes abounding in history and Indian legends, and last but not least, a cool, healthy atmosphere, when inland towns are suffering from summer heat.

Negotiations are now pending for the acquirement of Fort House Hill as a site for the proposed building. This was a military post commanding the entrance to Minas Basin in the times of the French wars.

The services which two teachers, the late Mr. John A. Purdy and Miss Bessie Wilson, gave to the schools of Cumberland, warrant a mention in this report. Mr. Purdy was connected with the Springhill schools for 15 years. Hundreds who have passed under his tutorship testify to his goodness of heart and ability as a teacher. Miss Wilson had been on the Amherst staff for several years, when ill health necessitated her resignation. Her popularity as a teacher was shown on the day of her burial, when many floral offerings were cast upon her grave by scores of little hands.

In conclusion, I desire to acknowledge your kindness and courtesy in our official relations. Also, the cheerful co-operation of teachers, to whose fidelity and general efficiency the prosperity of the schools is largely due.

Your obedient servant,

INGLIS C. CRAIG.

To A. H. MACKAY, ESQ., LL.D.,
Superintendent of Education.

APPENDIX C.

REPORT OF THE BOARD OF SCHOOL COMMISSIONERS

OF THE

CITY OF HALIFAX,

(YEAR ENDED JULY 31st, 1895.)

(I.)

CHAIRMAN'S REPORT.

OFFICE OF SCHOOL COMMISSIONERS,
Halifax, December, 1895.

A. H. MacKay, Esq., LL. D.,
   Superintendent of Education.

SIR:—

I have the honor to submit herewith, for the information of the Council of Public Instruction, the annual report of the Supervisor of Schools.

The members of the Board have devoted a great deal of time and energy to the ordinary duties devolving upon them in the past year, and have given prompt attention to all matters coming before them. Every effort has been made to keep the expenditure within reasonable bounds, at the same time endeavouring to maintain a high standard of efficiency in the schools.

The expenditure for the year ended April 30th, 1895, was $98,445.70 ; the estimate was $98,200.00.

The expenditure for the year ended Nov. 1st was $101,062.79, against $101,488.16 last year ; a saving of $425.37.

The expenditure for the common schools was $91,298.55 ; the attendance, 7,241 ; giving an average per pupil of $12.60, or 18 cents less per pupil than last year.

The commissioners have given more especial attention to examinations in the past year than heretofore, and have been able almost uniformly to report very satisfactory work. The teaching staff, as a whole, consists of ladies and gentlemen well educated and most devoted to their duties, a large proportion of them holding first-class licenses.

The Academy under the new Principal, Mr. Kennedy, has lost none of the prestige it acquired under his able predecessors. As the result of the recent Provincial Examination will show, it has led the Province in both the quantity and quality of its work.

The Board was called together in the past year on two occasions to record its regret at the death of two of its former members, who did eminent service to the country as well as to the Board. I refer to the late Right Hon. Sir John S. D. Thompson and Hon. M. J. Power.

An addition of two rooms, with four cloak rooms, to Bloomfield School has just been completed at a cost of $3,145.70, which includes architect fees, making six rooms in this building, and affording abundant accommodation to the pupils in this rapidly increasing district.

The large attendance pressing into Morris Street and LeMarchant Street Schools will necessitate an addition to the latter in the very near future.

Arbor Day.—A change in the method of observing " Arbor Day," by which each large school was placed in charge of a commissioner, was found to be a considerable improvement upon former methods. In nearly all the schools the teachers and pupils took great pains in having their rooms and play grounds properly decorated with plants, and otherwise, in which considerable taste was displayed. I might suggest to my successors that " Arbor Day " can be utilized, even more extensively than in the past, in educating the rising generation to the beauty and value of trees and plants.

Calisthenics.—The " Ling" system of Calisthenics was introduced this year into most of the school departments by Miss Holmstrom, who evidently has a scientific and practical knowledge of her work. For use in schools, this system seems to be better adapted than the old one to produce harmonious physical development. Many of the teachers have taken it up with great enthusiasm, and the effect on their classes has been most beneficial.

Truant Officer.—The truant law has been non-effective for some time on account of the Board not having a regular truant officer of its own. The defect has now, however, been happily remedied by the appointment of policeman Webster, whose efficiency was abundantly demonstrated in former years. Since his appointment, in June, he has taken the census of all children of legal school age in the city. These returns, having been tabulated and compared with teachers' returns, showed that about five hundred children had failed to make the requisite number of days, while many children had never attended any school. It was the object of the Executive who had to deal with this matter, to see that the children got the benefit of the expenditure made for their education.   To do this was a matter of very great difficulty, and required their most careful consideration for several successive meetings.   Every valid excuse was readily accepted, so that the number of actual delinquents was reduced to about fifty. By this means, and by the careful daily vigilance of the truant officer, the regular attendance has been greatly improved.

Buildings and Furniture.—The special committee from the " School Sites and Buildings," appointed to inspect school buildings, furnishings and grounds, devoted more than the usual time and attention to this important work before the closing of schools for summer holidays.   In addition to the usual repairs, which about equalled that of former years, the committee recommended not only the general tinting and painting of the walls and wood work, but also a thorough cleansing and renovating of the furniture, including all school desks, which were varnished. Upon the reopening of schools, the teachers and pupils were delighted to find their respective departments cleaner and brighter than ever before, a condition in which they were admonished to spare no pains in keeping them.   Although the work was so well done, it was found that the committee had kept within the limits of their estimate.   It is to be hoped that the greatly improved surroundings will assist in developing the taste and improving the morals of the pupils.

In conclusion, I desire to express my sincere appreciation of the hearty assistance accorded me at all times by the members of the Board in all matters coming before us in the past year, and cannot close without adding my testimony to that of my predecessors as to the high standing and qualifications of the Supervisor, Mr. Alex. McKay, and the Secretary, Mr. R. J. Wilson, both of whom are hard worked officials, and who fill their important offices to the very best satisfaction.

I have the honor to be,

Your obedient servant,

WILLIAM E. BREMNER,
Chairman.

(II.)

SUPERVISOR'S REPORT.

To the Chairman and Members of the Board of School Commissioners for the City of Halifax:

GENTLEMEN :—

I herewith submit my Annual Report on the public schools of Halifax. In the statistical tables accompanying this report you will find, set forth very fully, detailed information regarding the attendance of pupils, their studies, and the efforts of the teachers towards self-improvement.

ATTENDANCE.

The number of pupils enrolled during the year was 7524, showing an increase of 112.

During the first quarter, the daily average was 5153; second quarter, 4702; third quarter, 4594; and fourth or Spring quarter, 4983.

The percentage of attendance was 73, which was 2 per cent. less than that of the previous year. This was partly owing to the prevalence during the last two quarters of mild epidemic diseases, which, though not causing many deaths, yet interfered seriously with school attendance. Some of these diseases still continue, and, in the form of measles, are reducing the attendance in some departments by 30 or 40 per cent.

But another cause was also operating. The services of a special truant officer having been withdrawn, the compulsory attendance law was inefficiently administered, was even held in contempt where it had previously a wholesome effect. Truants and careless parents began to smile at threats which were seldom executed, and at punishments long deferred. The result was as might have been expected, an increase of truancy and irregularity of attendance.

Now, that a thoroughly capable truant officer has been appointed many of these evils will doubtless disappear.

But it is to be feared that even under the present more favorable circumstances it will be impossible to render the compulsory attendance act effective. Experience elsewhere teaches that such laws lose much of their beneficent effects when not supplemented by parental schools.

Even among respectable people there are many children whose misfortune it is to have parents or guardians weak in discipline. But among the poor, on account of the very unfavorable circumstances that sometimes prevail, such cases are very common, especially in towns and cities. Many of these unfortunate children, who might otherwise become useful citizens, go to swell the criminal classes. The strict enforcement of the compulsory act would greatly lessen the number of those who would become habitual truants, and save many ;

but they would be saved partly at the expense of those who became the victims of the weakness of their parents, of their own waywardness, and of the false economy of the state.

From general apathy, and from fear of expense, these unfortunate children are made to consort with criminals, and often return to their homes worse than they left them.

But all are not wholly apathetic. The commissioners often have to choose the less of two evils, and hoping against hope, they give many a boy another chance rather than send him to the Industrial School or the Reformatory. And so likewise, it is with painful regrets and misgivings that the Stipendiary pronounces every sentence.

The fact is that this law, which is very good as far as it goes, will not be efficiently administered, until *parental schools* are established.

It is good homes, with strong and kindly control, that we need for the boys ; not prisons. Superintendent Seaver says:

" Truancy is not in itself a crime ; but it is the dangerous way that leads many a boy into crime. The boy who has broken away from the restraints of home and school is not by that act a criminal ; though he. is giving rein to tendencies that will soon make him one. He is in grave danger, but timely care may save him. Now if the truant is not a criminal it is an injurious mistake to treat him as if he were ; it is worse. it is a crime against society. His self-respect must be guarded and cherished as the very germ of that better life that is to be awakened and strengthened in him."

There are in Halifax many, perhaps 30. or 40, or 50 children, who are almost certainly going to become criminals if left to themselves, or if sent to some penal establishment to associate with the hardened and to lose caste.

In Massachusetts every county but one has a parental school. Some other states have them also. Toronto has a *model* school of that kind,—a school in which the children are brought up under the most elevating influences.

In England truant schools are kept entirely distinct from all kinds of penal schools, and are managed by the school boards. Many parents voluntarily send their children to them, paying their expenses ; just as some parents in this city, having partially lost control of their boys, send them away for a time to some private school, where by a good disciplinarian, they may be educated into habits of obedience and industry. It is not looked upon as a disgrace, for they are merely sending their children to a specialist.

Now the establishment of a school of this kind is plainly necessary for Halifax ; for if our education is to be universal it must be free and compulsory. Other parts of the province need such a school as well as Halifax. This has become evident in every town where the compulsory law has been honestly tried, as in the town of Dartmouth.

It would then be economical, if at the beginning, a parental school were established for the whole Province by the Council of Public

Instruction. Such a school would, for several years, develop by experience the best methods, and serve as a model for other similar schools which, no doubt, will be established in every county within the next twenty years.

Now as to the character of the school to be established. It should be in a country district, and should consist of one cottage, or more than one, according to requirements, each with a few acres of land. Each cottage should be large enough to accommodate about 25 pupils. There should be a neat schoolroom having a department for manual training. There should be a well kept garden, and the whole establishment should be entirely home-like, with no high fences or other jail-like appurtenances. The cottage should be in charge of a male teacher, his wife, and one male assistant, and perhaps one or two servants. And here arises the chief difficulty, that of obtaining a suitable teacher. He should thoroughly understand human nature, should be apt to teach, should be gentle and strong, and should be familiar with many forms of manual labor, and his wife should be like-minded. Such teachers can be found, for we have them in the Halifax schools.

In this parental home the utmost regularity would prevail, and good habits would soon be formed. So far as the number of pupils would admit of it, they should be grouped in the different cottages according to age and moral conditions. All housework would be done by the pupils under competent direction. Three hours each day would be spent in school instruction. A few hours each day would be devoted to manual training and to gardening, and a few hours to play.

The cost of such an establishment would not be great, and would be borne in part by the parents according to their ability to pay; in part by the municipality to which the pupils belonged; and in part by the Provincial Government. .

It may be said, why not let this work be done by the churches and by charitable organizations? For the very simple reason that they are unable to do it. For centuries they grappled with the subject of general education and did magnificent work, yet half the people were illiterate. The state, in every civilized country had to step in and aid them. The churches and various societies have been doing a great work in Halifax, and yet there are dozens of vagrants in the streets, and others not yet criminals, are being made to associate with criminals. The churches have neither the money nor the legal status to enable them to cope fully with this crying evil. Experience everywhere shows that the work will not be done unless the state does it.

Prevention is better than cure,—nobler, and a hundred times more economical. Let us urge upon the government the necessity for such schools as I have described above, and aid it in their establishment. We may pattern after many successful experiments in England, the United States, and our own country; and can scarcely make a mistake.

This subject was introduced to the Teachers' Association, and advocated in a very able and thoughtful paper by Principal Miller,

7

and it was decided that Inspectors of Schools should be asked to collect information as a basis for the consideration of the government.

As corroborating what has been said above, my attention has been called to the fact that in England, between 1870 and 1893, juvenile crime has decreased nearly 70 per cent., and this in spite of the fact that acts are now classed as crimes that were formerly overlooked. This wonderful improvement is attributed partly to social conditions, but chiefly to the S. P. C. C., the truancy laws, and the moral and religious training in the schools. To quote from the *Independent*:

"Education has had its share in this good work ; the school laws punish truancy by sending the offenders to truant schools, where the little runaways, washed and clothed, are kept constantly at work witn a little study and no play, for two months for the first conviction, four for the second, and six for the third ; about half the truants are reformed during their stay in these schools. Industrial schools care for those who are not brought into line by the truant schools, and the reform schools set themselves the task of making bad boys and girls good. That they have succeeded so well and turned the tide of crime merits our hearty rejoicing."

There is another subject somewhat related to this to which I must refer. By the improvements in the compulsory act of last winter, pupils have to attend school between the ages of 14 and 16, unless properly at work. Now this change increases the number of large boys in the primary classes. They dislike school because they are humiliated by being placed in competition with very young pupils who have outstripped them in learning. The two classes have but few sympathies in common. The same motives do not appeal to them, nor do the same methods of teaching. Even the same subjects are not the most useful to them. The older boys are an injury to the younger, and their management too great a strain on the teacher, who would do excellent work with the younger children, were the older ones absent. I would therefore recommend the establishment, in some central locality, of one or two special departments for older boys who need to get the essentials of an education in as little time as possible. Establish such a department, place it under a superior male teacher, and you will materially lessen the number of truants, while at the same time adding largely to the comfort and efficiency of many other departments.

Before leaving the subject of attendance, I would call attention to the fact that 325 pupils are reported as attending 20 days or less ; 699 as attending between 20 and 50 days ; and 891 between 50 and 100. Now as the minimum required is 120, there must have been considerably over 2000 who failed to make the attendance required by law. While this is a matter for serious regret, and calls for some active remedy, it also shows the vast amount of work required of the Executive Committee, and its prudence in selecting only two or three per cent. of the cases presented, for investigation before the court. The public will surely not accuse it of inconsiderate harshness.

In reporting the attendance, it is sometimes a difficult matter to get at the proper enrolment. In such a school as Alexandra, for instance, where the primary departments are numerous and large, and pupils are transferred and sometimes re-transferred during the year, inexperienced teachers find it difficult to keep correct returns. The mistakes of this kind, though serious in only one instance, were more numerous than usual. It will be necessary for principals to be, more careful hereafter, even if it should cause the delay of a week in sending in the returns.

In this connection I may remark that much more care should be exercised in reporting the amount and value of apparatus in the schoolrooms. For the present year ten schools report libraries with an aggregate of 1710 volumes. Of these 720 belong to the Academy, and 400 to Summer St. school. That leaves 8 schools with an average of 75 volumes each, and 13 schools without any libraries.

The number of wall maps and globes are reported as being 411, which is, I believe, considerably below the correct number. All books, maps, globes, and scientific apparatus and collections, are reported as being worth only $1673, whereas they are doubtless worth three or four times that amount. Evidently the reports on these subjects are in many cases mere guesses. It is desirable that in every school there should be an inventory of all apparatus, with its cost ; so that the reports from year to year might be more reliable.

Table C. is interesting, as giving the average number of minutes devoted each week to each subject. I find that for the last year more time has been given to recreative studies, and less to temperance, patriotism, and other moral duties. Spelling and reading have each gained a little, but arithmetic has gained over an hour. In High School studies, Latin, Greek, French, and German combined, have lost over three and a half hours. Notwithstanding the discontinuance of Grade A, the High School students have increased in number by 13.

THE ACADEMY.

Of the excellent work done by the Academy, you can obtain a very correct idea from Principal Kennedy's report, which follows, and from the results of the Provincial examinations published elsewhere. These results show most conclusively that, taken as a whole, the common schools are doing most thorough work, such work as they never did before, in all the subjects tested by these examinations. Those in charge of the Academy are unquestionably superior teachers, but they could not achieve such results without good material, and that good material is almost wholly from the public schools,—about 85 per cent. of it from the public schools of Halifax,—from such teachers as Miss Creighton, Miss Miller, Miss Cunningham, Miss McGregor, Sr. DeChantal, Messrs Creighton, Marshall, E. J. Ross, O'Hearn and others.

But it was more in the way of criticism that I intended to speak of the Academy. In Classics the work was not quite equal to that of former years. This cannot be said to the discredit of the teacher, for he succeeded two remarkably able teachers, and did the classical work of both. That his pupils should have passed their examinations, though with slightly lower marks, shows that you could not have made a better appointment to that department. With the help of last year's experience he will leave nothing to be desired.

In modern languages, particularly French, the work was unsatisfactory. This was partly owing to the fact that Latin was made to displace French in the first year's work. This arrangement, although necessary when made, and though still greatly to the advantage of the Academy, scarcely gives French a fair chance. The resignation of Von der Groeben was a loss to the Academy, for he was a faithful, honorable and industrious teacher. However, with the new text-books and the new teachers, and new methods, aiming more directly for the examinations, we may expect more passes.

Of Miss Mackintosh and Miss Peters I cannot speak too highly The Board is fortunate in having two teachers in their positions, who can with such perfect ease control so large mixed classes, and inspire them all with the highest enthusiasm for study, with self-respect, and with noble motives.

It is in the science department that we find the greatest defects. Mr. Morton has about 120 students, who are expected to take a course in practical chemistry. For all of these there are 14 practice stands, of which not one is properly fitted up. About all that can be done in the circumstances is to cram from the text-book, and to have chemical principles illustrated by occasional experiments which can scarcely be seen by those at the further end of the room. This is little more than a pretence of science teaching. Amherst Academy, New Glasgow High School, and other institutions have adequate and modern appliances for real science teaching, where the pupil's powers of observation and induction as well as his memory are cultivated. Pictou Academy is devoting a special and well-equipped room to science work. The fact is that we are behind other places in this respect. Unfortunately a student who is well crammed in science can pass nearly as well as one who is well taught; but the effect on the student is most injurious.

As soon as possible, we should have a room in the Academy fitted up as a laboratory, and thus give Mr. Morton an opportunity to do the work properly for which he is so well qualified.

In drawing, the work has been very satisfactory, considering the large numbers, and the short time given to one teacher.

As a Principal, in the general management of the Academy, Mr. Kennedy has been most successful, and in the ability to prepare his pupils to pass with high marks, he is perhaps without a rival. It is difficult to be superior in all things, but if, in the Academy, more attention could be given to form, to physical culture, to music, to voice culture, to practical science, and to manual training, it is probable that the students would be more successful in after life, if not in examinations. Halifax is, notwithstanding, proud of its Academy, and with good reason.

Principal Kennedy reports as follows :—

A. McKay, Esq.,

Supervisor of Schools, Halifax :

During the past school year, Sept. 1894, to July, 1895, our Academy did quiet, steady and efficient work. The conduct of the students was invariably good, and the very best of feeling prevailed both among the students and between students and teachers The teachers' sympathy and anxiety to aid were always met by the pupils' confidence and willingness to co-operate.

The attendance was larger than in any previous term. The number registered was 283, of whom 126 were young men, and 157 were young women.

The number of students from outside of the city and county was somewhat smaller than usual. For this there are at least two causes :— First, the discontinuance of the A class ; and, second, the very marked improvement within the last few years, in the different Academies and High Schools throughout the province. The latter, while depriving us to some extent of a very desirable class of students, is yet a cause of sincere gratulation to all who have the right kind of interest in education and in our common country. And it is possible, too, that the resolution of the School Board disallowing grade A work in our Academy may be in agreement with the principle of the greatest good to the greatest number.

Although instruction is given in only three grades, namely, IX, X, and XI. of the Academic Course, we have five distinct classes,—two D classes, two C classes, one B. The two D classes do exactly the same work, as also the two C's ; and the existence of the two classes doing collateral work is purely a matter of accommodation, and is wholly due to the number of students in each of those grades being larger than can be seated in one class room.

The grading of the Academy is done entirely by the annual Government examinations, a circumstance for which teachers, who might otherwise run the risk of being charged with partiality, are properly grateful. Although those who make the highest aggregates in entering the Academy, or at the said government examination, are placed in the D^1 or C^1 classes, it has happened, in more than one instance, that the first prize was captured by a student of the D^2, or C^2 classes.

At the government examinations in July, 140 of our students succeeded in obtaining the certificate for which they applied, while 38 others obtained a lower grade The names or aggregates of the B, or graduating class, are as follows :—

Jennie Elizabeth Williston	858.	Alexander David Cook	553.
Charles Fowler Lindsay	836.	John Stanley Burgoyne	546.
Alice May Gilmore	835.	Daniel John Nicholson	555.
James Carlyle Fyshe	823.	Estella Mabel Burris	543.
George Herbert Sedgewick	815.	John Charles Morrison	535.
Henry Stewart Murray	779.	Alma Helene Hobrecker	513.
Samuel James Allen	752.	Georgina Maude Moody	503.
Janie McKenzie	656.	Walter Allan Black	500.
Gertrude Louise Lawlor	654.	Maggie Henry	500.
Gertrude Conrod	650.	Florence Elizabeth Blackwood	496.
Grace Dean Burris	604.	John Lorne Allan	491.
Katie Wetmore McKay	601.	Albert Lorne Macdougall	483.
Bertie Rogers	601.	Robert Louis Ellis	464.
Luther Burns McKenzie	597.	Amalie King	422.
Donald Keith	564.	Florence Bentley	418.
James Barnes	562.	Maude Chisholm	416.
Annie Bowden Rankine	562.	James O'Brien	405.
Ralph Simpson Gates	557.		

Six others made more than the required aggregate of 400, but failed on account of going below 25 on one or more subjects.

Besides those whose aggregates are given above, 50 of our students took C, and 94 took grade D certificates. Edward Manning McLeod led in the C class, with an aggegate of 732, and Thomas Albert Wilson in the D class, with an aggregate of 725.

Several of our students took the Minimum Professional Qualification Examination, with marks as follows :—

Grace Dean Burris......................203. First Rank.
Maude Chisholm ....195. Second Rank.
Georgina Maude Moody ....195.   "
George Herbert Sedgwick...............190.   "
John George Hockin ....189.
Jane Wallace Mortimer.................161.
Jane Isabel Sutherland..................154.
Emilie Francis Alcorn ....153.   "
Maggie Henry.................. .....145. Third Rank.
James Carlyle Fyshe....................136.   "
Minnie Povoas   .. ..136.   "

In the Dalhousie College entrance examinations, the first and second places, of those entering the first year, were taken by Charles Lindsay and Stewart Murray, Mr. Lindsay taking the MacKenzie Bursary, worth $200, and Mr. Murray the Professors' Scholarship, entitling him to free tuition throughout his course.

Respectfully submitted,
W. T. KENNEDY, *Principal.*

ST. PATRICK'S GIRLS' SCHOOL.

Here we have the same grades of work as in the Academy. There are 69 pupils, taught by three teachers.

During the past year much attention was given to Chemistry. The most of the practical work in Williams' Chemistry was covered very thoroughly.   In History, and in English Literature also, superior work was done.

These departments labor under the disadvantage of insufficient accommodation,—one of the cap-rooms, 25 feet by 7, forming one of the class-rooms.

One of the teachers, Sister Evaristus, obtained at the last provincial examination a grade A, while ,another missed on only two subjects.

Five students from this school attended the Normal School last year, and all took first rank diplomas.   The High School graduates have also supplied about a dozen teachers to the county schools for the current year.

Sister Angela reports as follows :—

The High School departments of St. Patrick's Girls' school show a fair average attendance for the year ended July, 1895.

Three gold medals were awarded, as follows :—

1. For Deportment, to Miss Maude Fanning, from ex-Commissioner Craig.
2. For Good Work, to Miss Jean Egan, from ex-Chairman Blackadar.
3. For Home Exercises, to Miss Carrie Henrion.

Four pupils went up for B scholarships, of whom two, one seventeen years of age, the other sixteen, obtained the grade applied for, while the other two received C and D respectively.

The High School departments, having no laboratory, and only two out of the three class-rooms being originally intended as such, the work cannot be as effectively carried on as it would under improved conditions.   A High School building with ample class-room accommodation, a library, laboratory, and proper assembly hall, would do much towards increasing the ardour of the pupils, and lessening and rendering more effective the labours of the teachers, and securing better results, as well as a larger attendance.

Entrance examinations were held during the first week in July, at which 45 passed. The candidates were from St. Mary's, St. Patrick's, Young Street, and Dutch Village schools.

The highest number of girls enrolled in the grammar school departments was 524, giving an average of 58 to each permanent teacher for the year. A temporary department was opened about the middle of May, and continued until the summer holidays.

The average attendance during the year was very encouraging. The number increased steadily from September to December, decreased in January, when an average of about 45 was reached, which continued until April, at which time a steady increase set in. A large proportion of the falling off in attendance was due to disease and stormy weather.

Tonic Sol-fa received a little extra attention during the past year, and the system of vertical writing, which had been generally adopted throughout the school, showed very satisfactory results. In grade VIII. much useful and interesting manual work was done, such as modelling in clay and plaster of Paris, making production maps, etc.

The heating apparatus put in during the summer vacation of 1894 proved excellently well adapted to make the building comfortable, with the exception of the two east rooms, where the prevailing north-easterly winds of our Nova Scotia winter made themselves masters, and occasioned much discomfort. Double windows placed in those departments from December to May would, however, overcome the difficulty, and render that part of the building as warm as the rest.

The ventilation of the school is rather good, although it is entirely effected by transoms and judiciously opened windows and doors. A distinguished visitor remarked on entering the building, that it was the first school he had been in where he did not perceive the school odor."

ST. PATRICK'S BOYS' SCHOOL.

In St. Patrick's Boys' School, Principal O'Hearn has had in grade D, 10 boys; and in grade C, 5. In addition to this work, he has single-handed to do the work of grade VIII. and of grade VII.

It is always found, however, that when his boys grade into the Academy, or go abroad, they are well grounded, and show good mental development and thorough training.

He reports as follows :—

"Although the work during the past year has been, on the whole, better than in any preceding year, yet there is much room for further advance. Where there are nine teachers besides the principal, the teacher of the second department should be doing grade VIII. work. If the present teacher of that department could have graded into his room only pupils who have finished grade VII., I am sure he would do the work of the eighth grade satisfactorily. At present he has a voluntary class, selected from his own pupils, attending on Saturday mornings and doing part of that work.

After the first of May next there will likely be enough pupils to warrant the employment of another teacher. I would strongly urge that no one be employed unless furnished with the very best recommendations. Indeed, I think it would pay the Board to employ a first-class male teacher. Such an appointment would materially aid the High School department, and would be of great advantage to those pupils who leave school before getting into the first department."

CALISTHENICS.

During a part of last year Miss Holmstrom was employed by the Board to give a course of lessons in Swedish gymnastics to the teachers. For the accomplishment of the end in view,—the harmonious physical development of pupils in the ordinary school, all who studied the exercises were convinced of the superiority of this system to any other with which we are familiar.   By the infinite variety of its exercises, and the peculiarity of the words of command, it escapes the monotony of other systems, and develops attention and good order as *they* cannot do.   I felt that some of the exercises were not the most graceful possible, but this feeling was, no doubt, caused by prejudice and want of knowledge on my part, for, upon investigation, I found that this system was introduced into fastidious Boston by the accomplished and refined Mrs. Hemenway,—that a special committee of the Boston School Board, after visiting several cities and examining other systems, gave the Swedish gymnastics their unqualified approval,—that it was adopted for Boston, aristocratic Brookline, and all the leading cities in the Eastern States.

In the words of one of its exponents, "it is a rational system, for there is a scientific reason for everything that is adopted and used; it is practical, for it is independent of apparatus, and can be applied anywhere and everywhere."

It is true that free and unrestrained play gives the best physical recreation, if not the best physical development.   Popular games in which all the boys or girls engage give the best general results.   But, unfortunately, such games are giving way to games played only by experts, who injure themselves by too great exertion ; while the great majority are mere onlookers, whose health or morals are not thereby improved.   Nor in most schools do we have playgrounds suited for out-door games.   In this respect, such schools as Acadian, St. Mary's Boys', St. Patrick's, and others, are lamentably deficient.   In the meantime the present system of education, as usually carried out, is making enormous demands upon many constitutions.   The ambition of teachers, and of parents as well, often leads them, while pressing for higher mental attainments, to overlook the physical ruin that they are bringing upon the children committed to their care, until it is too late, and body and mind are both sacrificed.   Is it not, then, the duty of this Board, entrusted by the State with the responsible duty of seeing that the young are suitably prepared for all the duties of citizenship, to provide for physical as well as for intellectual and moral culture.   It will not do to leave this to chance.   The Greeks, the Romans, the Germans, and the English, owe much of their greatness to the attention they paid to physical culture.   It does not matter so much what system we adopt, as that we adopt some system that will reach all.

I submit the following report from the teacher of the class of last year :—

"The classes in Swedish gymnastics for the teachers of the Halifax public schools, for the maintenance of which the School Board paid about one-third—the teachers themselves paying the rest,—commenced Feb. 12th, 1895, ending May 30th, with an attendance of sixty-six pupil teachers.

The idea with the classes being to interest the teachers so as to make them competent in their turn to instruct the school children, both theory and practice were taught,—the former, in necessarily elementary form ; and the practical gymnastics were those specially adapted to the schoolroom, as taught in the public schools of Boston and other cities.   The schools, not having had Swedish gymnastics before, and consequently not knowing much about the merits or demerits of the system, (although it was known that the exercises had after due trial been accepted elsewhere and been eminently successful), it was understood that these classes were an experiment, which, if demonstrating their utility, would of course cease to be an experiment, and become part of the school curriculum, as long as it was known that the need for physical training among the school children was becoming more and more apparent.

The lessons were given in the High School twice a week, and although this was extra work for the teachers, often involving long walks back and forth, the attendance was very regular, and among those regularly attending, a good deal of intelligent interest was manifested.

Indeed at the close of the lessons when there was an opportunity of seeing and judging, in the children, of the teachers' understanding and application of the work, it was found that, particularly in one school of boys, it had already improved the discipline, general carriage and bearing, and several of the teachers had improved distinctly in health as the result.

It was found that the children readily took to the exercises, and should the teacher happen to forget or otherwise omit them, — would clamor for their gymnastics.

These results, from only four months instruction, might surely be called encouraging.

At the same time there was formed a girls' class of thirty-six, under my own personal instruction, who really all showed decided improvement in health and bearing, this being the more noteworthy as they only had thirty lessons. The parents expressed their satisfaction as to the improvement of their children, and there was a generally felt and uttered desire for the permanency of the system in the schools.

This term,— 1895-1896,—the teachers wished to go on with gymnastics at their own expense, and there is now in progress an enthusiastic teachers' class, as well as another school-girls' class, which also defrays its own expenses.

The School Board has, however, as yet not taken any decided and definite steps towards making the Swedish system what it is in so many other cities besides Boston,— an acknowledged and permanent part of the daily instruction.

V. M. HOLMSTROM.

MANUAL TRAINING.

Manual training as a school subject is quietly winning its way everywhere. The best educationists no longer speak of it as a fad. In many countries it occupies as honorable a place on the curriculum as spelling, writing, or drawing.

We are fortunate in having for our teacher of this department such a man as Mr. Gardner,— a man who adds to his manual skill, literary ability and scholarship of no mean order. What the boys learn from him in modesty, gentlemanly deportment, and industrious habits, is quite as important as the knowledge they gain of the use of tools and of working drawings.

This department, which was begun as an experiment, has been so far successful as to justify its extension by the addition of a turning-lathe. The expense would be slight.

I would like to see every boy obliged to take this course, unless excused for very good reasons.

The young ladies do not need such training to the same extent, because much of it comes to them incidentally in their homes. Instrumental music is in a slight degree a substitute. Yet every young lady should be called upon to give proof of a certain proficiency in needle-work, or be required to take sewing lessons in school.

Mr. Gardner reports as follows:

" This school has been under my care for over two years. I have continued the training on pretty much the same lines as my able predecessor, Mr. Lee Russell, The system of training is a modified Sloyd, or rather a combination of the Russian system and Sloyd. To explain :— At first an exercise is given involving some principle of construction, then when the exercise is well understood and executed, some article of use or ornament, involving the principle of instruction given in the exercise is designed, and worked out in wood. This system seems the best suited for the training of our pupils. Interest is aroused and sustained by the making of articles of use, etc., while tools and their uses, principles of construction, etc., are introduced through the series of exercises.

That the pupils are interested no one can doubt who sees them hurrying here from their schools. That the school is becoming more popular is proved by the interest that parents are evincing. Parents, who a year ago would not allow their boys to attend the school, are now quite anxious that they should take the training. While the parents of several boys are giving stronger proof of their interest by giving their boys tools and opportunities for extending their training outside of school hours.

The attendance from the common schools has increased. This is not clearly shown in the monthly reports, but is evidenced by the fact that schools from which I had classes last year are excluded this year, and yet the enrollment is nearly as high as this time last year, while the attendance is better. The attendance from the High School has decreased. This is due to the fact that many of the High School boys have had two or more terms at the manual training before entering the High School, and to continue the training means only to become better acquainted with the carpenter's tools, and not to get much of "anything new." Until we have added to our apparatus a couple of turning-lathes and several setts of wood-carving tools, we cannot expect large numbers from our High School, nor the best results from the training given those who do come from there. Another drawback to the training of boys from that school is the mixed nature of the classes (i. e., boys who had no manual training with boys of one, two, or more terms of the training), making class instruction impossible "

N. H. GARDNER.

TEXT-BOOKS.

In accordance with your instructions, I invited teachers to send me the text-books, donated by the pupils for the benefit of the poor. In this way quite a number of pupils were supplied with books who would not otherwise have had them. I have been asked to give some information regarding free school text books.

I find that the system is adopted in about 200 American towns, and that it is extending. It was adopted in Toronto upon a vote of the rate-payers, the majority in its favor being about 4000. I have not learned that it has been discontinued anywhere.

The arguments used in favor of the system are numerous and cogent. It is urged that the cost of school books to the town, as a whole, is very much reduced, sometimes as much as 50 per cent.; that two or three weeks are saved in beginning school work ; that the attendance is greatly improved ; that pupils are thereby taught to take care of things not their own ; that the system helps to do away with painful and humiliating class distinctions ; that thus the schools become in reality what they are in name,—free schools.

Of course the old arguments, that were of so little avail against free tuition, are used against free text-books No one disputes the right of the state to protect itself from the effects of ignorance, by taxing all, so as to provide free tuition: nor can any one logically object to a slight further tax that tends to add, as it is claimed, 25 per cent. to the efficiency of that tuition. It seems very absurd to tax a man one or two hundred dollars on the plea that you are rendering his property more valuable by indirectly protecting it from the evil effects of illiteracy, and then neglect to compel the attendance at school, in the most favorable circumstances, of the very individuals who are most likely to endanger the security of that property.

Cost and Method of operating the Free Text-Book System.

In the United States, where text-books are much more expensive than here, the cost varies from an average per pupil of 57 cents to one dollar per year. In Halifax the average cost would probably go no higher than 60 cents. It might go as low as 40.

In introducing the system, all pupils who prefer supplying their own books are allowed to do so, all other pupils are asked to make over to the Board their present supply of school-books. These are supplemented by the Board, as need requires.

The books are given out under some such rules as the following :—

1. The book must not be marked with pencil or ink, or otherwise defaced, and it must be kept clean.

2. If it be lost or injured, it must be paid for by the pupil to whom it was loaned.

3. It must be returned when called for by the teacher.

4. It is not to be taken from the school-room except by permission of the teacher, for the purpose of studying lessons at home. .

From the central store-room a supply is sent to each principal. The principal keeps an account against each teacher, who, in turn, keeps a record with each pupil.

To sum up :—The introduction of the system into Halifax would save to the ratepayers over $2000, and to those who attend the public schools over $3500 a year; it would increase the attendance about 5 to 10 per cent., and the efficiency 10 to 15 per cent. On the other hand there would be some disadvantages which I am unable properly to estimate.

PROMOTIONS.

The new system of promotions was tried last year, and gave general satisfaction. Pupils are no longer promoted as the result of examinations held by the principal during the last week of the year. Promotions depend upon the judgment of the teacher of the pupil. In order to arrive at a correct judgment she is required to watch more carefully the daily progress of her pupils, to notify their parents each month of the cause of their failures, and to hold several teaching examinations during the year. Many serious evils arise when the results of a whole year's work depend upon one examination.

In Germany, where teaching is a science, if it is anywhere, there are no grading examinations in the lower classes. The teacher is looked upon as being as much of a specialist as a medical man ; and his decision as to the fitness of a pupil is rarely questioned.

It is, of course, desirable that the poorest pupils in every room should, at the beginning of the year, be in advance of the best in the next lowest room, but it is a less evil to have two grades in one department than to make any pupil again go over the work that he has once done fairly well.   He has lost interest, and without interest there is no assimilation.

SUPPLEMENTARY READING.

For the same reason that twice over the same grade is generally an evil, twice over the same book is, in primary classes, also an evil. There should be several sets of interesting supplementary readers authorized, so that reading by rote, and dull monotony, may be avoided.   An application should go from this Board to the Council of Public Instruction asking for this privilege.

LIBRARIES.

More encouragement should be given to teachers and pupils in the formation, and regular and methodical use of school libraries, especially in the study of history, geography and science.

The Council of Public Instruction is empowered to expend the sum of $1600 per annum for the establishment and support of school libraries,—this sum to be supplemented by an equal sum from the sections.

If Halifax City received its share of this grant, say about $75 each year, our large schools would very soon have very serviceable libraries.   Already we have two or three fairly good libraries. Whether we can succeed in obtaining a Government grant or not, I hope that we will not lose sight of the necessity of supplying our school children with an abundance of good reading matter.

Principal Kennedy deserves much credit for his care and system in the management of the Academy library, and for the use made of it by the pupils.

Here let me refer to the beginning of a library at Dutch Village school.   It owes its inception to the encouragement and support of ex-Commissioner Mitchell.   It will be most useful to the boys and girls of this suburban school,—so remote from the libraries and other literary advantages of the city.

Our pedagogical library has been sadly neglected for the last few years.   If our teachers had the use of a proper reading room, where they could see the leading educational periodicals, and the best and latest professional books, it would be of the greatest benefit to them, and indirectly to the schools.   Such a room would also be valuable for teachers' meetings.   It is, indeed, a prime necessity ; for now they have no room where they can meet, where they can have a library, or where they can consult with me, without inconveniencing some one else.

SUPERANNUATION.

A committee has been appointed by the Provincial Educational Association to formulate a scheme of superannuation for teachers. The subject was introduced by Principal O'Hearn. The most valuable thoughts in the discussion that followed were contributed by Commissioner McKerron.

If successful, the superannuation of teachers would benefit us chiefly by raising the standard required for their admission to our city schools, and by the retiring of the inefficient. I bespeak for this committee the helpful co-operation of this Board.

In closing, let me say that the past year has been a successful one in the history of the Halifax schools. The teachers have been untiring and faithful. Never before have the School Commissioners devoted more time or energy to their duties, or shown a greater interest in the schools.

All of which is respectfully submitted.

A. McKAY, *Supervisor.*

Halifax, 5th December, 1895.

SPECIAL PROVINCIAL INSTITUTIONS.

(I.)

HALIFAX INSTITUTION FOR THE DEAF AND DUMB, 1895.

The total attendance for the year was seventy-two, viz.: forty-one boys and thirty-one girls, of whom sixty-three belong to Nova Scotia seven to Newfoundland, one to P. E. Island, and one to New Brunswick. The following table gives in detail the whole attendance:

	Boys.	Girls.	Total.
Pupils of previous years still in attendance..	38	29	67
New pupils from January, 1895............	2	..	2
Absentees expected to return.............	1	2	3
	41	31	72

Number of pupils under 15 years of age 43
"   "   over   "   "   29
Average age of pupils 13
Number of pupils less than one year at school............... 14
"   "   one year and less than two at school........ 12
"   "   two years and less than three at school...... 9
"   three years and less than four at school 10

HEALTH.

In spite of a great deal of sickness of an infectious nature throughout the city, it is gratifying to be able to report that the health of the pupils of this Institution has remained good throughout the year.

NEW BUILDING.

On account of the unsuitable character of the old building and its dilapidated condition, the directors found that it was necessary to erect a new building without delay if the work was to be carried on successfully. The pupils were, therefore, sent to their homes earlier in the spring than usual, the old structure removed, and the erection of a new building commenced on the old site. The building, when completed, will be one of the most suitable of its kind in the Dominion. The length will be 200 feet, and it will afford accommodation for 150 pupils. The play rooms, sitting rooms, and dormitories will be large, airy, and well-lighted apartments; the plumbing will be of the best description, and the whole will be arranged with a view to the health and comfort of the pupils.

THE SCHOOL-ROOM.

The work of the school-room has been going on satisfactorily, and encouraging results have been obtained both on the oral and manual systems. The unavoidable interruption caused by the erection of the new building is to be regretted, but it is to be hoped that when the pupils and teachers return with renewed energies correspondingly good results will be obtained. A greater number than heretofore has been taught speech and lip-reading, and with the improved facilities the new builaing will offer, a still larger number will be so taught in the coming session. The teachers have been painstaking and conscientious in their work, and the pupils have one and all conducted themselves to the entire satisfaction of the directors and staff.

J. FEARON,

Principal.

.(II.)

HALIFAX SCHOOL FOR THE BLIND, 1895.

TWENTY-FIFTH ANNUAL REPORT OF THE BOARD OF MANAGERS.

The Board of Managers have much pleasure in submitting to the members of the Corporation, to the Governments and Legislatures interested, and to the friends of the blind, the twenty-fifth annual report of the school, and in doing so they desire to express their deep sense of gratitude to Almighty God for the manifold blessings of the past year, and for the success which has continually marked the work of this Institution.

The Superintendent's report deals at length with the several departments of the school, all of which are in a high state of efficiency. The thorough character of the training which we are now able to give to the blind of the Maritime Provinces and Newfoundland is a source of satisfaction to your Board, and while we recognize our ever-increasing responsibilities, we feel that the success which has attended the graduates of the school is a guarantee that with the hearty co-operation of its friends the Institution will be kept fully abreast of the times, will prove a blessing to very many young blind persons, and will be a credit to the Governments, Legislatures, and benefactors, by whom it is supported.

Your Board desires to express its appreciation of the excellent work performed by the members of the teaching staff, each of whom in his or her special way has contributed in no small degree to the successful work carried on during the past year.

Every care has been taken to make the sanitary conditions of the school as perfect as possible, and the physical welfare of the pupils has received constant attention. The food supplied, while plain, is of excellent quality, the dormitories are large and airy, and the bathing facilities are all that can be desired. The general health of the

pupils is good, and physically speaking, their status is far above that
of the average of the blind.   Wholesome diet, regular hours, and
physical training are more important to those deprived of sight than
to those who can so easily combine exercise with pleasurable pastimes.

Since the publication of our last report Miss Bowman, the matron
of the school, has, owing to ill health, felt obliged to resign her position, much to the regret of all within the establishment.   Your Board
desires to express its appreciation of Miss Bowman's long and faithful
services both as teacher and matron, and to hope that she may speedily
be restored to health.

Owing to the growth of the school and the increased domestic
duties, a sub-division of the work has been arranged; Mrs. Dudley,
the acting matron, having charge of the cleanliness of the Institution
and the clothing of the pupils, while Mr. G. N. Towell, as acting
steward, has assumed the entire management of the culinary, dining
room, and laundry departments.   The new arrangement has so far
worked admirably, and will doubtless continue to do so.

The thanks of the friends of the blind are due to the Government
and Legislature of Nova Scotia for amending the Act respecting the
Education of the Blind, so as to admit into the school children
between the ages of six and ten years.   The parents of nine little
boys and girls have availed themselves of the privileges secured
under this amended Act, and the education of the children has commenced at an age when they are best fitted to receive instruction, as
a visit to our Kindergarten will unquestionably prove.

The Government and Legislature of New Brunswick have ever
been mindful of the needs of the blind of that Province, and have
made statutory provision for the education of their blind youth in
this Institution.   The present New Brunswick Act makes provision
for the admission of children between the ages of ten and twenty-
one years, but we have every reason to hope that during the coming
session of the N. B. Legislature the Act will be amended so as to
provide for the admission of children between the ages of six and
ten years.

During the past year a deputation consisting of the clergymen of
all denominations in Charlottetown, His Lordship Bishop Macdonald,
and the Superintendent of this school, waited upon the Government
of Prince Edward Island, and strongly urged the claims of the blind
to a free education. This deputation was cordially received by
Premier Peters and his colleagues, and while no definite promises
were made, the deputation retired with the assurance that the matter
would receive full and earnest consideration.   As a result of this
interview the Legislative appropriation of P. E. Island to the school was
doubled.   While this increase in the grant gives a measure of satisfaction to your Board, it does not meet the wishes of the friends of the
blind of P. E. Island ; it makes no statutory provision for the education
of those deprived of sight, and recognizes no claims of those who are
blind to be educated like other children at the public expense.

The Government, Legislature and people of Prince Edward Island should see to it that the blind, who are already handicapped in the race of life, should have at least equal opportunities with those who are fully equipped for the struggle for self-maintenance.

The Government and Legislature of Newfoundland have, notwithstanding the crisis through which that colony has passed, fully met their obligations with respect to the Newfoundland pupils in this Institution ; and while it has not been thought advisable to at present increase the number of pupils from Newfoundland, we believe that the Government and Legislature will, at the earliest possible date extend the blessings of the school to an increased number of the blind youth of the Island colony.

As foreshadowed in our last report, the need for increased accommodation in the school has been more and more felt, and your Board has found it a most difficult matter to provide accommodation for all the young blind persons seeking admission to the school. The following table will give a clear idea of the growth of the school during the past five years :

Pupils registered Dec. 1st, 1890.................. 31
      "   "   " 1891.................. 39
      "   "   " 1892.................. 46
                          1893.................. 47
                          1894.................. 52
                          1895.................. 70

Our present buildings were planned for the accommodation of sixty pupils, but by utilizing our music rooms for bedrooms, and making other changes, we have been able to provide accommodation for all the pupils that have so far been received. Several other applications have been accepted, and with the information in our possession we believe that the minimum number of the school will in the near future reach one hundred. Under these circumstances an extension of our present school building has become an urgent necessity, and during the coming year we purpose presenting the matter fully to the Government and Legislature of Nova Scotia, and to our friends in the Maritime Provinces. The deep interest that has ever been evinced in the education of the blind in these Provinces makes us confident that when our needs become fully known we shall not be wanting the means to make provision for them.

Your Board regretfully record the death of the Hon. S. L. Shannon, who for a long time was identified with the work of the Institution, and who for many years was associated with the Board of Managers.

In addition to the donations elsewhere acknowledged, your Board gratefully acknowledges the receipt of $200 from the estate of the late Miss Elizabeth Heales, St. John, N. B. ; also the receipt of $500 from the estate of the late Rev. Thos. N. DeWolf, Windsor, N. S. Such bequests enable your Board to extend the work far beyond the limit which the funds at command would otherwise warrant.

8

The treasurer's statement shows the receipts to have been $9,963.99, and the expenditure $9,604.86, leaving a small balance to the credit of the school.

The Superintendent, Mr. C. F. Fraser, continues to discharge the manifold and ever-increasing duties of his responsible office to the entire satisfaction of the Board.

The thanks of the Board of Managers are hereby tendered to Drs. Lindsay, Dodge, Kirkpatrick and Cogswell, for their kindly attention to the pupils; to H. B. Clarke, lessee of the Academy of Music, for tickets to entertainments; and to the railway, steamship, and coach proprietors, for the privileges granted to our pupils.

All of which is respectfully submitted.

W. C. SILVER,
President.

SUPERINTENDENT'S REPORT.

To the President and Board of Managers of the School for the Blind:

GENTLEMEN :—

The table of attendance herewith submitted shows that 74 blind persons have been under instruction during the past year, 52 of whom were males and 22 females; 4 of these have since graduated or left the school, making the total number in attendance on Dec. 1st, 1895, 70; of whom 50 are males and 20 females. Of these 41 are from the Province of Nova Scotia, 17 from New Brunswick, 4 from Prince Edward Island, and 8 from Newfoundland.

TABLE OF ATTENDANCE.

	Boys.	Girls.	Adults.	Total.
Registered Dec. 1st, 1894	36	15	1	52
Entered during year	15	7	. .	22
Graduated or remained at home	2	2	. .	4
Registered Dec. 1st, 1895	49	20	1	70

LITERARY DEPARTMENT.

Steady, solid and satisfactory progress has marked the work in our school rooms during the past year, and it has been the aim of our teachers to hold before the pupils the highest ideals of perfection, and to stimulate them to apply themselves with earnestness to their studies. With scarce an exception, it may be said that our pupils have worked to advantage, and the results are as creditable to themselves as they are gratifying to their teachers and myself.

Since the amendment of the Act respecting the Education of the Blind, referred to in the report of the Board of Managers, our kindergarten department has been very greatly improved, and has now become separate and distinct from the third division or primary department with which it had previously been associated.

"The education of a child should commence at its mother's knee," but the little blind child, even when the family is in comfortable circumstances, seldom receives any training whatever, and hence it is of the utmost importance that little blind children should be sent to the Institution as soon as they reach six years, the age of admission. Parents may rest assured that the little ones they send to us will receive special care, and that every effort will be made to promote the very best interests of such children.

Four teachers are now steadily engaged in the work of the literary department. Miss Fletcher, the enthusiastic and successful kindergartener, finds ample work for her head, hands and heart in the training of the children of the kindergarten department. The assistant, Miss Josie Howe, who first entered upon her duties in September last, has been both zealous and painstaking in her work. In the other divisions of the school, Miss C. R. Frame has sustained her reputation as a most successful teacher of the blind ; while Mr. S. R. Hussy has proved our estimate of his capabilities as a teacher to have been well founded.

In addition to our regular teaching staff, Professor Lanos, teacher of French, and Fraulein Œllars, teacher of German, have been conducting language classes in the school, and have both done excellent work.

Musical Department.

Of the seventy pupil in the schools, thirty-five are receiving lessons on the pianoforte or cabinet organ, while twenty-seven others are under training preliminary to the study of instrumental music.

This department is much appreciated by the pupils, not merely on account of the natural attractiveness of music, but because it opens up to them a field of occupation in which the lack of sight offers no obstacle to success—a field in which rich harvests are the result of patient, persevering work. Our register contains the names of many graduates of the school who now occupy good social positions in the communities in which they reside, and hold leading places as teachers of music.

Mr. A. M. Chisholm, the musical director, received a long training in this school, and subsequently in Scharwenta's Conservatory of Music, Berlin. This thorough training has enabled him to occupy his position with credit to himself and to the school, and to the great advantage of those under his instruction. It is gratifying to find an old pupil of the school filling with such signal success one of the most important positions in the Institution.

At the close of the last school year, Mr. F. Campbell, of Sussex, N. B., graduated from the tuning department of the school, and has since found steady and growing occupation in Moncton and the outlying districts. Mr. D. M. Reid, the instructor, who, like Mr. Chisholm, is a graduate of the school, has won a first-class reputation as a pianoforte tuner, and the pupils under his instruction never fail to succeed if success is in them.

The following is a complete list of the classes in the Literary and Musical departments :—

Kindergarten Department.—Object lessons and lives of famous men, games and recitations, songs and musical exercises, clay modelling, physical drill, gifts and occupations, number work, multiplication tables, reading and spelling.

Third Division.—Object lessons, spelling, reading, Braile point writing, arithmetic, geography, grammar, history, clay modelling, knitting, Sloyd work, musical training.

Second Division.—Spelling, reading, Braile point writing, round hand pencil writing, arithmetic, geometry, geography, history, grammar, composition, English literature, musical notation, Braile point music.

First Division.—Spelling, reading, round hand pencil writing, arithmetic, geometry, algebra, book-keeping, geography, history, grammar, composition, English literature, French, German, musical notation, Braile point music, theory of music, singing, band music.

TECHNICAL DEPARTMENT.

A visit to the technical department of the Institution is alwayf appreciated by the visitor. Entering the larger workshop, a class os boys between ten and twelve years of age is found busily engaged in light carpentry work. This manual training, which is based upon the Sloyd system, is especially adapted to the needs of the blind, and develops in them great precision and dexterity in the use of edged tools. A little further down the room are to be seen several young men busily employed in recaning chairs, which they do easily and well. Crossing the workshop, the visitor enters the compartments set aside for the manufacture of willow baskets and chairs. Here the work of splitting, shaving, sizing and weaving the willow wands into pretty and useful articles is carefully explained by the competent instructor, Mr. D. A. Baird. A number of young men are quietly working, some at simple, others at more complicated articles. Among them the visitor finds Willie Heulin, the deaf, dumb, and blind boy from Bay St. George, Newfoundland, and judging from the bright, intelligent face and the keen interest shown in his work, Willie's constructive faculties are as fully developed as those of other lads of his own age. Passing along the visitor is shown a number of finished baskets manufactured by the blind, which all display creditable workmanship. In speaking of those who have graduated from the workshop, the instructor mentions a young man belonging to Belleville, Yarmouth County, named Sylvain Lefave, who left the school last June. "Young Lefave, he says, "will make his way in the world. Since leaving us he has manufactured a large quantity of willow work, and has sold it as fast as made. He should, with his knowledge of the willow basket trade, make a comfortable living for himself."

Leaving the workshop the visitor enters a small room set apart for light electrical work. Here a quartette of young men are actively at work in manufacturing electric bells, telephones, etc. The visitor is particularly interested in the work of a young man who is operating a metal turning lathe with ease and skill. Mr. J. S. Harivel, the enthusiastic instructor of this department, explains to the visitor that the field of light electrical work offers a new and profitable occupation to the blind, and that the Halifax School for the Blind is the pioneer in this work.

Passing on to the main building the visitor enters the girls' work department, where is mingled the hum of the sewing machine with the great buzz of many merry voices. Each girl is busy, and upon each face is an expression of conscious confidence, the outcome of systematic training. The work of these girls is certainly very credit- able, and well deserves the Diploma of Honorable Mention received at the World's Columbian Exposition. It includes plain and fancy knitting, crocheting, sewing, bead and jet work, etc., etc.

GENERAL.

The physical training of the pupils continues to receive systematic attention, and every effort has been made to provide suitable appliances both in the gymnasium and the play grounds. The classes in gymnastics and calisthenics, conducted by Sergt.-Major Kelly, have been thoroughly appreciated by the pupils, and have aroused a spirit of enthusiasm and a desire for more perfect physical development; the outcome being volunteer athletic clubs, walking, skating, and coasting parties, and a general improvement in the physical standard of the school.

While the pupils have, generally speaking, enjoyed good health, and no serious case of illness has occurred during the past year, Scarlet fever has twice made its appearance, and measles once; but owing to the prompt and untiring attention of the attending physician, Dr. A. W. H. Lindsay, no serious results ensued, and the regular work of the school went on with scarce an interruption.

Each year new graduates go forth from the school prepared to take an active part in life's work, and each year the circle of those who appreciate the practical character of the training given to the blind in this school is widened. The outcome of this growth of appreciation is a natural desire upon the part of the parents of the youthful blind to have their children participate in the advantages which the school affords. As a consequence, each year has brought us an increased number of applications for admission.

During the present year the new applications have been supple- mented by those for children between the ages of six and ten years, so that the number of pupils has at once increased from fifty-two to seventy. Up to the present time the Board of Managers has been able to accept each application as it was made, although they have found it a very difficult matter to provide accommodation for more than sixty pupils. As, however, the final limit of accommodation has unquestionably been reached, and as there are still very many blind children not enjoying the blessings of an education, it is evident that a strong and vigorous effort should at once be made to extend the present building. This probably involves an expenditure of $20,000, and I have faith to believe that when the needs of the blind are properly placed before their friends in the Maritime Provinces and elsewhere, the response will be as liberal and as cordial as it has been on former occasions. The school is endeavoring to perform a truly noble work. Its managers, officers, and teachers have but one aim in view, namely, the welfare of those who are destined to fight the battle of life in the dark. It may truly be said that the school gives eyes to the blind, and in the desire to extend this beneficent work it is deserving of the support, encouragement, and practical help of every man and every woman who knows how to appreciate the inestimable blessing of sight, and who can realize that by assisting the blind to assist themselves they are helping forward a work that is at once practical, philanthropic, and noble.

Within the coming year I trust to be able to present the claims of the school to the Government and Legislature of Nova Scotia, and to the many friends of the blind throughout the Maritime Provinces, and I feel confident that with such a cause to espouse, and with such a broad minded constituency to appeal to, the necessary funds will be secured, so that before the issuing of our next report an extension to our present building may be under construction.

In conclusion, gentlemen, allow me to thank the members of the Board of Managers for their cordial support and hearty co-operation in carrying forward the work of educating the blind, and to express the hope that with increasing responsibility and increased experience, our mutual relations will continue to be as in the past, pleasant and satisfactory.

All of which is respectfully submitted.

C. F. FRASER,
Superintendent.

(III.)

VICTORIA SCHOOL OF ART AND DESIGN.

To. A. H. MacKay, Ll.D.,
Superintendent of Education.

Sir:—I have the honor to submit herewith the report of the Treasurer of the Victoria School of Art and Design; also, abstracts of the reports of the teachers of Mechanical and Architectural Drawing.

CONSPECTUS OF CLASSES FOR 1894-95.

Freehand and Object Drawing.....	Tuesday and Wednesday evenings	28 pupils.
Clay Modelling. ...!..............	Monday afternoon	9 "
" "	.Monday evening................... ...	4 "
Freehand and Object Drawing, and } Life Class................. }	Tues., Wed., and Thur. afternoons....	15 "
Children's Drawing Class..........	Saturday forenoon	16 "
Class for Deaf and Dumb.....	Friday...........	9 "
Mechanical Drawing	Mon., Wed., and Friday evenings	25 "
Architectural Drawing........	Tuesday and Thursday	9 "
Total..................................		115 "

I wish to call attention to the fact that of these about 75 are free pupils. The evening and mechanical classes are almost wholly composed of apprentices and artisans, who are entitled to free tuition by the rules of the school.

The Art School is quietly doing good work in supplying intelligent workmen to the various mechanic arts, in educating the young away from the overcrowded professions, and perhaps in raising the standard of public taste in several directions.

Mr. J. T. Larkin, teacher of Mechanical Drawing, in his report, *inter alia:* "The pupils are first taught a short course in Practical Geometry; then follow lessons in Orthographic Projection, the study of points and lines projected on different planes. Then they are given cards of different shapes and in different positions, and are shown how to make correct drawings of the same. The next course is in solids of different shapes and in various positions, showing how they should be drawn. This gives a thorough ground work for plotting the planes of projection. Then simple drawings are taken up. This includes studies in cutting planes, development of surfaces, how to obtain the curve of intersection, of cylinders passing through variously shaped solids, how to draw a working plan of a steam boiler, and how to shape and cut the plates so as to form the different members of the same; then come lessons in metal work, such as laying out a bath-tub so as to form it without cutting stock to waste. A short time ago a prominent member of an engineering firm in our city told me that he noticed a decided improvement in his apprentices after they attended our classes."

Mr. C. H. Hopson, C. E., teacher of Architectural Drawing, reports *inter alia:* " The students, with two or three exceptions, are engaged in the building trades, and find the draughting experience gained at the school of particular benefit to them in their work. At present most of them are making full size and scale details of carpentry and brickwork. Several of them are designing and drawing stair-cases, and detailing the several parts, while others are projecting spiral stairs, hand-rails, detailing sashes and frames, describing elliptical arches for masonry, calculating lengths of hip and valley rafters, making raking molds which will intersect with horizontal ones, and getting the curves of circular and other structures, etc."

I may add that for the current year there is a gratifying increase of interest and students.

All of which is respectfully submitted.

A. McKAY, *Secretary.*

VICTORIA SCHOOL OF ART AND DESIGN, HALIFAX.
(Incorporated 1888.)

DIRECTORS, 1894-95.

Ex-Officio: { THE SUPERINTENDENT OF EDUCATION,
{ THE MAYOR OF HALIFAX.

MRS. LEONOWENS,	MR. J. M. SMITH,
MRS. H. H. FULLER,	MR. J. C. MACKINTOSH,
MRS. J. F. KENNY,	MR. E. P. ARCHBOLD,
MISS E. RITCHIE,	MR. GEO. HARVEY,
MISS H. ALLISON,	MR. D. KEITH,
MR. J. DEMPSTER,	HON. SENATOR POWER,
DR. J. G. MacGREGOR,	MR. M. DWYER.
MR. A. McKAY,	

Auditors.

MR. THOMAS BROWN,
MR. R. J. WILSON.

President .... MAYOR KEEFE,
Vice-President .... DR. MacKAY,
Treasurer .... MR. J. M. SMITH,
Secretary .... MR. A. McKAY.

TEACHING STAFF, 1894-95.
Head Master.
MR. C. C. WOODBURY.

Assistant Teachers.
Mechanical Drawing .... J. T. LARKIN, *Engineer.*
Architectural Drawing ....

Saturday Class.
MISS M. GRAHAM.

TEACHING STAFF, 1895-96.
Principal.
MISS M. N. EVANS.

Teachers.
Object Drawing, Life Work, Painting......MISS EVANS.
Mechanical Drawing ...........*........J. T. LARKIN, Engineer.*
Architectural Drawing ....C. H. HOPSON, *C. E.*
Elementary Drawing.................... MISS M. GRAHAM.

TREASURER'S REPORT.
THE TREASURER IN ACCOUNT WITH VICTORIA SCHOOL OF ART AND DESIGN.

Endowment Fund :—
    Amount from 1894...........................$ 7,702 40

Building Fund :—
    Amount from 1894........................... 8,000 00

Current Account Receipts :—
    School Fees...........................$316 41
    Local Government Grant................ 800 00
    Proceeds of lecture by Mr. J. Knight...... 55 00
    Interest 530 87
                                         1,702 28

                                                 $17,404 68

Disbursements :—
    Salaries............................ $1,370 01
    Rent 200 00
    Fuel and Light...................... 91 24
    Advertising and Printing............. 18 50
    Models, Squares, etc................. 69 10
    School Supplies...................... 12 96
    Janitors 117 50
    Exhibition 26 71
    Sundries 5 37

                       $1,911 39
    Balance, September, 1894............. 3,355 51

                       $5,266 90

Town of Kentville Bonds..........$5100 00
City of Halifax Consols........... 4950 00
Deposit Receipts Bank N. S......... 2000 00
Open Account   " 81 41
Cash on hand.................... 6 37
                     12,137 78
                       $17,404 68

    JOHN M. SMITH, *Hon. Treasurer.*
HALIFAX, N. S., *September, 1895.*

(IV.)

HALIFAX MEDICAL COLLEGE, 1895.

A. P. REID, M. D , ETC........................*President.*
G. L. SINCLAIR, M. D., ETC....................*Dean.*

No. of regular Professors, *fifteen ;* Lecturers, *eleven.*

No. of Undergraduates: First Year, 21; Second Year, 10; Third Year, 7; Fourth Year, 5.   Males, 40 ; females, 3.   Total Undergraduates, 43.   General students, 2 ; regular students in Pharmacy, 3 ; total students, 48.   Forty-five males, 3 females.

Institution founded in 1867 as a Faculty of Dalhousie College and University.   Separated in 1876.

Total number of graduates in Medicine (M. D. C. M.), 57 ; in Pharmacy (Ph. M), 5.   Total graduates, 62.

APPENDIX E

EDUCATIONAL INSTITUTES.

(I.)

SUMMER SCHOOL OF SCIENCE FOR THE ATLANTIC PROVINCES.

To A. H. MacKay, Esq., Ll. D.,

Superintendent of Education.

Sir:—

I respectfully submit the following report of the Ninth Session of the Summer School of Science for the Atlantic Provinces of Canada, which met at Amherst, N. S., July 3rd to July 18th, 1895.

The session was opened by a public meeting, held in the spacious Assembly Hall of the Amherst Academy, Mayor Curry presiding. Interesting and enthusiastic addresses were given by Councillor Chapman of Amherst, Inspector Craig of Cumberland County, N. S., Dr. MacKay, Superintendent of Education for Nova Scotia, Dr. Inch, Superintendent of Education for New Brunswick, Prof. Coldwell of Acadia College, and Prof. Andrews of Mount Allison University. This session of the school was characterized by the diligence of the students, and the marked improvement made by them. Greater prominence than usual was given to *field work*, the success of which was largely due to the presence and assistance of Dr. MacKay, Superintendent of Education for Nova Scotia, and Mr. Hickman of Pictou; the latter gentleman conducting the early morning walks to study birds.

The subject of permanently locating the school at some suitable summer resort was discussed, and committees were appointed to procure information regarding the project, and report at the next annual meeting.

The following were awarded Certificates of Proficiency:

Botany.—Annie L. Darling, Jennie McManus, Minnie A. Weir.

Mineralogy.—Willard S. Carter, Winnie Freeman, Maretta Angus, Ida Crowe, Daniel A. Matheson.

Zoology.—Sarah J. Patterson, Minnie A. Weir.

Music.—Junior Certificate: Jennie S. Johnston, Sarah Harris, Clara
M. Coates, Chas. E. Reid, Bella Henderson, Fred A. Dixon,
Ella J. McKay, Lizzie R. Kirkpatrick, Bessie L. Gregor, Flora
Embree, Mabel Acorn, Minnie A. Weir.
Elementary Certificates: Clara M. Coates, Sarah J. Patterson,
Flora Embree, Mabel Acorn, Sarah C. Ross.

There were in attendance 63 students. From Nova Scotia, 42 ;
New Brunswick, 18 ; Prince Edward Island, 3.

The next session of the School will be held at Parrsboro', N. S.,
July 9th to July 24th, 1896.

OFFICERS FOR THE ENSUING YEAR.

Patrons.

LIEUT.-GENERAL MONTGOMERY MOORE......Halifax, N. S.
HON. SIR S. L. TILLEY, K. C. M. G.; C. B..St. John, N. B.
HON. JUDGE FITZGERALD ....Charlottetown, P. E. I.

President.

A. CAMERON ....County Academy, Yarmouth, N. S.

Vice-Presidents.

G. J. OULTON, B. A............High School, Moncton, N. B.
W. R. CAMPBELL, M. A........County Academy, Truro, N. S.
EWEN STEWART...............Supervisor Schools, Ch'town, P. E.I.

Secretary-Treasurer.

J. D. SEAMAN ....Prince St. School, Ch'town, P. E. I.

Executive Committee.

INSPECTOR CRAIG ....Amherst, N. S.
MRS. S. B. PATTERSON.........Normal School, Truro, N. S.
PROF. J. BRITTAIN ....Normal School, Fredericton, N. B.
MISS BESSIE L. GREGOR ....Prince St. School, Ch'town, P. E. I.

FACULTY.

Botany.

CHAS. B. ROBINSON, B. A.......County Academy, Pictou, N. S.
JOHN M. DUNCAN ....Kent St. School, Ch'town, P. E. I.

Chemistry.

W. H. MAGEE, PH. D..........High School, New Glasgow, N. S.

Civics.

PROF. TUFTS ....Acadia College, Wolfville, N. S.

Elocution.

MISS MINA A. READ............Acadia College, Wolfville. N. S.

English Literature.

A. CAMERON ....County Academy, Yarmouth, N. S.

Geology and Mineralogy.

PROF. A. E. COLDWELL..........Acadia College, Wolfville, N. S.

Kindergarten.

MRS. S. B. PATTERSON ....Normal School, Truro, N. S.

Music (Tonic Sol-Fa.)

REV. JAMES ANDERSON, M. A.....Toronto.

Psychology.

J. B. HALL, PH. D.............Normal School, Truro, N. S.

Physics.

S. A. MORTON ....County Academy, Halifax, N. S.

Physiology and Hygiene.

PRINCIPAL E. J. LAY ....County Academy, Amherst, N. S.

Zoology and Entomology.

G. J. OULTON, B. A ....High School, Moncton, N. B.

I have the honor to be,

Your obedient servant,

J. D. SEAMAN,

Secretary.

To A. H. MACKAY, ESQ., LL. D.,
    Superintendent of Education.

(II.)

TEACHERS' INSTITUTES.

ANNAPOLIS AND DIGBY.

The sixteenth annual meeting of the Teachers' Institute of Inspectoral District No. 4, convened in the school house at Bridgetown on Thursday, May 30th, was duly called to order at 9.30 A. M. by the President, L. S. Morse, M. A. The minutes of the last meeting held at Weymouth were read and adopted.

The following officers were elected for the ensuing year :

Vice-President	A. D. Brown.
Secretary-Treasurer	A. L. Bishop.
Executive Committee	{ O. P. Goucher. S. C. Shaffner. W. M. McVicar. Mrs. I. M. Benson.

It was suggested that persons be appointed to correspond with the press regarding the proceedings of the Institute ; accordingly, Mr. A. E. McCormick was appointed reporter to the *Halifax Herald ;* Mr. H. W. Messenger to the *Morning Chronicle ;* and Mr. J. H. Crowe to the *Ed. Review.*

The President called the attention of the Institute to the new regulation regarding the appointment of delegates to the Provincial Educational Association ; but, as there was not a full representation of the teachers at the morning session, the matter was laid over for a future session.

The annual membership dues were then collected.

The programme arranged by the Executive Committee was then taken up. The first was a paper presented by Mrs. I. M. Benson of the Bear River schools, entitled, " Practical Teaching." In this paper the old and new methods of teaching were contrasted. The writer related her experience with both, and set forth in a forcible manner the advantages of practice over theory. The various subjects on the " Course of Study " were then taken up and dealt with in an able manner, the writer setting forth her methods in teaching certain subjects practically. Time might be economized by combining lessons. Teaching was regarded by some as a gift, but the writer strongly believed it to be a science. The paper throughout was interesting and valuable, and undoubtedly left lasting impressions from which much good will result. At its close remarks were made in favor of certain points in it by A. E. Dunlop of Middleton, and Dr. MacKay, Superintendent of Education. The latter highly commended the paper. He regarded its grand point to be concentration of study.

Concentration was especially needed in miscellaneous schools if anything was to be done. Good work, he believed, in the country, could only be done by the inspiration of the pupils with an intelligent interest in their work. If this was manifested in school work, it would follow the pupils in after life.

The next on the programme was an illustrative lesson on Botany taught by Miss Belle Redding. In order to show her method of teaching this subject she called in a number of her scholars, to whom a lesson on the Lily of the Valley was taught. The manner of her procedure showed that she was fully capable of dealing with the subject before her. The different parts of the plant were studied from observation and botanically named. The lesson formed the text of many comments on the methods of teaching botany by I. M. Longley, A. E. Dunlop, L. M. Denton, and Dr. MacKay.

Miss Jennie A. Hall then read an interesting paper on the " Tonic Sol-Fa " system of music. Some of the important ideas set forth were : The necessity of doing our work cheerfully ; cast aside all prejudice and look at the system in its true light ; other branches were taught that we may *know* more, but music was taught that we may *be* more ; the necessity for its culture ; it is a stepping stone to the staff notation. The desirability of the system was then set forth under different heads, viz. : (1st) its simplicity ; (2nd) its time advantages as compared with other methods ; (3rd) it affects a change in school work ; (4th) it cultivates expression and purity of tone ; (5th) through its hand signs pupils are compelled to keep their attention on the teacher, and thus attention is strengthened ; (6th) its powerful effect through the children on home life.

At its conclusion Mr. A. D. Brown expressed himself fully in sympathy with the paper. He had experienced difficulties in teaching "Tonic-Sol-Fa " music. He was, however, willing to do the best he could towards teaching it. Mr. R. Elliott spoke briefly concerning the paper, after which meeting adjourned to 1.30 P. M.

AFTERNOON SESSION.

Meeting was called to order at 1.45 P. M. The programme was continued by Mr. A. E. Dunlop teaching an interesting lesson on Botany. He confined it to the study of the apple, taking the same course as he would with his pupils. The parts of the plant were taken up and studied from observation, and a synopsis of the same represented on the blackboard. Mr. Dunlop gave a number of valuable hints regarding the teaching of this important subject, and proved himself competent to teach it.

At the close of the lesson Mr. G. B. McGill was called upon for a few remarks. He took great pleasure in endorsing the lesson as presented to them, and knew that all must agree that Mr. Dunlop's method of teaching this subject was the true way. Ideas were what they must develop in the child. He had been pleased with the lesson, and thought it must commend itself favorably to the teachers present.

Mr. A. D. Brown followed with a lesson on Goldsmith's "Traveller." He said his purpose was to teach as Mr. Dunlop had, viz.: as he would in school, and to this end called in his class of "C" scholars. The lesson from beginning to end was listened to with the greatest interest by all present. The excellent manner in which the exercise was conducted, and the prompt and plain expression of the pupils' original answers, showed that Mr. Brown was well calculated to develop the minds of the young, and called forth at the close favorable remarks from W. M. McVicar, O. P. Goucher, Mr. McGill, and A. McN. Patterson, of Acacia Villa School.

Mr. Patterson, on rising to speak, was greeted with applause, and made a pleasing address. He thought the grand secret of teaching was the power to bring out the thought. Mr. Patterson threw out many valuable hints as regards teaching, which, if put into practice, would undoubtedly result in much good.

Miss Hattie Congdon then favored the Institute with an interesting lesson on "Tonic Sol-Fa" music. Miss Congdon proved herself to be thoroughly acquainted with her subject, and also proved her aptness to teach it. This lesson called forth approbation from Dr. MacKay, A. E. Dunlop, Mr. Patterson, and others in their remarks which followed. Meeting adjourned to 8 P. M.

EVENING SESSION.

The public educational meeting was held in the Baptist Church. The meeting was duly called to order by the President at 8 P. M., and opened with a piece of music rendered by the scholars of the Bridgetown school. Prayer was then offered by Rev. John Cameron, followed by music from the choir entitled, "Abide with Me." The President, Mr. L. S. Morse, M. A., with a few well-chosen remarks, explained the object of the Institute, and highly complimented the people of Bridgetown for their past and present interest in educational matters. The speakers of the evening were Dr. MacKay, Mr. Patterson, W. M. McVicar, I. M. Longley, S. C. Shaffner, G. B. McGill, A. E. Dunlop, and Prof. Geo. Tufts of Belfast, Me.

The address of Dr. MacKay was listened to with the greatest attention. He spoke of the educational affairs of this Province as compared with those of Ontario, and while he believed the high school system of that province to be superior in some respects to our own, yet he thought the common school system of this Province was better than that of Ontario. He spoke at length of the *old* system of education and of the *new*, and emphasized the necessity of instilling in the minds of the pupils the spirit of patriotism. His address was practical and well calculated to inspire an educational spirit in all present, and to encourage and strengthen the teachers in their work.

Mr. Patterson's address was full of spirit, and was exceedingly interesting. He spoke of the "Course of Study" and its object—to develope a practical knowledge useful in all relations of life. He believed teaching to be a great and noble work.

Mr. McVicar, in a few well directed remarks, spoke of the position of the teacher as standing between the educational powers and the people, and he thought it well to mingle with both. He believed that teachers should come together to find the out the different methods of each.

The other speakers mentioned made appropriate addresses, which were interspersed with pleasing selections of music rendered by the choir. Votes of thanks were tendered to Dr. MacKay and Mr. Patterson for the able and instructive manner in which they had entertained the meeting ; to the people of Bridgetown for the courteous manner in which they had received the Institute ; and to the choir of the Baptist Church for the excellent music rendered.

FRIDAY MORNING SESSION.

The Institute was called to order by the President at 9.30. The matter regarding the appointment of delegates to the Provincial Educational Association was again brought before the Institute, and the following persons were elected to attend the same : A. D. Brown, W. M. McVicar, I. M. Longley, and Mrs. I. M. Benson.

A letter was read by the President from the secretary of trustees of the Bear River school, inviting the Institute to hold their next annual meeting at that place. It was resolved that the communication be left in the hands of the Executive Committee for consideration.

Resolved, That the Secretary be paid the sum of $3.00 as a remuneration for performing the duties of the office.

The financial statement was rendered by the Executive Committee, and all bills were ordered to be paid.

Resolved, That instead of having an afternoon session, the Institute prolong the session of the morning and finish the work of this year.

The programme was then continued by Mr. J. H. Crowe favoring the Institute with an interesting address on " Tardiness and Irregular Attendance." The subject was dealt with in an able manner, and several good points were made. He referred to the " Compulsory Attendance Act," and believed compulsory attendance to be a good thing. He thought the habit of punctuality should be cultivated in school. Mr. Crowe's address was practical and aroused considerable discussion.

Principal McGill believed after all that tardiness was regulated to a great extent by the teacher, and related his method of preventing it. He believed irregular attendance could be prevented by co-operation of teachers, trustees, and parents.

Mr. Denton thought that tardiness could be prevented to a great extent by making the opening exercises so very interesting that all would wish to be present. He knew of no other way of preventing irregular attendance than by getting pupils interested in their work. Other interesting and valuable remarks were made by Rev. Mr. Tufts, Principals Banks, Patterson, and Dunlop, and Mrs. I. M. Benson

9

Mr. W. M. McVicar was then called upon to give his lesson on Physical Geography. He chose as his subject the "cause of unequal length of day and night." It is needless to say that Principal McVicar was at home on this subject, and for over half an hour was listened to with the greatest attention. Many valuable points relating to this subject were clearly set forth, and the pleasing and forcible manner in which they were presented undoubtedly left lasting impressions on the minds of all present.

The President announced that Principal Longley, on account of sickness, would not be able to give his valuable lesson on the "Metric System."

Votes of thanks were tendered to Principal Brown and his colleagues for their efforts, which had brought the meeting of the Institute to a successful issue; to the trustees of the school section for the free use of the building; and to the railway authorities for reduced rates of travel.

Thus closed one of the most interesting and largely attended meetings ever held by the Institute, from which much good must surely result to educational matters in Annapolis and Digby Counties.

AVARD L. BISHOP, *Secretary.*

GRANVILLE FERRY, N. S., June 8th, 1895.

HANTS AND KINGS.

The Teachers' Institute of Inspectoral District No. 5, convened at Windsor on April 25th, 1895, and occupied two entire days. Inspector Roscoe, *ex-officio* President, occupied the chair. J. A. Smith, Principal of Windsor Academy, was elected Secretary-Treasurer. There were enrolled 104 teachers, one of the largest conventions ever held in this district. The programme was as follows:—

Opening address, C. W. Roscoe, Inspector of District.
"The relation of the Teacher to the moral well-being of the Pupil," Miss Ida A. Parker, Berwick.
"The Minor Mode of the Tonic Sol-Fa," Miss E. C. Begg, Windsor.
A lesson to Grade VI. Pupils on Patriotism," Miss Theresa Farrell, Kentville.
"History and Patriotism," Mr. Ernest Robinson, Selma, Hants Co.
"Solution of Problems in Mathematics," A. McLeod, Prin. Kentville Academy.
"Illustrative Teaching in Grade I. Work," Miss A. M. Freeman, Primary Department Windsor Schools.
"Grammar—a Method of Teaching it," Mr. C. W. Brown, B. A., Prin. Maitland Schools.

In addition to the above programme a public meeting was held in Reform Club Hall, April 25th, at which addresses were delivered by C. W. Wilcox, Esq., M. P. P., Mayor of Windsor, Prof. C. G. D. Roberts.

of Kings College, Rev. Henry Dickie, M. A., Prof. Haley, Acadia College, and A. H. MacKay, Superintendent of Education. The meeting was largely attended. The music was provided by 100 pupils of the Windsor schools under the supervision of Miss N. A. Burgoyne, teacher of Grade VII. of said school, and was a convincing proof of the adaptability of Tonic Sol-Fa Notation to the schools of the Province. Addresses were also delivered at the closing session by the Superintendent of Education on matters relating to the Course of Study, and responses to various questions in connection with the school work, and also by Prof. C. G. D. Roberts, Kings College, on Canadian History.

According to Regulation of C. P. I., *four* delegates were elected to the Provincial Association, to be held in Truro in the month of October. The following were elected : A. McLeod, Principal Kentville Academy ; J. A. Smith, Principal Windsor Academy ; Miss C. Willett, Kentville ; and Miss N. A. Burgoyne, Windsor.

The officers elected for the next Institute were :

C. W. ROSCOE, Esq., Inspector, District No. 5, *President (ex-officio).*
E. H. NICHOLS, B. A., Kentville Academy, *Vice-President.*
J. A. SMITH, B. A., Principal Windsor Academy, *Secretary-Treasurer.*
L. D. ROBINSON, Esq., Berwick ; C. W. BROWN, Esq., Maitland ; MISS H. BENNETT, Windsor ; and MISS T. FARRELL, Kentville, with the officers form the Executive Committee for the next year.

On motion, it was resolved to hold the next Institute, to be called by the Executive, at Berwick, Kings Co.

The Institute, after listening to addresses by the Superintendent of Education and President, closed *sine die.*

J. A. SMITH,
Secretary Institute, District No. 5.

WINDSOR, Jan. 6th, 1896.

CUMBERLAND COUNTY AND WEST COLCHESTER.

The Teachers' Institute for District No. 10 met in session at Amherst on Thursday and Friday, the 8th and 9th of November, 1894. [For a full account of the different sessions see Inspector Craig's Report, page 90].

(III.)

OUTLINE MINUTES OF THE TWELFTH CONVENTION OF THE PROVINCIAL EDUCATIONAL ASSOCIATION.

Held at Truro, N. S., 16th, 17th, 18th October, 1895.

[The proceedings are being published in detail by the Association for general circulation ; hence, but an outline is required here].

1ST SESSION, WEDNESDAY 16TH.

9.15 a. m. The President, Dr. MacKay, Superintendent of Education, took the chair, and opened the meeting with a few appropriate remarks.

Alexander McKay was re-elected Secretary, and H. S. Congdon Assistant Secretary.

An hour was devoted to the enrolment of members. The number enrolled was 250. On motion of Principal Miller, Dr. MacKay vacated the chair in favor of Principal Calkin. Principal McKeen then read the following address :—

To A. H. MACKAY, ESQ., LL.D. :

Respected Sir,—We, the inspectors and teachers of Nova Scotia assembled in convention, desire to greet you with warmest welcome on this the first occasion of your occupancy of the chair of our Provincial Association. We have greatly appreciated your earnestness in the work of education while engaged as a teacher in our public schools, and especially have we marked with pleasure your work in promoting the study of science in this Province. Although there may be differences of opinion as to ways and means of effecting this object, all recognize the zeal which you have evinced in this matter. We recognize, too, your unwearied efforts as Superintendent of Education in giving greater fulness and efficiency to the educational system of our Province, so well inaugurated by your predecessors. It is my pleasing duty now to give expression to the sentiment of the teaching staff of this Province towards yourself—sentiments of respect, of honor, of good will. The inspectors and teachers of Nova Scotia wish to acknowledge through me the uniform kindness, care and interest which they have always found in all their intercourse with you, and as a mark of their appreciation, a visible token of their esteem, they wish you to accept this cane. We hope that you may live long to preside over us, and to exert your great energies on behalf of the educational interests of Nova Scotia.

Dr. MacKay expressed his appreciation of the elegant gift in a few well-chosen happy sentences, after which he resumed the chair and delivered his opening address.

Principal Miller, of the Dartmouth public schools, read a paper entitled, " A Provincial Reformatory for Incorrigible Pupils." This paper was discussed by Comr. McKerron of Halifax Miss Graham, A. McKay, Principal McKeen, Professor McDonald, and others.

The following resolution was then passed :

Resolved, That the Superintendent of Education, through the Inspectors, collect statistics and information regarding the subject, and report at the next meeting of the Association.

Professor Lanos, of Halifax Academy, read a paper on the teaching of French in Nova Scotia The paper was read in French and the leading ideas explained in English. Discussion : Rev. Alph. B. Parker, D. D., Principal O'Hearn, and others. The meeting then adjourned.

2ND SESSION.

2 p. m. Discussion on Professor Lanos paper continued—Principal Calkin, Inspector Morse, Professor McDonald, Principal Kennedy, and others.

The following resolution relating to the subject was passed :

Resolved, That in the opinion of this educational convention, it would seem desirable that the Council of Public Instruction for this Province should allow such change to be effected in the books in use in schools in French speaking districts as would give to pupils in said schools text books in their own language, at least in Reading and Grammar, in order to facilitate their acquiring a knowledge of English.

A paper by Inspector Roscoe on District Institutes was read. Discussion by Inspectors Morse and Craig, Principals Lay, Kennedy and McVicar, and others. The following resolution passed :

Resolved, That this Association record its sympathy with the sentiments expressed in Inspector Roscoe's paper, and that we commend the matter of District or County Institutes to the earnest attention of any inspectors who have not already established such.

Dr. Hall, of the Provincial Normal School, read a paper on " Concentration." Discussion followed.

By permission of the Association, Miss M. J. Graham read a paper advocating " a closer relation between the home and the school." The following was then moved, discussed by Inspector Craig, Mr. Andrews, Principal McLeod and Principal Kennedy, and lost ; 23 for, and 28 against.

" Believing that a closer relationship between home and school is desirable, and that much good will result from having the mothers of our public school children take a more active interest in the school, this Association endorses every effort made to amend Section 44 of the Statutes of Public Instruction, by adding the words ' and female.'"

Mr. N. H. Gardner, of the Halifax Manual Training School, read a paper on " Manual Training in the Public Schools." An interesting discussion followed, in which Professor Russell of the Normal School, and Commissioner McKerron of Halifax, took the lead.

3RD SESSION.

8 p. m. The third session took the form of a public meeting in the Y. M. C. A. hall. Addresses were delivered by President·Forrest of Dalhousie College, Rev. Dr. Parker of St. Ann's College, President Allison of Mt. Allison College, Rev. Dr. Chisholm, President of St. Francis Xavier's College, Hon. W. S. Fielding, Provincial Secretary, and Hon. Speaker Lawrence, M. P. P. The Superintendent of Education, Dr. MacKay, presided and opened the session with general remarks, outlining the philosophy of his educational policy.

THURSDAY 17TH—4TH SESSION.

9.30 a. m. The President, Dr. MacKay, read a lengthy paper " On the correlation of the studies of the High School and the best method of testing its work." He was followed on the same subject by the Rev. Dr. Chisholm of St. Francis Xavier's College, and Principal Calkin of the Provincial Normal School, who read carefully prepared papers. Some discussion followed, in which Inspector Maclellan and the President took part.

Owing to the want of time, a paper " On the General Characteristics of a good school text-book," by F. H. Eaton, A. M., of Kentville, was taken as read.

5TH SESSION.

2 p. m. During this session the convention was divided into two sections.

Common School Section, Inspector Morse presiding.

Miss O. A. Smith of the Normal School, read a paper on " Drawing in the Public Schools." Discussed by Mr. Andrews, Miss Graham, and Mr. McArthur.

Miss Mary B. King of the Normal School, read a paper on " Music in the Public Schools." Instead of discussion there followed a practical lesson on Tonic Sol-Fa, given to a class composed of pupils of the Normal School.

Mrs. Patterson, of the Truro Kindergarten, read a paper on " Kindergarten—How can its principles be made to vitalize primary work (*a*) in town schools, (*b*) in country schools." This paper was discussed by Miss Hamilton, Dr. Hall, Mrs. Condon, and others.

High School Section, Principal Calkin presiding.

Professor Haley of Acadia College, read a paper on " The conditions under which the study of Natural Science becomes a better mental discipline than the study of the Ancient Classics." He was followed by another paper on " Science and Classics as school subjects," by Professor Thompson, of St. Francis Xavier's College.

An animated discussion arose from these papers, in which several took part, among them Dr. Chisholm, Principal Kennedy, Principal Soloan, Professor Eaton, Principal Campbell, and Professor McDonald.

In the absence of Professor Andrews, of Mt. Allison College, his paper on this subject was taken as read.

Prof. MacDonald, of the Normal School, read a paper, " What qualifications should the Head Master of an Academy possess ?" He gave a consensus of the opinions of 45 prominent educators of Nova Scotia in reply to a circular in which questions were asked on the various phases of the subject. This paper was also followed by a lively discussion.

6TH SESSION.

8 p. m. Principal Campbell, of Truro Academy, read a paper entitled, " Nature studies in the school ; the best preparation for industrial occupations." This was discussed by Principal McVicar, Principal Smith, Professors Haley, Eaton, Smith, Dr. Hall, President Forrest, and Principal Kennedy.

Commissioner McKerron, of Halifax, gave an address on the " Ideal Product of the Common School Grades." He was followed by Principal Lay of Amherst Academy, on the same subject.

FRIDAY 18TH—7TH SESSION.

9.30 a. m. Prof. W. C. Murray, of Dalhousie College, read a paper on " The relations of Teachers to Morals and Citizenship." This paper led to a valuable discussion by Prof. McDonald, Principal Calkin, Inspector Maclellan, Principal Kennedy, Miss Burgoyne, Miss Graham, and many others.

Inspector Craig read a paper " On the Characteristics of the Periodical best calculated to aid the Teacher." Discussed by Professor W. C. Murray, Inspector Roscoe, Miss Hamilton, and Principal Campbell.

Aside from the regular work of the Association, Miss Graham, by permission, read a paper on " The Necessity for a Teachers' Union." She was followed by A. McKay, Mr. Congdon, and Commissioner McKerron, after which the following resolution passed :—

Resolved, That the principle of the formation of a Teachers' Union, as expressed by Miss Graham and Supervisor McKay, be approved by this Association.

A number of teachers and others became enrolled as members of the Teachers' Union of Nova Scotia. The Union was organized with officers as follows :—

President .... INSPECTOR MACLELLAN.
Vice-President .... " CRAIG.
Secretary-Treasurer .... PRINCIPAL KENNEDY.
Executive Committee .... { PRINCIPAL O'HEARN,
                 " McKEEN,
                 MISS BURGOYNE,
                 PRINCIPAL LAY,
                 INSPECTOR MORSE.

8TH SESSION.

2 p. m.   Principal O'Hearn, of Halifax, read a paper on "Superannuation of Teachers." Commissioner McKerron spoke at some length on the same subject. In the discussion that followed, Mr. Andrews, Principal McLeod, Principal Miller, and Principal McVicar, took part. A committee, consisting of A. McKay, Principal O'Hearn, Principal Miller, Principal Lay, and Mr. C. M. Moore of Pictou Academy, was appointed to formulate a scheme of superannuation.

The President read a letter from the Educational Association of Prince Edward Island, asking for a joint meeting of the Maritime Educational Associations. The following motion passed : —

Resolved, That the Committee of Management be empowered to convene the Association for next year at the same time, and that if the Executive of the Prince Edward Island Association can make it convenient to meet with us, we will be glad to meet them.

On motion of Prof. McDonald and Principal Kennedy, the following resolution was passed in reference to the late Inspector Congdon :—

Resolved, That this Association place upon its minutes an expression of their high esteem and admiration for the many eminent virtues of the late Inspector Congdon, and the great services rendered by him to the cause of education, not only in the Inspectoral District in which he so ably discharged the duties of Inspector for 23 years, but in the Province at large ;

Resolved, further, That a copy of this resolution be sent to his bereaved family.

A ballot was then taken for the appointment of the Executive Committee of the Association. It resulted in the election of Inspector Roscoe, Principal Kennedy, Professor McDonald, Principal Hebb, Principal McVicar, Inspector Maclellan, Inspector Morse, Principal McLeod, and Commissioner McKerron.

A vote of thanks was passed to the provincial papers for their excellent reports of proceedings, and to the railway and steamboats for travelling facilities. The meeting then adjourned *sine die.*

A. McKAY, *Secretary.*

HALIFAX, 6th Jan., 1896.

APPENDIX F.

STATISTICAL INFORMATION FROM INSTITUTIONS RECEIVING NO PROVINCIAL GRANTS.

(I.)

EDUCATIONAL INSTITUTIONS HAVING DEGREE-CONFERRING POWERS.

Educational Statistics for the School Year ended Summer of 1895.

Name of Institution	Place	Name of Principal	Staff: Professors	Staff: Lecturers	Undergrad 1st year	2nd year	3rd year	4th year	Males	Females	Total	General Males	General Females	General Total	Total in Arts	Science Under-graduates	(General)	Males	Females	Total	Med. Males	Med. Females	Total	Law Regular	Partial	Total	Theol. Regular	Partial	Total	Grand Total Students	Institution—when founded?	Total Graduates to date	B.A.	L.B.	B.A.	B.Sc.	B.Eng.	M.Eng.	LL.B	B.C.L.	B.C.L.	Ph.D.	M.D., C.M.	D.D.	R.D.	D.D.	Total
Kings Coll.	Windsor	Rev. C. E. Willits, M.A., D.C.L.	a 6	4	5	5	4	14	15	1	1			1	16	b 9		9		9				c				12		12	26	1790	443	4		3	1	1	1		5	5					4	20
Presbyter'n College	Halifax	Rev. A. Pollok, D.D.	4	1																								48		48	48	1820 e	285														9	9
Acadia Coll.	Wolfville	Rev. A. W. Sawyer, D.D.	9		31	32	29	28	96	24	120				120																190	1838	415	21		10	2				1							34
Dalhousie College	Halifax	Rev. John Forrest, D.D.	11	12	31	35	25	40	111	20	131	45	12	57	188	8		19	22	5	27	42	3	45	39	14	53	8		8	301	1863	532	26	2	9	3	1	1	13								58
St. Francis Xavier Coll.	—	Rev. H. McD. A. Chisholm, D.D.	10	i																											j	1854	100	9		1													10
St. Anne's College	Church Point	Rev. G. Blanche.	15	2																											k	1890																
Totals			**55**	**19**	67	58	69	221	45	296	45	13	55	**324**	17	19	31		5 36		42	3 45		39 14	53	68		68	**495**		**1778**	60	2	23	3	1	1	13	5	5		7			4	**135**

(a) Lecturers in Theology non-resident.   (b) Science and Engineering.

(c) The Law School being situated in St. John, N. B., is not included here.   (d) Eleven of these are included in "Arts."

(e) Opened first in Pictou, 1820, under Dr. McCulloch. Re-organized at West River, Pictou, in 1848. Removed to Truro, 1858. Removed to Gerrish Street, Halifax, 1860, and afterwards to "Pine Hill," on the North West Arm, Halifax.

(f) Eleven of these are taking a "Post Graduate" course, leaving 29 undergraduates in the 4th year.   (g) Three of these are registered in "Arts" or "Science." The Medical Students take nearly all their classes in the Halifax Medical College.   (h) Nine of these are registered in "Arts."

(i) Four of these are returned as instructors in the Antigonish County Academy.

(j) The great majority of students (106), were registered in the County Academy with which the institution is affiliated.   (k) Eighty are in attendance of whom eighteen have been admitted to the first and second year of the Clare County Academy with which the institution is affiliated.

(II.)

EDUCATIONAL INSTITUTIONS not HAVING DEGREE-CONFERRING POWERS.

Educational Statistics for the School Year ended Summer of 1895.

County	Name of Institution	Place	Name of Principal	No. of Teachers	Kindergarten	No. of Pupils corresponding in general attainment to each of the Public School Grades of Nova Scotia, as given below:												Males	Females	Total	Average Daily Attendance
						Gr. I	Gr. II	Gr. III	Gr. IV	Gr. V	Gr. VI	Gr. VII	Gr. VIII	IX (D)	X (C)	XI (B)	XII (A)				
Colchester	Snell's Business College	Truro	S. G. Snell																		
	Truro Kindergarten		Sara B. Patterson		48																
	Miss Bryden's School	Tatamagouche	Elizabeth Bryden																		
Digby	St. Mary's Convent	Church Point	Sr. H. Patricia																		
Halifax	Halifax Ladies' College	Halifax	Margaret S. Ker																		
	LaSalle Academy		Bro. Castorius																		
	Arnold School		W. H. Waddell																		
	Whiston & Frazee's Commercial Coll.		S. E. Whiston																		
	St. Patrick's Home		Bro. Lawrence																		
	Miss Marshall's School		J. Marshall																		
	Miss Forbes Day School		Mary F. Forbes																		
	Miss Davis' School		S. E. Davis																		
	Academy Mt. St. ...cenn		M M Bonaventure																		
Hants	Church School for Girls	Rockingham	Hannah Machin																		
Kings	Acadia Seminary	Windsor	Adelaide F. True																		
	Horton Collegiate Academy	Wolfville	B. Oakes																		
	Acacia Villa School	Horton Landing	A. McN. Patterson																		
Pictou	Stella Maris Convent	Pictou	Sr. St. Pamphilius		15																
	St. John Baptist Academy	New Glasgow	Sr. St. Alexander																		
	Our Lady of Lourdes	Lourdes	Sr. M. Josephine																		
Yarmouth	Yarmouth Business College	Yarmouth	J. W. Walsh																		
	Miss Tooker's School		Florence Tooker																		
	Miss Hilton's School		Eudora E. Hilton																		
	Totals			102	66	10	121	121	130	119	63	97	120	134	127	80	51	765	407	1012	1140

(a) Averages in brackets,), are estimates made in the Education Office in order to make an approximate sum total possible.

(b) The classification into grades is only approximate, in some cases based on the age of pupils, in others on the English, or Mathematics, or Classics principally, by the various Principals.

(c) Forty partial students ungraded.

In some other institutions no classification is given, therefore the totals will not be expected to check.

HIGHEST MARK AND AVERAGE OF MARKS MADE IN EACH SUBJECT AT EACH STATION.

PROVINCIAL EXAMINATION.   IMPERATIVE, GRADE D.--1895.

OPTIONAL, GRADE D. 1895.

Columns: Station | No. of Candidates | Eng. Lang. (Highest Mark, Average Mark) | Eng. Gram. (Highest Mark, Average Mark) | Hist. and Geog. (Highest Mark, Average Mark) | Science (Highest Mark, Average Mark) | Draw. & B. K. (Highest Value, Average Mark) | Arith. (Highest Mark, Average Mark) | Algebra (Highest Mark, Average Mark) | Geometry (Highest Mark, Average Mark) | Latin (No. of Candidates, Highest Mark, Average Mark) | French (No. of Candidates, Highest Mark, Average Mark) | Aggregate (Highest Mark, Average Mark)

Stations:

- Amherst
- Annapolis
- Antigonish
- Arichat
- Baddeck
- Barrington
- Bridgetown
- Canso
- Cheticamp
- Clare
- Digby
- Guysboro
- Halifax
- Kentville
- Liverpool
- Lockeport
- Lunenburg
- Maitland
- Margaree Forks
- New Glasgow
- Parrsboro
- Picton
- Port Hawkesbury
- Port Mulgrave
- Shelburne
- Sherbrooke
- Springhill
- Sydney
- Tatamagouche
- Truro
- Windsor
- Yarmouth

Average Provincial Mark

Highest Provincial Mark

(II.)

EDUCATIONAL INSTITUTIONS *not* HAVING DEGREE-CONFERRING POWERS.

Educational Statistics for the School Year ended Summer of 1895.

County	Name of Institution	Place	Name of Principal	No. of Teachers	Kinder-garten	Gr. I.	Gr. II.	Gr. III.	Gr. IV.	Gr. V.	Gr. VI.	Gr. VII.	Gr. VIII.	IX (D.)	X (C.)	XI (B.)	XII (A.)	Males	Females	Total	Average Daily Attendance
Colchester	Snell's Business College	Truro	S. G. Snell	3														10	10	30	15
"	Truro Kindergarten	"	Sara B. Patterson	3	48													21	27	48	21
"	Miss Bryden's School	Tatamagouche	Elizabeth Bryden	1														6	4	10	9
Digby	St. Mary's Convent	Church Point	Sr. H Patricia	2															10	10	9
Halifax	Halifax Ladies' College	Halifax	Margaret S. Ker	6															123	123	(100)
"	LaSalle Academy	"	Bro. Castorius	7		7	0	12	13		7			1	13	13		117		117	110
"	Arnold School	"	W. H. Waddell	8										2	7	5		23		23	22
"	Whiston & Frazee's Commercial Coll.	"	S. E. Whiston	3					13	13	14	15	10	23	7	4		198	62	260	(75)
"	St. Patrick's Home	"	Bro. Lawrence	2		3	7	19	4	2	3	3	12	13	3			46		46	40
"	Miss Marshall's School	"	J. Marshall	1		2	4	3	4		4			3				10	10	20	16
"	Miss Forbes Day School	"	Mary F. Forbes	2		1	2	2	8	10	3	4	14					9	20	29	16
"	Miss Davis School	"	S. E. Davis	1		3	9	10	2	4	3								12	12	9
Hants	Academy Mt. St. Vincent	Rockingham	M. M. Bonaventure	15	3					7	8		3	16	8	7		105		105	103
Kings	6th School for Girls	Windsor	Hannah Machin	14					11	6	5			20	20	10		84	84	84	(80)
"	... Seminary	Wolfville	F. True	12									14	11	16	15	10	70		70	58
"	Horton Collegiate Academy	Horton Landing	I. B. Oakes	5										6	41	5	16	68	2	70	70
"	Acacia Villa School	"	A. McN. Patterson	6						11		4		24					6	74	74
Pictou	Stella ... Convent	Pictou	Sr. St. Pamphilius	3	15	12	23	15	19	14	8	24	10	9	6	5			116	116	88
"	St. John Baptist Academy	New Glasgow	Sr. St. Alexander et	4		11	19	14	20	23	8	10	11	7	7	1		69	83	152	94
"	Our Lady of Lourdes	Lourdes	Sr. M	3				40	44	15		2		4				91	79	170	180
Yarmouth	Yarmouth Business College	Yarmouth	J. W.	2											5			12	10	22	(10)
"	M...	"		1		5	3											5	3	P	8
"	Miss Hilton's ... School	"	Eulora E. Hilton	1															(21)	21	(10)
			Totals	**102**	**66**	**10**	**121**	**121**	**180**	**119**	**63**	**97**	**120**	**134**	**127**	**85**	**96**	**755**	**857**	**1612**	**1156**

(a) Averages in brackets,), are estimates made in the Education Office n order to make an approximate sum total possible.

(b) The classification into grades is only approximate, in some cases based on the age of pupils, in others on the English, or Mathematics, or Classics principally, by the various Principals.

(c) Forty partial students ungraded.

In some other institutions no classification is given, therefore the totals will not be expected to check.

APPENDIX J.

HIGHEST MARK AND AVERAGE OF MARKS MADE IN EACH SUBJECT AT EACH STATION.

PROVINCIAL EXAMINATION. IMPERATIVE, GRADE D.—1895. OPTIONAL, GRADE D.—1895.

Station	No. of Candidates	Eng. Lang. Highest	Eng. Lang. Average	Eng. Gram. Highest	Eng. Gram. Average	Hist. and Geog. Highest	Hist. and Geog. Average	Science Highest	Science Average	Draw. & B.K. Highest Value	Draw. & B.K. Average	Arith. Highest	Arith. Average	Algebra Highest	Algebra Average	Geometry Highest	Geometry Average	Latin No.	Latin Highest	Latin Average	French No.	French Highest	French Average	Aggregate Highest	Aggregate Average
Amherst	30	68	41.1	83	51.1	82	40.7	67	36.4	45	27	88	32.7	90	34.7	100	47.8	12	53	28.1	4	45	21.5	597	324.1
Annapolis	28	62	43	73	44.6	75	36.4	33	33	11	29.3	85	31.7	87	48.7	82	44.5	1	25	16.6	15	80	44	473	309.6
Antigonish	28	23	38.6	69	42.7	69	33.3	45	30.8	33	20.3	87	37	95	38.9	70	41.8	1	15	38				451	300.9
Arichat	19	57	37.5	71	44.7	60	34	43	26.5	38	22.4	84	36.1	70	30.2	65	42.8			8.3				510	397.0
Baddeck	31	68	43.7	73	49	62	43.9	49	34.3	35	19.6	86	46.8	70	34.1	67	49.6	4	15					509	319.7
Barrington	21	64	40.1	72	40.1	70	33.3	52	33.2	38	21.1	80	43.5	85	57.2	63	38.8							488	315.8
Bridgetown	5	43	33.4	66	28.5	73	43	57	37.4	63	21.4	80	31.9	50	29.6	62	38.6				2	79	76	470	273.1
Canso	3	45	35.3	58	11.8	60	33.3	22	22	65	8.7	90	51.2	60	16	63	36.6				19	90	79.2	387	270.6
Chebucamp	2	72	39	72	39.7	50	57.1	57	57.1	66	3.1	90	28.3	61	55	74	38							470	303
Clare	21	61	31.2	79	48.6	50	48.6	61	33.3	63	15.7	95	26.7	82	36.9	80	37.3	4	73	53.3	31	64	17.3	724	361.1
Digby	16	48	42.8	81	42.6	65	41.7	53	57.1	61	31.2	100	36.3	61	32.3	98	21.3	4	18	11.3	2	31	30	650	288.3
Guysboro	165	46	41.3	90	40.9	80	42.5	78	35.9	46	31.1	57	29.3	100	40.2	100	65.5			33.7	3	57	38	725	351.9
Halifax	73	63	35.7	90	42.5	95	35.5	73	32.4	61	25.7	91	50.3	100	42.2	60	21.3	15	78	12.3	2	35	5	508	412.2
Kentville	63	71	35.7	91	52.5	90	43	65	30.5	40	24.6	93	28.9	100	33.4	100	37.3	9	55	20.2	1	33		629	282.1
Liverpool	21	71	40.9	83	55.3	90	43	65	36.7	50	30.3	91	47.3	100	51.4	95	41.7			15.8				494	373.2
Lockeport	36	68	39.7	83	47.7	80	45	60	42	41	29	87	44	100	44.6	98	55.3							521	289.9
Lunenburg	12	79	43.2	62	45.2	80	50.2	46	36.2	56	29.2	47	43.8	100	37.4	96	60.2	21	11	14	6	31	15	570	359.5
Maitland	12	73	33.7	82	27.3	60	33.5	26	34.7	58	29.2	49	26.7	74	19.4	92	31.8	6	41	22.8				558	226.8
Margaree Forks	18	58	45.6	60	43.5	80	37.6	49	24.5	36	27.4	63	28.2	96	36.9	31	34.3	5	47	29.6	9	50	26.8	552	306
New Glasgow	84	61	31.2	85	44.9	90	36.7	49	32.7	56	27.1	60	28.8	98	42	90	12.5	10	88	29.8				477	288.3
Parrsboro	22	74	39.9	67	41.9	60	31.4	50	30.5	41	20.3	73	35.2	78	34.8	90	38.6			35.2	9	73	26.8	645	284.3
Pictou	25	71	28.1	65	11.9	75	38.4	41	22.9	53	25.6	96	42.9	98	31.5	60	41.7							448	290.6
Port Hawkesbury	13	64	50.0	77	47	75	44	46	44.2	44	22.9	91	43.3	97	50.5	84	29.5			27.7			29.1	604	315.1
Port Hood	16	58	34.1	82	48	70	30.3	54	37.6	51	27.3	80	47.2	100	32.9	80	39.9	5	32	19.6	5	30	21	568	409.1
Shelburne	17	60	40.4	85	56.5	65	30.3	45	20.6	41	19.6	91	32	95	50.5	98	38.9							557	277.3
Sherbrooke	40	62	37.9	77	46.5	80	33.8	54	28.8	16	25.6	82	43.2	91	41.8	91	38.0			26.1	25	83	12.6	452	330.4
Springhill	15	72	51.1	84	51.1	91	49.1	73	40.4	96	28.3	89	43.3	95	66.3	91	48.6	7	80	12.9	1	82	60	477	296.2
Sydney	78	72	47.7	91	57.7	90	46.3	56	40.1	40	38.3	73	46.7	100	60.3	98	57.9	72	51	26.1	21	32		535	345
Tatamagouche	31	73	40.7	92	57.7	90	36.3	50	35.5	48	31.7	90	46.7	100	63.3	94	46.1	8	51	33.2	2	32		780	411.4
Truro	—	—	—	—	—	—	—	—	—	—	—	—	—	—	—	—	—	—	—	—	—	—	—	—	—
Windsor	31	72		78		91		56		35	28.5	90	47.4	100		94	44.9	11	58		21	93		564	325.3
Yarmouth	50	81		78	50.9	73	36.3	61	35	35		90		100		94								681	364.3
Average Provincial Mark	1165		43.7		40.7		38.5		33.6		25.2		39		40.7		43.9			23.5			33.8		319.3
Highest Provincial Mark		86		92		95		79		96		97		100		100		88			96			730	

HIGHEST MARK AND AVERAGE OF MARKS MADE IN EACH SUBJECT AT EACH STATION.—(Continued).

Stations listed:

Amherst
Annapolis
Antigonish
Arichat
Baddeck
Barrington
Bridgetown
Canso
Chéticamp
Clare
Digby
Guysboro
Halifax
Kentville
Liverpool
Lockeport
Lunenburg
Maitland
Margaree Forks
New Glasgow
Parrsboro
Picton
Port Hawkesbury
Port Hood
Shelburne
Sherbrooke
Springhill
Sydney
Tatamagouche
Truro
Windsor
Yarmouth

Av. Prov. Mark

Highest P. Mark

HIGHEST MARK AND AVERAGE OF MARKS MADE IN EACH SUBJECT AT EACH STATION.—(Con

PROVINCIAL EXAMINATION. IMPERATIVE—GRADE B.—1895.

OPTIONAL—GRADE B. 1895.

Subjects (column headings): Eng. Lang., Eng. Gram., Hist. & Geog., Physiology, Physics, Prac. Math., Algebra, Geometry, Latin Composit'n, Latin Authors, Greek Composit'n, Greek Authors, French, German.

Stations (rows):

Amherst
Annapolis
Antigonish
Arichat
Baddeck
Barrington
Bridgetown
Canso
Cheticamp
Clare
Digby
Guysboro
Halifax
Kentville
Liverpool
Lockeport
Lunenburg
Maitland
Margaree Fks.
New Glasgow
Parrsboro
Picton
Port Hawkesbury
Port Hood
Pubnico
Shelburne
Springhill
Sydney
Tatamagouche
Truro
Windsor
Yarmouth

Average P. M.
Highest P. M.

AVERAGE OF MARKS MADE IN EACH SUBJECT AT EACH STATION.

PROVINCIAL EXAMINATION. GRADE A.—1895.

STATION.	No. of Candidates	ENG. LANG. No. of Can.	ENG. LANG. Average Mark	ENG. LIT. No. of Can.	ENG. LIT. Average Mark	BRIT. HIST. No. of Can.	BRIT. HIST. Average Mark	PSYCHOLOGY No. of Can.	PSYCHOLOGY Average Mark	SAN. SCIENCE No. of Can.	SAN. SCIENCE Average Mark	LAT. COMP. No. of Can.	LAT. COMP. Average Mark	CÆSAR No. of Can.	CÆSAR Average Mark	CICERO No. of Can.	CICERO Average Mark	VIRGIL No. of Can.	VIRGIL Average Mark	HORACE No. of Can.	HORACE Average Mark	ROM. HIST. No. of Can.	ROM. HIST. Average Mark	GREEK COMP. No. of Can.	GREEK COMP. Average Mark	GREEK XENOPHON No. of Can.	GREEK XENOPHON Average Mark	DEMOSTHENES No. of Can.	DEMOSTHENES Average Mark	EURIPIDES No. of Can.	EURIPIDES Average Mark	GREEK HIST. No. of Can.	GREEK HIST. Average Mark
Annapolis	6	6	39	6	71	6	74.2	6	43.2	6	56.8	1	30	4	62.5	3	53	4	50.5	5	56	5	70			1	46	1	44	1	56	5	64
Antigonish	4	3	49	3	59.5	4	63.8	3	53	4	50.3	2	47	4	65.5	3	78.3	4	52.3	3	68.3	4	60	2	28	4	40	3	67.3	3	59	4	65
Arichat	2	1	55	1	73	1	75	2	52	2	47	1	37	1	53			1	38	1	30	1	70	1	40	1	58					1	85
Digby	5	4	45	4	70	4	63.8	4	51.5	5	45	2	45.5	4	53	3	52	4	48	3	52.3	3	58.3	2	27.5	3	58	3	47.3	2	63	5	50
Halifax	8	5	51.4	5	60.6	5	62.5	4	58.5	3	45	3	40.7	2	50	1	52	2	52.5	1	43	3	61.7	6	36.2	4	66.8	3	61	4	65.3	3	66.7
Kentville	2	2	44.5	2	49	2	50	2	47.5	2	50	1	31	2	56	1	53	2	50	2	49	2	65	1	28	1	53	1	47	1	57	2	62.5
Liverpool	1	1	29	1	62	1	70	1	39.5	1	51	2	25	2	72	1	55	2	52.5	2	60	2	60	2	27.5	2	46.5	1	25	1	36	2	55
Lunenburg	1	1	30	1	51	1	66.4	1	43	1	33	2	27	1	42	1	43	1	36	1	46	1	50	3	20	1	41	1	39	1	41	1	50
Pictou	8	7	45.9	7	64	7	67.5	6	51.5	7	40.3	6	29.3	7	54.4	4	52.5	7	46.3	6	56.5	6	63.3	3	25	4	43	3	43.7	3	56.3	6	69.2
Sydney	2	2	50	2	61.5	2	67.5	2	47.5	2	51	1	40	2	68.5	2	66.5	3	64	2	66.5	1	45	1	37	1	42	1	57	2	64.5	1	60
Truro	12	12	60.6	12	76.1	12	77.1	12	54.9	12	57.1	11	41.5	11	66.9	10	61.8	10	61.1	10	60.8	12	71.5	11	37.1	10	57.4	10	59	11	66	12	75.4
Windsor	2	2	62.5	2	69.5	1	80	1	54	2	51.5			2	64			1	48	1	54	1	65					1	42			1	75
Yarmouth	10	7	62.6	9	65.4	7	67.9	7	49.3	9	65.6	2	39	3	64.3	2	73	2	65	1	66	9	62.2	1	32	1	71	1	42	1	77	8	61.9
Av. Prov. Mark	64	55	47.2	56	64	53	68.2	52	49.8	56	48.7	33	35.2	44	60.1	31	58.2	42	51.8	38	54.9	50	61.7	31	30.8	32	51.9	28	48.4	30	57.4	51	65.3

AVERAGE OF MARKS MADE IN EACH SUBJECT AT EACH STATION.

PROVINCIAL EXAMINATION. GRADE A.—1895.—(Continued).

STATION.	PHYSICS No. of Can-didates	PHYSICS Average Mark	CHEM-ISTRY No. of Can.	CHEM-ISTRY Average Mark	BOTANY No. of Can.	BOTANY Average Mark	ZOO-LOGY No. of Can.	ZOO-LOGY Average Mark	GEO-LOGY No. of Can.	GEO-LOGY Average Mark	ASTRO-NOMY No. of Can.	ASTRO-NOMY Average Mark	NAVI-GATION No. of Can.	NAVI-GATION Average Mark	THIG. No. of Can.	THIG. Average Mark	ALGE-BRA No. of Can.	ALGE-BRA Average Mark	GEOM-ETRY No. of Can.	GEOM-ETRY Average Mark	FRENCH COMP. No. of Can.	FRENCH COMP. Average Mark	FRENCH AUTH. No. of Can.	FRENCH AUTH. Average Mark	GER. COMP. No. of Can.	GER. COMP. Average Mark	GER. AUTH. No. of Can.	GER. AUTH. Average Mark	AGGREGATE Highest Mark	AGGREGATE Average Mark
Annapolis	6	24	4	26	5	47.4	4	51.5	4	41.8	-5	40.2	4	27.8	4	30.8	4	31	4	47.5		68	1	67	1	28	1	48	1441	879.3
Antigonish	2	45.5	2	53.5	1	33	1	51		38			1	44	4	55	4	50	3	45.3	1	85	2	85					1314	976
Arichat	1	54	2	35	1		1		3	34	1	25	1	44	3	51	2	39.5	2	67		80	4	80			1		976	709.5
Digby	2	29						46	1	43	1	81	3	50.7	3	37.3				58	3								1180	749.4
Halifax	2	28.5	2	17	1	46	2	46.5	1	28		27	2	41.5	2	67	2	4	1	59	4	56.7	4	82.3				92	1019	520.6
Kentville	2	46.5	1	40	1	30	2	39	1	28	1		1	55	2	67.5	2	66		74.5			1		1	24	1		1121	1034.5
Liverpool												86	3	36	1	80			5	43	3	30	1	90	1	24	1	86	960	762.5
Lunenburg										33.3		52.8		57.3		57				48									889	889
Pictou	4	23	5	30.6	4	43.8	3	46	3	13	5	48	3	57.3	4	43	2	25.5	5	39	3	28	3	61	1	29	1	90	1233	825.3
Sydney	1	82	1	96	2	18	1	25	1		3		2	60.5	2	79.5		40	2	70.5	3	28	1	61					1139	1137.5
Truro	7	37.1	3	26.33	1	46.5	1	35	3	47.3	3	57.7	6	45.7	7	57.9	3	31.3	10	44.7	4	59.3	4	94	1	61	1	95	1466	1151.4
Windsor	2	45	1	47	1	25	1	33	1	56.	1	60	1	38	1	66	1	57	1	74					1	36		87	1131	703
Yarmouth	8	25.5	7	21.4	8	37.8	6	43.3	7	38.4	8	55.6	8	36.9	9	55.4	7	28.4	10	51.1	8	53.3	9	81.1	1	36	6		1103	881.5
Average Prov. Mark	39	33	28	32.3	34	30.5	21	41.6	25	30.6	27	54.2	33	45	41	58.3	24	37.9	44	55.7	30	46.1	26	84.5	6	33.6	11	83	1466	963

N. B.— It must be remembered that the candidates at each station do not necessarily represent the local institutions there, as the stations are centres for the surrounding country. Also, for example, Pictou Academy students have presented themselves at various stations throughout the province, while in the Halifax Academy (by order of the Board of Commissioners), no grade A work is now done. The same will apply to several other stations.

DISTRICT No. 7.—RICHMOND AND CAPE BRETON.

M. J. T. MACNEIL, B. A., *Inspector.*

(Received too late for insertion in regular order).

SIR:

The following brief report on the general condition of the schools, and the educational work done, in District No. 7 during the scholastic year ended 31st July, 1895, is respectfully submitted.

The number of school sections in operation in the County of Cape Breton was 107, leaving 25 vacant the whole year, being two more than the previous year, though the number of teachers employed was greater by one—158 as against 157. This is accounted for by increases in the staffs of two of the graded schools, to which reference will be made in the sequel.

The number of sections having school in Richmond County was 59 as against 60 the previous year, but in this case the number of schools in operation remained the same by the employment of an extra teacher at River Bourgeois, where the school was graded into two departments at the beginning of the year. The number of sections remaining vacant was 11.

The teachers employed were of the classes and sexes shown in the following table in comparison with the previous year :—

CAPE BRETON COUNTY.

	MALE.				FEMALE.				TOTAL.		
	A.	B.	C.	D.	A.	B	C.	D.	M.	F.	Total.
1894..................	3	21	23	19	..	6	42	43	66	91	157
1895..................	4	18	18	21	..	8	45	44	61	97	158

RICHMOND COUNTY.

	MALE.				FEMALE.				TOTAL.		
	A.	B.	C.	D.	A.	B.	C.	D.	M.	F.	Total.
1894.....................	..	9	22	12	..	..	12	15	43	27	70
1895.....................	..	7	13	20	..	..	12	18	40	30	70

The returns for both counties show a gratifying increase in the number of pupils enrolled, as well as in the attendance, as indicated in the following table, the proportion of population at school during the year having been one in 4.6 in Cape Breton County, and one in 4.4 in Richmond, as against one in 4.9 in both counties last year, although, as already stated, the number of sections in operation was less.

CAPE BRETON COUNTY.

	Under 5 years	5 to 15.	Over 15.	Total annual enrollment	Total days' attendance for year.	Daily present on an average.
1894	87	6386	414	6887	687,701	3438.1
1895	117	6798	476	7391	768,901	3766.1
Increase	30	412	62	504	81,200	328.0

RICHMOND COUNTY.

1894	73	2683	172	2928	282.592	1368
1895	61	2776	197	3034	309,208	1732.8
Increase	....	93	25	106	26,616	364.8
Decrease	12	.....	.....	.....	.....	.....

The number of High School pupils in Cape Breton County was as follows :

	1895.	1894.
Taking full course	284	235
" partial course..............	35	90
Total	319	325

And in Richmond County :

Taking full course	44	27
" partial course..............	7	22
Total	51	49

The average of salaries paid to teachers of the different grades in both counties, indicates a slight advance over that of last year, as the annexed table shows, with one or two trifling exceptions. I wish I could believe that this advance, small as it is, was due to some fixed principle of annual increase, or to a recognition of the inadequacy of the salaries generally paid, especially in rural sections. We could then look forward hopefully to the time when it would be comparatively easy to keep all the schools in operation. My correspondence proves to me that it is not owing to the scarcity of teachers that 36 sections in this inspectorate remained vacant last year, but that the people needing their services were either unable or unwilling to pay the figures demanded by teachers recommended to them. When the local supply of teachers cannot be induced to remain, it is not to be expected that people can be attracted from abroad, except by more liberal wages.

10

CAPE BRETON COUNTY.

	MALE.				FEMALE.		
	A.	B.	C.	D.	B.	C.	D.
1894	$866.66	$377.50	$212.81	$154.46	$323.55	$242.16	$148.64
1895	850.00	394.82	235.84	161.58	327.64	250.63	153.51

RICHMOND COUNTY.

1894	$231.88	$307.99	$220.44	$161.63	......	$168.10	$142.08
1895	......	328.62	230.97	163.13	......	167.23	152.28

The above table does not take the salaries of County Academy principals into account. The ordinary Government grant to teachers, however, is included.

The amount of local expenditure for school purposes for the two years, compares as follows :

CAPE BRETON COUNTY.

	Total amount voted at last annual meeting for all School purposes.	Portion voted for building and repairs.	Total amount of salaries paid during year by section.
1894................	$25,095.00	$2228.00	$24,124.00
1895................	25,545.00	3341.00	22,248.00
Increase	$450.00	$1113.00	....
Decrease	....	....	$1,876.00

RICHMOND COUNTY.

1894................	$6,507.00	$ 990.00	$7000.50
1895................	7,530.00	1975.00	6743.65
Increase	$1,023.00	$985.00	....
Decrease	....	....	$256.85

Having received many enquiries as to the cause of the reduced amount of the County Fund apportionment to the different sections of the County of Richmond, as compared with former years, it may be as well to give the explanation here. In the first place, for reasons unknown to me, it was the first year that the amount of the fund was fixed upon the basis of the reduced census of 1891, which diminished the total by $216.00. (2.) There was a first charge against the fund of (a) $180.00 for the Halifax Institution of the Deaf and Dumb as against $60.00 the previous year, and (b) a new first charge of $75.00 for the "School for the Blind," and (3) there were other first charges amounting to $97.74 as "refunds" under section 89 of the School Act; all of which contributed to reduce the scale of distribution from $9.62 per 1000 days in 1894, to $7.06 per 1000 days in 1895.

The school house at Benacadie section, No. 104, Cape Breton Co., was destroyed by fire on the evening of November 15th. The school was continued under very unfavorable circumstances in a small and very ill-adapted building the remainder of the term, but it is feared that a greater portion of the ·current term will have elapsed before school can be resumed. The section is a large one, and the difficulty of locating the new school house in a convenient and central place has given rise to an agitation for dividing the section, which is likely to retard building operations. However, I am in hopes that better counsels may yet prevail, and that the "unity" of the section may be preserved, in which case I should expect to see a graded school of two departments established there ere long. It is difficult to persuade the average ratepayer, especially if he be at what he considers an inconvenient distance from the school house (and that, now-a-days, is not very long) or from the proposed site of one, of the unwisdom of subdividing large sections into small and consequently weak ones. The advantages of the division of labor secured by the graded system do not enter into his calculations, but the baneful results of the policy of division are ever painfully present to the "mind's eye" if not to the physical optic of the inspector, who encounters in this tendency to disruption, an element which calls for the expenditure of a great deal of time, and the exercise of as much patience, tact, and diplomacy as he may be possessed of to combat it.

Quite a number of new school houses were occupied about the beginning or during the course of the term. In Cape Breton County, —No. 76, Gabarus; No. 76½, Gabarus Bay; No. 77, Gull Cove; No. 97, McAdam's Lake; No. 129 Brickyard; and No. 122, Little Pond, were all found rejoicing in the possession of new school buildings, the last two named having lost their old ones by fire as mentioned in previous reports. These are all unfinished interiorly but are sufficiently comfortable to meet present exigencies. The one at Gabarus is supplied with good patent desks. It is situated on a good site, commanding a fine view, and when finished and properly equipped, with the grounds tastefully improved, will be a source of honest pride to a thriving village. The people are to be congratulated on the final outcome of a long-standing difficulty. The building at Gabarus Bay is not as conveniently planned, nor so pleasantly situated, but the one at Gull Cove has been placed upon a site not officially approved— perched among rock on the very edge of the highway. The trustees have been notified of the illegality of their action, and requested to remedy the mistake at the earliest opportunity. The school is recognized conditionally in the meantime. Here also is another instance of a fairly good building which might have been made more convenient and of more modern design without much, if any, additional expense. The necessity for having officially prescribed plans is made apparent from time to time by cases of this kind.

At Glace Bay, No. 11, three departments were opened under the direction of the Sisters of Charity in a new building, comprising six elegant rooms which throw the other class rooms of this large and growing town completely into the shade. But, I think that at last both trustees and ratepayers generally have awakened to the necessity of providing such accommodation for the remaining departments, including the high school, as the growing importance of the section demands, and I hope to be in a position at the next opportunity to report accordingly.

In the County of Richmond, two good buildings have been added to the growing list of new school houses. Port Richmond, as foreshadowed in last year's report, opened school this term in a new house of respectable and convenient dimensions, and of modern design. This fills a want long felt, as the last school house owned by the section was destroyed by fire as long as six years ago. Poirierville, No. 66, was found to be also enjoying the advantages of a fine new school house in place of the antiquated little cabin, which was too long permitted to bring discredit upon so thrifty a community, where the tidy dwellings of the people indicate the possession of so much taste and the enjoyment of so much comfort.

The foregoing references only indicate a small portion of the building operations found to be going on throughout the district, but as many of the new school houses were either only under construction, or not as yet occupied at the time of my last visit, a more particular reference to, or description of them will more properly belong to the report for the current year, as doubtless they will all be found occupied by the time of my next visit.

I am pleased to report that Sydney Academy, still under the efficient management of Principal MacKeen, ably assisted by Vice-Principal Stewart, and supported by an energetic and public spirited school board, has passed through what was probably, in many respects, the most successful year in its history. The total annual enrollment was 63, and the average daily attendance for the year was 45.3. This does not include 14 high school pupils registered in one of the departments of the public schools, under the direction of the ladies of the Congregation of Notre Dame, and under the able tuition of Rev. Sister St. Leonard. In the results of provincial high school examinations, Sydney high schools compare favorably, I think, with those of other counties, having turned out 3 B's, 6 C's, and 4 D's. A red-letter day for the Academy and its pupils, was the occasion of the visit of His Honor the Lieutenant-Governor in June last, who was accorded an enthusiastic reception. A new and interesting feature in the work of the year was the systematic instruction in music of all the classes excepting those under the direction of the sisters, by Miss B. M.

Ormond, one of the regular auxiliary staff, the great success of which aroused the interest of all classes of the community. An exhibition of the results achieved was given at a concert in Temperance Hall, where some two or three hundred juvenile voices, executing music, harmonized in two, three, and four parts, entertained, during a whole evening, a packed audience containing many connoisseurs whose delighted surprise and warmly expressed enconiums were sufficient guarantees of the character of the work. And this was the result of only a few months' work, all done after the regular school hours. It is to be hoped that the school board will see their way clear at an early day to engage Miss Ormond's services exclusively in a line of instruction for which she displays such marvellous tact and talent, and of which the citizens of Sydney generally have shown such keen appreciation.

An addition was made to the auxiliary staff in the person of Miss A. L. Beaton, Grade B, a native of the town and erewhile a pupil of the Academy. The full staff now numbers eleven teachers. The buildings have been put in thoroughly good repair, freshened and embellished with paint inside and out, and equipped with a complete system of sewerage and steam heating apparatus. All interested look forward to the continued and increasing success of an institution which has already accomplished incalculable good.

I regret to state that the prospects of resuscitating the Richmond County Academy at Arichat are not very promising. A movement was set on foot at St. Peter's, at the last annual school meeting, looking to the possibility of securing the grant for the county academy for that village. The people are prepared to make reasonable sacrifices for the attainment of that desirable end, but it will take some time before they can put themselves in a position to claim the grant. In the meantime it is a pity that said grant could not be made available for the encouragement and assistance of some of the leading schools of the County. Or better still would it be, perhaps, could the necessary legislation be secured to apply the grant towards strengthening the staff and improving the appliances of the one institution in Cape Breton whose field of usefulness is not restricted by county limits—Sydney Academy.

Excellent work in the high school curriculum is being done in several high schools throughout the inspectorate. Without going into details, I may particularize those of North Sydney, Sydney Mines, Glace Bay, Gowrie (Port Morien) and Bridgeport—schools comprising from eleven to four departments; and very many of the less pretentious schools, even of the miscellaneous class, have contributed to raise the number of high school pupils to the figures given in a preceding paragraph of this paper.

The progress being made in the schools from year to year may not, to a casual visitor, appear very marked, but to one acquainted with their general status in the years before we had a course of study, the development cannot but be very apparent. The introduction and extension of oral instruction in place of the old-time recital from the text-book, and the levelling up of subjects in the various grades, have brought about changes which can only be appreciated by comparison with what may be called the ancient state of things. If, therefore, it is true that "The teacher makes the school," the truism is more applicable to the modern·than to the ancient school and it should be the aim of every intelligent and wide-awake board of trustees to secure the very best teaching talent available. It should also be their.aim to place within the reach of the teacher as many aids as possible, not only the apparatus prescribed by law as of obligation, such as maps, dictionaries, gazetteers, &c., but other good books and periodicals. The generality of our teachers are not, unfortunately, overburdened with this world's goods, and the acquisition of needed literature is, to them, not always easy. History is making every day, and in order to keep himself *au courant des choses*, so as to be in a position to let his pupils know what is going on in the world, the industrious and earnest teacher must read current literature. And yet, how many teachers do we not find who do not receive even a local newspaper ! Now, if the suggestion thrown out in my last report were only acted upon and the *Educational Review* subscribed for by every board of trustees, that excellent periodical would receive such a start, and be placed on such a footing as would enable it, I feel confident, to be transformed into a weekly instead of a monthly magazine, containing, in addition to its usual wholesome and instructive bill of educational fare, such notes on current events as would make it fill the place, to the general run of teachers, of a first class newspaper. Its usefulness would be immeasurably extended,—it would become a convenient medium of inter-communication and correspondence on subjects germane to the profession, and we would have an organ whose influence could be made a power in the land. *And who would feel the expense ?*

The publication of the new school manual, with the " Comments and Regulations of the Council of Public Instruction " revised and re-arranged under convenient and indexed headings, fills a long felt desideratum. With a copy placed in the hands of every board of trustees, the necessity for a large amount of the correspondence heretofore addressed to inspectors in the way of questions on the school law, ought now to be obviated. Still, it is surprising to find how slow people generally are to notice changes in the law and to act accordingly. While the manual was in the hands of trustees early in May, and the annual school meetings were only held on the 24th June, so few sections complied with the requirements of the law on the " Compulsory Attendance" clauses, that it was found necessary, according to your directions, to suspend or withhold payment of the County Fund to the great majority of sections in both counties until measures were taken to comply with the law by holding special meetings. Another instance is the fact that at present writing only *seven* school secretaries' bonds have been received from the County of Cape Breton, and *nineteen* from the County of Richmond, to be filed in this office in compliance with section 33 of the School Act, and of the latter number *fifteen* were received through the clerk of the municipal council.

The number of candidates presenting themselves at the Provincial High School Examination at the different stations was: at Sydney, 128, and at Arichat, 33; but as the different grades of applicants with the general results will doubtless be tabulated in the usual place in the second part of your general report, it does not seem necessary to insert them here.

I have the honor to be, Sir,

Your obedient servant,

M. J. T. MACNEIL.

A. H. MacKay, Esq., Ll. D.,
Superintendent of Education.

Lightning Source UK Ltd.
Milton Keynes UK
UKHW041200300119
336362UK00017B/269/P